NATIONAL ACADEMIES *Sciences Engineering Medicine*

NATIONAL ACADEMIES PRESS
Washington, DC

Reducing Racial Inequality in Crime and Justice

Science, Practice, and Policy

Committee on Reducing Racial Inequalities in the Criminal Justice System

Bruce Western,
Khalil Gibran Muhammad,
Yamrot Negussie, and Emily Backes,
Editors

Committee on Law and Justice

Division of Behavioral and Social Sciences and Education

Consensus Study Report

NATIONAL ACADEMIES PRESS 500 Fifth Street, NW Washington, DC 20001

This activity was supported by contracts between the National Academy of Sciences and Arnold Ventures (20-05123), Bill & Melinda Gates Foundation No. INV-025407, The Joyce Foundation (SG-20-43354), National Academy of Sciences Cecil and Ida Green Fund, National Academy of Sciences W.K. Kellogg Fund, Robert Wood Johnson Foundation (78590), Russell Sage Foundation (2010-28361), and William T. Grant Foundation (201726). Any opinions, findings, conclusions, or recommendations expressed in this publication do not necessarily reflect the views of any organization or agency that provided support for the project.

International Standard Book Number-13: 978-0-309-69337-0
International Standard Book Number-10: 0-309- 69337-3
Digital Object Identifier: https://doi.org/10.17226/26705
Library of Congress Control Number: 2023930738

This publication is available from the National Academies Press, 500 Fifth Street, NW, Keck 360, Washington, DC 20001; (800) 624-6242 or (202) 334-3313; http://www.nap.edu.

Printed in the United States of America.

Suggested citation: National Academies of Sciences, Engineering, and Medicine. 2023. *Reducing Racial Inequality in Crime and Justice: Science, Practice, and Policy*. Washington, DC: The National Academies Press. https://doi.org/10.17226/26705.

The **National Academy of Sciences** was established in 1863 by an Act of Congress, signed by President Lincoln, as a private, nongovernmental institution to advise the nation on issues related to science and technology. Members are elected by their peers for outstanding contributions to research. Dr. Marcia McNutt is president.

The **National Academy of Engineering** was established in 1964 under the charter of the National Academy of Sciences to bring the practices of engineering to advising the nation. Members are elected by their peers for extraordinary contributions to engineering. Dr. John L. Anderson is president.

The **National Academy of Medicine** (formerly the Institute of Medicine) was established in 1970 under the charter of the National Academy of Sciences to advise the nation on medical and health issues. Members are elected by their peers for distinguished contributions to medicine and health. Dr. Victor J. Dzau is president.

The three Academies work together as the **National Academies of Sciences, Engineering, and Medicine** to provide independent, objective analysis and advice to the nation and conduct other activities to solve complex problems and inform public policy decisions. The National Academies also encourage education and research, recognize outstanding contributions to knowledge, and increase public understanding in matters of science, engineering, and medicine.

Learn more about the National Academies of Sciences, Engineering, and Medicine at **www.nationalacademies.org**.

Consensus Study Reports published by the National Academies of Sciences, Engineering, and Medicine document the evidence-based consensus on the study's statement of task by an authoring committee of experts. Reports typically include findings, conclusions, and recommendations based on information gathered by the committee and the committee's deliberations. Each report has been subjected to a rigorous and independent peer-review process and it represents the position of the National Academies on the statement of task.

Proceedings published by the National Academies of Sciences, Engineering, and Medicine chronicle the presentations and discussions at a workshop, symposium, or other event convened by the National Academies. The statements and opinions contained in proceedings are those of the participants and are not endorsed by other participants, the planning committee, or the National Academies.

Rapid Expert Consultations published by the National Academies of Sciences, Engineering, and Medicine are authored by subject-matter experts on narrowly focused topics that can be supported by a body of evidence. The discussions contained in rapid expert consultations are considered those of the authors and do not contain policy recommendations. Rapid expert consultations are reviewed by the institution before release.

For information about other products and activities of the National Academies, please visit www.nationalacademies.org/about/whatwedo.

COMMITTEE ON REDUCING RACIAL INEQUALTIES IN THE CRIMINAL JUSTICE SYSTEM

KHALIL GIBRAN MUHAMMAD (*Co-Chair*), Harvard Kennedy School
BRUCE WESTERN (*Co-Chair*), Columbia University
DARYL ATKINSON, Forward Justice
ROBERT D. CRUTCHFIELD, University of Washington
RONALD L. DAVIS, 21CP Solutions, LLC (committee member through 9/22/2021)
HONORABLE BERNICE DONALD, United States Court of Appeals for the Sixth Circuit
FRANCIS (FRANKIE) GUZMAN, National Center for Youth Law
ELIZABETH HINTON, Yale University
NIKKI JONES, University of California, Berkeley
TRACEY MEARES, Yale University
DEREK A. NEAL, University of Chicago
STEVEN RAPHAEL, University of California, Berkeley
NANCY RODRIGUEZ, University of California, Irvine
ADDIE C. ROLNICK, University of Nevada, Las Vegas
ROBERT J. SAMPSON, Harvard University
JEFFREY SEDGWICK, Justice Research and Statistics Association
MARÍA B. VÉLEZ, University of Maryland

Study Staff

YAMROT NEGUSSIE, *Study Director*
ELLIE GRIMES, *Research Associate*
DARA SHEFSKA, *Communications Specialist (through March 2022)*
AARON WARNICK, *Communications Specialist (from June 2022)*
STACEY SMIT, *Program Coordinator*
EMILY P. BACKES, *Deputy Board Director*
NATACHA BLAIN, *Senior Board Director*

COMMITTEE ON LAW AND JUSTICE

ROBERT D. CRUTCHFIELD (*Chair*), University of Washington (*retired*)
SALLY S. SIMPSON (*Vice Chair*), University of Maryland
ROD K. BRUNSON, University of Maryland
SHAWN D. BUSHWAY, University at Albany
PREETI CHAUHAN, John Jay College of Criminal Justice
KIMBERLÉ W. CRENSHAW, University of California, Los Angeles
MARK S. JOHNSON, Howard University
CYNTHIA LUM, George Mason University
JOHN M. MACDONALD, University of Pennsylvania
KAREN J. MATHIS, American Bar Association (*retired*), University of Denver
THEODORE A. MCKEE, United States Court of Appeals for the Third Circuit, Philadelphia
SAMUEL L. MYERS, JR., University of Minnesota
EMILY OWENS, University of California, Irvine
CYNTHIA RUDIN, Duke University
WILLIAM J. SABOL, Georgia State University
LINDA A. TEPLIN, Northwestern University Medical School

Study Staff

NATACHA BLAIN, *Senior Board Director*
EMILY P. BACKES, *Deputy Board Director*
STACEY SMIT, *Program Coordinator*
YAMROT NEGUSSIE, *Senior Program Officer*
ELLIE GRIMES, *Research Associate*

Acknowledgments

This report would not have been possible without the contributions of many people. First, we thank the sponsors of this study: Arnold Ventures, Bill & Melinda Gates Foundation, The Joyce Foundation, National Academy of Sciences Cecil and Ida Green Fund, National Academy of Sciences W.K. Kellogg Fund, Robert Wood Johnson Foundation, Russell Sage Foundation, and William T. Grant Foundation.

Special thanks go to the members of the study committee, who dedicated extensive time, thought, and energy to the project on a compressed timeline under unprecedented conditions during the coronavirus pandemic.

In addition to conducting systematic literature reviews and drawing from its own research and expertise, the committee received input from several outside sources, whose willingness to share their perspectives and experience was essential to the committee's work. The committee began its work with a series of public information-gathering sessions, where committee members engaged with a diverse set of researchers, practitioners, and representatives directly impacted by the criminal justice system.[1] The committee and project staff thank the many speakers and discussants who provided research, data, and testimony to inform the committee's study process.

The committee and project staff also thank the group of stakeholders and officials who shared their practiced-based expertise: Nicole Banister (National Governors Association), Edwin Bell (National Center

[1]For more information on the committee's public information-gathering sessions, including agendas and video recordings, see https://www.nationalacademies.org/our-work/reducing-racial-inequalities-in-the-criminal-justice-system

for State Courts), Michael Buenger (National Center for State Courts), Jae K. Davenport (Virginia Secretary of Public Safety and Homeland Security), Amanda Essex (National Conference of State Legislatures), Elizabeth Glazer ([*former*] Mayor's Office of Criminal Justice, New York), Kalyn Hill ([*former*] National Governors Association), David Hureau (University at Albany), Jacquelyn Katuin (Virginia Secretary of Public Safety and Homeland Security), Alison Lawrence (National Conference of State Legislatures), Jeffrey Locke (National Governors Association), Brett Mattson (National Association of Counties), Karhlton Moore (Ohio Office of Criminal Justice Services), Anne Teigen (National Conference of State Legislatures), and Andy Wilson (Office of Governor Mike DeWine, OH).

To inform its report, the committee built on a synthesis of research on the social drivers of racial disparities in policing. The committee would like to thank Roland Neil (University of Pennsylvania) for contributing this valuable resource to the committee's process.

The committee also elicited input from "listening sessions" where perspectives were shared regarding direct work with barriers and innovative solutions to reducing racial inequalities in the criminal justice system. The committee thanks the following individuals: Donald Anthonyson (Families for Freedom), Shelby Chestnut (Transgender Law Center), Currey Cook (Lambda Legal), Christina Gilbert (National Juvenile Defender Center), Annita Lucchesi (Sovereign Bodies Institute), Amber Miller (Yurok Tribal Court), Ravi Ragbir (New Sanctuary Coalition), Paromita Shah (Just Futures Law), Sirine Shebaya (National Immigration Project of the National Lawyers Guild), Jane Shim (Immigrant Defense Project) and, Toni-Michelle Williams (Solutions Not Punishment Collaborative).

This Consensus Study Report was reviewed in draft form by individuals chosen for their diverse perspectives and technical expertise. The purpose of this independent review is to provide candid and critical comments that will assist the National Academies of Sciences, Engineering, and Medicine in making each published report as sound as possible and to ensure that it meets the institutional standards for quality, objectivity, evidence, and responsiveness to the study charge. The review comments and draft manuscript remain confidential to protect the integrity of the deliberative process. We thank the following individuals for their review of this report: Amanda Y. Agan (Department of Economics and Program in Criminal Justice, Rutgers University), Phillip Atiba Goff (Department of African American Studies and Center for Policing Equity, Yale University), John M. MacDonald (Department of Criminology, University of Pennsylvania), Theodore A. McKee (United States Court of Appeals for the Third Circuit, Philadelphia, PA), Daniel S. Nagin (H.J. Heinz School of Public Policy, Carnegie Mellon University), Victor M. Ríos (Department of Sociology, University of California, Santa Barbara), Cassia Spohn (School of Criminology and Criminal Justice, Arizona State University), Heather A. Thompson (Departments of Afro-American and African Studies and Department of History, University of Michigan), and Jeffery T. Ulmer (Criminal Justice Research Center, Pennsylvania State University).

Although the reviewers listed above provided many constructive comments and suggestions, they were not asked to endorse the conclusions or recommendations of this report nor did they see the final draft before its release. The review of this report was overseen by Bradford H. Gray (Urban Institute) and Anne Morrison Piehl (Rutgers University). They were responsible for making certain that an independent examination of this report was carried out in accordance with the standards of the National Academies and that all review comments were carefully considered. Responsibility for the final content rests entirely with the authoring committee and the National Academies.

The committee members were fortunate to have the additional research support from staff in their respective institutions and provide thanks to the following individuals: Teresita Cruz Vital (University of California, Berkeley), Madison Dawkins (The Square One Project), Evie Lopoo (The Square One Project), Toryn Sperry (University of Maryland, College Park), and Caroline J. Zhai Lefever (Yale Law School).

The committee also wishes to extend its gratitude to the staff of the National Academies, in particular to Yamrot Negussie for her expert direction of this study from beginning to end as well as Emily Backes who made critical substantive contributions in the conception, writing, and editing of the report. Ellie Grimes provided essential coordination and research alongside writing support throughout the consensus study process. Stacey Smit provided key administrative and logistical support and ensured the committee process ran efficiently and smoothly. Throughout the project, Natacha Blain, director of the Committee on Law and Justice, provided oversight. From the Division of Behavioral and Social Sciences and Education, we thank Kirsten Sampson-Snyder, Douglas Sprunger, and Ron Warnick who shepherded the report through the review process and assisted with its communication and dissemination. Thanks are also due to Dara Shefska for her skilled contributions to the communications of the report and to Abigail Allen and Briana Smith for their fact-checking assistance. We also thank Marc DeFrancis for his skillful editing and Christopher Lao-Scott for providing research and fact-checking assistance.

Khalil Gibran Muhammad, *Co-Chair*
Bruce Western, *Co-Chair*
Yamrot Negussie, *Study Director*
Committee on Reducing Racial Inequalities
in the Criminal Justice System

Contents

Boxes, Figures, and Tables

BOXES

FIGURES

TABLES

Preface

The history of the U.S. criminal justice system is marked by racial inequality. Across time and space numerous racialized populations from the Indigenous tribes of North America to Central American immigrants at today's southern U.S. border have been a focus of attention for the nation's police, courts, and prisons. The most researched among these groups are African Americans, whose enslavement stood as a visible exception to the founding principles of universal liberty, liberal democracy, and natural rights. W.E.B. Du Bois's (1899) study of Philadelphia's Seventh Ward at the end of the 19th century was among the earliest studies to link high rates of crime and arrest in Black neighborhoods of the city with structural inequalities and discrimination. Thorsten Sellin (1928) documented the high rates of conviction and prison sentencing among Black defendants in the mid-1920s, and also traced the historic connections of chattel slavery to chain gangs and prison farms in the American South (Sellin, 1976). The high rate of imprisonment among Black Americans has been well documented for the entire 20th century and into the 21st century. As we will see in the following chapters, today's researchers—like Du Bois a century ago—trace disparate incarceration to conditions of crime, poverty, and segregation and a punitive policy response that flourished under such conditions. Racial disparity in incarceration was a major theme of an earlier National Research Council (NRC) report (NRC, 2014), and shortly before this committee first met, in 2020, the nation had experienced its largest racial justice protests in opposition to police brutality.

Since the 1990s, various members of the National Academies of Sciences, Engineering, and Medicine's Committee on Law and Justice, which oversaw this report, have made efforts to support a consensus study on racial inequality in the criminal justice system. While many of these efforts were unsuccessful, the 2014 publication of the NRC report on high rates of incarceration helped build the research case for a more targeted examination of race and racism. The committee was compelled by the urgent need to respond to the disproportionate numbers of police stops, court appearances, and prison and jail admissions among Black, Latino, and Native American people.

Earlier NRC reports had sometimes examined research on racial inequality in the criminal justice system, but they had concentrated on specific stages of criminal processing, and racial inequality was never the main focus. For example, a report in 1983 on sentencing policy made an important and detailed examination of research on racial discrimination in sentencing and incarceration. The report concluded that there was a large racial disparity in imprisonment, but "factors other than racial discrimination in sentencing account for most of the disproportionate representation of blacks in U.S. prisons" (NRC, 1983, p. 13). Another NRC report in 2004, on policing, found that the "class and gender of suspects" have little influence on police behavior, but "more research is needed on the complex interplay of race, ethnicity, and other social factors" (NRC, 2004b, p. 3). In 2018, a National Academies report was published on proactive policing, including a close examination of research on racial bias in hot spot and other proactive policing tactics. The 2018 report described the testimony of a community advocate who asked: "Why aren't you doing anything to invest in the reasons why this is a hot spot in the first place?" (the National Academies of Sciences, Engineering, and Medicine, 2018, p. 274). The report went on to observe, "The choice of policing as a response to crime problems is in itself a policy decision that has implications for communities." The charge to the proactive policing committee, however, was not broad enough to consider how policing functions within a broad social system of racial inequalities, inclusive of the criminal justice system, and the greater system's impact on crime.

The current report should be understood to stand in this line of work by the National Academies on race and the criminal justice system, and as the most comprehensive effort to date. In this study, because of the pioneering efforts of Jeremy Travis and Ruth Peterson, racial inequality is the central focus of the statement of task, and the committee's charge takes in the whole criminal justice system in relation to a broad consideration of societal factors. The criminal justice system does not operate in a vacuum and never has.

We are asked to review research to explain why there are such large racial inequalities in crime, victimization, and criminal justice involvement, and to offer evidence-based advice on reducing inequality. The topic is vast and in places we have necessarily traded breadth for depth. In the committee's perspective, the criminal justice system is a complex interlocking apparatus and part of the challenge of understanding racial inequality involves understanding the operation of the system as a whole. Large crime policy projects, like the War on Drugs and the War on Crime that were mounted in the 1960s and 1970s, involved thousands of agencies including state legislatures, police departments, prosecutors, and prison authorities. Racial inequality is not produced by any one stage of the system but is the combined product of each stage in the sequence.

In addition to institutional complexity, police, courts, and prisons are deeply embedded in a racially unequal society that has denied opportunity to communities of color (e.g., Black, Hispanic/Latino, and Native American communities) and preserved socio-economic advantages for White Americans. Through segregation, unequal public investment, and a political acceptance of enduring and spatially concentrated poverty, White Americans have mostly lived in vastly different social worlds than people of other racial groups. In Black, Latino, and Native American neighborhoods and communities where crime and poverty are more prevalent, the criminal justice system is the dominant response to crime. In White neighborhoods and communities, the public policy approach to safety does not depend chiefly on the threat of arrest and incarceration.

The committee has tried to absorb the lessons of research on racial inequalities in crime and the criminal justice system to propose policies that might reduce both. Criminal justice reform has a fundamentally important role to play in reducing racial inequality. Hundreds of policy initiatives are currently unfolding around the country that aim to reduce the burden of unnecessary or harmful state supervision in Black, Latino, and Native American communities, while also reducing crime. We have tried to learn from some of the most important of these examples in proposing future directions for policy. The committee also studied many of the efforts undertaken through community-led initiatives and social policies that try to build a different kind of safety and well-being that relies less on police and prisons. We have also tried to draw lessons from these examples, while acknowledging the political challenges. The committee acknowledges the importance of the inclusion of lived experience with the criminal justice system throughout this process, which we have integrated through committee perspective, our information-gathering process, and dissemination efforts (see below for artwork created for the report). Finally, we see a critical role for the federal government to seed new initiatives and help promote a paradigm shift that can change the relationship of citizens of color to the American state. Instead of depending mostly on punitive measures by the state to deliver safety, a United States without racial inequality would find safety in greater prospects of opportunity, healthier communities in which to live, and accountability for harm would involve setting relationships right. In such a world, the criminal justice system might even be deserving of its name. We offer this report in the hope of such an outcome.

Khalil Gibran Muhammad, *Co-Chair*
Bruce Western, *Co-Chair*
Committee on Reducing Racial Inequalities in the Criminal Justice System

Title: Untold
Artist: Jemaell Riley
Year: 2022
Artist statement:

I am unfortunate to be one of those cast away by society. The decade removed from my life are the pages of some untold story that most will never know and a story I never wish to relive. This is not unique—in this art is a picture of those lost pages, scattered, full of lives from every community, race, and creed who will struggle to find the meaning of being forgotten.

Acronyms and Abbreviations

BID	Business Improvement Districts
BJS	Bureau of Justice Statistics
BTB	ban the box
Byrne JAG	Byrne Justice Assistance Grant Program
CAHOOTS	Portland, Oregon's Crisis Assistance Helping Out on the Streets
CCD	Houston's Crisis Call Diversion
CDC	Centers for Disease Control and Prevention
CIA	Central Intelligence Agency
ECE	early childhood education
EMS	emergency medical services
FBI	Federal Bureau of Investigation
FFPSA	Family First Prevention Services Act
IDD	intellectual and developmental disability
LAPD	Los Angeles Police Department
LEAA	Law Enforcement Assistance Administration
LGBQ/GNCT	lesbian, gay, bisexual, queer/gender nonconforming, transgender
LGBTQ2S+	lesbian, gay, bisexual, transgender, queer or questioning, two-spirit, and other identities

MTO	The Moving to Opportunity project
MTSS	multi-tiered systems of support
NCVS	National Crime Victimization Survey
NIJ	National Institute of Justice
NYPD	New York (City) Police Department
OEO	Office of Economic Opportunity
OJJDP	Office of Juvenile Justice and Delinquency Prevention
OLEA	Office of Law Enforcement Assistance
PHS	Pennsylvania Horticultural Society
RCT	randomized controlled trials
RIPA	Racial Identity and Profiling Act
SBI	Sovereign Bodies Institute
SRO	school resource officers
TCN	Transitions Clinic Network
UCR	Uniform Crime Reporting

Summary

A large research literature has documented substantial racial and ethnic disparities at each stage of the criminal justice process. Black American, Latino, and Native American people have all been found to experience relatively high rates of arrest, pretrial detention, incarceration, and community supervision compared to White people. At the same time, community violence poses a significant risk to health and well-being for disadvantaged communities. Researchers have wrestled with the complex relationship between racial disparities in crime and disparities in criminal justice involvement. Racial inequality can drive disparities in both crime and system involvement; racial differences in criminal victimization, offending, and incarceration can further exacerbate racial inequality in socioeconomic life.

In 2020, the Committee on Law and Justice of the National Academies of Sciences, Engineering, and Medicine convened an expert ad hoc committee to review and assess the scientific evidence on how racial inequalities in criminal justice might be reduced through public policy. The Committee on Reducing Racial Inequalities in the Criminal Justice System was assembled to carry out this study and produce a consensus report. The committee reviewed and synthesized a diverse body of evidence from a variety of disciplines, including criminology, sociology, law, economics, psychology, history, and public policy, and it gathered public testimony from a variety of community participants in the course of three public workshops. Box S-1 includes key definitions and terminology derived from these efforts.

This report builds on the work of researchers, practitioners, policy makers, and community representatives who have been working to address racial inequality in the criminal justice system for decades. It was prepared

BOX S-1
Key Terms and Definitions

Racial disparity, in the context of this report, refers to group-based average differences in criminal justice outcomes. It is important to keep in mind that an average difference does not imply that all members of one group are more likely to experience an adverse outcome relative to another. It is also important to note that the existence of a disparity is simply a descriptive pattern and absent further analysis provides no information as to the source of the disparity.

Racial inequality refers to group-based differential treatment or access to valued resources rooted in law and public policy as well as in individual behavior and institutional practices. Racial inequalities can result from multiple sources, including both historic and contemporary oppression, structural racism, and prejudice, whether or not intended. Racial inequalities are thus multidimensional, compounded, intergenerational, and enduring over the life course. They also evolve in ways that make singular or point-in-time policy interventions challenging.

in the contemporary context of a global pandemic, the police killings of George Floyd, Breonna Taylor, and other Black Americans, and subsequent protests against racial injustice. Moreover, gun violence—often concentrated in low-income Black communities—increased sharply in 2020 and 2021, posing an additional threat to racial equity. The current moment is thus marked by opportunity and urgency. The report offers an account of the research evidence that can inform the public conversation and the policy discussion over reducing racial inequality in the criminal justice system and advancing racial equity.

Given the complexity and deep historical roots of contemporary racial inequality in the United States, the committee has considered both policy reforms to the criminal justice system and policy reforms that address social, economic, and environmental conditions that give rise to inequalities in crime and justice. Criminal justice reforms that can reduce the scale of police stops and prison admissions, the duration of long sentences, and the duration and intensity of community supervision are likely to produce large absolute reductions in criminal justice involvement in minority communities. However, the criminal justice system does not operate in a vacuum, and reductions of criminal justice inequalities also depend in part on social and economic policy. Criminal justice reform can be buttressed by reducing the socioeconomic disadvantages that disproportionately increase the risks of criminal justice contact among the residents of low-income communities, who are disproportionately Black, Latino, or Native American. Given this context, the report considers both criminal justice reforms and alternative strategies that lie outside the criminal justice system for reducing violence and other crime. The committee also found significant limitations in the available data and research evidence and offers recommendations for their development that might also help in overcoming racial inequality.

KEY TRENDS IN CRIMINAL JUSTICE INEQUALITIES

Large racial and ethnic disparities exist across the several stages of criminal legal processing, including in arrests, in pretrial detention, and in sentencing and incarceration, with Black Americans and Native Americans typically experiencing the greatest criminal justice involvement. Despite this pattern, racial disparity in incarceration and the absolute size of the total correctional population (including prison, jail, probation, and parole) have substantially declined in the 12 years from 2008 to 2020. Nevertheless, large racial disparities in criminal justice involvement remain, and they are extremely high in some jurisdictions. Racial inequalities in the impacts of criminal justice contact on Black, Latino, and Native American communities also persist.

Key trends in criminal justice inequalities are detailed in Chapter 2 of this report. Here the committee highlights key data that informed its understanding of racial inequalities in the criminal justice system:

- *Homicide victimization.* With the exception of homicide victimization, racial disparities in victimization have narrowed considerably over the past three decades. However, racial disparities in homicide rates have *grown wider* since 2010, with Black Americans, American Indian people, and Latino people at higher risk of homicide victimization than White and Asian Americans. These disparities grew as overall homicide rates rose sharply during 2014 to 2016 and again from 2019 to the present.
- *Police interactions and arrests.* Police officers stop and search Black individuals at rates that are higher than for other racial and ethnic groups.
- *Pretrial detention.* Between 2005 and 2019, the rate of detention in jail, per-capita, was more than three times higher for Black Americans than for either White or Latino people. A growing literature attributes part of this racial disparity in jail populations to the common practice of requiring defendants to post cash bail in order to be released from jail between their preliminary hearings and the resolution of their cases.
- *Sentencing and corrections.* The absolute Black/White disparity in incarceration rates narrowed between 1999 and 2018, and the Black/White incarceration rate ratio also declined, from 6.23 to 4.24. Over

this same period, the Latino-White incarceration rate differential narrowed, while the Latino/White incarceration rate ratio declined from 2.18 to 1.56. For American Indians, however, there was a *widening* in absolute as well as relative incarceration rates relative to White people, with the absolute incarceration rate differential increasing and the corresponding ratios increasing from 2.18 to 3.02.

- *Community supervision.* The probation population dropped by almost 20 percent between 2007 and 2019. Despite that drop, the racial makeup of the population under probation supervision changed little from 2007 to 2019.

THE DRIVERS OF RACIAL INEQUALITY IN CRIMINAL JUSTICE

Historical and Social Drivers of Racial Inequalities

Current racial inequalities in community violence and lethal criminal justice contacts are tied to historical and social processes of racial exclusion. The history of the criminal justice system in the United States is inextricably linked to the history of slavery and settler colonialism in early America, in which Black and Indigenous people—free, enslaved, and self-emancipated—were segregated, confined, and incarcerated. Inequalities in the criminal justice system in the contemporary period thus descend from a longer and larger history defined by processes of separation and social control in non-White communities (see Chapter 1).

Connections between historically rooted structural inequalities and racial disparities in crime and criminal justice system involvement can be seen in a variety of ways. For example, patterns of racial residential segregation, discriminatory housing policies, and spatially concentrated poverty are closely associated with high rates of serious violence in Black communities. Large American cities remain highly segregated by race, despite the nation's growing diversity and the suburbanization of certain racial groups (e.g., Black Americans). Rising income inequality coupled with drivers of residential segregation, like racial discrimination in the housing market and racially structured residential preferences, perceptions, and knowledge, tend to foster concentrated racial disadvantage. Concentrated disadvantage and racial segregation also expose communities to toxic inequalities like lead exposure and airborne pollution, which themselves have been linked to crime and criminal justice contact. In this way, racial inequality gets into the minds and bodies of individuals from an early age, reinforcing disadvantages over the life course and driving criminal justice outcomes.

Social processes like these indicate how race-based contextual disadvantage—regardless of individual characteristics—continues to characterize the U.S. demographic landscape, allowing relatively few Black or Native American children to grow up in environments that enable upward economic mobility. Indeed, very few White communities experience the concentrated disadvantage that typically confronts Black communities. Racial inequality in neighborhood environments is so deep that the most disadvantaged urban contexts in which White people reside are generally better off than the conditions of life in the most common context of Black communities. Neighborhood racial inequalities are multidimensional, compounded, enduring over the life course, and transmitted from one generation to the next. Singular or point-in-time policy interventions may therefore be ineffective at reducing inequalities that are entrenched in this way, and policy reforms to reduce racial inequality in crime and criminal justice involvement must tackle the contexts in which inequality emerges.

Racial disparities in serious violence—in both victimization and offending—are also spatially patterned, with high rates of violent crime being concentrated in communities that face longstanding and ongoing patterns of segregation and concentrated poverty. Segregation and neighborhood poverty themselves are closely associated with local pockets of joblessness, patterns of family complexity, disinvested infrastructure, a shortage of social services, and depleted collective efficacy, creating obstacles to safety while inviting policing and incarceration. Research indicates that these conditions of social structural disadvantage are highly correlated with violent crime.

In sum, both racial inequality in serious crime and criminal justice contact emerge in broader contexts of socio-economic inequality. Such contexts contribute to racial differences in criminal offending and criminal justice involvement. Eliminating racial inequalities in the criminal justice system will depend in part on addressing the legacy of historic inequalities and cumulative, racially based disadvantages over the life course. Criminal justice reforms are essential for reducing criminal justice inequalities, but their effects may be multiplied by addressing the societal inequalities in which the criminal justice system is embedded (see Chapter 3).

Criminal Justice Drivers of Racial Inequalities

Racial inequalities in neighborhood environments and crime combine with cumulative disadvantage through the stages of criminal processing to produce racial inequality in the criminal justice system and deepen structural racism in society more generally. Enduring and spatially concentrated patterns of racial inequality in residence, poverty, violent crime, and enforcement provide a context for racial inequality in criminal justice involvement. As a result, criminal justice system contact—including police stops, arrests, incarceration, and community supervision—tends to be highly spatially concentrated.

Socio-economic disparities, coupled with the bias of criminal justice officials and the routine operations of police and courtrooms that intensively regulate low-level offenses, generate large disparate impacts. Once individuals are ensnared in the criminal justice system, strong perpetuating effects continue criminal justice involvement and, in some cases, diminish life chances.

Three key processes are important contributors to this racial inequality in criminal justice involvement. First, the early stages of the system—including police stops, jail confinement, misdemeanor courts, and fines and fees—generate vast numbers of contacts (relative to White communities) between the police and courts on the one hand and Black, Latino, and Native American communities on the other. Second, sustained criminal justice involvement is produced through a cumulative process that may increase disparity with movement through the system. Third, the criminal justice system ensnares large segments of a disproportionately minority population on the front end for whom social problems related to concentrated poverty, including but not limited to serious crime, engender a criminal justice response involving arrest and penal control.

Criminal justice policies that broaden system surveillance and enforcement, combined with key points of discretion (for example, at arrest, pretrial detention, sentencing, parole release, and parole revocation), contribute to racial inequality by increasing the likelihood of criminal justice contact among low-income Black, Latino, and Native American populations. Moreover, criminal justice policies exacerbate the harm of criminal justice contact among these populations, particularly those who live in settings that have suffered the most harm from historical patterns of residential and economic exclusion based on race and ethnicity. These consequences extend to youth, for whom early exposure to policing in certain contexts has been associated with harmful outcomes in health and overall well-being.

Criminal processing—the sequence from police contact through arrest and incarceration—magnifies these preexisting inequalities. At each point, a person may be directed out of the system, treated more leniently, or treated more harshly. Racial disparities at each stage may compound across the system, creating greater racial inequality at the end, in imprisonment and re-imprisonment through parole revocation, than at the beginning with police contact.

A variety of institutional routines and decision points contribute to a system that casts a wide net to ensnare low-level offenders at the front end, keeps those offenders in the system, and metes out punitive responses to violence and other crime often apprehended in contexts of poverty and racial inequality. Two overall themes emerge from this sequential perspective: (1) Many policies operate to expand initial contact with the system through, for example, traffic stops, misdemeanor arrests, or fines and fees. (2) Later stages of the system can prolong criminal justice involvement, often with few options for diversion. For example, pretrial detention is associated with increased risks of criminal conviction; fines and fees commonly lead to warrants for non-payment; after sentencing, determinate sentencing jurisdictions provide limited opportunities for parole release; and community supervision is associated with an elevated risk of re-incarceration often for non-criminal technical violations.

Racial inequality that is produced in a cumulative way in the social context of structural disadvantage may be unyielding to narrow policy interventions that target specific points of discretion identified in discrimination studies. Research on arrest, sentencing, incarceration, and community supervision indicates that disparity can result from a range of factors, including biased decision-making by line officials, social structural inequalities, and inequalities produced through institutional design. Racial inequality is the cumulative effect of the procedures, decisions, and rules governing the interlocking agencies from police to corrections that comprise the criminal justice system. Analysis of disparities at any one point in the system is too narrow. To understand the impact of the criminal justice system on racial inequality, a more holistic understanding of contact across multiple points is necessary.

REDUCING INEQUALITIES AND ADVANCING EQUITY

Amid a changing political climate and an increase in homicide rates in U.S. cities since 2020, some policy makers have become more resistant to criminal justice reform. Our review of research finds that it is possible to reduce unnecessary and harmful criminal justice contact without increases in crime. In fact, we find that improving outcomes for such populations can help increase public safety. Empirical evidence on racial disparity and crime trends suggests no inherent trade-off between reducing racial and ethnic disparities and improving public safety. In key examples described in the report, large reductions in police stops (e.g., in New York City) and incarceration (e.g., in California) were adopted without corresponding increases in crime. Many other examples from the research literature similarly indicate that racial inequality in the criminal justice system has been reduced without increasing crime. Furthermore, violent victimization and criminal justice contact are often co-occurring in ways that disproportionately affect Black, Latino, and Native American communities. To safely achieve racial equity, it is critical to understand the key contributors of racial inequalities in the criminal justice system and to implement policies and practices that target these inequalities while accounting for the broader social conditions in which inequalities emerge.

As the nation seeks options for addressing longstanding racial inequalities in the criminal justice system, many communities have begun to embrace concrete policy reforms. The current system, with its outstanding inequalities, was itself built through investments and policy choices over many years, and the scientific evidence on criminal justice reform suggests that changes in policy can help to reduce racial disparities across stages of the system. The committee offers some guiding principles, drawn from the research and its expert judgment, for implementing such public policy approaches; see Box S-2.

Community-Driven Approaches to Safety and Reducing Harm

Calls for a larger role for impacted communities to participate in improving safety have become prominent in contemporary conceptions of criminal justice reform. Rather than relying on the police or other formal institutions of control, local community residents and community-based organizations can take a leading role in the definition and production of

BOX S-2
Guiding Principles to Reduce Racial Inequality in the Criminal Justice System

Informed by the committee's expertise, these principles are meant to inform decision makers as they consider strategies and policy levers for reducing racial inequalities in the criminal justice system though they are not exhaustive or meant to be narrowly prescriptive.

Reckoning and Reconciliation: *Criminal justice policies and reform should be informed by an understanding of the harms perpetrated by the system against specific racial and ethnic groups. Reforms that involve reconciliation can help repair relationships between criminal justice agencies and impacted communities that have been marked by historical tensions, grievances, and misconceptions.*

Participation, Accountability, and Transparency: *Efforts to reduce racial inequalities in the criminal justice system should include mechanisms for public participation and accountability as well as transparent data and evaluation methods. Above all, these efforts need to be accountable to the communities they serve.*

Impacted Community Voices: *Communities that are disproportionately harmed by racial inequality in the criminal justice system need to be partners in knowledge generation and implementation of policy solutions. Communities themselves have multifaceted needs, diverse perspectives, and unique contexts; the fact that community voices are so varied calls for extensive opportunities for outreach and consultation with policy makers, adequate survey tools, and other measures of community representation in decision-making.*

Heterogeneity: *Criminal justice decision makers must understand the heterogeneity of contexts across jurisdictions and communities and take this into account when considering public policy solutions that have been shown to work in other contexts.*

safety. The organizers of these efforts often view their work as not just reducing crime but also reducing racial inequality in crime and criminal justice involvement. In the scientific literature, research on neighborhood social organization, community-based organizations, and residents' collective efficacy has also emphasized informal social controls enacted under conditions of social trust and shared expectations. Providing organizational resources and harnessing the power of citizens can, at least in theory, enhance safety in ways that law enforcement alone cannot.

Community initiatives show enormous variation in their implementation and in the environments in which they operate. A community can be involved in the production of safety in at least two ways: by taking a leading role in the definition and production of safety and by providing oversight of criminal justice agencies. Community input in the definition and production of safety helps build trust and legitimacy and aligns with democratic values. Researchers can support these goals by creating a better science of assessing the nature of community members' views and preferences.

RECOMMENDATION 6-1: Cities and localities should partner with researchers to implement an ongoing system of data collection and omnibus surveys to provide data on the views of resident safety and to develop reliable and valid measures of the full range of residents' viewpoints.

Building healthy communities and reducing crime require investments in community capacity to define and advance safety and reduce harm and inequality associated with criminal justice involvement. Such efforts appear promising for promoting safety, buffering communities from violence, and reducing racial inequality. Moreover, it is necessary to expand the types of evidence from which we judge the success of these programs. Encouraging investments in community capacity building, not simply crime fighting, may be promising, and when such investments are made in people and relationships, not just in programs, they may be more sustainable in the long-run. Just as accountability to the public is needed for criminal justice interventions, community-based efforts also need accountability mechanisms when setting up funding sources, allocating resources, and specifying evaluation metrics for crime reduction.

RECOMMENDATION 6-2: Given suggestive but incomplete results from a burgeoning literature on community-based anti-violence and related initiatives, federal and state agencies should explore the significant expansion of community-driven pilot programs that are fielded in combination with strong evaluation strategies.

Many Indigenous communities rely on traditional systems of accountability, justice, and healing. Because of their emphasis on community definitions of safety, healing, and restorative practices, Indigenous-led efforts to reform justice systems suggest potentially promising models, though there are few rigorous evaluations of such programs and models.

RECOMMENDATION 6-3: In order to better understand the potential for Indigenous approaches to be transferred to other communities (Indigenous or otherwise) and the potential for such models to reduce racial inequalities, federal agencies and philanthropic organizations should support research examining and evaluating tribal models of justice. Such evaluations may need to pay attention to conceptions of success to ensure that outcomes are aligned with community needs and priorities.

Non-Criminal Policy Approaches to Reduce Inequality in Crime and Justice

As described above, eliminating racial inequalities in the criminal justice system must include addressing longstanding inequalities and cumulative, race-based disadvantages experienced over the life course. Policies and programs that improve the material well-being of communities characterized by concentrated disadvantage have the potential to reduce racial inequalities. For example, place-based interventions can target the economic and environmental conditions that can give rise to crime, such as housing insecurity, deficits in the built environment, lack of labor market opportunities, and inadequate public transportation.

In addition to addressing the underlying causes of concentrated disadvantage and segregation, this report also identifies promising sites of intervention in adjacent social policy institutions that can either perpetuate and compound or else mitigate racial inequality in and outside of the criminal justice system, such as education, child welfare, and health systems. Though that list is not exhaustive, the committee examined these systems with a life-course approach and with the understanding that the cumulative nature of racial inequality is intergenerational for families and children. The committee highlights select strategies for reforming social policy institutions with overarching principles that seek to strengthen families and protect children from system involvement, to enhance opportunities for youth learning and healthy development, and to promote health and well-being. Another central tenet of these strategies is the recognition of the role that biases and institutional racism can play in shaping outcomes for youth and families. Without meaningful structural reform that addresses these underlying mechanisms of inequality, decision makers run the risk of shifting the responsibility to address social problems but perpetuating racial inequality in different systems.

The committee also examines gun violence through a racial equity lens and explores potential policy solutions and public health approaches to minimize harm and advance equity. Given the enormous social cost and racial inequality associated with gun violence, proven measures for reducing the supply of guns may contribute to reducing serious crime that is concentrated in disadvantaged communities.

While this report does not make an exhaustive review, its identification of select strategies addressing longstanding inequalities and cumulative, race-based disadvantages over the life course emphasizes that reducing criminal justice inequalities also depends in part on social and economic policy.

Reforming the Criminal Justice System

The committee views reforms to police, courts, and corrections as part of a larger process needed for significantly reducing inequality. In addition to developing community-based strategies for safety, achieving a reduction in arrests, incarceration, and other criminal justice contact in communities of color will require changes to criminal justice agencies. The criminal justice system should work to holistically respond to harm, including both the harms attributable to crime and the harms for which the criminal justice system is itself responsible.

Consistent with a constitutional vision of the relationship between state and civil society, the state's powers of arrest and incarceration should be applied parsimoniously, kept at a minimum consistent with the purposes of public policy. An approach grounded in parsimony would rule out enforcement strategies such as widespread stop-question-and-frisk in minority neighborhoods—which have been found unconstitutional by the courts—or frequent querying of citizens about their probation/parole status during minor traffic stops, or pretextual traffic stops for minor equipment violations, all practices for which there is little evidence of abating serious crime but ample evidence of undermining public trust. Moreover, such a constitutional vision would likely preclude extremely harsh sentences that weigh any crime-reducing effect against social costs to individuals, families, and communities. On the other hand, the goals of harm reduction with parsimony would likely justify *enhanced* policing efforts to clear homicides, reduce gun violence, and reduce the incidence of robbery, burglary, and other serious crimes that are disproportionately experienced in disadvantaged communities.

Given the much larger presence of the criminal justice system in all its forms in minority communities, such a policy change would disproportionately impact affected communities and likely reduce disparities in involvement and victimization. Moreover, a refocusing of the objectives of criminal justice policy would explicitly take into account the impact of the criminal justice system on inequality, racial inequality in particular. A key strategy to reduce racial inequality involves reducing the scale of police contact, incarceration, and other criminal justice involvement that will tend to produce the largest reductions among Black, Latino, and Native American populations. Reducing the overall scale of criminal justice contact is somewhat different from many reforms that aim to reduce differential treatment, for example through anti-bias training or oversight.

Synthesizing the Evidence on Criminal Justice Reform

A wide variety of measures—including judicial bans on unconstitutional policing and incarceration, sentencing reform for drug offenses and de-felonization, bail reform, and reductions in the intensity and duration of probation and parole—have already reduced the overall level of criminal justice contact, incarceration, and community supervision. Although in many cases relative disparities have not been reduced, these measures have had large effects on reducing absolute racial disparities, with little evidence across specific cases of an adverse effect on crime.

More targeted initiatives to reduce relative disparities—for example, through federal oversight, diversity hiring, anti-bias training, or quantitative risk assessment—have been less clearly effective. In part this is due to limitations of the research evidence, which should be further developed to effectively guide policy. The research and policy experience reviewed in this report has often involved piecemeal and uncoordinated reforms that have affected *racial disparity* at specific stages of criminal processing, but have had less effect on the *racial inequality* that emerges across stages and in community contexts of racial inequality. Reducing racial inequality must involve coordinated reforms across stages of the criminal justice system that will reduce the racial disadvantage that accumulates from police contact, to court processing and sentencing, to correctional supervision.

Reducing Racial Inequalities in Criminal Justice Outcomes

Although some jurisdictions have significantly reduced specific kinds of criminal justice contacts that have, in turn, reduced absolute disparities, wide racial inequality in the criminal justice system remains.

> RECOMMENDATION 8-1: **Subject to the main goals of parsimony and community safety, states, localities, and the federal government should explore ways to reduce police stops and searches, jail detention, prison admissions, and long sentences, which would further reduce racial disparities. Examples of such efforts could include limiting jail**

detention to only those charged with serious crimes who pose a serious and immediate risk of harm or flight, pursuing further drug sentencing reform, establishing second-look provisions for long sentences, eliminating revocations of community supervision for technical violations, and eliminating the death penalty.

RECOMMENDATION 8-2: Given evidence of how racial inequality in the criminal justice system partly results from structural inequalities in society and the cumulative effect of criminal processing, states, localities, and the federal government should explore reducing racial inequality through coordinated reforms that work across the stages of the criminal justice system and also address structural inequalities in society.

ENHANCING GRANT-MAKING STRUCTURES, DATA SYSTEMS, AND RESEARCH

The federal government has an important role in shaping the narrative around criminal justice reform efforts. The Department of Justice and similarly situated federal agencies with charges to support justice-involved populations should use their bully pulpit to disseminate findings about evidence-based programs that work to reduce racial and ethnic disparities, promote model jurisdictions implementing effective reforms, and highlight innovative solutions that could be tested, evaluated, and scaled. In doing so, they can emphasize that the pursuit of public safety requires addressing racial and ethnic disparities throughout the criminal justice system. To improve the grant-making process for communities, the report also highlights the need for enhanced performance measures, transparency mechanisms, and specified program areas while allowing for flexibility in some settings (Recommendation 9-1).

In the past decade, several private foundations have provided incentives, taken risks, seeded innovation, and added value to existing efforts in order to accelerate progress toward system reform. It is incumbent upon private organizations and the federal government to coordinate their activities so that investments can be used more effectively to reduce racial and ethnic disparities and promote public safety. The committee identifies the following three areas as ripe for federal and philanthropic support:

1. Research support to evaluate policies and programs for reducing racial inequalities;
2. Support to better address the needs of communities; and
3. A robust data infrastructure to monitor, track, and assess progress toward reducing racial inequalities in the criminal justice system.

RECOMMENDATION 10-1: Federal agencies and private foundations that support criminal justice research examining racial inequalities in the criminal justice system should draw upon the best available research—including quantitative, qualitative, and mixed methods—to maximize knowledge and avoid the problem of limiting scientific research where empirical methods are not possible or constrained by the lack of quantitative data.

Without a viable data infrastructure, researchers and policy makers will be unable to track, monitor, and evaluate the effectiveness of new policies and their effects on racial and ethnic disparities. To this end, this report outlines opportunities for building a data infrastructure that promotes integration across the criminal justice system and serves to better assess and support efforts to reduce racial inequalities. These efforts include improving the quality and consistency of reporting data on race and ethnicity.

CONCLUSION

The historical legacy of racial exclusion and structural inequalities in housing, education, and socio-political forces forms the social context for racial inequalities in crime and criminal justice. Enduring socio-economic inequalities in combination with inequalities in the criminal justice system together comprise a process of structural racism, involving a wide variety of mutually reinforcing and interacting institutional domains. While observed racial disparities in outcomes such as incarceration have declined in the past few decades, disparities persist, as do the enduring consequences of racial inequality in the criminal justice system.

This report highlights two evidence-informed approaches that are needed to eliminate racial inequities in crime and justice: (1) policy reform to the criminal justice system itself—reforms to law enforcement, courts, corrections, and community supervision; and (2) innovations outside the criminal justice system to support community-led efforts at safety as well as policy reforms to address racial inequality at the neighborhood level and within adjacent social policy institutions. Furthermore, reversing structural racism and severing the close connections among racial inequality, criminal harms such as violence, and criminal justice involvement will involve fostering local innovation and evaluation, and coordinating and consolidating local initiatives with state and federal leadership. The report synthesizes the evidence on community-based solutions, non-criminal policy interventions, and criminal justice reforms, charting a path toward the reduction of racial inequalities by minimizing harm in ways that also improve community safety.

1

Introduction

A vast body of research has documented large racial disparities at each stage of the criminal justice process. Black American, Hispanic, and Native American people have all been found to experience relatively high rates of arrest, pretrial detention, incarceration, and community supervision compared to White Americans. Over the past decade, 2010–2020, racial disparity in incarceration has declined for most racial and ethnic groups and the total prison population has shrunk, but large disparities remain in police contact, court involvement, and correctional supervision. At the same time, violence poses a significant risk to the health and well-being of those same communities. Since the COVID-19 pandemic began, there have been recent increases in violence nationally across communities of various sizes and locations—rural, suburban, and urban.[1] The weight of the increased violence has fallen disproportionately on racial and ethnic minorities, though White communities have experienced increases as well. The urgent need to address this recent violence is one of many aspects of reducing racial inequality in the criminal justice system, the main focus of this report, and begs the question of how to address public safety and increase community well-being while continuing to reduce racial disparities in the system.

Disproportionate contact with police, courts, and prisons indicates one way in which people of color have a distinctive relationship to the state that often involves being watched, incarcerated, or otherwise subject to

[1]Provisional data from the Centers for Disease Control and Prevention indicate that the recent increase in gun violence extended into 2021, as firearm-related homicide and suicide rates increased by 8.3 percent from 2020 (Simon et al., 2022).

government oversight. (Chapter 2 provides a detailed discussion of racial disparities throughout the criminal justice system.) While racial inequality marked the founding of the republic and permeates American social life—from health care and housing to education and employment—this report takes aim at a specific question: By drawing on historical, legal, and social science research, how can racial inequality in the criminal justice system be meaningfully reduced?

The problem of racial inequality in the criminal justice system has gained great urgency and attention over the last few years. Criminal justice reforms, often motivated by the goal of racial justice and the reduction of disparities (Cox, 2015), have been wide-ranging. At the state level, the National Center for State Legislatures reports that in 2020 alone, 36 states and the District of Columbia introduced more than 700 bills on police accountability, of which almost 100 were passed into law (Mintz, 2021). Incarceration has been another key focus of reforms. States and localities have curtailed cash bail, ended mandatory minimum sentences, and capped periods of community supervision. At the federal level, in 2021 the administration identified racial equity and criminal justice reform as an immediate priority.[2]

At this writing, following the tumult of a global pandemic, a dramatic rise in homicides and gun violence, the killings by police of George Floyd, Breonna Taylor, and many others, and subsequent protests against racial injustice, the committee takes this moment to infuse research evidence into public discourse and inform the current wave of public policy reform to address racial inequality in the criminal justice system and to advance racial equity.

THE COMMITTEE'S CHARGE

To this end, the Committee on Law and Justice of the National Academies of Sciences, Engineering, and Medicine convened an expert ad hoc committee to review and assess the research evidence on how racial inequalities in criminal justice might be reduced through public policy (see Box 1-1 for the committee's full statement of task). The Committee on Reducing Racial Inequalities in the Criminal Justice System was assembled to carry out this study and produce this consensus report. The committee included experts in the areas of criminology, criminal justice, law, sociology, public policy, political science, history, racial equity, and economics. Arnold Ventures, the Bill and Melinda Gates Foundation, The Joyce Foundation, the National Academy of Sciences Cecil and Ida Green Fund, the National Academy of Sciences W.K. Kellogg Fund, the Robert

---

[2]See https://www.whitehouse.gov/priorities

BOX 1-1
Statement of Task

An ad hoc committee of the National Academies of Sciences, Engineering, and Medicine will be appointed to review and assess existing evidence on how observed racial differences in criminal justice might be reduced through public policy. As appropriate, the committee will make evidence-driven policy and research recommendations for key criminal justice stakeholders with the ultimate goal of identifying ways to reduce racial disparities in the criminal justice system. The panel will examine:

1. What societal forces have given rise to current inequalities in criminal behavior, victimization, and criminal justice involvement? How effective are efforts to reduce racial differences in criminal justice involvement, criminal behavior, and victimization (e.g., through education, housing policy, employment initiatives, illicit drug intervention)?
2. How has the criminal justice system exacerbated racial inequality in the United States? How effective are efforts to reduce racial differences in criminal justice involvement (e.g., implicit bias training, bail reform policies, risk assessment tools, etc.)?
3. Which policies or approaches for reducing racial differences in crime and justice have suggestive evidence of effectiveness or appear promising but require further study? What areas of research and policy should scholars and practitioners explore to broaden the nation's options to address racial inequalities in the justice system?

Wood Johnson Foundation, the Russell Sage Foundation, and the William T. Grant Foundation provided support for the study.

In undertaking its charge, the committee was asked to inform "key criminal justice stakeholders," a group defined broadly to include a wide network of policy makers, local elected officials, law enforcement officers, state legislatures, court officials, data scientists and researchers, community-based organizations, and individuals and communities directly involved in the criminal justice system. To speak to this broad audience, the committee enlisted a broad array of perspectives and aimed to be forward looking. The report provides key principles and concepts for policy makers, researchers, community representatives, and practitioners to address longstanding racial inequalities in the criminal justice system.

STUDY APPROACH

While racial equity and criminal justice reform are now pressing topics of policy and public conversation, this report builds on the work of researchers, practitioners, and communities that have been striving in many ways to reduce racial inequalities in the criminal justice system for decades. Building on earlier work has meant reviewing and synthesizing diverse bodies of evidence to distil key findings concerning ways public policy can reduce these inequalities. The criminal justice system does not operate in a social vacuum. Criminal justice inequalities are produced in part by longstanding socioeconomic inequalities and cumulative, racially based disadvantages that emerge over the life course and across generations.

Given the complex and deeply rooted nature of racial inequality in the United States, the committee acknowledges the need to examine policy changes within the criminal justice system and to address broader social, economic, and environmental conditions that give rise to inequalities in criminal justice. Addressing racial inequalities will require examining changes in criminal justice policy and examining changes to social and economic policy as well. Given this context, the report encompasses reforms that can occur within the criminal justice system, as well as reforms to public policy that shape the social context in which law enforcement, courts, and prisons operate. The committee explores public policy topics that have a scientific evidentiary basis for addressing racial inequalities in crime and justice outcomes. For those areas in the broader social and economic policy domains, the committee synthesizes the available evidence but does not make recommendations (see Chapter 7).

COMMITTEE METHODOLOGY

The committee met and deliberated over the course of 18 months to address the questions presented in its charge and reach the conclusions and recommendations presented in this report. To augment its own expertise, the committee organized wide-ranging information-gathering activities to inform the consensus study process and address the statement of task.

The committee conducted an extensive critical review of the literature pertaining to racial inequalities in the criminal justice system. This review began with an English-language search of online databases, including ProQuest and HeinOnline. Committee members and project staff used online searches to identify additional literature and other resources. Attention was given to consensus and position statements issued by relevant experts and professional organizations. Research reports in peer-reviewed journals of the disciplines relevant to this study received priority. The report also builds on recent publications of the National Academies, including *The Growth of Incarceration in the United States: Exploring Causes and Consequences*; *Proactive Policing: Effects on Crime and Communities*; and *Decarcerating Correctional Facilities during COVID-19:*

Advancing Health, Equity, and Safety (the National Academies, 2020, 2018; NRC, 2014).

The committee also engaged perspectives from academic researchers, criminal justice system actors, community-based organizations and activists, and community members directly impacted by racial inequalities in the criminal justice system. To further its outreach, the committee received materials from the greater public for its consideration at meetings and public workshops and throughout the course of the study.[3] Additionally, a website was created to provide information to the public about the committee's work and to facilitate communication between the public and the committee.[4]

The committee undertook its work in two phases. Phase I consisted of six closed committee meetings, three public information-gathering sessions, three community listening sessions, and additional information-gathering calls with community members, experts, and stakeholders. The public information-gathering sessions were not intended to reflect the full range of expertise or approaches to reducing racial inequalities in the criminal justice system and were not a representative sample; rather, they were meant to augment the committee's own expertise, solicit opinions from community representatives and key stakeholders, and facilitate exchanges among parties that otherwise might not have the opportunity to disseminate information and ideas. They were open to the public and live-streamed online.

The first public information-gathering session was held in January 2021 and focused on community safety and policing. The committee heard from academics, law enforcement officers, county officials, and community activists on the history and contemporary contexts of policing, police reform and accountability, and community-driven safety strategies. The second public information-gathering session was held in March 2021 and focused on the drivers of criminal justice involvement to advance racial equity, with an emphasis on health and well-being, opportunity contexts and neighborhood conditions, and education and youth-serving systems. The third public information-gathering session was held in April 2021 and focused on data, courts, and systems of supervision. Experts spoke about data gaps and research perspectives, policies and practices in the court system that drive racial inequalities, levers for change, and different systems of supervision and their impacts. Following each public information-gathering session, a "Proceedings of a Workshop—in Brief" was published.[5] While

---

[3]Public access materials can be requested from claj@nas.edu

[4]See https://www.nationalacademies.org/our-work/reducing-racial-inequalities-in-the-criminal-justice-system

[5]See https://www.nationalacademies.org/our-work/reducing-racial-inequalities-in-the-criminal-justice-system#sectionPublications

Box 1-2 highlights themes that emerged from the public sessions, it should be noted that all communities are heterogeneous in their make-up and their needs, and one voice alone cannot fully represent the diversity of perspectives within a community of people.

BOX 1-2
Perspectives from Public Information-Gathering Sessions

The Committee on Reducing Racial Inequalities in the Criminal Justice System convened a series of information-gathering sessions in 2021 as part of its exploration of ways to reduce racial inequalities in criminal justice outcomes in the United States. The committee identified several themes from the perspectives presented across the sessions that were particularly applicable to the study charge:

- It is important to couple scientific data and evidence with the experiences and expertise of impacted communities to inform policy solutions;
- Solutions can emerge from community-driven and community-centered approaches. There is no single response appropriate for all circumstances; each community response is uniquely tailored for its members (the National Academies, 2021c);
- Transparency, oversight, and accountability of law enforcement agencies can repair harm in communities (the National Academies, 2021c);
- The criminal justice system can take a public health approach, which tends to be "non-blaming," by addressing individuals as people rather than victims and offenders (the National Academies, 2021a);
- There is an overwhelming focus of the criminal justice system on low-income communities and Black, Latino, and Native populations (the National Academies, 2021a);
- Intersectionality is an important organizing framework for incorporating the multiplicative effects of socially constructed identities into criminological theory and research, criminal justice policy evaluation, and crime analyses (the National Academies, 2021c; Murray and Eastwood, 1965); and
- The way racial inequalities in the criminal justice system are measured matters. There is a lack of consistent, reliable data as well as data transparency and accountability. There is a need for scientific infrastructure, research funding, and guidance on data collection and analysis to ensure that reforms are based in science (the National Academies, 2021c).

NOTES: This summary of perspectives is based on a factual accounting of what was presented at public information-gathering sessions for the committee's consideration. The public sessions were one mechanism that the committee used to gather information on the perspectives and experiences of communities that are disproportionately affected by racial inequalities in the criminal justice system, though the sessions did not feature a random representative sample of community members. The statements reflected here are those of the presenters and do not represent the views of the committee or the National Academies.

In the committee's information-gathering process, particular attention was given to those who have had contact with police, courts, and prisons, often as family members or neighbors, or through the direct experience of incarceration. Many communities—particularly those that have been historically marginalized—continue to feel disconnected from the research enterprise and often question the relevance of research to their lives (Barry et al., 2017). Those who would purportedly benefit from a study are rarely consulted for their diagnosis of the problem or for their assessments of what needs to be further understood and what interventions may be available. The committee's approach reflects a growing understanding on the part of the research community that the individuals and communities that have been arrested and incarcerated, or those with close proximity as neighbors and kin, have a distinctive kind of expertise that can enhance understanding and widen the policy conversation (Smith and Kinzel, 2021; Epperson and Pettus-Davis, 2015). In some cases, widening the conversation moves beyond meetings and consultations to include partnerships among practitioners, community representatives, and researchers, where all parties work to identify gaps, discuss challenges, and together create strategies and solutions (Sturm and Tae, 2017).

People who have direct experience of racial inequality in the criminal justice system often have a unique understanding of the problems and avenues for solutions. However, their voices are regularly left out of the decision making process for reform. The committee sought to elevate direct experience and community voice through listening sessions, where committee members joined with community representatives who described how they worked toward racial equity, the challenges they faced, data and research gaps, and how the criminal justice system has affected them and their communities. These community listening sessions included tribal and Indigenous communities, LGBTQ2S+ communities, and immigrant and undocumented communities.[6] Community listening session participants and their affiliations are listed in the Acknowledgments section of this report (see page vii). Additional information-gathering calls were held with criminal justice state officials, police executives working on criminal justice reform, and policy makers and groups, including the National Governors Association, the National Conference of State Legislatures, the National Association of Counties, and the National Center for State Courts.

Phase II of the committee's work focused on committee deliberations and the production of this report. It consisted of seven additional closed committee meetings from May 2021 through May 2022, a review of the

---

[6]LGBTQ2S+ is an acronym that stands for lesbian, gay, bisexual, transgender, queer or questioning, two-spirit, and other identities.

existing scientific literature and information related to the study's charge, and report writing.

KEY TERMS AND CONCEPTS

Since this report addresses disparities and inequalities based on racial status, it is important to clarify what is meant by race, inequality, disparity, and racism (see Box 1-3 for a list of brief definitions of these terms). Relatedly, the terms used to describe specific racial and ethnic groups in

BOX 1-3
Key Terms and Concepts

Race *is a social construct created through relations between groups (Perry, 2011; NRC, 2004b). Racial groups are therefore socially and historically constructed categories. Although socially constructed, race is nonetheless real in the sense that it is a central principle of social organization and a central axis of inequality in the United States (Bonilla-Silva, 1999). This report takes as its starting point the claim that racial categories are socially constructed but important in explaining the distribution of legal, material, social, and psychological advantage and disadvantage.*

Racial disparity *refers to group-based average differences in criminal justice outcomes. It is important to keep in mind that an average difference does not imply that all members of one group are more likely to experience an adverse outcome relative to another. It is also important to note that the existence of a disparity is simply a descriptive pattern and absent further analysis delivers no information as to the source of the disparity.*

Racial inequality *refers to group-based differential treatment or access to valued resources rooted in law and public policy as well as in individual behavior and institutional practices. Racial inequalities can result from multiple sources, including both historic and contemporary oppression, structural racism, and prejudice, whether or not intended.*

Racial discrimination *refers to the differential treatment of two people who are similarly situated but differ with respect to race. For example, a sentencing judge engages in racial discrimination if, when faced with a Black and a White defendant who both present identical facts, he or she treats one defendant unfavorably compared to the other.*

Structural racism *refers to a system in which historical and (or) contemporary public policies, institutional practices, cultural representations, and other norms work in different, often reinforcing ways to maintain or compound racial inequalities.*

this report defer to the data cited in the studies presented throughout the presentation of the evidence. The term "community" can refer to "any configuration of individuals, families, and groups whose values, characteristics, interests, geography, and/or social relations unite them in some way" (the National Academies, 2017, p. xxiii). For the purpose of this report, communities can refer to specific racial or ethnic groups or geographically defined communities, and the term is explicitly labeled as such when used. As language is constantly evolving, the key terms used throughout this report are offered with specificity, precision, and justice in mind.

Race

In the social science perspective, race is not a biological category but a social construct created through relations between groups (Haney López, 1994). Racial categories have shifted, historically, and racial identities have been the objects of political and legal conflicts. Nevertheless, while race is socially constructed, it is nonetheless real in the sense that it is a central principle of social organization and a central axis of inequality in the United States (Bonilla-Silva, 1999, 1997). This report therefore takes as its starting point the claim that racial categories are socially constructed but important in explaining the distribution of legal, material, social, and psychological advantage and disadvantage.

The theory of race as a social construction incorporates a rejection of earlier pseudo-scientific approaches that treated race as a biological category (Winant, 2000). In medicine and genetics, scientists continue to debate the validity and utility of race as a biological category. Researchers agree that there is greater genetic variation within racial groups than between them (American Anthropological Association, 1998). Some argue that race is still an important scientific category, pointing to genetic differences that correspond to socially constructed racial groups and potential implications of the difference for health and medicine (Akinyemi et al., 2021; Burchard et al., 2003). Others argue against the use of race as a scientific category because it reinforces the rejected notion that socially constructed racial categories are biologically real (Yudell et al., 2016; Yudell, 2014; Cooper et al., 2003). This debate has particular resonance in the criminal justice context because of research that seeks to identify genetic predispositions to behaviors that have been criminalized, from violence to addiction (Duster, 2004; Carey, 1994). Given the entrenched problem of racial inequality in the criminal justice system, scholars have argued persuasively that any potential benefit of adopting a biological model of race in behavioral genetics research is outweighed by the harm of entrenching racial stereotypes (Rothenberg and Wang, 2006). This report's focus, therefore, is on race as a descriptive measure of inequality, not on race as a biological explanation for criminal justice involvement.

Racialization is a discursive process in which a group is categorized as non-White, individuals are mapped into those groups, social and legal meanings are attached at the group level, and those meanings regulate access to or undergird a hierarchical distribution of freedom, power, land, and wealth (Omi and Winant, 2014; Haney López, 2006). Although race itself is not a natural or biological fact, biological characteristics (such as eye shape, skin color, and hair texture) are frequently, but not exclusively, used to categorize groups and map individuals. Race is an unstable and evolving concept (Omi and Winant, 2014). Neither the categories nor the mapping rules are static, so racial inequality may operate differently over time or across place. Viewed this way, race is a category that gains meaning only as it is used to mark inclusion and exclusion (Goldberg, 1992).

Race can overlap and become entangled with other concepts, such as ethnicity, ancestry, religion, and indigeneity. In sociology, race and ethnicity are distinct but related concepts. Race refers to social meanings attached to physical or biological characteristics and is often associated with ascribed identity. Ethnicity refers to cultural differences and is often associated with self-identification (Cornell and Hartmann, 2006). Ethnicity is also used to refer to subcategories within racial groups (Clair and Denis, 2015). This distinction between race and ethnicity can easily collapse once the shifting, flexible nature of racial categories is acknowledged (Eipper, 1983). For example, the number and description of racial and ethnic categories on the census have shifted over time, reflecting political, academic, and ideological changes (Hochschild and Powell, 2008). Cultural, linguistic, or religious differences have also been used to map people into racial categories and define the boundaries of those categories (Beydoun, 2014; Rolnick, 2011; Tehranian, 2000). The committee's broad understanding of race as a social construction encompasses the experiences of these groups, even if they may be described elsewhere in terms of ethnicity, culture, or nationality. On the other hand, some groups, such as Black Americans, are commonly labeled as racial groups and rarely categorized in any other way. The "race" label is no less socially constructed for those groups.

Data used to measure racial disparities in criminal justice reflect the racial categories created by decision makers, including U.S. Census categories and classifications created by local officials. This report relies heavily on federal criminal justice data, which employ the five census racial categories (American Indian/Alaska Native, Black or African American, Asian, Native Hawaiian and other Pacific Islander, and White). Some federal data sources rely on reports from local officials, who may use other classification systems or define categories in different ways.[7]

[7]In this report, we predominantly use the following terms: Black American, Latino, Native American, and White. However, where reporting demographic categories used in particular data sources, we use the terms used in the corresponding data source.

Due to the shifting nature of racial categories, the overlap between race and other concepts, and the practice by decision makers of ascribing race to a person based on visual cues, the data are often an imperfect reflection of how racial inequality actually operates. For example, Pacific Islanders have been classified in a variety of ways, potentially masking significant criminal justice disparities (Office of Hawaiian Affairs, 2010). Hispanic or Latino people may not be counted as a racial group at all because the census considers "Hispanic or Latino" an ethnicity, making it difficult to measure criminal justice disparities (Subramanian et al., 2018). Where the population of a particular group is relatively small, as happens with Native Americans in many states, they may not be included in the data at all. When the Native American population is counted, it is defined in different ways, presenting additional difficulties for measuring disparities (see Chapters 2 and 10; National Congress of American Indians, 2021).

Acknowledging and addressing racial inequality requires attention to variations within racial groups. Race interacts with gender, sexual orientation, socioeconomic status, and disability in a way that compounds inequality (Nanda, 2019; Crenshaw et al., 2015; Harris, 2000). Some groups experience racial inequality while also experiencing inequality along another axis, such as class, religion, or citizenship status. Capturing how these other categories intersect with race is difficult because datasets do not always measure other variables or do not capture how they overlap with race. Measuring disparities by race also obscures the problem of skin tone inequality, or colorism. Researchers have documented differences in stops, arrests, incarceration, sentence length, and imposition of the death penalty between darker phenotype Black Americans compared to lighter skinned Black Americans (Monk, 2022; Kizer, 2017; King and Johnson, 2016; Eberhardt et al., 2006). This is consistent with research documenting color discrimination in other areas, such an employment, school discipline, and jury selection (Harpalani, 2020; Norwood, 2014; Banks, 1999).

Racial Disparities and Inequality in Criminal Justice

Involvement in crime, victimization, and contact with the criminal justice system varies greatly from person to person, from place to place, and across demographic groups in the population. Differences, between men and women for example, usually tell us about group averages. Since individual experience varies—often greatly—around the average, group averages by themselves tell us little about specific characteristics of individuals. Instead, averages offer a way of describing the status of one group compared to another.

Racial differences in crime, victimization, and criminal justice contact have been a longstanding interest of policy makers, researchers, and the general public. For example, Black men are more likely to be arrested and incarcerated than White men relative to their representation in the population. This example rests on a benchmark comparison. In general, for any measurable outcome where information pertaining to race is recorded (e.g., arrest, pretrial detention conditional on arrest, jail and prison incarceration, police stops), researchers commonly measure group disparities against chosen benchmarks. Most often these benchmarks are population totals (for example, arrests per 100,000 and incarcerated per 100,000) for racial groups, sometimes cross-classified with demographic characteristics such as age and gender.

Racial disparities like these are descriptive statistics that are uninformative about their underlying causes. They are a kind of "warning light," an indicator that life conditions in the population may have diverged or perhaps that authorities are treating or responding differently to different groups. Group-based disparities, in other words, are merely a starting point for multifaceted investigation. In the view of the committee, research to date on racial disparities in the criminal justice system has often narrowly focused on just one institutional component, such as the courts or prisons. In the next section, we focus on the various ways disparities have been defined and interpreted. That is followed by a discussion of racial inequality, which we argue is a more general framework that encompasses and expands the explanation of racial disparities in criminal justice.

Disparity Definitions and Their Limitations

A comprehensive assessment of average racial disparities (or more generally, differences in underlying distributions of key outcomes conditional on race) requires consistent definitions and strategies, which to date have not commanded widespread consensus. Empirical research often focuses on the details of criminal justice practice with an eye toward understanding whether otherwise similar individuals experience differential treatment based on race. Such research also focuses on the extent to which certain practices disparately impact one group relative to another.

As noted above, for the purposes of this report, we define racial disparity in general terms as follows:

> ***Racial disparity*** *refers to group-based differences in average criminal justice outcomes (often called absolute disparity) or group-based ratios of average criminal justice outcomes (often called relative disparity).*[8]

[8]The term disparity is often used in the research literature to refer to what the committee has called "relative disparity," and the committee follows that general usage in the report. The committee refers to absolute disparity specifically to refer to a difference in rates, unless it is clear from the context. This is an important distinction because criminal justice reforms that decrease the overall reach of the system will have disproportionately positive impacts on affected populations even when relative disparities are not reduced.

The literature on racial disparities has focused largely on comparisons of Black and White Americans and outcomes measured at the various stages of criminal justice processing—including police stops, arrests, charges, bail decisions, prosecutions, findings of guilt, sentencing, incarceration, or parole. The dominant conceptual framework for studying racial disparity in specific kinds of criminal justice involvement seeks to divide disparity into two components: one component related to race differences in legally relevant factors including crime, and another component related to differential treatment by line officials (e.g., Beck and Blumstein, 2018; Tonry, 1997; and Blumstein, 1982, discuss this framework; Chapter 4 provides a more detailed account). Although there are significant practical challenges to estimating these quantities in empirical analysis, racial disparity attributable to crime is often described as legally justifiable or warranted, and the residual disparity, which may be due to racial discrimination by officials, has been described as unjustifiable or unwarranted (Spohn, 2015a).

From Disparity to Racial Inequality

Researchers have described race differences in criminal justice contact variously as "racial disproportionality" (Blumstein, 1982), "racial disproportion" (Tonry, 1994), "racial disparity" (Muller, 2012; Mauer, 2011a), and "disproportionate minority contact" (Piquero, 2008), but the statement of task asks the committee to address "racial inequalities in the criminal justice system." In the committee's view, "racial inequality" encompasses a broader range of processes than the research on racial disparity alone can identify. Racial inequality includes differences in criminal justice involvement that may be rooted in social structures of racial stratification outside the criminal justice system. Racial differences in criminal justice contact that are closely linked to the social structure of stratification may be sustained and amplified across the stages of criminal processing.

Racial stratification—including historic patterns of neighborhood segregation and differences in socioeconomic well-being—can be a cause of both involvement in crime and involvement in the criminal justice system. Individual experiences in the system can drive further racial inequalities. Racial inequalities in the criminal justice system are thus related to racial inequalities in society and may be produced cumulatively across the stages of criminal processing (see Chapters 3 and 4). From the perspective of understanding racial inequality, research on disparity should be complemented by examining the links among socioeconomic inequality, structural racism, crime, and criminal justice and by examining disparities across stages of criminal processing.

A vast body of research examines racial inequality that lies beyond crime and justice. Racial inequality in housing, education, the labor market, income, wealth, health, politics, and other areas is a documented fact of social life in the United States (see Chapter 3). A large literature also examines the criminogenic effects of socioeconomic inequality (see Burt et al., 2017; Peterson and Krivo, 2010; Sampson, 2009; Sampson and Wilson, 1995; Massey and Denton, 1993; Wilson, 1987). By these accounts, racial inequality outside the criminal justice system can lead to racial inequality in crime and system involvement. Furthermore, criminal justice involvement has been shown to lead to both increased inequality (see Pager, 2003; Western et al., 2001) and ongoing racial differences in criminal justice involvement (see McGlynn-Wright et al., 2022; Geller et al., 2014).

This report therefore uses the following definition and orienting framework:

> ***Racial inequality*** *refers to the combination of race-based differential treatment and unequal access to valued resources rooted in law, public policy, individual behavior, institutional practice, and social structures of segregation. Racial inequality is often the product of a number of mutually reinforcing social processes, including both historic and contemporary oppression, structural racism, and prejudice, whether or not intended.*

Racial inequality, in this framework, can lead to racial differences in criminal behavior, which may in turn contribute to legally justified disparities in criminal justice outcomes, such as incarceration. Racial inequality can also lead to a racially differentiated criminal justice response that includes differential treatment of the public both by line officers and by policy design. For example, command decisions about police deployment and tactics, prosecutorial policy, and the design of penal codes have all concentrated criminal justice attention on Black, Latino, and Native American communities.

Racial disparity in criminal justice involvement can also further contribute to social and economic racial inequality. Racial inequality also exists in a wide variety of domains, in addition to the criminal justice system, including neighborhoods, schools, and governmental agencies. A focus on racial inequality can help explain the racially varied relationships between the public and the criminal justice system that go beyond a focus on racial disparity in, say, incarceration or sentencing. Including racial inequality in the conceptual framework for examining the criminal justice system helps to move the analysis beyond a focus on racial disparity to include the following, for example:

- ***Burdensome policing*** *(sometimes referred to as "over-policing")—police action whose costs in terms of community experience and* *resources exceed any improvements in community safety; over-policing is a form of inequality measured by the lack of political efficacy, the abuse of civil rights and civil liberties, and harmful incentives;*

- ***Lack of police responsiveness**—a failure to act by police in a way that would improve community safety more than any costs to the community experience or resources; under-protection is a form of inequality reflecting police indifference, discrimination, inefficiency, and lack of political accountability; and*
- ***The War on Drugs**—a multipronged policy agenda dating from the 1960s and 1970s, which combined sentencing policy, enforcement, and prosecution for drug-related offenses concentrated in low-income Black and Latino neighborhoods, that confronted wide-spread and poorly treated problems of drug addiction.*

There are several advantages to studying race and the criminal justice system within this larger framework on inequality. First, the decomposition of racial disparities into differential offending and differential treatment is placed in a larger social context in which the social structure outside the criminal justice system may influence offending, differential treatment within the system, and criminal justice policy design.

Second, in the inequality framework, a reduction in disparity at a particular point may not reduce racial inequality in the broader community. Large racial inequalities in housing, jobs, and quality education can persist even if racial disparities in criminal justice contact are reduced. For example, while absolute racial disparity in imprisonment is highest in southern states compared to those in the Northeast, relative disparities are sometimes lower due to harsher sentencing in the South for both Black and White people not because of less overall racial inequality in socio-economic outcomes (C. Muller, 2021, 2012; Crutchfield et al.,1994). In short, the task of reducing racial inequality is distinct from that of reducing racial disparity at a particular stage of the criminal justice system. Understanding racial inequality may also involve multiple levels of analysis and a variety of data sources including historical, anthropological, and qualitative evidence. The analysis of racial inequality may also motivate new systems of data collection for monitoring racial inequalities in criminal justice and assessing efforts at ameliorating those inequalities.

Structural Racism

The term "racism" has often been reserved to describe individual dispositions linked to a belief in racial stereotypes and anti-Black sentiment. Thus, survey researchers have designed scales to measure racism among individual respondents (NRC, 2004b), and psychologists have designed experiments to detect racial bias among research subjects, including members of law enforcement (see, for example, Geller et al., 2021; Eberhardt et al., 2004). For this research, belief, sentiment, and cognition operate at the individual level to drive decision making and other behavior in a direction that is harmful to non-White people. The discussion of racial inequality indicates that social organization (in neighborhoods, families, or markets, for example) and institutions are often patterned in a way that is harmful to non-White people, even in the absence of widespread individual-level racism. Scholars have described this configuration of social relations as "structural racism." While quantitative social science has traditionally focused on understanding these situational levels of racism, an examination of broader notions of structural racism is also critical to inform policymaking (Prowse and Goff, 2022).

"Structure" in this context conveys a set of social processes in which "causation is understood as cumulative within and across domains. It is a product of reciprocal and mutual interactions within and between institutions" (Powell, 2008, p. 796). Some scholars emphasize the historical character of structural racism in which "whiteness, a privileged racial category justified by negative racist stereotypes, [is] passed down from generation to generation, so as to become acceptable, normal, and part of the public common sense" (Marable, 2001, p. 13; see also Rucker and Richeson, 2021).

Whereas racial inequality describes (perhaps enduring and multidimensional) group-based differences, structural racism attributes such inequality to social organization and institutions. Against this background, structural racism is defined as the operation of race as an organizing social force to enact, codify, or enable the oppression of one or more groups. Once a society becomes racialized, invidious racial distinctions affect "social relations and practices" at "all societal levels" (Bonilla-Silva, 1997). Structural racism is not defined by individual bigotry, prejudice, or discrimination but rather is based on how social, economic, and political institutions of government and civil society are organized by law, policy, practice, and norms. In this way, the argument that posits structural racism as a force contends that the inequalities by race occur specifically because of social and institutional factors that perpetuate racial inequality.

Understanding the historical roots of structural racism is crucial to recognizing its effects today and how it has evolved over time (Glenn, 2015; Harris, 1993). Structural racism is reflected in the distribution of political power, economic wealth, material conditions, and equal access to, or fair treatment by, social systems over time, from housing to health care and, in particular, the criminal justice system (see below; Feagin and Elias, 2013). These impacts are, however, neither linear nor constant. Since laws change and social forces are dynamic, shifting with politics, demographics, economics, and social movements, structural racism has evolved over time.

Structural racism is built into policies and practices and does not depend on individual racial animus or discrimination, though racial animus or discrimination may also be intended. A classic example of structural racism is the passage of voter disenfranchisement laws after the passage of the Fifteenth Amendment. Laws establishing poll taxes, literacy tests, and grandfather clauses disproportionately excluded Black men from registering and casting a vote (Manza and Uggen, 2006). Though written in race-neutral language, these laws produced large racial disparities in voter participation between White men and Black men.

These disparities, as we understand today, were the evidence and mechanism for the problem of racial inequality resulting, for Black people, in second-class citizenship and an extremely low level of democratic participation for much of the 20th century. The Voting Rights Act of 1965 was a second attempt to address the structural racism of racially neutral disenfranchisement laws. Later policies, such as partisan redistricting or voter identification restrictions, continued to entrench the status quo of Black disenfranchisement. Thus, structural racism encompasses both those neutral policies that are motivated by racist intent and those that reinforce racial hierarchies resulting from past intentional racism, regardless of motivation (Roithmayr, 2014).

Contemporary scholars view racial inequality as largely structural, cumulatively generated through the mutual and reciprocal interaction of institutions (Ray, 2019; Sampson, 2012; Powell, 2008; Williams and Collins, 2001; Wilson, 1987). The mechanisms of structural racism today can be (although they are not always) found in an array of public policies such as zoning laws, the pricing of goods and service, as well as credit risk scoring to limit access to loans or rental housing (using income, zip codes, and arrest records). Still, it is often the case that contemporary forms of structural racism can be traced back to racially exclusive or racially targeted policies and practices of earlier moments in history. The National Academies noted the following in a 2017 report on racial health disparities:

> Though inequities may occur on the basis of socioeconomic status, gender and other facts, we illustrate these points through the lens of racism, in part because disparities based on race and ethnicity remain the most persistent and difficult to address (Williams and Mohammed, 2009). Racial factors play an important role in structuring socioeconomic disparities (Farmer and Ferraro, 2005); therefore, addressing socioeconomic factors without addressing racism is unlikely to remedy these inequities (Kaufman, et al., 1997, p. 104)

For the purpose of this report, the primary populations of focus with respect to racial inequalities in crime and justice are Black, Latino, and Native American populations. These are the racial and ethnic groups where the committee finds the most evidence connecting mechanisms of structural racism and history to racially disparate outcomes in crime and criminal justice system involvement. Where applicable, other populations or distinct subgroups, such as Asian Americans or immigrants, are discussed in subsequent chapters.

HISTORICAL ROOTS OF RACIAL INEQUALITY IN CRIME AND JUSTICE

To elaborate on structural racism in the criminal justice system, the persistent racial and ethnic disparities in crime and justice that are documented in this report can be better understood when placed in historical context. This section briefly recounts the historical evidence of U.S. policies that created and maintained surveillance, policing, and punitive incapacitation of various racialized populations. Indian wars, removal, and dispossession were the foundations of early American policies of land acquisition as European colonizers and later settlers moved westward people of Mexican ancestry and Indigenous tribes, whose presence on or possession of land and property lay in the path of White people, and who were often defined as savages or bandits by nature and criminal by law or custom (Hernández, 2017).

Colonial and Antebellum America

Since the origins of modern American policing and imprisonment, Indigenous people and Black people—free, enslaved, and self-emancipated—have consistently been the targets of unique forms of policing and confinement (Schrader, 2019; Hernández, 2017; Camp, 2016).

Historian John Grenier, in his study of the first wars against Native populations, found that colonial leaders empowered non-military White men as rangers to destroy Indigenous villages, fields, and food supplies. According to Grenier:

> Successive generations of Americans, both soldiers and civilians, made the killing of Indian men, women, and children a defining element of their first military tradition and thereby part of a shared American identity. Indeed, only after seventeenth- and early eighteenth-century Americans made the first way of war a key to being a White American could later generations of "Indian haters," men like Andrew Jackson, turn the Indian wars into "race wars." (Grenier, 2005)

With violence came a culture of impunity such that even when settlers or military personnel murdered innocent people, as in the Sand Creek massacre near Fort Lyon in southeastern Colorado in the winter of 1864, no one was prosecuted. By the second half of the 19th century, after two million square miles of land had been taken from them, Indigenous populations increasingly faced incarceration on reservations and in boarding schools—where children were forcibly removed from parents. The first of the boarding schools was Carlisle Indian Industrial School in Pennsylvania, which opened in 1879 and was modeled on the Fort Marion military prison (Dunbar-Ortiz, 2014).

In the 17th and 18th centuries, slave codes emerged across the 13 colonies to regulate the lives and labor of Black and Indigenous people. A Massachusetts Act in 1703 imposed a curfew for Indian, Black, and Mulatto[9] slaves and servants after 9:00 p.m. unless on special errand. A 1730 New York slave code prohibited any socializing of groups:

> No Negro, Mulatto, or Indian Slaves, above the Number of three, do Assemble or meet together on the Lords Day Called Sunday, and Sport, Play or Make a Noise or Disturbance, or at any Other time at any place from their Masters service within this City. (Osgood et al., 1905, p. 79)

Many of these codes, such as the South Carolina Slave Act of 1722, authorized the deputization of all White male citizens to police Black people and Indians (Hadden, 2003, p. 21). "Controlling slaves was one of the major purposes of the criminal justice system," as Samuel Walker wrote in his comprehensive history of American criminal justice (Walker, 1998, p. 24).

Jails and prisons in the southern United States also emerged as critical mechanisms to reinforce the institution of slavery, though few enslaved women and men interacted with the formal criminal justice system (Henderson, 2016; Johnson, 2013).

In colonial New England, settlers organized early law enforcement bodies known as Indian Constables to monitor Native Americans and protect White residents from their possible retaliation. By the early 19th century, police forces had emerged in St. Louis (MO) and other frontier cities for this purpose (Hadden, 2003; Rousey, 1996).

In the antebellum South, patrols made up of White citizens had legal authority over Black people (Hinton and Cook, 2021; Hadden, 2003). Armed White men of various socioeconomic backgrounds policed the areas

---

[9]Mulatto is defined by the Jim Crow Museum as "the first general offspring of a black and white parent; or, an individual with both white and black ancestors. Generally, mulattoes are light-skinned, though dark enough to be excluded from the white race." For more context see https://www.ferris.edu/HTMLS/news/jimcrow/mulatto/homepage.htm

surrounding plantations and supplemented the general surveillance sustained by overseers, slaveholding families, and local officials. Any person of African descent in the slave states who appeared to be outside of the control of a White master and failed to otherwise prove their free status could be seized and imprisoned by nearly any capable White civilian (Hadden, 2003). Charged with the responsibilities of slave management, insurrection suppression, and the maintenance of White racial and social order, slave patrollers served as the pre-modern predecessors for law enforcement practices that have shaped American history.

From the early Republic to the Civil War, slave patrols enforced planters' control over the personhood and labor of their slaves by maintaining three primary duties: raiding slave dwellings looking for weapons and educational contraband, dispersing slave gatherings, and patrolling the areas around plantations and towns to apprehend suspects for cruel and corporal punishment (Hadden, 2003). Patrollers tended to concentrate these tasks at the largest plantations, where it was easier to monitor slaves and where slaveholders' power was concentrated at the county level. As a result, the wealthiest slaveholders single-handedly molded the legal and penal system of the slave South by giving civilian patrollers enforcement authority (Schwarz, 1988).

Although most law enforcement and criminal justice institutions were idiosyncratic and decentralized during the antebellum period, law-and-order systems in the southern, western, and northern free-state regions of the United States were all tightly bound to the enforcement of slavery, especially after the passage of the federal Fugitive Slave Act of 1850. County sheriffs and town constables in the North operated similarly to slave patrols and militiamen in the South in order to quell mob uprisings and enforce a rigid "community ethos" of law and order based on strict moral guidelines that largely embodied the religious views and social expectations of the majority (Walker, 1998).

The Civil War and Its Aftermath

The mass criminalization of Black Americans profoundly shaped new developments of structural racism within the criminal justice system in the century between the end of the Civil War and the enactment of the Civil Rights Act of 1965. The only exception to this was the brief decade of Reconstruction, when Black elected officials, alongside White Republicans and the Freedmen's Bureau's federal agents, provided a measure of civil protection.

Following the emancipation of four million slaves, in 1865 and 1866, the former Confederate legislatures quickly enacted a new set of laws known as the Black Codes to maintain racial hierarchy. The Black Codes functioned to restore the power of former slaveholders to limit the economic independence of the formerly enslaved. Southern planters sought to reassert control over, and recapture the returns to, Black labor that they lost as a result of the Civil War. Although the Black Codes did recognize the new legal status of Black Americans under the provisions of the 13th Amendment, which extended the right to marry, enter contracts, and receive other basic legal entitlements, in most states these newly freedpeople could not vote, own arms, or testify in court without risk of racial violence. Local criminal systems enforced this racial hierarchy directly by criminalizing and punishing Black people and indirectly by failing to investigate or punish White civilians who committed violent crimes against Black victims (Hadden, 2003).

Across several former Confederate states, new vagrancy laws criminalized Black unemployment as well as the right to quit. When Black workers refused to work under abusive or exploitative conditions, their choice to pursue work elsewhere exposed them to arrest for vagrancy. In South Carolina, for example, Black Americans were prohibited from selling crops without permission from a White person. In Louisiana, newly freedpeople could publicly assemble only between sunrise and sunset. In Maryland, interracial marriage carried a penalty of seven years of servitude for both parties. In Florida, any person of color who "intruded" on a gathering of White citizens, or who even fell in the proximity of White residents in public, could be charged with a misdemeanor with a punishment of 39 lashes (Laws in Relation to Freedmen).

Moreover, criminal justice policies during this period disproportionately victimized Black youth, women, and families (Haley, 2016; Chatelain, 2015; Chavez-Garcia, 2012; Ward, 2012; Hicks, 2010; McGuire, 2010; Gross, 2006). Plantation owners turned to the Black Codes to reclaim the labor of Black youth, frequently accusing parents of being unfit. Vagrancy laws at the center of the Black Codes compelled newly freed men, women, and children to either enter into contracts with White employers as punishment or risk entering a system of incarceration administered by private industry, known as the convict lease system.

Congress repealed the Black Codes with the Civil Rights Act of 1866 and, later, with the citizenship, due process, and equal protection clauses of the 14th Amendment. However, southern slave states continued to implement statutes that gave rise to mass criminalization of Black Americans immediately after Reconstruction through convict leasing, which was allowed explicitly by the 13th Amendment. The convict lease system allowed planters to continue to control Black labor after slavery. Although a small percentage of Black southerners served as convict laborers, the southern criminal justice system functioned as a coercive regime to compel people to accept exploitative labor contracts and limited freedom as citizens. As the titles of two seminal books on the subject suggest, for Black Americans during this period the New South's punitive regime was "Worse Than Slavery" or could be called "Slavery by Another Name."

Moreover, the gradual abolition of slavery in northern states during the first half of the 19th century coincided with the birth of the modern penitentiary (McLennan, 2008; Rothman, 1971). Black Americans have suffered disparate rates of confinement from the very beginnings of imprisonment in America. At Newgate, the first state prison in New York, 25 percent of those confined between 1797 and 1828 were of African descent, even though free Black people only accounted for roughly 12 percent of the state's population. In Philadelphia (PA), home in 1816 to the largest community of free Black people in the nation at about 15 percent of the city's total population, 43 percent of the men and women incarcerated in the city's penitentiary at that time were identified as Negro or Mulatto (Mishler, 2016; Nash, 1988).

The Progressive Era to World War II

During the Progressive period of the early 20th century, criminal laws, policing practices, and legal-cultural customs increasingly targeted Black Americans. The entrenchment of Jim Crow laws before, during, and after Prohibition unleashed new mechanisms for spatial regulation and social control at the federal and local levels that subsequently compromised Black social and physical mobility, economic opportunity, and life prospects (Haley, 2016; Muhammad, 2010; Gross, 2006). Northern authorities frequently turned to jails and prisons as a means to control "undesirable" groups and, in the process, maintain public order as increasing numbers of Black Americans migrated from the rural south (Adler, 2019; Balto, 2019; Hernández, 2017; Gross, 2006).

The period also saw sustained collective violence leveled at Black communities throughout the South. Most vividly reflected in the statistics on lynching, a sustained campaign of terror was conducted through mob violence and a White criminal justice system. Estimates of anti-Black lynchings in the United States between Reconstruction and World War II range between four and five thousand, based on new archival discoveries and research efforts to revise the work of sociologists Stewart Tolnay and E.M. Beck (Tolnay and Beck, 1995). While the vast majority of documented lynchings against Black Americans occurred in southern states, recent research has found that such lynchings occurred in at least 33 states between 1883 and 1941, far surpassing the boundaries of the former Confederacy (Seguin and Rigby, 2019).

This form of racial violence and terror was directed not only at Black Americans but also at people of Mexican ancestry as well as Chinese immigrants and Native Americans (see Pfeifer, 2021). Estimates of the number of known anti-Mexican lynchings range widely, from 71 to 600, and they occurred primarily in the southwestern states of Arizona, California, New Mexico, and Texas (Seguin and Rigby, 2019; Martinez, 2018; Carrigan and Webb, 2013). Nevertheless, the circumstances of vigilante violence directed at Mexicans were comparable to the violence directed toward Black Americans. In both cases there are no known cases of prosecution for what often amounted to mob killings committed in broad daylight, in public venues, or with community consent such that the perpetrators were known and often heralded. Additionally, criminal justice actors often abided the mob, or refused to protect the victim from impending violence, or were unwilling to identify, arrest, or prosecute the killers. In the case of Mexican nationals, many of whom were ranchers and prominent landowners, the Texas Rangers were directly involved in some unlawful killings (Martinez, 2018; Carrigan and Webb, 2013).

Economic hardship and a climate of violence and terror were potent forces for Black migration. Muller (2012) found that the non-White population of the South fell by 3.2 million from 1870 to 1950. Muller's research shows that the migration of southern Black people to industrial centers in the Northeast and the Midwest was closely associated with a gradual widening of the racial disparity in imprisonment through the first half of the 20th century. In 1880, census data show that native-born non-White people were about 2.5 times more likely to be imprisoned than native-born White people. That racial disparity increased in each of the following decades, so that by 1950 the imprisonment rate of native-born non-White people exceeded that of White people by a ratio of 5:1. The largest increase in disparity was found in cities of the Northeast and Midwest.

Historians who have tracked the migration of racialized minorities in the 20th century have described how police regulated the boundaries of Black and Mexican-American citizenship, mobility, and political organizing (Balto, 2019; Thompson, 2010; Mumford, 2008; Biondi, 2003; Escobar, 1999). In a recent study of police contact among Black youth, for example, Carl Suddler (2019) details certain tactics found in New York City that date back to the 1930s that he calls "heightened surveillance." These encounters both inflated crime rates and "triggered racial antagonisms," which led Black youth to view police as a "repressive, unworthy authority" (Muhammad, n.d.).

As millions of Black Americans continued to migrate from southern farms and cities to northern and western cities, police surveillance, harassment, and violence intensified and often accompanied White vigilante violence. Blue-ribbon commissions studied racialized police brutality; for example, the *Negro in Chicago* riot report issued in 1922 found systemic evidence of discrimination by police and court officials. Additional commissions that covered discriminatory policing and violence were convened in

Harlem in 1935 and 1943, among others. These reports presented systemic evidence of structural racism in the criminal justice system before the War on Crime and the War on Drugs began in the 1960s and 1970s.

Given the importance of these latter developments, after the Civil Rights movement ended, to understanding the historical and social roots of structural racism in the criminal justice system and given the historically unprecedented use of incarceration beginning in the 1970s, these more recent historical forces will be discussed in greater detail in Chapters 4 and 5 of this report. Taken together, this historical context sets the stage for understanding the current state of the criminal justice system in the United States and its relationship to Black, Latino, and Native American communities.

THE CRIMINAL JUSTICE SYSTEM IN THE 21ST CENTURY

The criminal justice system is "not a monolithic, or even consistent, system": "[e]very village, town, county, city, and State has its own criminal justice system, and there is a Federal one as well. All of them operate somewhat alike. No two of them operate precisely alike" (President's Commission on Law Enforcement and Administration of Justice, 1967, p. 7). This description of the system appeared in the 1967 report *The Challenge of Crime in a Free Society*.[10] Over a half-century later, elements of this description still hold true. At the same time, there are also important differences between the criminal justice systems of the 1960s and the criminal justice systems of today that help to explain how system responses to crimes and misdemeanors drive racial inequality in the 21st century.

As is discussed in Chapter 9, federal involvement in criminal justice systems is greater today than it was 50 years ago; the federal system has grown alongside the federal government's increased investment in state and local systems; the reach of the state and local systems, where the bulk of what is described as "criminal justice" takes place, is more expansive; and even as concerns about the quality of data persist, criminal justice systems are far more integrated, collaborative, and technology-dependent than they were 50 years ago.

Today's federal system includes approximately 132,000 full-time federal law enforcement officers employed by 83 federal agencies, not including the U.S. Armed Forces, the Central Intelligence Agency, or the Transportation Security Administration. This number is dwarfed by the number of law enforcement agencies and agents in states and on tribal lands. The Bureau of Justice Statistics reports that there are nearly 18,000 state, county, and local law enforcement agencies in the United States with over a million total

[10] See https://www.ojp.gov/ncjrs/virtual-library/abstracts/challenge-crime-free-society

full-time employees, two-thirds of whom are sworn officers (Banks et al., 2016). There are also over 570 American Indian/Alaska Native tribes, with roughly half having formal criminal court systems that are partially funded by federal allocations pursuant to the United States' treaty and trust obligations and a greater number with traditional justice systems. In 2020, there were a reported "1,833 state prisons, 110 federal prisons, 1,772 juvenile correctional facilities, 3,134 local jails, 218 immigration detention facilities, and 80 Indian Country jails as well as military prisons, civil commitment centers, state psychiatric hospitals, and prisons in the U.S. territories" (Sawyer and Wagner, 2020, p. 1).

Criminal justice systems are also more deeply embedded in communities than they were 50 years ago. Criminal justice actors, including police officers and probation and parole officers, are entrenched in neighborhoods and schools (Shedd, 2015), and the use of new technologies like ankle monitors and on-the-spot drug testing has brought the system directly into the homes of people under correctional control. The concentrated visible presence of law enforcement along with the concentration of incarceration and community corrections among historically disadvantaged populations reinforces divisions between White and Black space in ways that are consequential for how people encounter and experience criminal justice in the 21st century (Anderson, 2022, 2015; Bell, 2020a).

Reuben Miller's research on reentry draws our attention to how restrictions that bar returning citizens (i.e., those under community supervision) from housing, employment, educational opportunity, and other social supports disparately impact Black men and, in turn, widen racial inequality in outcomes (Miller, 2021).

Moreover, viral videos of incidents with law enforcement like the one experienced by Christopher Cooper bring attention to the ways law enforcement may be deployed in a biased manner and to the way anti-Black racism can be aligned with attitudes about belonging, the law, and citizenship that structure the criminal justice system today. Sociologist Elijah Anderson describes this as the "provisional status" of Black people, as Black people are burdened with proving that they are law-abiding citizens and belong in a "white space" (Anderson, 2015).

ADDRESSING RACIAL INEQUALITIES THROUGH PUBLIC POLICY

Given this history and contemporary context, the question of how to address racial inequalities in the criminal justice system looms large. The social determinants of health framework, widely accepted in the scientific literature today, is a framework used to combat racial inequalities in the unequal risk of poor health outcomes, the lack of access to health care, and differential treatment by health care providers. Public health researchers understand that these are all to varying degrees outcomes of a racially stratified society rooted in historical and material conditions that remain imminently salient in the health care system itself (Jones, 2002). Change means fixing how the health care system works in relation to an unequal society. Identifying the mechanisms that drive racial inequality as a form of structural racism can help ensure that the policy or practice solutions are designed at an appropriate institutional or systemic level rather than at the individual level. It is this understanding that animates the committee's interpretation of its task and informs its recommendations for reducing racial inequalities in the criminal justice system through public policy.

Along with the preceding discussions of the terms of racial analysis and the way history informs our definitions, the social science of racial bias provides additional insight and also helps to explain why any attempt to reduce racial inequalities in the criminal justice system by addressing structural racism or moving away from punishment approaches to delinquency (and crime) is exceedingly difficult. (See Box 1-4 for a more thorough discussion of the psychological science of bias.)

Social psychologists recognize the role of "sociostructural forces in creating and maintaining racial bias and biased outcomes" (Richeson, 2018; see also Richeson and Sommers, 2016). This means that commitments to egalitarian values are not necessarily inconsistent with behaviors that support structural racism. The body of research explaining these behaviors, known as Aversive Racism Theory, demonstrates that White people who do not hold explicitly racist views can nevertheless behave in ways that reinforce the racist systems they oppose (see, e.g., Dovidio and Gaertner, 2004; Dovidio et al., 2002; McConnell and Leibold, 2001). Another theory that seeks to explain the continued existence of commitments to hierarchy that support racial inequality is Social Dominance Theory, a comprehensive conceptual framework that seeks to explain how group-based social hierarchies (not exclusively race-based ones) are maintained through individual and institutional discrimination. This latter theory posits that members of socially dominant groups will legitimize and maintain their dominance by supporting policies that reinforce their group advantage, seeking out social roles where they can police the interests of their group status (including, importantly, working as police officers) and engage in both overt and discrete acts of discrimination against nondominant groups (Sidanius et al., 1994; Sidanius, 1993).

Taken together, the prevailing understanding of these theories today is that they are natural as opposed to pathological. That is, behaviors and policy choices are driven by ongoing socio-structural forces and, indeed, by the history of structural racism itself. This means that eradicating the formal indicia of discrimination and racism in law would not inherently be adequate to break down those forces built over time (as shown in

BOX 1-4
The Psychological Science of Bias

A previous National Academies report on proactive policing summarized the psychological science of bias, which is excerpted in the following (the National Academies, 2018, pp. 284–286).

> Across the literature, what social psychologists define as "threats to self-concept" tend to produce biased responses when: (1) the threat is in a domain that is important (Branscombe et al., 1999; Fein and Spencer, 1997); (2) a stigmatized individual is an appropriate target for negative behavior (Richeson and Sommers, 2016; Goff et al., 2008; Frantz et al., 2004); and (3) negative behavior does not violate anti-racist norms (Dovidio et al., 2017; Dovidio, 2001). For instance, in experimental laboratory studies, researchers have demonstrated that the mere presence of a stigmatized group member often causes White participants to experience concerns with appearing racist (Shelton and Richeson, 2014, 2006, 2005; Richeson and Shelton, 2012, 2007; Trawalter et al., 2009; Goff et al., 2008; Shelton et al., 2006; Vorauer and Kumhyr, 2001; Vorauer et al., 2000, 1998). Subsequently, this concern predicts social distancing behaviors (Goff et al., 2008), negative evaluations of interracial interactions (Vorauer et al.,1998), and even negative evaluations of stigmatized group members (Frantz et al., 2004).
>
> More broadly, psychology has identified robust sets of dispositional (individual characteristics) and situational (related to the environment) factors that are associated with higher levels of racially biased behavior. A dispositional risk factor for bias is a relatively enduring personal trait that puts an individual at risk of biased behavior. For example, social dominance orientation measures individuals' support for hierarchies that disadvantage members of lower social strata; individuals who self-report higher levels of social dominance orientation are more likely to engage in biased behavior (Sidanius and Pratto, 1999).

Chapter 8 discusses the role of bias and bias interventions in the context of the criminal justice system.

the previous section). Historian Khalil Muhammad offers an example of this phenomenon by demonstrating how, in the period spanning the post-Reconstruction period to the 1960s, growing racial disparity coincided with a "statistical discourse" about the idea of "black crime" in the popular and political imagination. Reinforced by social science data, this discourse cast Black people as a uniquely dangerous and law-breaking group and justified the expansion of the U.S. prison system, sustained harsh sentencing practices, informed decisions surrounding capital punishment, and sanctioned racial profiling in general. Scholars, policy makers, and reformers analyzed the disparate rates of arrests of Black Americans and incarceration as empirical "proof" of the "criminal nature" of Black Americans. These statistical measures deeply informed ongoing national debates about racial differences and steered the politics of reform in the first half of the 20th century (Muhammad, 2010; Du Bois, 1899). While the problem of crime among poor White and immigrant communities was also concerning to elected officials and academics, accepted explanations of their deviance framed the problem as a socioeconomic issue, not a biological trait. By World War II, Irish, Italian, Polish, Jewish, and other European ethnic groups in the United States had shed these criminal associations, but the view of criminality as an inherent problem among citizens of African descent has long endured (Muhammad, 2010).

This history informs and contextualizes nearly 80 years of psychological research documenting stereotypical association in the United States between Black people and criminality well beyond the passage of legal structures designed to address formal discrimination. The advent of subconscious-processing research has taken this work a step further—even *thinking* about people who are Black can lead to thoughts of crime and to split-second misapprehensions of their behavior as more suspicious and more dangerous (Correll et al., 2007; Payne et al., 2002; Payne, 2001). Likewise, thinking about crime and violence (primed subconsciously with an image of a gun) can lead to thinking about Black people (Eberhardt et al., 2004). The research base on these associations for other groups is not as extensive, but, again, the long history of differential treatment of Latino and Native American groups, combined with conceptual frameworks such as Social Dominance Theory and Aversive Racism Theory, leads to the hypothesis that disrupting these dynamics would be extremely difficult without large policy investments.

The committee thus recognizes the historical antecedents that have created structures of inequality by race that may override personal and psychological orientations, but also that biases are examples of the enduring effects of racism that result in racial inequalities in criminal justice. It is necessary to address the structural factors that are endemic and driving forces behind differences in criminal behavior, criminal justice discretion, and policy choices on how to respond to crime. Racial inequalities in violence and lethal criminal justice contacts are tied to historical and social processes of racial exclusion that manifest today (see Chapter 3), and given this, remedies must include the social drivers of crime and criminal justice inequalities (see Chapter 7).

Relatedly, reducing racial inequality in the criminal justice system also holds the promise of improving safety from the harms of interpersonal violence and from the harms of policing and incarceration, which cycle to further reinforce social drivers of crime and criminal justice inequalities. In short, instead of a tradeoff between racial inequality and crime, the committee finds that reducing racial inequality can reduce crime and improve safety. Minimizing the overall harms from crime, including harms that result from society's responses to crime, expands the toolkit of criminal justice responses beyond retribution, deterrence, and incapacitation to include victim restoration, prevention through improved community relations, attention to unmet needs, and cross-system coordination beyond criminal justice agencies.

Given the large presence of the criminal justice system in minority communities, minimizing criminal and system harms would disproportionately impact Black, Latino, and Native American communities, and likely reduce disparities in system involvement and victimization. This understanding informs the committee's approach—which is also framed by the constitutional idea of parsimony (the minimal use of the state's power of coercion)—emphasizing two main strategies for reducing racial inequality in the criminal justice system: (1) by reducing the scope of criminal justice contact and (2) by reducing the disparate impacts of policy and differential treatment (see Chapter 8).

REPORT ORGANIZATION

The committee's report is organized into two parts: Part I sets the stage by exploring the causes and the nature of racial inequalities in the criminal justice system (Chapters 1–4). Chapter 2 documents key trends in racial and ethnic disparities across criminal victimization, offending, police contact and arrest, charging and sentencing, and community supervision. Chapter 3 explores the social drivers of racial inequalities in the criminal justice system, and Chapter 4 discusses the drivers of inequalities at each major decision point within the criminal system. Together, these chapters describe the nature, magnitude, and drivers of racial inequality in the criminal justice system as well as the role of historical legacies of slavery and settler colonialism, social-political forces, and criminal justice policies and practices in creating and maintaining racial inequalities.

Part II discusses how to address racial inequalities through social and criminal justice policy (Chapters 5–10). Chapter 5 introduces Part II of the report with a case example of civil rights, socialization, and the federal response to crime. Chapter 6 identifies and examines community-driven approaches to enhance safety and reduce harm. Chapter 7 delves into noncriminal policy approaches, including interventions in ancillary institutions that can interact with the criminal justice system to either perpetuate or mitigate racial inequalities. Chapter 8 synthesizes the evidence on reforms to the current criminal system and assesses their potential to reduce racial and ethnic disparities. Chapter 9 highlights the role of the federal government in grant making and supporting communities to promote safety and to reduce inequalities in crime and justice. Finally, Chapter 10 describes challenges and opportunities to enhance data systems to better identify and monitor racial disparities in criminal justice system involvement.

2

Racial Disparities in Victimization, Offending, and Involvement with the Criminal Justice System

Experiences with crime and the criminal justice system differ greatly by race and ethnicity in the United States. Whether one measures differences in victimization, in serious criminal offending, in homicide clearance, in being stopped by the police, in arrest rates, in pretrial detention, or in representation within the populations of those under community supervision, sentenced to jail, or sentenced to prison, in each case a clear racial hierarchy emerges. Crime and criminal justice outcomes are often worse for members of the nation's racial and ethnic minority groups, especially for African Americans. These differential outcomes are closely connected to structural racism across multiple domains in society.

Victimization rates show clear racial disparities. American Indian people and African Americans are the most likely to be victimized by serious violent offenses, followed by Hispanic people and, finally, by non-Hispanic White and Asian people. While inter-racial disparities in nonlethal violent victimization have narrowed considerably over the past decade, racial disparities in murder rates remain stubbornly high, with the murder rate for African Americans relative to other groups increasing sharply during the 2020 pandemic. Disparities and trends in disparities in property crime victimization are qualitatively similar. There are also racial/ethnic disparities in offending rates and arrest rates, with arrests for serious felonies higher among African Americans and to a lesser extent Hispanic people as compared to White people.

Explanations for observed disparities in victimization, criminal offending, and criminal justice involvement often focus on sources of structural socioeconomic inequality, including differences in neighborhood conditions, exposure to concentrated disadvantage, personal poverty, and other measures of socioeconomic status. To illustrate disparities in one such measure, Figure 2-1 displays patterns of poverty according to the proportion of a neighborhood's residents that are poor, using data for 2019, for the entire United States. The figure presents separate distributions for members of different racial/ethnic groups, ordered from groups with the highest average neighborhood poverty rates to those with the lowest average rates. It reveals large differences experienced by different racial and ethnic groups, with concentrated poverty particularly high in areas where African Americans, American Indian people, and Hispanic people disproportionately reside. Prior studies attempting to assess the degree to which racial disparities in victimization and offending are attributable to systematic inequality tend to find that inter-group differences in neighborhood characteristics, personal poverty, and exposure to high-risk peers explain a substantial part of Black/White disparities and often all Hispanic-White disparities (Light and Ulmer, 2016; Krivo and Peterson, 1996). See Chapter 3 for a fuller discussion. Later chapters further explore research on the socioeconomic determinants of the inter-racial/ethnic disparities in victimization and involvement with criminal justice.

In this chapter, we document the current levels of racial disparities in these outcomes as well as trends over recent decades. First, the chapter documents racial differences in victimization, offending, and arrests. It then discusses what is known about how police behavior as well as patterns of interaction between police and different communities may contribute to the observed disparities. After exploring data on public safety and policing, the chapter discusses racial disparities in criminal justice outcomes that reflect processes that occur after individuals are arrested. It documents racial disparities in time served in jail while cases are being resolved before documenting racial disparities in rates of imprisonment. It also addresses racial disparities in charging, plea bargaining, and sentencing, paying specific attention to historical and continuing disparities in death sentences and executions.

Finally, the chapter documents racial differences in rates of community supervision (i.e., probation or parole supervision), noting that a growing body of evidence suggests that, in many jurisdictions, probation and parole supervision do little to help the formerly incarcerated and recently convicted establish steady employment and stable housing while making great efforts to find technical reasons to re-incarcerate those under supervision. Throughout, we focus on careful documentation of existing disparities and trends and document evidence that the racial bias exhibited by some police officers, prosecutors, probation officers, parole officers, and other state actors in the criminal justice system contributes to these disparities.

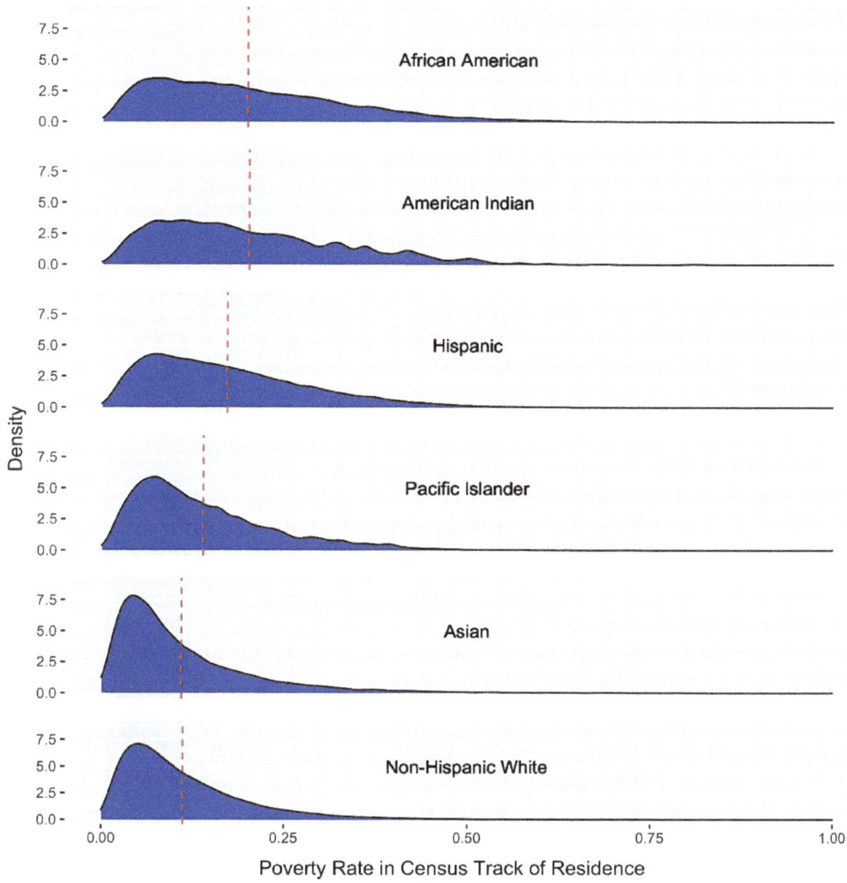

FIGURE 2-1 Distribution of all U.S. residents across census tracks classified by the proportion of residents who are poor, by race and ethnicity, during the 2015–2019 period.
NOTE: The dashed line indicates the proportion of poor in the neighborhood of the average resident.
SOURCE: Tabulations from the 2019 American Community Survey summary files, https://www.census.gov/programs-surveys/acs/data.html

Of course, the information presented in this chapter is necessarily incomplete. For example, if police agencies report crime rates separately by race and by gender, but not also by race and gender combined, it is difficult to track offending by and victimization against women of color disaggregated from those rates for men in the same racial group or for women overall. Similarly, detailed data are routinely reported for certain decision points (e.g., pretrial detention and death sentences) but not for others (e.g., diversion and informal processing), so the data give an incomplete picture of the points in the system where racial disparities occur.

Moreover, research on racial disparities is heavily focused on Black versus White; there is comparatively little research documenting and analyzing disparities faced by other racial groups. This is due to both researcher focus and data availability. American Indians and Pacific Islanders, in particular, are often left out of reported data even though the little available information suggests they face significant disparities in violent victimization, police encounters, and incarceration. Some of this data invisibility is due to small overall population numbers. American Indian people are one to two percent of the national population (their share increased to 2.9% in the 2020 census) and one to two percent of the population in most states. Observable disparities show up in states and localities with larger concentrations of American Indians but may not show up in national datasets. Another problem is inconsistency in how racial categories are defined and reported, a problem that is discussed in further detail in Chapter 10.

VICTIMIZATION

There are two principal measures of crime in the United States. First, the Uniform Crime Reporting (UCR) program relies on the reporting of crimes to individual police agencies, which subsequently report them in summary form to the Federal Bureau of Investigation (FBI). Second, the U.S. Census Bureau in conjunction with the U.S. Bureau of Justice Statistics (BJS) conduct the annual National Crime Victimization Survey (NCVS), which each year asks a representative sample of U.S. residents about criminal offenses they have experienced in the past year, including contextual information regarding the nature of the offense; whether the offense was reported to the police; and for violent offenses, characteristics of the person perpetrating the crime. Both sources tend to focus on more serious offenses, often referred to as Part 1 felony offenses (sometimes referred to as index crimes), though data pertaining to less serious offenses such as simple assaults and low-value larcenies (both offenses often charged as misdemeanors) are also collected.

Geographic variation in violent and property crime rates as measured in the UCR data has shown higher crime rates in urban areas relative to suburban areas, a positive correlation between the proportion of a jurisdiction's residents that are racial and ethnic minorities and crime rates, and a positive correlation between the proportion of residents who are poor and crime rates (Kneebone and Raphael, 2011). However, this research has also demonstrated that over the past three decades the strength of these associations has weakened considerably, as have the differences in crime rates between urban and suburban cities.

To focus more precisely on differences in victimization, in the subsequent sections we analyze data that allow us to identify the race/ethnicity of specific crime victims. The NCVS allows us to document inter-group differences in victimization for serious offenses using large-scale surveys of victims. In addition, we use data from the Supplementary Homicide Reports (a separate data series produced under the FBI UCR program) to study differences in murder rates.

First, we present data on property crimes and nonlethal violent crimes, and then we discuss homicide victimization. In doing so, we find clear racial disparities in victimization rates: American Indians and African Americans are the most likely to be victimized by serious violent offenses, followed by Hispanic people and last of all by non-Hispanic White and Asian people. While inter-racial disparities in nonlethal violent victimization have narrowed considerably over the past decade, racial disparities in murder rates remain large and some have grown wider, with the murder rate for African Americans relative to other groups increasing sharply during the 2020 pandemic. Disparities and trends in disparities in property crime victimization are qualitatively similar.

Property and Nonlethal Violent Crimes

Table 2-1 and Table 2-2 present property crime and violent crime victimization rates, respectively. The tables combine the 2012 through 2019 NCVS surveys to increase the sample size with an eye on generating more accurate estimates for smaller groups. The NCVS asks respondents about property crime experienced by anyone in their entire household (burglary, motor vehicle theft, other theft), so property crime victimization rates are typically reported as the number of incidents per 1,000 households. We use the race/ethnicity of the household head to classify the race/ethnicity of the household, acknowledging that race/ethnicity may vary within households. Violent crime victimizations are measured for all household members ages 12 and older; thus, violent crime victimization rates are measured as the number of incidents per 1,000 individuals.

Table 2-1 reveals that the lowest property crime victimization rates are among Asian/Pacific Islander and White households, and the highest rates are among American Indian and multi-racial households. Black households experience an overall property crime rate that is roughly 1.14 times that among White households, while Hispanic households experience an overall rate that is 1.28 times that among White households. The largest proportional disparities occur for motor vehicle theft, though this crime occurs relatively infrequently relative to home burglaries and other thefts.

Table 2-2 presents estimates for violent crime victimization rates. The NCVS defines serious nonlethal violent offenses to include the offenses of

TABLE 2-1 Property Crime Victimizations per 1,000 Households by Race/Ethnicity of the Household Head, All Offenses Occurring 2012 through 2019

	All Property Offenses	Burglary	Motor Vehicle Theft	Other Theft
White	111.8	21.2	3.4	87.2
Black	127.0	29.4	6.0	91.6
Amer. Ind./Aleut.	246.1	64.9	10.1	171.2
Asian/PI	85.1	12.7	4.0	68.4
More than one race	270.8	57.5	9.4	203.9
Hispanic	143.4	24.8	7.9	110.8

NOTE: The race/ethnicity categories used in this table are mutually exclusive.
SOURCE: Figures are tabulated from the concatenated National Crime Victimization Survey files, https://doi.org/10.3886/ICPSR38136.v1

TABLE 2-2 Serious Violent Crime Victimizations per 1,000 by Race/Ethnicity, All Offenses Occurring 2012 through 2019

	All Serious Violent Offenses	Rape	Robbery	Aggravated Assault
White	6.8	1.5	1.8	3.5
Black	8.9	1.0	3.4	4.5
Amer. Ind./Aleut.	16.5	3.8	6.6	6.1
Asian/PI	4.5	1.2	1.6	1.7
More than one race	22.8	6.9	5.6	10.4
Hispanic	8.6	1.4	3.0	4.2

NOTE: The race/ethnicity categories used in this table are mutually exclusive.
SOURCE: Figures are tabulated from the concatenated National Crime Victimization Survey files, https://doi.org/10.3886/ICPSR38136.v1

rape, robbery, and aggravated assault. American Indians and those classified as multi-racial experience by far the highest victimization rates for these offenses, with American Indian women having a uniquely high rate of sexual victimization. For example, among American Indians the number of rapes per 1,000 is more than double the number among White people, the robbery rate is more than triple the rate among White people, and the aggravated assault rate is 1.74 times the rate among White people. Black and Hispanic respondents experience higher rates of robbery and aggravated assault relative to White respondents as well, though the differences are smaller than those observed for Native Americans. Asian respondents experience the lowest violent crime victimization rates.[1] While most violent victimization is intra-racial, violent victimization of American Indians—including sexual violence—is more likely to be inter-racial.

Homicide Victimization

Figure 2-2 presents the national homicide rate for 1990 through 2020. Overall, the U.S. murder rate has declined considerably from a peak rate during that period of 9.8 per 100,000 in 1991 to the pre-pandemic level of five per 100,000 in 2019. The rate fell by more than a third during the late 1990s and fell roughly 20 percent between 2006 and 2014 before jumping up sharply between 2014 and 2016. However, the homicide rate increased by almost 30 percent between 2019 and 2020 to reach a high point for the 21st century.

Several sources of early counts suggest that homicide rates have stabilized at these higher levels. Rosenfeld and Lopez (2021) study 22 cities and find that homicide rates continued to increase during the first three quarters of 2021. Overall, they find that between the first nine months of 2020 and the first nine months of 2021, homicide rates in these cities increased by four percent. The FBI has posted preliminary homicide counts for 2021 for roughly 170 cities with populations over 100,000; the total population in these cities equals roughly 49 million. The population-weighted murder rate in these cities increased by one-tenth of one percentage point between 2020 and 2021.[2]

Table 2-3 presents homicide victimization rates by race and sex for 1990, 2000, 2010, and 2015. Men drive the racial differences in these rates. White and Asian people face the lowest risk of death from homicide, and for these groups the ratio of male-to-female homicide victimization rates is never more than 3:1 from 1990 forward. However, among Black people, Native Americans, and Hispanic people the rates of homicide victimization are higher, and the ratio of male-to-female rates is always above three; among Black people this ratio is roughly 5:1 or greater in every year.

In all racial groups, we see noteworthy declines in homicide victimization rates between 1990 and 2010 for both men and women. Among men, these rates fell by more than one-third within each racial group, and these steep proportional declines within all racial groups greatly diminished racial

[1]For both property and violent crime victimization rates, Black/White and Hispanic-White differences were much smaller in the 2010s than in the 1990s.

[2]These figures are based on tabulations of the FBI quarterly reports; see https://crime-data-explorer.fr.cloud.gov/pages/explorer/crime/quarterly

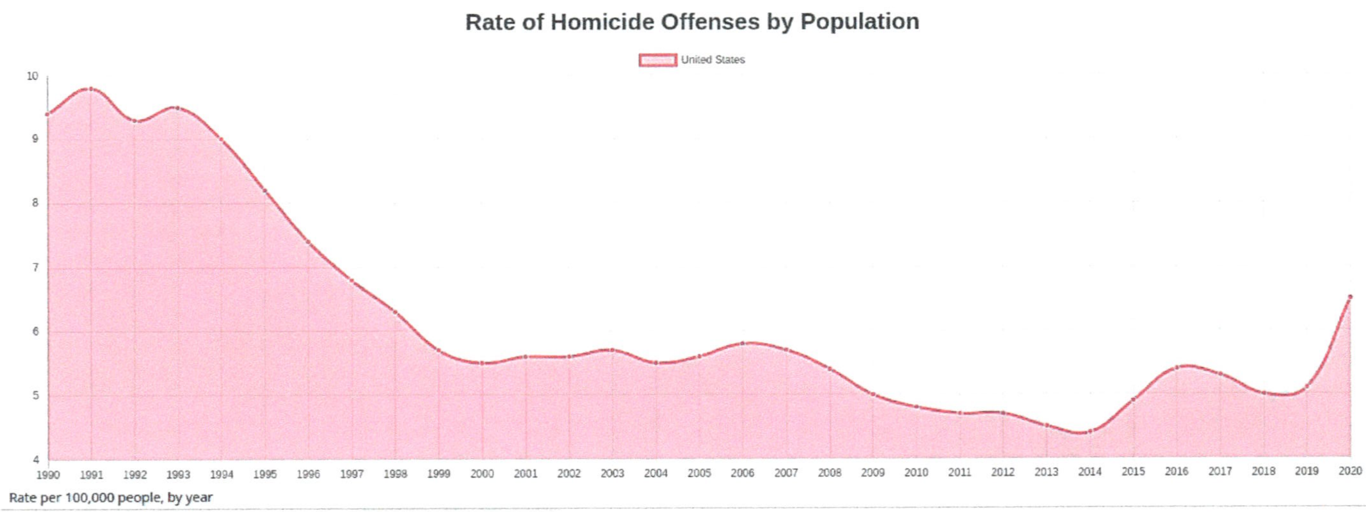

FIGURE 2-2 Rate of homicide offenses by population, 1990–2020.
SOURCE: Data from Federal Bureau of Investigation, Crime Data Explorer, https://crime-data-explorer.app.cloud.gov/pages/explorer/crime/crime-trend

TABLE 2-3 Homicide Rates for Males and Females, by Race (Age-Adjusted), 1990, 2000, 2010, 2015

Homicide Rates for Males by Race (Age-Adjusted)				
	1990	2000	2010	2015
White	5.6	3.6	3.3	3.6
Black	63.1	35.4	31.5	35.4
Native American	16.7	10.7	8.8	9.8
Asian	4.3	2.6	2.2	2.3
Hispanic	27.4	11.8	8.7	7.9
Homicide Rates for Females by Race (Age-Adjusted)				
	1990	2000	2010	2015
White	2.5	1.9	1.8	1.7
Black	12.5	7.1	5.0	4.9
Native American	4.6	3.0	2.5	2.5
Asian	2.8	1.7	1.2	1.0
Hispanic	4.3	2.8	1.8	1.8

NOTE: White is defined as White and not-Hispanic.
SOURCE: Data from National Center for Health Statistics, http://www.cdc.gov/nchs/hus/contents2016.htm#029

gaps in rates of homicide victimization. We see similar patterns among women, but the changes in these racial gaps are much less dramatic.

Nonetheless, Black men remain an outlier. In 2015, the Black/White ratio in homicide victimization rates was 9.8. This ratio is lower than the corresponding ratio for 1990 but higher than the ratio in 2010. Data from the Centers for Disease Control and Prevention (CDC) show that this increase can be attributed to a large jump in homicide victimization rates among Black men between 2014 and 2015 (from 30.6 to 35.4). It appears that the spike in the overall homicide rate between 2014 and 2016, which Figure 2-2 documents, involved a relative surge in homicide victimization among Black men. In 2014, the rates for Black and White men, respectively, were 30.6 and 3.3. Between 2014 and 2015, these rates rose to 35.4 and 3.6, which were also the rates in 2000. What this means is that in a single year, 14 years of declines in the Black/White gap in homicide victimization rates among men were reversed.

The most recent data on homicide victimization demonstrate two facts concerning the recent increase in homicide rates: (1) the increases were broad-based geographically, with similar patterns observed across the country, and (2) the increases were extremely concentrated among specific demographic groups. Table 2-4 presents data from the CDC Underlying Causes of Death file on homicide rates for 2019 and 2020 by gender, race, and ethnicity for five states: California, Florida, Illinois, New York, and Texas. While homicide levels vary considerably across states, we observe similar inter-group disparities within state and year as well as similar relative patterns of increase between 2019 and 2020. Within year and state, homicide victimization rates for males are multiple times those for females,

TABLE 2-4 Homicides per 100,000 by Race, Gender, and Hispanic Origin, 2019 and 2020 for Select States

Panel A: Non-Hispanic Black

	Male		Female	
	2019	2020	2019	2020
California	35.0	48.8	4.5	7.2
Florida	37.4	43.6	5.0	6.2
Illinois	69.8	104.3	8.4	11.2
New York	20.5	34.6	2.7	4.0
Texas	32.5	42.2	5.0	7.1

Panel B: Non-Hispanic White

	Male		Female	
	2019	2020	2019	2020
California	3.4	4.5	1.5	1.5
Florida	4.4	4.6	2.1	2.4
Illinois	2.7	2.5	1.5	1.0
New York	1.2	1.8	1.0	0.7
Texas	4.8	6.0	2.0	2.9

Panel C: Hispanic

	Male		Female	
	2019	2020	2019	2020
California	9.1	12.2	1.5	1.8
Florida	6.0	7.0	2.4	2.0
Illinois	8.9	15.1	-	-
New York	5.6	8.6	1.6	1.6
Texas	8.2	10.3	2.0	2.4

NOTE: Homicide rates are not reported for Hispanic women in Illinois by CDC due to small number of cases and lack of reliability.
SOURCE: Data from the Underlying Causes of Death 1999–2020 dataset and downloaded through a query from the CDC Wonder data tool, http://wonder.cdc.gov/ucd-icd10.html

and there are enormous racial/ethnic disparities. African American males experience the highest homicide rates by far for all states, followed by Hispanic males, and then African American females. Between 2019 and 2020 very large increases occurred in homicide victimization rates that were concentrated among African Americans, with especially large increases among Black males.

Murder rates are much higher in cities than in rural areas, and both Black and Hispanic citizens are overrepresented in urban centers relative to rural areas. Thus, the recent sharp rise in murder rates in U.S. cities may generate growing racial disparities in homicide victimization over time. Figure 2-3 shows that there are enormous differences in murder rates across cities, but since 2019 murder rates have grown in the vast majority of cities. Figure 2-3 presents a scatter plot of the 2020 murder rates against the 2019 murder rates for large cities (populations over 100,000) included in the most recent quarterly crime reports published by the FBI. The solid black line shows coordinates where the y-axis value equals the x-axis value. Hence, points above the line display cities where the homicide rate has increased, while points below the line display cities where the homicide rate has decreased. The blue line fits the observed relationship between city-level murder rates in these two years.

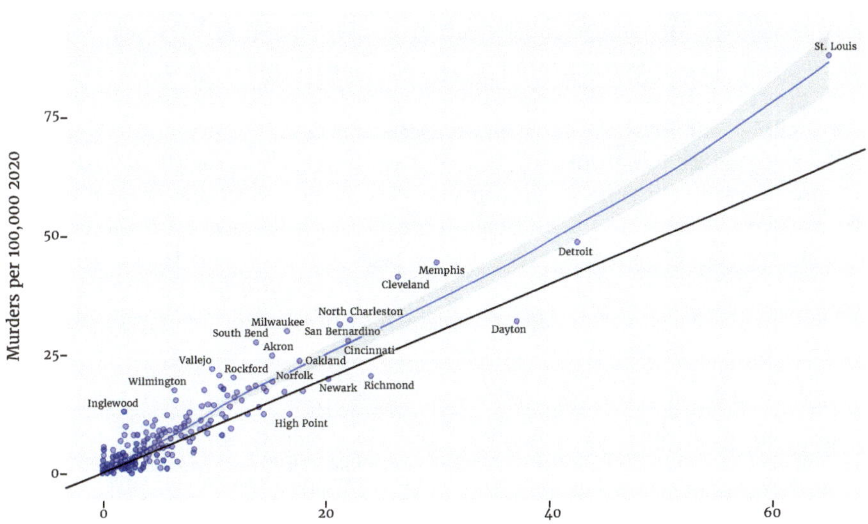

FIGURE 2-3 Scatter plot of 2020 murder rates against 2019 murder rates for cities with more than 100,000 residents in the Federal Bureau of Investigation's (FBI's) Quarterly Crime Report data.

SOURCE: Tabulations from the FBI Quarterly Crime Reports, https://crime-data-explorer.app.cloud.gov/pages/explorer/crime/quarterly

Several patterns stand out. First, the rise in the murder rate between 2019 and 2020 is broad-based, with most points lying above the black line. Second, the increases appear to be larger in cities that were already suffering from high murder rates. Third, while most cities have murder rates in both years below 10 per 100,000, there is a cluster of cities with extremely high murder rates by both national as well as international standards.[3]

In sum, racial and ethnic minority groups experience higher victimization rates in the United States. With the exception of homicide victimization, racial disparities in victimization have narrowed considerably over the past three decades. However, American Indians continue to face higher levels of violent victimization compared to all other groups. Racial disparities in murder rates have grown since 2010, including during the periods when overall homicide rates rose sharply, from 2014 to 2016 and again from 2019 to the present.

DIFFERENCES IN ARRESTS AND CRIMINAL OFFENDING

Arrest rates are consistently higher among African Americans than among other racial and ethnic groups. While these disparately higher rates may reflect differences in baseline offending rates by group (see Chapter 4), they may also be partly due to differences in enforcement, driven for example by greater police deployment in minority neighborhoods or by differential treatment of African American suspects by police. Several researchers have demonstrated that there are higher numbers of police per capita in cities with larger minority populations (Chen et al., 2022; Carmichael and Kent, 2014; Stults and Baumer, 2007). Moreover, Chen and colleagues (2022) demonstrate that within cities, officers spend disproportionate amounts of time in predominantly Black census blocks, relative to the population density and to limited measures of location-specific criminal activity.[4] Such differential exposure to policing may lead to higher arrest rates in minority neighborhoods relative to arrest rates for comparable behavior in White neighborhoods (see Chapter 4).

[3]The World Bank collects homicide data from around the world to facilitate international comparisons. While the data are incomplete and do not contain values for all years (often reporting the most recent complete year for a nation), the highest recorded value is for El Salvador (measured in 2018) with a murder rate of 52 per 100,000. The two other northern triangle Central American countries had murder rates in 2018 of 39 (in Honduras) and 23 (in Guatemala). Note that these are among the highest national murder rates in the world. See https://data.worldbank.org/indicator/VC.IHR.PSRC.P5?most_recent_value_desc=true

[4]Specifically, Chen and colleagues (2022) condition on distance to the nearest homicide in 2016 and total homicide by census block in addition to a number of other measures of block-level socioeconomic status and proxies for social cohesion. They still find a partial correlation with racial composition.

At the same time, clearance rates—the rates at which offenses are solved by an arrest or the identification of the offender via some other means—are *lower* for serious crimes that involve Black victims. To the extent that crimes are committed within race, these lower clearance rates may signal that, at least for some crimes, arrest rates understate the relative Black offending rates.

This section reviews the data on racial disparities in arrests. While we discuss disparities across racial and ethnic groups, we pay particular attention to evidence that high arrest rates in Black communities may reflect forms of over-policing and that, for some crimes, low clearance rates suggest that police are failing to provide accountability in Black communities. The number of stops by police in African American communities often appears to be greater than one would expect given the high relative proportions of stops that end with no more than a warning and the often-lower search discovery rates associated with these stops, providing evidence that minority communities are over-policed.

However, arrest rate differentials reveal very large disparities across groups in arrests for the most serious felony offenses, with the offense disparities aligning more closely with disparities in offender race as perceived by surveyed crime victims. African Americans are overrepresented among those arrested for Part 1 felony offenses. American Indian people are also overrepresented among arrests, though this largely reflects arrest disparities for less serious offenses.[5] Further, overall levels of violence by police against African American citizens are higher than expected given levels of contact with police. Added to this, we also find evidence that minority communities are under-protected, with data on clearance rates suggesting that serious crimes committed and reported in African American communities often going unsolved.

Moreover, American Indians are most heavily overrepresented in arrests for a handful of nonviolent, mostly alcohol- and drug-related offenses. When understood in context with the relatively high rates of detention and incarceration in this population, a picture emerges of Native people coming into the system at the front end for low-level offenses but being treated more punitively at the back end.

Several studies find evidence of either a differential likelihood of contact or a difference in the nature of contact with law enforcement, holding

---

[5]For example, using detailed arrest data by race/ethnicity and offense from the FBI for 2019 (https://ucr.fbi.gov/crime-in-the-u.s/2019/crime-in-the-u.s.-2019/tables/table-43) and population totals from the U.S. Census Bureau for 2019 (https://www.census.gov/newsroom/press-kits/2020/population-estimates-detailed.html), we tabulate that the numbers of arrests per 100,000 for drunkenness or disorderly conduct (both non-index offenses) stand at 669.7 for American Indians, 218.5 for African Americans, and 118.7 for White people. As a percentage of total arrests, arrests for these two categories account for 6.3 percent of White arrests, 5.4 percent of Black arrests, and 17 percent of American Indian arrests.

constant underlying behaviors. In a juvenile justice context, Crutchfield and colleagues (2012) find that African American eighth graders are nearly twice as likely to have contact with police as White eighth graders, a difference that is only partly explained by differences in self-reported criminal conduct. Raphael and Rozo (2019) find that arrests of Black youth are more likely (than arrests of other youth) to result in a formal booking as opposed to an informal disposition (e.g., counseling and a call to the parents), holding charges constant.

Disparities in arrest rates may be driven by (1) racial disparities in baseline offending rates, (2) disparities in reports to the police by the race of the perpetrator, (3) disparities in the arrest probability conditional on having committed an offense (i.e., members of one group more likely to get a pass relative to members of another group), and (4) disparities in the likelihood that an innocent person is arrested for something they did not do. Rather than disentangling these underlying contributors, prior efforts to assess the relative contributions to arrest rate disparities of differential offending rates as opposed to the other possible contributing factors have relied on comparisons of victim reports to official arrests. For example, Beck (2021) demonstrates that African Americans are overrepresented among people arrested for serious nonfatal violent offenses, comprising 12.5 percent of the resident population and 36.1 percent of arrests for nonfatal felony person offenses (33% if simple assaults are included). Beck also finds that while African Americans account for 28.9 percent of offenders as reported by victims, they constitute roughly 35 percent of offenses reported to the police, reflecting a higher likelihood that offenses where the perpetrator is perceived to be African American are officially recorded (Beck, 2021). Hence, comparisons of arrest compositions to results from victimization surveys suggest that both race disparities in offending as well as disparities in the likelihood of reporting contribute to differences in officially recorded arrests. Such comparisons are not possible for property offenses nor for drug offenses, as there are no victim reports that one could use to benchmark the racial composition of offenders.

Arrests

To examine patterns in arrests by race it is useful to see arrest rates broken down by offense category as well as race over a substantial period. Figure 2-4 presents arrests per 100,000 persons by race for the years 1980 through 2019.[6] The figure presents separate time series for adult index violent

[6]Tabulations from the Office of Juvenile Justice and Delinquency Prevention arrest tool; see https://www.ojjdp.gov/ojstatbb/crime/ucr_trend.asp?table_in=. The UCR arrest data do not present separate tabulations for Hispanic arrests.

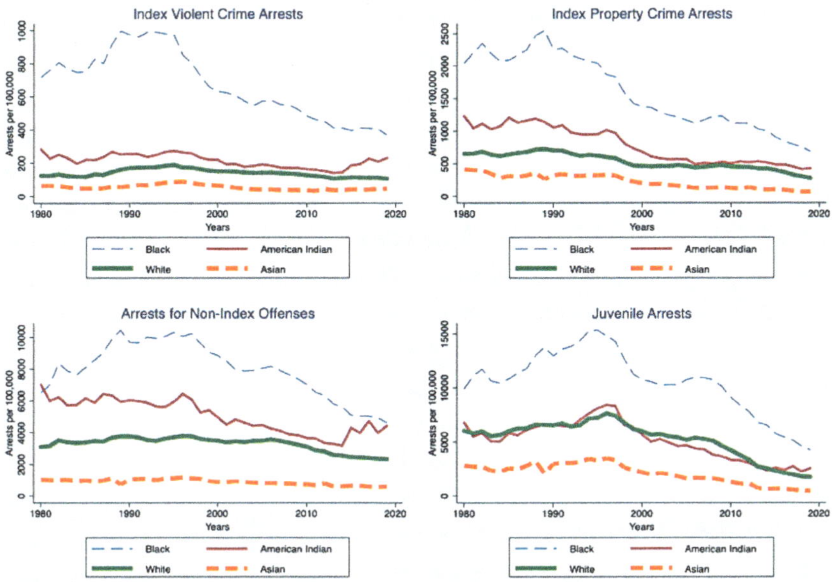

FIGURE 2-4 Trends in arrest rates by race for index violent offense, property offense, non-index crimes, and juvenile arrests, 1980–2020.
SOURCE: Data from Office of Juvenile Justice and Delinquency Prevention Statistical Briefing Book. Trends in the number of arrests by race for all offenses. Released on July 08, 2022. https://www.ojjdp.gov/ojstatbb/crime/ucr_trend.asp?table_in=2

offenses (murder, rape, robbery, and aggravated assault), adult index property offenses (burglary, larceny, motor vehicle theft), and adult non-index crime arrests (all the other categories, which are generally less serious offense categories). The figure also provides a separate time series for juvenile arrest rates (all offenses combined).

The patterns are fairly consistent across these arrest categories. For adults, non-index offenses are clearly the most numerous, followed by arrests for property offenses and violent offenses. Disparities in arrest rates between African Americans and all other groups are largest during the late 1980s and early 1990s but have narrowed over the past three decades. The decline in the Black/White ratio in arrest rates has accompanied a very large decline in the absolute disparity, reflecting a decline in the arrest rate for Black Americans, greater than 50 percent, in the two decades from the late 1990s. We see a similar narrowing in juvenile arrest disparities. Despite this narrowing, race disparities persist in 2019, with the highest arrest rate being that for African Americans, followed by American Indian, White, and Asian people.

Patterns of Offending by Race

While it is not possible to pin down the exact contribution of different factors to racial disparities in arrest rates, reported offense patterns from victimization surveys provide some insights. Table 2-5 presents the results from victim responses pertaining to the race/ethnicity of the offender as perceived by the victim. The NCVS asks this question only of victims who have experienced a violent crime. The table presents the distribution of offenses by the perceived race/ethnicity of the offender for all serious violent offenses as well as for those individual crimes that are defined as serious violent offenses. The final column presents the race/ethnicity distribution of survey respondents, which provides an estimate of the composition of the resident population of the country ages 12 and older. Here we use all offenses occurring from 2012 through 2019.

The numbers in Table 2-5 are quite similar to those reported in Beck (2021), with the small differences relative to Beck's tabulations likely attributable to our aggregation of multiple years of the NCVS surveys. African Americans are overrepresented among offenders for serious violent offenses, constituting 25.2 percent of all such serious offenses, while African Americans made up just 12.2 percent of survey respondents. White people are underrepresented as perceived by violent crime victims, while Hispanic people are roughly represented in proportion to their representation among the general population.

TABLE 2-5 Distribution of Serious Violent Criminal Victimizations across Race/Ethnicity of the Offender as Perceived by the Crime Victim, 2012 through 2019

	Serious Violent	Rape	Robbery	Aggravated Assault	Distribution of Survey Respondents
White	40.6	47.2	31.4	43.5	63.9
Black	25.2	15.8	35.3	22.9	12.2
Other	5.7	5.8	6.7	5.0	7.7
Hispanic	16.7	16.2	15.8	17.4	16.2
Unknown	11.9	15.0	10.8	11.2	—
Total	100.0%	100.0%	100.0%	100.0%	100.0%

NOTE: The race/ethnicity for perceived offenders accounts for incidents where there are multiple offenders and follows the coding scheme employed by the U.S. Bureau of Justice Statistics.
SOURCE: Figures tabulated from the concatenated National Crime Victimization Survey files for 1993–2019, https://doi.org/10.3886/ICPSR38136.v1

Table 2-6 presents a finer breakdown of these data by showing the fractions of offenders by race given the race of a victim. The columns in Table 2-6 sum to one. Among both Black and White people, most victims report that they were attacked by an offender of the same race. One would expect to see this pattern among White people even if all attacks were random, since they account for more than 60 percent of the population. However, attacks are not random. African American victims of serious violent crime report roughly 65 percent of the time that they are victimized by a Black person. White victims report being victimized by a White person roughly 56 percent of the time. Victims in other groups do not report that the majority of offenses are within group, but Hispanic victims report that 40 percent of those who attacked them were Hispanic.

Examining cross-group victimizations, we see that 16.6 percent of White victims report being victimized by a Black person, while 8.3 percent of Black victims report being victimized by a White person. The White victimization rate of 6.8 (per thousand) is just over three-fourths of the Black victimization rate (see Table 2-2). The White victimization rate attributable to Black offenders is about 50 percent greater than the Black victimization rate attributable to White offenders.

The White population is about five times larger than the Black population. Thus, there are (16.6 × .75 × 5) = 62.25 White victims of Black offenders for every 8.3 Black victims of White offenders—that is, about 7.5 times as many. Given that the Black population is about one-fifth the size of the White population, these results imply that Black people are roughly 35 times more likely to commit violent offenses against

TABLE 2-6 Distribution of Criminal Offenses across Offender Race/Ethnicity by Race/Ethnicity of the Victim and Offense Type, 2012 through 2019

All Serious Violent Offenses						
Offender race/ethnicity	Victim Race/Ethnicity					
	White	Black	Am. Ind	Asian/PI	More than one race	Hispanic
White	55.7	8.3	63.0	14.3	54.3	19.5
Black	16.6	64.8	7.4	24.6	21.3	22.9
Other	4.2	4.7	19.9	28.1	8.4	5.3
Hispanic	12.8	7.1	3.4	9.4	7.9	40.4
Unknown	10.6	15.1	6.2	23.7	8.1	12.0

NOTE: Columns sum to 100 percent.
SOURCE: Figures tabulated from the concatenated National Crime Victimization Survey files for 1993–2019, https://doi.org/10.3886/ICPSR38136.v1

White people than White people are to commit violent offenses against Black people.

We use the term "roughly" because the NCVS measures of victimization rates are noisy, and implied inter-racial victimization rates jump around from year to year. Even though we are using eight years of data, 2012–2019, our calculations should not yield a precise estimate of the ratio of inter-racial offending rates by race.[7] We also note that, in a world where all offenders choose victims at random, the ratio between the probability of a Black person victimizing a White one and the probability of the converse is simply the ratio of Black-to-White offending rates times the ratio of White-to-Black population shares. If we use Black/White arrest ratios associated with violent crime as proxies for Black/White ratios of violent offense probabilities, we expect this product to be at least 15 in recent years, and for earlier years to be often more than 20. In sum, we expect the likelihood that Black persons violently offend against White persons to be much larger than the probability of the converse simply because racial differences in offense rates are significant and racial differences in population shares are large (see, e.g., Messner and South, 1992, 1986; O'Brien, 1987; Sampson, 1984).

We have also analyzed inter-racial offense patterns by crime category. From this it is clear that one crime, robbery, drives the high overall rate of violent victimization by Black people against White people. Twenty-four percent of White robbery victims are robbed by a Black offender, but only five percent of Black robbery victims are robbed by a White offender.[8] This pattern may be expected, since White people in large cities are typically more affluent than the average resident. In addition, O'Flaherty and Sethi (2019) argue that racial stereotypes also play an important role. They argue that White people possess stereotypical beliefs that cause them to view Black people as more dangerous than they are. Furthermore, they argue that these fears make White victims less likely to resist Black robbers. Finally, they argue that Black robbers select White victims because they know White people have exaggerated fears of Black people and are therefore unlikely to resist robbery attempts by Black people. They argue that racial stereotypes

---

[7]We have made similar calculations using published reports from BJS. Using these results and weighting each yearly inter-racial offending rate equally, we estimate that Black citizens are 23 times more likely to victimize White people than White people are to victimize Black people. For some years, we could not find annual criminal victimization reports that cover the race of offenders. We did find suitable annual reports for 2018, 2019, and 2020. BJS also produced a special report, *Race and Hispanic Origin of Offenders, 2012–2015,* NCJ 250747; see https://bjs.ojp.gov/library/publications/race-and-hispanic-origin-victims-and-offenders-2012-15

[8]For other violent crimes, rape, simple assault, and aggravated assault, the fraction of Black offenders in the population of events involving White victims ranges from 10.5 to 15.6 percent, and the Black population share is more than 12 percent.

about Black men create excessive fear among White people, and this fear invites the encounters with Black robbers that White people want to avoid. They cite ethnographic work among Black robbers to support their claims.

Glenn Loury (2021) discusses models of the processes that transform biased perceptions into realized group differences in behavior. These models describe information traps. Members of a minority group may behave in a different way than a majority group but not because they are inherently different. Rather, they may find it in their own interests to behave differently because they know that the majority group believes they are different. However, this rational response to stereotypical beliefs may strengthen these beliefs.

White offenders do account for a large portion (63%) of the violent offenses against American Indians. Since the American Indian population is small, these offenses account for a small part of the overall White offense rate. This result may imply a high rate of White people offending against American Indian victims in border-town communities. Alternatively, because more than half of American Indian and Alaska Native people (78% in the 2010 census) do not live on reservations or tribal lands, and unlike other groups Native people living in cities tend not to live in spatially segregated communities, inter-racial offending may also reflect the experiences of Native people living among White people and other groups in cities. Or, if rates of inter-racial sexual and domestic violence are especially high, this may also reflect racial-sexual patterns, including both intermarriage rates and the use of sexual violence as a tool of racial domination.

Table 2-2 shows that American Indian people are almost twice as likely as Black people to report being the victim of violence, but Figure 2-4 shows that they are much less likely than Black people to be arrested for violent crimes. These large differences between relative arrest rates and relative victimization rates create a puzzle for those who view violent offenses as predominately intra-racial acts, but the fact that White people commit 63 percent of all violent crimes against American Indian people may help us understand these patterns. American Indian arrest rates for violent crimes may be low relative to their violent victimization rates because American Indian people are often the victims of White offenders.

Researchers cannot collect reports from homicide victims concerning the races of their attackers. However, the Supplementary Homicide Reports do provide information on the race and ethnicity of the offender when the offense is cleared by arrest or some other means. We use this information in Table 2-7 to document the distribution of murder victims by the race/ethnicity of the person committing the murder for each racial/ethnic group observable in the Supplementary Homicide Report data with available offender information. Again, we use all murders occurring between 2000 and 2019.

The results in Table 2-7 reveal that murders are even more likely to occur within race. Approximately 55 percent of incidents involving American Indian victims, 52 percent of those involving Asian victims, 90 percent of those involving Black victims, 74 percent of those involving Hispanic victims, and 79 percent of those involving White victims are intra-racial murders. African Americans are overrepresented among reported assailants when the murder victim is Asian (19.6% of offenders) and when the victim is White (16.34% of offenders). Similar to the results in Table 2-6, we see that 16.3 percent of White victims were murdered by a Black person while roughly eight percent of Black victims were murdered by a White person.

However, these results do not have the same implications for inter-racial offense rate differences. The raw count of White victims of violent crime is more than three times higher than the raw count of Black victims, but the raw number of Black homicide victims is significantly greater than the number of White victims. For example, in 2020, there were 9,913 Black homicide victims and only 7,029 White victims. Thus, the number of murders involving White victims and Black offenders is less than 50 percent greater than the number of murders involving Black victims and White offenders. Rates of homicide by Black offenders against White victims are greater than the rates of homicide by White offenders against Black victims, but the ratio of these rates is much smaller than the comparable ratio for all violent offenses.

Our comparisons of inter-group differences in arrest rates to patterns from victimization surveys and homicide incident reports suggest that the relatively high arrest rates in Black communities may reflect relatively high offending rates. However, as reported by Beck (2021), violent offenses

TABLE 2-7 Race/Ethnicity-Specific Distribution of Murder Victims by the Race/Ethnicity of the Offender for Murders Where Offender Race/Ethnicity Is Known (All Murders Occurring from 2000 to 2019)

	Offender Race/Ethnicity				
Victim Race/ Ethnicity	American Indian	Asian	Black	Hispanic	White
Amer. Indian	55.48	0.87	12.95	5.58	25.13
Asian	0.62	51.81	19.60	6.54	21.42
Black	0.13	0.40	89.18	2.33	7.96
Hispanic	0.39	0.89	12.20	74.27	12.24
White	0.72	0.78	16.34	3.56	78.59

NOTE: Rows sum to 100 percent.
SOURCE: Figures tabulated from the concatenated National Crime Victimization Survey files for 1993–2019, https://doi.org/10.3886/ICPSR38136.v1

where the victim indicates an African American assailant are more likely to be reported to the police and thus arguably more likely to result in an arrest. We conclude this section by documenting the proximate determinants of reporting rates for serious violent offenses.

Appendix Figures 2A-1 and 2A-2 present estimated disparities in the proportion of offenses reported to the police relative to offenses involving White offenders. We indeed see considerably higher reporting rates for offenses involving African American offenders, but the reporting rates given Hispanic offenders are not statistically different than reporting rates given White offenders. We examine potential reasons for this Black/White difference in reporting rates.[9] Since we only see statistically significant disparities relative to White offenders when the offender is perceived to be Black, we focus on the Black/White reporting disparities.

Controlling for victim race explains roughly half the disparity in reporting rates between incidents involving Black and White offenders. This reflects at least two facts: (1) as we discuss more below, African American victims are discretely more likely to report offenses to the police; and (2) offenders who are perceived to be African Americans are greatly overrepresented in incidents involving African American victims. Controlling for offense type, on the other hand, does not narrow the disparity.

In sum, African Americans are overrepresented among offenders for serious violent offenses; White people are underrepresented as perceived by violent crime victims; and Hispanic people are roughly represented in proportion to their representation among the general population. Inter-group differences in arrest rates to victimization rates suggest that the relatively high arrest rates in Black communities may reflect relatively high offending rates. However, variation in likelihood of reporting crimes to the police may also explain some of these differences. Moreover, a large body of evidence establishes the historical and contemporary social pathways through which racially inscribed inequality leads to both crime and criminal justice involvement, and assessments of offending, violence, and victimization need to be situated in an understanding of the social drivers of crime, which are discussed at length in Chapter 3.

[9]Specifically, the first set of disparities in Figure 2A-2 report the regression coefficients on race/ethnicity dummies from a linear probability model where the dependent variable is an indicator that the offense was reported and the explanatory variables are dummy variables for perceived offender race/ethnicity (with White offenders the omitted category). The second set of disparities are the coefficients on the offender race/ethnicity dummies after adding a complete set of indicators for the race/ethnicity of the crime victim. The final set of disparities report similar coefficients that additionally add indicator variables for the type of serious violent offense.

INTERACTIONS WITH POLICE OFFICERS

As described above, both victimization rates and offending rates tend to be higher among African American and American Indian people and to a lesser extent among Hispanic people. We also see higher arrest rates among African American and American Indian people, although we did not report arrest rates for Hispanic people. The arrest rates for African Americans remain quite high relative to other groups, and homicide victimization rates among African American men are likely more than 10 times the rates among White men and rising.

These patterns raise two concerns about interactions between police and Black communities: (1) Are high arrest rates in these communities, at least in part, the result of an excessive police presence? (2) Are police engaging with Black communities in ways that do not produce public safety? In sum, are Black communities both over-policed and poorly served?

Police officers frequently stop members of the public. In 2018, 11.1 percent of the U.S. population, 16 or older, were stopped by police (BJS, 2020). These stops may arise because officers observe suspicious activity, minor infractions like traffic violations, or serious crimes in progress. Police officers stop and search African Americans at rates that are higher than those observed for other racial and ethnic groups. While this pattern may be expected given higher rates of offending among African Americans, most stops do not result in arrests. Furthermore, although police rarely use force during stops, they are more likely to use force when they stop African Americans, even when the stop does not begin because police believe that a crime is in progress.

Over the past two decades, a large body of research has focused on understanding these stop disparities and the degree to which they reflect differential scrutiny applied to African American drivers and pedestrians. Much of this literature has focused on stops involving searches of either one's person or one's vehicle, focusing on whether observed differences in search rates reflect differential scrutiny or differential underlying base rates of offending across groups. An earlier National Academies of Sciences, Engineering, and Medicine report on proactive policing provides an extensive review of this technical research (the National Academies, 2018). While we will touch upon this specialized literature below, in this section we focus on documenting basic facts about differences in the incidence and nature of interactions between police and the public. A more extensive discussion of policing in minority communities can be found in Chapter 4.

Many state, county, and local law enforcement agencies routinely collect information about traffic and pedestrian stops and have specific reporting requirements pertaining to incidents where force is used. That being said, data collection is far from uniform, and departments vary considerably in terms of the data they collect, the degree to which data are publicly shared, and the level of disaggregation with which stop and incident data are shared with the public (e.g., summary data vs. incident-level records). Combined with the fact that there are over 19,000 law enforcement agencies in the United States, it is difficult to provide a complete portrait of disparities in interactions with law enforcement.

Nonetheless, there have been several efforts to compile and harmonize police stop and other incident data from various departments, sometimes by research organizations and sometimes by media outlets. Moreover, several state legislatures have now undertaken efforts to implement uniform reporting requirements for all law enforcement agencies in their states. Here we draw on these various projects to document what we generally know about differences in interactions with police. While we do not have data on all police agencies, the patterns we document are typical of the patterns documented in this body of research.

Basic Patterns Regarding Stops, Searches, and Search Outcomes

The Stanford Open Policing Project has compiled and harmonized stop-level data for several large city police departments as well as state police agencies for nearly half of all U.S. states.[10] We use these data to document differences in the rates at which Black, Hispanic, and White members of the public are stopped by police. The data cover various years during the 2010s and are averaged to generate average stops per year per 100 residents. Figure 2-5 presents a scatter plot of Black stops per 100 residents against White stops per 100 residents (blue dots) as well as Hispanic stops per 100 residents against White stops per 100 residents (red dots) for 34 large cities from across the country. Each point corresponds to a city, with the marker size proportional to the number of Black (Hispanic) stops made in the specific city. The scatter plot includes a diagonal black line marking coordinates that would indicate equal stop rates across groups. Hence, points that lie above the line indicate that the stop rate for African Americans (Hispanic people for the red markers) exceeds that for White people, while points lying below the line indicate relatively lower stop rates for Black or Hispanic people.

The plot reveals that Black stop rates are higher than White stop rates across nearly all included departments. The disparities range from slightly higher rates (e.g., in Albany [NY] and Louisville [KY]) to stops rates for African Americans that are nearly three to four times those for White people (e.g., in St. Paul [MN], Madison [WI], Los Angeles [CA], and San Francisco

[10]See https://openpolicing.stanford.edu/

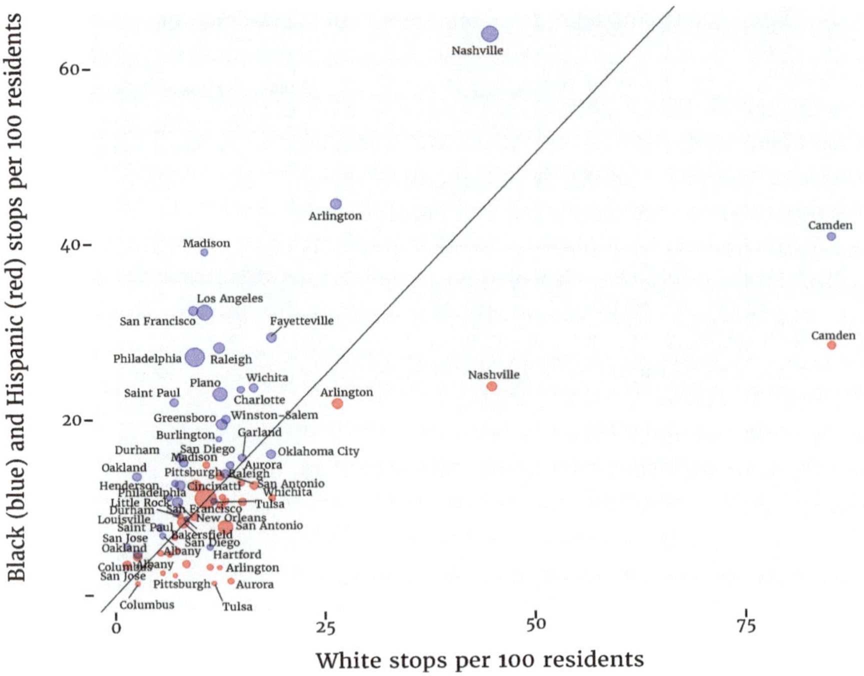

FIGURE 2-5 Scatter plot of police stops per 100 residents for Black and Hispanic residents against White stops for U.S. cities included in the Stanford Open Policing Project database.
SOURCE: Data from Stanford Open Policing Project, https://openpolicing.stanford.edu/

[CA]). In contrast, Hispanic stop rates tend to be lower than White stop rates in most cities, with a few exceptions. Figure 2-6 presents similar comparisons for 22 state police agencies. The patterns are similar: state police tend to stop African Americans at higher rates relative to White people and stop Hispanic residents at relatively low rates.

The Stanford data do not include detailed information regarding what occurred during the stops or their outcomes. However, the State of California is in the process of rolling out a uniform stop data collection form across all law enforcement agencies in the state that includes detailed information about the nature of stops, actions taken by officers during the stops, and the ultimate outcome. The most recent year of publicly available data (2019) includes stop records for the 15 largest agencies in the state, covering a large portion of the state's population and several of the country's top 10 largest

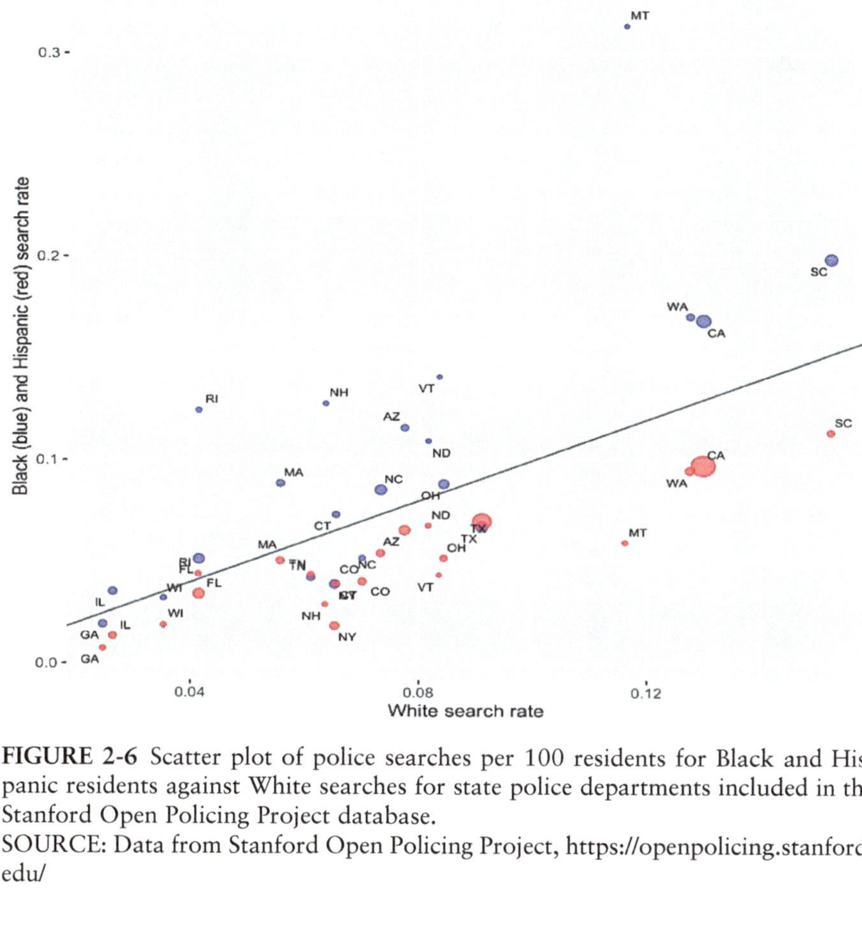

FIGURE 2-6 Scatter plot of police searches per 100 residents for Black and Hispanic residents against White searches for state police departments included in the Stanford Open Policing Project database.
SOURCE: Data from Stanford Open Policing Project, https://openpolicing.stanford.edu/

cities.[11] We use these data to dig into the details of what happens during traffic stops and the outcomes of these stops.[12] The committee restricts the analysis to traffic stops (basically excluding calls for service). In all tabulations

[11]As of 2019, the Racial Identity and Profiling Act (RIPA) data include all traffic stops made by the California Highway Patrol, the Los Angeles Police Department, the San Diego Police Department, the Oakland Police Department, the Sacramento Police Department, the Long Beach Police Department, the Fresno Police Department, the San Francisco Police Department, and the San Jose Police Department, as well as county sheriff departments for the counties of Los Angeles, Orange, Riverside, San Bernardino, Sacramento, and San Diego.

[12]Similar to the patterns observed in the Stanford Open Policing Project data, RIPA data for California reveal that the proportion of stops that involve African Americans is roughly 2.5 times the African American population share. Similarly, Hispanic and White people are underrepresented among those stopped relative to their population share.

to follow, we present separate estimates for the California Highway Patrol, the one statewide agency in the data that accounts for a large share of stops disproportionately on the state's freeway system, and other law enforcement agencies, primarily municipal police departments and county sheriffs that focus on local law enforcement. We also present separate tabulations for the broad race/ethnicity categories included in the data where stop totals are sufficient in number and interact race with gender in all of our tabulations.[13] Appendix Figures 2A-3 through 2A-5 present the results.

These data reveal a number of important patterns. Traffic stops for non-moving violations are highest for African Americans, both for California Highway Patrol stops as well as stops made by local agencies. To begin, the proportion of stops for equipment violations is particularly high for Black males when the stops are made by local law enforcement (nearly 30% of stops), exceeding the comparable rate for White males by nearly 10 percentage points. In addition, among stops made by local law enforcement, roughly 17 percent of Black males are ordered to exit their vehicles, compared to 12 percent of Hispanic males and slightly over five percent of White males. Further, fully one-fifth of local stops of Black males involve either a curbside or backseat detention, compared with approximately 16 percent of stops involving Hispanic males and 10 percent of stops involving White males. We see a similar pattern of disparities in the proportions of stops that involve vehicle searches or the use of handcuffs.

We see different patterns when we examine the ultimate outcomes of these stops. Here, we bin outcomes into four categories: (1) the stop resulted in no more than a warning; (2) the stop resulted in a traffic citation or a misdemeanor citation and release in the field; (3) the stop resulted in an actual arrest and booking; and (4) a residual category for other possible outcomes (e.g., contacted the legal guardian of the person stopped, referred the person to a school counselor, executed a psychiatric hold). Given the very small proportion of stops that fall under the fourth ("other" outcome) category, we focus our discussion on the first three outcome contrasts.

California Highway Patrol stops are most likely to result in a citation, but citation rates are lowest for Black males. Many California Highway Patrol stops end with no more than a warning, with the highest rates for White males and females (roughly 30 and 28% of stops), followed by Black males and females (roughly 28 and 25% of stops). For local law enforcement, more than 60 percent of stops of Black males result in no more than a warning.

[13]For gender, we focus on cisgender males and females, though the data do include information on whether the officer perceives the stopped citizen to be gender nonconforming. These latter stops are a very small percentage of stops made by officers in the data.

Local law enforcement stops Black men at high rates, and given these stops, local law enforcement is more likely (than other officers) to interrogate drivers, search vehicles, handcuff motorists, and so on. However, among the stops that occur, local law enforcement is also most likely to simply let the driver go with a warning if the driver is a Black man. In fact, Black men stopped by local law enforcement are about 20 percentage points more likely to be let go with a warning than White men who are stopped.

Hit-Rate Analyses of Stops Involving Searches

The differential stop rates documented above do not necessarily imply that police agencies across the country are discriminating against African Americans. There is a long literature on police stops discussing the likely problems associated with benchmarking stops against residential populations. Among the many issues that researchers and policy makers have raised in interpreting these data are: (1) differences in staffing and police deployment across areas of the city, (2) differences between the population at risk of being stopped by the police and the resident population of a given city, and (3) movement of individuals across city boundaries for work and recreational activities that may create disparities between the racial composition of the resident population and the racial composition of the daytime population of specific cities. For these reasons, research has focused on the results of stops in an attempt to detect differential scrutiny.

Appendix Figure 2A-5 shows that stops of Black and Hispanic drivers do result in arrests more often than stops of White drivers, but arrests may in part reflect subjective decisions made by officers. The principal outcome test explored in a larger research literature compares the contraband discovery rates of searches for Black and Hispanic people to the rates for White people. The logic behind this comparison is the following. Suppose that officers only search people when those people cross some internal suspicion threshold that the officer has regarding the likelihood that they possessed illegal drugs, weapons, or some other form of contraband. Suppose further that for some race/ethnicity groups, this internal threshold is lower; that is to say, there will be members of the lower threshold group whom the officer will search and individuals from another group who exhibit similar behavior who are not searched. This greater scrutiny should lead to relatively lower contraband discovery rates, as it takes less to arouse the suspicions of officers for members of the group being discriminated against. Hence, a simple empirical test of discrimination in searches against one group is to test whether contraband discovery rates (often referred to as the hit rate associated with a search) are lower for the group in question.

The annual reports of California's RIPA board consistently show hit rates for all stops in the dataset combined that are slightly lower (and statistically distinguishable) for racial and ethnic minorities relative to White hit rates (RIPA Board, 2020). Figure 2-7 illustrates this fact. The top panel presents a scatter plot of the contraband discovery rate for searches of Black people against the comparable rates for searches of White people, while the bottom panel presents the comparable scatter plot for Hispanic hit rates against White hit rates. The data reveal that, for most agencies, searches of Black and Hispanic people made during police stops are less likely to yield contraband relative to searches of White people. Figures 2-8 and 2-9 break the data down by type of contraband. The exception to the lower minority hit-rate rule involves firearms discoveries. For African Americans, firearm discovery rates are generally higher than the discovery rates for White people, though for most agencies these rates fall in the one-to-three percent of searches range. Firearm discovery rates also tend to be higher among Hispanic people who are stopped compared to White people, but here the difference is less pronounced.

Lofstrom and colleagues (2021) provide a more detailed analysis of racial disparities in hit rates conditional on being searched using 2019 RIPA data. The authors confirm the basic finding in the RIPA annual reports of a slightly lower hit rate for searches of Black and Hispanic stops (with the differences statistically significant). However, they also find that conditioning on the age and gender of the member of the public, the reason for the stop (e.g., moving violation, pedestrian stop), and the basis for the search (e.g., probation parole, reasonable suspicion) widens the disparities. This

FIGURE 2-7 Scatter plots of contraband discovery rates, Black and Hispanic rates against White rates for California agencies.
SOURCE: Data from Open Justice, California Department of Justice, Racial and Identity Profiling Act database, https://openjustice.doj.ca.gov/

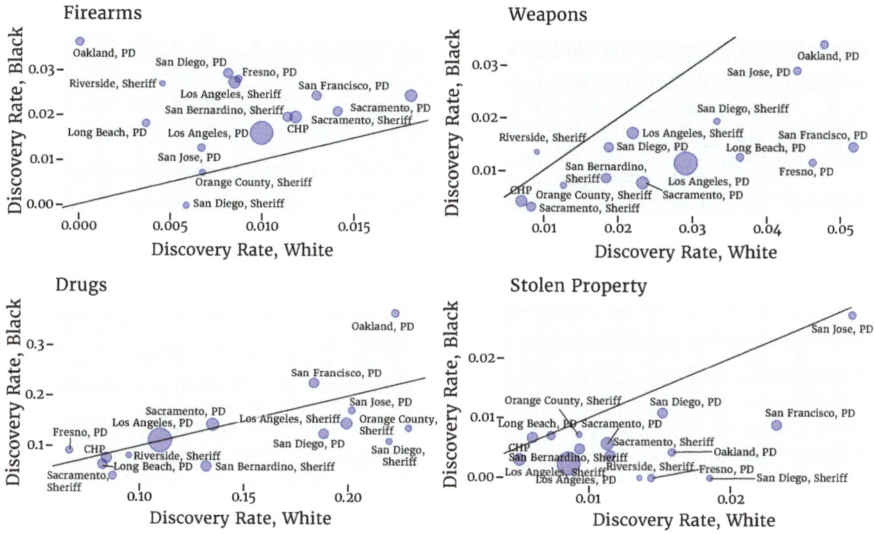

FIGURE 2-8 Scatter plots of Black contraband discovery rates against White discovery rates for specific contraband categories.
SOURCE: Data from Open Justice, California Department of Justice, Racial and Identity Profiling Act database, https://openjustice.doj.ca.gov/

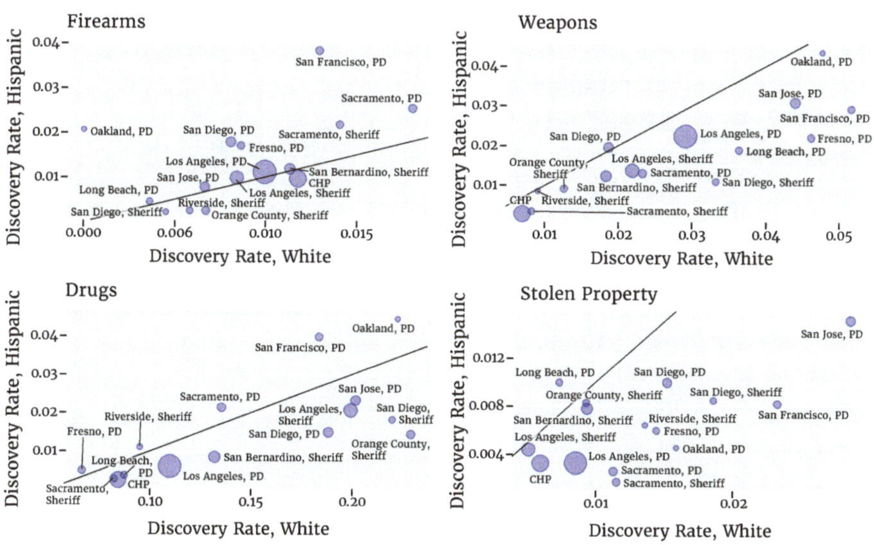

FIGURE 2-9 Scatter plots of Hispanic contraband discovery rates against White discovery rates for specific contraband categories.
SOURCE: Data from Open Justice, California Department of Justice, Racial and Identity Profiling Act database, https://openjustice.doj.ca.gov/

suggests that the hit rates for Black searches are even lower relative to White searches for similarly situated stop and search incidents.

Simoiu and colleagues (2017) produce similar hit rate comparisons using the city and state agencies from the Stanford Open Policing Project for stops of Black, Hispanic, and White people where searches are conducted. For Black/White comparisons, they document that there are agencies where hit rates are higher for searches of White people, agencies where they are higher for searches of Black people, and many agencies where they are comparable. A scatter plot of Black hit rates against White hit rates generally reveals similar rates on average across groups, despite the uniformly higher search rates for African Americans. By contrast, Hispanic hit rates for the departments analyzed are uniformly lower than the corresponding hit rates for White searches. The National Academies (2018) review a large literature of department-specific studies that find evidence both suggesting discrimination and suggesting no discrimination based on this particular test.

The hit rate test for search is of course imperfect, for both methodological as well as legal and policy reasons. Regarding methodology, many have pointed out that it is entirely possible for officers to hold African Americans to a higher level of scrutiny and still observe comparable hit rates for Black and White searches. This would be the case if the distribution of Black and White people across risk tranches were such that African Americans were more concentrated in higher risk categories beyond the reasonable suspicion thresholds used by officers.[14] Beyond this methodological contention, the hit-rate test is based on a behavioral model of policing that assumes that officers are attempting to maximize contraband discoveries by making group-based probabilistic assessments of the likelihood that someone is carrying. If this is indeed true, behavior aimed at maximizing discovery rates for a fixed number of searches may be unconstitutional, to the extent that Black individuals would otherwise not be searched if they were White. The chapter has documented that Black people are stopped by the police at much higher rates than White people, and among those stopped they are searched at much higher rates. With these two facts in mind, equal hit rates between Black and White searches still leave in their wake a larger swath of the African American population who have been searched by police officers, had nothing discovered, and then been released with just

[14]This is commonly referred to as the inframarginality problem and was first pointed out in the empirical literature debating whether differential mortgage default rates might be used to test for discrimination against Black borrowers by financial institutions. This inframarginality problem prompted Simoiu and colleagues (2017) to develop a methodology for directly inferring whether officers apply differential thresholds to Black motorists who are stopped. The authors find evidence of systematically lower thresholds applied to African Americans and Hispanic people (implying higher scrutiny of minority drivers) for nearly all municipal and state law enforcement agencies included in the Stanford Open Policing Project data.

a warning. Combined with differences in being asked to exit the vehicle, being detained on a curb, and so on, one would imagine that the differential incidence of unproductive searches might create worse relations between local police departments and minority community members.

These tensions between public safety and notions of fairness are not unique to the subject of police stops and vehicle searches. Persico (2009) provides an in-depth treatment of the statistical challenges that face researchers when they attempt to identify bias in police decision by using data that describe racial differences in the outcomes of police decisions, such as patrol locations, stops, searches, and arrests. He shows how difficult it is to formulate convincing statistical tests for bias.

Uses of Force and Police-Involved Shootings

Use-of-force incidents involving police vary in severity and the likelihood of lethality (Alpert and Dunham, 2004). Recent experience has demonstrated that uses of force that are commonly classified as "less serious" can and do result in the death of civilians. Nonetheless, use-of-force incidents are often categorized into less lethal uses of force (e.g., control holds, strikes, the use of chemical sprays or conducted-energy devices [tasers], deployment of a police dog) and lethal force (discharges of firearm).

Use-of-force incidents are relatively rare, with the most lethal uses of force very rare. For example, roughly 2.8 percent of U.S. residents ages 16 and older in 2018 reported experiencing a nonfatal threat or having force used upon them by a police officer in the past year (Harrell and Davis, 2020). However, the data that are available clearly indicate that racial and ethnic minorities are often more than twice as likely as others to experience official use of force (Harrell and Davis, 2020; see also Paoline et al., 2018).

The Police-Public Contact Survey (an addendum the NCVS)[15] permits a national-level characterization of these disparities. The most recent year for these data is calendar year 2018. In their analysis of these 2018 data, Harrell and Davis (2020) estimate that while two percent of non-Hispanic White people experience either a threat of force or a less lethal use of force, for minorities the comparable figures are 5.34 percent of Black people, 4.8 percent of Hispanic people, and 1.9 percent of people in an "other" category. For Black and Hispanic people, the relatively higher rates are statistically distinguishable from those for White people concerning experiencing a threat; being handcuffed, pushed, grabbed, hit, or kicked; and having a weapon pointed at them. Weisburst (2019) uses data on response-to-resistance reports for Dallas from 2013 through 2016. The data clearly reveal that African Americans are overrepresented relative to the resident

[15]See https://bjs.ojp.gov/data-collection/police-public-contact-survey-ppcs

population of Dallas among individuals who experience a nonlethal use-of-force incident with the police. Weisburst also notes that the proportion of these incidents experienced by African Americans exactly equals the proportion of arrests of African Americans, but this result is difficult to interpret. Weisburst's use-of-force definition involves more than simply detaining or handcuffing. She restricts attention to "pushing, grabbing, joint locks, takedowns, and taser use." If officers always arrest any person that they plan to document using this type of force against, possibly as a way of justifying their decisions to use such force, the patterns Weisburst documents do not constitute evidence against the hypothesis that officers are more likely to use nonlethal force against Black defendants, holding constant the nature of their encounters. Some arrests may be the result of the officer's decision to use force rather than an indicator that force was justified. These results add to the body of evidence showing high rates of police violence experienced by Black and Hispanic segments of the population (e.g., Geller et al., 2021; Paoline et al., 2018; Ross, 2015; Jacobs, 1998).

A variety of research strategies have been used to study more serious applications of force by police, including shooting and lethal force. Police shootings have been studied experimentally, and in observational studies with police and media reports. Experimental studies have examined "shooter bias," the tendency to shoot Black or other minority members of the public (Correll et al., 2002). Shooter bias studies examine the effect of race on shoot/don't shoot decisions in videogame-like simulations. A large number of studies find that experimental subjects are faster and more accurate when shooting an armed Black man compared to an armed White man, and they are faster and more accurate at choosing "don't shoot" for an unarmed White man compared to an unarmed Black man. Police officers show greater speed and accuracy in correct decision making than community members, but some studies nevertheless show significant levels of racial bias. While reviews conclude there is less bias among police than community members (Cox and Devine, 2016; Correll et al., 2014), shooter bias can be mitigated further by training but increases when police are short of sleep or placed under conditions of high cognitive load (Correll et al., 2014; Ma et al., 2013). While these results are suggestive, it is also true that no studies provide direct evidence that the biases identified in these experiments contribute directly to racial differences in observed rates of death associated with police shootings.

A number of studies compare the use of lethal and nonlethal force and analyze racial disparities in lethal force. Analyzing several sources of microdata on police encounters with members of the public from several cities, Fryer (2019) tests for racial disparities in the likelihood that less-lethal and lethal force are used conditional on a stop occurring. Using stop data from the New York City (NY) police department as well as national survey data that queries members of the public regarding recent interactions with the police, Fryer documents sizable racial and ethnic disparities in use of force that cannot be attributed to observable characteristics of the stop. In the analysis of the New York City data, Fryer finds that part of the relatively high rate of use of less lethal force when Black and Hispanic people are stopped is attributable to differences in practice across precincts combined with average differences in where Black, Hispanic, and White people are stopped in the city. This finding suggests that differential policing practices in predominantly Black and Hispanic precincts explain part of the higher use-of-force probability faced by Black and Hispanic people conditional on being stopped.

Using a random sample of arrests for relatively serious offenses (e.g., attempted murder of a police officer, resisting arrest, interfering with an arrest) combined with data on police shootings in Houston, Fryer finds relatively lower likelihoods that such incidents involving Black and Hispanic people result in an officer-involved shooting relative to incidents involving White people. Based on these findings, Fryer concludes that there is evidence of disparate use of less lethal force but no evidence of disparate use of lethal force.

Several authors have contested Fryer's interpretation of his findings, observing that police killings of Black and Hispanic individuals may result from police bias if the initial encounter with police resulted from bias (Durlauf and Heckman, 2020; Knox et al., 2020; Ross et al., 2018). In a comment on the study published in the *Journal of Political Economy*, Durlauf and Heckman (2020) note that Fryer's results effectively test for a differential likelihood of being shot conditional on having been stopped for a small subset of offenses. To the extent that there are race disparities in the likelihood of being stopped (and that this disparity may in itself be the result of discriminatory practices), Fryer's results do not rule out a relatively higher likelihood that Black people are at risk of being shot by the police relative to a White person with similar pre-stop and post-stop characteristics and behavior. From this perspective, a relatively low death rate conditional on incident characteristics "does not establish credible evidence on the presence or absence of discrimination in police shootings" (Durlauf and Heckman, 2020). The authors go on to note that a conclusion about the role of police bias requires data and an analysis of the process that leads to the police-public interaction in the first place.

Knox and colleagues (2020) provide a particularly nuanced analysis of the problems of testing for discrimination in administrative police data and the likely impact of the lack of information on the process generating stops. Suppose that stops can be grouped into (1) serious incidents where a stop will occur regardless of race, (2) incidents or activities observed by police where a stop will never occur regardless of race, and (3) incidents where Black people are stopped but otherwise similar White people exhibiting similar pre-stop characteristics and behaviors are not stopped. Analyses that condition on a stop occurring ultimately compare outcomes for stops of White people from group (1) only to outcomes for stops of Black people from groups (1) and (3), leading to selection bias and likely unobserved differences between the average stopped Black person as well as the average stopped White person. Hence, selection bias may lead to mis-estimation of the race disparity in the use-of-force probability conditional on being stopped. Knox and colleagues employ external estimates of the proportion of stops in New York City data that are discriminatory against Black citizens to reanalyze the data and findings in Fryer, providing corrected bound estimates that adjust for the differential stop probability and the likely selection bias in terms of who is stopped. While Fryer's original analysis finds substantial evidence of discriminatory use of less lethal force, the adjusted estimates presented in Knox and colleagues suggest substantially larger disparities.

There is at least one study that suggests that bias may be in part responsible for the relatively high relative rate at which Black people are shot by the police that avoids the selection bias issue. Hoekstra and Sloan (2022) analyze the outcomes of police who are dispatched through 911 calls in two large (unidentified) cities and test for differential use of force depending on the racial/ethnic composition of the area to which the officer is dispatched and how this interacts with officer race. Officers in these cities cannot turn down the dispatch request, and characteristics of the calls and the neighborhoods from which the calls for service originate are unrelated to officer characteristics. The study finds that calls from Black and Hispanic neighborhoods are more likely to result in the use of less lethal as well as lethal force. Moreover, they find evidence of a differential impact by officer race—that is, the effect of an increase in the proportion of the neighborhood that is minority on the likelihood of an officer-involved shooting is greater for White officers relative to Black officers.

At least part of the debate stems from the limited availability of data on the use of force and the reliance on police reports (Knox et al., 2020; Goff et al., 2016). A number of data collection efforts have emerged over the last few years that aim to independently record at the national level the number of police shootings and killings (Goff et al., 2016; Ross, 2015). A team of investigative reporters from the *Washington Post* maintain a database of all fatal incidents that involve police shooting citizens, beginning in January 2015. The committee employs the *Washington Post* data, in part because no national data source tracking killings by police is reliable. A 2019 study published in the *Lancet* indicates that the National Vital Statistics System does not provide data that allow researchers to construct accurate counts of citizens who die at the hands of police officers. Here, the chapter summarizes *Washington Post* data posted through the middle of July 2021.

The *Washington Post* data do not contain all incidents where citizens die as a result of encounters with police. For example, George Floyd is not one of the victims in this dataset because he was not shot. However, most citizen deaths during police encounters are shooting deaths. The results in Table 2-8 combine the *Washington Post* data on police shootings with population data from 2018 to create shooting deaths per 100,000 persons at the hands of police over the 6.5-year window covered in the newspaper's data. Table 2-8 presents results by census region, by race, and by race within regions.

The data reveal stark racial disparities. Overall, Black citizens are roughly twice as likely as Hispanic people to be shot and killed by police and two and one-half times more likely than White people. Further, in every region of the country, Black citizens are significantly more likely to die in a police shooting.

We also see striking regional variation in the incidence of police shootings. Police shootings are four times more common in the West than in the Northeast, despite lower relative police staffing levels on the West Coast. Further, there are large differences in the rates of fatal police shootings in the West versus the Northeast within every race category. Note that these regional differences are so large that the rate of fatal police shootings among Black people in the Northeast is only four percent greater than the rate of fatal police shootings among White people in the West.

Relative rates of fatal police shootings by race follow regional patterns that may surprise some readers. Black people in the Northeast are least likely to be fatally shot by police, but the ratio of fatal police shootings among Black residents relative to White residents is greatest in the Northeast at 4.31. The ratio of deaths from police shootings among Black versus White

TABLE 2-8 Persons Killed by Police per 100,000, by Region and Race/Ethnicity, 2015–2021

	All	White	Black	Hispanic
All	2.41	1.48	3.75	1.81
Northeast	0.93	0.54	2.33	0.55
Midwest	1.64	1.07	4.43	0.98
South	2.65	1.85	3.38	1.28
West	4.14	2.24	7.36	2.94

NOTE: The database includes incomplete information on race and ethnicity; for example, in the data for 2021, race and ethnicity is unknown for almost half of the entries.
SOURCE: Tabulations based on the *Washington Post* database, nationwide and by broad regions within the United States (2022), https://www.washingtonpost.com/graphics/investigations/police-shootings-database/

people is also greater than four in the Midwest. The South has, by far, the lowest Black/White ratio of deaths from police shootings: 1.83.

Hispanic people are equally or less likely than White people to be shot and killed by police in the Northeast, Midwest, and South, and are most likely to be fatally shot by police in the West. This result holds whether we measure risk in levels, relative to the comparable risk for White people, or relative to the comparable risk for Black people. This elevated risk in the West drives the national disparity between White and Hispanic people in the risk of becoming the victim of a fatal police shooting.

The *Washington Post* data only provide descriptions of encounters that involved a shooting death. Thus, these data do not allow an analysis like Fryer's (2019) that estimated the likelihood of police killing a Black or a White citizen conditional on characteristics of the encounter, nor can we assess whether the encounter itself resulted from police bias. However, the data we do have provide no evidence that contradicts Fryer. The data we review above indicate that Black citizens have much higher rates of violent offending. Furthermore, Black citizens are much more likely than White citizens to kill police officers. A 2020 report from BJS documents shootings of police by citizens during the period 2010–2019 (BJS, 2020). During these 10 years, 537 police officers were feloniously killed by citizens. In 303 cases, the assailant was White, and in 199 cases, the assailant was Black. Using 2015 estimates of national populations by race, we calculate the relative rates at which Black citizens versus White citizens kill police, and this ratio is greater than three. BJS does not report the Hispanic origin of offenders who kill police, so we cannot produce comparable results for Hispanic people. Further, the committee conjectures that most Hispanic assailants of officers are coded as White, which means that the report is likely overstating the relative rate at which White people kill police.

Table 2-8, describing population exposure to police shooting, indicates that, regardless of race, the risk of being shot is lowest in the Northeast, and among Black people the reduction in risk associated with relocation to the Northeast is quite large. In future work, researchers who seek to understand racial disparities in rates of police shootings need to confront the striking differences within race among different regions of the country.

The most complete data concerning the circumstances surrounding the shootings cover the incidents recorded in 2015. According to our correspondence, less than 10 percent of all police shootings occurred in settings where records document no threat to police officers. Furthermore, less than one percent of victims were fleeing from police on foot when they were shot.[16]

[16]The committee thanks Amy Brittain for providing these results and information about the data collection process.

Nature of Interactions between Police and the Public

Additional research examines the nature of interactions between police and the public, beyond lethal and nonlethal force. This literature is summarized in depth in a report by the National Academies (2018), which reviews the way people evaluate their experiences with and impressions about what police do, how policing affects the way people orient toward the police as an institution (i.e., do they view policing as legitimate?), and how policing affects the ways that people behave toward the police, the law, and their communities (i.e., do the police behave in ways that strengthen the community's collective efficacy and thereby facilitate the creation of social capital among members of the community? See the National Academies, 2018, p. 179).

A large literature finds that African Americans report more negative experiences in their interactions with the police than other groups (see, e.g., Voigt et al., 2017; Hetey et al., 2016; Epp et al., 2014). Across numerous studies, for example, African Americans report being treated less fairly and respectfully in their contacts with the police than White people (Peffley and Hurwitz, 2010; Tyler and Huo, 2002). Indeed, some have argued that racial disparities in perceived treatment during routine encounters help fuel mistrust of police. Using footage from body-worn cameras, Voigt and colleagues (2017) analyze the respectfulness of police officer language toward White and Black community members during routine traffic stops. They find that officers speak with consistently less respect toward Black versus White community members, even after controlling for the race of the officer, the severity of the infraction, the location of the stop, and the outcome of the stop. Similarly, Camp and colleagues (2021) use footage from traffic stops to examine how officers communicate to drivers and whether racial disparities in officers' communication erode institutional trust in the police. Specifically, they consider the cumulative effects of an officer's tone of voice, which is a subtle interpersonal cue, and demonstrate that nonverbal aspects of police interactions shape how individuals construe the police generally and that racial disparities in intonation undermine trust in institutions such as police departments. The authors further conclude that participants' trust in the police and their personal experiences of fairness correlated with their perceptions of officer prosody across studies, illustrating a cycle through which interpersonal aspects of police encounters erode institutional trust across race (Camp et al., 2021).

EVIDENCE CONCERNING PUBLIC SAFETY DELIVERY

Given the evidence that some African American communities are policed too aggressively, it is important to examine the impact of aggressive police practices on public safety. It is difficult to give precise answers to this question. Victimization rates for Black, Hispanic, and Native American people tend to be the same or higher than comparable rates for White people, but it is difficult to know what portion of these differences is due to failure by police or higher baseline offending rates in communities that have been historically disadvantaged. Moreover, it is difficult to precisely estimate the degree to which policing lowers crime rates, though existing empirical evidence (reviewed in Chapter 10) consistently finds that high police staffing levels reduce serious crime rates.

Data on clearance rates provide one benchmark for police performance. It is well known that murders involving White victims are considerably more likely to be cleared by arrest or by exceptional means[17] relative to murders involving Black victims (Fagan and Geller, 2018). We document this pattern in Figure 2-10. Specifically, using data from the Supplementary Homicide Reports for all reported murders occurring from 2000 to 2019, we tabulate the proportion of cases where information is reported for an identified assailant.[18] Technically, this does not necessarily mean that the case was cleared, since the assailant's characteristics may be known even when an arrest has not been made and the case has not been cleared via exceptional means. Moreover, cases reported in the Supplementary Homicide Reports may be cleared following reporting of the incident. However, the disparities we observe in these data are consistent with race disparities in clearance rates reported in other data sources.[19]

---

[17]Most homicides are cleared officially by the arrest of a suspect. In some instances, homicides are cleared without an arrest, often when the suspect dies on scene. This is called an exceptional clearance. Exceptional clearances also include, for example, declines to prosecute and refusals of cooperation by crime victims. Studies report that high rates of exceptional clearances have been reported for cases with female victims (e.g., Walfield, 2016; Jarvis and Regoeczi, 2009).

[18]Note that clearance requires an arrest of a suspect or a clearance by other means (e.g., when the perpetrator dies at the scene). We use the fact that information was reported about the assailant in the Supplementary Homicide Reports (SHR) as a proxy for arrest. Note also that SHR can be updated in subsequent years when arrests are made at a point beyond the initial reporting into the SHR.

[19]The Trace and Buzzfeed have assembled data on violent crimes inclusive of homicides in 22 cities along with information on whether the incidents are cleared by an arrest or exceptional means. These data cover violent offenses occurring roughly between 2010 through 2017. See https://github.com/the-trace-and-buzzfeed-news/local-police-data-analysis. We tabulated the percentage of homicides in these data cleared by arrest or some other means by the condensed victim-race category created by the Trace/Buzzfeed researchers. For the homicide incidents in these data, the percent cleared is approximately 48 percent for victims placed in the Black/Hispanic category, 60 percent for the victims placed in the other/unknown race category, and 65 percent for victims placed in the White category. While the clearance rates in these data are lower than the percentages of cases in the Supplementary Homicide Reports (SHR) with reports about offender characteristics, the cross-group disparities are quite similar. For example, the White-Black victim difference in the SHR data is 18 percentage points, while the White-Hispanic victim difference is 15 percentage points. By comparison, the difference in clearance rates between

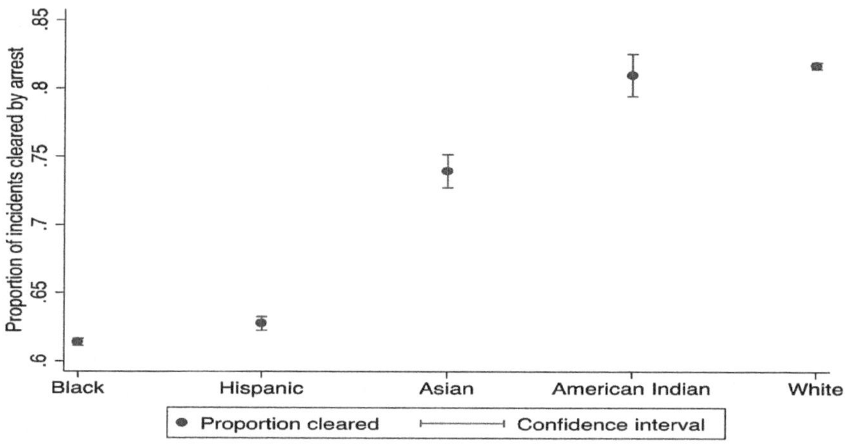

FIGURE 2-10 Clearance rates by race/ethnicity for all murders occurring between 2000 and 2019.
SOURCE: Tabulations from the Federal Bureau of Investigation Supplementary Homicide Reports, https://ucr.fbi.gov/crime-in-the-u.s/2019/crime-in-the-u.s.-2019/topic-pages/expanded-homicide

Murders involving African American victims have the lowest clearance rate (roughly 62%), with clearance rates for Hispanic people the second lowest (also below 65%). Murders involving American Indian and White victims have the highest clearance rates, with over 80 percent of cases for both groups cleared.

Some advocates and researchers argue that crime rates are higher in African American communities than official data indicate because African Americans are reluctant to report crimes to the police. Further, some argue that clearance rates are low in African American communities because local residents refuse to cooperate with police. The first argument suggests that the lack of protection in African American communities is greater than the data imply. The second implies that clearance rates are low in African American communities for reasons beyond the control of the police, although some might contend that better police-community relationship in predominantly minority communities would improve cooperation.

We find limited evidence in favor of either argument. Even though there is clear evidence that police employ aggressive tactics in African American communities, African American crime victims are by far the most likely to

homicides involving White victims and homicides involving Black victims for the 22 cities in the Trace database stands at 17 percentage points.

report what happened to them to the police. We again use victimization survey data (from the NCVS) to document this fact. Given that the NCVS bases victimization rates on individual-level survey responses and asks about follow-up actions to a crime, we are able to measure whether the person experiencing the crime reports the offense to the police. We are also able to observe the demographics of the perpetrator of the offense, an issue that we will discuss in detail in the next section. Tables 2-9 and 2-10 present estimates of whether households or individuals who experience crimes report them to the police by the race/ethnicity of the victim.

In Table 2-9 we observe within each racial/ethnic group familiar patterns regarding difference in reporting across the different categories of property offenses. Motor vehicle thefts are the most likely to be reported to the police. This is not surprising, since motor vehicle thefts often result in insurance claims and the need for official documentation of the incident. Burglaries and other thefts are reported at lower rates. African American households have the highest overall reporting rates for property offenses, with the largest positive differential in reporting rates between Black households and other households being the rate observed for burglaries.

In Table 2-10 we see that African American victims of violent crime also have the highest reporting rates both overall and for each of the serious violent offenses except for rape. For all violent offenses, 66 percent of African American victims report the crime to the police compared to 56 percent of Hispanic victims, 52 percent of White victims, and 49 percent of American Indian victims.

Hence, minority victims of serious violent offenses are generally as likely if not more likely to report the incidents to police. When we consider

TABLE 2-9 Proportion of Property Crime Incidents Reported to the Police by the Race/Ethnicity of the Household Head and the Offense Type (All Offenses Occurring between 2012 and 2019)

	All Property Offenses	Burglary	Motor Vehicle Theft	Other Theft
White	0.35	0.51	0.77	0.29
Black	0.37	0.60	0.78	0.27
Amer. Ind./Aleut.	0.33	0.50	0.62	0.25
Asian/PI	0.36	0.54	0.89	0.29
More than one race	0.29	0.38	0.55	0.25
Hispanic	0.34	0.52	0.77	0.26

NOTE: The race/ethnicity categories used in this table are mutually exclusive.
SOURCE: Figures tabulated from the concatenated National Crime Victimization Survey files, https://doi.org/10.3886/ICPSR38136.v1

TABLE 2-10 Proportion of Serious Violent Crime Incidents Reported to the Police by the Race/Ethnicity of the Victim and the Offense Type (All Offenses Occurring between 2012 and 2019)

	All Serious Violent Offenses	Rape	Robbery	Aggravated Assault
White	0.52	0.31	0.56	0.58
Black	0.66	0.46	0.69	0.68
Amer. Ind./Aleut.	0.49	0.66	0.39	0.49
Asian/PI	0.37	0.17	0.51	0.38
More than one race	0.37	0.13	0.49	0.47
Hispanic	0.56	0.29	0.57	0.64

NOTE: The race/ethnicity categories used in this table are mutually exclusive.
SOURCE: Figures tabulated from the concatenated National Crime Victimization Survey files, https://doi.org/10.3886/ICPSR38136.v1

racial differences in clearance rates, we must remember that clearance rates are incidents cleared divided by incidents reported. The low clearance rates we observe in minority communities are low rates of clearing crimes that someone, who was likely a member of the victim's community, reported to police. This pattern is consistent with historical evidence of racial bias in police neglecting to pursue accountability among crime victims in Black communities. We cannot rule out the possibility that low clearance rates in minority communities may reflect racial differences in levels of cooperation with police. Residents of minority communities that are plagued by gang violence may fear retribution if they cooperate, and even if the risks of retribution are small, residents who live in communities where police rarely clear crimes, even homicides, may reason that the returns from cooperating are low while the risks are high.

Whether police can affect clearance rates through increased effort and resources devoted to working cases is an active debate among criminologists. A highly cited early study by Greenwood and Petersilia (1975) concluded that whether a homicide is cleared by arrest or exceptional means tends to be a function of conditions beyond the control of the police, such as whether someone is apprehended at the scene, whether witnesses come forward and are cooperative, and the nature of the incident (for example, whether the homicide derived from a domestic dispute as opposed to resulting from a robbery or a gang related conflict). While researchers have challenged this conclusion over the previous four decades (see, for example, Wellford and Cronin, 1999), until recently there has been little by way of careful quasi-experimental or experimental research documenting a causal relationship between effort/resources and crime clearance.

However, a recent study by Cook and colleagues (2019) strongly suggests that policing and investigations are quite central to solving many homicides as well as nonfatal aggravated assaults involving a gun injury. Using detailed data for Boston (MA) on all gun homicides occurring between 2010 and 2014 as well as a random sample of cases where an aggravated assault victim is shot yet survives, the study first documents that these two sets of cases are statistically indistinguishable from one another along most dimensions, including characteristics of the victim and the nature of the incident. Their analysis implies that whether the victim of a gun assault dies is as good as random conditional on being injured by a firearm. However, incidents where the victim dies (or where it is deemed early on that the victim is likely to die) are treated differently. Homicide cases are worked by homicide detectives, who have lighter caseloads, have claim to crime laboratory and forensic investigatory resources that are typically not as available for nonfatal gun assaults, more carefully manage and collect evidence at crime scenes, and make more intensive efforts over the coming weeks, months, and sometimes years in pursing leads, identifying witnesses, and encouraging those with knowledge to come forward. The authors find very little difference in clearance rates between the two sets of cases occurring within two days or even two weeks of the incident. However, between two weeks and six months, and also between six months and a year following the incident, very large differences in clearance rates emerge, suggesting that the initial differences in resources devoted to the case as well as the sustained investigatory efforts increase the likelihood of an arrest.

The study by Cook and colleagues relies on data originally collected for a quasi-experimental evaluation of an effort by the Boston Police Department to increase homicide clearance rates. In 2011, the department conducted an extensive assessment of its homicide investigations with the aim of generating and implementing a set of recommendations that would increase department-level homicide clearance rates, which were far below the national average. Braga and Dusseault (2018) compare homicide investigation before and after the reforms were implemented and document that relative to the pre-reform period, post-period investigations had more homicide detectives assigned to each case, were more likely to have a homicide supervisor on scene, had more crime-scene response unit officers on the crime scene, increased the number of witness interviews after the crime scene investigation, were more likely to find latent prints on the scene, were more likely to have the forensic unit on the scene, were more likely to collect DNA evidence, and were more likely to use follow-up computer searches as part of the investigation. The study finds a notable pre-post increase in homicide clearance rates as well as an increase relative to clearances for all other homicides in Massachusetts over the same period.

This latter research suggests that while incident circumstances are clearly important determinants of the likelihood of a clearance, there are factors under the control of police that—through sustained effort, careful crime scene processing, and careful and systemic management of the investigation and follow-up activities—can increase the likelihood of an arrest. Cook and colleagues (2019) additionally argue that devoting more resources to clearing nonfatal shootings (given the large disparity in clearance rates) may go long a way in reducing gun violence overall through a stronger deterrent and through interruption of retaliatory violence.

PRETRIAL DETENTION

According to BJS, the average jail population for 2019 was about 740,000 U.S. citizens. This large population of jail inmates is an important source of racial disparities in the criminal justice system. Between 2005 and 2019, per-capita jail populations for Black people averaged well over three times the rates for both White and Hispanic people.[20] Further, a growing literature attributes part of this racial disparity in jail populations to the common practice of requiring defendants to post cash bail in order to be released from jail between their preliminary hearings and the resolution of their cases. A growing body of research indicates that the existing Black jail population would be significantly smaller in absolute and relative terms if the pretrial detention decisions generated by courts reflected only the relative risks that defendants will fail to appear in court or commit a new crime while waiting for their court dates. Cash bail expands jail populations, especially among economically disadvantaged groups, because it links release directly to a defendant's capacity to pay bail, even in cases where defendants are charged with minor crimes and have no desire to flee prosecution. Monetary sanctions have been studied as being linked to broader patterns of racial and economic inequality (Harris et al., 2022; see Chapter 4 for more on fines and fees).

In 2019, the roughly 740,000 people in jail on any given day represented more than one-third of the roughly 2.1 million persons who were incarcerated on that day.[21] Some of these jail inmates were serving short sentences associated with convictions for relatively minor offenses, but Sawyer and Wagner (2020) report that more than 500,000 of these persons

---

[20]See Figure 1 in *Jail Inmates in 2019* (Zeng, 2021). We draw on this report for the several descriptive statistics we discuss below.

[21]See Table 1 in Correctional Populations in the United States, 2019–Statistical Tables (Minton et al., 2021).

had not yet been convicted of the charges brought against them.[22] Thus, roughly one-fourth of the persons incarcerated in the United States were in a local jail or in the custody of the U.S. Marshals Service waiting for the resolution of a case.

This 500,000-person count for 2019 is a stock measure for the jail population on an average day. The total number of people who spent weeks or months in jail waiting for a verdict is likely much greater. Further, a significant fraction of those who spent weeks or months in jail waiting for a verdict were not denied bail outright. In many cases, judges set a cash bail amount that defendants are not able to raise. One of the challenges facing researchers in this area is the fact that researchers have no clear way to label cases where the judge set a cash bail expecting that the defendant would likely be released versus cases where the judge intended the bail amount to prevent release. However, in some jurisdictions, the majority of defendants in jail waiting for a verdict could be waiting at home if they had greater access to cash.[23] Given the significant income and wealth differences between White defendants and Black or Hispanic defendants, cash bail is an institution that, by design, exacerbates racial disparities in incarceration.

In addition, research suggests that pretrial detention systems built around cash bail do not effectively detain the defendants who are most likely to flee or commit new crimes if released, and Kleinberg and colleagues (2018) claim that it is possible to shrink jail populations by at least one-fourth without increasing the rates at which defendants facing charges either fail to appear in court or commit new crimes. The authors employ data from New York City and argue that these gains are possible if New York courts replace cash bail systems with a pretrial system that bases release decisions on statistical measures of the risks associated with releasing each defendant. The authors study pretrial detention using data from late 2008 to late 2013. They use a machine learning algorithm to predict the probability that a given defendant will fail to appear in court or will commit a new crime if the court grants pretrial release. This estimation problem is challenging, because the data only contain the outcomes of interest for the select sample of defendants that bail judges released directly or set bail amounts such that the defendants were able to post the required amount and gain release.

Nonetheless, the authors provide compelling evidence that some judges release many risky defendants. Failure-to-appear rates and crime rates are high among defendants whom judges release even though the authors'

[22]See https://www.prisonpolicy.org/reports/pie2020.html

[23]For example, Cook County, IL, has been reforming its pretrial detention rules for several years. Yet, around 2010, judges in Cook County assigned cash bail to more than 80 percent of felony defendants.

algorithm correctly labels them as "risky." It is impossible to determine whether these judges fail to understand that certain types of defendants are "risky" or whether they often guess wrong concerning a defendant's capacity to pay a certain bail amount. However, these mistakes are so infrequent that the authors claim it is possible to shrink jail populations significantly without any costs to public safety by basing release decisions on algorithmic risk scores. This reform would result in the detention of more high-risk defendants and the release of a much greater number of low-risk defendants, who now often remain in jail because they do not have the resources to post even modest bail amounts.

At least four states, including New York, have recently begun or completed efforts to reform pretrial detention rules, and the elimination of cash bail is central to many of these reform efforts. Researchers are also actively studying the optimal way to create the risk scores that serve as the key input in proposed systems that are alternatives to cash bail. In Chapter 8, we return to these reform efforts and discuss how a growing research literature on pretrial detention can inform these efforts.

While there is little research on the racially disparate impacts of bail reform, there is existing research suggesting that reductions in pretrial detention are likely to disparately impact case outcomes for African American defendants. MacDonald and Raphael (2020) study the disparate impacts of a reform that narrowed the definition of felony offenses. In late 2014, California voters passed Proposition 47, which redefined a set of less serious felony drug and property offenses as misdemeanors. The authors examine how racial disparities in criminal court dispositions in San Francisco changed in the years before (2010–2014) and after (2015–2016) the passage of Proposition 47. The study decomposes racial disparities in court dispositions into components due to racial differences in offense characteristics, involvement in the criminal justice system at the time of arrest, pretrial detention, criminal history, and the residual unexplained component. Before and after Proposition 47 case characteristics explain nearly all of the observable race disparities in court dispositions. However, after the passage of Proposition 47 there is a narrowing of racial disparities in convictions and incarceration sentences that is driven by lesser weight placed on criminal history, active criminal justice status, and a reduction in the racial disparity in pretrial detention in effecting court dispositions. The findings from this study suggest that policy reforms that scale back the severity of punishment for criminal history and active criminal justice status for less serious felony offenses may help narrow racial inequalities in criminal court dispositions. Efforts to reduce the impact of racial inequalities in incarceration in other states should consider reforms that reduce the weight that criminal history, pretrial detention, and active probation status have on criminal defendants' eligibility for prison for less serious drug and property offenses (Jordan et al., 2022).

PLEA BARGAINING, TRIALS, AND SENTENCING

After defendants are arrested, several outcomes are possible. The state's attorney may drop the charges due to lack of evidence. A judge may dismiss the case because it fails to meet some legal standard. A trial may produce a verdict of guilty or not guilty. Yet, the most common outcome involves a plea agreement. The state's attorney typically offers each defendant a promise that, if he or she enters a plea of guilty, the judge will assign a sentence that is known ex ante and much less severe than the expected sentence if the defendant insists on a trial and loses.

Many researchers worry that prosecutors offer less generous plea deals to Black defendants than to White defendants. This concern arises, at least in part, because Black defendants are much more likely to remain in jail between arrest and sentencing. Thus, in any court where it takes significant time to schedule and conduct trials, Black defendants are likely to find it more costly to demand a trial, and this gives prosecutors extra leverage when making plea bargain offers to Black defendants. The power of prosecutorial discretion in plea bargaining may be strongest in jurisdictions with presumptive sentencing guidelines (Piehl and Bushway, 2007).

Rehavi and Starr (2014) provide compelling evidence that prosecutors in federal courts discriminate against Black defendants by selecting initial charges that are both inflated and associated with long mandatory sentences. This practice gives them extra leverage that allows them to get Black defendants to accept less favorable plea bargains, which typically involve entering a guilty plea to slightly less serious charges. Tuttle (2019) also finds evidence that federal prosecutors discriminate against Black defendants facing drug charges, and similar to Rehavi and Starr (2014), he finds that prosecutors discriminate by manipulating the initial charge.

Jordan (2021) examines data from Cook County (IL). Here, the charging decision is not made by the prosecutor who constructs plea bargain offers, but Jordan still finds some evidence that is consistent with the view that prosecutors make less favorable plea bargain offers to Black defendants. However, Jordan also concludes that banning plea bargains and forcing all cases to be resolved through bench trials would likely harm Black defendants. Plea deals are a form of insurance, and Black defendants in Cook County often face initial charges that result in significant prison time if they are found guilty at trial.

Jordan (2021) concludes that, in Cook County, the most important source of racial bias in the plea-bargaining process is that police bring more weak cases against Black defendants. Cases that are so weak that the defendant would stand a good chance of winning at trial are much more common among Black defendants. However, because defendants are risk-averse, state's attorneys can often get these defendants to plead guilty to some charge.

SENTENCING AND CORRECTIONAL TRENDS

The previous sections have shown that arrest decisions by police, charging decisions by police and state's attorneys, and plea-bargaining practices by state's attorneys all play a role in shaping the sentences that judges assign to convicted offenders. However, the priorities and preferences of judges also constrain the types of deals that a state's attorney can offer, and the laws that govern sentencing constrain the sentencing decisions of judges whether a case ends with a guilty plea or a guilty verdict following a trial. Here, we discuss corrections populations while paying specific attention to the development of laws that govern sentencing.

Correctional populations in the United States fall into two broad categories: (1) people physically detained in either a local jail or state or federal prison, and (2) people who have been sentenced and are under some form of community corrections supervision. The former category includes both individuals who are detained while awaiting trial (commonly referred to as pretrial detainees) as well as sentenced individuals serving time in jail or prison. People in the latter category include both individuals who have been sentenced directly to community supervision, usually under threat of a prison or jail term should they violate the conditions of their sentence, as well as people who have been released from a prison or jail sentence yet are still under correctional supervision, effectively serving the remainder of their sentence in a non-carceral setting.

The steep increase in U.S. correctional populations during the last quarter of the 20th century has been widely studied (Neal and Rick, 2016; NRC, 2014; Raphael and Stoll, 2013). The principal factors driving the steep increase in prison, jail, and community corrections populations were punitive shifts in sentencing policy that both increased the proportion of felony sentences punished with a prison term and increased the length of prison terms for specific offenses. The specific forms these policy shifts took varied across correctional systems—that is, the various state and federal criminal codes governing sentencing—though there are common elements. Sentencing generally became more determinate (fixed rather than open terms with minimum and maximum sentences); more severe for defendants with a criminal history; laden with enhancements for factors such as using a firearm, being affiliated with a gang, or crossing a quantity threshold for controlled substances; and more subject to binding constraints associated with various mandatory minimum sentences.

Rates of incarceration grew for all groups during the late 1970s and 1980s as prison time became more likely given arrest for a broad range of offenses, and this shift in policy had a clear disparate impact on African Americans, who are arrested at higher rates than other groups. Figure 2-11 presents incarceration rates per 100,000 for several racial/ethnic groups

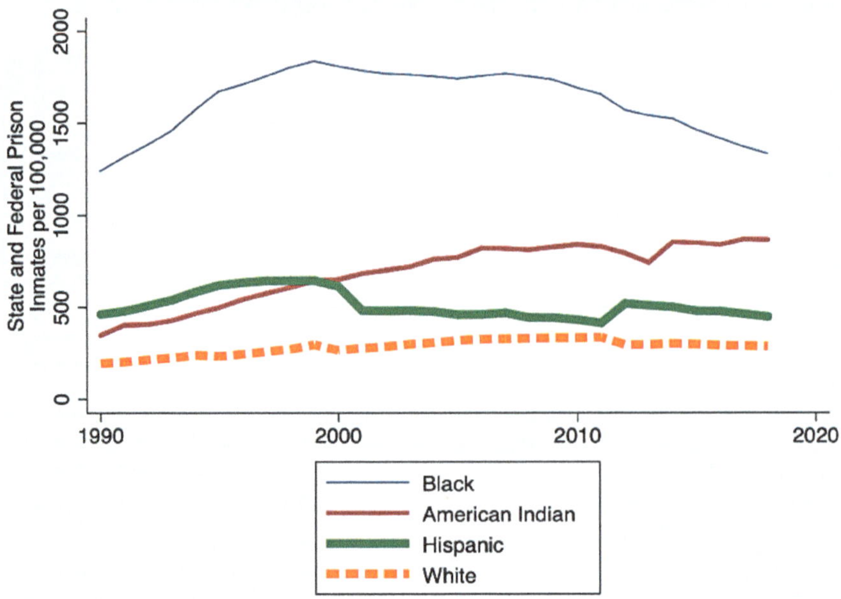

FIGURE 2-11 Number of state and federal prisoners per 100,000 residents by race and ethnicity, 1990 through 2018.
SOURCE: Data from the Bureau of Justice Statistics. Generated using the Corrections Statistical Analysis Tool, https://csat.bjs.ojp.gov/

reported in the National Prison Statistics database for the years 1990 through 2018.[24] The Black prison incarceration rate peaks in 1999 at 1,837 per 100,000 and then declines each year until it reaches 1,333 per 100,000 by 2018, a 28 percent decline relative to the peak year. Over this period, the absolute Black/White disparity in incarceration rates also declines, from 1,524 per 100,000 in 1999 to 1,047 per 100,000 in 2018. Moreover, the Black/White incarceration rate ratio declines from 6.23 to 4.24.

Over this same period, the Hispanic/White incarceration rate differential narrows from 349 per 100,000 to 141 per 100,000, while the Hispanic/White incarceration rate ratio declines from 2.18 to 1.56. The one group for whom we see a trend in the opposite direction is American Indian people. For American Indian people we see a widening in both absolute and relative incarceration rates relative to White people, with

[24]We tabulated incarceration rates, combining incarceration totals from the National Prison Statistics database for each year with population estimates of race interacted with ethnicity tabulation and publicly posted by the CDC.

the absolute incarceration rate differential increasing form 348 in 1999 to 579 in 2018 and the corresponding ratios increasing from 2.18 to 3.02.

As with arrest and victimization trends, trends in correctional population skew heavily toward males and people with less formal education. Prison populations tend to be older relative to the composition of arrests, given that many in prison are serving long terms for offenses committed at a relatively young age. While these patterns exist within racial groups, the gender and educational disparities are largest among African Americans, with less educated Black men experiencing the highest incarceration rates in the country.

EXECUTIONS

In 1972, the Supreme Court ruled in *Furman v. Georgia*[25] that the death penalty as applied in Georgia law and in many other states was unconstitutional. A key argument against the existing statutes centered on the observation that juries had great discretion and little guidance when deciding whether to assign death or a term of confinement in prison as a punishment. Further, the history of death penalty verdicts left no doubt that jurors could and did use their discretion to discriminate against Black defendants. Steiker and Steiker (2016) report that between 1930 and 1967, state corrections systems executed 455 inmates convicted of rape.[26] Of that total, 405 inmates were Black, even though the Black population was roughly 12 percent of the U.S. total over this period. Wolfgang and Riedel (1973) in their analysis of capital sentencing for rape concluded that "there has been a patterned systematic, and customary imposition of the death penalty... sentences of death have been imposed on blacks, compared to whites, in a way that exceeds any statistical notions of chance or fortuity" (p. 133).

Between 1972 and 1976, 35 states passed new death penalty laws that sought to address the process requirements spelled out in *Furman v. Georgia*. The U.S. Supreme Court, in a series of 1976 decisions, upheld most of these new laws. In 1977, the Supreme Court held in *Coker v. Georgia*[27] that the death penalty for the rape of an adult woman was grossly disproportionate and excessive, and thus unconstitutional under the Eighth Amendment. In the years following *Furman*, the country moved from an abolition to a regulation regime. The death penalty enjoyed robust support in many state legislatures, but these new laws applied only to cases of murder with aggravating circumstances and required courts to reach

---

[25]408 U.S. 238 (1972); see https://supreme.justia.com/cases/federal/us/408/238/

[26]Our account of the legal history of death penalty litigation draws heavily on Chapter 2 of Steiker and Steiker (2016).

[27]433 U.S. 584 (1977); see https://supreme.justia.com/cases/federal/us/433/584/

each death penalty verdict in a separate post-trial proceeding where judges or juries received guidance concerning the details of the crime and the characteristics of the defendant that should be considered when deciding whether to assign the extreme penalty of death.

In one of the 1976 decisions, *Woodson v. North Carolina*,[28] the Supreme Court also ruled that states could not make the death penalty mandatory for any offense. The High Court argued that North Carolina could not simply make the death penalty mandatory as a way of addressing the concern it had raised earlier in *Furman v. Georgia*—about the capricious use of the death penalty—because the North Carolina law imposed the same death penalty on individuals who had committed crimes under greatly varying circumstances and given varied criminal histories. Since Black people are arrested for murder more than other groups, mandatory death penalties would likely have created even larger racial disparities in execution rates.

Further, even if one examines only the population of persons arrested for murder, allowing mandatory death sentences could have increased conditional racial disparities in the use of the death penalty. Prosecutors have discretion when choosing charges to file, and if juries feel any affinity for a defendant, they may be reluctant to find him (or her) guilty if he faces the death penalty. Thus, mandatory death sentences could have generated racially biased behavioral responses that made racial disparities in executions worse, holding constant racial disparities in homicide arrest rates.

Given the tighter regulation of death penalty cases after 1976, researchers have tried to determine whether racial bias still drives disparate application of the death penalty. Since 1976, corrections systems in the United States have executed 1,542 people.[29] Thirty-four percent of these people were Black, and 56 percent were White. Over this period, Black persons were, on average, just over 12 percent of the U.S. population, meaning Black citizens have been overrepresented in the sample of executed persons by a ratio of almost 3:1. White and Hispanic people have been underrepresented. As of the fall of 2021, racial disparities in the number of people on death row are even more striking. More than 40 percent of the almost 2,500 people facing an execution sentence are Black; and both White and Hispanic persons are underrepresented. These ratios suggest racial bias in the application of the death penalty, but as we note above, arrest rates for violent crime are much higher among Black people than other racial groups, and no data exist on aggregate counts of arrests for offenses that are death penalty "eligible."

However, a significant research literature addresses the question of racial bias using more granular data. The Supreme Court heard part of this

---

[28]428 U.S. 280 (1976); see https://supreme.justia.com/cases/federal/us/428/280/

[29]See www.deathpenaltyinfo.org

evidence in *McCleskey v. Kemp*[30] (1987). Warren McCleskey, a Black defendant, received the death penalty for murdering a White police officer in Atlanta (GA). McCleskey later challenged the constitutionality of his death sentence on the grounds that statistical work by Baldus and colleagues (1983) showed that the races of both defendants and victims predicted the use of the death penalty in Georgia even after *Furman*. The Supreme Court's 5–4 majority said that statistical patterns could not prove racial bias in the administration of the defendant's particular sentence. Several years later, Baldus and colleagues (1990) published their findings from Georgia and other states. Using regression models that control for case characteristics, they conclude that *Furman v. Georgia* reduced but did not eliminate disproportionate use of the death penalty as a sentence for Black defendants, and evidence for this disparity is quite robust in cases involving White victims. Baldus and colleagues concluded that racial disparities in the capital cases they examined were concentrated in the middle of their seriousness scale—where prosecutors and judges had more discretion to decide whether to charge a case as a capital case or impose a death sentence.

Reviews of research on death penalty sentencing report that many studies find evidence that Black defendants are more likely than White defendants to receive the death penalty. However, the vast majority of credible studies find that the presence of a White victim enhances the likelihood of a death sentence, and this effect is stronger when a Black defendant is accused of killing a White victim (see, e.g., Baumgartner et al., 2015; U.S. General Accounting Office, 1990). Prosecutors have been found to be more likely to seek the death penalty in the case of Black defendants and White victims (Paternoster, 1984). Phillips and Marceau (2020) also argue that conditional on receiving a death sentence, prisoners are more likely to be executed if their victim was White. Some indication of how bias may be working against Black defendants is provided by psychological research. Among those accused of killing a White victim, Eberhardt and colleagues (2006) find that defendants with stereotypically Black features (e.g., broad nose, thick lips, dark skin) are more likely to receive the death penalty.

Existing evidence that the differences in the race of victims and defendants predict the use of the death penalty in otherwise comparable cases is particularly noteworthy, given the growing awareness that a nontrivial number of persons have been sentenced to death who are innocent. Since 1973, 186 persons on death row have been exonerated (Death Penalty Information Center, 2022a). In 2003, George Ryan ended his term as governor of Illinois by commuting 167 death sentences to life in prison. Ryan acted in response to evidence that a number of persons sentenced to death in Illinois were innocent persons who gave false confessions while being

[30]481 U.S. 279 (1987); see https://supreme.justia.com/cases/federal/us/481/279/

tortured by police. Further, Gross and colleagues (2014) examined the arrival rate of exonerations for persons on death row and concluded that at least four percent of all persons sentenced to death are innocent.

Paternoster and colleagues (2003) examine death penalty cases in Maryland over the period 1978–1999. They find enormous variation across different counties in the willingness of prosecutors to seek the death penalty for similar cases. Significant county variation in the prosecution of capital murder cases has also been reported in Pennsylvania (Ulmer et al., 2020). Given the spatial segregation of population by race in the United States, such geographic variation in death penalty use could generate important racial disparities in execution rates given the characteristics of cases, even if no prosecutors exhibit racial bias when seeking the death penalty.

COMMUNITY SUPERVISION

In most states, probation and parole supervision are legal substitutes for incarceration. In some states, a probation sentence is legally a sentence that takes away an offender's freedom but assigns him (or her) to serve the sentence in the community under the supervision of a probation officer rather than in a prison under the supervision of guards.

Probation populations have fallen since the Great Recession. The national population under community supervision reached a peak of almost 4.3 million in 2007 and then declined each following year. In 2019, just under 3.5 million persons were on probation. Thus, the probation population dropped by almost 20 percent between 2007 and 2019. However, the racial makeup of the population under probation supervision changed little from 2007 to 2019. In 2007, 55 percent of probationers were White, 29 percent were Black, and 13 percent were Hispanic. The racial composition of probationers in 2019 was almost identical (see Oudekerk and Kaeble, 2021). Still, the absolute reduction in rates has been favorable to Black men and women because they have a relatively high probation rate compared to White people.

The fall in probation populations is not surprising given the fall in arrest rates over this same period. However, probation populations did not fall quite as sharply as prison populations. This difference may, in part, reflect the fact that the *Brown v. Plata*[31] (2011) Supreme Court decision placed limits on how many inmates could be housed in a single prison, given its size and design. Following this decision, states faced higher costs due to expanding prison populations during a period when many states faced budget problems. Hence, probation may be increasingly serving as a substitute for custodial sentences.

---

[31] 563 U.S. 493 (2011); see https://supreme.justia.com/cases/federal/us/563/493/

In contrast to prison and probation populations, parole populations have grown steadily in recent decades. Table 2-11 shows that parole populations continued to grow through the Great Recession and beyond. As the parole population grew, the fraction of White individuals grew slightly, while the fractions of Black and Hispanic individuals remained roughly constant. In both 2001 and 2019, Black men and women accounted for roughly 37 percent of parolees, which means that, as the parole population has grown, Black persons have remained more than twice as likely to be on parole as other groups.

The growth of parole populations stands out because the recent experiences with policy reform in California (the largest state in the nation) suggest that it is possible to (1) reduce incarceration rates, (2) narrow racial disparities, and (3) not increase crime rates by reforming parole practices as well as dialing back the punishment for lesser felonies. Between 1970 and 2000, prison incarceration rates in the state increased in lockstep with the overall national rate for the United States (see Figure 2-12). From the early 2000s on, however, there are notable departures with large relative decreases in California's incarceration rates post 2010. Figure 2-13 presents long-term trends for California's overall violent and property crime rates. Similar to national trends, California's violent crime rate peaks in the early 1990s before declining to current historical lows. While the historical peak for property crime occurs in the early 1980s, the largest declines in property crime occur post 1990, with the rate declining by roughly 50 percent over the subsequent 26 years. In both figures, the years 2011 and 2014 (years of reform to parole and sentencing) are marked with vertical lines. Notably,

TABLE 2-11 Parole Populations by Race/Ethnicity, 2001 through 2019

	2001	2006	2011	2016	2019
Total	731,147	798,210	855,458	874,777	876,921
White	274,015	319,392	323,263	341,163	344,999
Black	299,708	304,484	305,297	323,667	324,461
Hispanic	130,755	143,012	138,104	157,460	157,845
Amer. Ind.	4,828	7,000	8,502	—	—
Asian	4,391	5,147	5,600	—	—
Unknown	15,672	13,402	68,508	—	—

NOTES: In 2016 and 2019, the fractions with unknown race were quite high. We use the racial composition of the parole population in 2018, which is well measured, to create race specific counts for the larger racial groups.

SOURCE: Data from Annual Probation Survey and Annual Parole Survey and Probation and Parole in the United States–2019, https://bjs.ojp.gov/data-collection/annual-probation-survey-and-annual-parole-survey

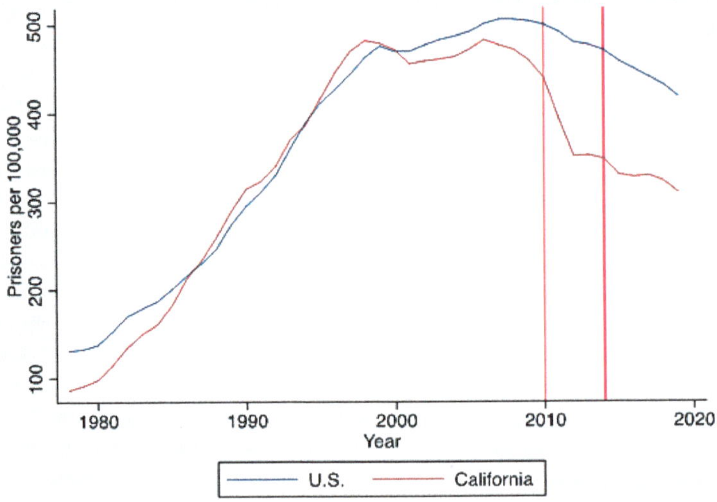

FIGURE 2-12 Long-term trends in U.S. and California incarceration rates, 1980–2020.
SOURCE: Data from the Bureau of Justice Statistics. Generated using the Corrections Statistical Analysis Tool, https://csat.bjs.ojp.gov/

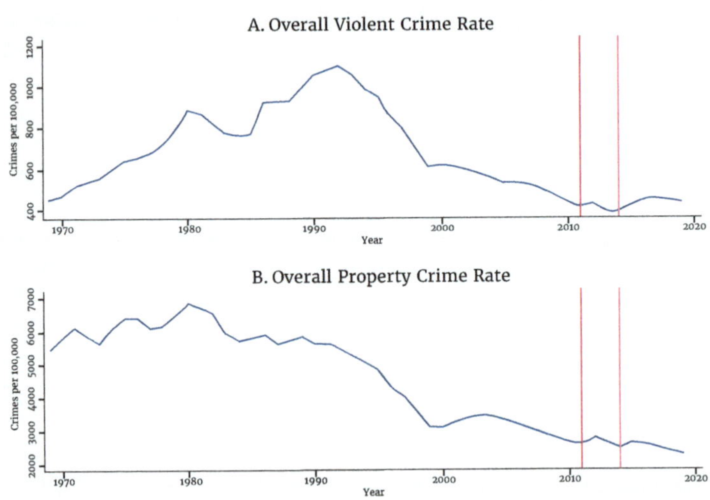

FIGURE 2-13 Long-term violent and property crime trends in California, 1970–2020.
SOURCE: Data from Crime in California 2020, California Department of Justice, https://oag.ca.gov/cjsc/databases

these reforms reduced the state's prison incarceration rate to early-1990s levels with little evidence of an impact on crime rates.

Here we ask several questions pertaining to the California experience. First, what drove the departure of California's prison trend from that of the nation? Second, did the reforms impact public safety? Finally, were there racially disparate impacts of this change?

Two broad factors converged to generate the reduction in the state incarceration rate. First, decades of litigation pertaining to conditions of confinement and the availability of health and mental health services in the state prison system culminated in a federal court order to reduce state prison overcrowding, an order ultimately affirmed by a 2011 U.S. Supreme Court ruling. Second, public opinion pertaining to sentencing severity and the use of incarceration in particular softened, resulting in several notable ballot measures aimed at undoing much of the stringent sentencing practiced in past decades.

Regarding the response to the federal court order, in 2011 California enacted broad corrections reform legislation under the banner of corrections realignment. The legislation was prompted by pressure from a federal three-judge court overseeing the California prison system, impaneled as a result of legal decisions in two lawsuits against the state filed on behalf of California prison inmates. In one lawsuit (*Coleman v. Brown*),[32] it was alleged that California was providing inadequate health care services to its prison population. In the other lawsuit (*Plata v. Brown*), it was alleged that the system was providing inadequate mental health services. Both resulted in rulings in favor of the plaintiffs, finding that prison overcrowding was the primary cause of the inadequate services and that the poor health and mental health care systems violated the Eighth Amendment prohibition against cruel and unusual punishment.

Assembly Bill 109[33] (referred to in the state as "corrections realignment") was passed and implemented under threat of a federal court order to release up to 35,000 inmates if the state failed to act on its own. The legislation eliminated the practice of returning parolees to state prison custody for technical parole violations for all but a small set of the most serious offenders. It also defined a group of nonserious, nonsexual, nonviolent offenders who upon conviction serve their sentences in county jails. The act generated an immediate reduction in weekly prison admissions from roughly 2,100 per week to 600 per week and a steady, permanent decline in the prison population of over 20 percent. While this decrease was partially offset by an increase in jail populations, the overall incarcerated population in California (combined prison and jail) fell by roughly 25,000 people within six months of the reform.

---

[32] 563 U.S. 493; see https://www.law.cornell.edu/supremecourt/text/09-1233

[33] See https://probation.lacounty.gov/ab-109/

Regarding the change in public opinion, in recent years California voters passed several state ballot initiatives aimed at reducing the use of prison along both the intensive and extensive margins. In 2012, voters approved a ballot measure to narrow the definition of felonies that would qualify for second- and third-strike sentence enhancements, limiting these felonies to serious and violent offenses (Proposition 36). More recently, voters passed a proposition that incentivizes prison inmates to engage in rehabilitative programming and refrain from institutional misconduct in exchange for shorter prison terms (Proposition 57, passed in November 2016).

Proposition 47, passed in November 2014, is the most far-reaching sentencing reform passed by way of ballot initiative and had immediate impacts on the operations and practices of several arms of the state's criminal justice system. Put simply, the proposition redefined a subset of "wobbler" offenses, those that can be charged as either a misdemeanor or felony, as straight misdemeanor offenses. Regarding property offenses, the proposition redefined shoplifting, forgery, crimes involving insufficient funds, petty theft, and receiving stolen property offenses where the value of the property theft falls below $950 as misdemeanors. The proposition also eliminated the offense of petty theft with a prior. Regarding drug offenses, a subset of possession offenses was redefined as misdemeanors. These new charging protocols apply to all new cases with the exception of instances where the individual in question has certain prior convictions. The proposition also included a provision for individuals currently serving sentences for reclassified offenses to file a resentencing petition, as well as a provision for those convicted in the past to file a petition to have the prior conviction reclassified as a misdemeanor (California Judicial Council, 2016). The passage and implementation of Proposition 47 reduced jail populations by about 10 percent, the state prison population by about 3.5 percent, policing, and the actions associated with specific offenses (Dominguez-Rivera et al., 2019).

Evaluations of these reforms find little evidence that the documented impacts of these reforms on jail populations, prison populations, the likelihood of being arrested, and the sanctions one faces in the event of arrest and conviction also impacted crime rates. Regarding the effects of the 2011 realignment reform, Lofstrom and Raphael (2016) find no impact of the large discrete reduction in the state's prison population on violent crime and modest short-lived effects on property crime. Similarly, two separate evaluations of Proposition 47 find no evidence of an effect of the reform on violent crime (Dominguez-Rivera et al., 2019; Bartos and Kubrin, 2018) and some suggestive evidence of a small impact on larceny theft.[34]

[34]One might note in Figure 2-13 what appears to be a slight increase in violent crime in California in 2014. Dominguez-Rivera and colleagues (2019) demonstrate that this increase is almost entirely attributable to the Los Angeles Police Department expanding its formal

By contrast, these reforms did impact racial disparities in criminal justice involvement both in terms of incarceration rates as well as arrests. Tables 2-12 and 2-13 present the proportion of California residents institutionalized (largely in jail or prison) by race, gender, age, and level of educational attainment (from Lofstrom et al., 2020). The tables present figures for the years 2011 (realignment was implemented at the end of 2011), 2014 (Proposition 47 goes into effect at the end of 2014), and 2017. While large disparities exist across racial groups in all years, there is a notable narrowing in overall race disparities especially among men and among lesser educated and younger men.

In addition to disparate impacts of these reforms on incarceration rates, researchers have also documented disparate impacts on arrest rates as well as pretrial processing and criminal case disposition. Mooney and colleagues (2018) present an analysis of California arrest rates before and after the passage of Proposition 47. They demonstrate a sharp decline in felony drug arrest rates for African American, White, and Hispanic people, with the larger decline for African Americans narrowing the disparity relative to White people. They also find comparable declines and narrowing racial disparities for other offenses reclassified as result of the proposition. Lofstrom and colleagues (2020) find similar effects on arrests, with particularly large declines in race disparities in felony drug arrests among younger men. MacDonald and Raphael (2020) study administrative data on criminal cases processed by the San Francisco District Attorney before and after the passage of Proposition 47. The authors find a narrowing of racial disparities in case outcomes largely attributable to lessening of the adverse effects of pretrial detention and criminal history on case outcomes.

Given that parole populations have grown as other forms of supervision have decreased, it is important to note that a growing literature finds that parole supervision generates many re-admissions to prison for violations of parole conditions that are technical. For example, in Illinois, violations fall under one of 15 rules. Rule 1 violations are the only ones that involve new criminal charges. However, those under supervision may be returned to prison for changing residence without approval, possessing a firearm, using drugs, associating with known gang members, or doing anything that violates approved conditions established by a parole agent.[35]

---

definition of aggravated assaults to include incidents where someone brandishes a firearm. The change occurred in response to an internal inspector general's report noting that the department was undercounting aggravated assaults. The change in reporting methods coincides exactly with the passage of Proposition 47.

[35]See 730 ILCS 5/3-3-7, https://www.ilga.gov/legislation/ilcs/fulltext.asp?DocName=073000050K3-3-7. In Illinois, the parole system is called Mandatory Supervised Release because release dates from prison are not determined by parole boards, and post-release periods of supervision are fixed at one, two, or three years, given good behavior.

TABLE 2-12 Proportion Institutionalized for California Men, 18 to 55 Years of Age, by Race/Ethnicity, Age, and Educational Attainment, 2011, 2014, 2017

Panel A: White Men			
	2011	2014	2017
All	0.015	0.013	0.012
18–25	0.013	0.008	0.006
26–30	0.017	0.013	0.015
31–40	0.016	0.015	0.014
41–55	0.015	0.014	0.012
Less than HS	0.086	0.071	0.070
HS grad	0.023	0.022	0.020
Some college	0.011	0.011	0.011
College +	0.001	0.001	0.001
Panel B: African American Men			
	2011	2014	2017
All	0.093	0.078	0.065
18–25	0.076	0.056	0.050
26–30	0.094	0.089	0.072
31–40	0.106	0.089	0.075
41–55	0.097	0.082	0.064
Less than HS	0.337	0.285	0.295
HS grad	0.109	0.093	0.075
Some college	0.054	0.040	0.038
College +	0.007	0.008	0.005

TABLE 2-12 Continued

Panel C: Hispanic Men			
	2011	2014	2017
All	0.024	0.022	0.022
18–25	0.023	0.020	0.019
26–30	0.028	0.023	0.027
31–40	0.026	0.028	0.028
41–55	0.019	0.019	0.016
Less than HS	0.036	0.035	0.041
HS grad	0.024	0.023	0.022
Some college	0.011	0.011	0.010
College +	0.003	0.003	0.002
Panel D: Asian Men			
	2011	2014	2017
All	0.005	0.006	0.005
18–25	0.006	0.002	0.002
26–30	0.007	0.008	0.003
31–40	0.005	0.009	0.008
41–55	0.004	0.005	0.004
Less than HS	0.021	0.034	0.039
HS grad	0.012	0.010	0.010
Some college	0.004	0.005	0.003
College +	0.001	0.001	0.000

SOURCE: Data from Table 7 in Lofstrom and colleagues (2020).

TABLE 2-13 Proportion Institutionalized among California Women, 18 to 55 Years of Age, by Race/Ethnicity, Age, and Educational Attainment, 2011, 2014, 2017

Panel A: White Women			
	2011	2014	2017
All	0.002	0.002	0.002
18–25	0.002	0.002	0.001
26–30	0.003	0.002	0.001
31–40	0.003	0.002	0.002
41–55	0.003	0.002	0.003
Less than HS	0.026	0.012	0.017
HS grad	0.004	0.002	0.004
Some college	0.003	0.003	0.002
College +	0.000	0.000	0.000
Panel B: African American Women			
	2011	2014	2017
All	0.010	0.008	0.007
18–25	0.009	0.004	0.002
26–30	0.009	0.008	0.012
31–40	0.013	0.011	0.010
41–55	0.010	0.008	0.004
Less than HS	0.048	0.050	0.043
HS grad	0.012	0.008	0.006
Some college	0.007	0.005	0.006
College +	0.002	0.000	0.000

TABLE 2-13 Continued

Panel C: Hispanic Women			
	2011	2014	2017
All	0.002	0.002	0.002
18–25	0.002	0.002	0.002
26–30	0.004	0.003	0.003
31–40	0.003	0.002	0.003
41–55	0.002	0.002	0.002
Less than HS	0.005	0.003	0.004
HS grad	0.002	0.002	0.002
Some college	0.001	0.001	0.002
College +	0.000	0.001	0.001
Panel D: Asian Women			
	2011	2014	2017
All	0.001	0.001	0.001
18–25	0.001	0.000	0.001
26–30	0.001	0.001	0.000
31–40	0.001	0.001	0.001
41–55	0.001	0.001	0.000
Less than HS	0.002	0.007	0.003
HS grad	0.002	0.001	0.001
Some college	0.001	0.001	0.001
College +	0.001	0.000	0.000

SOURCE: Data from Table 8 in Lofstrom and colleagues (2020).

In Illinois and other states, parole agents have great discretion and considerable power to start proceedings that generate readmissions for people recently released from prison. Jordan and colleagues (2022) examine formerly incarcerated individuals during and just after fixed periods of post-release supervision. They find that post-release supervision has only minor impacts on the likelihood that a given formerly incarcerated individual faces a new felony charge but large impacts on the likelihood that a formerly incarcerated individual returns to prison. The resolution of this apparent contradiction is that more than one-third of prison admissions among persons under post-release supervision are associated with technical violations and not new crimes.

Franco-Paredes and colleagues (2021) and Harding and colleagues (2017) find that the parole agents in Michigan use technical violations to readmit large numbers of formerly incarcerated individuals back to prison. However, they also find that the incapacitation effects created by these readmissions and any other services these agents provide have little impact on rates of severe crime.

In some states, a single agency governs both probation and parole supervision, and research on the impacts of probation supervision contains findings that parallel findings in recent studies of parole. For example, Hyatt and Barnes (2017) review a recent experimental evaluation of a program known as Intensive Supervision Probation. The program involved more intensive supervision and more frequent contact with probation officers. The program had no impact on recidivism, but it did increase rates of technical violations and prison reentry.

Rose (2021) examines a reform of probation in North Carolina that made it more difficult for probation officers to start proceedings that would send probationers to prison. By comparing offender characteristics and recidivism rates in the pre- and post-reform periods, he shows that in the pre-reform period probation officers were not using technical violations to incapacitate offenders who were significantly more high risk than others on probation.

Many probation and parole systems appear to be designed in ways that maximize the opportunities for agents or officials with implicit or explicit bias to use discretion in ways that harm certain groups of offenders. Defenders of these systems argue that parole and probation agents possess information that allows them to act to protect society from dangerous persons who are likely to reoffend. However, the literature offers little evidence that this is true.

SYNTHESIZING THE EVIDENCE

This chapter has broadly documented what is known about racial and ethnic disparities in victimization, offending, and criminal justice interactions and processing in the United States. The following section summarizes the findings from this analysis.

CONCLUSION 2-1: *There are clear racial disparities in victimization rates. American Indians and African Americans are the most likely to be victimized by serious violent offenses, followed by Hispanic, non-Hispanic White, and Asian people. While inter-racial disparities in nonlethal violent victimization have narrowed considerably over the past decade, racial disparities in murder rates remain stubbornly high, with the murder rate for African Americans relative to other groups increasing sharply during the 2020 pandemic. Disparities and trends in disparities in property crime victimization are qualitatively similar.*

CONCLUSION 2-2: *The most recent data on homicide victimization, for 2020, demonstrate two facts concerning the recent increase in homicide rates, which have reached the highest levels since the mid- to late 1990s: (1) the increases were broad-based geographically, with similar patterns observed across the country; and (2) the increases are extremely concentrated among specific demographic groups, particularly among Black men.*

CONCLUSION 2-3: *There are large racial disparities in arrest rates for serious felony offenses as well as for less serious offenses. Salient patterns include very high relative arrest rates among African Americans for robbery and relatively high arrest rates for American Indians for alcohol-related offenses. Regarding race disparities in arrests for serious offending, the racial composition of arrests aligns with the racial composition of offenders as reported by crime victims, though there is also evidence that offenses where the victim identifies the perpetrator as being Black are somewhat more likely to be reported to the police.*

CONCLUSION 2-4: *Black people are considerably more likely to be stopped by the police while driving, riding a bike, or walking relative to members of other racial groups. Vehicle stops often occur due to equipment violations rather than moving violations and often do not result in a citation. Among those stopped, Black people are considerably more likely to be searched by police and are more likely to be asked to exit a vehicle, to be handcuffed, to be ordered to sit on a curb, or to experience a backseat detention during the duration of the stop. Again, such stops often do not end with a citation or an arrest, and for African Americans they are relatively less likely to result in arrest or citation.*

CONCLUSION 2-5: *While most interactions between the police and the public do not involve a use of force, there are sizable racial disparities in use of force of all sorts. Black people are the most likely to report experiencing force or the threat of force during police stops. Moreover, Black people are overrepresented among instances where police shoot and kill members of the public. There are large regional disparities in fatal police shootings, with the highest rates in West Coast states and the lowest rates in the Northeast.*

CONCLUSION 2-6: *The higher rate at which police shoot Black persons does not necessarily imply that, holding the conditions of citizen encounters constant, police are more likely to shoot Black people. Black individuals are much more likely to be arrested for violent crimes and also more likely to shoot police, although this is a relatively rare event. However, existing studies do not rule out the possibility that police behaviors that shape interactions with Black citizens create circumstances that make the use of lethal force more likely. This in particular qualifies the findings from the one study (Fryer, 2019) that tests for and fails to find racial disparity in the likelihood that serious incidents result in an officer-involved shooting. There is evidence of a higher likelihood that emergency calls for service originating from Black and Hispanic neighborhoods are more likely to result in an officer-involved shooting, and that this appears to be driven in its entirety by outcomes involving White officers. This finding in particular provides evidence that racial bias is likely a factor in differential use of force. Moreover, there is clear evidence that police are more likely to use less lethal force against Black defendants. The higher rates at which police stop, search, and apply nonlethal force to Black citizens cannot be explained by the rates at which Black citizens engage in crime.*

CONCLUSION 2-7: *Black people consistently report being treated with less respect in their interactions with police officers. Moreover, research analyzing the content of interactions recorded by body-worn cameras confirms these reports.*

CONCLUSION 2-8: *Murders involving Black and Hispanic victims are notably less likely to be cleared by arrest relative to murders involving White victims. Recent research suggests that police efforts and resources have considerable impacts on the likelihood of clearing such offenses, especially during the weeks and months following the initial few days following the incident. Research recently has focused on gun assaults that generate nonfatal injuries and suggests substantial reduction in violence could be achieved by paying more attention and devoting more effort to clearing these nonfatal but serious assaults.*

CONCLUSION 2-9: *Black criminal defendants are more likely to be detained pretrial and are more likely to be convicted as a result. Existing research on bail setting indicates that the practice releases many high-risk defendants while simultaneously detaining low-risk defendants due to their inability to make bail. Research suggests that eliminating cash bail and replacing the system with an actuarial system where detention depends more directly on risk of pretrial misconduct could both reduce jail populations and not increase crime rates. Such a change would likely have a disparate impact on African American defendants, who are more likely to be detained pretrial, often for less serious offenses.*

CONCLUSION 2-10: *Incarceration rates in state and federal prisons have declined since their peak in the mid-2000s, but they still remain high by historical and international standards. Black people, especially Black men, have very high incarceration rates relative to other groups. Prison incarceration rates have declined for all groups in recent decades, and by nearly 30 percent for Black Americans. While absolute and relative race disparities have declined for Black Americans, there are still large racial disparities in prison incarceration rates.*

CONCLUSION 2-11: *Black people are heavily overrepresented among people currently condemned to die for their conviction offense. Moreover, the historical application of the death penalty has been disproportionately applied to Black defendants, not only for the offense of murder but also for the offense of rape for much of the 20th century. Empirical research consistently finds that case factors such as whether the victim was White, the quality of the defense effort, the state, and the time period significantly impact the likelihood of being sentenced to death for a capital offense. Finally, advances in DNA evidence analysis and targeted legal advocacy have revealed that a nontrivial portion of those sentenced to death were innocent.*

CONCLUSION 2-12: *Combining data from all states and the federal system, incarceration rates and probation populations have fallen in recent years, with consequent reductions in absolute racial disparities, but the population of formerly incarcerated people on parole has expanded steadily since 2000. California's experience with corrections suggests that it is possible to shrink correctional and parole populations, and to use less punitive and more local forms of community supervision, without adversely impacting public safety. Moreover, the state's experience suggests that doing so narrows racial disparities in criminal justice involvement.*

CONCLUSION

The committee finds strong evidence of high rates of violent victimization in minority communities, high rates of police contact, and large racial disparities across the multiple stages of the criminal justice system, including in arrests, pretrial detention, sentencing and incarceration, application of the death penalty, and probation and parole. The statistical portrait indicates a variety of harms reflected in high rates of homicide mortality and robbery victimization, and at the hands of the criminal justice system through police use of force, police shootings, and imprisonment. The statistical portrait shows the extent to which Black, Latino, and Native American communities must confront the dual challenges of high rates of interpersonal violence and the pains of criminal justice system contact.

The evidence indicates that interpersonal harm and the injuries of criminal justice contact are related. High rates of criminal offending in Black and Brown communities help explain criminal victimization and disproportionate contact with police and the courts. Still, beyond the damage caused by serious crime, there are a vast number of low-level police contacts that are racially disparate and often characterized by disrespect and harsh treatment by police.

The review of statistics on crime and the criminal justice system also revealed limitations of the data. Race and ethnicity in the criminal justice system are measured inconsistently across agencies, making it difficult to get a national picture of racial disparity. One critical area, the police use of force—a longstanding issue of public interest and policy significance—is not measured by any federal agency, and independent efforts have emerged to fill the gap. While relatively good data exist on Black Americans' and White Americans' interactions with the criminal justice system, crime, and victimization, data on Latino and Native American populations are often lacking.

Although the disparities in crime and criminal justice contact paint a picture of significant racial inequality, the data also indicate substantial improvement in some areas over the last two decades. Despite the increase in homicides over the last two years, crime is generally substantially lower than in the early 1990s, and this has conferred enormous improvements in quality of life in Black and Brown communities. Incarceration rates have fallen from 2008 to 2020, and this has accompanied large reductions in absolute and relative racial disparity.

From the statistical portrait of racial inequality in this chapter, we will turn next in Chapter 3 to review research on the high rates of crime that concentrate in racially segregated and low-income neighborhoods. These neighborhoods often form the context for the high levels of victimization and disproportionate criminal justice contact reported in this chapter. We will then examine in Chapter 4 how spatially concentrated patterns of crime combine with an accumulation of racial disparities throughout the stages of the system from arrest to sentencing to incarceration.

CHAPTER 2 APPENDIX FIGURES

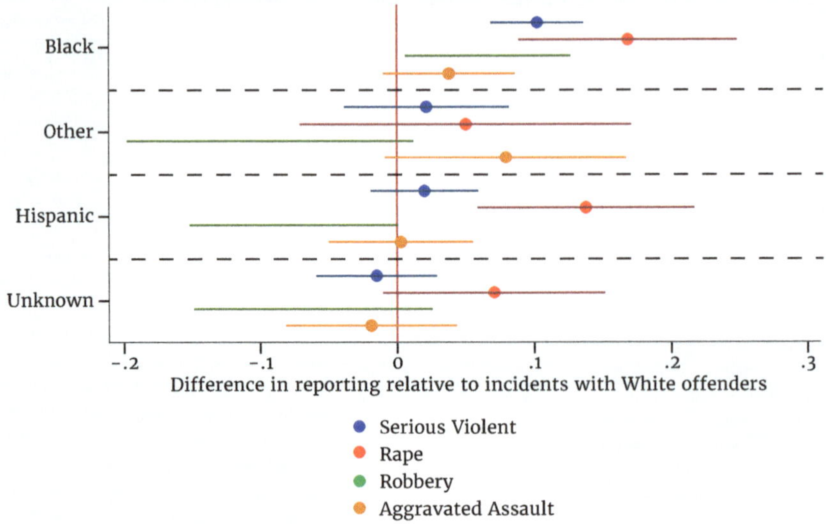

FIGURE 2A-1 Difference in the proportion of serious violent incidents reported to the police by the race/ethnicity of the offender relative to incidents involving White offenders: all offenses 2012 through 2019 for all serious and specific offense types.
SOURCE: Tabulations from multiple years of the National Crime Victimization Survey, https://bjs.ojp.gov/data-collection/ncvs

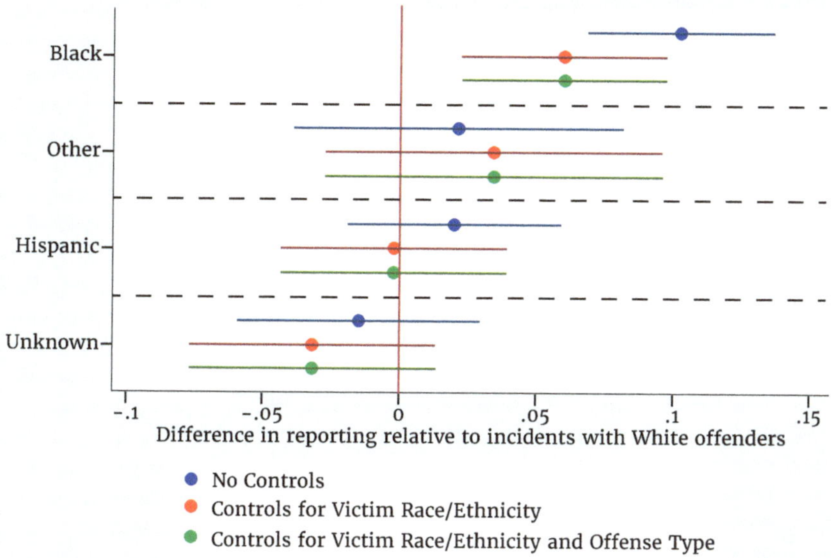

FIGURE 2A-2 Difference in the proportion of serious violent incidents reported to the police by the race/ethnicity of the offender relative to incidents involving White offenders: raw difference, adjusting for victim race/ethnicity, and adjusting for offense type.
SOURCE: Tabulations from multiple years of the National Crime Victimization Survey, https://bjs.ojp.gov/data-collection/ncvs

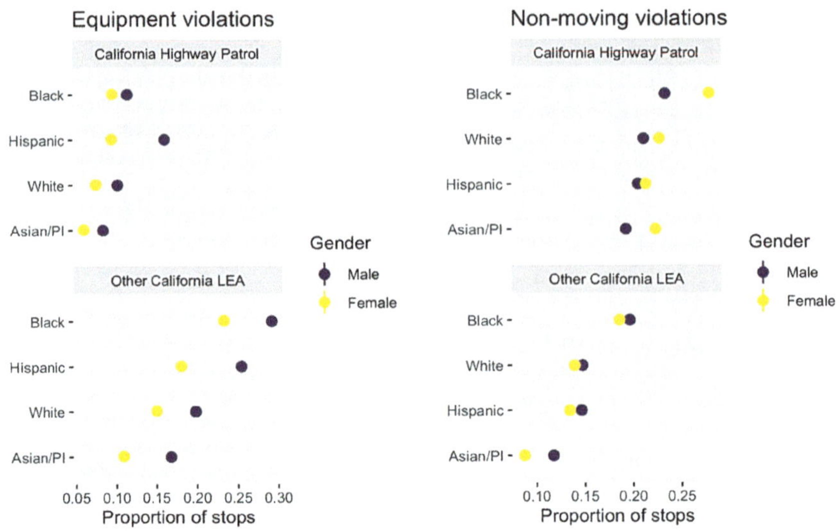

FIGURE 2A-3 Proportion of stops for equipment and non-moving violations by agency type, race, and gender, California.
SOURCE: Data from Open Justice, California Department of Justice, Racial and Identity Profiling Act, https://openjustice.doj.ca.gov/

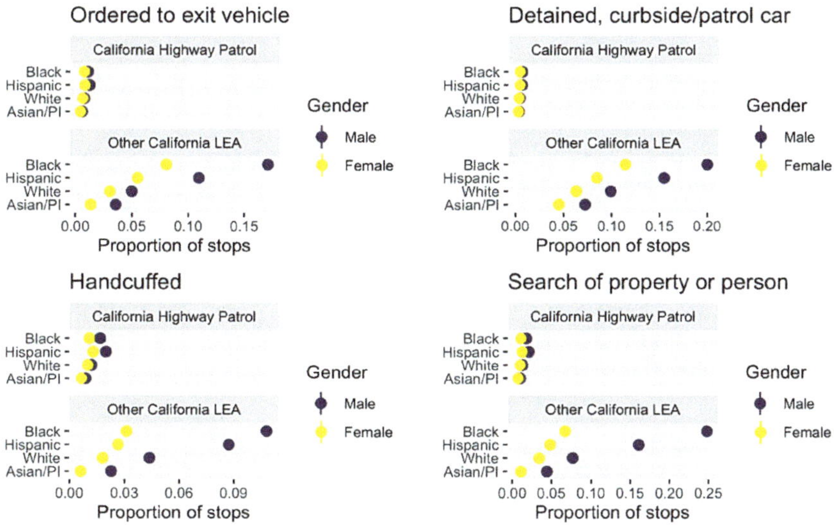

FIGURE 2A-4 Incidence of actions taken by officers during traffic stops by agency type, race, and gender, California.
SOURCE: Data from Open Justice, California Department of Justice, Racial and Identity Profiling Act, https://openjustice.doj.ca.gov/

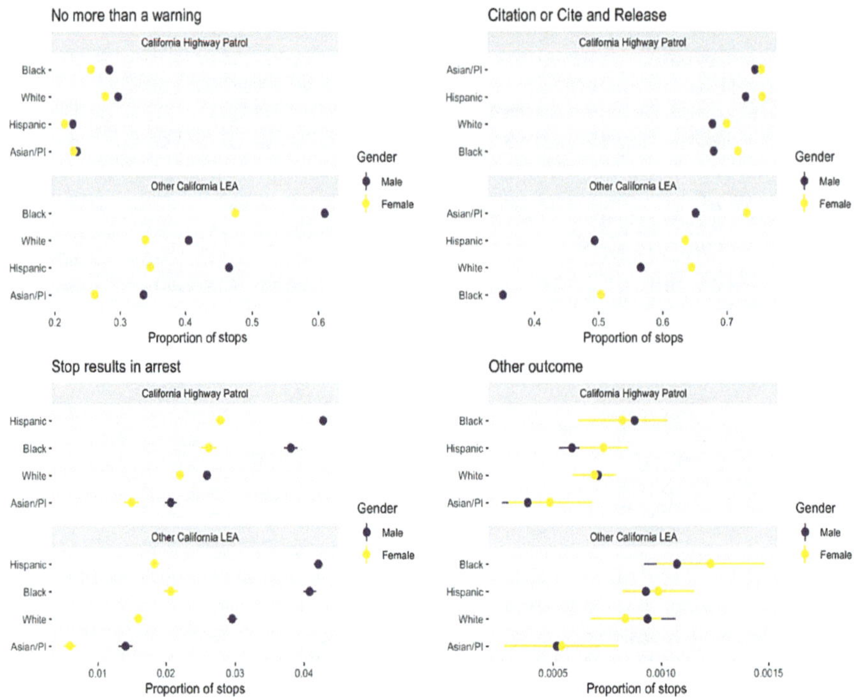

FIGURE 2A-5 Traffic stop outcomes by agency type, race, and gender, California. SOURCE: Data from Open Justice, California Department of Justice, Racial and Identity Profiling Act, https://openjustice.doj.ca.gov/

3

Social Drivers of Racial Inequalities in Crime and Justice

Knoxville (TN) is not often in the national news, but, like many American cities, it experienced a surge in homicides in 2020. In early 2021, the tragedy of gun violence escalated further in ways that stunned residents and leaders alike, drawing national attention. The *New York Times* reported that in one Knoxville high school, five students were fatally shot over the course of two months. One of these students was killed by the police and the other four were killed by their peers. The streets surrounding that high school are characterized by the entrenched poverty that pervades the wider neighborhood, according to residents (Rojas, 2020).

The violent incidents in Knoxville happened days before the shooting deaths of other young people across the country, including Ma'Khia Bryant, 16, who was wielding a knife when she was killed by a police officer in Columbus (OH; K. Williams et al., 2021), and a seven-year-old girl who was fatally shot sitting in her father's car in a drive-through lane at a McDonald's restaurant in Chicago (IL; Kenney et al., 2021). All these victims were young and Black. In this regard, Knoxville is neither an outlier nor unusual. Rather, it is typical of American cities large and small, reflecting racial inequalities in crime, victimization, policing, and incarceration that are documented elsewhere in this report and elaborated further in this chapter.

Sadly, the concentration of violence in African American and other non-White urban communities is not new. While rates of violence declined dramatically over the last quarter century (Baumer et al., 2018; Zimring, 2006), homicide remains the leading cause of death among young Black men (CDC, 2019) in the United States. In 2020, homicides spiked from

30 to 50 percent in many of our major cities, threatening the gains in life expectancy among Black Americans that have been made through reductions in violence (Sharkey and Friedson, 2019). In fact, there is evidence that racial disparities in violent victimization have *increased* after years of steady decline, explained by the rise of violence in U.S. cities in the late 2010s and in 2020 (Sharkey and Marsteller, 2022).

Many homicides also go unsolved, increasingly so in recent years and disproportionately so in poor Black and Latino communities (Brunson and Wade, 2019; Petersen, 2017; Roberts and Lyons, 2011), a direct indication that minority communities are underserved by the criminal justice system. Furthermore, police killings are the sixth leading cause of death among Black men under age 44 (Edwards et al., 2019), often tied to the same disadvantaged settings that experience heightened interpersonal violence (Siegel et al., 2021). While far fewer young Black men lose their lives to police shootings than from other causes, the social consequences of these deaths on families and already disadvantaged communities should not be understated.[1]

In Knoxville, as is the case elsewhere, the explicit racism that created racial segregation and the concentration of disadvantage alongside the structural racism that has maintained these conditions have long been connected to each other and to racial inequalities in community violence and lethal criminal justice contacts. Police killings are now highly visible because of cell phone videos and police body cameras; but disproportionate police shootings of non-White Americans are not new, nor is interpersonal violent victimization in non-White communities. Many more individuals are killed in acts of community violence than by the police, at a rate of about 20:1, but any life lost is a tragedy and the victims of both types of violence are disproportionately drawn from the same types of disadvantaged communities (Ross, 2015). In other words, there is an enduring and compounded burden of violence.

Accordingly, this chapter highlights the historical and contemporary social pathways through which structural racism leads to both crime and criminal justice involvement, with a focus on the role of violence as a key ingredient of racial inequality and its persistence over time. Through this social-pathway view, it is possible to see how racial inequalities in violence

[1]According to Centers for Disease Control and Prevention data from the National Vital Statistics System, 23,210 young Black men (age 44 or younger) died in 2020 (see https://www.cdc.gov/nchs/products/databriefs/db456.htm#section_2). The top three leading causes of death were suicide and homicide with a firearm (10,981), drug poisoning (5,313), and vehicle accidents (3,694). By comparison, according to the *Washington Post's* police shooting data collection effort (see https://www.washingtonpost.com/graphics/investigations/police-shootings-database/?itid=sf_Investigations_sn_police-shootings-database_1), 190 of these deaths were police killings.

and lethal criminal justice contacts are tied to historical and social processes of racial exclusion that manifest today in multiple forms, such as durable patterns of public and private underinvestment and toxic exposures in poor Black neighborhoods. Such a view implies that remedies must include tackling the social drivers of crime and criminal justice inequalities. In an important and under-appreciated sense, non-criminal justice factors drive criminal justice outcomes.

HISTORICAL LEGACIES

At the turn of the 19th century, W.E.B. Du Bois (1899) noted the link between concentrated urban disadvantage and differences in crime by racial groups in his classic *The Philadelphia Negro*. Later, in the mid-20th century, the sociologists Shaw and McKay (1942) highlighted three key facts about this relationship that have proven prescient: (1) overall rates of delinquency were higher for Black boys than for White boys in Chicago; (2) rates of delinquency among both Black and White boys varied by neighborhood; and yet (3) it was impossible to determine empirically if delinquency among Black boys was more prevalent than among White people living in comparable neighborhoods. "Even if it were possible to parallel the low economic status and the inadequacy of institutions in the White community," Shaw and McKay wrote elsewhere, "it would not be possible to reproduce the effects of segregation and the barriers to upward mobility" (1949, p. 614). Among other factors, these scholars cited the structural predicates of racial segregation that included racially discriminatory laws and housing policies, which in turn spurred the social isolation and physical deterioration of African American neighborhoods (Hirsch, 1983).

In the 1960s, the Kerner Commission issued a report whose findings were not materially different in substance, concluding that the Black and White communities of urban America were worlds apart because of racial segregation, severe economic disadvantage, and police violence (National Advisory Commission on Civil Disorders, 2016). By tracing crime to racial inequalities and structural racism, this body of work set the stage for explanations that eschewed pathologizing Black, Latino, and Native American communities as inherently or culturally disposed to violence. Rather, political economy and structural ecology constitute a self-amplifying feedback loop that produces exceptional disadvantage in African American neighborhoods along multiple dimensions (e.g., housing, education, physical environment). For example, neighborhoods that had been subjected to redlining in the first half of the 20th century were typically the same neighborhoods that, over the course of later decades, would have the greatest concentrations of both poverty and vulnerability to violence (Mehranbod et al., 2022; Jacoby et al., 2018). As South and colleagues (2021) note, a consequence of this cycle of concentrated racial disadvantage is the lack of neighborhood investment, which in turn is a factor in deteriorated housing stock, blighted vacant lots, and a lack of green space—environmental conditions that disproportionately occur in Black urban neighborhoods and that are associated with stress, fear, poor mental health, and violence (see also Branas et al., 2018).

In proposing a theory of race, crime, and urban inequality, Sampson and Wilson (1995; see also Sampson et al., 2018) pushed the logic of historical and contemporary observations like these to pose two questions on crime and violence in America. To what extent do Black and White rates of crime vary by type of ecological area? In American cities during the late 20th and early 21st century, is it possible to find in White communities the structural circumstances under which many Black people live?

The first question signals that Black communities are heterogeneous, as are White, Latino, and other communities. In earlier eras, White ethnic groups (native as well as foreign born) were highly involved in crime and criminal justice contacts. While stereotypes developed tagging some groups as prone to criminality (e.g., Italians and organized crime), this did not result in a popular attribution to whole White communities of inherent criminality. Most immigrant communities were seen as White and deserving of second chances, so they were not ascribed criminality (Muhammad 2011). To imagine Black people (or Black neighborhoods) as carrying a distinct or homogeneous "criminogenic" character is a distinct form of racial stereotyping.

In fact, there is substantial variation in the crime rates of both Black *and* White people—and this variation systematically corresponds to variation in community and other social contexts. According to this perspective, race is not a direct cause of violence. Instead, race is a marker for the accumulation of social and material adversities that both follow from and constitute racial status in America (Sampson, 2012, p. 248).

On the second question, more than 80 years after Shaw and McKay's assessment and 50 years after the Kerner Commission, Black and White people still do not share similar socioeconomic environments. As Chapter 5 notes, the societal remedies proposed by the Kerner Commission more than 50 years ago were a road not taken. To the contrary, as we document more in the next section, racial differences in concentrated urban poverty remain large, so much so that the most deprived urban contexts in which White people resided are considerably better off than the average context of Black communities (Sharkey, 2013; Peterson and Krivo, 2010). (See Chapter 7 for a discussion of the Moving to Opportunity experiment, which illustrates the durability of the structure and history of housing markets.) What most research on racial segregation emphasizes is not that living among White people is a necessary condition for reducing crime or improving well-being;

rather, it is the social inequalities that confer concentrated advantages and disadvantages through racialized social practices that are seen as primary (Massey and Denton, 1993).

In short, historical continuities in racial inequality, reinforced by racist policies, helped solidify and reproduce these divergent social worlds. Associated social inequalities manifested in individual actions, institutional practices, and public policies—both historical and contemporary—combined to concentrate urban Black poverty and its myriad social dislocations (Rothstein, 2017; Sugrue, 1996; Sampson and Wilson, 1995, p. 43; Wilson, 1987; Hirsch, 1983).[2] By this account, racial residential segregation is a lynchpin of racial inequality in America (Massey, 2016), a key structural factor linking the past to the present. Consistent with the focus of most research on racial inequality and crime, and for reasons of data availability, we focus primarily on Black/White differences.

CONTEMPORARY RACIAL INEQUALITIES

As with racial disparities in violent crime and criminal justice contact, racial disparities in residential and other social contexts continue to plague the United States. Large American cities remain highly segregated by race despite the nation's growing diversity, suggesting that people of the same race still tend to live in neighborhoods where they form the majority (Massey et al., 2009). Modest declines in residential segregation among smaller cities stem largely from the growth of multiethnic neighborhoods rather than integration between White and Black people (Elbers, 2021; Friedman, 2008). Rising income inequality coupled with dynamic forces that sustain residential segregation, like racial discrimination in the housing market (Rothstein, 2017; Pager and Shepherd, 2008) and racially structured residential preferences, perceptions, and knowledge (Krysan and Crowder, 2017), create a feedback loop of concentrated racial disadvantage. Faber (2020), for example, finds that in the mid- to late-20th century, the actions of federal housing institutions directly contributed to both Black ghettoization and

[2]This perspective is consistent with an explanatory role for how slavery and Jim Crow laws formed and perpetuated concentrated racial disadvantage. For example, while African Americans are uniquely exposed to concentrated disadvantage for unique historical and contemporary reasons owing to structural racism (Unnever, 2018), and while there is some disagreement across studies, there is considerable evidence that the pathway from structural disadvantage to crime operates similarly across racial groups (Sampson et al., 2018; Sampson and Wilson, 1995). What differs the most is differential exposure to disadvantage by race. As a matter of theory, any group that faces high levels of disadvantage would exhibit elevated levels of crime: this logic has been called the racial invariance thesis. From this perspective, what drives crime (and other human behaviors) remains rooted in fundamental historical and structural conditions that are differentially experienced by racial groups (see also Light and Thomas, 2019).

White flight to the suburbs, in turn contributing to the persistent racial segregation and racialization of poverty that continues to this day. Not only do individually poor Black people (i.e., those in low-income households) have higher neighborhood poverty than any other subgroup, but "*even blacks who are not individually poor* have higher mean neighborhood poverty rates than Latinos and whites who *are* individually poor" (Perkins and Sampson, 2015, p. 44). Black people also face much greater odds than White people of experiencing compounded (i.e., simultaneous individual and neighborhood level) poverty, even controlling for individual differences in rarely measured factors such as self-control, aggression, anxiety, depression, and cognitive ability (Perkins and Sampson, 2015), and they are much more likely to experience such deprivations over multiple generations (Sharkey, 2008).

These findings underscore the fact that race-based contextual disadvantage—regardless of individual characteristics—continues to characterize the U.S. demographic landscape, despite demographic shifts in spatial inequality (Bartik and Mast, 2021). In support of this general pattern and based on a nationwide longitudinal study of over 20 million children, Chetty and colleagues (2020) find that very few Black children grow up in environments that foster upward economic mobility across generations. They report that "less than 5 percent of black children currently grow up in a Census tract with a poverty rate below 10 percent and more than half of black fathers present" (p. 718). In contrast, 63 percent of White children grow up in areas with analogous conditions. Although sample sizes are small and causal estimates are always difficult to prove (and have been challenged), Chetty and colleagues (2020) argue that exposure to "good neighborhoods" influences upward mobility for both Black and White boys.

Chetty and colleagues (2020) also find that American Indian people are extremely disadvantaged, with low rates of intergenerational mobility. Two recent reviews lay the groundwork for a better understanding of American Indian and Indigenous people. Ulmer and Bradley (2019) argue that American Indians often face a unique criminal justice system that has often been ignored by criminologists. They provide a framework to begin to understand the consequences of tribal, state, and federal agencies' actions for Indigenous communities. Cunneen and Tauri (2019) argue that negative interactions between Indigenous people and criminal justice systems are fueled by the settler-colonial state and that they will remain this way until Indigenous peoples are empowered. Again, the key problem is the differential exposure by race to such (dis)advantaged environments, as was starkly portrayed in the last chapter.

Racial inequalities are thus multidimensional, compounded, intergenerational, and enduring over the life course. They also evolve in ways that make singular or point-in-time policy interventions challenging. African

Americans in particular are disproportionately exposed to what we might call durable "criminogenic conditions." The differential distribution of concentrated disadvantage is a key example of a criminogenic condition that follows a racialized gradient. As we review below, an important body of work examines the influence of this key factor on violence and criminal justice contact. We caution that tremendous differences in disadvantage by race make it difficult to compare Black and White neighborhoods, which leaves analyses incomplete and, in some cases, makes predictions outside the bounds of everyday experiences. In addition, given that disadvantage is a hypothesized cause of crime and criminal justice contact, scholars have assessed how well it explains relative racial *gaps* in important outcomes, such as homicide victimization or police killings. This strategy helps to identify which social drivers explain the most variation in racial gaps in crime and criminal justice. Both research approaches to understanding the racial patterning of violence and criminal justice contact have been tried. We briefly assess each approach in turn.

CONCENTRATED DISADVANTAGE AND VIOLENCE

Most evidence supports the observation that structural disadvantage at the social level is an important predictor of violence and well-being in general. We give greater weight in our assessment to research on racial disparities and inequalities conducted in the last two decades or that postdate recent reviews. We also highlight violence, in *all* its forms, both because violence is measured better than other types of crimes and because the toll it takes on society is greatest. Also, while all felonies put individuals at risk of coming into contact with the criminal justice system, violence increases that risk substantially. Homicide is of specific interest not only because of its severity in the loss of human lives but also because it is widely accepted as a reliable indicator of violent crime.[3]

The disadvantage-crime link emerges intact from "virtually all prior research" (Krivo et al., 2009). This linkage is geographically robust as well; empirical work conducted in a wide range of cities points to a strong and positive relationship between disadvantage and violent crime. The cities studied include Atlanta (GA; McNulty, 2001); Baton Rouge (LA; Shihadeh

[3]Although our focus is on violence and homicide, the evidence of racial differences is mixed for property crimes, with some finding more modest Black/White differences (Hindelang et al., 1981) and other studies reporting few if any significant racial differences (Crutchfield and Pitchford, 1997). Differences are often measured using arrest statistics (LaFree, 1995), which are likely better measures of police activity than behavior for these types of crimes. While there are often no significant racial differences in drug crime involvement for drug use and possession, or even for drug sales, differences emerge in how Black and Latino drug offenders are treated by the system (Beckett et al., 2005; Tonry, 1995).

and Shrum, 2004); Chicago (IL; Morenoff et al., 2001); Cincinnati (OH; Wooldredge and Thistlethwaite, 2003); Cleveland (OH), Seattle (WA), Washington (DC; Crutchfield et al., 1999); Columbus (OH; Krivo and Peterson, 1996); Miami (FL); San Diego (CA); El Paso (TX; Lee et al., 2001); St. Louis (MO; Kubrin and Wadsworth, 2003); and Washington (DC; Johnson and Kane, 2018). The relationship between concentrated disadvantage and violent crime also extends to work utilizing the National Neighborhood Crime Study, which covers neighborhoods across 87 cities (8,931 neighborhoods) in the year 2000 and 71 cities in 2010 (8,557 neighborhoods; Krivo et al., 2021; Peterson and Krivo, 2010). Scholarship tracing racial inequalities in violence to disadvantage covers a range of aggregate units: census tracts and block groups, cities and the surrounding metropolitan areas, resident-defined neighborhoods, and simultaneous combinations of the above.

Neighborhoods do not exist in social or physical isolation, however. Due to pronounced spatial segregation in the United States, a neighborhood is often surrounded by other neighborhoods that are socioeconomically similar. These extra-local but proximate spatial processes matter because the socioeconomic conditions of nearby neighborhoods are important predictors of violence in a given neighborhood. For example, Mears and Bhati (2006) show that resource deprivation in one community promotes more violence in communities that are socially proximate. Moreover, research shows that Black neighborhoods, and to a lesser extent Latino and other non-White neighborhoods, often share borders with both higher-disadvantage and higher-crime areas (Peterson and Krivo, 2010; Morenoff et al., 2001; Pattillo, 1998). Johnson and Kane (2018) also draw upon spatial data to argue that highly disadvantaged communities that are positioned at the center of a contiguous ghetto have significantly higher violent crime rates than other very underprivileged areas. In this sense, neighborhoods are not islands, as traditional models implicitly assume. Racial inequalities in spatial exposure to crime should help explain ethno-racial inequality in crime and crime change.

A qualitatively different form of neighborhood inequality is forged when residents visit other neighborhoods throughout a city in their everyday routines, including neighborhoods that are not spatially proximal. Levy and colleagues (2020) integrate the literature on urban mobility and neighborhood networks with research on neighborhood effects to develop the concept of "triple neighborhood disadvantage"—the notion that for any given neighborhood, its vitality is a function not only of its residential (or nearby) socioeconomic conditions but also of the conditions in the neighborhoods its residents visit and are visited by. Most research considers a neighborhood to be socioeconomically disadvantaged if it scores highly on just one measured trait—commonly "disadvantage" is indexed by measures like poverty, unemployment, or public assistance receipt. A neighborhood that scores highly on such a residential socioeconomic disadvantage measure as well as on the two metrics of mobility-based disadvantage (in-degree visitation from other poor areas and out-degree visitation to other poor areas) is considered triply disadvantaged. Analyzing nearly 32,000 neighborhoods and 9,700 homicides in 37 of the largest U.S. cities, Levy and colleagues (2020) show that neighborhoods' triple disadvantage independently predicts homicides, accounting for traditional neighborhood correlates of violence, spatial proximity to disadvantage, prior homicides, and city fixed effects. Not only does triple disadvantage improve explanatory power over traditional measures, but it also explains a sizable portion of the association between residential neighborhood disadvantage and homicides.

Directly relevant to our concerns with racial inequalities, the distribution of triple disadvantage is highly uneven, most often experienced by Black and Latino neighborhoods compared to White neighborhoods. Conversely, White communities enjoy triple advantage while Black and Latino communities rarely do. In fact, almost no White neighborhoods are triply disadvantaged, and essentially no Black or Hispanic neighborhoods are triply advantaged.

Moreover, if we use a simple and traditional indicator of neighborhood poverty—neighborhoods in which at least 30 percent of households are in poverty—Black neighborhoods are at much higher risk for being in poverty than White neighborhoods across the 50 largest American cites—almost 11 times greater. But Black neighborhoods are over *35 times* more likely than White neighborhoods to have triple disadvantage: to be poor, to have residents who visit other poor neighborhoods, *and* to be visited by those from other poor neighborhoods (Sampson, 2019, p. 19). Hence, when we account for urban mobility flows, Black neighborhoods are substantially more exposed to compounded poverty and disadvantage than White neighborhoods. Hispanic neighborhoods fare a bit better than Black neighborhoods, followed by mixed neighborhoods, but the patterns are similar. These racial differences reveal a previously overlooked dimension of racial inequality that plausibly explains racial disparities in the experience of crime and violence. These patterns also bring into sharp relief the divergent social worlds occupied by White and non-White communities.

Krivo and colleagues (2009) examine another kind of inequality beyond individual neighborhoods, finding that city-level racial segregation accounts for some of the unexplained racial gap across neighborhoods. The authors posit that city segregation contributes to neighborhood violent crime by making it difficult for separate and unequal groups to address shared problems and indirectly by creating structural disadvantage and isolation in predominantly minority areas (Krivo et al., 2009, p. 1792). Vélez and colleagues (2015) adopt a similar approach, finding (1) that there is variation by city in the relationship between a neighborhood's percentage of Black residents and the prevalence of violence there; and (2) that this "average positive relationship often is attenuated, and reduced to statistical insignificance, in cities with favorable political contexts" (p. 93). These favorable contexts, Vélez and colleagues argue, yield benefits that are both substantive and symbolic, providing a footing for neighborhood-based organization against violence.

Concentrated Disadvantage and Gun Violence: A Closer Look at Trends

The relationship between high rates of neighborhood poverty and high rates of crime is reflected in rates of serious violence—particularly gun violence among young people. As was shown in Chapter 2, homicide risk is not distributed equally in the United States, and Black Americans are exposed to the greatest risk. In 2010, Black people comprised 55 percent of all U.S. homicide victims despite making up just 13 percent of the U.S. population. While guns are used in more than two-thirds of U.S. homicides, between 1999 and 2009, 81 percent of homicides among men ages 15–34 (N = 85,643) involved the use of guns; among Black men this figure rises to 91 percent (Hennekens et al., 2013). Although nationwide crime declines since the early 1990s appear to have reduced the Black/White disparity in exposure to overall violent crime until around 2014 (Friedson and Sharkey, 2015), Black people still experience approximately 11 times the gun homicide rate as their White counterparts (calculated from CDC-WISQARS tables 2010).[4] Box 3-1 outlines different types of and recent trends around gun violence.

For young men ages 15–34, the rate of gun homicide mortality for Black people is roughly 23 times that of White people: 67 per 100,000 compared to 2.9 per 100,000 (calculated from CDC-WISQARS tables 2019). Such inequality in homicide victimization not only affects the life chances of Black people but meaningfully alters the expectation of the longevity of life at the population level. While the Black/White disparity in life expectancy has shrunk to its lowest level ever recorded, homicide still explains more than 18 percent (more than one full year) of the life expectancy gap between White and Black men (Harper et al., 2012).[5] Over the last three decades, homicide has accounted for 15.6 to 18.8 percent of the overall disparity in

[4]For all homicides (not just gun) the current Black/White disparity in homicide at the population level is approximately 8:1.

[5]The current Black/White life expectancy disparity is 5.44 years among men and 3.71 years among women. Homicide's role in explaining this gap among women is much more modest than for men, representing between 3.4 percent and 5.8 percent over the past three decades.

BOX 3-1
Gun Violence: Different Types and Recent Trends

It is important to note that gun violence takes on different forms, including intimate partner violence, mass shootings, and violence motivated by racial animus, and at times there is overlap among these types. In 2020, more than half (54%) of all gun-related deaths in the United States were suicides and 43 percent were homicides; the remaining proportion (3%) were either unintentional, involved law enforcement, or had undetermined circumstances. It's also worth noting that between 2009 and 2018, at least 54 percent of mass shootings, defined as shootings in which more than three people are killed in one event, were related to domestic or family violence (Everytown for Gun Safety, 2022). The problem of gun violence victimization is pronounced for children and youth, ages one to 19, with Black and Native youth experiencing disproportionate rates of mortality. From 2019 to 2020, the relative increase in the rate of firearm-related deaths of all types (suicide, homicide, unintentional, and undetermined) among children and adolescents was 29.5 percent—more than twice as high as the relative increase in the general population (Goldstick et al., 2022). Black youth in particular have seen an upward trend in suicide rates: between 2003 and 2017 they rose by 4.9 percent among 15–17-year-olds and by 6.6 percent among Black girls (Sheftall et al., 2022). See Chapter 7 for a discussion around policy interventions for firearm violence.

life expectancy between Black and White men (Harper et al., 2012, 2007).[6] Virtually any way they are analyzed, these data demonstrate that the risk of violent death among Black and White people, at the population level, is practically incommensurable.

From 2014 to 2020, gun violence steadily increased, with the increase in shootings being disproportionately concentrated in poor and predominantly Black neighborhoods (Sharkey and Marsteller, 2022). Analysis of data on fatal shootings at the census tract level in the 100 largest cities, excluding accidents and suicides, shows that the rate of gun violence increased by 87 percent in predominantly Black neighborhoods compared to a 64 percent increase in White neighborhoods. The recent increase in gun violence follows a similar pattern for poverty. Gun violence increased 91 percent in high-poverty neighborhoods from 2014 to 2020, compared to 58 percent in non-poor neighborhoods (Sharkey and Marsteller, 2022, pp. 375–376). A keen understanding of gun violence trends, both spatially

[6]It is worth noting that in these analyses, homicide's contribution to explaining the homicide gap among Black and White men was the same in 2008 as in 1993 (18.8%). In 1993 this percentage equated to 1.59 years; in 2008, it equated to 1.03 years.

and demographically, is important for understanding and addressing the social mechanisms of crime and victimization.

COMPOUNDED ADVERSITIES AND SOCIAL MECHANISMS

Just as neighborhoods do not exist in isolation, concentrated poverty does not operate in isolation either—it is closely connected to many of the correlates commonly emphasized in studies of crime and violence involvement, especially as they interact over the life course. While people leave neighborhoods, the effects of neighborhoods do not necessarily leave them. For example, unstable family structures, dropping out of high school, and labor market detachment are both causes of poverty and consequences of living in disadvantaged neighborhoods. Disrupted family life, poor academic achievement, bad school experiences, and problematic labor market participation have all been linked to higher levels of criminal involvement, including in crimes of violence, and to contacts with the criminal justice system.

Concentrated disadvantage and racial segregation also expose residents to physically toxic inequalities, such as in lead exposure and airborne pollution, that have been linked to crime and criminal justice contact (Manduca and Sampson, 2021; Muller et al., 2018). In this way, structural racism gets into the brains and bodies of disadvantaged children (Sampson and Winter, 2018; Winter and Sampson, 2017), reinforcing disadvantages over the life course (Massey, 2004).

On employment, ever since Wilson's (1987) seminal work, *The Truly Disadvantaged*, researchers have moved beyond the simple examination of unemployment as defined by people out of work and currently searching for positions. Wilson (1987) found that Black neighborhoods characterized by high levels of joblessness had substantially elevated violent crime rates, and those places also had high delinquency rates as well. Controlling for income inequality, poverty, race, and several other social indicators, census tracts with more marginalized workers, namely those in secondary-sector jobs (low wage, unstable, and with few if any benefits), and with more unemployed have higher homicide rates and higher rates of other forms of violence (Crutchfield, 2014; Crutchfield et al., 1999). Krivo and Peterson (2004) found that racial residential segregation concentrated the negative influence of marginal employment's effects on neighborhood crime rates.

Furthermore, young adult males who are marginally employed are more likely to engage in criminal behavior, both violent crime and property crime (Crutchfield and Pitchford, 1997), even after controlling for income and education. It is notable that this association tends to appear where individuals live in places with higher levels of unemployment, precisely the kinds of places where Black people live because of segregation. Low-end employment also explains modest racial differences in the violent crime involvement of individuals (Crutchfield, 2014) and helps to explain higher violent crime rates in neighborhoods populated by more people of color (Crutchfield et al., 2006). Similar patterns are reported elsewhere (Apel and Horney, 2017; Uggen, 2000). Researchers have found that children whose parents are out of work or who do "low-end jobs" and those living in communities with more adults who are marginally employed are more likely to engage in delinquency than other children (Crutchfield and Wadsworth, 2013; Bellair et al., 2003; Bellair and Roscigno, 2000; Wadsworth, 2000). The operating mechanism for these observations appears to be indirect; children in such situations do not do as well in school, and that outcome in turn is related to heightened likelihood of delinquency.

Other social mechanisms that have been hypothesized to translate macro disadvantage and racial inequalities into violence are legal cynicism and estrangement from the criminal justice system (Bell, 2020b; Sampson, 2012; Kirk and Papachristos, 2011; Sampson and Bartusch, 1998), competition for local political power, municipal resources, and representation (Vargas, 2016), community-based institutions such as churches and recreation centers, and weakened social controls (Sampson et al., 1997). Much of the national conversation today about community alternatives to criminal legal institutions in fact finds its intellectual origins in sociological research on communities and crime. It is especially derived from the social disorganization tradition (Kornhauser, 1978), revised in more recent work on the role of informal social controls and neighborhood cohesion, or what has been conceptualized as collective efficacy in reducing violence (Sampson et al., 1997).

A large body of research in the United States has examined collective efficacy and crime rates, especially rates of violence, indicating that while causality is difficult to pin down, the associations are typically negative and significant (for reviews, see Lanfear et al., 2020; Pratt and Cullen, 2005).[7] There is also evidence that the efforts of community-based organizations to mobilize around community safety and social supports for youth played an important role in the drop in crime (Sharkey et al., 2017), an example of organizational-based collective efficacy. The presence of and participation in religious organizations also have the potential to blunt the deleterious consequences of disadvantage on violence in general and particularly on Black and Latino levels of violence (Harris and Ulmer, 2017; Ulmer and Harris, 2013). For example, a recent paper by Harris and Ulmer (2017) finds that counties with a relatively large share of adherence to Black

[7]There is more variability in findings from other countries that use different community-level units of analysis, such as in Australia (Wickes and Hipp, 2018; Mazerolle et al., 2010), the Netherlands (Steenbeek and Hipp, 2011), and Latin-American countries (Villarreal and Silva, 2006). Longitudinal associations are also sometimes different than cross-sectional ones.

Protestantism, the dominant Black religion, have less violence, and this protective relationship is enhanced in counties that are disadvantaged. Another mechanism by which collective efficacy and organizational mobilization can reduce crime is through the built environment, such as the remediation of toxic wastes, vacant homes, and abandoned lots (Branas et al., 2018; Kondo et al., 2018). See Chapter 7 for a discussion on reducing harmful environmental exposures to influence crime and justice contact.

Politicians, the general public, and some academics have long held that higher rates of violence in Black communities are a consequence of subcultures (Curtis, 1975; Banfield, 1970; Woolfgang and Ferracuti, 1967), another potential mechanism. Such arguments have largely given way as a result of the evidence we have provided here, but they persist in some corners (see Crutchfield, 2015, for a review). What has emerged are new cultural contributions to our understanding of violence, which define cultural adaptations as emerging from structural disadvantage. Anderson (2000), for example, argues that a "code of the street" develops in disadvantaged Black communities, resulting from long-term isolation of residents from important institutions, especially the labor market, when combined with the same communities being ignored by city government and denied effective policing. Certainly, teenagers everywhere develop attitudes, beliefs, and behaviors that are contrary to those of conventional adults, but Anderson argues that this is different, deeper, and not simply juvenile rebellion in severely, inter-generationally disadvantaged Black communities (Matsueda et al., 2006).

In addition to Anderson's ethnographic evidence from Philadelphia neighborhoods, Duck (2015) finds that the same kind of ongoing marginalization in a Black community led to patterns of drug dealing, and neighbors' reaction to it, in a small city suffering from deindustrialization. Stewart and Simons (2010) similarly find that Black people who adhere to this kind of street code are more likely to engage in violent delinquency; this vulnerability is magnified in neighborhoods where many residents uphold a street code. Miller's (2008) and Jones's (2010) studies document the devastating effects of criminal involvement, especially the victimization of Black girls and young women, from these patterns of long-term marginalization, isolation, and poverty. They find that young women's behavior, identities, beliefs, and expectations are affected by the disadvantage and victimization that are central to their daily lives. Finally, Sampson and Wilson (1995) refer to cognitive landscapes and shared expectations about violence in highly disadvantaged communities, but in their view this sort of adaptation has been a result of cumulative and compounded racial disadvantages and the existential realties of everyday life in communities underserved by the criminal justice system (see also Kirk and Papachristos, 2011; Sampson and Bartusch, 1998).

MODELING RACIAL GAPS IN CRIME

As we have seen, research on urban inequality points scholars to the wide disparity in community conditions as one of the sources of racial inequality in serious crime, and it suggests that these disparities are plausible mechanisms for explaining the association. Accounting empirically for these stark ecological differences has been the dominant strategy to explain racial differences in crime. Work on communities and crime generally finds support for this approach, especially spotlighting concentrated disadvantage as an important source of racial gaps in serious crime at the cross-section and over time (Krivo et al., 2020, 2018; Peterson and Krivo, 2010; Stults et al., 2010).

For example, many studies find that simply adjusting for degrees of disadvantage explains most, and sometimes all, of the racial gaps in property crime at the neighborhood level (Peterson and Krivo, 2010; Shihadeh and Shrum, 2004; McNulty and Holloway, 2000). Krivo and colleagues (2020), studying neighborhoods in 71 cities in 2010, find that adjusting for disadvantage accounts for a large portion of the Black/White gap in violence and property crime (see also Lyons et al., 2022). In the same study, adjusting for ecological variation in disadvantage accounts for much of the Latino/White gap in violence and the entire Latino/White gap in property crime. In a study of neighborhoods across 19 cities, Hipp (2007) explains away much of the race effects for violence. Researchers also find that proximity to disadvantage or advantage (sometimes measured as the percentage White) helps explain differences in crime between White and Black or Latino neighborhoods (Peterson and Krivo, 2010, 2009). Feldmeyer and colleagues (2013) report that structural disadvantage helps explain the influence of percent-Black and percent-Latino on violence arrest rates but note that the strength of this correlation depends on the size of the census place. In smaller places, disadvantage explains more of the influence of racial composition on violence.

Scholarship also links racial residential segregation to the explanation of racial differences in crime. Vélez and colleagues (2003) find that racial segregation lies at the heart of Black/White inequality in homicide offending at the city level. Light and Ulmer (2016) point to structural disadvantage and segregation as strongly (but not perfectly) predictive of both the cross-sectional racial disparities in homicide rates and the changes in those disparities over time at the metropolitan level (for a review, see LaFree et al., 2010). Light and Thomas (2019) examine large metropolitan areas and argue that racial residential segregation is related to higher Black homicide victimization rates but lower risk for White people. They conclude that segregation plays an important role in creating and maintaining the racial gap in victimization.

Bank investments in housing that are conventional or prime in nature are considered lucrative and have the potential to inhibit or at least curtail a spiral of neighborhood decline and shore up a neighborhood's ability to fight crime. High cost or sub-prime lending, however, has the potential to destabilize a community, and evidence mounts on the racialized nature of its distribution. Specifically, the distribution of subprime loans, which can include predatory loans, was greater in segregated areas and was allocated disproportionately by banks to disadvantaged minority communities (Rugh et al., 2015; Hyra et al., 2013; Rugh and Massey, 2010). We focus the review here on the body of work that assesses the implications of ecological differences in prime lending by race for understanding racial differences in neighborhood crime. In Chicago, Vélez (2009) finds that controlling for race-based differences in home mortgage lending (measured in both dollars and number of loans) accounts for a significant share of the gap in homicide between Black or Latino communities with White communities. Studies using the first and second waves of the National Neighborhood Crime Study (NNCS) find that home mortgage lending explains important shares of the gap in violent and property crime between Black and White neighborhoods and between Latino and White neighborhoods as well. Applying this more concretely based on findings from the second wave of the NNCS, equalizing home mortgage dollars would reduce the gaps in violent crime levels between White and Black or Latino communities by approximately 30 percent (Krivo et al., 2021).

A large literature in economics explores the causes of longstanding and significant racial differences in rates of homeownership and mortgage borrowing. Five-year estimates centered on the 2015 American Community Survey yield the following homeownership rates by race and ethnicity: non-Latino Black people, 45 percent; Latino people, 46 percent; and non-Latino White people, 74 percent. Compared to the rates implied by 2000 census data, these rates are slightly lower for Black people, slightly higher for White people, and about the same for Latino people.

While there is some evidence that lenders discriminate against minorities, in particular against Black applicants for home mortgages, well over 90 percent of those seeking mortgages are able to obtain one regardless of race. Racial differences in rates of *applying for* mortgages are large and are a key driver of racial differences in rates of homeownership. Charles and Hurst (2002) conclude that the Black/White gap in applications is driven primarily by "income, family structure, and in the ability and willingness of parents to provide down-payment assistance." These Black/White differences are rooted in historical discrimination. Slavery, Jim Crow restrictions on education and employment opportunities, and racist housing policies (e.g., red lining) have all contributed.

The most recent study utilizing the NNCS finds that home mortgage lending has emerged as a key factor in helping explain racial differences in neighborhood crime using two time periods of data, likely because of how the Great Recession deepened a reluctance to extend mortgage credit to Black and Latino communities (Faber, 2018; Woodstock Institute, 2010). New work also explains how evictions, foreclosures, and vacancies may help account for ethno-racial differences in neighborhood crime and crime change. Work by Kirk (2022, 2020) in Boston, for example, finds an association between inequality in eviction rates and home-mortgage denials and the concentration of crime in disadvantaged communities. Given the vast legacies of racial discrimination in lending and current inequalities, addressing these long-standing inequalities has the potential to reduce racial inequalities in crime and criminal justice.

Immigration is another social process that has been hypothesized to have an influence on crime, in this case a protective influence (Ousey and Kubrin, 2018; MacDonald and Sampson, 2012; Sampson, 2012). Although the literature on crime rates is vast, only some research has assessed whether immigration explains racial gaps in crime. Immigration patterns vary notably across neighborhood ethno-racial profiles, with Latino and multiethnic areas having much more immigration than Black areas.[8] Research finds that accounting for varying levels of immigration helps to explain some of the differences in crime, particularly between Latino and White communities (Peterson and Krivo, 2010) but also between Black and Latino communities (Vélez, 2006). The ability of immigration to explain racial gaps may depend upon city-level experiences with immigration (Ramey, 2013).

Exploring gaps in Black/White and Latino/White homicide rates over time, Light and Ulmer (2016) find that differences in levels of immigration help explain these evolving gaps. Moreover, changes in immigration help to explain decreasing gaps between Black and White homicide rates. Light and Ulmer (2016) speculate that an increase in foreign-born residents in metropolitan areas may be associated with strengthened informal social control, reducing interracial homicide gaps. Their observations indicate that not only is immigration a protective factor against violence, a claim consistent with a large body of work, but that the broader communities into which immigrants move also benefit from less homicide and lower racial

[8]A small body of work explores whether the protective influence on violence extends to all racial/ethnic groups and their neighborhoods. For instance, Martinez and colleagues (2016) find that changes in immigration levels bring about reductions in homicide levels from 1970 to 2010 in San Diego neighborhoods. But when homicide is racially disaggregated, immigration loses some of its protective influence for Black homicide levels across neighborhoods (though it remains negative and significant). To make sense of this finding, Martinez and colleagues (2016) suggest, "A likely explanation for this result is the fact that newcomers from abroad are not settling into traditionally Black neighborhoods in numbers that would have a meaningful impact on levels of homicide." Xie and Baumer (2018) find that immigration concentration protects against victimization risk for Latino, Black, and White people, but this protection is particularly enhanced for Latino people given that they are most likely to live in close proximity to the foreign born.

homicide disparities. Ironically, politically charged arguments that lead to greater immigration enforcement attenuate the positive effect of having more immigrants in communities (Kirk et al., 2012).

A smaller body of research demonstrates how analyzing individuals and neighborhoods simultaneously allows for a fuller understanding of individual-level racial disparities in crime. Such multi-level approaches allow for an accounting of how vulnerabilities to crime are brought about by the risk and protective factors at the individual level alongside contextual adversities, such as the structural disadvantages individuals face because of their immediate surroundings. As an example, using the National Longitudinal Survey of Adolescent Health, a nationally representative school-based sample, Bellair and McNulty (2005) document that concentrated disadvantage explains the *entire* gap between Black and White reports of engaging in serious violence. Notably, they find that indicators of verbal ability and academic achievement are not as potent as community-level disadvantage in explaining race differences in violent behavior (see also McNulty and Bellair, 2003). Sampson and colleagues (2005) analyzed individual, family, and neighborhood factors to assess competing hypotheses regarding racial/ethnic gaps in perpetrating violence among 2,974 individuals ages eight to 25 living in 180 Chicago neighborhoods. The odds of perpetrating violence were 85 percent higher for Black people than for White people, whereas Latino-perpetrated violence was 10 percent lower. Yet the majority of the Black/White gap (over 60%) and the entire Latino/White gap were explained primarily by the marital status of parents, immigrant generation, and dimensions of neighborhood context, including socioeconomic status, concentrated immigration, and legal cynicism.

Appreciating the multifaceted nature of the forces explaining racial gaps in offending, newer work tries to advance an integrated model of the race difference in violence. Specifically, this work sees individual-level risk factors like verbal ability or school attainment as "best conceived as originating from the segregation of Blacks in disadvantaged contexts" (McNulty et al., 2013, p. 140). For example, McNulty and colleagues (2013) find that part of the reason residence in disadvantaged contexts is related to violence is that it is related to low verbal ability and poor school attainment. Lauritsen and colleagues (2018) find that the national Black/White gap in serious violent victimization drops considerably (from 71% to 22% greater) but is not entirely eliminated once controls for poverty, urban residence, age, and employment are introduced.[9] In this sense, risk factors for

[9]The authors write, "Nearly all of the factors that are significantly related to between group differences in risk are also associated with heterogeneity in risk within race and ethnic groups. Black and White males who are younger, living in poverty and urban areas, and not employed are most likely to become victims of serious violence" (p. 84).

offending that are more pronounced for Black people than White people are better thought of as differential exposure to neighborhood disadvantage, which, as noted above, has a long history rooted in social policies.

RESEARCH GAPS

Though the study of racial inequality in crime and justice has accumulated more than a century of academic attention, key questions remain that should guide work in the future. To achieve this, a diverse set of methodologies and theories must be engaged. First, as discussed in this chapter, there is a rich theoretical tradition for understanding racial differences in crime. Particularly needed is scholarly attention on how racialized inequalities in socioeconomic conditions play out to produce differences in crime. Mechanisms such as collective efficacy, legal cynicism, and the code of the street suggest particularly fruitful lines of study. Second, given the durability of heightened crime and of exposure to toxic neighborhood environments in Black and Latino communities, especially in their linkage with violence, research should also investigate the toll these factors play in neighborhood viability and general well-being. What are the long-term consequences of such heightened levels of violence?

Third, a key methodological issue that needs further study is how to better account for the fact that Black and White populations do not reside in comparably disadvantaged places. This presents deep methodological challenges that researchers should try to address. Fourth, the weight of past literature has focused on comparisons of Black and White communities. Scholars today are more frequently comparing experiences in Latino and Asian communities, reflecting the increasing diversity of America (Alba, 2020). These efforts should be continued and expanded. Like Black communities, Asian Americans are disproportionately concentrated in urban and suburban settings. In areas with substantial Asian populations, researchers should avail themselves of that opportunity to examine to what extent the processes described in this chapter are similar or different.

Fifth and finally, as stated earlier, Black, Latino, and Native American communities are heterogeneous. Even in some disadvantaged places examples of resiliency can be found, for instance the "decent families" described by Anderson (2000) in areas of profound disadvantage in North Philadelphia or the many vibrant economic districts that exist within otherwise disadvantaged, segregated spaces within some cities. How pockets of resiliency emerge and thrive in these communities in ways that undercut vulnerability to crime is an important question, worthy of more research attention. At the same time, we need to focus research on the various ways that White privilege, for example in exposure to advantaged residential environments, is maintained over time (Candipan and Sampson, 2021).

Concerning Indigenous people, there are two pressing issues. First, while urban American Indian populations may be growing, they remain relatively small, which creates a problem for much quantitative research along the lines of what has been done. Ethnographic research can fill some of the resulting gap, but new quantitative data efforts are needed in areas with large American Indian populations such as Albuquerque (NM), Phoenix (AZ), and Oklahoma City (OK). Second, much of the country's Indigenous population resides in nonurban places, which raises important questions about how criminogenic forces and processes work in rural areas. These are important research questions that should be addressed more fully than they have been.

Existing social and economic disadvantage experienced by Black, Latino, and Native American communities can also be addressed by focusing more directly on educational and labor market inequalities. Increasing class and educational stratification is the underappreciated story of contemporary differential punishment (Muller and Roehrkasse, 2020).

CONCLUSION

This chapter has sought to illustrate the key social drivers of racial inequalities in violent crime and homicide, which are key sources of racial justice differences. Structural racism rooted in historical patterns of residential segregation set the stage for the vast inequalities we see today in socioeconomic conditions and crime. Extant work highlights racially inscribed inequalities, especially disadvantage, in explaining dramatic differences in crime across racialized areas. These same disadvantaged contexts also contribute to lethal criminal justice contacts, further compounding inequality. This chapter cautions that racial inequality in both serious crime and criminal justice contact is driven by broader systems that perpetuate racial inequality more generally. Thus, to study one without the other misses the larger picture. Racial inequalities in the American criminal justice system begin before individuals enter that system. In fact, they begin before persons of color have any differential experience with police,[10] as soon as early childhood.

> *CONCLUSION 3-1: Race-based contextual disadvantage—regardless of individual and family characteristics—continues to characterize the U.S. demographic landscape wherein neighborhood and social conditions for Black and White households remain highly divergent. The most deprived urban contexts in which White people reside are considerably better off than the average context of Black communities.*

[10]Social drivers of criminal justice, such as policing, are covered in Chapter 4 of the report.

CONCLUSION 3-2: *Racial disparities in serious violence—both victimization and offending—are also spatially patterned, with high rates of violent crime concentrated in Black, Latino, and Native American communities that face longstanding and ongoing racial exclusion leading to enduring patterns of segregation and concentrated poverty.*

CONCLUSION 3-3: *Racially inscribed inequalities, especially disadvantage, explain most of the dramatic differences in crime across racialized areas. These same disadvantaged contexts also contribute to racial disparities in criminal justice contacts, further compounding inequality. However, the fact that Black and White populations do not reside in comparably disadvantaged places presents deep methodological challenges to the study of racial inequality and crime.*

CONCLUSION 3-4: *Elimination of racial inequalities in the criminal justice system must include addressing longstanding inequalities and cumulative, racially based disadvantages over the life course. Policies that focus solely on inequalities within the criminal justice system, failing to consider larger, societal systemic inequalities, will have limited chances of success.*

4

Criminal Justice Drivers of Racial Inequalities

Researchers find strong evidence of large racial differences in exposure to violence, serious offending, police contact, and incarceration (Chapter 2). They also find that violence and other crime is spatially concentrated in racially segregated neighborhoods that experience high rates of poverty (Chapter 3). This chapter brings these two lines of empirical evidence together to explain high levels of criminal justice contact and control in Black and other non-White communities.

Highly segregated low-income neighborhoods provide social environments in which crime and police contact are concentrated. Criminal processing—the sequence from police contact through arrest, conviction, and incarceration—can magnify these preexisting environmental disadvantages. Criminal processing is itself shaped by policies governing the deployment of police resources, procedures for arrest, prosecutorial procedures for charging and sentencing, and prison and parole administration. The criminal justice system does not simply reflect race differences in crime and social conditions; it also *contributes* to inequality in criminal justice outcomes.

Over the last two decades, researchers, policy makers, practitioners, and advocates have worked to reduce racial disparities, often within institutions of criminal legal processing. Reform efforts include developments in prisoner reentry policy from the early 2000s to address the collateral consequences of incarceration and more recent policy changes that abolish money bail, eliminate court-ordered fines and fees, reform sentencing policy, and end solitary confinement in prisons. For example, the combined effects of research, advocacy, and investigation through the U.S. Sentencing Commission helped reduce (but not eliminate) the crack-cocaine disparity in federal sentencing in 2010; states and localities have ended arrests and incarcerations for cannabis possession; hundreds of people have been exonerated through DNA evidence; and the rate at which Black people have been imprisoned has declined over the last two decades. While these trends and reforms represent changes to a vast system consisting of thousands of agencies and departments, neighborhood segregation and concentrated poverty are enduring. Despite reform, police, courts, jails, and prisons remain a substantial presence in Black communities.

The sequential character of criminal processing can compound inequalities both within the criminal justice system and in social life more broadly. One way to understand how the criminal justice system itself affects inequalities is to focus on disparities at each stage of the system and key decisions at each stage. These decisions may divert a person out of the system, treat them more leniently, or treat them more harshly.

This chapter examines the evidence for racial disparities in criminal justice monitoring and processing at three key stages: entry into the system, primarily through policing; court processes, including pretrial detention; and post-conviction, including sentencing. Procedures and decision making at each stage suggest how disparities at one point are consequential for subsequent phases. If non-White people are treated relatively harshly, racial disparities grow larger across stages, resulting in high rates of incarceration of Black, Native, and Latino people.

To underscore why racial inequality in the criminal system is such a significant concern, this chapter also considers how people are harmed by involvement in the criminal system. Much of the research on racial disparities in the criminal justice system conceives of continued court and correctional control as the main outcome to be explained. However, greater racial disparities in ultimate outcomes—such as imprisonment or police killings—are not the only way inequality harms people. Since police contact, criminal conviction, and incarceration may negatively affect health, family structure, education, and employment, the inequalities produced by the criminal system may have a broader impact on socioeconomic inequality. Even early-stage criminal justice contact that does not result in continued correctional control can harm psychological and economic well-being. For example, a day or two spent in pretrial detention causes measurable damage even when the person is released and never tried or sentenced (Meares and Rizer, 2020; Dobbie et al., 2018). Similarly, racial disparities in incarceration are especially harmful in view of the prison experience, which increases vulnerability to violence, sexual abuse, solitary confinement, and poor health care.

CONCEPTUALIZING RACIAL INEQUALITY

A large research literature has wrestled with the complex relationship between racial disparities in crime and racial disparities in criminal justice involvement. The dominant approach aims to divide racial disparities in criminal justice involvement into two components: one for race differences in crime and a residual component that is often interpreted as discrimination by judges or other officials. While researchers often acknowledge the empirical limitations of interpreting a residual as a measure of discrimination, the underlying conceptual framework views disparity in criminal justice outcomes such as arrest or incarceration as the combined result of disparities in crime on the one hand and discrimination by officials on the other. In this review of research on racial disparity across stages of the system, we extend the crime-discrimination approach by considering the social and historical context of criminalization and the accumulation of disparities across stages.

Sentencing has been a longstanding focus of the analysis of racial inequality. Studies dating from the 1920s find Black defendants across a range of crimes were more likely to be convicted and given heavier sentences particularly compared to native-born White people (Sellin, 1935, 1928). In that wave of research, from the 1930s to the 1970s, severe court outcomes for Black defendants were taken by some researchers as evidence of discrimination. While researchers at the time often acknowledged racial differences in crime, the absence of controls for a prior criminal record, for example, clearly weakened the claim of discrimination (Kleck, 1981; Hagan, 1974).

A new line of research, beginning in the 1970s, incorporated information about crime into the analysis through statistical controls for a wide variety of case characteristics. Criminal history and offense severity are legally relevant considerations in sentencing and were found to explain much of the variation in sentence outcomes. Once these case characteristics were considered, evidence of racial discrimination became much weaker, and many concluded that Black overrepresentation in the criminal justice system was chiefly the result of serious criminal involvement within the Black population. Summarizing these studies, a National Research Council panel concluded in 1983 that "factors other [than] racial discrimination in sentencing account for most of the disproportionate representation of blacks in U.S. prisons" (NRC, 1983, p. 13).

Importantly, the research consensus at that time did not conclude that there was no race discrimination in U.S. courts, just that most of the observed disparity in sentencing outcomes was related to offense severity, prior record, and other legally relevant case characteristics. Subsequent research turned away from decomposing disparity into crime and discrimination components to instead make a more detailed study of discrimination.

This later wave of research found that, controlling for case characteristics, harsh sentencing outcomes were associated with the defendant's race in combination with other attributes (e.g., age, education, or employment), or in certain kinds of social and institutional contexts. We review the main empirical findings from this research below.

The Explained versus Unexplained Racial Differences Framework

Parallel to the sentencing studies, another line of research examined racial disparities in incarceration. An early paper on imprisonment by Blumstein (1982) calculated the Black population's share of arrests across 10 offense categories and estimated the expected share of Black prisoners given the racial disparity in arrests. Blumstein's (1982, p. 1261) goal was to "explore the racial disproportionality of prison populations to discern... the degree to which it is likely to have emerged as a consequence of racial discrimination in the criminal justice system compared to the alternative explanation that the racial disproportionality might have emerged as a consequence of disproportionate involvement in criminal activity." Data from the 1979 prison population showed that the Black share of arrests for murder and attempted murder was then 59 percent, and those offenses account for 14 percent of all people in state prison. Given the racial composition of arrests, the expected percentage of Black prisoners in the prison population who were incarcerated for murder or attempted murder is $0.59 \times 0.14 = 0.081$, or 8.1 percent. Summing across all offense categories, Blumstein (1982, p. 1266) calculated that the prison population would be 42.7 percent Black if it simply reproduced the racial distribution of arrests. The observed Black share of the prison population, Blumstein found, was 48.3 percent, suggesting that 80 percent ($42.7 \div 48.3 = 0.8$) of the total was accounted for by the differential involvement in arrests. The explanatory power of arrests varied across offense categories being larger for crimes of serious violence, like homicide, but smaller for less serious crime like drug offenses. A number of papers elaborated on this framework, replacing arrests with survey data on the race of offenders (Langan, 1985), updating the analysis from 1979 to 2004 (Tonry and Melewski, 2008), and then making further adjustments for the Hispanic population (Beck and Blumstein, 2018). The most recent estimates indicate that from 1979 to 2011, between 70 and 80 percent of the Black/White disparity in imprisonment is statistically accounted for by the racial disparity in arrests. Summarizing the research, Beck and Blumstein (2018, p. 863) write that "differential involvement in crime remains a significant factor that should be accounted for when considering racial disproportionality in prison."

Criminalization

The explained and unexplained racial differences framework has dominated research on racial inequality in the criminal justice system, but the approach has been subject to two kinds of criticisms. First, in the crime-discrimination framework, discretionary decision making is often treated as the sole source of disparity for which authorities are responsible. The process of criminalization is excluded from the analysis. The term "criminalization" acknowledges that conduct treated as "crimes" by the state is necessarily a product of state-sponsored efforts of labeling, enforcement, surveillance, and punishment. This is true whether the conduct includes behaviors for which there may be wide agreement concerning the propriety of collective condemnation (homicide is the clearest case), or behaviors for which consensus may be less stable (such as sex work, drinking alcohol in public, or playing radios too loudly).

Criminalization thus describes how the law, police, and court officials classify and act upon some kinds of conduct, but not others, as criminal. Criminalization is a precondition for punishment, so treating some behaviors as criminal can magnify or attenuate the consequences of behavioral disparities across racial groups (Naidoo and Karels, 2012). Social norms, prejudices, electoral politics, and power relations at a given point in time can influence this process, potentially codifying and locking in definitions of crime that have a disproportionate impact (Lacey et al., 2018; Lacey and Zedner, 2017). Subsequent to this classification, how state officials carry out the identification and punishment of people who commit these enumerated offenses may also have disproportionate impact, compounding the biases created in the first instance by conduct categorization.

Criminalization has been used to regulate and control racial groups. For example, the Bureau of Indian Affairs created criminal codes and reservation court systems as part of the federal government's campaign to forcibly assimilate Indigenous people in the late 1800s to early 1900s. The codes criminalized traditional religious and cultural activities that the U.S. government sought to eradicate. Agency-run criminal courts imposed sanctions on American Indians who resisted assimilation, local officials were given wide discretion to punish Indigenous cultural practice, and the courts were viewed as educational instruments in the campaign to "civilize" Native communities (*U.S. v. Clapox*).[1] In this context, the criminal law and its administration was used to control and change Indigenous people, not to ensure public safety or address violence or social harm (Ross, 2010). Criminal system involvement by Native people, in this example, followed

---

[1] 35 F. 575 (D. Or. 1888). See https://law.resource.org/pub/us/case/reporter/F/0035/0035.f.0575.pdf

from the government's choice to criminalize new behaviors, not from a change in behavior.

Law is fundamental to the process of criminalization (Jenness, 2004). Vagrancy laws have long criminalized poverty by subjecting people who appear to be unemployed to surveillance, arrest, and/or sanction. These laws also allowed for the policing of space, limiting the right to move freely, congregate, or to otherwise occupy public streets and sidewalks. In the United States after slavery ended, vagrancy laws were commonly used to criminalize Black southerners and Black migrants in northern cities (Muhammad, 2010). The proliferation of drug felony laws and a broad array of newly defined possession offenses adopted in the 1980s and 1990s illustrate widening the net of criminalization through the enactment of new criminal offenses in state penal codes (Tonry and Melewski, 2008; Dubber, 2001). If drug dealing is more likely to take place in public places in primarily Black and Latino communities, such communities become more vulnerable to arrest and incarceration when drug laws become more punitive. A legal framework that places few constraints on police discretion, or sentencing guidelines that punish criminal history, might also foster disparities (Engel et al., 2019; Frase and Roberts, 2019; Reiter, 2015; NRC, 2004a).

A more expansive idea of criminalization includes the social and historical context in which the law, police, and prosecutors operate, acknowledging that the law and criminal justice operations punish some social contexts or conduct more harshly than others. For example, the law penalizes crack cocaine more heavily than powder cocaine, and because crack is disproportionately used in Black communities, so the law itself generates disparities in imprisonment that could be traced to differential offending in the crime-discrimination framework. Similarly, Chapter 3 showed that in cities and tribal communities, residential segregation and spatially concentrated poverty were associated with the concentration of crime and other social problems in small geographic areas. Police contacts—stops, calls for service, and arrests—are also spatially concentrated, so criminalization follows the contours of geographic and social space (Simes, 2021; Sampson, 2012). If police were deployed disproportionately to Black communities through proactive policing strategies, which can include targeted traffic enforcement to generate public revenue, this would likely produce large racial disparities in the volume and nature of police contacts (the National Academies of Sciences, Engineering, and Medicine, 2018, p. 301) that could again be attributed to differential offending in the crime-discrimination analysis. High rates of interpersonal violence and victimization in Black communities (see Chapters 2 and 3), for example, may intensify police suspicion or enforcement, magnifying racial disparity in criminal justice contact.

Second, but equally important, empirical studies in the crime-discrimination approach focus only on a single stage of the system and neglect how inequality may accumulate across a sequence of stages. Analysis of a single stage of the process of criminalization may underestimate disparate treatment by neglecting how disparity might grow from policing, to sentencing, to incarceration, to parole release (Kurlychek and Johnson, 2019; Spohn, 2015a; Rehavi and Starr, 2014; Sutton, 2013). Hagan (1974, p. 379) describes this dynamic perspective, writing that racial disparities result from "transit through the criminal justice system" that operates "cumulatively to the disadvantage of minority group defendants." Researchers have thus examined cumulative racial disadvantage in criminal court processing and sentencing (Wooldredge et al., 2015; Kutateladze et al., 2014; Baumer, 2013; Sutton, 2013; Ulmer, 2012; Brennan and Spohn, 2008; Schlesinger, 2005).

The crime-discrimination framework is particularly limited in its ability to capture the ways the criminal system harms Indigenous people. American Indian individuals may be subject to the criminal jurisdiction of tribal, federal, or state governments—and often to the concurrent jurisdiction of two or three governments (see Box 4-1 describing jurisdictional structure). While a race-comparison approach is helpful in assessing the experiences of Indigenous people in state systems, it is less useful in the federal system, where American Indians may be prosecuted based on the location of their crimes, and it is irrelevant to tribal systems, which (with very limited exceptions) exercise jurisdiction over only Indian people. Any assessment of criminal justice disparities affecting Indigenous people as a group needs to consider information from multiple jurisdictions—information that is not included in most datasets. Moreover, because definitions and counts of Native people vary across jurisdictions and stages of the system, it is difficult to determine the implications of single-stage disparities or to link those disparities to an assessment of cumulative disadvantage.

We examine racial inequality in the criminal justice system by considering each stage of criminal processing, how the stages operate together, and how they operate in poor and highly segregated communities, which account for a disproportionate share of serious crime, arrests, and incarceration. Two overall themes emerge through this analysis. First, policy decisions made at the early stages of criminal processing have increased the level of police contact, particularly in Black and Latino communities. High rates of arrest for low-level drug offenses, for example, put large numbers of people at risk of sustained criminal justice contact through continuing court obligations, pretrial supervision, violations of release conditions, diversion, or probation. Second, in cases of prosecution for serious violence, criminal justice contact is sustained through long sentences and a surveilling style of parole and supervision that leaves parolees vulnerable to re-incarceration. Both patterns of criminal justice involvement reflect policy

BOX 4-1
Indigenous People and Criminal Jurisdiction

Chapter 2 describes how Indigenous people are disproportionately criminalized, under-protected, and punished compared to their representation in the population. However, many Indigenous people are subject to special rules of criminal jurisdiction that complicate efforts to measure and address racial inequality in their treatment. These jurisdictional rules determine whether the tribal, federal, and/or state government is responsible for criminal policing, investigation, prosecution, and sentencing. Application of the rules depends on where the crime occurred (in Indian country,[a] Indian country where state jurisdiction applies, or outside Indian country); the identity of the defendant (whether Indian[b] or non-Indian); the identity of the victim (whether Indian or non-Indian); and the type of crime (whether it is a "major" crime covered by 25 U.S.C. § 1153 or not). In many cases, Indians in Indian country will be subject to the criminal jurisdiction of at least two governments (federal and tribal, or state and tribal), with minimal guidelines to guard against duplicative prosecutions or conflicting dispositions. Federal criminal law and federal agency policy thus disproportionately affect Indigenous people. Tribal criminal law and policy are also important, although tribal systems are rarely included in datasets or assessed in studies.

Indian tribal governments exercise criminal jurisdiction over Indian defendants for offenses committed in Indian country, regardless of victim or type of crime (*Talton v. Mayes*;[c] *United States v. Wheeler*;[d] 25 U.S.C. § 1301(2)[e]). Some tribes also exercise criminal jurisdiction over non-Indian defendants for certain covered crimes under 25 U.S.C. § 1304,[f] such as domestic violence, child violence, and assault of tribal justice personnel. In some places, the federal government exercises concurrent jurisdiction over so-called inter-racial crimes (Indian against non-Indian, and non-Indian against Indian) and over "major" crimes between Indians (18 U.S.C. § 1152-1153).[g] In these federal jurisdiction areas, tribes are the only governments with jurisdiction over non-major crimes between Indians (Newton et al., 2012). States have jurisdiction over crimes committed by non-Indians, exclusively if the victim is non-Indian and—according to a 2022 U.S. Supreme Court decision—concurrently with the federal government if the victim is Indian (*United States v. Castro-Huerta*; *United States v. McBratney*).[h] In other places, including Alaska and areas where the federal government has delegated its criminal jurisdiction to states under Public Law 280 or similar laws, states exercise concurrent jurisdiction (along with tribes) over all crimes committed by Indians in Indian country, regardless of victim or type of crime (25 U.S.C. § 1162;[i] *Alaska v. Native Village of Venetie Tribal Government*;[j] Goldberg et al., 2007).

Jurisdictional rules are further complicated by the role of federal agencies in carrying out the responsibilities associated with federal and tribal criminal jurisdiction. For example, federal criminal jurisdiction includes the FBI's investigatory responsibilities, the U.S. attorneys' prosecution responsibilities, federal courts' sentencing responsibilities, and the Bureau of Prisons' incarceration responsibilities. In addition, the Bureau of Indian Affairs provides law enforcement and incarceration services to many tribes (either as a direct provider or with the tribe as a federal contractor), and its Courts of Indian Offenses are the primary

TABLE 4-1-1 Criminal Jurisdiction for Indian and Non-Indian Defendants

Defendant	Place	Crime type	Indian victim	Non-Indian victim
Indian	Indian Country	Major	Tribal and Federal	Tribal and Federal
		Non-major	Tribal only	Tribal and Federal
	PL 280 Indian country	Any	Tribal and State	Tribal and State
Non-Indian	Indian country	Any	Federal and State (and tribal if exercising jurisdiction under 25 U.S.C. § 1304)	State
	PL 280 Indian country	Any	State (and tribal if exercising jurisdiction under 25 U.S.C. § 1304)	State

SOURCES: 18 U.S.C. section 1152; 18 U.S.C. section 1153; 25 U.S.C. section 1301(2); 25 U.S.C. section 1162; 25 U.S.C. section 1302; 25 U.S.C. section 1304; Rolnick (2016c,d); Felix Cohen's Handbook of Federal Indian Law, section 9.04 (see Newton et al., 2012); *Oklahoma v. Castro-Huerta*, 597 U.S. (2022); *Talton v. Mayes*, 163 U.S. 376 (1898); *United States v. McBratney*, 104 U.S. 621 (1881); *United States v. Wheeler*, 435 U.S. 313 (1978); *Walker v. Rushing*, 898 F.2d 672 (8th Cir. 1990); *Wetsit v. Stafne*, 44 F.3d 823, 825 (9th Cir. 1995).

criminal courts on a handful of reservations. Tribal governments also rely heavily on Bureau of Indian Affairs formula funding and Department of Justice grant funding to run their criminal justice systems because they lack the local tax base that other governments use to generate revenue. Where state criminal policy is the most important site of reform for most groups, for Indigenous people federal law, federal agency policy, and federal funding priorities are important sites of intervention (e.g., Ulmer and Bradley, 2018). This jurisdictional maze can lead to underenforcement—for example, under-prosecution of sexual and domestic violence crimes—and slow law enforcement investigative response to crime (Braithwaite et al., 2019; Riley, 2016; Eid et al., 2013; Washburn, 2006a,b). At the same time, efforts to bolster federal and tribal responses to crime may fall disproportionately on Indian defendants because of jurisdictional limitations, differences in federal and state sentencing practices, and greater federal law protections for non-Indian defendants in tribal court (Ulmer and Bradley, 2018; Riley, 2016; Rolnick, 2016b; Eid et al., 2013).

continued

BOX 4-1 Continued

These special jurisdictional rules apply only to Indigenous people defined as "Indians" under federal or tribal law. As described in Chapter 2, this generally excludes Native Hawaiians, Indigenous Pacific Islanders, and individuals who may be racially identifiable as Indigenous people but are not affiliated with a federally acknowledged tribal government. The rules also apply only to offenses committed in areas defined as "Indian country" under federal law—generally reservations and similar communities. Indigenous people who are not Indians or who are outside Indian country are subject to state jurisdiction to the same extent other groups are (except that many Indigenous Pacific Islanders are prosecuted in territorial courts, which may not be counted in national datasets). Most of the disparities described in this report are based on reports from state criminal justice systems and therefore include only those Native people subject to the jurisdiction of state systems.

---

[a]Defined in 18 U.S.C. § 1151 to include reservations, trust allotments, and other restricted lands known as "dependent Indian communities."

[b]The term Indian is defined by federal law and based on tribal citizenship or affiliation; it does not include all Indigenous people.

[c]163 U.S. 376 (1896). See https://supreme.justia.com/cases/federal/us/163/376/

[d]435 U.S. 313 (1978). See https://supreme.justia.com/cases/federal/us/435/313/

[e]https://www.law.cornell.edu/uscode/text/25/1301

[f]https://www.law.cornell.edu/uscode/text/25/1304

[g]https://www.law.cornell.edu/uscode/text/18/1152

[h]104 U.S. 621 (1881). See https://supreme.justia.com/cases/federal/us/104/621/

[i]https://www.law.cornell.edu/uscode/text/18/1162

[j]522 U.S. 520 (1998). See https://supreme.justia.com/cases/federal/us/522/520/

decisions to respond with incarceration to social problems that include drug use, delinquency, and violence. As described in Chapters 5 and 6, this accompanies a choice by policy makers not to proportionally invest in public health or social welfare.

THE FORMS AND EXPANSION OF RACIAL CRIMINALIZATION

Changes in criminal justice policy and the disproportionate impact on Black, Latino, and Native American communities since the early 1970s have been widely documented by political scientists, sociologists, and policy researchers (C. Muller, 2021; Beckett and Francis, 2020; Beckett, 2018; Gottschalk, 2014; NRC, 2014; Raphael and Stoll, 2013). In presidential races, from the Goldwater campaign of 1964, to the 1968 campaigns of Nixon and Wallace, through the Trump campaign of 2016, political language has long invoked images of Black communities as "jungles" (Murakawa, 2012), personified crime through the use of Black faces in political advertising (Mendelberg, 2017), and conflated social protest with crime (Weaver, 2007).

"Law and order" became the dominant policy response to a racialized crime problem (Hinton, 2017; Miller, 2016; Campbell and Schoenfeld, 2013; Flamm, 2005). Black communities experiencing high rates of crime often supported law-and-order politics, along with the rest of the electorate (Enns, 2016; Fortner, 2015), but they also demanded greater investment in social services (Forman, 2017). While the currents of public opinion were often complex, the crime problem in political rhetoric was often cast as a problem of Black criminality that posed a broad threat to community order and safety. As the National Research Council panel on the growth of incarceration wrote, "A uniquely American combination of crime, race, and politics...shaped the adoption of more punitive criminal justice policies" (NRC, 2014, p. 104).

Researchers have discussed three policy changes developing out of the politics of law and order that have been important for how structural racism evolved in the criminal justice system. The first policy change, collectively known as the War on Drugs, intensively criminalized drug use and drug sales (Provine, 2011; Tonry and Melewski, 2008; Tonry, 1996). The War on Drugs encompassed a wide variety of policy changes that included the revision of state and federal penal codes and the development of new police tactics. Beginning in the early 1970s, mandatory prison sentences for the possession and sale of drugs were widely adopted in state penal codes. Federal statutes also established mandatory prison sentences for drug crimes. As penal codes criminalized a broad range of drug-related activities and intensified punishment, police increased both the number and racial disparity in drug arrests in the 1980s (NRC, 2014, pp. 60–61). The punitive effect of the War on Drugs can be seen in the increasing probability of imprisonment given a drug arrest and the growing share of people in prison convicted of drug crimes (Beck and Blumstein, 2018, 1999; Tonry and Melewski, 2008). Given the large racial disparity in drug arrests and prison admissions, the growth in drug incarceration also tended to increase the racial disparity in incarceration through the 1980s and 1990s.

The second major policy change contributing to racially disparate criminalization was the War on Crime. Like the War on Drugs, the War on Crime was not a single policy reform but a variety of changes in sentencing policy at the state and federal levels that increased the duration of prison sentences, particularly for violent offenses. In many cases, sentences were simply increased in length by statute. In other cases, sentence enhancements were added that increased prison time for people with prior violent felony convictions, or sometimes just for having prior convictions of any kind. The most notable example is California's Three Strikes enhancement, passed in 1994, which doubled the sentence for a second felony conviction given one prior felony conviction for a residential burglary or violent offense. A felony conviction of any sort for someone with two prior serious or violent felony convictions carried a mandatory 25 years to life sentence (the law was modified in 2012 to apply only when the third strike was a serious or violent felony; Zimring et al., 2001; Tyler and Boeckmann, 1997).

Similar second-and-third strike enhancements were passed in nearly half of the remaining states, though few states enhanced as many people with these provisions as did California (Chen, 2008). At the same time, nearly half the states passed "truth-in-sentencing" provisions. These provisions, often focused on violent felonies, required that people serve 85 percent of their sentence. The resulting increase in the length of stay for violent crimes in the 1990s also increased racial disparity because Black men were more likely to be admitted for the violent crimes of murder, rape, and robbery. In this example, racial disparity in offending contributed to a racial disparity in incarceration that was amplified by an increase in the criminalization of violent offenses through the truth-in-sentencing provisions.

Third, policing strategies and organization changed in the final decades of the 20th century to focus more on crime prevention and to allocate resources more intensively to areas and people who were viewed as high risk. National Research Council panels described these changes in policing as "focused policing efforts" (NRC, 2004a) and "proactive policing" (the National Academies, 2018). Policy change took a variety of forms, but they commonly involved more police-initiated contacts with the public and the intensive allocation of police resources in low-income minority communities. Among these efforts, for example, "order maintenance" or "quality-of-life policing" cracked down on low-level violations for public order and drug offenses. Such efforts have been found to produce large numbers of racially disparate police stops and other police contacts (e.g., Howell, 2016; Fagan et al., 2010). The National Academies (2018) concluded that, although the causal pathway from proactive policing to racial disparity is not well understood, large racial disparities in police contacts and the nature of police contacts are likely to follow from proactive strategies.

Policy changes that propelled an increase in incarceration from 1972 to 2008 also tended to increase racial disparity at least until the end of the 1990s. As a result, very high levels of criminal justice contact, including imprisonment, were sustained in Black and Hispanic communities through the first decades of the 2000s. The degree of criminal justice contact and racial disparity is indicated by a variety of period prevalence estimates that shows the cumulative risk of different kinds of criminal justice contact over the life course. Period prevalence estimates are helpful for thinking about racial inequality by describing race differences in the exposure of specific birth cohorts to criminal justice contact and its consequences.

The Bureau of Justice Statistics has published estimates of the lifetime likelihood of imprisonment. Using 1991 data, it reported that 28.5 percent of Black men, 16 percent of Hispanic men, and 4.4 percent of White men would be imprisoned in their lifetime, if admission rates remained fixed at the level of the 1991 survey data (Bonczar and Beck, 1997). The early Bureau estimates have since been refined to measure the experience of specific birth cohorts and to reflect a variety of forms of criminal justice contact (Table 4-1). Work by Pettit and Western (Pettit, 2012; Western and Pettit, 2010; Pettit and Western, 2004) found that the cumulative risk of imprisonment more than doubled for Black men in a single generation, comparing birth cohorts born in the late 1940s to those in the late 1970s. They also reported a steep educational gradient, in which the cumulative

TABLE 4-1 Cumulative Risk Estimates of Criminal Justice Contact, by Race

Criminal Justice Contact	Birth Cohort	By Age	Black	Hispanic	White	Native American
Men						
1. Prison	1945–49	30–34	10.4	2.8	1.4	—
2. Prison	1975	30–34	26.8	12.2	5.4	—
3. Solitary confinement (prison)	1986–89	32	11.1	3.4	1.4	—
4. Jail, New York City	Synthetic	38	26.8	16.2	3.4	—
Women						
1. Prison	1945–49	30–34	1.1	0.4	0.1	—
2. Prison	1975–79	30–34	2.7	1.3	0.8	—
3. Solitary confinement (prison)	1986–89	32	0.4	0.2	0.2	—
4. Jail, New York City	Synthetic	38	4.9	2.3	0.7	—
Children						
1. Parent charged with felony	1999–2000	18	41.6	23.5	16.1	34.2
2. Parent in prison	1999–2000	18	19.8	11.4	6.1	14.9

SOURCES: Prison risks are taken from Pettit (2012); solitary confinement risks are from Pullen-Blasnik and colleagues (2021) and are for Pennsylvania; jail risks are from Western and colleagues (2021); and parental felony and prison risks are from Finlay and colleagues (2022b).

risk of imprisonment is 68.0 percent for Black men with less than a high school education born between 1975 and 1979 (Western and Pettit, 2010).

Pullen-Blasnik and colleagues (2021) find that an extreme form of imprisonment, solitary confinement, had been experienced by 11.0 percent of Black men in Pennsylvania by age 32. Over a quarter of Black men in New York City had been incarcerated in jail by age 38 in the 2000s, a time when the jail population was less than half its peak in 1991 (Western et al., 2021).

Finally, greater exposure to incarceration means greater exposure of children to parental incarceration. Recent estimates indicate that more than 40 percent of all Black children have caregivers who have been charged with felonies, and nearly 20 percent have caregivers who have been imprisoned. Figures are similarly high for American Indians/Alaska Natives (Finlay et al., 2022a).

CRIMINAL JUSTICE CONTACT AS CUMULATIVE DISADVANTAGE

Racial inequality can increase through the sequential stages of criminal processing from police contact through arrest, sentencing, and incarceration. Racial inequality in the criminal justice system is not just a disparity occurring at a discrete stage that can be decomposed into components related to crime and discrimination. Racial inequality includes the spatial concentration of crime and poverty in low-income Black, Latino, and Native American communities, in which criminal justice resources are disproportionately deployed; it encompasses penal codes and police tactics that surveil and penalize those communities more intensively than White communities; and it encompasses the sequential character of criminal processing, in which disproportionate representation may increase from stage to stage.

In the framework of this report, therefore, the idea of "inequality" is conceptually distinct from that of "disparity." Racial inequality within the criminal justice system in the current sense is rooted in structural racism, manifested in continued segregation and poverty, and sustained and magnified through the sequence of criminal justice processing (see Chapters 1 and 3).

Turney and Wakefield (2019) describe criminal justice contact as fitting into one of three categories: transitory contact (e.g., police stops, arrests, and tickets and fines); sustained contacts (which include felony conviction, pretrial detention, and correctional supervision); and spillover consequences of the criminal justice system (as in the foster care system for children with incarcerated parents). Research has also shown that vicarious contacts—for example, witnessing police stops, hearing stories of negative police encounters, and being exposed to media coverage of police brutality—also have significant impacts on people's attitudes toward law enforcement (Desmond et al., 2016; Brunson and Weitzer, 2009; compare to Zoorob, 2020). These forms of contact can be co-occurring and are often concentrated in Black and Hispanic communities (Jones, 2018). In the following sections, we document and explain how racial inequality is produced across system stages, and how criminal processing may amplify and concentrate the negative consequences of criminal justice contact among racial minority populations.

Early Exposure to the Criminal Justice System

Well before they experience police stops, arrests, or incarceration, Black and other non-White children are disproportionately in contact with the criminal justice system. The adult criminal justice system impacts the lives of children, adolescents, and young adults in Black and Latino communities, and while a number of aspects of growing up in densely poor areas may contribute to worse developmental outcomes for children and youth, the criminal justice system itself can also contribute to a distinct developmental experience qualitatively different from the life pathway for children and adolescents in White communities. In some cases, these contacts with the authorities can create direct and indirect pathways to the criminal justice system.

Under conditions of racial segregation, where crime and poverty are concentrated in minority neighborhoods, a pervasive police presence can cause adverse childhood experiences from police encounters (Geller, 2021). Surveys of children and parents indicate that African American youth are about twice as likely to have contact with the police as White youth (Turney, 2021), a difference that is only partially explained by difference in self-reported criminal conduct (Crutchfield et al., 2012). Police are more likely to treat Black children with suspicion and intervene more forcefully because they perceive children and adolescents as older than they really are (Goff et al., 2014; Rattan et al., 2012; Graham and Lowery, 2004). In regressions studies with controls for delinquency, police contact has been found to be associated with depressive symptoms and reduced future orientation among adolescents, and sleep problems and health limitations among mothers (Testa et al., 2022; Turney, 2021; Turney and Jackson, 2021). Moreover, researchers have documented that living in areas with a high level of police presence is associated with higher rates of preterm birth, stress, anxiety, and depression through correlational studies (Sewell et al., 2021; Hardeman et al., 2020; Boyd et al., 2016; Geller et al., 2014; Shedd, 2012). This is the case for both police presence and exposure to violence. Sharkey and colleagues (2012) found an association between decreased cognitive functioning and the ability to self-regulate behavior in children and homicides that occurred near their home. Additionally, surges in police contact through stop-and-frisk policing in New York, for example, were associated with decline in test scores among Black boys ages nine to 15 (Legewie and Fagan, 2019). Exposure to police violence can be traumatic, which puts children at risk for later involvement in the juvenile and criminal justice systems (the National Academies, 2021a).

Routine interactions with police can also influence development more subtly, effectively preparing children to expect policing and contact with the criminal system as a regular part of life (Gardner, 2020; Jones, 2014). Some research thus suggests that police contact is itself criminogenic. Following a sample of Black and White juveniles in Seattle until they were 20 years old, McGlynn-Wright and colleagues (2022) found that those who had early childhood police contacts (by eighth grade) had profoundly different likelihood of arrests as young adults. Controlling for self-reported criminal behavior, they found that police encounters in childhood increased the risk of arrest in young adulthood for Black but not White students. Black young adults who had early contact with police were 11 times more likely to have been arrested than Black students who had not had an encounter with police.

Individual contact with the criminal justice system may also occur through the school disciplinary process and the presence of police in schools. In their review of research on disparities in school discipline, Welsh and Little (2018, p. 771) write that "the federal government has endorsed school resource officers (SROs) as a means of improving school climate, school safety, and student achievement," but research provides mixed evidence of effectiveness. Schools that serve a greater share of non-White children are more likely to respond to student behavior issues with punitive discipline (Keels, 2021b; Losen et al., 2015; Welch and Payne, 2010). The presence of police in schools amplifies this response; schools with a greater police presence are more likely to impose exclusionary discipline and to criminalize violations of school rules (Keels, 2021b; Kupchik, 2016; Morris, 2015). While school security measures are commonplace, exclusionary discipline and criminal punishment are concentrated in schools that serve poor and non-White students (Kupchik and Ward, 2014; Welch and Payne, 2010). Research indicates that teachers who reduce suspensions and improve attendance can reduce the risk of later arrest and incarceration (Rose et al., 2021).

School policing is just one example of an approach to controlling youth misbehavior that brings children into the system instead of directing them out. Another example is status offenses: young people may be directed into the juvenile justice system for non-criminal infractions like skipping school or fighting with their parents. Consequences for status offenses vary along race, gender, and class lines. Normal adolescent misbehavior in Black children is more likely to be labeled as pre-criminal behavior (e.g., "willful defiance") and to result in entry into the juvenile system (the National Academies, 2021a). Indigenous children and girls of all races are more likely than others to be referred to the juvenile system and to be detained for status offenses (Tribal Law and Policy Institute, 2015; Chesney-Lind, 1988). For these youth, juvenile system involvement is the price of receiving intervention services.

In addition, while juvenile courts were created to prevent children from experiencing the consequences of involvement in the adult criminal courts (Tanenhaus, 2004), modern juvenile systems can feed directly into the adult criminal system. A number of studies and national data show that Black youth, and minority youth more generally, are 30–50 percent more likely to be transferred to the adult criminal court system (Hockenberry, 2021; Zane et al., 2016), but most of the raw disparity is related to legal factors such as the severity of the offense (Zane et al., 2016). Finally, under modern rules, prior juvenile system involvement may also be used as a mitigating or enhancing factor in later adult prosecutions, affecting the consequences of criminal justice involvement for youth later in their lives. Disparity in youth incarceration presents a mixed picture. Absolute disparity has declined as the overall number of youth in secure confinement has declined, but relative disparity has worsened: in 2013, Black youth were 4.3 times more likely to be incarcerated than White youth, up from 3.7 times as likely in 2003 (see, e.g., the National Academies, 2019a). By 2019, the Hispanic/White disparity in residential placement rates had shrunk, but the Black/White disparity persisted and the American Indian-White disparity had worsened (OJJDP, 2022).

These examples demonstrate both the direct and indirect consequences of early contact—whether formal or informal—with the criminal justice system. The decisions that place higher concentrations of police in particular neighborhoods or in particular schools, and the decisions that condition services on involvement in other systems of surveillance, pull people into the system and open them up to more formal contact and associated harms, and disparities in these initial experiences will be compounded as people move deeper into the system.

Policing

The police are the main entry point for the public's interaction with the criminal justice system. People come into contact with police as victims of crime, as perpetrators, as those who call for service, as motorists, and as pedestrians going about their daily routines where proactive policing strategies have been deployed.

Policing in the United States has evolved in significant ways over the past 50 years. Police departments in large and mid-sized cities in the United States are among the most professionalized, well-funded, and well-armed police departments in history. The nation's response to the urban unrest of the 1960s and its later investments in criminal justice led to policy changes, innovations, and experiments in police tactics at the local, state, and federal levels. The expanding role of the federal government in funding state and local criminal justice initiatives from the 1960s provided successive administrations and the Department of Justice with growing influence over local policing policy. National trends in policing policy are described in a National Research Council (2004a) report on the fairness and effectiveness of police and in a National Academies (2018) report on proactive policing.

As the 20th century came to a close, and with the support of both popular and scholarly arguments for place- and person-based policing, spatially focused policing tactics came to be used routinely in historically disadvantaged neighborhoods. These tactics aimed to deter crime through elevated police presence at locations that were identified as at high risk of violence (Manski and Nagin, 2017; Meares, 2014), and evidence reviewed in the National Research Council (2004a) report finds evidence for the crime-reducing effect of these intensive policing tactics. These changes, however, also increased the likelihood of individuals' exposure to police contacts and sometimes amplified the negative consequences of police contact among people living in low-income and racially segregated neighborhoods.

Racial Differences in Police Contacts

Racial differences in police-initiated contacts are associated with the pattern of stops, for which police are constitutionally required to have a "reasonable suspicion" that the person stopped has been or is involved in the commission of a crime. Most commonly reported by the public are motor vehicle stops for speeding, but police stops also arise in the context of stop-question-and-frisk policies in some departments, pretextual traffic stops in others, and in general officers' practice of justifying stops by having a "reasonable suspicion" that a crime has been or is about to occur.

Figures on the relatively high rates of police interaction among Black and Hispanic members of the public are reported in Chapter 2. The most widely cited national statistics on racial differences in police stops come from the Police-Public Contact Survey, a Bureau of Justice Statistics data collection based on a nationally representative sample of roughly 50,000 people. Recent years of the survey, in 2015 and 2018, showed that around 11 percent of U.S. adults were stopped by police each year, about 10 percent in traffic stops and one percent in street stops. Data from 2015 showed that Black members of the public were more likely to be stopped than White people, although in 2018 rates of police stops were roughly equal for Black and White people. In both survey years, Black respondents reported police use of force at roughly twice the rate of White respondents (Harrell and Davis, 2020; Davis et al., 2018).

An alternative approach to studying racial differences in police contact analyzes police records. Police records indicate larger racial disparities in police-public contact than self-reports in social surveys. A research team at Stanford used public records requests to compile a dataset of approximately 95 million traffic stops conducted by 56 state police agencies and local police departments from 2011 to 2018 (Pierson et al., 2020). They found that the annual per capita stop rate for Black motorists was about 40 percent higher than for White motorists. Black and Hispanic motorists were also more likely to be searched than White people, given that they were stopped. Similar analyses of large data files of police records also report high rates of stops and searches among Black members of the public in California (Lofstrom et al., 2021), Connecticut and North Carolina (Shoub, 2022), and New York City (Gelman et al., 2007).

A longstanding line of research finds that Black survey respondents under-report arrests, compared to official arrest records, more than White respondents (Kirk, 2006; Huizinga and Elliott, 1986; Hindelang et al., 1981), and the mode of data collection may contribute to a divergence between administrative records and self-reports on police contacts. Whether such measurement errors in surveys apply to police contacts is an important question for further research.

Research from the field of social psychology has explored the role of stereotype threat with respect to racial differences in police encounters.[2] This literature builds on a body of psychological research that has documented evidence of a cultural stereotype of Black criminality, which has been shown to have a biased effect on how individuals process information and form judgments, even when there is no conscious bias apparent (see, e.g., Eberhardt et al., 2004; Devine, 1989). Najdowski and colleagues (2015) conducted two studies where they investigated how Black and White participants experience and interpret police encounters. The first study used self-reported survey data to assess the presence of stereotype threat during police encounters, and the authors found that Black participants (in particular Black men) reported concern that police officers would stereotype them as criminals because of their race. The second study examined perceived consequences of stereotype threat and revealed that anticipated stereotype threat among Black participants was associated with anxiety, self-regulatory attempts, and behaviors that are often perceived as suspicious by officers. Kahn and colleagues (2018) further explore the consequences of stereotype threat by conducting a content analysis of police training videos and find that the pre-attack or danger indicators that police are trained to detect

[2]Stereotype threat can be defined as the "concern one experiences when at risk of being perceived in light of a negative stereotype that applies to one's group" (Najdowski et al., 2015, p. 464).

overlap significantly with stereotype threat indicators (e.g., anxiety, arousal, and reduced cognitive capacity). Theoretical research has also investigated the relationship between stereotype threat and racial differences in false confessions (Najdowski, 2011). Collectively, this body of research points to an important mechanism for racially disparate police encounters that requires further study and integration into police interventions.

Neighborhood Context

Interactions between police and the public can be thought of as nested encounters. Interactions take place within neighborhoods, which are located in cities or towns that are embedded in states. Due to high rates of residential segregation by race and income, these nested social contexts are important for understanding how policing contributes to racial inequality in the criminal justice system. Social context has been found to influence the likelihood of police contact and racial differences in police contacts. Researchers have studied social context in a number of ways in neighborhoods, based on police organizational and operational practices and based on wider law and policy regimes.

Patterns of policing vary greatly across neighborhoods (Smith, 1986), and adjusting for the fact that people of different races tend to be encountered in different places can account for large portions of observed racial disparities in stops and searches (e.g., Goel et al., 2016; Ridgeway, 2007). A long tradition of scholarship highlights the importance of neighborhood-level processes in influencing policing (e.g., Terrill and Reisig, 2003; Klinger, 1997; Herbert, 1996).

Much of the research on neighborhood influences on policing examines the role of the racial composition of residential populations. The fraction of residents who are Black has been found to be significantly associated with a variety of types of police contact—including stops, searches, and arrests—after conditioning on other neighborhood-level factors (e.g., Gaston et al., 2020; Hannon, 2020; Gaston, 2019; Lautenschlager and Omori, 2019; Morrow et al., 2018; Levchak, 2017; Fagan et al., 2016, 2010; Geller and Fagan, 2010; Kane, 2002). These research findings are sometimes interpreted through the prism of racial threat theory in which police are used instrumentally to control populations that pose a threat to the dominant racial order (Novak and Chamlin, 2012; Parker et al., 2004). Research also appeals to the idea of "neighborhood stigma" (Sampson and Raudenbush, 2004) to explain why racial context leads officers to perceive people as especially suspicious in certain areas, as has social disorganization theory to indicate that policing may be more aggressive in low-income, minority areas where there is weaker informal social control to respond to problems or to counteract police excesses.

In contrast to theories of racial composition, an alternative hypothesis argues that individual and neighborhood race interact such that minorities face elevated rates of policing in non-minority contexts, where they seem out of place (Carroll and Gonzalez, 2014; Novak and Chamlin, 2012; Rojek et al., 2012; Gelman et al., 2007; Meehan and Ponder, 2002). In contrast to the out-of-place theory, Neil's (2021) analysis of the New York Police Department's stop-and-frisk tactics finds strong main effects of individual race that existed in all contexts and that officers applied lower standards of suspicion in deciding to stop people of all races in minority neighborhoods, an effect that did not vary by race.

The neighborhood sources of disparities in police contact may not result from discrimination but may be associated with patterns of residential segregation, which shape police behavior. Most obviously, police deploy officers and resources in response to crime, and several types of crime are more common in minority neighborhoods than in others. This reflects the persistent consequences of structural racism, most especially in segregation and concentrated disadvantage. There is disagreement as to how important this "deployment hypothesis" is in explaining disparities (Gaston, 2019; Briggs and Keimig, 2017; Petrocelli et al., 2003). For example, Beckett and colleagues (2006) find that neighborhood crime does not explain racial disparities in drug delivery arrests in Seattle, but Engel and others (2012), using data slightly different from those used a few years later in Seattle, find that those disparities are overwhelmingly explained by calls for service.

Neighborhood violence was found to be the key driver of racial disparities in the New York Police Department's stop-and-frisk practice (Neil, 2021). However, the effect of neighborhood crime reflects organizational decisions that may ultimately induce officers to stop large numbers of innocent minorities. Thus, finding a strong neighborhood crime effect on disparities could indicate a rational bureaucratic, proportional response to crime—a major function of policing—but it could also be that an organizational fixation on crime statistics, and of conceptualizing and responding to problems at the neighborhood level, influences unconstitutional policing of racialized minorities.[3] Under the law, individuals who commit acts of

[3]Lum and Nagin (2017, p. 1) argue that 21st century efforts to reinvent American policing need to be guided by two principles: (1) crimes averted, not arrests made, should be the primary metric for judging police effectiveness; and (2) citizens' views about the police and their tactics for preventing crime and disorder matter independently of police effectiveness. They go on to argue that "seven steps are essential to reinvention of democratic policing: Prioritize crime prevention over arrest. Create and install systems that monitor citizen reactions to the police and routinely report results back to the public and police supervisors and officers. Reform training and redefine the 'craft of policing.' Recalibrate organizational incentives. Strengthen accountability with greater transparency. Incorporate the analysis of crime and citizen reaction into managerial practice. Strengthen national-level research and evaluation."

violence are subject to criminal sanctions, not individuals who happen to live in communities where violence occurs.

Many other neighborhood-level processes may also influence racial disparities. Parker and colleagues (2004) discuss how theories of neighborhood poverty and crime—involving social disorganization and concentrated disadvantage—may be associated with racial profiling. Other work has argued that neighborhood class context is an important determinant of police behavior (Neil, 2021; Weitzer and Tuch, 2002; Fagan and Davies, 2000; Sampson, 1986), that public housing projects may be policed in ways that are linked to race (Fagan et al., 2012), and that gentrification may influence policing patterns (Beck, 2020; Lanfear et al., 2018; Laniyonu, 2018). Typically, in such studies scholars discuss the relation of these topics to racial stratification without directly modeling racial disparities. Some research focuses on the notion of policing social marginality (Herring, 2019; Herbert et al., 2018; Stuart, 2016; Beckett and Herbert, 2009).

Little of such scholarship comes in the form of quantitative tests of racial disparities, but the research draws attention to the fact that it is not only the policing of poor, segregated communities that may drive disparities but also the high levels of enforcement in areas of extreme deprivation, such as Skid Row (Bittner, 1967), and against certain people—such as the homeless—in certain spaces.

These theories linking neighborhoods, race, and policing share two similar mechanisms. First, context influences officers' cognition, such as their perceptions of people encountered in certain places, which in turn affects their behavior. In this way, racial differences in exposure to relevant contexts could yield racial disparities. For example, Werthman and Piliavin (1967) detail a process of "ecological contamination" where the police come to view all people encountered in "bad neighborhoods" with suspicion. More recently, Forman (2017) argues that the presumption of innocence is flipped in high-crime, segregated areas: guilty until proven otherwise. This form of collective guilt lowers the standard for police contact, surveillance, investigation, and arrest for individuals in these communities. Such arguments find support in historical patterns in the Jim Crow South and in northern and western cities during the decades of the Great Migration from 1920 to 1970 (Balto, 2019; Muhammad, 2010; Curtin, 2000; Oshinsky, 1997) as well as in social psychological research (Bonam et al., 2016; Correll et al., 2011), but the impact of context on cognition has received much less attention than that given to implicit bias based on individuals' race.

Second, because the police are more present and active in certain areas, this will produce higher rates of police contact for whichever racial groups are in those areas. Some theories detailed above emphasize that this reflects racialized processes, whereas others portray it more as collateral damage from police responses to other demands. Such accounts are not mutually exclusive, nor are they truly independent: how the police choose to respond to a given set of problems across space does not exist independent of—or a priori to—the racialized society in which policing occurs. The implication is that race might affect organizational decisions about how to police neighborhoods (Gordon, 2020), even if in turn there is actually a proportional enforcement concerning whatever problem the police are confronting with their strategy.

In racially segregated low-income and working-class neighborhoods like those described in the previous chapter, researchers have found that police are more likely to view community members as problematic, dangerous, or criminal. Residents of these neighborhoods report receiving less respect and higher levels of aggression in police encounters (Gaston and Brunson, 2020; Lanfear et al., 2018; Boyles, 2015; Brunson and Weitzer, 2009; Terrill and Reisig, 2003; Mastrofski et al., 2002; Klinger, 1997). In contrast, residents in whiter and wealthier neighborhoods typically receive a form of service-oriented policing. Bell (2020a,b) has written about how residents in the latter neighborhoods sometimes pay police departments directly to secure the resources of police protection. The delivery of (at least) two different types of policing across racial and spatial lines helps to reinforce racial inequality by maintaining the spatial and psychic boundaries of racially segregated space. Moreover, as argued by Braga and colleagues (2019, p. 536),

> inappropriate police focus on ambiguous people and places—where the police, in isolation from the community, identify areas of focus and where entire neighborhoods are defined as trouble zones—can contribute to racial disparity and mass incarceration problems that further exacerbate disadvantaged neighborhoods.

Stops and Arrests

Beyond increased police presence in neighborhoods, entry into the formal criminal justice system most often comes through police in the form of an arrest or citation. The changes in law enforcement policies and practices noted above have affected the frequency, quality, and consequences of police encounters between the police and minority members of the public, especially minority young adults who live in settings most impacted by histories of racial and economic exclusion and exploitation. As Chapter 2 noted, police officers stop and search Black individuals at rates that are higher than those observed for other racial and ethnic groups, and they are more likely to use force when they stop Black individuals, even when the stop does not begin because police believe that a crime is in progress.

At the individual level, the decision of police officers to stop and question can reflect conscious and unconscious racial biases (Swencionis and Goff, 2017). While disparities vary across localities, Black and Latino individuals have been widely found to be more likely to be stopped by police (Fagan et al., 2010; Geller and Fagan, 2010); Gorsuch and Rho (2019) report similar evidence for searches of Native Americans in Minnesota. Racial disparities in police stops persist in part because the law permits stops as long as an officer can point to a non-racial reason for the stop, even if that reason is pretextual (Johnson, 2010; Carbado, 2002). Because not all stops result in further action recorded by law enforcement, available data may underestimate levels of racially biased policing (Knox et al., 2020).

The concentration of proactive policing tactics in poor and non-White neighborhoods suggests the need for further understanding of the collateral consequences of police-civilian contact. Current research assesses the consequences of imprisonment for health, employment and earnings, and families, communities, and society writ large (see, e.g., NRC, 2014). An emerging literature suggests that involuntary police contact may be harmful to health. The adverse health effects may arise from the physical nature of some stops, which present risks of physical injury. Contact with police may also cause trauma associated with unwarranted accusations of wrongdoing, and the stress and stigma of racism (see, e.g., Bylander, 2015; Jee-Lyn García and Sharif, 2015; Nordberg and Wrede, 2015; Shedd, 2015; Geller et al., 2014; Jones, 2014). Another emerging body of research considers the indirect effect of policing practices on civic and institutional engagement and political life. Scholars have analyzed and assessed the dynamics through which, and impact of the manner in which, criminal justice system involvement detracts from an individual's civic engagement (see, e.g., Brayne, 2014; Justice and Meares, 2014; Lerman and Weaver, 2014a,b; Weaver and Lerman, 2010).

Pretrial Decision Making and Charging

Pretrial processes can also play a role in creating or worsening disparities. Initial decisions about how to proceed are made by prosecutors, with judges exercising final decision making authority. While judges exercise ultimate authority, the principle of prosecutorial discretion and the practical demands of an overloaded court system mean that the pretrial process is largely driven by prosecutors, who exercise tremendous power in the criminal justice system. Prosecutors decide whether and what to charge, whether to plea bargain, whether to ask for pretrial detention, and how much to request as bail. Prosecutors are also responsible for presenting charges to a grand jury, shaping the presentation of evidence, coordinating with law enforcement, managing the discovery process, and making sentencing recommendations. Beginning in the pretrial phase, prosecutors are responsible for a series of decisions that can exacerbate or reduce racial inequality.

Discretion is an important feature of the criminal system as a whole, and prosecutorial discretion is protected by the constitutional principle of separation of powers: as part of the executive branch, prosecutors are tasked with making decisions about how to enforce laws; judges are required to approve their decisions at specific moments in the process (for example, a judge must review and decide whether to accept a guilty plea), but judges are not permitted to second-guess discretionary decisions that are within the legal bounds of a prosecutor's authority. This feature of the system can make it difficult to address racial disparities. For example, a prosecutor's decision to file charges against some people but not others is generally not reviewable by a court (*Inmates of Attica v. Rockefeller, 1973*). Selective prosecution based on race is illegal, but making such a claim requires evidence of a pattern of express race-based decision making that is rarely present in modern criminal courts (*United States v. Armstrong, 1996*).

A meta-analysis of 26 studies of prosecutorial decisions on charging and full prosecution that were published between 1960 and 2012 found that minority defendants were about nine percent more likely to be charged or fully prosecuted than White people (Wu, 2016). A quasi-experimental analysis of federal prosecutors also found that Black and Hispanic defendants were disproportionately charged at the mandatory-minimum threshold for crack cocaine following the introduction of a sentencing reform, conditional on criminal history and crime characteristics (Tuttle, 2019). A similar result was reported in the observational study of federal sentencing by Rehavi and Starr (2014), who trace most of the Black/White gap in sentence length to prosecutors' charging decisions and charging mandatory minimum sentences in particular. Controlling for the arrest offense and criminal history, federal prosecutors were found to charge mandatory minimum sentences 65 percent more often against Black defendants compared to White defendants. Two decades earlier Berk and Campbell (1993) reported similar findings for federal mandatory minimums. They reported that Black people accounted for 58 percent of federal crack cocaine arrests in Los Angeles but 83 percent of federal crack cocaine charges, whereas White people accounted for three percent of arrests and were never federally prosecuted for crack related offenses over a two-year period. In contrast to these results, an experimental vignette study by Robertson and colleagues (2019) found that a sample of 467 prosecutors charged felonies at the same rate for minority defendants and White defendants when presented with identical fact situations. In short, there is relatively little research on prosecutorial discretion, but several studies find that Black and Latino defendants are charged more severely than White people, conditional on arrest.

A variety of policies that expanded police contact and low-level enforcement with misdemeanor arrests also exposed members of the public to the discretionary decision of prosecutors and judges (Kohler-Haussmann, 2018). While large racial disparities in the criminal courts are well documented, there is also moderate evidence that prosecutors treat minority defendants more harshly in charging decisions.

Pretrial Release and Detention

After charging but before trial, a criminal defendant may be either released (with or without conditions of release) or detained. In most jurisdictions, pretrial detention is legally appropriate only where the defendant poses a danger to others or is likely to flee the jurisdiction. However, commonly used money bail systems condition release on the ability to post a monetary bond. The bond amount is set by judges and reflects the relative danger and flight risk as well as the amount of money needed to ensure that a particular defendant will not risk losing it by fleeing. Facially equal bail systems will affect people differently depending on their ability to pay, leaving poor defendants (who are disproportionately non-White) to serve time in pretrial detention because they cannot make bail.

Some research suggests that judges set higher bail amounts for Black and Latino criminal defendants. Ayres and Waldfogel (1994) compared the flight risk assessments of judges and private bail bond companies and found differences suggesting that courts overestimate Black and Latino defendants' flight risk, resulting in higher bail amounts.

A growing body of evidence suggests that pretrial detention leads to worse case outcomes for those who are held in jail as compared with similarly situated people who are able to secure pretrial release, and as discussed in Chapter 2, Black defendants are much more likely to remain in jail (Dobbie et al., 2018; Stevenson, 2018b). These effects may be attributed to a strengthening of bargaining positions before trial for people who are released—they are both less likely to plead guilty, and thus less likely to be convicted, and more likely to receive favorable deals when they do plead, as compared with people who are detained (Dobbie et al., 2018; Leslie and Pope, 2017). Pretrial detention, even for a relatively small number of days, may also have negative implications for future involvement with the criminal justice system and lead to more punitive treatment in juvenile settings (Zane et al., 2021), as well as negative implications for housing, employment, and access to health care. For example, under the Inmate Exclusion Policy, some states terminate Medicaid enrollment for individuals held in pretrial detention (see, e.g., the National Academies, 2020).

In summary, pretrial detention harms defendants in at least three ways. First, pretrial detention pulls a person further into the criminal system, increasing the likelihood of continued involvement and worse outcomes at later decision points. Second, detention disrupts all aspects of life, including employment and family responsibilities, housing, and health care access. Where money bail is used, families suffer additional financial consequences to post bond and larger losses if bail is forfeited. These disruptions can compound existing inequalities for people and for the larger communities of Black, Latino, and Native American people. For example, Black defendants are more likely than others to have unaffordable bail amounts or be denied bail, and therefore are more likely to be detained. Since Black people are more likely than White people to enter the system from conditions of concentrated disadvantage (see Chapter 3), and are more likely to have more precarious finances, housing, employment, and childcare, they have less of a safety net to accommodate the disruption of a few days in detention.

Plea

Once a charge is filed, a defendant may choose to plead guilty, usually in exchange for a reduced charge or sentence, or to plead not guilty and proceed to trial. The vast majority of felony criminal cases are resolved through defendants pleading guilty, not by jury trial, and the rate of guilty pleas continues to increase. Between the 1960s and 1990s, about 80 percent of federal cases were resolved by guilty pleas. Since the 1990s, 90–95 percent of federal cases have been resolved by guilty pleas. State plea-bargaining rates are similar overall (Devers, 2011).

Prosecutors play an important role in this process by deciding whether to offer a plea deal or to accept a proposal from a defendant. Defense attorneys advise clients whether to accept a plea or proceed to trial. These decisions may be influenced by a variety of factors beyond guilt or innocence, including the strength of available evidence, witness cooperation, defense attorney caseload, and an assessment of how a judge or jury would perceive the defendant. In theory, plea bargaining has a judicial backstop; a judge must review and accept a guilty plea, determining whether it was knowing and voluntary. However, in practice, especially in large urban jurisdictions, arraignments may be brief and tightly scheduled, leaving the judge little time to carefully consider whether to accept a plea (Bogira, 2005). This practice can contribute to racial disparities by effectively rubber stamping the guilty pleas of non-White defendants who may have had little choice but to plead guilty (Van Cleve, 2016).

Johnson (2019) notes that what has been called a "trial tax" (for electing to decline a plea deal and take a case to trial) increases the likelihood of imprisonment two to six times compared to if a defendant accepts a plea deal.

It is not clear that the practicing of plea bargaining itself produces racial disparities, though there is some evidence that prosecutors make less favorable plea bargain offers to Black defendants (see Chapter 3 and Jordan, 2021). Plea bargaining, though, interacts with other decision points to increase disparities. The widespread use of plea bargaining contributes to the growth of incarceration by making it possible for prosecutors to charge more people and by making punishment more predictable, certain, and efficient (Hessick, 2021; Pfaff, 2017).

For example, Rehavi and Starr (2014) find that Black and Latino defendants are charged with more serious crimes than White defendants. Plea bargaining means those charges are more likely to be resolved with guilty pleas, which makes Black and Latino defendants more likely to face imprisonment even if the plea-bargaining process itself is not administered in a disparate manner. In a study of Delaware courts from 2012 to 2014, Donnelly and MacDonald (2018) found—after controlling for measured differences in a variety of case characteristics, including severity of charges and criminal histories—that cash-only bail and pretrial detention increase a defendant's likelihood of conviction and pleading guilty, being incarcerated, and receiving a longer incarceration sentence, thus contributing to disparities as individuals proceed further in the system. Moreover, while Kutateladze and colleagues (2016) find that most race differences in plea bargaining are explained by legal factors and case characteristics, they also find that Black individuals are more likely to be offered custodial sentences in plea bargaining, even after controlling for legal and case specifics.

Sentencing and Incarceration

Shifts in sentencing and incarceration policies over the last 50 years have also affected racial inequality, both by increasing the incarceration of minority populations and by worsening its long-term effects. American sentencing policies, practices, and patterns have changed dramatically during the past 40 years, with three distinct discernable phases.

During the first phase, principally from 1975 to the mid-1980s, the reform movement aimed primarily to make sentencing procedures fairer and sentencing outcomes more predictable and consistent. The second phase, from the mid-1980s through 1996, aimed primarily to make sentences for drug and violent crimes harsher and their imposition more certain. The principal mechanisms to those ends were mandatory minimum sentences, three-strike laws, truth-in-sentencing laws, and guidelines for life without possibility of parole. As described in Chapter 2, these changes increased the number of people in prison overall, including a dramatic increase in the number of Black and Latino people in prisons. While the number of imprisoned White people also increased during this time, the growth in incarceration disparately affected non-White people, with an especially heavy impact on Black Americans, especially on Black American males (see, e.g., NRC, 2014).

The third phase, since the mid-1990s, has seen many jurisdictions make policy changes intended to reduce the incarcerated population, including changes in drug policy and a retreat from inflexible sentencing schemes. According to annual reports issued by the National Conference of State Legislatures, several hundred state laws have been enacted since 2000 that in various ways make sentencing less rigid and less severe. Most of these laws are relatively minor and target less serious offenses. With overall reductions in imprisonment, racial disparities have also fallen in some states. However, policies intended to reduce incarceration overall have not always resulted in a decrease in the relative imprisonment rate of Black versus White populations. As noted in Chapter 2, while absolute disparities have narrowed, Black Americans of all ages and educational levels remain considerably more likely to be institutionalized relative to other racial groups.

Research on racial differences in sentencing in U.S. courts dates to the first decades of the 20th century (Spohn, 2015b; for reviews see also King and Light, 2019; Ulmer, 2012). For this research, "no issue has received more attention in the scholarly literature on sentencing than whether non-white defendants are treated more harshly than similarly situated whites," write King and Light (2019). Early scholars concluded that observed differences resulted from discrimination, but later reviews observed that the older studies failed to take into account racial differences in criminal involvement and prior record. Indeed, as noted in the conceptual discussion of racial inequality above, the National Research Council's (1983) review of sentencing research found that offense seriousness and prior record were key determinants of sentences, and the overrepresentation of Black men and women in prison was mostly explained by factors other than discrimination (see also Kleck, 1981; Hagan, 1974). Research over the last two decades continues to observe large race differences in the likelihood of prison sentence given a felony conviction and reports evidence of small but significant race differences in the likelihood of imprisonment when crime severity and prior record are accounted for (King and Light, 2019). Disparities of this kind have been reported for Black and Hispanic defendants compared to non-Hispanic White people (more modest evidence has also been found for race differences in sentence length). Two other themes also emerge from recent research: that the effects of race on sentencing outcomes may be indirect and lie upstream of the sentencing decision; and that discrimination may vary across other characteristics of respondents, such as demographics or neighborhood residence.

To study upstream or indirect racial effects, only a few studies have traced criminal processing from arrest through sentencing. Much of the recent research on sentencing follows what Baumer (2013) has called the "modal approach" that seeks to estimate race differences in the likelihood of a prison sentence, say, in a sample of defendants with felony convictions. Usually, controls are introduced for offense severity, criminal history, and demographics. In this design, the prosecutor's charging decision, the conviction itself, and the race of the victim are all typically uncontrolled but may be subject to racial disparities that are associated with racial disparities in sentencing outcomes. For example, if prosecutors charge Black defendants more severely than White defendants, and offense severity is controlled in an analysis of imprisonment decisions, racially differential treatment by prosecutors is missed in the analysis of racial disparity. King and Light (2019) suggest that research designs should encompass variability in penal policy, prosecutorial discretion, race of victim, and citizenship status that is missed in the "modal approach." In an important example of an alternative approach, Rehavi and Starr (2014) analyze a linked dataset that traces federal criminal cases from arrest to charging to sentencing. They find that much of the racial disparity in sentencing outcomes can be explained by racial disparities in the prosecutor's decision to charge a mandatory minimum offense. These results are consistent with other research showing that race differences at pre-sentencing points of discretion—at pretrial detention (Wooldredge et al., 2015; Sutton, 2013), plea offers (Kutateladze et al., 2014), and parole status (Hickert et al., 2022)—ultimately contribute to the relatively high probability of prison sentences among Black defendants.

Sentencing research has also examined variability in disparity across the dimensions of demography and socio-legal context. Studies focused on demography report on the "high cost of being black, young, and male" (Steffensmeier et al., 1998, p. 789). Several regression studies report on the relatively high likelihood of prison sentences among convicted male defendants who are Black or Hispanic and under age 30 (Wooldredge et al., 2015; Spohn and Holleran, 2000). Contextual studies have examined how disparity may vary with county-level characteristics and the characteristics of the court working group. Although theories of racial threat suggest that sentencing disparities are larger in localities with large Black or Hispanic populations, the evidence is inconsistent (King and Light, 2019). More proximate to the sentencing decision, greater racial diversity in the courtroom (more Black or Hispanic judges and counsel) has been found to be associated with less racial disparity in sentencing outcomes (King et al., 2010; Ward et al., 2009; Johnson, 2006).

Judicial discretion lies at the center of many analyses of racial disparity in sentencing, but another line of research examines how disparity varies with limitations on discretion through statute or sentencing guidelines. Tonry (2019) reports that states with presumptive sentencing guidelines, imposing the greatest limitations on judicial discretion across a wide variety of offenses, reduced racial disparity. Thus, studies of federal sentencing guidelines find that disparities in sentence length are mostly explained by legally relevant factors prior to the point of judicial discretion at sentencing (Ulmer et al., 2016; Rehavi and Starr, 2014). Studies of presumptive state sentencing guidelines in Pennsylvania, however, find a larger role for the sentencing stage where, for example, Black and Hispanic defendants were less likely to receive downward departures to non-custodial sanctions (Painter-Davis and Ulmer, 2020; see also Ulmer et al., 2016). Research on sentencing structures remains relatively underdeveloped. Frase (2019, p. 112) observes that there are no national studies comparing racial disparity in states with and without guidelines. More generally, King and Light (2019) find that while racial disparities in sentencing, resulting in longer sentences for Black and Hispanic people, have declined in some jurisdictions, the actual level and source of disparities cannot be accurately known at this time (see also Light, 2022). To better understand the sources of declining disparity in sentencing they argue for data collection that tracks cases from point of arrest through case disposition.

Research on sentencing guidelines exemplifies a larger point that racial disparity can be built into the structure of sentencing itself. For example, Johnson and colleagues (2021) review seven years of federal sentencing data and find racial disparities in life without parole sentences, and the authors find these differences to be attributable to mechanisms built into the sentencing system (e.g., mode of conviction, mandatory minimums, and guideline departures). Moreover, Tonry (2019, pp. 11–12) observes that long and mandatory sentences were adopted in many jurisdictions that increased in incarceration disproportionately in Black communities: "Legislature enacted laws that mandated especially severe sentences for crimes of which disproportionately large numbers of minority offenders are convicted." The mandatory minimum sentence, three-strikes, dangerous offender, truth in sentencing, and life without parole laws enacted in the 1980s and 1990s targeted violent and drug crimes. Rates of violence are higher in Black communities, though we saw evidence in Chapter 2 that disparity is declining, and Black communities face more intensive policing of drug offenses than White communities.

Conditions of Imprisonment

Prisons in the United States are generally remote, highly segregated, and closed environments that are difficult to access and challenging to study. For the most part, prisons are categorized and run very differently on the basis of their security or custody levels. This is further explored in Box 4-2. But even among prisons at the same level of custody, conditions of confinement can vary widely along critical dimension, including physical layout, staffing

BOX 4-2
Sentencing in Federal Court

In the federal system, approximately 20 percent of all defendants are convicted on charges that carry a mandatory minimum (prison) sentence. Over 99 percent of federal sentences include some form of deprivation of liberty—either probation or prison (United States Sentencing Commission, 2018a). This is not because federal statutes require imprisonment; most do not. However, the Federal Sentencing Guidelines (hereafter, the Guidelines) operate in such a way as to promote increased reliance on imprisonment.

1984 Sentencing Reform Act. In 1984, Congress passed the Sentencing Reform Act to try and reduce these disparities in sentencing, setting mandatory minimums for certain crimes. The Act had the effect of circumscribing judicial discretion, expanding prosecutorial power and discretion, and increasing sentence lengths.

The U.S. Sentencing Commission promulgated the *Sentencing Guideline Manual,* which set forth a uniform sentencing policy for federal offenders, with factors and formulas for calculating sentencing. The manual was intended to create uniformity among offenders sentenced for the same offense type and with the same criminal history. However, operating in tandem with statutory mandatory minimum sentences, federal sentencing guidelines have accompanied an increase in racial disparity (Hofer, 2019; Rehavi and Starr, 2014; McDonald and Carlson, 1993). Almost 20 years after the Guidelines were first announced, the United States Supreme Court held that they were no longer mandatory (*United States v. Booker*, 2005). While *Booker* held that judges must still "consult [the] Guidelines and take them into account when sentencing," the decision expanded the possibility of departures from the Guidelines' sentencing ranges and excised the enforceability of the Guidelines on appeal. Empirical research indicates that Booker had little impact on judges' sentencing decisions, though racial disparity was greater among judges appointed after *Booker*, and prosecutors became more likely to charge Black defendants with mandatory minimums (Light, 2022; Hofer, 2019; Yang, 2015).

Almost all (97%) federal defendants plead guilty instead of taking a chance and going to trial. As a result, the sentencing process typically begins with a plea hearing before a judge. At the plea hearing, a defendant establishes the factual basis for the specific offense or offenses, facts that then become relevant at sentencing. During the process, the court will also inform the defendant of the court's statutory obligation to calculate the relevant range under the Guidelines and examine factors that may justify departure from the calculated range, and to consider other statutory factors (United States Sentencing Commission, 2018a).

Role of the Probation Officer. In addition to the roles played by prosecutors and courts, federal probation officers also play a central role in the sentencing process. Following a conviction, a federal probation officer conducts a presentence interview in which the probation officer asks the defendant questions regarding the circumstances of the offense, their criminal history, their personal history (e.g., family circumstances, employment, and history of substance abuse), financial circumstances, and a variety of other topics (United States Sentencing Commission, 2018a).

After the presentence interview, the probation officer conducts an independent investigation of the defendant's criminal offense and personal background, and then compiles the information obtained during that investigation and from the interview into a presentencing report. In addition to information regarding a defendant's background and the offense of conviction, including the range of punishment prescribed by the statute, the report also contains a calculation of the applicable Guidelines range (United States Sentencing Commission, 2018a).

Calculating Sentences Using the Guidelines. The Guidelines range is based on two key components: offense level and criminal history. The offense level is determined by first identifying the base level for the offense prescribed by the Guidelines, then adjusting it according to specific facts of the case, such as the defendant's role in the offense, whether the defendant possessed a deadly weapon during the offense, and whether there were victims. If a defendant has prior offenses, the offenses are each given a numerical value, and these values are added together to determine the defendant's criminal history score, which places the defendant within an established criminal history category (United States Sentencing Commission, 2019, pp. 1–2). The offense level is the vertical axis on the sentencing table and the criminal history category is the horizontal axis. The intersection of these axes determines the defendant's recommended sentencing range (18 U.S.C. § 3553(a)).

At the sentencing hearing that follows, the court is charged with determining the applicable guidelines range and imposing the defendant's sentence. In addition to the presentencing report, the court will also consider the parties' arguments, which typically address whether to sentence a defendant to a term within the Guidelines range. The court may also permit the parties to present evidence and call witnesses, which can aid the court in settling disputes of fact and in examining mitigating or aggravating factors (United States Sentencing Commission, 2020). A defendant may also submit letters from family and community members as mitigating evidence. Finally, the defendant may make an allocution—a formal statement to the court—before being sentenced.

The sentencing hearing, with the presentation of evidence, witness testimony, and allocution, is comparable to trial procedure but with key differences. The burden of proof during sentencing is not the same as it is at trial. The Federal Rules of Evidence do not apply, nor does the Confrontation Clause of the Sixth Amendment. At trial, the government is required to prove every element of the charged offense beyond a reasonable doubt. At sentencing, the only facts that must be proven beyond a reasonable doubt are facts used to increase a sentence beyond the statutory maximum (*United States v. Booker*, 2005). Facts that will not raise the guidelines range are typically reviewed under a less demanding standard (preponderance of the evidence). The lower burden of proof at sentencing means defendants are without one of the key safeguards of the trial process. Because most federal defendants skip the trial phase, the sentencing hearing may be the only proceeding at which facts must be proven.

Departure from the Guidelines. A *departure* refers to the imposition of a sentence outside of the calculated Guidelines range based on the district court's application of a particular Guidelines provision (*United States v. Grams*, 2009).

continued

BOX 4-2 Continued

Various bases for departures—including ones related to the offense or to the defendant's criminal history—are permitted, however (18 U.S.C. § 3553(b); United States Sentencing Commission, 2018b). The Supreme Court has indicated that factors such as race, sex, national origin, religion, socioeconomic status, drug or alcohol addiction, and lack of guidance as a youth can never serve as a reason for departure (*Koon v. United States,* 1996), although research regularly finds that Black defendants receive, on average, slightly longer sentences than White people even when the offense characteristics and criminal history are controlled (Yang, 2015; Rehavi and Starr, 2014; Ulmer et al., 2011). One of the most common methods for departure is located within Chapter 5 of the *Sentencing Guidelines Manual* and allows for a downward departure when the defendant provides the prosecution with "substantial assistance in the investigation or prosecution of another person." Courts may award this "substantial assistant" departure only upon a motion by the prosecution during the sentencing proceedings. Notably, a defendant does not have to cooperate with the government, and "a defendant's refusal to assist authorities in the investigation of other persons may not be considered as an aggravating sentencing factor."

levels, resources, correctional philosophy, and administrative leadership, which may render one facility fundamentally different from another.

Along some dimensions—overcrowding, the availability of some rehabilitative programs—aspects of prison life changed in ways that adversely affected individual prisoners. For example, once legislatures and prison systems deemphasized the rehabilitative rationale, and as they struggled to deal with unprecedented overcrowding, they were under much less pressure to provide prison rehabilitative services, treatment, and programming (e.g., United States Government Accountability Office, 2012; California Department of Corrections and Rehabilitation Expert Panel on Adult Offender Reentry and Recidivism Reduction Programs, 2007).[4] A variety of trends in the conditions of penal confinement have been documented indicating that the experience of incarceration has become more severe during the period

[4]The rejection of rehabilitation is captured in figures on prison program participation. Data on program participation from the Survey of Inmates of State Correctional Facilities (renamed the Survey of Prison Inmates in 2016) show that participation rates in drug programs, education, job training, and work assignments were highest in the Northeast, and lower in the South and the West. The survey data shows broad reductions in program participation in U.S. prisons across the country and across program areas. Participation in drug treatment programs in the Northeast and the Midwest fell from highs of 30 to 50 percent in the 1980s to below 20 percent by 2016. Educational programming was also reduced in all regions except the West. Job training became less common.

of prison population growth. An increase in prison overcrowding from the 1980s to 1990s is indicated by national statistics on prison capacity. In the mid-1980s, state prisons operated on average at 105 percent of the most generous measure of capacity, compared to 115 percent in the mid-1990s.[5] By another measure of crowding, under two percent of the prison population was held in local jails in 1980, compared to 4.6 percent by 2000. At the peak of the prison population in 2008, 5.2 percent of prisoners were held in local jails, and prison populations in 20 of the 50 states exceeded the maximum capacity. The California prison system, the site of landmark court rulings on overcrowding, operated at *204 percent* of designed capacity in 2008.[6]

As the U.S. prison population grew, the availability of correctional programming declined. Participation in the system's education, work, and job training programs fell from the 1980s to the 2000s. Researchers described the emergence of "warehouse" prisons that were stripped of recreation facilities and rehabilitation activities (Phelps, 2011; Lynch, 2009). Prison security levels also increased in the period of prison growth. According to the periodic census of prison facilities, about half of all prisons were minimum or low-security in both 1979 and 2005. However, there were no prisons at the super-maximum level of custody in 1979 compared to 22 of them in 2005.

The census also shows that the prison population in solitary confinement had nearly doubled between 1979 and 2005, from 3.0 percent to 5.7 percent. In the most recent data, from 2016, 4.4 percent of a national sample of the U.S. prison population were held in solitary confinement on any given day, and about 20 percent of the prison population were in solitary confinement at some point during a prison stay.

Although the severity of prison conditions increased on average during the period of the prison boom from 1972 to 2008, there has been substantial variation in conditions across jurisdictions and prison facilities. Thus, conditions of overcrowding and programming, for example, vary greatly. Despite this variation, the disproportionate incarceration of Black, Latino,

[5]Overcrowding is measured as a percentage of the designed, rated, and operational capacity of the prison. Each of the capacity yields a different estimate of the number of prisoners that can safely be incarcerated. The Bureau of Justice Statistics regularly reports prison counts as a percentage of the maximum and minimum prison capacities.

[6]Currently, California's prison population is 58 percent of the peak level in 2008. This large reduction was achieved through a wave of reforms starting in 2011 that (1) eliminated most technical revocation back to custody for people on parole supervision, (2) limited the application of life sentences under the state's three-strikes law to the most serious felonies, (3) redefined many drug offenses and theft offenses as misdemeanors, (4) increased ability to earn time off sentence for certain cases, and (5) eliminated some commonly imposed sentence enhancements. We discuss the case of California in greater detail in Chapter 8.

and Native segments of the population is found in all states, so the pains of incarceration are disproportionately experienced by people of color.

The deterioration of prison conditions on the dimensions of overcrowding, programming, and levels of secure custody is associated with reduced opportunities for challenging conditions in court. As part of the larger civil rights movement, a period of active prisoners' rights litigation began in the late 1960s and continued through the 1970s, which resulted in many of the most important improvements in the quality of prison life. This continued through the 1980s and early 1990s with at least 49 reported court cases decided between 1979 and 1990 addressing jail and prison overcrowding, a majority of which resulted in court-ordered population "caps" or ceilings to remedy unconstitutional conditions (Cole and Call, 1992). In 1995, Congress passed the Prison Litigation Reform Act, which greatly limited prisoners' access to the courts to challenge their conditions of confinement. As a result, by the late 1990s, the average person in prison could find much less recourse in the courts than the early years of prison litigation had appeared to promise (Schlanger and Shay, 2008, p. 140; Cohen, 2004).

Beyond the general pattern of prison conditions, researchers have consistently identified three key areas of racial inequality in which the experience of minority prisoners differs from the experience of White prisoners. First, people of color and Black prisoners in particular are incarcerated at higher levels of custody and are more likely to be locked in solitary confinement than White prisoners. Second, White prisoners are more likely to report violent victimization than non-White prisoners. Third, mortality risk is relatively high among White prisoners.

Solitary Confinement

Solitary confinement refers to a very high level of penal custody where prisoners are locked in their cells for 22 hours each day, with one or two hours out of the cell for showers or recreation. Conditions of solitary confinement often include heavily restricted opportunities for programming, visits, or phone calls (Frost and Monteiro, 2016). Solitary confinement is used for two purposes: for punishing misconduct, often known as disciplinary segregation, and for controlling and managing the prison population, often known as administrative segregation. Administrative segregation might be used to control conflicts such as gang rivalries, or for the protective custody of those who are unsafe in the general prison population—for example, due to their youth or gender identity (Kapoor and Trestman, 2016, p. 200). Solitary confinement is regularly found to be closely associated with a high level of psychological distress (Reiter et al., 2020; Haney, 2018).

Although the conditions and procedures for solitary confinement vary greatly, researchers consistently find relatively high rates of solitary confinement among Black prisoners. A study of Pennsylvania prisoners, using data from 2007–2018, found that Black men were 22 percent more likely to have been in disciplinary or administrative segregation than White men, and that Black women were more than 50 percent more likely to have been in solitary confinement than White women. Research on misconduct and disciplinary segregation finds that Black prisoners are more likely to experience solitary confinement than White prisoners (Pullen-Blasnik et al., 2021). Similar racial disparities have been reported in analyses of state prisoners in Florida (Cochran et al., 2018), and in Kansas (Sakoda and Simes, 2021), and in national survey data (Logan et al., 2017; Olson, 2016).

In analyses in the crime-discrimination framework, misconduct studies find that race differences are largely explained by the number and severity of prison infractions (Cochran et al., 2018; Logan et al., 2017). However, one regression discontinuity study using Kansas state prison records finds that when solitary confinement capacity is increased, the risk of solitary confinement disproportionately increased among young Black incarcerated men. This analysis suggests that race differences in prison isolation also depend on the punitive capacity of the state penal system.

Violence in Incarceration

Prisons and jails are violent settings, where the risks of assault and sexual violence are much higher than in free society. Prison researchers report that violence and the fear of violence are central concerns for incarcerated people and constitute one of the main "pains of imprisonment" (Haney, 2006; Bottoms, 1999; Toch, 1978; Sykes, 1958). Rates of violent infractions in prison have been found to be about five times higher than community-based rates of violent victimization (Western, 2021; Bottoms, 1999).

Sexual assault in prison is also much more prevalent than in free society, although estimates of sexual assault vary greatly with protocols for measurement. For example, a self-administered questionnaire sent to seven prisons in the Midwest in the mid-1990s yielded a rate of coerced sexual activity during the current incarceration of 210 per 1,000 (Struckman-Johnson and Struckman-Johnson, 2000). In the early 2000s, survey estimates of the six-month prevalence of nonconsensual sex acts ranged from 15–30 per 1,000 (Wolff et al., 2006). Despite the great variability, even the low-prevalence estimates in prison exceed by an order of magnitude the community estimates of rape or sexual assault where the 12-month prevalence is one to two per 1,000 (Morgan and Truman, 2020). Women prisoners are more likely to be the targets of sexual abuse by staff (e.g., Jenness et al., 2019; Buchanan, 2007).

The evidence concerning lethal violence paints a more complicated picture but still indicates the climate of violence in U.S. incarceration. Similar to community trends, the prison homicide rate declined significantly between 1980 (54 homicides per 100,000) and 2000 (three per 100,000). Since 2000, the rate has more than doubled, reaching eight per 100,000 in 2016, which exceeded the community rate in that year of 5.2 per 100,000 (Carson and Cowhig, 2020; Mumola, 2005). The relatively high rate of prison homicide is related to the age, race, and sex distribution of the prison population, but the absence of firearms in prison also protects against the risk of homicide mortality. When the prison homicide rate is compared to the community non-firearm homicide rate, adjusting for age, race, and sex, the incidence of homicide in prison is about twice as high as that in the community (Western, 2021).

Although the risk of violent victimization is very high in prison compared to community rates, victimization risks are relatively higher for White prisoners. Theories of prisoner victimization emphasize vulnerability and a lack of guardianship. Thus age, mental health status, and sexual identity are correlated with race and associated with greater vulnerability and lower levels of guardianship (Steiner et al., 2017; Wooldredge and Steiner, 2012).

Health and Incarceration

Incarcerated people are generally in poor health, suffering from relatively high rates of chronic conditions, infectious disease, and mental illness. Courts have decided that the constitutional prohibition against cruel and unusual punishment establishes a minimal right to health care. As a result, prisons and jails face the significant challenge of managing medical services for a high-needs population. Injuries sustained through accidents or assaults, the cumulative effects of incarceration-related stress, and the inadequate treatment of preexisting conditions may all impair the health of incarcerated people. Research points to two areas in which prisons and jails appear to clearly affect the physical health status of incarcerated people: mortality risk and infectious disease.

Despite the relatively high burden of disease, mortality rates in prison are not uniformly high. Standardized mortality ratios for White men have been estimated at around 1.2, indicating an age-standardized mortality risk in prison about 20 percent higher than in the general population (Rosen et al., 2011; Patterson, 2010). But standardized mortality ratios estimated for Black incarcerated men have been estimated at around 0.5, indicating that the death rate for Black men in prison is about *half* the death rate for those in the general population (see also Wildeman et al., 2016). Patterson (2010) examines the contribution of violence to prison and community mortality rates and finds that the low prison homicide rate of Black men could not explain the mortality gap between prison and community. Analysis of cause-specific mortality data for men incarcerated in North Carolina found that the excess risk was associated with cardiovascular disease, cancer, and infectious disease (Rosen et al., 2011).

Although correctional health services may reduce mortality for Black men with chronic conditions, research on health and incarceration finds that prison impairs health by elevating the transmission of infectious disease. High rates of HIV, hepatitis B, and hepatitis C have been widely documented in U.S. prisons. Recent estimates indicate that HIV prevalence in prison exceeds community rates by a factor of three to five, and hepatitis B and hepatitis C prevalence exceeds community rates by five to 10 times (Gough et al., 2010; Bick, 2007). Although precise numbers are difficult to estimate, screening at prison intake suggests that 80–90 percent of cases were present before incarceration, with the remainder transmitted in prison, mostly through sexual activity and needle use.

A related line of research studies outbreaks of infectious disease, focusing on the spread of tuberculosis, influenza, and varicella (Beaudry et al., 2020). Each of these infections is airborne and spread through aerosol transmission (droplets) and contact with surfaces. The congregate living areas, dining halls, and recreation areas that make up the physical plant of prisons facilitate the spread of airborne pathogens, particularly in overcrowded conditions. Population turnover raises the risks of both bringing infections in from surrounding communities and also transmitting disease back to the communities from which the incarcerated population is drawn.

The significance of correctional facilities for the transmission of infectious disease was strikingly illustrated by the novel coronavirus pandemic. Prisons and jails were consistently among the leading hot spots for COVID-19 outbreaks throughout 2020 (the National Academies, 2020). Facilities such as Rikers Island (New York City, NY), Cook County jail (Chicago, IL), and Marion Correctional Institution (OH) suffered outbreaks that resulted in dozens of fatalities among staff and incarcerated people.

The Consequences of Conviction and Incarceration

Labor Market Consequences

A wide range of evidence points to the negative effects of criminal conviction and incarceration on later employment and earnings. People with criminal records and histories of incarceration experience high rates of unemployment and low earnings, both before and after incarceration (Kling, 2006; Western et al., 2001). Both having a criminal record and experiencing incarceration may reduce economic opportunities. A criminal record may signal untrustworthiness, unreliability, or dangerousness to a prospective employer. The experience of incarceration itself—the risks of violence, isolation, and infectious disease—may contribute to disability and erode human capital.

Several studies have tried to isolate the causal effect of incarceration by capitalizing on the random assignment of judges to criminal cases. Judges vary in their propensity to hand down prison sentences, so random assignment induces variation in incarceration that is unrelated to other factors, such as criminal involvement or a lack of soft skills, that are associated with poor labor market outcomes. Among the studies based on the random assignment of judges, an early analysis by Kling (2006) finds no effect of prison incarceration on earnings, and this result was replicated by Loeffler (2013). On the other hand, Mueller-Smith (2015) finds that incarceration did cause a reduction in earnings. Studying pretrial jail detention, Dobbie and colleagues (2018) also found a reduction in earnings associated with incarceration. Audit studies conducted by Pager (2007; see also Pager et al., 2009) also indicate the clear reluctance of employers to hire job applicants with prison records (see also Decker et al., 2015). Audit evidence also indicates the aversion of employers to job applicants with misdemeanor arrests and no conviction (Uggen et al., 2014) and felony convictions without incarceration (Agan and Starr, 2018). Employer surveys yield similar results.

Labor market experiences after incarceration also appear to clearly differ by race. In an analysis of what they called compounded disadvantage, Lyons and Pettit (2011) examine the wage trajectories of Black and White men before and after incarceration and find that the racial gap in earnings became wider after incarceration. Field studies also find that employment outcomes after incarceration have been found to be worse for Black youth and men compared to White people (Western and Sirois, 2019; Sullivan, 1989). Consistent with these findings, Pager (2007; see also Pager et al., 2009) also finds that the stigma of a criminal record in the labor market is larger for Black jobseekers than for White ones.

Parental Incarceration

As incarceration rates increased, more families and children had direct experience with the imprisonment of a parent (see NRC, 2014, Figure 9-1). About half of the 2.2 million people incarcerated in the United States today are parents; 2.7 million children have at least one incarcerated parent, and about 10 million children have had a parent incarcerated at some point (Underwood, 2021). Black children are nine times more likely than White children to have an incarcerated parent, and Latino children are three times more likely (Underwood, 2021).

The number of children with a mother in prison increased 131 percent from 1991 to 2007 (see NRC, 2014, Figure 9-1), while the number with a father in prison increased 77 percent (Glaze and Maruschak, 2008). Parental incarceration has been found to affect many aspects of children's well-being, including increasing the risk of later system involvement by those children (Wildeman et al., 2018; Ruiz and Kopak, 2014; Kjellstrand and Eddy, 2011; Foster and Hagen, 2009). Against a large literature finding evidence of the negative effects of parental incarceration on children and the intergenerational persistence of incarceration risk, researchers also caution that removing a parent from the home who is violent or otherwise harmful can improve children's well-being (Turney and Wildeman, 2015). Consistent with this finding, a study of Ohio correctional data finds that parental imprisonment reduces the risk of children's imprisonment in adulthood by about five percentage points, and the reduction in the risk of imprisonment is found to be significantly larger for Black children (Norris et al., 2021).

Parental incarceration can also precipitate removal and foster care, and, under federal laws that set limits on the time children can remain in foster care, it can lead to fast-tracked adoption (Zavez, 2008). Child welfare involvement also increases the likelihood of later criminal system involvement for these children (Tasca et al., 2011). Incarcerated mothers are more likely than incarcerated fathers to have lived with their children prior to incarceration. In a 2004 survey of incarcerated persons, 55 percent of females in state prisons who were parents, compared with 36 percent of males, reported living with their children in the month before arrest. Parents incarcerated in federal prisons are more likely than those in other facilities to report living with their children before arrest (73% of females, compared with 46% of males). In addition, incarcerated mothers are more likely than incarcerated fathers to have come from single-parent households (42% vs. 17% in state prisons and 52% vs. 19% in federal prisons; Glaze and Maruschak, 2008). The significant racial disparities in adult incarceration therefore translate into earlier introduction of Black, Native, and Latino children to the criminal system; see discussion above about the harmful effects of early exposure to the criminal justice system on child development.

Sustaining a relationship between an incarcerated parent and their child can be difficult due to several factors, not limited to visitation restrictions, difficulty navigating the criminal justice system, transportation challenges, and lack of consistent communication. Visitation rules for incarcerated individuals vary across the United States, for example. Correctional facility visits can be challenging as facilities may require pre-clearance, approved adult supervision for children younger than 18, and proof of identification; visits may be canceled without notice; and it may be a financial burden to travel to the facility (Boppre et al., 2022). Depending on where the parent is incarcerated, visitation may require the child to be transported a significant distance to reach the facility, thus requiring reliable transportation from a supervising adult. Moreover, incarcerated individuals face significant communication barriers as they are not able to accept incoming calls and they must pay for all outgoing calls, often at significant cost. Without easy, consistent access to a phone and affordable calls, it can be difficult for an incarcerated parent to maintain consistent communication with their child. Box 4-3 discusses some strategies for addressing these challenges.

BOX 4-3
Protecting Ties between Incarcerated Parents and Their Children

Providing incarcerated parents with opportunities to participate in parenting courses can promote strong ties with their children and families. Parenting classes can "provide parents the opportunity to expand their understanding of child development and learn and practice effective and appropriate communication, discipline, problem-solving, and other parenting techniques" (Peterson, Cramer, and Fontaine, 2019; Peterson et al., 2019). Parenting Inside Out[a] is one such program that teaches both mothers and fathers involved in the criminal justice system parent management training, facilitated by parenting coaches. In 1998, the New Hampshire Department of Corrections established the Family Connections Center,[b] which provides a variety of services and programs to incarcerated parents, including parenting education classes, parenting support groups, and healthy relationship classes. Vocational and life skills programs can help prepare incarcerated individuals for life outside of correctional facilities. For instance, the Life Skills[c] project is a combination of the Iowa Department of Corrections' Going Home Re-Entry project and the Des Moines Area Community College's Training Academy-Career Link. This program provides training on job readiness preparation, career development, vocational trades, and financial responsibility to enable those who are incarcerated to successfully reenter the community and obtain employment.

Creating more welcoming environments and providing accessible information about correctional facility policies and rules can also reduce the burden on families trying to connect children with incarcerated parents. For example, in Washington County (MN), the jail division has a webpage dedicated to visiting with children,[d] which outlines visitation times and rules for visiting with minors. Creating more family-friendly visitor areas, such as the one in the Allegheny County (PA) Jail,[e] can create a more welcoming environment for children in what can otherwise be an intimidating or tense environment.

---

[a]See http://www.parentinginsideout.org/
[b]See https://www.nh.gov/nhdoc/fcc/programs.html
[c]See https://www.dmacc.edu/outreach/Pages/lifeskills.aspx
[d]See https://www.co.washington.mn.us/3214/Inmate-Information
[e]See https://www.alleghenycounty.us/jail/visitors/visitor-waiting-area.aspx

Collateral Consequences

Collateral sanctions are typically located outside the penal code, implemented by non-criminal justice institutions, and interpreted by courts as civil regulations rather than criminal penalties. Among other limitations, these include restrictions on occupational licensure (Aukerman, 2005) and on parental rights, access to housing and education, public benefits, and voting rights (Manza and Uggen, 2006). Today, approximately 5.2 million U.S. adults remain disenfranchised due to a felony conviction, representing about 2.3 percent of the total U.S. voting-eligible population and 6.2 percent of the Black voting-eligible population (Uggen et al., 2020). Although these legal and informal restrictions are separable for analytic purposes, people experience them in combination as compounding challenges (Uggen and Stewart, 2014).

People who have been released from prison are also required to navigate the stigma and negative reactions of those in their community. This arises in both immediate face-to-face interactions and in what Lageson calls "digital punishment," a product of the widespread public availability of criminal records in the information age, which can further restrict opportunities and enhance the stigma of a criminal record (Lageson, 2020, 2016).

Ineligibility for certain welfare benefits also adds to the financial insecurity of formerly incarcerated individuals. Some states subject people with a felony drug conviction to restrictions or complete bans on food assistance under the Supplemental Nutrition Assistance Program, cash assistance through Temporary Assistance for Needy Families, or both.

In addition, due to federal policies and local practices that deny assistance to individuals convicted of a drug felony offense, many justice-involved individuals face unique barriers to obtaining housing assistance. For example, the law allows family members who house relatives or friends engaged in criminal activity to be evicted themselves, even if the tenants "did not know of, could not foresee, or could not control the behavior of other occupants or guests" (Love et al., 2021).

Incarceration also deepens the social disadvantages that have resulted from racial disparities in poverty rates and educational attainment. For example, data show that despite sharing a similar criminal history and generally very low levels of schooling, Black men are far less likely than White men to be employed during the 12 months after prison. Moreover, the Black men who are employed during that period earn less than their White counterparts (the National Academies, 2018).

Researchers have taken evidence of racial disparities in incarceration, the exposure to harm during imprisonment, and the negative socioeconomic effects that may flow from conviction and incarceration to investigate the possibility of community-level effects associated with high rates of incarceration that are spatially concentrated in low-income Black and Hispanic neighborhoods. There is strong evidence of the spatial concentration of incarceration in minority communities, even accounting for, or contributing to, local crime rates (Simes, 2021; Sampson, 2012). Under these conditions, some scholars believe that these adverse impacts fed inequality in Black communities, furthering a cycle of inequity that saw societal conditions such as those outlined in Chapter 4 feed into criminal justice contact and involvement, which further perpetuated and exacerbated structural racism impacting non-White communities (Clear, 2009; Rose and Clear, 1998). They hypothesize that the resulting "coercive mobility" is itself criminogenic, increasing crime rather than decreasing it. Assessing the community-level effects of incarceration that are also closely associated with crime, poverty, and segregation poses a steep challenge for causal inference (NRC, 2014), but even in the absence of causal evidence from experimental designs, researchers conclude that the spatial concentration of incarceration contributes to a multidimensional disadvantage of which criminal justice intervention is a significant part (Simes, 2021; Sampson and Loeffler, 2010).

Probation, Parole, and Supervision

Community supervision remains the largest segment of U.S. correctional control with 4.4 million people under community supervision in 2018 (Carson, 2020; Kaeble and Alper, 2020; Zeng, 2020). The term "community supervision" encompasses both probation and parole. Modern probation is a type of supervised community release determined by a court, sometimes prior to sentencing, or as part of a criminal sentence. A probation sentence is often given to defendants with relatively short criminal records and for low-level offenses. A probation sentence often involves regular meetings with a probation officer and compliance with the conditions of the community-based sentence, which might involve programming, work, or educational activities. Whereas probation is often ordered in lieu of incarceration, parole follows a period of prison incarceration. Parole's origins date back to the indeterminate sentence, created in the 19th century, in which a judge specifies a range for the period of incarceration, for example from one to five years. Under an indeterminate sentence, prison release is determined at a parole hearing. If parole is granted, a prisoner is able to return to the community subject to conditions of release. If those conditions are violated, parole can be revoked resulting in a return to prison.

Several studies find that probation and parole supervision create a recidivism trap, one that increases the risk of incarceration even in the absence of new criminal conduct. Probation and parole are both a type of conditional release, where supervision in the community depends on complying with a few conditions, such as maintaining employment and a stable address, avoiding drinking and drug use, and avoiding association with others who have criminal records. For an economically insecure population, often living in poor neighborhoods and struggling with substance use problems, compliance with such conditions of supervision can be challenging. In many cases, noncompliance may reflect life circumstances much more than involvement in crime. The response by probation and parole officers to noncompliance varies greatly across agencies, but parole and probation clients can be returned to incarceration for so-called technical (non-criminal) violations of release conditions. Strong evidence of an elevated risk of re-incarceration has been reported by Franco-Paredes and colleagues (2021), Rose and Shem-Tov (2021), Harding and colleagues (2017), Hyatt and Barnes (2017), and Lofstrom and colleagues (2014).

Do the risks of revocation vary with race? There are relatively few studies of racial disparities in probation sentencing and revocation. A four-county study examined racial differences in probation revocation in Dallas County (TX), Iowa's Sixth Judicial District, Multnomah County (OR), and New York City (NY) from 2007 to 2010 (Jannetta et al., 2014). Black probationers experienced relatively high revocation rates in all four jurisdictions, being 18 to 36 percent more likely to be placed in custody than White probationers. Of the observed Black/White disparity in revocation, between 20 and 49 could not be explained by demographics, offense type, criminal history, or other covariates. Similar results were obtained in the analysis of probation revocation from a large southwestern state. Black probationers there were found to have relatively high rates of revocation but were less likely to be discharged early or to successfully complete the probation sentence, net of demographic characteristics, a risk score, and offense type (Steinmetz and Henderson, 2016; see also Olson and Lurigio, 2000).

Research on racial disparities in parole has examined both the parole release decision and the revocation decision. A number of papers find that minorities are less likely to be paroled than White people (Huebner and Bynum, 2008; Proctor, 1999; Bynum and Paternoster, 1984; Heinz et al., 1976). Research on parole violations has found that Black people are between 50 percent and over 100 percent more likely to be charged with parole violations than White people, even when controlling for relevant demographic and legal factors (Steen et al., 2013; Grattet et al., 2009; Steen and Opsal, 2007). Black people are also more likely to be returned to prison for a parole violation, which contributes to racial disparities in incarceration overall (Curry, 2016; Vito et al., 2012). Finally, a report by the Brennan Center for Justice finds that Black and Latino people remain on probation and parole longer than similarly situated White people, which other research suggests may generate increasing disadvantages for people of color over time (Eaglin and Solomon, 2015; Steen and Opsal, 2007).

It's possible that observed disparities in parole are a mechanical effect of prison release policies from earlier cohorts that received lengthier prison sentences for violent and repeat offenses that are still on parole, as well as requirements of releasing inmates. These studies indicate that community supervision, among the many stages from arrest to release, is a major driver or racial inequality in the criminal justice system.

Legal Financial Obligations

Monetary sanctions and court-ordered fees resulting from contact with the criminal justice system can result in ongoing criminal justice supervision, especially for poor people. Non-payment of court fines and fees can result in continuing court supervision until payment is made in full. A randomized controlled trial in a misdemeanor court in Oklahoma showed that court fines and fees led to warrants for non-payment, debts in collection, and state garnishment of tax refunds (Pager et al., 2022). Researchers argue that fines and fees exacerbate inequality, creating a two-tiered system—one for people with the means to pay their fines and move forward and one for people who cannot afford to pay their fines (Harris, 2016). Studies show that these sanctions are both disproportionately imposed on and are associated with the adverse treatment of people of color by police and other officials (Bing et al., 2022; Shoub et al., 2021).

There is evidence that the financial, social, and health-related consequences of this system of monetary sanctions are substantial. Debt accumulates through interest, surcharges, and collection costs, which add to the financial burden on poor people. These monetary sanctions also disrupt families, especially when people are incarcerated for non-payment, and fear of re-incarceration can lead to significant stress (Harris, 2016).

CONCLUSION

This chapter describes how racial inequalities in neighborhood environments and crime combine with cumulative disadvantage through the stages of criminal processing to produce racial inequality in the criminal justice system and deepen structural racism in society more generally. Research indicates that the concentrated neighborhood disadvantage contributes to racial disparities in criminal offending and criminal justice involvement. These disparities coupled with the bias of criminal justice officials and the routine operations of police and courtrooms that intensively regulate low-level offenses generate large disparate impacts. Once individuals are ensnared in the criminal justice system, strong perpetuating effects continue criminal justice involvement and, in some cases, diminished life chances.

The combined effects of crime and poverty, punitive criminal justice policy focused in poor non-White communities, and racial bias put Black, Hispanic, and Native populations at high risk of initial criminal justice contact and severe treatment and at high risk of the negative consequences of criminal justice system involvement. This inequality is produced at a number of decision points and involves a large number of officials that comprise a criminal justice system that produces long-lasting consequences that are spatially concentrated and may stretch across generations. The expansion of the criminal justice system in low-income Black, Hispanic, and Native American communities from the 1970s to the early 2000s became a new and salient dimension of racial inequality in the post-Civil Rights period since the 1960s.

The collective effect of spatially concentrated crime and poverty, a penal code that has intensified punishment for drugs and violence, and criminal processing that has amplified racial disproportion comprises a social structure of racial inequality, with historical roots in institutions designed for racial exclusion and domination (see Chapter 1).

The social structure of racial inequality that emerges from this review of the research contrasts with the dominant analysis, which decomposes criminal justice disparity into components for crime and discrimination.

The idea that criminal processing creates growing disproportion in a context of structural disadvantage raises challenging questions for science and policy. For science, where the focus has often been on estimating discrimination, the question is: What do we control for? For example, sentencing studies routinely control for the prior criminal record to assess racial discrimination. But if prior discrimination tainted the criminal record, controlling for the prior record defines bias more narrowly. Arnold and colleagues (2020), in their analysis of pretrial detention, observe that in some analyses, "the definition of bias is so narrow that it rules out many plausible forms of racial bias."

A similar issue is raised in studies of policing. Knox and Mummolo (2020) critically review studies of police use of force that have found no racial differences in the victimization of civilians by police once characteristics of the police encounter are controlled. The authors argue that in a context in which there are large racial differences in the likelihood of a police encounter, conditioning on characteristics of the encounter controls away the relevant bias in police behavior.

For policy, racial inequality that is produced in a cumulative way in the social context of structural disadvantage may be unyielding to the narrow interventions that target specific points of discretion identified in discrimination studies. Examination of research on arrest, sentencing, incarceration, and community supervision indicates that disparity can result from a range of factors, including possible biased decision-making by line officials, social structural inequalities, and inequalities produced through institutional design. Arnold and colleagues (2020) appear to be pointing to this larger policy challenge when they argue that "economists must critically examine the notion that there must exist 'relevant differences' across groups that can 'explain' away observed racial differences when studying bias and discrimination." Reducing racial inequalities in the criminal justice system that are cumulatively produced from a starting point of structural inequalities in crime and poverty may require changes inside and outside the criminal justice system that are implemented in a comprehensive and coordinated way.

> CONCLUSION 4-1: *Enduring and spatially concentrated patterns of racial inequality in residence, poverty, violent crime, and enforcement provide a context for racial inequality in criminal justice involvement. As a result, criminal justice system contact—including police stops, arrests, incarceration, and community supervision—tends to be highly spatially concentrated.*

> CONCLUSION 4-2: *Three key processes are important for racial inequality. First, the early stages of the system—including police stops, jails, misdemeanor courts, and fines and fees—generate vast numbers of contacts between police and the courts and racial and ethnic minority groups. Second, sustained criminal justice involvement is produced through a cumulative process that may increase disparity with movement through the system. Third, the criminal justice system ensnares large segments of a disproportionately minority population for whom social problems related to concentrated poverty, including but not limited to serious crime, engender a criminal justice response involving arrest and penal control.*

> CONCLUSION 4-3: *The criminal justice system produces racial inequality through the cumulative impact from policing through community supervision; a focus on disparities or trends at any one point in the system will tend to underestimate the systemic effect of inter-related stages. Understanding the impact of the criminal justice system on racial inequality will require a more holistic analysis of contact across multiple stages of the system.*

5

Introduction to Part II

Part I of this report describes the nature, magnitude, and drivers of racial inequality in the criminal justice system. There we examined the roles of the historical legacies of slavery and settler colonialism, sociopolitical forces, and criminal justice policies and practices in creating and maintaining racial inequality. In Part II, we explore policies and programs to reduce racial inequalities in crime and criminal justice involvement. We examine community-based strategies, interventions in social policy areas adjacent to the criminal justice system, and criminal justice reform.

This current chapter outlines guiding principles for policy solutions and presents a historical example of a potentially promising policy agenda that was not fully developed to highlight lessons for decision makers and policy makers as they work to achieve reductions in racial inequalities in the criminal justice system.

GUIDING PRINCIPLES TO REDUCE RACIAL INEQUALITY IN THE CRIMINAL JUSTICE SYSTEM

This section outlines a set of guiding principles to the application of public policy solutions to address racial inequality in the criminal justice system. Informed by the committee's expertise, these principles are meant to inform decision makers as they consider strategies and policy levers for reducing racial inequalities in the criminal justice system, though they are not exhaustive nor meant to be prescriptive.

Reckoning and Reconciliation

Criminal justice policies and reform need to be informed by an acknowledgment of the harms perpetrated by the system against specific racial and ethnic groups. Reforms that involve reconciliation can help repair relationships between criminal justice agencies and impacted communities that have been marked by historical tensions, grievances, and misconceptions. For example, the Stockton (CA) police department implemented a racial reconciliation intervention that required the department to acknowledge the past harms of the criminal justice system, to truly listen to the community about their experiences, and then to make policy decisions based on what was learned in the process (National Academies of Sciences, Engineering, and Medicine, 2021b).

Participation, Accountability, and Transparency

Any effort to reduce racial inequalities in the criminal justice system needs to include mechanisms for community participation, accountability, and transparent data and evaluation methods. Impacted communities need to be resourced and trained to participate in the research process if their voices are absent in leadership positions. Above all, these efforts need to be accountable to the communities they serve.

Impacted Community Voices

Communities that are disproportionately harmed by racial inequality in the criminal justice system need to be partners in knowledge generation and in the implementation of policy solutions. Communities themselves have multifaceted needs, diverse perspectives, and unique contexts; the fact that community voices are heterogeneous across contexts calls for adequate survey tools and other measures of community representation in decision making.

Heterogeneity

Criminal justice decision makers must understand the heterogeneity of contexts across jurisdictions and communities and take this into account when considering public policy solutions that have been shown to work in other contexts.

Engaging communities and impacted populations is a central theme across each of these principles. While community engagement can take a variety of forms, ensuring that the perspectives of all key partners are taken into consideration throughout research development and design is critical to increasing the relevance and effectiveness of any resulting intervention programs or reform efforts and can help to empower populations that have been stigmatized, marginalized, and ignored (the National Academies, 2022a). For example, the Burns Institute has worked to center community voices in reform efforts in Los Angeles County (the National Academies, 2021b). Other examples in public health and climate adaptation rely on using structured decision making processes, facilitating partnerships between decision makers and community organizations, and encouraging public ownership of responses (the National Academies, 2022b,d).

APPLYING A HISTORICAL LENS TO INFORM CRIMINAL JUSTICE POLICY

Chapter 2 presents an overview of the profound disparities among different groups categorized by race and ethnicity at every level of criminal justice system processing. Chapter 1 locates these disparities in historical context; Chapters 3 and 4 place them in contemporary contexts. Demands for strategies, policies, and new conceptual frameworks for organizing the work of the various institutions that comprise the criminal justice system emerge from these contexts.

Evidence concerning the relationship that a policy has on a desired outcome, what Gelman and Imbens (2013) refer to as "forward causal inference," is critical to future policy making that can address the serious issues detailed in this report. Equally important is a deeper understanding of the reverse of forward causal inference—that is, seeking to uncover the causes of an outcome, such as racial inequality in the criminal justice system. History as a discipline provides insight on questions such as these.

Criminal legal institutions in the United States have a shape, orientation, and function that are dictated in part by laws and legal structures, the organization of the political economy, and cultural contexts. This means that to understand the shape of what these institutions should be, one must first understand what they *could* be.

In this vein, this section offers an historical account of the first substantial efforts of the federal government to address racial inequality at the intersection of social policy and criminal law enforcement at the national level. During the 1960s, national policy makers recognized the devastating impact of historical discrimination and sought to use national resources to end racial inequality. Guided by social science research, the policies of the Kennedy and Johnson administrations offered a response to the problems of poverty and crime through a preventative framework that stressed community empowerment. Yet despite unparalleled federal attention to the larger socioeconomic drivers of delinquency, by the end of the 1960s it was clear that racial disparities still existed and were growing rather than abating.

The federal government investments in a promising conceptual framework put forth in the 1960s never reached the scale that some advocates recommended. The failure of national policy makers and social scientists to follow their own research and policy recommendations was due, in part, to the influential view that "cultural pathologies" of broken families and bad behavior were among the root causes of poverty and crime, to which policing and incarceration were often assumed to be appropriate responses. By the early 1980s, federal and state policy makers adopted increasingly punitive responses to the problems of unemployment, failing school systems, housing insecurity, and public health problems, such as gun violence, that involved greater oversight and more intensive enforcement of behavioral standards (Kohler-Hausmann, 2017; Soss et al., 2011; Mead, 1997). Social spending increased greatly in the 1960s, and absolute poverty declined in the 1960s, but the growth in the anti-poverty effort was not sufficient to substantially reduce relative disparities in well-being that had alarmed many policy makers and social scientists at the beginning of the 1960s. Crime-control budgets, particularly at the federal level, began to grow quickly. Ultimately, rising crime rates in the 1960s and 1970s were interpreted as proof that the War on Poverty had failed and that the War on Crime did not go far enough (see Box 5-1).

This history helps us understand the range of alternatives for reducing racial inequality in the criminal justice system today. The Kerner Commission—formally the National Advisory Commission on Civil Disorders, chaired by Illinois Governor Otto Kerner—established by President Lyndon Johnson's executive order during the unrest in Detroit in July 1967 called for large social policy investments to address underlying structural factors. This call was broadcast to a national audience through the Commission's final report, release in February 1968. The report recommended the creation of two million jobs for "disadvantaged" Americans, continued federal intervention to ensure school desegregation, year-round schooling for low-income youths, the construction of hundreds of thousands of public housing units, and a guaranteed minimum income. Notably, the Commission looked beyond policing and incarceration to address problems of safety in disadvantaged communities. While spending in several of these areas did increase during the 1970s, anti-crime policy at all levels of government also came to rely more on the modernization of urban police forces. Further, changes in sentencing policy at the state level, from the mid-1970s forward (NRC, 1983, Chapter 3), drove significant growth in prison populations, amplifying racial inequality.

BOX 5-1
Case Study: Juvenile Delinquency and Youth Offenses and Control Act of 1961

In the 1960s, the federal government launched a substantial national effort to combat crime based on an analysis of racial inequality for the first time in the history of the United States. This undertaking was notable for two reasons. First, it was national in scope, in contrast to notions of federalism that relegated crime policy to the states. Second, it targeted social conditions that gave rise to crime and juvenile delinquency—a preventive approach, in contrast to the more typical reactive, punitive approach to addressing crime. Under the influence of scientific theories that traced delinquency to the failures of educational and labor market institutions to support youthful development in a meaningful way through job training, education, and equal opportunity programs, the Kennedy administration framed its urban social programs as anti-delinquency measures.

Based on the "systemic barriers" conception of urban problems that Lloyd Cloward and Richard Ohlin described in their 1960 book, *Delinquency and Opportunity*, the federal government's anti-delinquency program represented a moment when research-based criminological theory was used to design policy aimed at solving problems of racial inequality. The federal government sought to legitimize its approach to fighting delinquency by grounding it in scientific research. Federal officials had previously relied heavily on the opinions of agency officials and bureaucrats in shaping national programs, but the proliferation of academic research after World War II had produced a diverse body of knowledge. With research at hand, the envisioned anti-delinquency program of the 1960s articulated a theory of the sources and solutions to delinquency supported by statistical evidence provided by Cloward and Ohlin, Daniel Patrick Moynihan, James Q. Wilson, and other scholars (Hinton, 2017; O'Connor, 2001).

Cloward and Ohlin had both been strongly influenced by sociologist Frank Tannenbaum's theory of delinquency (Flamm, 2005; Terte, 1963; Cloward and Ohlin, 1960). They had worked with prisoners in the 1950s—Ohlin as a researcher for the Illinois Parole and Pardon Board while pursuing a doctorate in sociology at the University of Chicago, and Cloward as a social worker at an army prison in Pennsylvania—and, following Tannenbaum, became convinced that law enforcement programs should focus on social systems rather than individuals in order to be effective. Writing about the criminalization of young European immigrants in *Crime and Community*, Tannenbaum (1938) argued that when authorities treated actions such as playing games in public or playing truant at school as criminal or delinquent, they further isolated already marginalized youth from mainstream society, increasing the resistance of that marginalized group to formal social institutions and exacerbating delinquency. Under Tannenbaum's theory, the decision to arrest teenagers for offenses such as cursing, shouting, or skipping school reflected more the failings of traditional social welfare systems and public institutions than individual behavior. Labeling activities as delinquent that the teenagers themselves likely saw as adventuresome began a process Tannenbaum called the "dramatization of the evil" and inadvertently encouraged criminality in the future.

continued

BOX 5-1 Continued

As Tannenbaum (1938) wrote, "The person becomes the thing he is described as being" (see also Hinton, 2017; Terte, 1963).

Building from Tannenbaum's ideas about the sources of crime and the impact of criminal labeling and applying them to Black and Puerto Rican youth in New York City (NY), Cloward and Ohlin devised "opportunity theory" in the late 1950s. They argued that criminal "pathology" did not stem from culture or individual traits but was the result of inadequate resources for neglected children and punitive responses to their everyday behavior, making it more likely that low-income youth would fail in school, be unable to gain employment, and eventually engage in criminal activity. Thus, effectively controlling delinquency meant changing "opportunity structures" by strengthening the institutions in which poor young people interacted with education, training, and development programs. Paraphrasing Tannenbaum, Ohlin and Cloward explained, "The target for preventive action should be defined, not as the individual or group that exhibits the delinquent pattern, but as the *social setting* that gives rise to the delinquent" (Cloward and Ohlin, 1960, p. 211). According to Cloward and Ohlin, these preventative measures could effectively break the cultural pathologies that bred delinquency.

Administration officials considered opportunity theory a significant breakthrough in understanding and responding to urban problems and incorporated the concept into the federal government's juvenile delinquency program. "The best solution to the delinquency problem is prevention," David Hackett, the executive director of the President's Committee on Juvenile Delinquency and Youth Crime (hereafter, the President's Committee), declared at the Institute of Juvenile Delinquency in the fall of 1961. The committee, which was created by executive order on May 11, was chaired by then-Attorney General Robert Kennedy and included the secretaries of Labor and Health, Education, and Welfare.

The Juvenile Delinquency and Youth Offenses and Control Act of 1961[a] sought to address the problems of "youth unemployment, poor housing, poor health, inadequate education, and the alienation of lower-class communities and neighborhoods," as Attorney General Kennedy explained. He and other federal policy makers believed that the racial discrimination Black families confronted within school systems and workplaces was the root cause of this "alienation." Drawing from Cloward and Ohlin's work, the preamble to the Act itself argued that "delinquency and offenses occur disproportionately among school dropouts, unemployed youth faced with limited opportunities and with employment barriers, and youth in deprived family situations" (Hinton, 2017).

The Juvenile Delinquency and Youth Offenses Control Act would focus on young people who had come into contact with law enforcement or criminal justice authorities, as well as groups of youth who lived in impoverished neighborhoods and whom federal policy makers believed to be susceptible to delinquency. Hackett and other Kennedy officials believed that if the social and behavioral problems they attributed to urban youth of color remained unaddressed, crime and delinquency would continue to escalate, among Black youth especially. With funding and broad discretion under the terms of the 1961 legislation, which passed in late September with an initial allocation of $10 million a year (equivalent to nearly $100 million today) for three years to support experimental programs, the

President's Committee focused its efforts almost explicitly on Black youth and emphasized prevention as a key goal in controlling crime.

Indeed, despite the President's Committee's awareness that "delinquency has increased in the suburbs and rural areas," policy proposals focused on concentrated poverty in Black central city neighborhoods, a harbinger of contemporary scholarly attention to communities of triple disadvantage described in Chapter 3. Concern for residents in the "decaying core of the inner city" strongly influenced the committee's decision to target Black youth for the vast majority of juvenile delinquency appropriations. In the opinion of policy makers, researchers, and professional staff, Black urban neighborhoods contained "the most imposing array of social pathology" (Hinton, 2017).

In Harlem and other segregated Black communities with median family incomes well below the national average and high levels of unemployment, the committee faced "a challenge and an opportunity" to remedy the "broad, established, pathological base" that appeared to be the source of the community's problems. In Detroit (MI), Philadelphia (PA), and Cleveland (OH), at least 80 percent of youth served by the federal anti-delinquency programs were Black. In Washington (DC) "undoubtedly all the youth involved" were Negro, as Hackett wrote to Kennedy. And in cities like Syracuse (NY) and New Haven (CT), where Black residents represented five percent and 15 percent of the population, respectively, half of the participants in the anti-delinquency demonstration programs were Black (Hinton, 2017).

Cloward and Ohlin's delinquency prevention strategy opened up two policy domains for the federal government: forming partnerships with community-based organizations and addressing the plight of racially marginalized citizens. As a 1965 progress report produced by the Office of Juvenile Delinquency and Youth Development stated: "The delinquency program has... supported projects aimed primarily at changes in social situations affecting target area youth rather than changes in the personality of the individual delinquent. The program stresses a simultaneous focus on the many social conditions believed to cause delinquency" (Hinton, 2017).

Along these lines, the administration aimed to foster a community transformation, framed as an anti-delinquency program, which required a simultaneous attack on the institutional barriers to inclusion.

When Lyndon Johnson assumed the presidency in 1963, he soon expanded the pre-kindergarten, remedial education, family intervention, and job training initiatives of Kennedy's anti-delinquency program as part of a "War on Poverty," which began in 1964 under the administration of the Office of Economic Opportunity (OEO).[b] But rather than continuing to combat crime through the preventative framework developed by his predecessor, in 1965 Johnson also began a separate investment in policing, courts, and prisons as part of a "War on Crime," to be prosecuted by the Office of Law Enforcement Assistance (OLEA). Soon, federal support for local law enforcement through the OLEA supplanted social welfare programs through the OEO as the main channel for a national anti-crime policy. Thus, the approach to local communities as the main centers of anti-poverty and crime control programs was short-lived. The scale of this community-based approach remained limited. It also faced resistance from local officials who bristled at the expanded role of community members in shaping municipal programs and

continued

BOX 5-1 Continued

at the way it challenged widely held assumptions among policy makers that participants in social welfare programs were unworthy and incapable.

New community action, secondary education, and housing and urban development programs far surpassed crime control in terms of their proportion of federal expenditures during the Johnson administration. Anti-poverty policy developed quickly as many of the main safety net programs of the Great Society were established at this time, including food stamps (now the Supplemental Nutrition Assistance Program), Medicare, Medicaid, Head Start, and expanded Social Security. Each of these programs became mainstays of the current social safety net. In line with the anti-crime predictions of opportunity theory, recent research finds that children's access to food stamps is associated with reduced incarceration in adulthood (Bailey et al., 2020), that Supplemental Security Income benefits for disabled youth are associated with reduced criminal court charges (Deshpande and Mueller-Smith, 2022), and that Medicaid coverage is associated with a reduction in arrests (Simes and Jahn, 2022). Despite the evident success of these social programs at reducing crime and criminal justice contact, large racial inequalities in socioeconomic well-being endured, and crime rates escalated through the 1960s and 1970s.

During this period, assistance to local law enforcement became a key instrument of national crime policy through the 1960s and beyond. While Congress expanded and transformed the OLEA into the Law Enforcement Assistance Administration (LEAA) within three years of its creation, the OEO never grew into a larger, more permanent agency. Criminal justice agencies also began to administer social welfare programs. The LEAA came to fund some job training, after-school, and neighborhood service programs that had once been supported by the OEO. The choice to use criminal justice actors as agents of social policy tied the delivery of services to the surveillance of criminal risk, which was at odds with the Kennedy administration's initial approach.[c] The federal government gained a significant role in crime policy through the 1960s, and the LEAA became a forerunner of the many offices and programs at the Justice Department that implement a national crime policy by providing federal grants and technical assistance to local law enforcement agencies.

In short, throughout the 1960s and 1970s, federal policy makers' expansion of the social safety net was insufficient to substantially reduce racial inequality in socioeconomic status or to stem rising crime, and federal funding of local criminal justice agencies became the dominant instrument of federal anti-crime policy. By the mid-1970s, Black and Latino groups combined began to approach majorities in state and federal prisons for the first time in American history (Black Americans had previously amounted to about one-third of the nation's prison population). During the same period, state and federal prison populations ballooned, rising from just under 200,000 by 1970 to just over 300,000 by 1980—a 50 percent increase in a decade (Minor-Harper, 1986; Nagel, 1977).

---

[a]Public Law No. 87-274, 75 Stat. 572.
[b]Economic Opportunity Act of 1964 (Public Law No. 88-452. 78 Stat.).
[c]On the criminalization of welfare during this period, see Kohler-Hausmann (2017).

CONCLUDING OBSERVATIONS

In the 1960s, the Kerner Commission carried out just one of several high-level reviews during the Kennedy and Johnson administrations that found that serious crime in low-income Black neighborhoods was rooted in a deep racial inequality and that addressing it required significant investment in Black communities. The President's Commission on Law Enforcement and Administration of Justice (1967) drew parallel conclusions in its report, *The Challenge of Crime in a Free Society*. Although the War on Poverty quickly expanded social safety net programs that benefited all low-income Americans, socio-economic disadvantage endured in minority communities.

At the same time, crime was transformed into a national political problem that demanded a federal response. Despite the social analysis of the time, federal crime policy came to rely heavily on grants to local law enforcement. Turning crime into a national political issue that demanded a national response in this way was not the only or even the main driver of high incarceration rates. But it was part of a trend in crime policy that greatly expanded the use of police and prisons disproportionately impacting primarily Black and Latino communities.

That the criminal justice system remains a significant dimension of racial inequality more than 50 years after the nation embarked on its most substantial investment in modernization, professionalization, and reform provides important context for the challenge of reducing racial inequality today. While policy makers should investigate criminal justice reforms that can directly reduce the harms associated with policing and incarceration, reducing racial inequality may also require changes outside the criminal justice system in social policy and community life. Moreover, the decentralized nature of criminal justice policy points us to states and local jurisdictions for policy innovation that can inform or drive change at the state and federal levels.

It is often observed that there is no one criminal justice system but a complex patchwork of agencies and jurisdictions at three different levels of government. Policy innovation and experimentation often happen at the local level, though sometimes buttressed and coordinated through state and federal budgets and legislation. Deep reform that addresses structural racism and severs the close connections between race, criminal harms, and criminal justice involvement may involve facilitating local innovation and coordinating and consolidating local initiatives with state and federal leadership.

The remainder of this report delves into community-driven approaches to safety and reducing harm, non-criminal policy interventions in adjacent social policy domains, criminal justice reform, and the federal role in supporting communities to address inequalities. The committee's recommendations set forth in the subsequent chapters offer evidence-based guidance on how public policy might reduce racial inequalities in crime and justice.

6

Community-Driven Safety and Reducing Harm

Calls for a larger community role in improving safety have become prominent in contemporary conceptions of criminal justice reform. Rather than relying only on police and the legal system, community efforts promote a larger role for local residents and organizations in both the definition and production of safety. The organizers of these efforts often view the aim of their work as not just reducing crime but also reducing racial inequality in crime and criminal justice involvement by increasing a community's capacity, through the community's own methods of decision making, to determine what safety is and how it is achieved.

This chapter builds on findings from Part I of this report by exploring ways that community members, community-based organizations, and community representatives (formal and informal) can help to minimize the likelihood of contact with the criminal justice system among racial and ethnic minority groups and mitigate the harm of that contact when it does occur. The chapter highlights opportunities and strategies for strengthening the capacity for community organization in ways that build collective efficacy while mitigating harms associated with racial inequalities in criminal justice.

Although the evidence base from causal research designs is not large, we seek to identify community strategies that hold promise as a means to reduce racial inequality in a variety of ways. Community interventions are typically place-based and preventive. Notable examples have emerged through the efforts of activists and organizers in Black, Latino, and American Indian communities who view violence—whether at the hands of community members, intimate partners, or criminal justice authorities—as a key dimension of racial inequality. For example, the successful prevention of retaliatory gun violence and homicide would reduce harm overall while also narrowing racial gaps in violent offending, violent victimization, and criminal justice contact. Such strategies typically involve intervention by community residents rather than police, offering the possibility of reduced police contact, particularly for young men who are the focus of intervention efforts.

Some community strategies also target "root causes"—the physical environment and economic opportunity, for example—that are related to the legacy of historical racial inequities and racial inequalities in victimization, offending, and community well-being. For example, community-led efforts at reducing levels of lead exposure, as well as efforts to green vacant lots and turn them into small public spaces in communities that have historically seen disinvestment, can lead to reductions in crime and greater collective efficacy in those communities (Cui et al., 2022; Sampson, 2022). Finally, local community safety efforts are often framed as projects of empowerment that aim to expand the control of local organizations or community residents over their own neighborhoods; see Box 6-1 for a discussion of community-driven response through mutual aid programs.[1]

At the most basic level, community safety is concerned with the security of persons and property. Threats to safety include both interpersonal violence in families and within communities and harms perpetrated by the criminal justice system itself (see Chapter 4). To this end, community safety is concerned with buffering people, especially young people, from interpersonal violence of all forms and from unwarranted surveillance and violence at the hands of criminal justice officials. From this perspective, community safety is centered on capacity building and non-coercive social controls, not merely crime fighting.

A community can be involved in the production of safety in at least two ways: by taking a leading role in the definition and production of safety, and by providing oversight and accountability for the criminal justice agencies. This chapter assesses the state of the literature on collective efficacy and neighborhood social organization, including "bottom up" approaches that seek to build informal social controls and cohesion among residents in the community. It then reviews several community initiatives for defining and producing safety and assesses their implications for reducing racial inequality in the criminal justice system. The main efforts reviewed include systems of accountability for law enforcement and

[1]Recent efforts to develop community-driven and survivor-centered approaches to safety have roots in strategies developed by sex workers, historically marginalized women, and queer people of color who found themselves as either targets of or otherwise outside the protection of traditional forms of law enforcement. See Richie (2012) and Ritchie (2017).

BOX 6-1
Community-Driven Response: Mutual Aid Programs

Mutual aid is broadly regarded as the practice of reciprocal aid, cooperation, and building and sustaining of social relations, by which people can have their basic needs met without reliance on governed systems. Spade (2020) identifies three key elements of mutual aid projects: (1) they work to meet survival needs and build a shared understanding about why people do not have what they need; (2) they mobilize people, expand solidarity, and build movements; (3) they are participatory in nature, solving problems through collective action rather than waiting for external intervention.

While mutual aid groups have an extensive history (Katz, 1981), they have recently been an important component of community-based responses to the coronavirus pandemic (Mao et al., 2021). Community solidarity during emergencies and disasters is common; however, previous studies have shown that such solidarity behaviors tend to decline over time, even when needs remain high (Fernandes-Jesus et al., 2021).

Mutual aid groups that support people affected by violence or criminal justice system involvement have also been documented. For example, groups have been formed for survivors of parental intimate-partner violence (Molina and Chapple, 2017) and for mothers who are incarcerated (Howard et al., 2020). In response to the increase in race-based violence perpetrated against Asian Americans during the coronavirus pandemic, mutual aid groups have been reported to provide escorts for those who feel unsafe in their neighborhoods (Lang, 2021). Although more research is needed to evaluate effects and potential unintended consequences, mutual aid groups provide an example of community-driven responses to violence and criminal system involvement.

community organizations, community-based anti-violence initiatives, and crisis-response and community-driven programs to reduce the harms of system involvement. Finally, this chapter discusses the definition and measurement of safety and norms around crime, the criminal justice system, and community-based solutions.

In many cases, community-driven initiatives are locally organized and independent of any government involvement. In some cases, they are organized and funded by municipal or county government, often in close collaboration with local organizations. Due to their local character, community initiatives vary enormously in their implementation and in the environments in which they operate. Considering this heterogeneity, the committee draws some general principles that might effectively be adapted to local conditions, with the goal of reducing racial inequality in the criminal justice system. These principles include centering and respecting the needs and experiences of both crime survivors and people who have caused harm, while acknowledging these two identities as not mutually exclusive.

The chapter also addresses potential unintended consequences of community-driven interventions for crime and racial inequality and the need to build systems of accountability. The committee characterizes programs or practices as "promising" if they approach the work in ways that are known to build informal social controls and cohesion among residents in a community. Further evaluation is needed to determine whether or how such programs/practices do so and the impact of these programs/practices on producing safety and mitigating racial inequalities.

The discussion of community-driven approaches in this chapter focuses on urban areas and, to a lesser extent, tribal lands. In the case of tribal communities, we are concerned with the role that local residents and organizations can play in strengthening Indigenous systems of accountability and redemption and the role of tribal members, representatives, and organizations in mitigating harms done to victims and perpetrators when tribal, state, and federal justice systems intersect. More research is needed to explore the applicability of community-driven approaches described in this chapter to more suburban or rural settings.

DEFINING COMMUNITY AND COMMUNITY WELL-BEING

One of the first challenges is to clarify what is meant by "community" in the context of crime and criminal justice policy. A prior National Academies of Sciences, Engineering, and Medicine study on community-based interventions to advance health equity defined community as "any configuration of individuals, families, and groups whose values, characteristics, interests, geography, and/or social relations unite them in some way" (the National Academies, 2017, p. 50). "Community" may thus be applied to a particular geographic area, such as a village, town, or city. But within geographic areas, there may be multiple distinct communities (or, perhaps, sub communities, such as ethnic, racial, and religious communities). In this chapter, we focus primarily on geographic communities, such as neighborhoods in a city, suburban communities, small cities, and tribal communities.

Across communities and over time, different governance structures come into being, each structure amplifying some voices and suppressing others. The choice among governance structures thus has significant consequences in terms of outcomes. A complicating issue is the resulting specialization of distinct functions, accompanied by distinct methods, approaches, and professional identities, that arise within a particular geographic space. When it comes to the criminal justice system, specialization and the siloes it creates out of different policy domains can obscure the influence of public health, economic security, education, and family on offending and victimization. People affected the most need to have a voice in how the systems of public safety and punishment work. They experience the failures of the system and can inform policy making and reform efforts since they have traveled the system's breadth.

Further compounding these "horizontal" divisions among communities in each geographic space is a vertical division between local, state, and federal communities of similar definition whether they are based on matters of public health or public safety. Is the best way to address social issues like racial inequality in the distribution of public services and goods a federal (i.e., national) leadership/initiative? Or is it best addressed through state or local capacity building? Within this context of both horizontal and vertical differentiation, focusing attention on community well-being or wellness as essential to public safety can prevent the narrowing of focus to professional/disciplinary boundaries, since community well-being arises from a wide variety of factors. Public health researchers typically include socioeconomic indicators of health and wellness in definitions of the term. For example, community well-being is the combination of social, economic, environmental, cultural, and political conditions identified by individuals and their communities as essential for them to flourish and fulfill their potential (Wiseman and Brasher, 2008, p. 358).[2]

COLLECTIVE EFFICACY AND NEIGHBORHOOD SOCIAL ORGANIZATION

As introduced in Chapter 3, the theory of collective efficacy is based on a "bottom up" approach to community anti-violence, grounded in informal social controls and cohesion among residents in the community rather than in "top-down" law enforcement by the state (Sampson et al., 1997). Researchers have measured collective efficacy by asking community residents questions such as: How likely is it that your neighbors would take action if children were skipping school? What about if there was a fight in the neighborhood? How much do residents trust their neighbors? Are people willing to help their neighbors?

Although causation is always difficult to estimate in observational studies, research results in the United States tend to show that among neighborhoods that are otherwise similar, including in prior levels of crime, those with higher collective efficacy tend to have lower rates of violence (Lanfear

[2]Although some institutional domains may be preferred over law enforcement—for example, in producing community well-being and wellness—it is important to acknowledge that all social institutions in the United States are influenced by the historical forces identified in Part I of this report. Without attention to these histories and lingering impacts, any institutional response runs the risk of reproducing or exacerbating preexisting racial inequalities.

et al., 2020; Maxwell et al., 2018; Pratt and Cullen, 2005; Morenoff et al., 2001; Sampson et al., 1997). Collective efficacy is also relatively stable over time, and it predicts lower crime after adjusting for community characteristics like concentrated poverty, racial composition, and traditional forms of neighbor networks, such as friend/kinship ties. Further, the more heterogeneity there is in norms of collective efficacy in a neighborhood, the more crime that neighborhood tends to experience (Brunton-Smith et al., 2018). However, evidence from reciprocal models and trajectories of collective efficacy and crime, and studies from outside the United States, both yield more mixed and sometimes null results (see, e.g., Wickes and Hipp, 2018; Sampson, 2012, pp. 173–177; Steenbeek and Hipp, 2011; Mazerolle et al., 2010).

As Bell (2021, p. 33) has argued, the theoretical framework and measurement strategy of collective efficacy theory has the advantage of forming the basis of an alternative set of metrics for public safety outcomes. Rather than starting with the long-held assumption that the police and official crime statistics should be the primary objects of inquiry, community-based theories like collective efficacy focus on alternative forms of social control and peacekeeping efforts rooted in a broader conceptualization of safety and, at its most general level, human flourishing (Bell, 2021). There is emerging (though incomplete) evidence on the success of localized efforts to promote informal social controls and build community capacity, especially among minority youth, absent the police (see discussion below). In an era when alternatives to the criminal justice system are being demanded, such efforts deserve further scrutiny in future research and evaluation.

A challenge, then, is to address such structural conditions and increase collective efficacy without unintended consequences and to identify community-driven interventions that reduce crime and racial inequality without undue reliance on the criminal justice system. This involves understanding how community action can create conditions that foster collective efficacy, and how collective efficacy may be undermined by violence, the harms of system contact, and racial inequalities generated by increased vulnerability to the system. Yet very few, if any, experiments exist that test collective efficacy or community social organization efforts, especially those that take into account reciprocal relationships with crime or that seek to address racial inequities. An additional challenge is that community crime prevention is hard to implement in the areas that need it the most—poor, unstable neighborhoods with high crime rates—and participation levels tend to fall off once interventions are removed. Efforts to reduce crime are most likely to succeed if they are embedded in more comprehensive programs for neighborhood stabilization that local residents support, but most interventions are single-site or time-constrained. Interventions that are externally imposed and simply try to reduce crime in the short run without confronting durable aspects of a neighborhood's vulnerability are, unsurprisingly, highly susceptible to failure (John Jay College Research Advisory Group on Preventing and Reducing Community Violence, 2020; Branas and MacDonald, 2014; Hope, 1995; Skogan, 1988).

As Bell (2021, p. 35) puts it, "There has never been a robust, well-funded, and consistently supported network of community organizations that engage in violence reduction and public safety efforts." Whether the limited track record of community interventions in building community capacity and reducing crime and racial disparities is due to a failure of theory or a programmatic failure of stable implementation is therefore unclear, but on balance there is enough evidence to recommend a program of new research and evaluation. It is important to note that, comparatively considered, substantially more resources have been devoted to criminal justice programs despite the similar absence of clear evidence of their effectiveness.

What Is Needed for Success

The data on persistent and compounded inequality also point to the need for sustained community interventions in order to provide a fair test. Durable investments in disadvantaged urban neighborhoods that match the persistent and longstanding nature of institutional disinvestment that such neighborhoods have endured over many years can take many forms (Sharkey, 2018). Community-based safety efforts such as Advance Peace; Chicago's Rapid Employment and Development Initiative; Safe Streets; Communities That Care; and Portland, Oregon's Crisis Assistance Helping Out on the Streets (CAHOOTS) all share the goal of reducing violence through informal mechanisms of control and local organizational partnerships. While the evidence is mixed, some of these efforts offer strategies that deserve further testing and evaluation (Urban Labs, 2022; Bell, 2021; John Jay College Research Advisory Group on Preventing and Reducing Community Violence, 2020).

While community residents are central to the definition and production of safety—city representatives like the police or housing officials cannot do it all—local nonprofit organizations are also crucial. Sharkey and colleagues (2017), for example, examine national data and find that community-based organizations that fought against rising crime in the 1990s were responsible for a significant portion of the crime drop in subsequent years. This finding is important because it suggests that it is not a single program but the general strategy of community organization that is most effective in improving safety (see also Sampson, 2012, Chapter 8).

Further research on collective efficacy and community-based organizations is especially needed in lower-income communities, where residents, especially racial minorities, are disproportionately burdened with both interpersonal and criminal justice violence. A promising idea is to build upon organic community-care work by giving residents and local organizations a greater stake in their communities, possibly through "community shareholder tasks," where residents are supported for contributing to public safety and community improvement (Jones, 2018; Sharkey, 2018). Community shareholder tasks that might foster collective efficacy include (1) organizing community supervision of leisure-time youth activities, (2) parent/guardian supervision and involvement in after-school and night-time youth programs, and (3) adult-youth mentoring systems and forums for parental acquaintanceship (Bell, 2021; John Jay College Research Advisory Group on Preventing and Reducing Community Violence, 2020; see also Jones, 2018; Anderson, 1999).

When addressing problems of violence, which most often involve young people, it is especially important to center community-based efforts on capacity building, not simply the punitive objectives of crime fighting (Jones, 2018). In short, there are promising signs that community-based organizations, as well as community-building work on the part of residents, play an important role in improving the quality of life in minority neighborhoods, reducing crime and criminal justice contact, and reducing racial inequality. This role should be further investigated (Bell, 2021).

Federal or large-scale interventions are also needed to support and evaluate such efforts—local collective efficacy is not enough. In many cities, programs such as Choice Neighborhoods and Promise Neighborhoods are, to date, relatively small-scale and unevaluated (Sharkey, 2018), but they may prove useful in informing the next generation of place-based interventions (Whitehurst and Croft, 2010). Educational reforms and support for healthy child development in high-risk, poor communities are also crucial to these efforts, as seen for example in the implementation of the Harlem Children's Zone in New York City (NY; Dobbie and Fryer, 2011). Moreover, initiatives to provide permanent, affordable housing for diverse low-income people, such as the Bay Area Community Land Trust, are also important for creating social environments in which collective efficacy might grow.

COMMUNITY-DRIVEN INITIATIVES

In this section, we review community-driven initiatives aimed at defining and producing safety and assess their implications for reducing racial inequality in the criminal justice system. The main efforts reviewed include:

- Creating systems of accountability for both law enforcement and community organization efforts;

- Community-driven anti-violence initiatives and crisis response; and
- Community-driven efforts to mitigate the harms of system involvement.

Initiatives in these areas are non-criminalizing interventions or responses that aim to improve safety in localities while minimizing harmful interventions of the police or other criminal justice agencies.

Interventions in neighborhood ecology and local social service efforts are also community-driven approaches with similar goals, and they are discussed in more detail in Chapter 7. This section examines how community members take a leading role in providing safety and reducing racial inequality. In this role, community actors and institutions take on a function that is complementary to some of the goals of law enforcement (e.g., reduction in violent crime) but with more independence than has historically been the case in collaborations between law enforcement and the community (Gascón and Roussell, 2019; Jones, 2018).

The capacity of community action to promote safety and reduce racial inequality has a long history. In American Indian communities, traditional dispute resolution mechanisms predate modern law enforcement and criminal court systems. Indigenous approaches often reflected what are now called "restorative justice" principles, in which offender and victim are joined by other members of the community and the focus is on helping the offender and repairing the harm done to the victim and to the community (Yazzie, 1994).

Various forms of community action have aimed to couple local knowledge of social problems with local empowerment, as far back as the 1930s with the Chicago Area Project, whose goal was to empower communities to reduce crime and enhance local well-being; including the work of Black churches that acted as social service providers in the civil rights era; as well as the Community Action Programs established under the War on Poverty. There is also a documented history of government efforts to undermine community empowerment among marginalized groups in the United States. The federal government used federal and state criminal jurisdiction to undermine Indigenous justice systems (Rolnick, 2016a; Washburn, 2006a). This was especially acute in the 1960s and early 1970s, when such groups were labeled by the Federal Bureau of Investigation and local law enforcement as threats to law and order (Bloom and Martin, 2013).

In the scientific literature, research on neighborhood social organization, community-based organizations, and resident collective efficacy has also emphasized informal social controls enacted under conditions of social trust and shared expectations. Providing organizational resources and harnessing the power of citizens have been hypothesized to enhance safety.

Community-Centered Approaches to Justice

Many of the community interventions described in this chapter operate in the shadow of pervasive law enforcement and criminal court systems. Some interventions focus on reducing the harm done by those systems by reducing contact between community members and police, by making police accountable to the community, or by providing support to reduce the long-term harm of criminal system involvement. Others operate in tandem with formal systems by diverting individuals away from law enforcement or formal court proceedings. When compared to the principles of control, confinement, and retribution that animate formal criminal systems, many of the community approaches described in this chapter are premised on fundamentally different understandings of justice and safety. However, the transformative potential of most community-centered efforts is limited by government investment in formal systems.

American Indian tribal communities are uniquely situated in this regard because, as sovereign governments with criminal jurisdiction over their territories and their people, tribes have greater authority than other communities to define and shape local criminal systems. Indeed, modern tribal criminal systems are characterized by ongoing efforts to reconcile formal American models of safety and justice with Indigenous approaches to safety and justice.[3] An Indigenous justice system is one that incorporates that community's customary approaches to safety, justice, and conflict resolution. While each system is unique, Indigenous approaches generally incorporate non-adversarial approaches, holistic treatment, and a rejection of punishment in favor of accountability, healing, and repairing harm to the community. As such, Indigenous approaches have served as models for restorative practices in other communities.

In some communities, Indigenous justice systems operate parallel to formal criminal systems (Melton, 2005). For example, the Navajo Nation's Peacemaking Program, *hózh óji naat'aah*, originated as a way to incorporate customary Diné dispute resolution practices into the Navajo Nation's judicial system (Nielsen and Zion, 2005), but it was bifurcated from the courts in 2012 out of concern that formal Anglo-American court rules were changing its core principles (Peacemaking Program of the Judicial Branch of the Navajo Nation, 2012). The current program is voluntary and accepts referrals from both courts and non-court sources. A non-judicial

[3]This reconciliation is critical because federal support of tribal criminal jurisdiction has typically required that tribal courts resemble state and federal courts. For example, recent legislative expansions of tribal jurisdiction require that tribal courts operate according to an adversarial model with due process protections based on the U.S. Constitution (Riley, 2016). Federal grant funding for tribal governments has also heavily favored American approaches, including construction of detention facilities and support for police training (Rolnick, 2016b).

peacemaker—a "community leader whose leadership depends on respect and persuasion and not a position of power and authority"—hears from offenders, victim, relatives, and other affected community members (Zion, 1998). Peacemaking is based on Navajo justice concepts, including an emphasis on healing and a "horizontal," or non-hierarchical, process (Gross, 1999; Zion, 1998; Yazzie, 1994).

In other Indigenous communities, formal systems are structured to divert individuals into traditional courts (the National Academies, 2021b, pp. 6–7). For example, several tribal governments operate Healing to Wellness Courts, specialty courts that serve adults, juveniles, and/or families referred from formal courts for drug- or alcohol-related behaviors, usually as part of a diversion or plea agreement (Flies-Away et al., 2014). While similar to drug courts in non-Indigenous communities, the Wellness Court model has been developed by Indigenous communities specifically to serve their people. Since the introduction of federal grants to support tribal Wellness Court development, beginning in 1997, the use of Healing to Wellness Courts has expanded in tribal communities. Healing to Wellness Courts are supported by a community of tribal justice experts who have refined the Healing to Wellness approach (Cordero et al., 2021; Garrow et al., 2018; OJJDP, 2017; Flies-Away et al., 2014; Flies-Away and Garrow, 2013; Gottlieb, 2005; Riggs, 2002).

These courts "utilize a non-adversarial approach, integrating traditional concepts of healing and community involvement toward healing, rather than punishing, their addicted tribal members" (Flies-Away et al., 2014, p. 10). For many tribes, Healing to Wellness Courts have been a cornerstone of their efforts to expand alternatives to detention and incarceration (Flies-Away et al., 2014). Though little formal evaluation is available, a 2005 evaluation of four Wellness Court programs found a statistically significant effect of intervention for adults but not for juveniles (Gottlieb, 2005). Tribes have increasingly adopted a family court model that enables entire families, including juveniles and adults, to be treated together (Gottlieb, 2005).

Other tribes exercise their jurisdiction primarily through an Indigenous system, while federal and/or state courts exercise limited jurisdiction to formally prosecute some offenders and offenses. For example, the State of California exercises criminal jurisdiction over Yurok Territory under a federal law called Public Law 280.[4] In building its own system, the Yurok have disinvested in incarceration and directed financial resources to a restorative system, including a Wellness Court. Through an agreement with the state, Yurok tribal members may be removed from the state court system and redirected into the tribe's system (Clarren, 2017).

[4]18 U.S.C. § 1162, 28 U.S.C. § 1360. See https://oag.ca.gov/nativeamerican/pl280

While their precise character and their relationship to formal systems varies, research on Indigenous approaches to justice highlights key principles. According to Melton, Indigenous justice approaches differ significantly from Anglo-American court systems.

> Conflicts are not fragmented, nor is the process compartmentalized into pre-adjudication, pretrial, adjudication, and sentencing stages. These hinder the resolution process for victims and offenders and delay the restoration of relationships and communal harmony. All contributing factors are examined to address the underlying issues that precipitated the problem, and everyone affected by a problem participates in the process. This distributive aspect generalizes individual misconduct or criminal behavior to the offender's wider kin group, hence there is a wider sharing of blame and guilt. The offender, along with his or her kinsmen, are held accountable and responsible for correcting behavior and repairing relationships. (Melton, 2005, p. 110)

Hand and colleagues (2012, p. 452) contrast Indigenous systems with Anglo-American criminal systems: "whereas the former seeks to reduce crime through punishment, restorative justice seeks to re-establish balance and harmony within each individual affected by an offensive act, within the perpetrator as well as the victim and the community."

Due to their emphasis on community definitions of safety, healing, and restorative practices, Indigenous-led efforts to reform criminal and juvenile systems offer alternative approaches to traditional models of criminal justice that deserve evaluation (Braithwaite, 2000). For example, many non-tribal courts have adapted a practice called Family Group Conferencing, a restorative justice program for juveniles and families based on traditional Māori approaches (Rolnick, 2021). More research is needed to determine how to measure success under such an approach and whether specific models deliver on their goals. As with any community-based approach, a particular Indigenous system will not be immediately transferrable to another community (Indigenous or otherwise).

Moreover, to the extent that these principles are based on a relationship between individual and community that is unique to small, kinship-based Indigenous communities, or to the extent they rely on shared religious beliefs and commitments, they may not be readily transferrable to non-Indigenous communities (Goldberg, 1997).[5] They do suggest, however, that local, community-centered approaches may be better able to ensure safety and justice, particularly for marginalized communities, than top-down outsider approaches.

---

[5]The practice of non-Indigenous communities adopting Indigenous approaches has also been criticized because of potential negative impacts on the communities and the practices (Moyle and Tauri, 2016; Tauri, 2014).

Community-Driven Accountability Efforts

A historic imbalance of power between law enforcement and the community that privileges the paradigm of law enforcement (especially concerning how problems are defined and the tools available to solve problems), along with law enforcement mistrust of the community, help to explain why community-driven approaches to police accountability can face strong resistance from police unions, local police, and even the community they serve (Gascón and Roussell, 2019; Jones, 2018). Cid Martinez noted to the committee, "How can we expect police to protect and serve the very communities that they are supposed to care for?" (the National Academies, 2021b, p. 8). Yet, community-driven approaches to police accountability can play an important role in building collective efficacy and trust in government more broadly. Such efforts are an important part of an ecosystem of accountability (the National Academies, 2018).

Community organizations have led efforts to analyze police budgets and explore alternative public expenditures to promote safety. Such community-led efforts propose increasing investments in community-based programs and other initiatives that aim to improve public safety at relatively low cost. For example, Oakland (CA) created a task force to create a roadmap for what it would look like to shift a portion of its law enforcement budget toward community-based programs. Since the creation of that task force, the sustained increase in murder rates has shifted local politics surrounding this issue, with several local city officials critically reconsidering this proposition. The Oakland City Council embraced a holistic approach—one that includes prevention, intervention, and concentrating on crime's root causes, as well as an adequately staffed police department (Har, 2021).

Community organizing in Chicago (IL) also led to the first-of-its-kind reparations for police torture. Chicago activists succeeded in 2002 in getting a state special prosecutor appointed to investigate the torture by police of more than 100 African-American men in Chicago through the 1970s and 1980s. Local community-led organizations called for the passage of the Illinois Reparations for Police Torture Victims Act, the establishment of a Chicago-based Center for Torture Victims and Families, and the appointment of an Illinois Innocence Inquiry Commission to adjudicate the innocence of torture victims. Such efforts seek to acknowledge past harms and pursue accountability and redress while also implementing political education efforts intended to prevent future harms (Hagan et al., 2022).

Civilian review boards are another example of accountability efforts. Citizen review was revived in the early 1970s as urban Black Americans gained more political power and as more political leaders came to see the need for improved police accountability (Finn, 2001). Most oversight procedures have come into existence after a high-profile case of alleged police misconduct (usually a shooting or other use of excessive force), often involving White officers and suspects from racial and ethnic minority groups. A 2001 report from the Department of Justice's Office of Justice Programs reviews approaches and implementation strategies for civilian oversight, in addition to their potential costs and benefits (see Finn, 2001).

In 2021, the Council on Criminal Justice's Task Force on Policing published *Policy Assessment on Civilian Oversight*, in which it reviewed a variety of models and the potential merits of civilian oversight. In this assessment, the task force concluded that rigorous empirical research on the impact of civilian oversight and the relative merits of different models does not exist, and that other research has yielded mixed findings about the ability of civilian oversight to reduce excessive use of force and other forms of police misconduct (Council on Criminal Justice, 2021). Specifically, the report notes many methodological problems, including failure to account for other policy changes during the research period. The result is a characteristically mixed message: civilian oversight has promising aspects and is helpful as a matter of public relations and transparency, but robust empirical evidence evaluating its effectiveness at reducing police misconduct or the use of force is lacking (the National Academies, 2022c). While potentially promising, additional testing and evaluation are needed.

Community-Based Anti-Violence Efforts

In 2021, the United States recorded the highest number of mass killings in nearly 50 years. Most mass killings, in which four or more persons are killed not including the perpetrator, involved people who knew each other: family violence, retaliatory street violence, or workplace violence. Since the start of the COVID-19 pandemic, the number of mass killings has continued to increase along with other forms of violence, including homicides in general and fatal shootings by police. A spike in gun violence in urban settings following the start of the pandemic, and in the wake of uprisings over the police murder of George Floyd, has drawn particular attention from media, policy makers, and politicians. Reflecting the local heterogeneity of violent crime, rates of lethal gun violence have since dropped in some cities that saw increases in 2020, while other cities have seen additional increases.

These recent patterns indicate a large increase in serious violence concentrated in Black and Latino communities. Addressing the persistent problem and concentration of gun violence in historically marginalized communities in the United States requires evidence-informed approaches grounded in an informed understanding of both the historical harm done by the criminal justice system over time as well as the documented impacts of criminal justice interventions on interpersonal and in particular lethal violence (see Chapter 8 for a more detailed discussion of criminal deterrence approaches). Such approaches took root years prior to recent increases in gun violence and provide promising models for community-driven and noncoercive models of gun violence prevention, especially in cases of retaliatory gun violence involving youth. These models can co-exist with other strategies for reducing gun violence, especially legislative efforts that have shown promise in regulating the supply of the most lethal firearms (see Chapter 7 for discussion of other approaches to gun violence).

In this section, we address the prevention of harm inflicted by interpersonal forms of violence and predatory victimization, including what is traditionally described as "street violence" and intimate partner violence. Community-based anti-violence initiatives recognize that the risk of involvement in serious violence, both for victims and for perpetrators, is distributed unevenly across the population. Individuals who are most likely to cause serious harm to others and face the highest risks of victimization are likely to be embedded in social networks that are highly exposed to violence. The networks themselves are located in social contexts of demography and neighborhood ecology in which serious violence tends to be most prevalent. Those who face the highest risks are likely to be highly marginalized. That is, they are "likely to be chronically alienated, disconnected, and distrustful of traditional structures and systems of support" (John Jay College Research Advisory Group on Preventing and Reducing Community Violence, 2020). At least since the 1980s, "the community" has been called on to participate with police in crime-fighting efforts, especially gun violence in urban settings. The current chapter focuses on community-based anti-violence initiatives, while Chapter 8 examines initiatives that involve coordination between community groups.

Community outreach or street outreach offers one proposed way of positively intervening with those at greatest risk of serious violence, although evaluations to date of street outreach programs provide mixed evidence of their effectiveness. Since the programs depend on the development of trusting relationships, often in the face of threats to safety, successful implementation can be difficult to achieve. In the sections that follow, we describe three violence prevention programs that have drawn great interest in recent years: Operation Ceasefire, Cure Violence, and Advance Peace. While the committee notes that only preliminary evidence of the programs' effectiveness is available, this section highlights some key components across programs that emphasize the building of community capacity to advance safety and reduce harm and inequality associated with criminal justice involvement.

Operation Ceasefire

Operation Ceasefire, first fielded in Boston in the 1990s, provides a model of police-community initiatives that rely on the "focused deterrence" of a small number of people identified as being at high risk of serious violence (Braga et al., 2001). Focused deterrence refers to the strategy to deter criminal behaviors by focusing on the consequences of participation in criminal behavior as well as the benefits of not participating in criminal behavior. For this, the community and the police work together with those at high risk of engaging in violence (RAND Corporation, 2022).

Operation Ceasefire is a program where law enforcement collaborates with identified community leaders to work with individuals most involved in violent activity, in neighborhoods across the country, to reduce gun violence. While the program typically relies on a zero-tolerance message for shootings, recently it has made more of an effort to provide resources and services to those targeted by law enforcement and has placed a greater emphasis on the importance of police departments acknowledging and apologizing for past racial harms. While there have been some successful results from Operation Ceasefire and other programs modeled after it, there are still major drawbacks to this type of collaboration with law enforcement, as it can exacerbate already present disparities and exploit already vulnerable populations (Jones, 2018).

Cure Violence

Operation Ceasefire and Cure Violence are programs that attempt to stop the transmission of violence following a model that public health interventions use to curb epidemics (Corburn et al., 2020). Cure Violence initially began as a branch of Operation Ceasefire in Chicago; it later became Cure Violence as the organization changed the program to not involve the use of law enforcement. Several studies have shown success in both of these programs in reducing urban gun crime (Braga et al., 2018; S.A. Delgado et al., 2017; Corsaro and Engel, 2015). Some of the key focused deterrence strategies involve community mobilization, street outreach, and partnerships among frontline staff in police, probation, corrections, and social services sectors. This model sees gun violence as a learned, transmissible behavior, one that can be interrupted through the training of community partners and local "credible messengers" to detect and interrupt conflict. This promotes safer and healthier behaviors and life directions among high-risk individuals and builds healthy social norms (Cure Violence Global, 2021); see Box 6-2 for a more detailed discussion of credible messengers.

The Cure Violence model uses three strategies to stop violence:

1. **Detect and interrupt potentially violent conflicts.** Violence interrupters are a new category of health workers who prevent violence by identifying and mediating potentially lethal conflicts in the community and following up to ensure conflict does not reignite.

BOX 6-2
Credible Messengers

Credible messengers are defined broadly as accepted members of a community who can support and influence others toward reducing violence. These messengers have become integral actors in community-based programs that provide social support to target populations, diverting young people who face the highest risks from violence.

This chapter discusses program models that rely on credible messengers in the context of violence prevention and racial and ethnic minority groups. For example, the perspectives of street workers with life experiences around violence or system contact can make them trustworthy and credible as well as protective of information that authorities might find incriminating. Street workers often operate as credible messengers, providing introductions to programs and social services, and addressing the personal needs of youth and their families. Outreach workers and violence interrupters are credible messengers in the communities they serve, as this allows them to reach out to at-risk individuals and connect with them in ways that others cannot.

SOURCE: Adapted from Butts, J. A., Roman, C. G., Bostwick, L., and Porter, J. R. (2015). Cure Violence: A public health model to reduce gun violence. *Annual Review of Public Health, 36*, 39–53.

2. **Identify and treat individuals at the highest risk.** Outreach workers help those at the highest risk to steer them away from violence by speaking to them in terms familiar to them, discussing the costs of using violence, and helping them to obtain support and social services (e.g., education, job training, drug treatment) to foster long-term behavior change and changes in life course.
3. **Mobilize the community to change norms.** Workers engage community leaders, local business owners, residents, faith leaders, and particularly individuals at high risk to shift the messages, expectations, and norms around violence for the long term (Cure Violence Global, 2021).

An additional key piece to this strategy is the use of credible workers. Public health outreach regularly employs workers who share the same background and come from the same neighborhood as those who are the most at risk for violence. Cure Violence hires and trains violence interrupters and outreach workers who already have the trust of community members and are able to influence and change behavior. The program's perspective is to view people who use violence as potential "patients" who are in need of a health-based intervention, not punishment. This allows the program to operate with an understanding that social networks and social relationships matter when it comes to influencing the behaviors of those most likely to be involved in violence.

Using this model, one solution to the problem of violence may be capacity building at both the individual and the community levels, and the delivery of services that rely on a network of community members and street outreach workers who work to strengthen both the individual capacity of community participants and the community's infrastructure. In contrast, programs that rely on the external threat of a punitive response from law enforcement run the risk of weakening a community's infrastructure by legitimizing targeted forms of law enforcement and removing individuals from the community via arrest and incarceration (Jones, 2018). Community outreach and violence interruption programs vary in their implementation, investment, and management strategy, and further research is needed to understand these contextual and implementation factors and their potential for reducing racial inequalities in crime and victimization.

Advance Peace

Advance Peace is a community outreach model that was created to interrupt gun violence and has been implemented in a number of cities, including Richmond and Stockton in California. While it was partly inspired by the Cure Violence model in Chicago, Advance Peace (also known as the Richmond model) is unlike the traditional Operation Ceasefire model. Instead of collaborating with law enforcement, its programs operate *in parallel* with them, thereby maintaining a separation between law enforcement officers and participating individuals.

The focused deterrence approach and the Advance Peace model both begin with a similar premise: that a large share of the risks of serious offending and serious victimization are concentrated among a small number of young people who are known to the police (Kennedy, 2011). The two differ in important ways on how to address this. Operation Ceasefire-style programs that partner with law enforcement typically demand change within a short window of time—if someone engages in criminal activity again, they are severely punished. By contrast, the Advance Peace model operates from an engagement paradigm, one that is informed by an appreciation of the time that relationship-building takes. Advance Peace makes an investment in the lives of youth most vulnerable to becoming perpetrators or victims of violence. Perhaps the most significant distinction is that, instead of a focused deterrence framework, Advance Peace relies on the concept of "the beloved community." It is a program that is based on engagement and encouragement instead of the threat of incarceration (Jones, 2018).

Another key difference between the Advance Peace–style programs and many other violence-intervention models is that Advance Peace workers are *city employees*. The founding director of the program in Richmond (CA), DeVone Boggan, elevated the status of street outreach workers by creating a new classification for city employees that would leverage the mark of an official criminal record for applicants. Preferred qualifications for the outreach positions would include past experience of incarceration *and* a felony gun charge. The "Neighborhood Change Agents," as they are officially categorized, must also be familiar with the neighborhoods in which they intervene. They are unionized. Their jobs come with benefits and, in general, a level of stability that other intervention models lack (Jones, 2018).

Although the Advance Peace program focuses solely on gun violence and interrupting violent retaliation, its approach is holistic in nature. Specifically, it views the young people it works with as at-risk people rather than criminals. The approach relies not on law enforcement to change behavior but on the motivating and transformative nature of mentoring relationships. These relationships are centered not just on accountability but also on respect, dignity, love, care, and compassion. The change agents are trained to meet young people where they are and to push them to expand their geographical and psychological boundaries. The program uses an 18-month fellowship (called a LifeMAP) that is not mandated by any law enforcement agency. The fellowship has seven components:

1. The development of a life management action plan;
2. Access to multiple healthy adults;
3. Connection to social services;
4. A LifeMAP milestone allowance that is paid after six months of participation in the program;
5. Transformative travel experiences (e.g., to colleges or international travel);
6. Access to an elder circle; and
7. Job preparation (a component that has been added since the start of the program) (Jones, 2018).

Outcomes

Programs organized around these sets of practices show some promise in preventing the involvement of participants in future gun violence and reducing harm done by the criminal justice system, though these results remain mixed and vary based on the program, location, and time frame of the evaluation. These programs invest in capacity building and in people and relationships, providing opportunities to build community safety and prevent criminal justice involvement. For example, an evaluation of the

Advance Peace program's impact in Stockton (CA) from 2018 to 2020 showed a 21 percent reduction in gun homicides and assaults as compared to the 2015–2018 averages. The majority of the street outreach fellows in the Stockton program were Black, with 32 percent previously incarcerated. Of those fellows, 71 percent had no new arrests during the course of the program (Corburn and Fukutome, 2021). In 2020, Advance Peace Sacramento intervened in 84 firearm incidents, which saved an estimated $36.5–84 million (Corburn, 2021a), and Advance Peace Richmond intervened in 28 firearm incidents, which saved an estimated $12.2–28 million in deaths and injuries (Corburn, 2021b).

Such initial findings and evidence from ethnographic research suggest that encouraging investments in capacity building, not simply crime fighting, may be promising. These investments made in people and relationships, not just programs, may be more sustainable in the long run (Jones, 2018; see also Anderson, 1999). Of course, a closer examination of the implementation and contextual factors that influence program effects is needed, as initial findings from the Safe Streets program in Baltimore (MD), which is based on a Cure Violence model, show an association with significant *increases* in violence in three locations in the city (Buggs et al., 2022; Webster et al., 2018, 2013). These findings may also suggest that program modifications are needed to achieve significant reductions in firearm violence, as the initial potentially positive effects of the program may have attenuated over time. Prior studies found that the Safe Streets program increased youth's preferences for nonviolent conflict resolution (Milam et al., 2016) and was associated with increases in preferences for nonviolent responses to interpersonal conflicts (Milam et al., 2018). The Cure Violence model has also been associated with reductions in youths' willingness to use violence to settle conflict (S. Delgado, 2017), improved confidence in police (Butts and Delgado, 2017), and increased confidence in a community's ability to reduce firearm violence (Picard-Fritsche and Cerniglia, 2013).

Other anti-violence programs exist outside of these three popular models, shaped to target other specific needs. One example is hospital-based violence interruption programs, in which social service providers make contact with victims of violence in the hospital setting and work to meet an individual's basic needs and to prevent retaliation (see the National Academies, 2019b). Many of these programs partner with community organizations to incorporate social services into the medical care offered in the hospital setting, hiring members of the community who are able to best treat and relate to those they serve. Results of effectiveness in future violence prevention are suggestive but inconclusive due to the lack of scale in the evaluations currently available (the National Academies, 2019b; Strong et al., 2016). This is also true regarding effectiveness for reducing future criminal justice contact (Shibru et al., 2007; see Chapter 7, Box 7-3).

Community-Driven Responses to Intimate Partner Violence

Historically, rates of domestic violence, including intimate partner violence, have disproportionately impacted marginalized and vulnerable populations. In the 25 years leading up to the start of the pandemic, rates of intimate partner violence, like rates of serious violence overall, steadily declined along with racial disparity (Raphael et al., 2019). However, during the pandemic, rates of intimate partner violence spiked (see, e.g., Piquero et al., 2021). Analyses of municipal reporting from Los Angeles and Indianapolis (IN), for example, reveal an increase in intimate partner violence incidents in the period immediately following the declaration of social restrictions in response to the pandemic, as compared to the period immediately prior (Mohler et al., 2020). Rosenfeld and Lopez (2021), using data across 13 cities, find that roughly the same number of domestic violence incidents occurred in the first nine months of 2021 as the year before; however, the authors note that these data should be interpreted with caution.

Intimate partner violence is a risk factor for criminal justice involvement among victims, who come into contact with the system as "offenders." The processes that transform victims into offenders are the criminalization of women's survival strategies; entrapment into crime by abusers and by gender, race, and class oppression; and enforcement through coercive laws, immigration policies, social welfare policies, and law enforcement practices. For example, some women are coerced to engage in crime by battering partners or by partners' financial abuse, some are arrested for defending themselves against abuse, and others are arrested for not protecting their children from domestic violence (Gilfus, 2002). Interventions that focus solely on enforcement and punishment of the offender (and often victims) exacerbate racial inequalities in the criminal justice system and more broadly.

Like community-led efforts for preventing gun violence, community-driven responses to intimate partner violence seek to address the mechanisms that drive these processes. New Hour for Women and Children, for example, addresses the intersection of intimate partner violence and criminal justice system involvement by providing incarcerated women who are survivors of domestic abuse with a variety of services, including reentry programming, parenting and wellness guidance, and support for those who have babies while incarcerated (the National Academies, 2021a).

These issues are particularly acute for Indigenous people, particularly those living in Indian Country, who are vastly under-protected by police. Murder is the third-highest cause of death for Native American and Alaska Native women, and the number of missing and murdered Indigenous women and girls is drastically undercounted. For example, in 2016, 116 cases were reported by the Department of Justice, while the National Crime

Information Center reported that the actual number was 5,712 (Lucchesi and Echo-Hawk, 2018). Several organizations highlight the role that the community can play in strengthening Indigenous systems of accountability and redemption and the role of tribal members, representatives, and organizations in mitigating harms done to victims and perpetrators when tribal, state, and federal justice systems intersect.

Sovereign Bodies Institute (SBI) is one example of a community-based, survivor-led organization that provides support services to Indigenous survivors of violence and the families of missing and murdered Indigenous women, girls, and two-spirit people.[6] SBI builds on Indigenous traditions of data gathering and knowledge transfer to create, disseminate, and put into action research on gender and sexual violence against Indigenous people.

SBI works to give the community more power and emphasizes the importance of having third-party advocates that can build trust with those that have been impacted and uplift those that can be an authoritative advocate for people in the system, as well as having larger roles for independent community-based advocates. The organization's governance is unique in that it is survivor led. SBI has a Survivors' Leadership Council that is comprised of Indigenous survivors of trafficking and survival sex work. The council advocates for victims and survivors, provides peer support to movement leaders who are survivors, and creates a platform for survivor voices, so that the world can learn from them directly. SBI and the Survivors' Leadership Council advocate for the importance of giving the community more power, having third-party advocates who can build trust with impacted people, and having meaningful roles for independent community-based advocates (the National Academies, 2021b).

One critical component of justice that can be practiced by all justice system stakeholders is deep, authentic, collaborative, and genuine listening. As an example, SBI facilitated this type of authentic listening in a circumstance where a sexual assault survivor felt unsafe with local law enforcement. In that case, the district attorney agreed to send investigators to meet with the survivor, listen to the story, explain the process, and answer questions. This type of deep listening is healing and conveys humility, service, generosity, and a survivor-centered sense of justice (the National Academies, 2021b). SBI reimagines the justice system as truly serving communities by putting the most vulnerable at the center of the conversation, focusing on healing the hurt individual, addressing the root causes of the crime, and addressing the impact on the community.

---

[6]Two-spirit people are traditionally Native Americans who are "male, female, and sometimes intersexed individuals who combine [gender identities] of both men and women with traits unique to their status as two-spirit people." See https://www.ihs.gov/lgbt/health/twospirit/ for more information.

Community-Led Crisis Response Efforts

Some jurisdictions are searching for ways to expand behavioral health diversion to earlier points in the criminal justice system process in order to reduce system contact and to connect people to services sooner. An example is 911 dispatch diversion, which connects people in a behavioral health crisis to mental health professionals rather than to law enforcement; this ensures the individual is connected to needed social services. Mental Health First: Community First Response Oakland (M.H. First) is an example of a community-driven model for non-police response to mental health crisis. M.H. First operates a weekend hotline with the aim of interrupting and minimizing the need for law enforcement in mental health crisis first response by providing mobile peer support, de-escalation assistance, and non-punitive and life-affirming interventions.[7] Additionally, one study conducted in Denver (CO) that diverted mental health emergency responses from law enforcement to health care providers found a 34 percent reduction in non-serious crimes, with no impact on serious crimes (Dee and Pyne, 2022).

Other communities have adapted non-punitive responses and diversionary models for mental health crisis. Houston, for example, implemented its Crisis Call Diversion (CCD) program in 2015 in response to a steady increase of mental health crisis calls to 911. Working with the Houston Emergency Center and the Harris Center for Mental Health and IDD, the police department determined that a high percentage of these calls could be more effectively resolved by quickly connecting callers to mental health professionals rather than dispatching police officers or emergency medical services (EMS) personnel. CCD now includes the Houston Fire Department (which joined the collaboration in 2017) and uses embedded professional tele-counselors within the 911 call center to help link people to non-emergency services when a call does not require police or EMS (Houston Police Department, 2021). In 2020 alone, CCD diverted 2,116 calls from the Houston Police Department and Houston Fire Department, and the program resulted in an estimated $1,666,732 annual savings to first responders (Council of State Governments Justice Center, 2021; Houston Police Department, 2020). Similarly, CAHOOTS, a program in Eugene (OR), has shown success in diverting behavior health crisis and related calls from the Eugene Police Department. These responders answer some calls from 911 that have been rerouted to them, as well as answer calls made directly to them. The diversion rates for CAHOOTS calls from the Eugene Police Department are between five and eight percent (Eugene Police Crime Analysis Unit, 2020). In Tucson (AZ) where crisis line staff are embedded within 911 dispatch to divert appropriate calls to the crisis line, 80 percent of calls are able to be

---

[7]See https://www.antipoliceterrorproject.org/mh-first-oakland

resolved over the phone. Of the remaining calls, the majority are resolved by a mobile crisis team in the community (Balfour et al., 2020). In addition to the community-run M.H. First, the City of Oakland is also establishing its Mobile Assistance Community Responders of Oakland program that is informed by the CAHOOTS model, which is targeted to help the people most impacted where they are with obtaining the referrals for assistance they need.[8]

Taken together, these approaches seek to reduce formal interaction with the criminal justice system and address health and behavioral health needs through other systems, including community services. As discussed in Chapter 4, increased exposure to criminal justice surveillance and enforcement among poor and racial and ethnic minority groups and decision making in key phases of the system reinforces and exacerbates racial inequality within and outside of the system. As such, diversionary programs, at the outset, have the potential to be preventive and reduce further racial inequalities.

Community-Led Efforts to Mitigate System Harm

As discussed in Chapter 4, the harms of contact with the criminal justice system are amplified among historically marginalized groups. Community-driven efforts seek to mitigate individual and intergenerational harm and to increase the capacity of the community to seek redress for harm.

One group most at risk of intergenerational harm from the criminal justice system are the approximately 10 million children and young adults in the United States who have had a parent incarcerated at some point in their lives. Recent estimates indicate that over 40 percent of all Black children have caregivers who have been charged with felonies, and nearly 20 percent have caregivers who have been imprisoned. Figures are similarly high for Native Americans (Finlay et al., 2022b).

Organizations like We Got Us Now exemplify a more general approach to disrupting intergenerational harm by amplifying the issues that children of incarcerated parents face through leadership by people who have been directly impacted by incarceration. The organization runs an "actionist" leadership program, which trains children who are directly impacted by parental incarceration to become leading subject matter experts committed to reforming the criminal justice system in their communities. We Got Us Now also builds public awareness; for example, the organization highlights the fact that incarcerated people who maintain close contact with their family members while incarcerated have better post-release outcomes and lower

[8]See https://www.oaklandca.gov/projects/macro-mobile-assistance-community-responders-of-oakland

recidivism rates. It also uplifts the resiliency and ingenuity of the families of incarcerated people and uses encouragement, empowerment, and support to help families thrive (the National Academies, 2021a, p. 4).

Transitions Clinic Network (TCN), a national consortium of more than 40 primary care centers that serves the primary health care needs of individuals returning from incarceration (Shavit et al., 2017), is another example of a community-led organization working to mitigate the harm of the criminal justice system. TCN programs include interdisciplinary primary care teams with community health workers with personal histories of incarceration. In a randomized controlled trial (RCT), participants in the TCN program in San Francisco had 51 percent fewer visits to the emergency department in a year compared with those who were assigned to receive expedited primary care in safety net systems (Wang et al., 2012). TCN participation also impacts future criminal justice contact, specifically being associated with lower rates of returning to prison for a parole or probation technical violation and fewer incarceration days compared with the control group (Wang et al., 2019). The involvement of previously incarcerated people is particularly critical to the TCN's success.

EXPANDING THE EVIDENCE BASE

Many of the community-led efforts discussed above are designed as non-punitive interventions for reducing contact with the criminal justice system, and thus reducing racial inequality, though many lack rigorous evaluation. A major barrier to the expansion of effective community solutions and continued innovation is the mismatch between what may be the most promising solutions and the knowledge base that is available for communities to draw on. In seeking "solutions," some jurisdictions and decision makers prioritize the use of experimental methods of evaluation, especially randomized controlled trials (RCTs), to inform policy-related decisions (the National Academies, 2017). The RCT, often regarded as the "gold standard" of scientific methods, has numerous strengths when applied in the right circumstances. However, it may not be an optimal or practical approach for evaluating multifaceted social programs, such as community-based programs for safety.

The RCT method may be insufficient for evaluating community programs for a number of reasons (Nagin and Sampson, 2019), including that they may be infeasible, expensive, or, in certain cases, ethically unadvisable (the National Academies, 2019a). The community programs discussed in this chapter exist in complex and variable public systems and community contexts that involve social interactions. These contextual factors are not simply variables to be controlled for purposes of experimental design. Rather, they determine how program services develop, how community members make use of programs, and what outcomes are possible (Goodman et al., 2018; Blamey and MacKenzie, 2007). Furthermore, such community programs are intentionally responsive to variable local community needs, values, strengths, and limitations. The services provided in a particular community are influenced by the specifics of local politics and cultural practices, civil and criminal justice systems, transportation systems, and the availability and quality of public and affordable private housing, mental health and substance abuse treatment programs, educational opportunities, and services for children and families (Goodman et al., 2018). Therefore, an RCT-based study of one program may have limited general applicability. A program based in another substantially different community context could not implement the RCT-evaluated model and expect similar success (Hess and Henig, 2008). An overemphasis on RCTs may result in a widening disparity between research and practice over time. That is, promising programs for which RCTs are appropriate will continue to be researched, highlighted, and disseminated, and will therefore improve. Promising programs not amenable to RCTs, in contrast, will receive less research funding, will be less highlighted, and will have far fewer opportunities to advance (Goodman et al., 2018; Whitesell, 2016).

In addition, there is a need to broaden the research paradigm for community safety programs to be more inclusive of other research methods. For example, researchers can employ methods from public health, sociological, and qualitative and participatory action research with directly impacted people. Moreover, the incorporation of lived experience through the participation of directly impacted people in research design and evaluation is critical, as they are often excluded from public policy making and yet have direct knowledge of how existing systems cause and fail to prevent harm.

Measuring Community Social Organization and Views on Safety

Part of these efforts would include taking seriously the input of community members in the definition and production of safety. To do so, researchers will need to create a better science of assessing the nature of those members' viewpoints. As we have noted, researchers have measured norms of informal control, social trust, and views on the criminal justice system by leveraging community surveys and what has been termed the "ecometrics" of community measurement (Raudenbush and Sampson, 1999). Drawing on the longstanding success of systematic measurement of individual properties, known as psychometrics, ecometrics focuses on metrics for assessing social ecologies, such as community surveys that aim to provide systematic data on whole neighborhoods. There is no such thing as a monolithic community, and we know historically that some voices have been silenced in marginalized communities. In others, the loudest voices are not necessarily representative. In one recent study, increased heterogeneity in the viewpoints of residents on collective efficacy was an important predictor of higher levels of crime (Brunton-Smith et al., 2018).

Taking heed of what community members want is not risk free nor does it necessarily imply agreement. "Defended" communities, for example, have in the past sought to keep out members of racial minority groups, often through vigilante forms of violence (Suttles, 1972). Independent of "what works," or even prior to considering what works, there is a need for an ongoing measurement system, ideally across entire cities, to assess and monitor the views of community residents and organizations, with a focus on racial equality rather than social exclusion.

Moreover, contemporary calls to involve the community in problems that are typically the primary domain of law enforcement need to acknowledge and address the limitations and unintended consequences of efforts to involve "the community" in this work, including how such collaborative efforts may privilege certain voices over others and exacerbate preexisting political fault lines and expose efforts that contribute to personal interests rather than the broader public good. Corruption and lack of accountability are age-old issues that have long bedeviled criminal justice agencies like the police. Indeed, much has been written about past corruption in policing, and the recent crisis of criminal justice in the United States has unsurprisingly led to calls for increased accountability mechanisms for the police and other agencies of formal social control. These are needed, as Chapter 8 discusses further.

Although a similar history of corruption does not exist with regard to community organizations, a parallel need nonetheless exists when setting up funding sources, resource allocation, and evaluation metrics for community-based efforts to address crime outside the purview of criminal justice. For example, a leading anti-violence community organization in Boston was recently indicted on federal fraud charges of misuse of funds for personal gain (Murphy et al., 2022). These may be the rare cases, but political legitimacy and public trust require transparency and accountability mechanisms across the board. Because community organizing efforts have historically been underfunded and in an ad hoc way, it is perhaps understandable that accountability mechanisms have taken a back seat.

We therefore recommend an integrated system of ongoing data collection and analysis sharing, transparency in methods, and accountability in assessing community-based interventions to promote human flourishing and collective efficacy as a means of addressing crime and violence. As one review puts it, existing research has "data blinders" that result from the fact that too much of the knowledge base for reducing violence depends on studies that measure public safety with data generated by law enforcement and subsequent processing within the criminal justice system (John Jay

College Research Advisory Group on Preventing and Reducing Community Violence, 2020, p. 21).

> **RECOMMENDATION 6-1: Cities and localities should partner with researchers to implement an ongoing system of data collection and omnibus surveys that would provide data on the views of resident safety and develop reliable and valid measures of the full range of residents' viewpoints.**

This measurement tool needs to be representative and designed to capture the full spectrum of racial diversity of community populations and for a broad representation of the cities or other areas in question. Although limited in geographic scope, an example of an approach rooted in community ecometrics of the sort recommended is "NeighborhoodStat," developed by the Mayor's Office of Criminal Justice in New York City. Its approach to community social organization and data collection centers the views of residents themselves and interactions with city decision makers. COMPSTAT became famous in New York City for prioritizing the collection and mapping of crime statistics by the police and using official metrics. NeighborhoodStat flips the script by prioritizing a community-based, problem-solving process grounded in the belief that public safety cannot exist without the public.[9] It is an acknowledgment that safe and thriving neighborhoods require resident leadership, community and government support, and resources to produce sustainable change. To support that goal, NeighborhoodStat employs a series of local meetings that engage residents in sharing, analyzing, and using data to identify public safety priorities and implement solutions.

Importantly, the kinds of neighborhood data collected by NeighborhoodStat include nontraditional measures like housing and food insecurity, trust, environmental hazards, and perceptions of safety. These data are provided by the community and can be analyzed or viewed by community members and discussed in meetings involving city decision makers. An example of how what the community values can lead to concrete efforts different than simple crime metrics is seen in the example of vacant homes and environmental toxins. Residents appear to be keenly aware of the numerous costs to the degradation of neighborhood environments and toxic inequalities like lead exposure. Vacant homes are a strong correlate of crime rates and residents have demanded their remediation. One recent study suggests that collective efficacy leads to lower crime in part because of its influence on the built environment, specifically fewer vacant homes (Lanfear, 2022). Collective efficacy can also lead to efforts to reduce lead in the environment

[9] For more information, see https://map.cityofnewyork.us/neighborhood-stats

and green vacant lots, with potentially important crime reduction effects (Branas et al., 2018; Kondo et al., 2018). Because toxic inequalities are disproportionately concentrated in Black, Latino, and Native American communities, more so than poverty (Sampson, 2022), reductions in them are a mechanism for reducing racial inequalities in crime. These pathways are examined in more detail in Chapter 7. The point here is that neighborhood social organization and the physical environment are connected and need to be integrated into the kinds of data that we consider. Crime statistics are but one measure of the health, well-being, and flourishing of communities.

Finally, when the public is allowed to express their opinions, however divergent they may be, and those views are measured systematically over time and made public, public trust will arguably be enhanced. Similarly, the communities on the receiving end of interventions deserve access to information about community-based organizations in terms of their intervention effectiveness, spending of resources, and accountability mechanisms when public trust is violated. Just as criminal justice agencies are subject to scrutiny and need to earn their legitimacy through just social actions, so too do community-based organizations and citizens.

CONCLUSION

Investments for community capacity appear promising in some cases, but additional research on implementation and contextual factors driving effects are needed, as results are heterogeneous across studies and locations. Such investments need to be paired with accountability mechanisms for spending to ensure evaluations to measure outcomes are conducted and resources are shared appropriately across and within communities.

> *CONCLUSION 6-1: Building healthy communities and reducing crime require investments in community capacity to define and advance safety and reduce harm and inequality associated with criminal justice involvement.*

Expanding the type of evidence from which we judge the success of these programs is critical for innovation, and investments in this type of research and evaluation is needed to continue to identify promising solutions and approaches to such a complex problem as racial inequality. Capacity building and investments made in people and relationships, not just programs, may be more sustainable in the long run.

> **RECOMMENDATION 6-2: Given some suggestive but incomplete results from a burgeoning literature on community-based anti-violence and related initiatives, federal and state agencies should explore the**

significant expansion of community-driven pilot programs that are fielded in combination with strong evaluation strategies.

The aim of such an initiative would be to expand community capacity to implement local strategies for safety together with a robust model for policy learning. Such efforts at each individual site would ideally be led by local community representatives and organizations. A lead agency could provide funding and oversight as well as field the pilots in a coordinated way to facilitate collective learning and accountability across sites; and given the sometimes burdensome nature of conducting such rigorous evaluation, federal and state agencies and philanthropic organizations could make investments to support such efforts, so that the burden is not on communities. For example, investments could link communities with academic institutions to partner and apply for grants and conduct evaluations, such as efforts like the Carnegie Community Engagement Classification.

In addition, many Indigenous communities rely on traditional systems of accountability, justice, and healing. Because of their emphasis on community definitions of safety, healing, and restorative practices, Indigenous-led efforts to reform justice systems suggest potentially promising models, though evaluations of such programs and models is especially limited.

RECOMMENDATION 6-3: **In order to better understand the potential for Indigenous approaches to be transferred to other communities (Indigenous or otherwise) and the potential for such models to reduce racial inequalities, federal agencies and philanthropic organizations should support research examining and evaluating tribal models of justice. Such evaluations may need to attend to conceptions of success to ensure that outcomes are aligned with community needs and priorities.**

Any investments in community initiatives will need to acknowledge and address the limitations and unintended consequences of efforts to involve "the community" in this work, including how such collaborative efforts may exacerbate preexisting community fault lines. A need for accountability for community-based efforts, like criminal justice responses, exists when setting up funding sources, resource allocation, and evaluation metrics for community-based efforts to address crime outside the purview of criminal justice. Finally, taking seriously the input of community members in the definition and production of safety is needed, and to do so, researchers will need to create a better science of assessing the nature of those community members' viewpoints.

7

Non-Criminal Policy Approaches to Reduce Racial Inequalities in Crime and Justice

Eradicating racial disparities in the criminal justice system, as has been documented in part one of this report, necessitates eliminating racial differences in criminal involvement. To do that, it is necessary to eliminate the systemic racism that underlies racialized disadvantage and racial residential segregation. With that in mind, in this chapter we address the noncriminal policy approaches (i.e., in systems outside of the criminal justice system) that hold promise for reducing racial inequality in the justice system. In addition to addressing the underlying causes of concentrated disadvantage and segregation, we seek to identify promising sites of intervention in adjacent social policy systems or institutions that can perpetuate, compound, or mitigate racial inequality in and outside the criminal justice system, such as education, child welfare, and health systems.

The non-criminal justice topics covered in this chapter reflect complex public policy issues that have been explored extensively in the social science literature. Here the committee synthesizes some of this evidence using high-quality studies with rigorous methodologies, systematic reviews, and authoritative sources to highlight potential strategies that can mitigate the relationship between the drivers of inequality and racial inequalities in crime and justice, consistent with the Statement of Task. When the evidence is mixed or findings are based on studies with a correlational research design, it is explicitly noted. The chapter begins with a discussion of strategies to improve the material well-being of communities, such as through economic supports and environmental interventions, reviews the evidence on related public health approaches to reduce crime and victimization, and ends with a discussion of individual system interventions, such as in child welfare, education, and health care.

IMPROVING THE MATERIAL WELL-BEING OF COMMUNITIES

The eradication of hyper-disadvantage is a long-term goal, one that policy makers need to immediately begin taking steps toward. In the meantime, certain steps might be taken to attenuate the negative consequences of the racialized patterning of social life in the United States through policies and programs to improve the material well-being of communities. This section addresses some possibilities toward that end, with a focus on economic and environmental interventions at the local level.

Policies and Programs to Address Underinvestment

This report takes a historical view on racial inequalities in crime and justice. It is a perspective that informs the need for structural policies and programs to address decades-long patterns of disinvestment (including underinvestment) from communities that have experienced disproportionately high rates of crime and criminal justice contact. The impacts of these policies and practices have been well documented by the social science literature (e.g., Faber, 2020; Lipsitz, 2011; Massey, 2007; Fullilove, 2001). For example, Faber (2020) traces the long-term consequences that redlining has had on segregation and patterns of spatial inequality, such as the enduring Black/White wealth gap. Benns and colleagues (2020) document an association between redlining and increased levels of gun violence in Louisville. The development of subsidized housing projects that concentrated low-income households in largely racially isolated groups has also been studied in relation to neighborhood effects and inequality (Freeman and Botein, 2002). For example, Popkin and colleagues (2000) use qualitative data to paint a portrait of public housing projects in Chicago (IL) in the 1990s, which were characterized by violence, crime, and hopelessness among residents as well as dysfunction in the Chicago Housing Authority. Massey and Kanaiaupuni (1993, p. 120) assert that public housing

> ...represents a key institutional mechanism for concentrating large numbers of poor people within a small geographic space, often within dense, high-rise buildings. Because low-income projects were systematically targeted to Black neighborhoods in a discriminatory fashion...this institutional mechanism greatly exacerbated the degree of poverty concentration for one group in particular—blacks.

In short, historical patterns of housing policy, such as segregation and redlining practices, have had cascading consequences for a variety of contemporary outcomes (e.g., wealth, neighborhood demographics, segregation, and crime). Investing in communities with concentrated disadvantage and high rates of crime and victimization is one promising mechanism for addressing the harms perpetuated by historical policies and practices.

Private Investments

Broadly speaking, investments from private sources such as banks directed at fortifying a community's housing stock can stimulate community social organization and help end the spiral of underinvestment and decline. As Vélez and Lyons (2014, p. 225) write, "External capital investments, ranging from bank lending to resources for public services, make or break the ability of neighborhoods to control crime." This form of investment offers important potential for remedying the relatively higher levels of neighborhood crime in Black and Latino communities than in White ones.

Investments that contribute to homeownership have also been explored in relation to reducing crime and racial inequalities, as large gaps in neighborhood crime rates exist between White and minority communities (see Chapter 3). A small but important body of work points to the important relationship between home mortgage lending and crime, which offers some suggestive evidence about the race-crime link at the neighborhood level. Controlling for a number of neighborhood-level characteristics (e.g., socioeconomic disadvantage, residential instability, immigrant concentration, and prevalence of young males), Saporu and colleagues (2011) use a multilevel Poisson model to establish the relationship between residential lending and violent and property crime among neighborhoods of different racial composition. The authors find that "residential lending has the greatest payoff in areas that suffer the most from criminal conduct: African American, Latino, and more disadvantaged neighborhoods" (Saporu et al., 2011, p. 96). A study of Cleveland neighborhoods employs time-series Poisson models and finds that relatively large shares of home mortgage loan dollars were associated with a reduction in rates of intimate-partner violence, and this correlation is enhanced as neighborhood disadvantage increases (Boggess and Chamberlain, 2021).

Relatedly, a body of work largely concerned with the fallout of the Great Recession, including the housing crisis, has focused on the consequences of neighborhoods losing homeownership through foreclosures and evictions. When homeownership loss spreads across a community, the community becomes vulnerable to crime and related processes. Minority communities, given their disproportionate share of these housing losses, become particularly vulnerable to public safety concerns. For instance, Kirk (2021) finds that neighborhoods with relatively large shares of evictions observed an increase in violent crime rates, and that such eviction levels help explain the increased risk of violent crime in Boston neighborhoods with relatively large shares of Black residents and high levels of concentrated disadvantage. Boessen and Chamberlain (2017) find that among Cleveland neighborhoods, being surrounded by foreclosures is associated with an increase in violent crime rates.

Some work has begun to explore what blocked access to lending capital means for neighborhood safety. In a study of Boston neighborhoods, Kirk assesses the geographic distribution of denials for home mortgage lending and the relationship between this patterning and violent crime. She finds that disadvantaged neighborhoods with large shares of Black residents have high rates of mortgage denials. Multivariate analyses also indicate that neighborhoods characterized by high levels of mortgage denials have higher levels of violent crime, partly because these denials increase resident perceptions of neighborhood social problems. Kirk (2021, p. 119) posits "that mortgage denials are a continuation of past acts of housing discrimination."

One limitation posed by these studies is the correlational nature of the analysis and findings. There may be unobserved or unaccounted-for neighborhood characteristics that could confound the relationship between investments and crime rates, which makes it difficult for researchers to establish a causal relationship. One significant caution to apply in interpreting these research findings is that evidence suggests the housing crisis that drove the Great Recession was largely the result of programs that incentivized subprime loans and an increase in household debt (Mian and Sufi, 2015). Nevertheless, policies that encourage private investments by banks into communities, especially policies that provide resources for home purchase or home retention, require further study as they could provide an opportunity to curb racial inequality in neighborhood crime, especially violence. Negative externalities associated with losses of homeownership, like eviction and foreclosures, would also potentially be thwarted with such place-based solutions.

Public Capital Investments

Cities can provide matching grants to community-based organizations for neighborhood improvement projects or services, which have been linked to reductions in crime and by extension in racial inequalities because of the focus on disadvantaged neighborhoods (Ramey and Shrider, 2014). Ramey and Shrider (2014) find that matching funds from a Seattle city program were associated with reductions in violent crime for all neighborhoods, and that this form of public capital is strongly correlated with reductions of violence in disadvantaged neighborhoods.[1] While the Seattle program relied on community-based organizations to plan, organize, and execute the projects, it also built a coalition among public agencies and local organizations to help build capacity to address social control and crime prevention. In more disadvantaged neighborhoods with relatively high levels of cumulative funding, the authors estimate that the expected violent crime rate dropped from almost 40 violent crimes per 1,000 to just over 15 violent crimes per 1,000 in 2007. This contingent finding suggests that neighborhoods with relatively high levels of concentrated disadvantage benefit the most from this form of investment.

A second paper, by Shrider and Ramey (2018), continues to document the importance of public capital in relation to violence in Seattle neighborhoods. In particular it finds that neighborhood matching funds could help to reduce violence by increasing local levels of mortgage lending. This indirect relationship is pronounced in Seattle's most disadvantaged neighborhoods. Neighborhood matching fund programs are an example of a type of community social control identified in Carr's (2005) study of a neighborhood in Chicago. Carr found that people are often too busy or fearful to engage in direct interventions in local problems, so residents worked to address local problems by engaging in a new parochial social control based on partnerships between the people living in the neighborhood and public agencies. See Chapter 6 for a discussion of social control and collective efficacy as principles of community-driven safety and responses to harm.

Such public investments may foster long-term commitments to, and investments in, communities as residents see the successes of their tangible efforts, and this in turn might lead to subsequent reductions in crime and better neighborhood conditions overall (Krivo, 2014). Vélez and Lyons (2014) note that the documented relationship between the Neighborhood Matching Fund program and violent crime reduction in Seattle underscores the significant role that external investments can play in facilitating neighborhood well-being, social control, and crime. However, researchers caution that before forming partnerships, local organizations need to consider who they are investing in, who is being neglected, whether the investments are beneficial or harmful (e.g., subprime loans), and how the political

[1]The Seattle Neighborhood Matching Fund was established to provide matching funds for neighborhood improvement, organization, or projects developed and implemented by community members. A central component is the community match, which requires recipients to match their award with contributions from the community (e.g., as volunteer time, materials donated, professional services donated, or cash). The program also contains a stipulation that at least 51 percent of the total Neighborhood Matching Fund funding must go to moderate-to-low–income neighborhoods and project sites. For more information see http://www.seattle.gov/neighborhoods/programs-and-services/neighborhood-matching-fund

context might affect everyone involved (Krivo, 2014; Leverentz, 2014; Vélez and Lyons, 2014).

Public-Private Partnerships to Promote Community Development

Cities and municipalities can collaborate with local businesses to fund Business Improvement Districts (BIDs). BIDs are self-taxing districts created by property owners to provide local public goods, typically for community service. BIDs allocate resources to enhance a variety of services, such as sanitation and public safety, which are typically provided by public agencies. In the case of BIDs, these services are funded by increased tax burdens on commercial properties that have been approved by local residents (Meltzer, 2012). A primary goal of BIDs is to improve the built environment as well as public safety; hence, they are often termed "clean and safe" initiatives (Hoyt, 2004). Studies document that this type of public capital intervention is linked to reductions in serious street crime (MacDonald et al., 2010; Brooks, 2008; Hoyt, 2004).

MacDonald and colleagues (2010) find that BID implementation was associated with a 12 percent reduction in robberies and an eight percent reduction in total violent crimes in Los Angeles neighborhoods. Brooks (2008) finds that neighborhoods with BIDs in Los Angeles have between six percent and 10 percent less crime than otherwise similar neighborhoods. Additional research indicates that the introduction of BIDs in Los Angeles was associated with a decrease in crime and police arrests over time, with a corresponding increase in criminal justice cost savings and minimal displacement of local crime to neighboring areas (Cook and MacDonald, 2011). However, Clutter and colleagues (2019) find that in Cincinnati, BIDs played a role in the spatial distribution of robberies at the level of street blocks. That is, street blocks within the BIDs observed *higher* robbery counts, after controlling for street factors. More research is needed in different neighborhood contexts to parse the mechanisms or mediating factors that might influence the relationship between BIDs and violent and nonviolent crime.

Place-Based Approaches

Shaping the Built Environment

As noted in Chapter 3, crime can be influenced by the built environment as well as the socioeconomic environment, and both differ across racial groups. Broadly, the built environment reflects the physical conditions of a community, including human-made physical components, design, and permitted use of space, including transportation, parks, and open space (the National Academies of Sciences, Engineering, and Medicine, 2017). Place-based interventions that modify features of the built environment have been the subject of experimental studies to examine how crime might be reduced in communities.

One such intervention is the "greening" of spaces, which entails the remediation of vacant lots or spaces by removing trash and debris, grading the land, planting trees and grass, and/or installing fencing. A review by Kondo and colleagues (2018) indicates that housing and blight remediation of buildings and land are the interventions that most consistently reduce violence, as compared to interventions addressing alcohol availability, transit changes, and school opening. Another systematic review, which covers 10 empirical studies, finds that while there is evidence to support the positive impact of green space on crime, comparisons across the studies are difficult due to variations in study design and mixed measurement and results (Bogar and Beyer, 2016). Shepley and colleagues (2019) synthesize some of the quantitative and qualitative evidence on the impact of green space on violent crime (i.e., on murder and non-negligent manslaughter, forcible rape, robbery, and aggravated assault). Their review of 45 publications indicates that a limited evidence base suggests that the presence of parks and green space reduces urban crime; however, many papers paid insufficient attention to confounding variables. Among the papers included in their review, Boessen and Hipp (2018) examine nearby demographics as moderators and find some protective influence of parks on Latino neighborhoods. Shepley and colleagues (2019) also point to a few hypothesized mechanisms by which green space might influence crime: social interaction and recreation, community perception, nature-induced stress reduction, climate modulation, and spaces with territorial definition (Shepley et al., 2019).

Recent research identifies the demolition of vacant or abandoned buildings as a promising strategy to reduce crime in the immediate vicinity, but effects are limited spatially (Wheeler et al., 2018). Other systematic reviews reinforce these findings on the association between modifying the built environment and reductions in crime (e.g., Inlow, 2021). MacDonald and Stokes (2020) trace reductions in crime to gentrification and subsequent changes to land use but note the need for a clearer analysis of how crime becomes spatially displaced in these processes. While these studies do not examine racial disparities in criminal victimization or offending as a primary outcome, there is a body of literature that suggests there are racial and socioeconomic inequalities in access to green spaces across the United States (Nesbitt et al., 2019; Wen et al., 2013).

Communities, particularly those with vacant lots, abandoned houses, and distressed commercial corridors, could consider strategic investment in these types of place-based programs. There is evidence to suggest that such programs are scalable, are cost effective, and reduce crime (MacDonald et al., 2021; Kondo et al., 2015). They could be concentrated in neighborhoods with the highest rates of crime and victimization, could be replicated across the country, and could employ individuals from the communities where they are applied. In seeking to improve public safety, communities need to examine not only how to "restore people, but also restore places" (MacDonald et al., 2021).

It's also important to note that revitalization initiatives can have unintended consequences, including gentrification. Undertaking such work is a balancing act. On the one hand, concentrated poverty can have a pernicious effect on communities, but on the other hand, gentrification can result in people being priced out of and displaced from their communities. Therefore, communities need to be mindful of these unintended consequences when undertaking such initiatives. See Box 7-1 for an example of a community urban greening program with promising results in crime reduction at relatively low cost.

BOX 7-1
"Greening" Cities: Pennsylvania Horticultural Society (PHS) LandCare Program

The PHS LandCare program, which began in a single neighborhood and expanded to incorporate the entire city, involves turning vacant lots into park-like settings that are cleaned and maintained through community partnerships. The program has been linked with reduced crime over the long term, including reductions in robberies, drug crimes, public order offenses, and total crime.

This program started as a pilot project with a neighborhood association in 1996. Vacant treatments consist of removing trash and debris, grading the land, planting grass and trees to create a park-like setting, and installing low wooden post-and-rail fencing. Interventions established focus areas, with clusters of "cleaned and greened" vacant lots throughout Philadelphia.

The PHS LandCare program has since expanded through partnerships with local contractors to the entire city, transforming more than 12,000 vacant lots and more than 18 million square feet of land. Approximately a quarter of the city's vacant lots have been remediated and maintained.

The program is funded by local community groups, the city, and private philanthropy. The program costs about $5 per square meter ($1,000–$3,000 per lot) for the initial transformation of property, and then $0.50 per square meter for annual maintenance ($150 per year).

BOX 7-1 Continued

LandCare's greening program reduces crime according to most measures: total crime was reduced by 5.59 percent, public order crime by 9.28 percent, drug crime by 10.88 percent, aggravated assault by 1.28 percent, and robbery by 20.75 percent.

The implications of remediating vacant lots and abandoned housing for gun violence include these:

- Every $1 in vacant lot remediation returns $26 in net benefits to taxpayers and $333 to society at large.
- Every $1 in vacant housing remediation returns $5 in net benefits to taxpayers and $79 to society at large.
- Sizable reductions in gun crimes could be achieved through citywide efforts.

NOTES: This summary is based on a factual accounting of what was presented at public information-gathering sessions for the committee's consideration. The public sessions were one mechanism that the committee used to gather information on the perspectives and experiences of communities that are disproportionately affected by racial inequalities in the criminal justice system. The statements reflected here are those of the presenters and do not represent the views of the committee or the National Academies.
SOURCE: J. MacDonald, *Changing Places: Renovating and Rebuilding Infrastructure to Reduce Racial Disparities in Victimizations and Arrests* (Committee on Reducing Racial Inequalities in the Criminal Justice System Workshop #2: Addressing the Drivers of Criminal Justice Involvement to Advance Racial Equity, Washington, DC, March 15, 2021).

Moving to Opportunity

The Moving to Opportunity (MTO) project exemplifies an important place-based study that randomly assigned families to rent-subsidized housing vouchers to explore the effects of concentrated poverty and neighborhood conditions on life outcomes. In 1994, more than 4,500 low-income families were randomly assigned to one of three groups: (1) those offered a housing voucher that could be used to move to a low-poverty neighborhood, (2) those offered a traditional Section 8 housing voucher, and (3) a control group. The MTO project featured a series of follow-up evaluations with the families—once for an evaluation four to seven years after a given family had been assigned (e.g., Ludwig, Duncan, and Hirschfield, 2001; Ludwig et al., 2001; Ludwig, Duncan, and Pinkston, 2000), and again from 2008 to 2010 for an evaluation 10–15 years post assignment (e.g., Ludwig et al., 2013, 2012; Sciandra et al., 2013). These evaluations examined the effects of the MTO project on adults and children, how these effects changed over time, and the potential mechanisms by which the outcomes were produced. The main categories of outcomes that were studied over time were adult economic self-sufficiency, mental health, physical health, education, and risky behavior (i.e., crime, delinquency), all of which have been documented in the evaluative literature cited above.

With respect to the crime and delinquency outcomes, the offer to relocate to lower-poverty areas was found to reduce arrests among female youth for violent and property crimes, relative to the control group. For males, the offer to relocate reduced arrests for violent crime, at least in the short run, but increased problem behaviors and property crime arrests. Ludwig, Duncan, and Hirschfield (2001) find a 30–50 percent reduction in juvenile arrests for violent offenses among the group of relocated families. Sciandra and colleagues (2013) document substantial initial reductions in violent-crime arrests along with sizable increases in property-crime arrests for experimental group males. These crime effects attenuate over time along with differences in neighborhood conditions.

The gender difference in treatment effects seems to reflect differences in how male and female youths from disadvantaged backgrounds adapt and respond to similar new neighborhood environments (Kling et al., 2005). Chetty and colleagues (2016) examine the long-term effects of MTO and find differential effects depending on the age of the children when they moved. Children who moved when they were younger (i.e., before the age of 13) saw increases in college attendance and earnings, while children who moved during adolescence experienced slightly negative effects. These findings corroborate the child development literature that emphasizes the importance of early intervention to shape life outcomes (the National Academies, 2019a).

The randomized nature of the MTO project has made a major contribution to the social sciences, as the authors were able to eliminate selection bias, a significant confounding variable in this area of research. However, despite the strong experimental design of the studies, scholars debate the generalizability and application of the findings to neighborhood-level theory broadly (Sampson, 2008). For example, the MTO project was an individual-level intervention for primarily Black families living in extreme poverty, which makes the findings limited to a specific segment of the population. Furthermore, the social mechanisms that explain the neighborhood effects observed in the MTO project are unknown, given the many correlates to neighborhood poverty (Sampson, 2012). Nonetheless, the MTO project provides important findings for reducing racial inequalities and directions for future research that integrates other important factors such as urban dynamics, social structure, and developmental neighborhood effects.

Labor Market Solutions

There is a well-developed literature on the relationship among race, labor markets, and crime (Lang and Kahn-Lang Spitzer, 2020; Crutchfield, 2014; Bushway and Reuter, 2002; Western et al., 2001). Wilson's (1996) theory of joblessness postulates that poor job prospects drive crime rates through the weakening of social ties, producing psychological strain, and through a reduced perceived cost of engaging in crime. This theory has been reinforced by research indicating that joblessness has a stronger effect on neighborhood violent crime than poverty itself (Dollar et al., 2019). Labor market discrimination has also been the subject of research, based on job application data, as differential treatment by race appears to still be prevalent (Bertrand and Mullainathan, 2004), particularly in areas with high crime rates (Mobasseri, 2019). In addition, qualitative research corroborates these findings of practices of racial discrimination in the labor market, particularly toward job applicants who are Black and/or from low-income backgrounds (Kirshenman and Neckerman, 2019). Labor market solutions offer one potential lever within a broader context of cumulative, intergenerational economic disadvantage for specific racial and ethnic groups (e.g., Black, Latino, and American Indian populations). This economic disadvantage can be traced in part to the patterns of policy investment in White populations that many other racial and ethnic groups did not benefit from (see Chapters 1 and 3 for discussions on structural racism and concentrated disadvantage, respectively).

This section explores labor market solutions as levers to provide opportunities for people living in disadvantage or those returning from incarceration to secure gainful employment. It is important to make a clear distinction between recommended efforts to improve the labor market prospects of adults living in disadvantaged neighborhoods and efforts to enhance the reentry of previously incarcerated persons. Both efforts are thought to be anti-criminogenic. However, while the former aims to improve the material well-being of disadvantaged communities and their residents and thereby reduce crime rates and racial inequalities, the latter aims to improve job prospects during reentry from prison, more specifically to reduce recidivism.

Employment Opportunities for Labor Market Success

Chapter 4 documents the consequences of criminal justice system involvement for racial inequality. One significant consequence is the impact that system involvement can have on future employment opportunities. While incarceration is often studied as a barrier to securing employment, research shows that even low-level offenses and/or history of arrest or conviction without incarceration can affect employment outcomes negatively (Agan and Starr, 2018; Uggen et al., 2014).

The effect of having a record of incarceration as a major barrier to securing employment is pronounced among Black job seekers (Decker et al., 2015). Moreover, Black people who have returned from prison have higher unemployment and recidivism rates when compared to White people returning from prison (Lockwood et al., 2015). The neighborhood conditions that a person who is formerly incarcerated returns to can also shape labor market outcomes (Schnepel, 2018; Yang, 2017; Morenoff and Harding, 2011; Raphael and Weiman, 2007). For example, returning to communities with high unemployment rates is a risk factor for violent recidivism among Black men (Wang et al., 2010). Given that unemployment is a strong predictor of recidivism, programs or policies that enhance employment opportunities in support of reentry efforts are a potential mechanism for reducing racial disparities in criminal just involvement (the National Academies, 2022a).

Programs and conditions designed to promote labor market success have been studied as interventions to support reentry efforts. Previous research indicates that programs aimed at shifting people in low-income settings from criminal activity and into employment need to reduce the attraction of crime and treat substance abuse problems, while providing social and educational supports to help high-risk individuals obtain gainful employment (Bushway and Reuter, 2002). Quality social ties (e.g., familial connections) have been shown to influence recidivism and job attainment (Berg and Huebner, 2011). Zhang and colleagues (2019) conducted a community-level review of reentry programs and found that programs that provide training and placement services to returning citizens using a holistic approach (i.e., with a focus on training and job placement) are the most effective in ensuring successful reentry into the workforce.

Research emphasizes the importance of placement into high-quality jobs with potential for upward mobility through educational (vocational and GED [General Educational Development Test]-based) and entrepreneurship programs (Zhang et al., 2019; Crutchfield et al., 2011). Lacoe and Betesh (2019) find that the long-term effectiveness of employment-focused approaches to improve employment outcomes or to reduce criminal justice system involvement is not consistent across studies; nonetheless, their review reinforces the value of vocational training as a prerelease intervention. Two randomized controlled trials (RCTs) suggest that transitional employment programs are not as effective beyond the initial implementation period and therefore have less success in terms of long-term employment outcomes (Cook et al., 2015; Valentine and Redcross, 2015).

In summary, a better understanding of the key mechanisms of reentry employment programs and contextual, protective factors to support sustained labor market success would inform a strong evidence base from which to build solutions. Box 7-2 presents an example of a policy intended to remove barriers to employment, for which evidence suggests there might be unintended consequences.

Homeboy Industries: Community-Building Reentry Services

Homeboy Industries is one example of a promising program that provides job training opportunities and free social services for people who are formerly gang involved and/or previously incarcerated. Each client is assigned a case manager who helps him or her set a goal plan, which might be obtaining a high school diploma or GED, following a course of action for release from parole or probation, or identifying needed services, classes, and skills in order to find outside employment. Many of the participants arrive into young adulthood with no support system and absent families. Homeboy Industries provides a supportive community, a sense of family, and a place where they can come to help find their strengths, learn job skills, get an education, learn new life skills, and become contributing members to their families and communities (Office of Justice Programs, 2021a). The program's efforts to transform the lives of its participants reflect an appreciation of the social nature of personal transformation and redemption, with a focus on building the capacity of its participants. In contrast to the "focused deterrence" framework, Homeboy Industries' efforts, described by sociologist Edward Flores (2013) as "integrative redemption," are shaped by a theory that emphasizes "recovery by way of reintegration into the mundane world."

Despite the challenges of evaluating the success of such a program within a dynamic environment, Leap and colleagues (2010) employed quantitative and qualitative methods to assess the program and identified the

BOX 7-2
"Ban the Box" Policies: Unintended Consequences

The "ban the box" (BTB) movement took hold in different jurisdictions to enact policies that would delay employers asking for information about an applicant's criminal record in order to increase employment opportunities for previous offenders and, ultimately, reduce racial disparities in employment outcomes. This is an example of a well-intended policy that, research suggests, had unintended effects that can be harmful for specific racial and ethnic groups.

A growing body of literature suggests that the BTB policies have led to labor market discrimination (Raphael, 2021; Schneider et al., 2021; Agan and Starr, 2018; Solinas-Saunders et al., 2015). Doleac and Hansen (2020) find net negative effects on employment for young, low-skilled Black men; specifically, this group is 3.4 percentage points less likely to be employed after the implementation of BTB than before. For young, low-skilled Hispanic men, BTB reduces employment by 2.3 percentage points. This effect is most pronounced for those job applicants with no high school diploma or GED, a group for whom previous incarceration is more likely. Shoag and Veuger (2016) also consider the effects of BTB and find that more people are employed in high-crime neighborhoods after BTB when compared to employment in low-crime neighborhoods. However, concerns about changes in neighborhood composition over time, controlling for demographic characteristics, and concerns about consistency in the way employment was measured during this time period[a] are highlighted and addressed by Raphael (2021).

Agan and Starr (2018) conducted a field experiment that tested the BTB policy's effect on the likelihood of securing a job interview by submitting job applications from fictional candidates. These authors find that before the policy was enacted, White applicants were called back at a slightly higher rate than Black applicants. This disparity increased *six-fold* after the policy went into effect, and White applicants with a criminal record appeared to benefit most from the policy. Schneider and colleagues (2021) discovered that after jurisdictions implemented BTB, some employers used strong warnings of criminal background checks later in the hiring process as an alternative method of "gatekeeping."

These studies show how well-intentioned policies that remove information about racially imbalanced characteristics from job applications can do more harm than good for job seekers from specific racial and ethnic groups. A better understanding of how employers interpret and use information in employment decisions is needed to inform employment policies in the future (Raphael, 2021).

---

[a]The American Community Survey changed the way employment was measured in 2008.

following mediators that shape program outcomes: improved self-esteem, attachment, self-efficacy, emotion regulation, coping skills, and prosocial orientation. In 2020, the program documented having 476 full-time trainee participants, 2,746 additional community members receiving program and service support, and $41,400 in fines and fees removed for participants

(Homeboy Industries, 2020). Taken together, community-building and re-entry programs such as Homeboy Industries and Cure Violence (discussed in Chapter 6) share a set of practices that encourage change. Jones (2018) notes that these programs appreciate "the importance of place, time, and community as well as the power of transformational relationships."

Crime Control Approaches through Employment Programs

The literature on jobs as a delinquency prevention strategy for youth is mixed in terms of practical application (Millenky et al., 2011; Schochet et al., 2008; Uggen, 2000; Bloom et al., 1997). It is worth noting, however, that there have been promising results from summer youth employment programs (Heller, 2021). For example, experiments in Chicago, New York City (NY), and Boston (MA) generally have led to similar findings, namely that summer youth employment programs resulted in large declines in criminal justice involvement and violence, although little improvement in future employment was found on average (Kessler et al., 2021; Davis and Heller, 2020; Modestino, 2019; Gelber et al., 2016; Heller, 2014). However, using a machine learning method Davis and Heller (2020) uncover some heterogeneity of effect: youth who benefit most from the summer employment program in Chicago are more likely to be younger, Hispanic, and female; more engaged in school; and less criminally involved than their counterparts, who are not predicted to experience positive outcomes. These data on subgroups could inform tailored approaches to employment programs for youth.

The Role of Public Transportation Systems and Spatial Mismatch in Labor Markets

A labor market problem for working class and low-income people in some locations is the spatial mismatch between where the jobs are and where potential employees live. This is part of the explanation for Black/White employment differences (Gobillon et al., 2007; McLafferty and Preston, 1996; Holzer, 1991). Historically, Black Americans and Latino people have tended to live in central cities, frequently in highly segregated neighborhoods (see Chapter 3), but increasingly industries and jobs have dispersed out of the central city into suburbs, thus contributing to racial labor market inequality. McLafferty and Preston (1996) find evidence that supports this thesis and note that African American and Hispanic women's experiences with mismatch result from their being more reliant on public transportation. However, it should be noted that more recent trends show that the suburbs are diversifying and that Black and Latino households in diverse suburbs have higher median incomes than the national average (Rastogi, 2021). Hellerstein and colleagues (2008) believe that spatial mismatch is less the problem than what they refer to as "racial mismatch," the proximity of jobs where people of color are hired to where people of color live. However the mismatch problem is conceptualized, it remains the case that residential segregation, combined with job and industrial dispersion, perpetuates Black/White and Hispanic/White employment inequalities.

Improving the routing and efficiency of public transportation may be another area of research to address this spatial mismatch between workers from disadvantaged neighborhoods and the locations of jobs. Workers need access to affordable, efficient transportation, as public transit that requires residents of poor neighborhoods to make multiple transfers and travel for hours between home and work is unlikely to improve their labor market prospects.

If designed and maintained properly, public transportation facilitates safe mobility and is accessible to all residents, regardless of geographic location. Moreover, transportation systems can play a role in mediating spatial disadvantage by providing residents with access to economic opportunity, social goods, and community services (Dodson et al., 2004). However, current research suggests that transportation costs are a barrier to mobility for households in poverty, which are disproportionately represented by African American and Hispanic people (Federal Highway Administration, 2014).

In addition, Andersson and colleagues (2018), assessing how improved job accessibility where a spatial mismatch is present might affect unemployment, find that it significantly decreases the length of unemployment among lower-paid, displaced workers. Their findings also revealed that Black workers, women workers, and older workers were more sensitive to the effects of job accessibility than the other subgroups studied. Although the evidence presented here does not directly connect transportation and job accessibility to racially disparate outcomes in criminal behavior and/or system involvement, this section presents a potential area for future research: if and how racial inequalities in crime and justice might be addressed given the disparities that are observed in job accessibility and access to quality transportation.

PUBLIC HEALTH APPROACHES TO VIOLENCE

Public safety and violence are significant indicators of health and community well-being. Violent victimization affects health by causing psychological and physical injury, which can lead to disability and, in some cases, premature death. Beyond the risk of injury and death, violent victimization also has far-reaching health consequences for individuals, families, and neighborhoods. Furthermore, research shows that simply being exposed to violence can have detrimental effects on physical and psychological well-being (Pinderhughes et al., 2015; Felitti et al., 1998). Violent victimization and exposure to violence have been linked to poor health outcomes among racial minority groups, including chronic diseases (e.g., ischemic heart disease, cancer, stroke, chronic obstructive lung disease, diabetes, and hepatitis), asthma-related symptoms, obesity, posttraumatic stress disorder, depression, and substance abuse (Prevention Institute, 2011). Some research also indicates a link between neighborhood crime rates and adverse birth outcomes, such as preterm birth and low birthweight (Egerter et al., 2011).

Given the connection between public health and violence, researchers have explored interventions that target unsafe environments to advance health and safety while also minimizing the harms of contact with the criminal justice system. Public health frameworks for addressing violence include efforts to advance data-driven policies that create environments that are less conducive to violence or that facilitate social conditions that constrain violence (Webster, 2022). The sections below discuss promising areas of public health policy, including firearm reduction policies, environmental exposure programs, and alcohol policies as they relate to racial disparities in violence, crime, and system contact. These are complex public policy issues that require careful consideration of the evidence, including study methodology, limitations of the available data, tradeoffs and unintended consequences, cost, and political will. The committee is not constituted to delve deeply into these issues or to provide recommendations in these areas; however, these areas warrant discussion as they are connected to racial inequalities in crime and justice. Here, the committee relies on systematic reviews, high-quality studies, and reviews of the literature from authoritative, evidence-based sources to synthesize some of the literature on public health approaches to violence.

Firearm Violence and Related Policies

To address the problem of racial disparities in crime, victimization, and criminal justice involvement, one needs to consider the issue of gun violence. As Chapter 2 discussed, the United States has observed a significant increase in firearm homicides in recent years. Gun violence is a racial equity issue, as marginalized racial and ethnic groups are disproportionately harmed by gun-related injury and death, by arrests and criminal charges, and by diminished community cohesion as a result of neighborhood-level gun violence (see Chapters 2 and 3 for more on firearm violence trends). Johns Hopkins Center for Gun Violence Solutions has developed a racial equity impact assessment tool to identify and assess the factors influencing racial equity that should be considered with firearm policy development and implementation (Educational Fund to Stop Gun Violence et al., 2022). The Center proposes a racial equity framework for gun violence prevention and recommends the following for a more equitable gun violence prevention movement:

- Identify and engage diverse members, and routinely ask who is missing and invite them to join;
- Identify the collective interest and allow for all collective members to provide ongoing input in developing a shared vision and goals;
- Commit to personal and collective growth and healing (i.e., truth and reconciliation);
- Prioritize inclusivity when identifying priority policies, programs, and strategies that address interests of all communities represented;
- Identify stakeholders, their resources, and influence to more effectively reach key policy decision makers;
- Engage in ongoing evaluation that is inclusive of all members;
- Make equitable collaboration sustainable; and
- Celebrate the victories and acknowledge the inevitable setbacks.

Previous reviews have examined firearm violence and policies (see, for example, American Psychological Association, 2013; NRC, 2005; Kaplan, 1984); this section highlights two more recent, comprehensive reviews of the evidence.

The John Jay College Research Advisory Group on Preventing and Reducing Community Violence (hereafter the John Jay research group) underscores the need to confront the issues of firearms as a comprehensive approach to reducing violence. Firearm availability is associated with rates of homicide across the United States (Siegel et al., 2014; Cook and Ludwig, 2006) and is also a reliable predictor of rates of fatal police violence (Hemenway et al., 2019). The John Jay research group reviews the evidence on reducing access to firearms as one potential mechanism to reduce homicides and other violence. For example, one recent study examined changes in state-level policies governing access to firearms, including child-access prevention, right-to-carry laws, and stand-your-ground laws (Schell et al., 2020). The results suggest that child access protection laws alone could lead to 11 percent fewer firearm deaths. Other research points to purchaser licensing laws with comprehensive background check requirements as being associated with lower firearm homicides and suicide rates in one state (McCourt et al., 2020).

In summary, the John Jay research group concludes that violence can be reduced through policies that limit access to firearms, increase restrictions for people with histories of violent crime, reduce access to firearms for young people, impose waiting periods, and increase required firearm training (John Jay College Research Advisory Group on Preventing and Reducing Community Violence, 2020). A 2020 review of the evidence, conducted by a collaborative of researchers as part of the RAND Corporation's Gun Policy in America initiative, examines the effects of firearm policies and how to improve the evidence on how such policies influence outcomes. The authors assessed the empirical literature on 18 categories of firearm policies related to eight different outcomes, including suicide, violent crime, unintentional injuries and deaths, mass shootings, officer-involved shootings, defensive gun use, hunting and recreation, and the gun industry. While the review does not offer findings specifically on race and ethnicity, the authors do find evidence to support the conclusion that child-access prevention laws (i.e., safe storage laws) reduce self-inflicted firearm injuries and deaths. They also report moderate evidence to suggest that laws prohibiting gun ownership for individuals subject to domestic violence restraining orders can decrease intimate partner homicides, and waiting periods can reduce firearm suicides as well as total homicides.

More research is needed to provide evidence-based policy guidance that takes into account political feasibility, racial equity considerations, and implications for Second Amendment rights. The RAND review supports this notion with a recommendation to Congress to consider appropriating significant funds for research on firearm policy and violence reduction at levels commensurate with other public safety and health investments.

Reducing Harmful Environmental Exposures

Chapter 3 draws a connection between concentrated disadvantage and toxic exposures such as lead and air pollution, which have been linked to crime and criminal justice contact. This section describes some of the literature that connects lead exposure as one toxic mechanism for influencing criminal outcomes and as an environmental pathway that contributes to racial inequalities (Sampson and Winter, 2016).

Lead exposure early in life has been shown to increase learning deficits and impulse control problems, which can increase the risk of criminal offending over the life course (Muller et al., 2018). Early studies have documented an association between lead exposure and impulsivity, violent behavior, aggression, and delinquency (Needleman et al., 2002, 1996; Byers and Lord, 1943). While most of the early literature provides cross-sectional analyses, more recent research provides longitudinal data showing a positive correlation between lead exposure and different measures of delinquency or criminal outcomes (e.g., school suspensions, antisocial behaviors, arrests; Reyes, 2015; Amato et al., 2013; Wright et al., 2008; Dietrich et al., 2001). Lead risk has been found to be associated with incarceration in adulthood, a risk that was found to vary substantially at the census tract neighborhood level (Manduca and Sampson, 2021). Children who live closer to busy roads within a neighborhood are more likely to have high blood lead levels, which in turn have been linked to increased likelihood of school suspension and juvenile incarceration (Aizer and Currie, 2019; see the section below on Enhancing

Opportunities for Youth Learning and Development for more on school disciplinary practices).

Muller and colleagues (2018) provide a review of the social causes and consequences of lead exposure, including future aggression and criminal offending, and conclude that "addressing the problem of lead exposure entails turning our attention away from explanations based on character deficiencies and toward durable investments" to repair harm done by harmful environmental exposures (p. 275). For example, early life interventions, such as lead remediation, nutritional assessment, medical evaluation, and developmental surveillance, have been shown to reduce negative outcomes due to lead exposure (Billings and Schnepel, 2018). Collective efficacy and community mobilization can catalyze the deployment of environmental interventions to reduce toxic exposures, thereby reducing crime and criminal justice contact (see Chapter 6 for discussion about collective efficacy).

Alcohol Outlets and Community Violence

Researchers have examined the relationship between alcohol outlet density—the number of physical locations where alcoholic beverages are sold either per area or per population—and neighborhood-level violence as a possible site of intervention to make communities safer. Communities characterized by concentrated poverty are also more likely to have both higher alcohol outlet density and higher rates of violence (Furr-Holden et al., 2019; Trangenstein et al., 2018). Spatial patterns of violence in cities show a clear relationship with public or off-premise alcohol consumption, regardless of racial composition (Furr-Holden et al., 2019). However, the nature of racial inequality in concentrated disadvantage imposes a disparate impact on primarily Black and Latino neighborhoods. The documented relationship between alcohol outlet density and violent crime has prompted researchers to explore policy solutions to mitigate this relationship (e.g., zoning policies). One cost-effectiveness analysis found that reducing alcohol outlet density in one mid-Atlantic city by one quintile is associated with a decrease of 51 homicides per year and 764 disability-adjusted life years (Trangenstein et al., 2018).

Policies that restrict the sale of alcohol in bars or restaurants during specific hours of the week have been studied as an intervention to reduce violence. Biderman and colleagues (2010) detected a 10 percent homicide reduction associated with legal provisions governing alcohol sales. The phased repeal of laws in Virginia that once prohibited the sale of packaged liquor on Sundays provided an opportunity for Heaton (2012) to examine that repeal; it led to the finding that increased alcohol sales were correlated with increases in serious crimes—including violent crime—by 10 percent. Similarly, using county-level variations in Kansas laws governing the sale and on-premises consumption of alcohol, Anderson and colleagues (2018) find that a 10 percent increase in the number of establishments licensed to sell alcohol by the drink increased violent crime by three to five percent. In a study of Chicago zoning codes, Twinam (2017) uses an instrumental variable strategy to find that in neighborhoods without high residential population density, the presence of liquor stores and late-hour bars was associated with higher levels of violent crime.

The Centers for Disease Control and Prevention's Task Force on Community Preventive Services conducted a systematic review on the effectiveness of limiting alcohol outlet density to reduce excessive alcohol consumption and alcohol-related harms, including violence (Campbell et al., 2009). The authors concluded that cross-sectional studies reveal a positive association between alcohol outlet density and crime and violence. Based on this evidence, the Task Force recommends "the use of regulatory authority (e.g., through licensing and zoning)" to limit alcohol outlet density and related harms (Task Force on Community Preventive Services, 2009).

INTERVENTIONS IN OTHER SYSTEMS

This section explores interventions that take place in the adjacent social policy systems or institutions—such as education, child welfare, and health systems—that can perpetuate, compound, or mitigate racial inequality in and outside of the criminal justice system. The strategies discussed here take a life-course approach with the understanding that the cumulative nature of racial inequality is intergenerational for families and children. The overarching principles of these interventions are:

- to improve systems to strengthen families and protect children from system involvement;
- to enhance opportunities for youth learning and healthy development; and
- to promote health and well-being.

Another central tenet of these strategies is the recognition of the role that biases and institutional racism can play in shaping outcomes for youth and families.

Without reforms that address the underlying mechanisms of inequality and structural racism, there is a risk of shifting the responsibility for addressing social problems (e.g., violence or poverty) onto non-criminal justice systems while perpetuating racial inequality. In short, the mechanisms of inequality operate in systems outside of the criminal justice system as well. For example, the social psychology, health, and education literature shows that explicit and implicit bias can operate in education and health care systems (Warikoo et al., 2016; Okonofua and Eberhardt, 2015; Paradies et al., 2014; IOM, 2003).

Strengthening Families and Protecting Children

Part I of this report documents how issues related to parenting and family stability, such as the loss of a child's relationship to a parent, can make *children* more vulnerable to later criminal justice system involvement. It also documents how the criminal justice system has been a primary strategy for addressing problems faced by children, parents, and families, bringing more *parents* into contact with the criminal justice system. Non-White families can be disproportionately likely to face criminal justice system consequences for family-related issues. Both non-criminal justice system inequalities and inequalities in criminal justice system referrals make non-White parents and children more likely to face criminal consequences. And as Part I also shows, criminal legal system involvement tends to worsen outcomes for children and families. The strategies outlined in this section address needs related to families and children without relying on criminalization or criminal consequences.

Family Preservation/Reunification in Child Welfare

Children of color and those from low-income households are disproportionately referred to the child welfare system and, once referred, are more likely than other children to be placed out of the home either temporarily or permanently.

An ongoing challenge in the child welfare field has been managing the potential conflict between collaborating with families to prevent out-of-home placement or reunifying children with their families and, at the same time, addressing safety concerns. Federal laws such as the Adoption and Safe Families Act and amendments to the Child Abuse Prevention and Treatment Act called for a better balance between protecting children and preserving families. More recent legislation and policy guidance have sought to refocus program and practice efforts on ensuring child well-being and family connections as well as attending to safety and permanency. The passage of the Family First Prevention Services Act (FFPSA) in February 2018 acknowledges the positive outcomes families and communities experience when child welfare systems devote more resources to preventing the need for foster care. Previously, resources were targeted to families who have had their children placed in foster care, but very few resources are available to strengthen families and prevent foster care. The FFPSA provides funding to states to increase such family preservation services.

Family preservation services are short-term and family-focused, designed to assist families in crisis by improving parenting and family functioning while keeping children safe. This approach grew out of the recognition that children need a safe and stable family and that separating children from their families is traumatic for them, often leaving lasting negative effects. Family preservation services vary by state but often include case management, individual and family therapy, and parenting skills training, as well as support services and referrals for families to community providers if they need help finding a job, securing housing, or accomplishing any other goal. Examples of evidence-informed intervention programs to keep children safe and promote permanency include the Nurse-Family Partnership, Safe Environment for Every Kid (SEEK), the Triple P Positive Parenting Program, and the Parent-Child Assistance Program (Casey Family Programs, 2018).

For those families whose preservation is not viable, kinship care may benefit children. Children who live in kinship families benefit from the ability to live with relatives when their parents cannot care for them. Research shows many benefits of kinship care. Compared to children in the general foster care population, for example, children in kinship care are better able to adjust to their new environments, less likely to experience behavioral and psychiatric problems, and less likely to change schools.

However, kinship families need more resources to support opportunities for the children in their care. Caregivers in kinship families may struggle, and many are grandparents living on fixed incomes. These caregivers may not have the financial resources to raise a child unexpectedly, especially children who face challenges because of their experience with abuse, neglect, and separation from their parents (Pittman, 2014). Programs and assistance to ensure that kinship caregivers access the benefits they are eligible for, such as Temporary Assistance for Needy Families, can help provide financial stability. Kinship caregivers tend to have higher poverty rates, less access to health insurance, and more physical or mental disabilities than other parents. Enhancing other community-based and government responses, such as promoting stable housing, ensuring that caregivers have health care and affordable legal representation, and easing barriers to school enrollment, could benefit both these children and their kinship families (Pittman, 2015).

Protecting Ties between Incarcerated Parents and Their Children and Families

Parental incarceration is one reason children may be fast-tracked to adoption under the Adoption and Safe Families Act, which requires states to file for the termination of parental rights for any child in foster care for 15 of the most recent 22 months (Children's Bureau, 2021). According to the Children's Bureau (2021),

> ...with the average prison sentence spanning more than 1 year—attributed in part to lengthy mandatory minimum sentences for common, nonviolent offenses—this requirement can be a significant barrier to reunification for incarcerated parents.

Some states' child welfare statutes, such as those in Ohio and Iowa, specify the length of parental incarceration as grounds for termination of parental rights (Office of the Assistant Secretary for Planning and Evaluation, 2021). States like New York and Washington have taken steps to allow for increased flexibility regarding placement for children of incarcerated parents (Walsh, 2016).

Beyond issues related to legal status and parental rights, sustaining a relationship between an incarcerated parent and their child can be difficult due to a number of factors, not limited to visitation restrictions, difficulty navigating the criminal justice system, transportation challenges, and lack of consistent communication. Visitation rules for incarcerated individuals, though they vary across the United States, are an example. Arranging visits can be challenging as facilities may require pre-clearance, approved adult supervision for children under 18, and proof of identification for visitors (e.g., birth certificate or driver's license; Annie E. Casey Foundation, 2011). Depending on where the parent is incarcerated, visitation may also require the child to be transported a significant distance to reach the facility, thus requiring reliable transportation from a supervising adult. Moreover, incarcerated individuals face significant communication barriers as they are not able to accept incoming calls and they must pay for all outgoing calls, often at significant cost. Without easy, consistent access to a phone and affordable calls, it can be difficult for an incarcerated parent to maintain consistent communication with their child. Providing incarcerated parents with a family conferencing model "can be extremely helpful in ensuring engagement and smoother communication between the parent, child, and child welfare agency" (Annie E. Casey Foundation, 2011).

Providing incarcerated parents with opportunities to participate in parenting courses can promote strong ties with their children and families. Parenting classes can "provide parents the opportunity to expand their understanding of child development and learn and practice effective and appropriate communication, discipline, problem-solving, and other parenting techniques" (Peterson, Cramer, and Fontaine, 2019; Peterson et al., 2019). Parenting Inside Out[2] is one such program that uses parenting coaches to teach both mothers and fathers involved in the criminal justice system. In 1998, the New Hampshire Department of Corrections established the

[2]See http://www.parentinginsideout.org/

Family Connections Center,[3] which provides a variety of services and programs to incarcerated parents, including parenting education classes, parenting support groups, and healthy relationship classes.

Vocational and life skills programs can help prepare incarcerated individuals for life outside of correctional facilities. For instance, the Life Skills[4] project is a combination of the Iowa Department of Corrections' Going Home Re-Entry project and the Des Moines Area Community College's Training Academy-Career Link. This program provides training on job readiness preparation, career development, vocational trades, and financial responsibility to enable those who are incarcerated to successfully reenter the community and obtain employment.

Creating more welcoming environments and providing accessible information about correctional facility policies and rules can also reduce the burden on families trying to connect children with incarcerated parents. For example, in Washington County (MN), the Jail Division has a Web page dedicated to visiting with children,[5] which outlines visitation times and rules for visiting with minors. Creating more family-friendly visitor areas, such as the one in the Allegheny County (PA) Jail,[6] can create a more welcoming environment for children in what can otherwise be an intimidating or tense environment.

Reducing the barriers to communication between incarcerated parents and children can support relationship development. These supports could include subsidizing or providing free phone calls to children, improving mailing practices to allow children to send their parents letters or drawings, and providing greater access to electronic communication such as emails or electronic messages (Peterson, Cramer, and Fontaine, 2019; Peterson et al., 2019). While incarcerated, parents can communicate with their children through phone calls, letter writing, or electronic communication.

Contact visits, when appropriate, can provide several benefits to both parents and children. They allow parents to practice parenting skills and can be "part of a larger family support program that may include parenting classes, coached telephone calls, case management, letter writing, and other activities" (Peterson, Cramer, and Fontaine, 2019; Peterson et al., 2019). Contact visits also enable children to better understand the incarcerated parent's circumstances and build a relationship with their parent. Organizations like Community Works[7] serve incarcerated parents to facilitate contact visits between parents and children.

---

[3]See https://www.nh.gov/nhdoc/fcc/programs.html

[4]See https://www.dmacc.edu/outreach/Pages/lifeskills.aspx

[5]See https://www.co.washington.mn.us/3214/Inmate-Information

[6]See https://www.alleghenycounty.us/jail/visitors/visitor-waiting-area.aspx

[7]See http://communityworkswest.org/program/one-family/#

Enhancing Opportunities for Youth Learning and Development

Providing access to high-quality education and opportunities for learning and development is an important policy solution to explore with the goal of interrupting pathways that drive youth from racial minority groups into the criminal justice system. A well-established literature documents how disparities in access to quality education mirror disparities in the criminal justice system. These disparities are prevalent across key education indicators, including access to high-quality early childhood education (ECE) programs, school readiness, Head Start, and high school graduation (the National Academies, 2019a). These racial disparities in performance and educational attainment (e.g., grades, standardized-test scores, dropout rates) have been studied as an enduring achievement gap in education policy research.

This section explores programs, strategies, and models that can foster academic achievement and provide supports or buffers for students from racial and ethnic minority groups that can be protective from crime and criminal justice involvement. To this end, the committee reviews some of the literature on providing high-quality ECE and care, investigating promising charter school models, and reforming school disciplinary practices.

Early Childhood Education and Care

The ECE literature identifies high-quality early learning and care as protective against future involvement in criminal behavior and criminal justice involvement (Lochner and Moretti, 2004). ECE programs increase children's cognitive, social, and health outcomes by enhancing children's motivation for school and readiness to learn and identifying problems that impede learning (the National Academies, 2019a). Head Start, the public preschool program for children from disadvantaged backgrounds, is one example of an ECE program that has been associated with reduced likelihood of criminal justice involvement. After studying the long-term effects of Head Start, Garces and colleagues (2000) find that African American children who attended Head Start are 12 percentage points less likely to report ever being charged or convicted of any criminal offense when compared to siblings who did not attend. This relationship is even stronger among African Americans whose mothers' level of educational attainment is high school completion. Head Start appears to have spillover effects as well; that is, individuals with an older sibling who attended Head Start are significantly less likely to report criminal activity as adults. Some research points to gender differences in treatment effects, with women showing greater reductions in crime than men after having participated in Head Start; conversely, men who participated tend to commit crimes that are more costly to society (García et al., 2018).

Some potential mechanisms that have been hypothesized to mediate the relationship between high-quality ECE and later criminal justice involvement are promotion of self-control, socio-emotional skills, reducing externalizing behaviors, and improved educational and labor market opportunities (García et al., 2019; Heckman et al., 2013). Not only do high-quality ECE programs reduce criminal justice involvement, but they also result in long-term societal cost-savings, which in large part can be attributed to crime reduction (García et al., 2020).

Charter School Models

Over the past 30 years, many states and school districts have expanded student access to charter schools. Charter schools are publicly funded, but they are not under the direct control of local school districts. They have additional freedom to experiment with educational programs and personnel policies.

In aggregate, the educational performance record of charter schools is not promising. Many appear to produce academic outcomes for students that are worse than the outcomes expected for similar students in traditional public schools. However, charter schools that serve disadvantaged urban communities have had noteworthy success, especially when these charters follow the "No Excuses" model. This model commits schools to additional time on task, extensive tutoring for students who are behind, the use of data to target students for additional help, the use of more intensive screening and accountability practices to hire and motivate educators, and cultural practices that communicate high expectations for all students. Neal (2018) summarizes a number of RCT evaluations of urban charters that follow this model. RCT evaluations are possible because these schools are often over-subscribed and districts use lotteries to ration admission.[8]

Studies conducted in Boston, Chicago, New York City, Texas, and Washington (DC) yield similar evaluation results for No Excuses charters, which all raise student achievement. The gains are typically larger in math than reading. Furthermore, more recent studies have shown that these schools increase future attendance and degree completion at four-year colleges. Dobbie and Fryer (2015) also examine nonacademic outcomes for students in New York City who applied to attend Promise Academy starting in middle school and find that attending Promise Academy reduced an index of risky behaviors among students in their late teens. They created the index using measures of teen pregnancy, criminal behavior, drug use, and

[8]See Dobbie and Fryer, 2020, 2013, 2011; Hassrick et al., 2017; Curto and Fryer, 2014; Angrist et al., 2013; Abdulkadiroglu et al., 2011.

incarceration. Although these follow-up samples are small, the treatment versus control differences in risky behaviors are statistically significant.

To date, the direct evidence that attending No Excuses charter schools reduces criminal justice involvement for minority youth in disadvantaged urban communities is limited. The students in many of these studies have not been followed into their adult lives. However, these schools are often able to take urban students from disadvantaged backgrounds and improve their academic outcomes substantially. Many models of criminal behavior suggest that these improvements are likely to reduce criminal justice involvement.

As with any other successful intervention, it is not obvious how school systems can scale this model and maintain fidelity in implementation. Teachers in No Excuses schools work longer hours than teachers in traditional public schools, and the model places stringent performance demands on educators. It could be expensive to hire enough teachers who are both willing and able to implement this model faithfully on a much larger scale. Further, these schools do not work for all students, as some students do not thrive in high-expectation environments. However, they demonstrate that it is possible to give many students who live in our nation's most challenging and distressed communities much better educations than they often receive from traditional public schools. Abdulkadiroglu and colleagues (2016) report that New Orleans (LA) had considerable success implementing No Excuses charters on a large scale as the city rebuilt its school system after Hurricane Katrina.

Another example of charter success is a network of schools operated by the University of Chicago. Hassrick and colleagues (2017) evaluate a cohort that applied for charter admission at (or near) the beginning grades of elementary school. These students had not already fallen below grade level nor were they switching from a public to a charter school to try to catch up. Therefore, the exceptionally long hours of individual tutoring that are so common in schools that follow the No Excuses model closely were not necessary. The vast majority of students who applied for admission to these schools came from Black families who were economically disadvantaged. Those who won lottery seats and entered these schools usually stayed. Attrition rates were low. Taken as a whole, the results suggest that attending these charters for grades K–5 raises a composite index of math and reading achievement by at least one half of a standard deviation, and Hassrick and colleagues (2017) find no evidence that these gains fade out as students move through higher grades.

It is difficult to compare test score impacts among studies that use different assessments, but the magnitude of the estimated learning gains produced by attending these University of Chicago charter schools is more than 50 percent of standard measures of the Black/White achievement gap among elementary school students. The cohort of students who attended schools in this charter network can expect to have academic and labor market opportunities that will simply be unavailable to most of their peers in traditional public schools. Given that educational attainment and employment are strongly associated with the absence of a criminal record, there are good reasons to believe that these expanded opportunities may reduce their involvement in the criminal justice system as well.

Neal (2018) notes that the literature on both voucher schools and charter schools shows that, in general, private schools and charters are not clearly superior to traditional public schools. However, most studies that document important gains for students who gain access to new schooling options in the private or charter sectors are studies that document gains from disadvantaged students of color who live in urban areas with above-average crime rates.

In many cities, legislation or organized political opposition limit the expansion of the No Excuses model as well as other alternatives to traditional public schools. Policy makers need to prioritize the expansion of new and better educational opportunities for students in distressed urban Black, Latino, and Native American communities. However, policy makers must make sure that new schools that operate under alternative organizational models and governance structures remain accountable for student outcomes.

Reforming School Disciplinary Practices

Measures of school discipline reveal significant disparities by race. For example, in 2013, 15 percent of Black students received an out-of-school suspension, compared with four percent of White students and six percent of Latino students. Moreover, a disproportionate number of Native American youth, LGBQ/GNCT youth, and youth with disabilities are suspended or expelled from school as a result of discretionary disciplinary practices (American Bar Association, 2018; Poteat et al., 2016). Much of the existing research on the "school-to prison pipeline" suggests that the disparities in school discipline by race and ethnicity are associated with the disparities seen in juvenile justice involvement, including the fact that Black youth are more than twice as likely as White youth to be arrested as juveniles (5.4% compared to 2.1%).

Researchers have theorized multiple ways school suspension or expulsion could be correlated with an increase in juvenile arrest and detention. First, with the presence of school resource officers (SROs), any disciplinary infraction could increase the probability of interacting with the police force (Owens, 2017). Second, suspension reduces time spent in school and might increase the probability of arrest during the days of suspension (Mowen and

Brent, 2016). Third, suspension and expulsion reduce attachment to school, and this in turn could reduce the probability of high school graduation, which can increase the probability of future criminal activity (Lochner and Moretti, 2004). The existing school-to-prison pipeline research is primarily correlational and often does not examine behavioral characteristics among youth and their family backgrounds, which criminology research has shown to be powerful predictors of violence and system involvement (Graf et al., 2021; Labella and Masten, 2018).

Disparate treatment of students when it comes to disciplinary actions, such as suspension or expulsion, is well documented (see, e.g., Gordon, 2018). Most of the previous work has focused on racial/ethnic differences, finding that Black and Latino high school students, for example, are only slightly more likely than White or Asian students to be "sent to the principal's office" for disciplinary infractions but are two to four times more likely to be suspended or expelled (Wallace et al., 2008). Interestingly, the reasons why White and minority students are reported for discipline differ significantly, with minority students being referred more often for more subjective reasons, such as "disrespect" and "perceived threat," and White students being referred more often for more objectively identifiable reasons, such smoking or vandalism (Skiba et al., 2002). Other research documents the bias that young Black girls face, which translates into their being perceived by adults as less innocent and more adult-like than their White peers (Blake and Epstein, 2019; Epstein et al., 2017). The higher rates of suspension for Black and Latino students for subjective infractions is consistent with differences in teacher and school personnel treatment of students based on race and ethnicity.

Experimental evidence confirms racial bias in disciplinary decisions. Okonofua and Eberhardt (2015) find that when presented with identical descriptions of student behavior, teachers viewed two minimal infractions as more troubling and deserving of harsher punishment when committed by a Black student than when committed by a White student. Mendez (2003) finds that unequal treatment based on race, ethnicity, gender, sexuality, or disability status results in disparate outcomes for children, as out-of-school suspensions are highly predictive of future involvement with the criminal justice system and reduced educational achievement. Recent initiatives have sought to reduce the suspensions and expulsions of youth of color from schools, but to date these initiatives have been small in scope.

Given the disproportionate filtering of students into the juvenile justice system from schools, one strategy to reduce disparities in the juvenile justice system is to invest in alternative school disciplinary strategies, such as the use of multi-tiered systems of support (MTSS; Ricks and Esthappan, 2018; Solomon et al., 2018). Two promising MTSS models include Integrated School Supports and Positive Behavioral Intervention

Supports, both of which work with parents, schools, and other community stakeholders to address the specific needs of the students and schools they serve. Evaluations of these models conducted by the American Institutes for Research, MDRC, and ICF International have resulted in mixed reviews that range from null to positive, with no negative findings. While these strategies hold promise for ending the pathway from school discipline to justice system involvement and, ultimately, reducing the disproportionate number of youth of color coming into contact with the juvenile justice system, ongoing evaluations are needed to monitor program outcomes and implementation fidelity if these programs are to be successful in supporting adolescent development and academic success (Solomon et al., 2018).

Another program that has shown promise in reducing racial disparities in the juvenile justice system is the Philadelphia Police School Diversion Program. This program, which was started by the Philadelphia Police Department in 2014, allows students with no prior criminal history who have been arrested for misdemeanor crimes the chance to avoid being officially charged with a criminal offense. Rather than enter the justice system, these adolescents are moved into a diversion program designed to help them change their behaviors and life trajectory. A key component of the program is the assignment of a social worker and provision of academic support, mentoring, social and emotional competency building, and other services. Since the program began in 2014, there has been a 54 percent drop in arrests in the city's schools. The program is currently participating in a three-year outcomes evaluation with funding provided by the Office of Juvenile Justice and Delinquency Prevention (Goldstein et al., 2019).

School Resource Officers

In addition to disciplinary practices, SRO programs have been subject to debate as they have been widely implemented and concerns about criminalizing student behavior have increased (Ryan et al., 2018). School security measures increased dramatically in response to high-profile incidents of lethal school violence (Theriot, 2009). One such measure has been the assignment of SROs to patrol schools and promote safety. Research in this area is limited, but there is evidence to suggest that the placement of SROs can criminalize youth, as it has been linked with increased arrests for non-criminal youth behavior and increased severity of punishment (King and Schindler, 2021; Weisburst, 2019; Na and Gottfredson, 2013). Gottfredson and colleagues (2020) examine effects of increased SROs in a sample of 33 public schools and find that the increase in SROs was associated with an increase in drug- and weapon-related offenses and exclusionary disciplinary practices. On the other hand, Theriot (2009), reviewing arrest rates in 13 schools with SROs, finds that having an SRO did not predict more total arrests, and having an SRO placed in a school decreased the arrest rate of assault and weapons offenses.

Fisher and Hennessy (2016) conducted a systematic review and meta-analysis of SROs and exclusionary discipline in U.S. high schools. The authors found that the pattern of results across the separate random effects meta-analyses provides evidence that the presence of SROs in high schools is associated with higher levels of exclusionary discipline using 10 effect sizes from seven different studies. One of the two models run by the authors was statistically significant, indicating that the presence of SROs was associated with approximately one additional exclusionary discipline incident per week in a school of 1,500 students.

Since serious crime occurs rarely on school campuses, SROs spend most of their time investigating minor incidents (King and Schindler, 2021). Time spent investigating minor offenses creates an environment where "schools subject students to strict scrutiny" for behavior that would not reach this threshold had it occurred outside of campus (p. 30). One study found that as schools increase their use of police, they record more crimes involving weapons and drugs, and they report a higher percentage of their nonserious violent crimes to law enforcement (Na and Gottfredson, 2013).

For schools in under-resourced communities, resources directed toward SROs may be better directed to other social supports for students. A report by the Brookings-AEI Working Group on Criminal Justice Reform documents some of the negative consequences of SRO programs and offers the following strategies for reforming these programs to promote safety and to reduce harm.

Over the short term, the Brookings-AEI group recommends these reforms:

- Providing staff training and resources so students have support services; and
- Having school leadership strictly limit the roles and responsibilities of SROs.

Over the medium term, the group recommends these reforms:

- Eliminating funding for police in schools; and
- Removing police from schools to invest in services that are proven to improve safety.

Over the long term, the group recommends these reforms:

- Breaking the school-to-prison pipeline by implementing alternatives to suspensions and expulsions;
- Creating healthy school cultures based on developmentally appropriate behavioral approaches;
- Integrating school and community-based restorative justice practices instead of punitive measures; and
- Positively engaging families of students (King and Schindler, 2021).

An additional set of questions regarding SROs remain to be addressed by the evidence: what is the optimal role of SROs in schools given concerns about mass shootings in schools? If embedded in schools, how might this influence disciplinary and criminal justice outcomes for youth of color? How can schools promote safety and protect students of color from disparate treatment by SROs? These questions outline next steps for the research on school safety. Schools are an optimal setting for shaping healthy socioemotional development, prosocial relationships, and conflict resolution when they provide the right climate and support services for students. By disrupting pathways that lead to criminal justice involvement, such as expulsions and SRO referrals for non-criminal behaviors, schools can be a promising site of intervention for reducing racial disparities in criminal justice contact and arrests for youth.

Promoting Health and Well-being

The racial inequalities in crime and justice that are discussed throughout this report are also reflected in health and well-being indicators. Relatedly, the health effects of criminal justice contact and prolonged involvement are well documented (for example, see NRC, 2014).

Health Disparities in the Context of the Criminal Justice System

Numerous health disparities exist between persons involved in the criminal justice system and the general U.S. population (Bui et al., 2019). People in state or federal prisons are 1.5 times more likely than people in the general U.S. population to report ever having a chronic condition, and half of all people in state or federal prisons report having a chronic condition such as asthma, heart disease, or diabetes. Rates of infectious diseases, such as tuberculosis, HIV, hepatitis B and C, and sexually transmitted diseases are higher among the incarcerated population than among the general U.S. population (Maruschak et al., 2015). In 2005, more than half of the incarcerated population had a mental health problem, including 56 percent of state prisoners, 45 percent of federal prisoners, and 64 percent of jail inmates (James and Glaze, 2006). Moreover, 58 percent of state prisoners and 63 percent of people sentenced in jail met the DSM (Diagnostic and Statistical Manual of Mental Disorders)-IV criteria for drug dependence or abuse during 2007–2009 (Bronson et al., 2017). Comparatively, 9.0 percent of persons ages 12 and older in the general U.S. population had a substance use disorder in 2009 (Substance Abuse and Mental Health Services Administration, 2015), and 11.3 percent of persons ages 18 and older had symptoms of serious psychological distress in 2005 (SAMHSA, 2006).

In addition to these disparities between the justice-involved population and the general U.S. population, health disparities among Black, Latino, and Native American populations that have been observed in the general U.S. population may also apply to the justice-involved population. These additional disparities may further compound the disadvantage of justice-involved Black, Latino, and Native populations compared with non-Hispanic White persons. With this complex relationship in mind, it is important to understand health disparities in the context of the criminal justice system and to explore potential interventions that mitigate the detrimental effects of criminal justice system involvement on health.

Health Care Policy and Crime

A small but important literature highlights a relationship between Medicaid expansion policies and crime. Aslim and colleagues (2022) found that increased health care access through Medicaid coverage expansion was associated with reduced recidivism among offenders who were convicted of violent and public order crimes. The authors postulate that an increase in referrals to addiction treatment with Medicaid coverage could reduce impulse behavior and, by extension, recidivism. Another study examines state-level crime data from 2009 to 2018 using a differences-in-differences design and reports that states that expanded Medicaid during this time period observed a 5.3 percent decrease in violent crime rates when compared to states that did not expand coverage (Vogler, 2020). The reduction in crime was also associated with an annual cost savings of approximately $4 billion. Moreover, there is evidence that Medicaid expansions were also associated with reductions in robbery, aggravated assault, and larceny theft, which have been theorized to be connected to increased substance use treatment. Simes and Jahn (2022) find evidence that supports this theory, with a differences-in-differences study that found that Medicaid expansion (2014–2016) was associated with 25–41 percent negative difference in drug arrests when compared to counties that did not expand Medicaid coverage. Additional research that explores the long-term effects of Medicaid expansion on crime as well as race-specific differences is needed in this area. Box 7-3 discusses health in the context of reentry and a community-based model for improving access to health care among justice-involved populations.

BOX 7-3
Transitions Clinic Network

The health system contributes to racial inequities, but it could also be a forceful solution to these inequities. Health care is constitutionally guaranteed in the correctional system, which is where a large proportion of incarcerated people first access health care and medications. Unfortunately, the quality of care in correctional institutions varies and does not always meet the needs of incarcerated individuals. Additionally, after a person leaves a correctional facility, they face significant barriers to accessing care. Getting an appointment or receiving appropriate medication can be difficult, and there can be bias against formerly incarcerated people or people of color.

The Transitions Clinic Network is a nationwide network of primary care programs for individuals with chronic health conditions who were recently released from prison. These programs rely on community health workers who have a history of incarceration themselves and who work alongside a primary care team to engage patients in primary care. Studies have shown that these programs increase patient engagement, reduce hospitalizations, and reduce future criminal justice contact (Wang et al., 2019; Shavit et al., 2017). The involvement of previously incarcerated people is particularly critical to the Transitions Clinic Network's success. The network's clinics are strategically located in the neighborhoods most impacted by incarceration, and each program assists individuals with successful and healthy re-integration into their lives and communities.

The health care system in correctional facilities has the potential to mitigate some of the health disparities in the United States, if care is equitable and of high quality. Because Black and Latino people are more likely than others to pass through correctional facilities, access to and quality of care in these facilities impacts these populations more than others. However, there are no data on how correctional systems influence racial disparities in health outcomes, due to a lack of systematic data collection. The United States has the highest reported incarceration rate in the world, and 95 percent of our nation's prisoners will return to society. That means more than 650,000 people a year will be released who have higher than average health risks and health care needs (Carson and Sabol, 2012; Visher et al., 2005). People released from prison are 12 times more likely to die in the first two weeks after their release than individuals who have never been incarcerated, even after controlling for participants' sociodemographic factors (Binswanger et al., 2007).

NOTE: See https://transitionsclinic.org/
SOURCE: The National Academies (2021a).

This summary is based on a factual accounting of what was presented at public information-gathering sessions for the committee's consideration. The public sessions were one mechanism that the committee used to gather information on the perspectives and experiences of communities that are disproportionately affected by racial inequalities in the criminal justice system. The statements reflected here are those of the presenters and do not represent the views of the committee or the National Academies.

Promoting Mental Well-being for Youth

As mentioned above, criminal justice disparities also exist for people with mental illness. Among youth, those with serious mental illness are more than three times more likely to come into contact with the criminal justice system than their peers without mental illness (Erickson, 2012). Youth with diagnosed mental health disorders are overrepresented in the juvenile justice system (Meservey and Skowyra, 2015; Teplin et al., 2015; Shufelt and Cocozza, 2006), and this prevalence increases the further a youth is within the system (Wasserman et al., 2010). Incarceration has been shown to worsen the behaviors in youth that are associated with undiagnosed mental health illnesses (Erickson, 2012). Co-occurring conditions predict worse outcomes; for example, youth with co-occurring behavioral problems and emotional problems are at elevated risk for recidivism (Hoeve et al., 2013; Cottle et al., 2001) and committing violent offenses during young adulthood (Copeland et al., 2007). Thus, juvenile justice programs are responsible for the care of a large number of youth who have complex mental health needs (Cocozza and Skowyra, 2000).

Youth struggling with mental health challenges need effective treatment, such as wrap-around and diversion programs, as well as community-based mental health care specialized for youth. Research suggests that the presence of mental health care offices in a county can be protective in terms of reducing crime rates (Deza et al., 2022). There is little information on evidence-based practices and policies specifically for justice-involved transition-age youth with mental health problems (NRC, 2014; Hoffman et al., 2009). Most of what is known is extrapolated from studies with adult or adolescent justice-involved populations. A variety of treatments have been well validated to target delinquency among justice-involved adolescents (e.g., Multisystemic Therapy, Multidimensional Treatment Foster Care; for review, see Henggeler and Sheidow, 2012), but far fewer are specifically designed to meet the unique developmental needs of transition-age youth or to address mental health problems among justice-involved youth. Evidence-based treatments for adolescents can be adapted for use with transition-age youth; however, they often rely heavily on parental involvement, an approach that may be less effective or feasible with transition-age youth who may be living independently, living with peers, or otherwise disengaged from their family of origin.

In a study of collaboration between child welfare and juvenile justice, two factors predicted successful coordination of mental health services: (1) having a single agency held accountable for the youth's well-being (i.e., either child welfare or juvenile justice) and (2) interagency sharing of administrative data (Chuang and Wells, 2010). Thus, effective coordination of care and agency accountability are necessary to ensure that youth do not fall through the cracks.

Other research suggests that youth and young adults with a co-occurring serious mental illness and substance use disorder require treatment that addresses the "whole person." Such person-centered services may include psychosocial interventions, family behavioral therapy, medication, proactive outreach, and use of specialized applications that can assist or provide an intervention and track symptoms (Brewer et al., 2017). In addition to targeted intervention for youth with mental illness, a more universal approach to promote well-being among youth who are exposed to violence is needed. As described above, living in areas characterized by high rates of violence is associated with poor mental health and well-being outcomes (e.g., anxiety, fear, posttraumatic stress disorder symptoms; Lee, 2016; Smith and Patton, 2016; Assari et al., 2015).

Diverting Youth with Mental Illness from the Justice System

Another promising strategy is the targeted diversion of youth with mental disorders to mental health treatment and other programs. Under mental health diversion programs, justice and social services agencies collaborate to divert youth offenders with mental disorders to mental health treatment in lieu of further court processing. It is hoped that—if mental health treatment is effective—diversion programs can help to reduce recidivism and the severity of crimes committed by offenders with mental disorders, thereby reducing the societal cost of crime.

One meta-analysis did not find significant reductions in recidivism, even for diversion programs that specifically targeted mental health needs (Schwalbe et al., 2012). However, when evidence-based interventions for adolescent delinquent behaviors (e.g., Multisystemic Therapy, Functional Family Therapy) were included in diversion plans, results were promising. Similar to these findings, preliminary results from Ohio's Behavioral Health Juvenile Justice program suggest that a diversion program that provides evidence- and community-based behavioral health treatment is effective in improving both delinquency and behavioral health outcomes (Kretschmar et al., 2016). Thus, diversion programs may be effective when evidence-based treatments are available in youths' own communities. Further, diversion programs reduce the time spent in locked settings, a contributor to developmental delays (Chung and Little, 2005). For these reasons, diversion programs need to be tailored to meet the needs of transition-age youth with mental health problems and examined as alternatives to formal sanctions.

CONCLUSION

Racial inequalities exist across the communities, institutions, and systems that shape and are shaped by the criminal justice system. As Chapter 3 asserts, structural policy reform that addresses the lasting effects of segregation, discriminatory housing policies, and other socioeconomic factors is needed to eliminate racial inequality. This chapter provides some promising strategies or policy solutions that, while situated outside of the criminal justice system, have the potential to mitigate the racial disparities that exist in crime, victimization, and criminal justice involvement. In summary, the committee offers the following conclusions that synthesize the evidence on promising approaches to address racial inequalities through non-criminal approaches.

CONCLUSION 7-1: Policies and programs that make progress toward eradicating disinvestment patterns show potential for reducing criminal justice system involvement and racial inequalities.

CONCLUSION 7-2: Improving the material well-being of people in disadvantaged neighborhoods (e.g., job opportunities, economic support) can reduce contact with the criminal justice system.

CONCLUSION 7-3: Ecological interventions that improve the quality of the built environment are a promising method of moderating the relationship between concentrated disadvantage and racially disparate outcomes in crime.

CONCLUSION 7-4: Given the enormous social cost and racial inequality associated with gun violence, measures for reducing the supply of guns, such as background checks and gun licensing, may contribute to reducing serious crime that is concentrated in Black, Latino, and Native American communities.

CONCLUSION 7-5: Evidence-based strategies in social policy institutions, such as education, health, and child welfare, to promote positive child and youth development and to promote the health and well-being of children and families are also needed to reduce racial disparities that exist in crime, victimization, and criminal justice involvement.

Addressing such "root causes" of racial inequalities is necessarily a long-term approach, one that will require commitment from a large swath of social institutions and stakeholders. Such approaches can be augmented by specific criminal justice system reforms that target reducing racial disparities at key points in the system. The committee turns to those strategies in the next chapter.

8

Criminal Justice System Reforms to Reduce Racial Inequality

Criminal justice policy has been an active area of reform over the last two decades. Proposals to reduce criminal justice disparities often focus on the specific stages of criminal processing. The committee views reforms to police, courts, and corrections as part of a larger transformation needed to significantly reduce racial inequality. Reducing arrests, incarceration, and other criminal justice contact in Black, Latino, and Native American communities will require reforms not only in criminal justice policy but also in other policy domains.

Research discussed in Part I shows that criminal justice contact, from police stops through arrests, prosecution, and incarceration, was disproportionately focused on predominately Black and Latino communities throughout the 20th century and became pervasive in the 1990s and 2000s. Arrest and incarceration became common responses to social problems related to concentrated poverty in communities marginalized by segregation. Chief among these problems is serious violence, which has taken a vast toll on disadvantaged communities, which are disproportionately Black, Latino, and Native American. But drug use, untreated mental and physical illness, failing schools, housing insecurity, and cumulative disadvantage over the life course and across generations have also created pathways into the criminal justice system. Part I also provided evidence that punitive policy disproportionately harmed Black, Latino, and Native American communities. Stops and searches and the use of force, sometimes fatally, by police combined with the communitywide effects of high rates of incarceration have transformed the relationship between state and citizen and undermined trust in authorities.

Reducing racial inequality in the criminal justice system holds the promise of improving safety by reducing the harms of interpersonal violence as well as the harms of policing and incarceration. Promoting racial equity will partly depend on abandoning a conception of community safety that relies mainly on punishment. In recent years, many communities and even criminal justice agencies have begun to move away from such a model, sometimes adopting alternative interventions where the threat of punishment becomes just one of several possibilities. As an example, specialty courts throughout the nation focus on the needs of people with severe mental illness, substance abuse problems, and veteran status, and others who are highly involved in the criminal justice system and have identifiable unmet needs. In another example, as discussed in Chapter 6, anti-violence strategies that rely on violence interrupters and other community members devoted to deescalating conflicts have been functioning largely independent of local law enforcement.

This chapter describes the implications of the committee's findings specifically for criminal justice system reforms. It reviews research on alternative interventions within criminal justice settings aimed at reducing violence and criminal justice contact, particularly in Black, Latino, and Native American communities. It pays close attention to recent changes in policy that have led to declines in police stops and correctional supervision. To be sure, eliminating racial and ethnic disparities in criminal justice involvement will require eliminating inequality in other domains. Hence, the criminal justice reforms discussed in this chapter should be viewed as one piece of a coordinated set of reforms that also extend beyond the criminal justice system.

Criminal justice agencies are charged with responding to and preventing serious interpersonal harm in communities. Traditional criminal justice policy in the United States pursues these objectives through retributive sentencing and a host of policies designed to either deter criminal activity or incapacitate the criminally active. Responding to harm runs through the history of policing and penal codes and is foundational to the jurisprudence of punishment. For its part, the process of punishment, decided by the courts and executed by correctional authorities, is treated as a form of accountability. Retributive theories of punishment contend that the pain of punishment proportionately imposed in the name of the people by the state restores moral balance after one person has harmed another.

Preventing crime is complex and difficult to assess, given the many determinants of criminal activity and the difficulty of specifying counterfactual levels of crime in the absence of a given policy. Social science research has focused largely on various strategies designed to either deter criminal activity or incapacitate individuals who would otherwise commit a crime. Deterrence strategies can be broad-based, such as through the imposition of severe sentences, or quite focused, such as through hot spot patrols or swift-and-certain sanctions. Incapacitation strategies rely on surveillance and the suppression of liberty, with intervention ranging from regular check-ins with a probation officer to solitary confinement. Empirical researchers have tried to estimate the deterrence and incapacitation effects of incarceration and other forms of punishment (e.g., Nagin, 2013; Paternoster, 2010; Hawken and Kleiman, 2009).

Our starting point for describing criminal justice reforms that can reduce racial inequality is the proposition that the criminal justice system should minimize the *overall harms* from crime, including harms that result from society's responses to crime. Minimizing the harms from crime expands the tool kit beyond retribution, deterrence, and incapacitation to include victim restoration, prevention through improved community relations, attention to unmet needs, and cross-system coordination with non-criminal justice agencies. Minimizing the harms caused by criminal justice officials would rule out indiscriminate, widespread, and unconstitutional stop-question-and-frisk practices in minority neighborhoods, frequent querying of citizens about their probation/parole status during minor traffic stops, and pretextual traffic stops for minor equipment violations, all practices that show little crime-reducing impact but which undermine community trust. Moreover, minimizing both the harms of crime and system harms would preclude long sentences that cannot be justified by incapacitation or deterrence. On the other hand, minimizing criminal and system harm may still yield a significant role for police in clearing homicide cases, reducing gun violence, and reducing the incidence of robbery, burglary, and other serious crimes that are disproportionately experienced in disadvantaged communities.

Given the large presence of the criminal justice system in minority communities, reducing both crime and system harms would have a disproportionate positive effect on impact, and likely reduce disparities in system involvement and victimization if implemented across the board or concentrated in Black, Latino, and Native American communities. However, if implementation is solely left to the discretion of criminal justice actors, it is possible to reduce average harm while not disproportionately reducing harm for affected racial and ethnic groups. One approach to reducing racial inequality has involved shrinking the scale of punitive impact of criminal legal processing—say, the numbers of arrests or prison admissions—in Black, Latino, and Native American communities. Shrinking the scale of punitive impact is different from many reforms that aim to reduce differential treatment, for example through anti-bias training.

We discuss criminal justice reform by first examining the structure of criminal processing and large-scale policy efforts focused on drugs and violence through the coordinated work of police, court actors, and the penal system. We then consider each of the main stages of criminal processing—by police, in the courts, and in sentencing and corrections—and explore how they might be reformed to reduce the scale of punitive impact and thereby reduce racial inequality in a way that serves the mission of responding to community violence and other harm.

INSTITUTIONAL STRUCTURE AND POLICY

Before examining each of the main stages of criminal processing, it is useful to consider the overall structure of interlocking agencies that comprise the criminal justice system and how they might operate together in a coordinated way to reduce racial inequality.

Part I of this report provides evidence of large racial disparities in involvement with the criminal justice system at all stages. Racial disparity preceded the increases in incarceration that occurred during the latter half of the 20th century and is certainly still with us today. In fact, policies that increased the punitiveness of sentencing have aggravated absolute racial disparities, while policies that reduced the severity of sanctions have narrowed them. Hence, one strategy for reducing disparities would be to reduce the overall punitiveness of sanctions and to exercise greater parsimony and proportionality.

Part I also provided evidence that, net of the general punitive level of the criminal justice system, racial and ethnic minorities, Black Americans in particular, experience greater scrutiny by and more frequent, intrusive, violent, and lethal interactions with police. Moreover, analysis of police stops finds that whereas Black Americans are the most likely to be stopped by the police, they are often the least likely to be ticketed or arrested, suggesting that many stops are effectively pretextual. Black Americans are also more likely to be searched yet in many jurisdictions are the least likely to be discovered to be carrying contraband. These disparities likely reflect both differential treatment of Black citizens by specific officers as well as more intrusive policing in cities with large minority populations. A second strategy for reducing racial inequality thus involves addressing bias by criminal justice officials and identifying seemingly race-neutral policies with racially disparate effects.

Constitutional Sources of Parsimony

In a discussion of sentencing policy, the legal scholar Morris (1974) outlined a theory of parsimony that held that the penal power of the state should be used minimally, just sufficient to achieve the goals of public policy. Excessive punishment, he wrote, amounted to state cruelty. Later writing expanded the idea of parsimony beyond sentencing and imprisonment to include policing, pretrial detention, and the manner of supervision on probation and parole (Atkinson and Travis, 2021).

The idea of parsimony—the minimal use of the state's power of coercion—although regularly overlooked in practice, has constitutional roots in the Bill of Rights and later amendments that embody a philosophy of limited government, especially in the area of criminal justice. Thus, policing power is specifically regulated through the Fourth Amendment, which requires police to justify intervention on the basis of probable cause or reasonable suspicion and establishes protections against unreasonable search and seizure (e.g., *Terry v. Ohio*;[1] *United States v. Cortez*[2]). Sixth Amendment rights to a speedy trial, to trial by jury, and to counsel also put limits on overreaching prosecution and provide the constitutional basis for indigent defense (e.g., *United States v. Wheat*).[3] The Eighth Amendment prohibits cruel and unusual punishment and has been applied to the conditions of incarceration, most notably to conditions of prison overcrowding and access to health care (e.g., *Hutto v. Finney*,[4] *Brown v. Plata*[5]). The Fourteenth Amendment's equal protection clause prohibits racially discriminatory laws and policies and has been applied by federal courts to limit racial profiling by police (e.g., *Floyd et al. v. City of New York et al.*[6]).

Throughout this chapter we will see two main strategies for reducing racial inequality in the criminal justice system. One strategy reduces the scope of criminal justice contact by reducing the number of police stops, arrests, court appearances, and incarcerations. The second strategy reduces the disparate impact of policy on and differential treatment of people of color. Although discrimination and disparate impact have been a focus for many reform efforts to reduce racial inequality, we also find strong evidence of reductions in absolute inequality by reducing the scale, duration, and intensity of criminal justice intervention. Proposals for reducing the overall extent of criminal justice contact are consistent with earlier research-based recommendations for reducing incarceration (NRC, 2014) and also align with founding commitments to constitutional limits on state power.

Assessing Decisions and Costs across Levels of Government

Like all public organizations, local, state, and federal criminal justice agencies operate subject to budget constraints and are often responsive to cost incentives. Moreover, police agencies are often called upon to enforce

[1]392 U.S. 1 (1968). See https://supreme.justia.com/cases/federal/us/392/1/
[2]449 U.S. 411 (1981). See https://supreme.justia.com/cases/federal/us/449/411/
[3]486 U.S. 153 (1988). See https://supreme.justia.com/cases/federal/us/486/153/
[4]437 U.S. 678 (1978). See https://supreme.justia.com/cases/federal/us/437/678/
[5]563 U.S. 493 (2011). See https://supreme.justia.com/cases/federal/us/563/493/
[6]959 F. Supp. 2d 540 (S.D.N.Y. 2013). See https://casetext.com/case/floyd-v-city-of-ny-2

regulations that often generate revenue for local and state government through fines and fees. To be sure, a fine or fee is often less severe than incarceration or community supervision, and fines and fees may have a greater role in a less punitive system. However, if generating fine and fee revenue motivates enforcement, these sanctions may distort police behavior, directing policing toward those activities that generate revenue.

Fine and fee revenue provides an example of how financial considerations create incentives for excessive enforcement or harsh sanctions. When police departments share in the revenues from enforcement actions, the incentives are quite clear. There are many instances, however, where the structure of public financing provides less obvious incentives. For example, a probation department that relies heavily on supervision fees will have incentives to surveil compliant individuals on probation who are current on their fees for as long as possible. Localities that pay none of the cost of sending someone to prison yet bear the full cost of a local sanction have an incentive to foist punishment costs onto the state, and perhaps to overuse state prisons.

A notable example of revenue generation distorting enforcement activity was provided by the Department of Justice's report on policing in the municipality of Ferguson (MO). Following the killing of a Ferguson resident, Michael Brown, by a local police officer in 2014 the Civil Rights Division of the Justice Department investigated the killing and the broader context of policing in the town. Like many U.S. towns (Graham and Makowsky, 2021), the local budget of Ferguson relied on municipal fines and fees (U.S. Department of Justice, 2015). Ferguson raised revenue with police-issued citations, and such efforts were focused on Black residents. Ferguson's "revenue-driven policing" increased contact between police and the public, and police stops often carried the potential of escalation. The proliferation of criminal justice fines and fees has been found to expand contact between the police and courts on the one hand and between police and the public on the other in a large number of jurisdictions (Shannon et al., 2020). The accumulation of criminal justice debt triggers warrants for non-payments, court appearances, and third-party debt collection, which can prolong court involvement well beyond the term of the initial sentence (Pager et al., 2022; Pattillo and Kirk, 2021). In Ferguson, the Justice Department found that pressures from city officials to raise revenue through citations led to an unconstitutional style of policing that demanded compliance in the absence of legal authority, led to stops without reasonable suspicion, and led to arrests without probable cause (U.S. Department of Justice, 2015, pp. 28–68). These examples of probation fees and municipal citations suggest that reducing the dependence of public financing on criminal justice contact could reduce the public's contact with police and the courts. Research has demonstrated that the political economy of law enforcement—the need to raise revenue through the criminal justice system—exacerbates racial bias and the expropriation of wealth from politically vulnerable subpopulations through the criminal justice system (Goldstein et al., 2020; Makowsky et al., 2019; Sobol, 2017; Makowsky and Stratmann, 2009; Blumenson and Nilsen, 1998).

Reducing criminal justice contact by altering cost incentives between different levels of government has been demonstrated in California with reforms to the juvenile justice system in the 1990s and to adult sentencing in the 2010s. Besides reducing correctional populations with no measurable change in crime rates, the reforms in California show that counties can respond to both fiscal savings and costs. Juvenile justice reform illustrates the effects of changes to local costs. In 1996, the state legislature passed a bill that increased the monthly costs for juvenile admissions to the California Youth Authority, the state agency that at the time ran state juvenile corrections facilities. Prior to the legislation, counties paid $25 per month for each of the agency's wards. Starting in 1997, the monthly payment increased to $150 per month for youth convicted of the most serious offenses. For those convicted of less serious offenses, counties were required to pay anywhere from 50–100 percent of the custody costs to the state. Subsequent legislation passed in 1998 capped the maximum annual per-ward payment from the counties to $31,200. Nonetheless, for all juvenile commitments, and especially for the commitment of youths convicted of less serious offenses, the increased cost to counties created by the reform was substantial. Shifting the costs of incarceration to counties, where incarceration decisions were made, caused an immediate and sustained drop in admissions to the California Youth Authority beginning in 1997. Further analysis showed little corresponding increase in incarceration in adult facilities, a greater propensity to divert cases to an alternative non-incarceration resolution, and no measurable effects on reported Part 1 crimes nor on youth arrests (Ouss, 2020).

More recent reforms in adult corrections illustrate the effects of aligning the cost incentives faced by counties with the actual cost of admitting people to prison. Under pressure from a federal court to relieve prison overcrowding and a U.S. Supreme Court ruling that overcrowding in California's prisons violated the Eighth Amendment rights of state prisoners, California enacted broad corrections reform legislation under the banner of corrections realignment in April 2011, with implementation beginning on October 1, 2011. The legislation halted the practice of revoking people under parole supervision back to prison for technical violations and diverted people convicted of many nonserious, nonviolent, nonsexual offenses to jail sentences or an alternative sanction to be served through some form of community corrections.

This realignment led to a relatively quick reduction in the California prison population, caused by a sharp and immediate reduction in prison admissions coinciding with the implementation of the legislation. By the end of 2011 (three months into the implementation of reforms) the prison population had declined by roughly 13,000 (an 8% decline). By May 2013, the prison population had declined by nearly 28,000 relative to September 2011 (a 17% decline). In terms of incarceration rates, by the end of 2012 California's incarceration rate stood at 348 per 100,000, a rate comparable to the rate in 1992, prior to the passage of the state's tough "Three Strikes" sentencing reform. This is in comparison to an incarceration rate on the eve of realignment's implementation of 426 per 100,000. The large decline in incarceration had minimal impact on California crime rates (Lofstrom and Raphael, 2016). In fact, despite subsequent reforms that reduced the prison population even further in subsequent years, crime rates continued to decline, with murder rates dropping below the national average for the first time in years in 2014. Little is known about longer-term effects, say a decade after the original policy change, and the committee sees this is as an important topic for further research.

Taken together, the implication of reforming fines and fees and California's realignment is not so much that financing and criminal justice decisions need to be aligned at the same level of government. After all, budgets and decision making had been aligned at the same level of government in Ferguson and in many county-court systems that levy fines and fees. Instead, the principle of parsimony is served when criminal justice decisions are taken with attention to the true cost of those decisions, both fiscally for the jurisdiction and socially for the communities that such decisions are intended to serve.

Costs and benefits have often been treated asymmetrically in criminal justice policy making and individual decision making, with the costs to government budgets and to communities often being overlooked. The implications of weighing costs are wide-ranging. At the level of statutes and penal codes, changes in sentencing could be scored in a manner similar to spending bills in state and federal legislatures. Policy researchers have also suggested that changes in sentencing policy include racial impact statements that account for the social costs of policy change.

Shifting Policy Approaches to Drugs and Violent Crime

The increase in incarceration rates in the four decades since the early 1970s largely resulted from changes in criminal justice policy (NRC, 2014; Raphael and Stoll, 2013). The proximate causes of the growth in imprisonment rates were an increase in prison admissions per arrest and an increase in the time served in prison (NRC, 2014). In state prison systems, tougher drug sentences accounted for one-fifth of incarceration growth from 1984 to 2004, while tougher sentences for violent crime account for roughly half

(Raphael and Stoll, 2013, p. 27). In federal prison systems, the growth of incarceration was driven primarily by tougher sentences for drug offenders and other public-order crimes. Across both the federal and state systems, legislatively driven policy changes largely drove incarceration grown in the latter decades of the 20th century (Raphael and Stoll, 2013).

Such policy changes largely took the form of state and federal sentencing policy that expanded the scope of criminalization and enhanced sentences for many offenses. Particularly relevant to the current discussion of policy change, the wars on drugs and crime involved the adoption of new rules and routines across many domains, from policing to corrections. These changes in criminal justice policy had large effects on racial inequality in criminal justice involvement. For example, drug arrest rates climbed sharply through the 1980s and are estimated to have contributed to about a third of the rise in imprisonment rates in the 1980s and 1990s (and likely to larger proportions of the increase in the population of people with prior felony convictions and prison time served; Blumstein and Beck, 2012). Increased policing and prosecution of drug offenses was also associated with increased racial disparities in both arrests and imprisonment.

Moreover, most states moved to determinate sentencing regimes, adopted mandatory minimum sentences, or enacted truth-in-sentencing laws that required individuals who are incarcerated to serve a specified minimum percentage of their original sentence. Some states passed repeat-offender statutes, such as "three strikes" laws (Raphael and Stoll, 2013). Nearly half of U.S. states passed sentence enhancements for second- or third-time violent felony convictions, with California's three-strikes law being particularly punitive (Chen, 2008). Following the lead of many states that passed "truth-in-sentencing" standards, in 1994 Congress passed the Violent Crime Control and Law Enforcement Act, which supplied federal funds for prison construction to states that required people to serve 85 percent of the sentence prescribed by statute (Ditton and Wilson, 1999). These examples indicate a broad shift toward more punitive treatment for offenders across every major crime category (Neal and Rick, 2016, p. 38). Since arrest rates for Black people are higher than for White people, this shift to more punitive sentencing policies was particularly devastating for Black communities (Neal and Rick, 2016, p. 38). Racial disparities in imprisonment are relatively large for drug and violent crimes, and these offenses account for a large share of the prison population. Tonry (2019, pp. 11–13) argues that changes in sentencing policy in these two areas have been important for the overall racial disparity in incarceration. In addition, in the federal system, the shift toward more punitive sentencing for drug crimes affected Black individuals more than White individuals (and drug offences accounted for a significant portion of growth in the federal prison population; Neal and Rick, 2016, p. 38).

According to Raphael and Stoll (2013, p. 28), "Collectively, these policy changes have driven the enormous increase in state incarceration rates since the mid-1970s. The increase in the federal prison incarceration rates can be traced largely to the incarceration of drug offenders and the minimum sentences mandated in federal sentencing guidelines."

The rate of incarceration for drug-related crimes has declined since around 2008, partly the result of drug policy reform over the last two decades that has revised sentencing statutes, policing practices, and prosecution. Sentencing reforms for drug offenses, enacted since the early 2000s, have focused on mandatory sentences (Mauer, 2011b), greater leniency for possession, and widespread decriminalization and legalization of cannabis (Beckett and Brydolf-Horwitz, 2020; Mikos, 2020). A number of jurisdictions have passed legalization statutes that provide for the legal cultivation and sale of cannabis (Mikos, 2020; Kreit, 2016), and in 2013 a Department of Justice memorandum advised federal prosecutors not to interfere with state marijuana legalization laws.

Decriminalization and legalization has been associated with large declines in arrests for cannabis possession (Plunk et al., 2019). Since 2000, the national-level decline in incarceration for drug offenses has been accompanied by a large absolute and relative decline in racial disparity. The prison population incarcerated for drug offenses has declined greatly for Black men and women, although it increased slightly for White people (Table 8-1). Of the total decline in the Black prison population (from 562,000 in 2000 to 399,000 in 2019), about 60 percent is attributable to the decline in the population convicted of drug offenses. Examining federal courts, Light (2022) also finds that racial inequality in length of sentencing between Black and White defendants decreased to less than six months from 2009 to 2018; among those convicted of drug offenses the Black/White gap decreased to zero over the same period. Light (2022) finds these trends to be driven by decreasing sentences for Black individuals and increasing sentences for White individuals, changes in observable case characteristics, and shifts in the prosecutorial use of mandatory minimums.

Like drug offenses, large racial disparities accompany arrest and incarceration for violent offenses. Unlike drug policy, however, sentencing for violent offenses has not become markedly more lenient in recent years, and racial disparities in incarceration for violence have not declined as much as for drug offenses. However, there is some movement in this direction as half of states have now banned life without the possibility of parole for juvenile offenders (a sentence generally meted out for serious violent offenses).[7] Moreover, the state with the harshest three-strikes law, California, narrowed the range of offenses for which a third felony carries a 25-to-life

[7]See https://www.sentencingproject.org/publications/juvenile-life-without-parole/

TABLE 8-1 State Prison Population by Race/Ethnicity and Offense, 2000, 2019

		2000	2019	Change	Percent Change
All Offenses	Black	562,000	399,000	–163,000	–29
	White	436,700	386,700	–50,000	–11
	Hispanic	178,500	266,500	88,000	49
Drugs	Black	145,300	48,600	–96,700	–67
	White	58,200	64,300	6,100	10
	Hispanic	43,300	31,100	–12,200	–28
Violent	Black	273,400	255,000	–18,400	–7
	White	212,400	192,600	–19,800	–9
	Hispanic	87,100	176,000	88,900	102
Property/ Other	Black	96,800	95,400	–1,400	–1
	White	108,600	129,900	21,300	20
	Hispanic	37,200	59,300	22,100	59

NOTE: The substantial increase in Hispanic state prison population for violent and property crime offenses observed in Table 8-1 is largely related to the growth of the Hispanic population in the nation as a whole and possible due to changing measurement of this population from 2000 to 2019 (see Beck and Blumstein, 2018).
SOURCE: Data from Sabol and colleagues (2009), Table 7; Carson (2021), Table 15.

sentence. The incarcerated population convicted of violent offenses also declined among Black people, but the reduction in imprisonment of nearly 20,000 contributed only about 12 percent of the decline in Black imprisonment from 2000 to 2018 (see Table 8-1).

Policy approaches to drugs and violence represent two distinct pathways for the criminal justice system. The liberalization of drug policy in the last two decades shrank both enforcement efforts and incarceration rates for the possession and sale of narcotics. Reducing drug arrest and prison admission rates, in turn, has been associated with a large decline in the incarceration of Black men and women. Nevertheless, the enduring pattern of long sentences for violent crimes has sustained racial disparities in incarceration. The two trends in policy suggest that alternative responses to violence that rely far less on long sentences would likely yield large reductions in racial disparity in incarceration.

POLICING

Research reviewed in Chapters 2 and 4 indicates that there remain significant racial disparities in police stops and searches, arrests, and use of force. In this section we consider research evidence on policing reforms that could reduce disparity. Racial disparities in policing are often seen as the outcome of two distinct processes (Pryor et al., 2020). First, there are policies and crime patterns that shape the context of police decision making and deployment. For example, there may be a more visible police presence in Black neighborhoods due to explicit enforcement strategies such as hot spot policing, responding to more emergency calls for service in Black neighborhoods, or differential policing employed in predominantly minority cities. This differential presence will tend to produce more contact between Black residents and police, regardless of the individual dispositions of officers. Second, officers may vary in their dispositions, and some may use their discretion to treat some racial groups differentially. This differential treatment may result in differential scrutiny of Black pedestrians and drivers, differential and harsher treatment during common police-citizen interactions, and a greater volume of stops and interactions that result in no actions taken by police officers.

Changing the Context of Policing through Oversight and Accountability

In this section we describe large-scale changes in the deployment of police resources obtained through civilian and Department of Justice oversight efforts. In some cases below, as in New York City's abandonment of an unconstitutional stop-and-frisk policy, racial inequality was the focal point of court oversight. In other cases, such as Washington State's experience with pretextual traffic stops, court oversight narrowed police discretion, and racial disparity declined as a consequence.

Stop-and-Frisk Practices

Notable recent cases of court oversight have focused on so-called *Terry* stops, named for the landmark U.S. Supreme Court decision in *Terry v. Ohio*. In that case, the court held that a police officer can temporarily detain a citizen if the officer has a reasonable, articulable suspicion that the detained person was engaged in criminal activity. The court also ruled that a citizen can be superficially searched (frisked) if the officer has a reasonable, articulable suspicion that the citizen is armed and dangerous. Guided by the broken windows theory that policing of low-level offenses serves to limit the perpetration of more serious crime, stops and searches became an important policing tool in many jurisdictions in the 1990s.

Policy developments and court action in New York City (NY) have been a key focus for researchers studying the connections between policing and racial inequality. In New York City, the New York Police Department (NYPD) had, since the early 1990s, embraced order-maintenance policing and enforcement actions against low-level offenses. The policy is reflected in the increased number of pedestrian stops and low-level arrests from the 1990s through the first decade of the 2000s. In 2003, the number of stops totaled around 150,000, and by 2011 it had climbed to nearly 700,000. Litigation around stop-and-frisk in New York began in 1999 in a class action lawsuit, which alleged that the NYPD targeted individuals on the basis of race and national origin without reasonable suspicion, in violation of the Fourth and Fourteenth Amendments (*Daniels v. City of New York*).[8]

A settlement in the case required, among other provisions, that the NYPD maintain an anti-racial profiling policy, engage in anti-profiling training, and maintain a database of stops. The settlement did not include an independent monitor, and police compliance with the settlement appears to have been poor. A second case was brought, *Floyd et al. v. City of New York et al.*, in which the court ruled in 2013 that the NYPD was continuing to engage in unconstitutional stop-and-frisk practices that were racially discriminatory, targeting Black and Latino New Yorkers. Among the remedies, an independent monitor was appointed to oversee policy changes that would bring the NYPD back into compliance with the law. The court also required body-worn cameras to be used in a number of police precincts and that community consultation be adopted for the process of policy change.

Immediately following the *Floyd* ruling, the number of stops, frisks, and arrests dropped precipitously. The top 10 precincts recorded 685,724 stops in 2011, compared to just 45,788 stops in 2014 (Table 8-2). The 93 percent reduction in stops in these precincts caused large declines in racial disparities in stop rates. While the differences among Black, Hispanic, and White New Yorkers in their likelihood of being stopped, questioned, and frisked by the police declined precipitously, the racial composition of the much smaller pool of post-*Floyd* stops is similar (Black New Yorkers accounted for 53% of all stops in 2014 in comparison to 51% of all stops in 2011). Among Black men and women, police stops in the top 10 precincts declined by 326,092 in three years, far exceeding the decline for any other racial group. We also observe a large decline in stops for Hispanic New Yorkers (White et al., 2016). This is an example of a reform that has disproportionately positive impacts on affected populations even when relative disparities are not reduced by much.

In these cases, a large across-the-board reduction in stops, frisks, and arrests, in a context with large preexisting racial disparities, greatly reduced police contact among Black and Hispanic residents. Court oversight resulting from private litigation in New York coupled with independent

[8]*Daniels v. the City of New York*, 99 Civ. 1695 (SAS) (S.D.N.Y. 2001). See https://casetext.com/case/daniels-v-the-city-of-new-york-sdny-2001

TABLE 8-2 Numbers of Stops, Frisks, and Arrests in the Top 10 Precincts in 2011, When *Floyd v. City of New York* Decided That the New York Police Department Policy of Stop and Frisk Was Unconstitutional, and in 2014, by Race

		2011	2014	Change	Percent Change
Stops		685,724	45,787	–639,937	–93.3
	Black	685,724	45,787	–639,937	–93.1
	Black-Hispanic	350,405	24,313	–326,092	–94.3
	White-Hispanic	17,545	9,707	–56,266	–94.5
	White	61,715	5,449	–45,846	–91.2
	Other	49,372	3,526	–45,846	–92.9
Frisks		381,704	30,345	-351,359	-92.1
	Black	203,067	16,993	–186,074	–91.6
	Black-Hispanic	28,246	1,912	–26,334	–93.2
	White-Hispanic	99,243	6,221	–93,022	–93.7
	White	27,483	3,065	–24,418	–88.8
	Other	23,666	2,154	-21,512	–90.9
Arrests		40,883	6,898	–33,985	–83.1
	Black	20,850	3,449	–17,401	–83.5
	Black-Hispanic	2,984	573	–2,411	–80.8
	White-Hispanic	10,221	1,759	–8,462	–82.8
	White	4,211	710	–3,501	–83.1
	Other	2,208	407	–1,801	–81.6

SOURCE: Data from White and colleagues (2016).

monitoring of unconstitutional policing significantly reduced absolute but not relative disparity in *Terry* stops, police searches, and arrests.

Pretextual Traffic Stops

Related litigation has focused on pretextual traffic stops. A pretextual stop occurs when an officer identifies an objective violation of traffic law and lawfully stops the motorist, but the officer's actual intention is to investigate a hunch that, by itself, would not amount to a reasonable suspicion or probable cause. The 1996 U.S. Supreme Court Case of *Whren v. United States*[9] ruled that the violation of a traffic law renders the stop reasonable

[9]517 U.S. 806 (1996). See https://supreme.justia.com/cases/federal/us/517/806/

under the Fourth Amendment, even though the true purpose of the stop, absent the traffic violation, would not be constitutional. Legal scholars argued that the *Whren* decision greatly enlarged police discretion in a way that allowed them to target motorists of color (Rushin and Edwards, 2021; Chin and Vernon, 2014; Maclin, 1998; Harris, 1997). Pretextual stops, like *Terry* stops, are a first point of contact generating vast numbers of interactions between police and the public.

Although state constitutions and state law may establish stronger protections against pretextual stops, few states have strayed from the core holding in *Whren* (Lawton, 2015). Unusually, the Washington State Supreme Court in 1999 imposed a ban on pretextual stops as violating the state constitution's provision that "no person shall be disturbed in his private affairs, or his home invaded, without authority of law" (Rushin and Edwards, 2021, p. 654). Thirteen years later, in 2012, another state supreme court effectively repealed the ban in Washington State by narrowing the restrictions on pretextual stops. Although racial profiling was not central to the Washington State Supreme Court decisions, in contrast to the *Floyd* case in New York, and neither decision was directly intended to affect racial disparity, a large body of legal scholarship has examined racial profiling by police in traffic stops, particularly since the *Whren* decision. Did the 13-year ban on pretextual stops in Washington State reduce racial disparity in traffic stops?

Rushin and Edwards (2021) studied the impact of legal changes in Washington State, comparing the number of stops of non-White and White motorists in the period during the ban to the number of stops made in the later period of its relaxation. In a difference-in-difference analysis of race × county × month counts of stops, non-White drivers experienced an additional 250 stops each month in a county, following the relaxation on the ban on pretextual stops. The average number of stops among Black and Hispanic drivers was approximately 2,500 each month. Racial disparity declined in night-time stops under the "veil of darkness" (Ridgeway and MacDonald, 2009). The analysis provides rare evidence of the causal effect of pretextual stops on racial disparity and the effectiveness of a legal ban on reducing disparity. Relying only on observational data, however, other changes in the legal and political environment that coincide with the relaxation of the ban on stops could threaten causal inference. Around the time of the ban, marijuana was legalized in Washington, a new governor and attorney general were elected, and Republicans won the state senate. Causal inference would be biased if one of these changes induced racially disparate changes in police behavior. Although it is unclear if changes in drug policy or state politics affected racially disparate police behavior, it is clear that that marijuana legalization coincided with a significant reduction in stops for Washington motorists in general. Similar to the reduction in the national imprisonment rate for drug offenses, the reduction in traffic stops accompanying marijuana legalization likely disproportionately reduced stops among non-White motorists, even as stops increased among minority motorists when the court narrowed the ban.

Federal Pattern or Practice Investigations

In a third example of changing police oversight, the Department of Justice since 1994 has expanded scrutiny of police departments through "pattern or practice" investigations. Under Section 14141 of the Violent Crime Control and Law Enforcement Act,[10] the Attorney General is authorized to initiate structural reform litigation against police departments suspected of systemic misconduct that "deprives persons of the rights, privileges, or immunities secured and protected by the Constitution or laws of the United States" (Stuntz, 2006, p. 798). This authorization, called the pattern or practice provision, is considered "the most important legal initiative of the past twenty years in the sphere of police regulation" (Stuntz, 2006, p. 798).

Investigative work under Section 14141 has been undertaken by the Special Litigation Section of the Justice Department's Civil Rights Division, which has specified a number of goals for the program, including ending unconstitutional policing by curbing officer use of force and curbing discrimination based on race, ethnicity, gender, or sexual orientation in an effort to establish "bias-free policing" (Walker, 2022). From 1994 to 2017, the Department of Justice initiated 69 investigations of local police departments, reaching settlements with 40 departments, involving 20 judicially enforced federal consent decrees (Walker, 2022). Settlements typically involve new procedures for investigations into use of force, searches and arrests, citizen complaints, and officer disciplinary actions. Several papers report comparative case studies of consent decrees in several sites. Rushin (2015, p. 1422) concludes that the "available evidence suggests that [systemic judicially enforced police reform] has been an effective tool for reducing misconduct in several police agencies." Chanin (2015) reviews pattern or practice investigations in Pittsburgh (PA), Washington (DC), and Cincinnati (OH) and generally finds evidence of reduced police misconduct, measured by statistics on use of force, citizen complaints, and disciplinary action in response to alleged misconduct.

In Los Angeles (CA), Stone and colleagues (2009) documented increased public satisfaction and decreased frequency of serious levels of force among the Los Angeles Police Department (LAPD) under a consent decree following the Rampart scandal. A consent decree in Newark (NJ)

[10]42 U.S.C. § 14141 (1994; re-codified as 34 U.S.C. § 12601). See https://www.justice.gov/crt/conduct-law-enforcement-agencies

was associated with fewer police stops among Black and Latino residents, although spatial concentration of field inquiries remained (Chillar, 2022). Walker's (2022) review of consent decree evaluations indicates reductions in use of force and sustained improvements in department operations, though many sites have gone unevaluated and there has been no general evaluation of the Department of Justice pattern or practice program.

Resistance to Change in Police Culture

Some researchers have argued that consent decrees have changed police behavior, but it has been more difficult to bring about lasting change to police organization and culture. A review by Alpert and colleagues (2017) reports that although consent decrees are often found to be effective while federal monitors are in place, temporary oversight has not produced enduring change. For example, qualitative data from Pittsburgh show that police officers met the 1997–2002 consent decree with resistance and negativity (Davis et al., 2005). The city implemented new systems to track the use of force, traffic stops, and searches, and established new procedures for officer accountability, new policies, and training. Officers noted increased accountability and oversight mechanisms during the period of the consent decree but also reported that changes in management made them less aggressive in fighting crime. The reforms remained intact one year after most of the consent decree requirements were lifted (Davis et al., 2005). Without additional provisions for enduring oversight, "there is no established mechanism or requirement to maintain any of the accountability features that were established under the consent decree" (Alpert et al., 2017, p. 243).

While there is evidence that federal oversight has reduced police misconduct, particularly while a court monitor was in place, oversight has often been resisted by police leadership and unions (Walker, 2022; Rushin, 2017). Police objections to oversight are well documented, and police leadership and middle management have regularly opposed and refused cooperation with federal monitors (Walker, 2022). Increasing the obstacles to effective oversight, police unions and their collective bargaining agreements frequently shield officers from public scrutiny. A review of police union contracts in 178 municipalities identified seven provisions that shield officers from accountability. These include the delay of investigative interviews in cases of police misconduct, limitations on the use of officers' disciplinary history in misconduct hearings, time limits for imposing discipline, and independent arbitration that regularly overturns terminations and reduces suspensions (Rushin, 2021, 2017). There is also evidence of countermovement organization among police and supporters in competitive opposition to protests for police reform (Solomon and Martin, 2019).

One line of research has examined whether police resistance to oversight and accountability has resulted in a withdrawal of police services that ultimately causes an increase in crime. Devi and Fryer (2020) examined this possibility in an empirical analysis of the effects of federal and state pattern or practice investigations on policing behavior and crime rates in 27 pattern or practice investigations. In 22 out of 27 cases, investigations are estimated to reduce overall crime rates, and to reduce homicides on average by 61 per investigation over 24 months following the investigation. In five of 27 cities, however, investigations were initiated following high-profile killings of Black citizens by police that sparked protests and gained national media attention. These "viral" incidents in Baltimore (MD), Chicago (IL), Cincinnati (OH), Riverside (CA), and Ferguson (MO) were followed by large increases in homicide and overall crime rates. An estimated 1,099 excess homicides and 31,293 excess felony crimes were recorded over the two-year period following an investigation in cities with a preceding viral incident. That being said, it is not clear whether the pattern or practice investigation or the high-profile incident preceding the investigation caused the additional crime. Evidence of declining police stops in four of the viral cities suggests that reduced police activity following the announcement of the federal investigation drove the increase in crime in those localities. Increasing crime as a result of reduced policing in response to oversight efforts was also reported in Los Angeles (Prendergast, 2021) and Cincinnati (Shi, 2009). In these cities, efforts to increase police accountability did not include close monitoring of police activities aimed at preventing and solving crime. The reduction in police services that accompanied federal oversight was associated with an increase in crime, including a jump in homicide rates in Los Angeles. In Los Angeles, Prendergast (2021) observed a 40 percent decrease in the arrest-to-crime rate and an increase in homicides (2000–2003) for the LAPD, and no corresponding changes in an adjacent department. The impacts were pronounced in predominantly Hispanic neighborhoods.

Related research has studied the so-called Ferguson Effect, where policing activities may have been reduced following the social protests and Justice Department investigation in Ferguson following the police killing of Michael Brown. Premkumar (2019) finds a decline in low-level arrests following protests in Ferguson that he associates with increased public scrutiny of the police, rather than the federal investigation, and an increase in homicides. Against this finding, Rosenfeld and Wallman (2019) find little evidence of de-policing measured by arrest rates, given homicides across 53 large cities following the killing of Michael Brown (Rosenfeld and Wallman, 2019).

Community-led efforts to reduce racial disparities in policing have focused on increasing social accountability measures through non-department oversight and engagement. An analysis of civilian oversight agencies in the period 1980–2014 found lower levels of racial disparity in the disorderly conduct arrests where oversight boards had broad authority to conduct investigations, although racial disparities in policing outcomes tend to grow as the oversight agency ages (Ali and Pirog, 2019). The Department of Justice's Office of Community Oriented Policing Services led a report on reconciliation efforts to acknowledge past harm in law enforcement practices while using historical context to inform solutions to reduce racial profiling and disparities (Mentel, 2012). Public scrutiny has led to a national reconsideration of the role of police officers and the responsibilities that should fall under their discretion. Judicial consent decrees are an example of efforts designed to reduce racial disparities with only evidence of temporary success.

Body-worn Cameras

One area of police operations that aims, in part, to improve police accountability involves the use of body-worn cameras. A significant literature now examines the effects of body worn-cameras on police behaviors. Body-worn cameras are intended to document interactions between police and citizens to improve transparency and accountability. The main mechanism by which cameras might affect behavior concerns the deterrence of wrongdoing. The effects of these cameras may be experienced by both police and the citizens with whom they interact. Hopes that body-worn cameras might reduce police misconduct were reflected in the recommendations of President Obama's Task Force on 21st Century Policing (2015, pp. 31–32) and the Leadership Conference on Civil and Human Rights (2015, Principle 4).

Lum and colleagues (2020) provide a thorough review of studies on this subject conducted between 2004 and 2018, examining the effects of body-worn cameras on outcomes including officer use of force, citizen complaints, arrests, and pedestrian and traffic stops. Their review examines 30 studies, 17 of which are known to have been fielded in the United States. Across a range of outcomes, the review indicates there is no consistent evidence that body-worn cameras are associated with either less or more enforcement action, officer injuries, or officer use of force. Against this general pattern of findings, however, body-worn cameras were found to be associated with significant reductions in complaints against officers and a significant increase in non-traffic citations. Given the relatively small body of research, meta-analysis results are sensitive to the included studies. M.C. Williams and colleagues (2021) add two more recent studies to the 30 examined by Lum and colleagues (2020) and report stronger evidence for a reduction in officer use of force.

The effect on racial disparities has been examined in New York City, where body-worn cameras were introduced following the *Floyd* case on stop-and-frisk. A randomized controlled trial evaluated the effects of cameras in an experiment involving 40 police precincts and 3,889 NYPD officers (Braga et al., 2021). In the design of the experiment, the 40 precincts were sorted into 20 pairs matched according to the number of complaints made to the Civilian Complaint Review Board, a civilian oversight body. Body-worn cameras were then assigned randomly to one precinct within each pair, and a random sample of stops was drawn for the one-year intervention period. The study found that body-worn cameras were not significantly associated with the numbers of arrests, arrests with force, summons, or crime complaints. However, officers in the treatment group experienced 21 percent fewer review board complaints and a 38 percent increase in the number of stops. An audit of a random subset of stops showed that New Yorkers in the treatment category were 10 percentage points more likely to be Black. Stops made by the body-worn-camera group of officers were significantly more likely to be evaluated as not meeting constitutional justifications for stops, frisks, and searches by the study team. The authors conclude both that the NYPD still has problems with unconstitutional stops of citizens made by its officers and that the presence of the body-worn cameras may be enhancing officer compliance with NYPD policy directives to document citizen stops (Braga et al., 2021).

Summary

Major efforts to change the context of policing to reduce racial inequality have been mounted through measures to expand judicial, federal, and public oversight. Significant reductions in the exposure of Black and Latino citizens to police contact have been obtained by regulating police discretion at the point of first contact between police and the public—in pedestrian stops and traffic stops. Evidence from New York City and Washington State shows that the elimination of stop-and-frisk and pretextual stops greatly reduced interaction between police and people of color. In New York City, relative racial disparity did not decline but the great reduction in police activity had substantial effects in minority communities. Pattern or practice investigations leading to Department of Justice settlements have been associated with reduced use of force, fewer citizen complaints, and declines in crime, but these effects are short-lived. Research on body-worn cameras shows that in some jurisdictions technological changes to improve accountability can reduce the use of force and citizen complaints against the police. However, other jurisdictions have obtained no benefit from body-worn cameras, and on average the results are not significantly positive.

Reducing racial inequality by improving oversight and accountability is often met with staunch resistance from police leadership, middle management, and line officers, although the evidence indicates this has more clearly stymied the implementation of reform rather than resulting in a withdrawal of police services. In some areas, particularly related to federal oversight of local police departments, research suggests that methods for accountability and oversight must be strengthened because constitutional compliance is short-lived, and in some localities police have withdrawn services, resulting in increases in crime.

Changing the Disposition of Officers

Whereas changes in oversight have affected the context of police decision making, direct efforts to change the use of discretion have focused on training and hiring policy. Recent training efforts directly aimed at racially unequal policing have focused on implicit bias. The idea of implicit bias rests on a social-psychological theory in which an individual's judgments and decisions are based on heuristics that simplify cognitive tasks to enable a speedy resolution. Stereotypes can inform judgments, even if the decision maker would reject the stereotype in a more deliberate decision process. This rapid decision making in combination with stereotypes is the basis for implicit bias.

As the historical discussion in Part I showed, longstanding and deep-seated stereotypes associate Black people with criminality and violence. Similar findings emerge from contemporary psychological research, in which experimental subjects are found to associate Black people with fears about dangerousness, threat, violence, and irredeemability (Donders et al., 2008; Eberhardt et al., 2004). Research shows that these deep-seated associations are just as prevalent among police officers as they are among the public. Stereotypes that associate people of color, and especially Black people, with violence and other criminality may lead police officers to act—perhaps even unconsciously—with bias.

Many police departments have responded to national pressure to address disparate outcomes by reforming officer training. Officer training has evolved to better equip officers in the field, including in their decision making processes. Implicit bias trainings aimed at reducing racial profiling (and therefore disparities) have been widely implemented in police departments throughout the country. There are few rigorous evaluations of the effects of such anti-bias training on racial disparities. Evaluations have found that trainees showed greater awareness of personal bias and a better understanding of how bias contributes to racial disparities. Still, there is no rigorous evidence base indicating that anti-bias training reduces racial disparity. For example, Worden and colleagues (2020) evaluated an implicit bias program for NYPD officers. They found that while the training had a moderate effect on officers' knowledge about implicit bias immediately after the training, a follow-up survey revealed a decay effect in terms of knowledge gained. Moreover, the authors report that they found insufficient evidence to conclude that racial and ethnic disparities in police enforcement actions were reduced because of the training.

Recently, some jurisdictions have passed legislation focusing on eliminating explicit bias from police departments, largely through enhanced screening during the hiring stage and by making evidence of explicit bias a separate articulated element of background investigations. For example, California's recently passed AB846 requires background investigators as well as psychological examiners to include explicit bias as a review criterion for new recruits.[11] While the law has yet to be implemented, the legislation will likely incorporate a routine review of past statements and social media activity for evidence of explicit bias.

The value of increasing diversity in the police ranks is supported by research showing that female police and people of color engage in less enforcement activity than male and White officers (Ba et al., 2021). Unusually for research on the effects of police diversity, Ba and colleagues analyze highly disaggregated data that allow comparisons of officers, who vary by race and gender and who are patrolling the same beats at the same time of year and at the same time of day. Earlier research had studied coarse geographic units (Legewie and Fagan, 2016; Donohue and Levitt, 2001). Analyzing data from the Chicago Police Department, they find that Black officers make fewer stops and arrests compared to White officers in the same settings. Notably, Black officers make significantly fewer stops for "suspicious behavior." The reductions in enforcement activity are largely due to fewer enforcement actions taken against Black citizens. The authors caution that further diversification of the police department is likely to have complex and heterogeneous effects, although they conclude that "the results strongly show that diversification can reshape police-civilian encounters" (Ba et al., 2021, p. 701). Similar results are provided in an analysis by Hoekstra and Sloan (2022) of 1.6 million 911 calls. They find that in Black neighborhoods (at least 80% Black), at the level of census blocks, White officers are about five times more likely to use gun force than Black officers. Another study exploits 25-year panel data on the race of U.S. sheriffs and shows that the ratio of Black-to-White arrests is significantly higher when a White sheriff is managing a department (Bulman, 2019). Relatedly, Harvey and Mattia (2022) found an association between the successful litigation over racially discriminatory practices within law enforcement agencies and

[11] See https://leginfo.legislature.ca.gov/faces/billTextClient.xhtml?bill_id=201920200AB846

a reduction in absolute and relative crime victimization among Black people without a corresponding increase in victimization among White people.

Implicit bias training, hiring procedures that foster diversity, and background checks for explicit bias can also be viewed as elements of a larger organizational context that promotes a department-wide culture of fairness and accountability. From this point of view, eliminating bias and building legitimacy is as much a challenge of culture change and organizational design as a challenge of shifting individual psychology (Tyler, 2017; Fridell and Lim, 2016). There is more research on individual police decision making (see, for example, Owens et al., 2018) than studies of multifaceted efforts at cultural and organizational change aimed specifically at reducing racial inequality, and the committee views this as an important area for future study.

Racial Inequality and Police Deterrence Tactics

Police tactics to deter crime have important implications for racial inequality in the criminal justice system. Deterrence-based tactics have been central to the evolution of crime-prevention strategies and a focal point for researchers. Chalfin and McCrary (2017) observe that deterrence-based strategies often involve the police in signaling the threat of sanctions, so policing necessitates close contact with the public. Deterrence-based tactics can also concentrate policing in predominately Black and Latino communities, where the risks of crime are assessed by police to be highest. Finally, deterrence-based tactics can also widen police discretion to stop and search the public. Due to close contact with the public, the concentration of resources in disadvantaged communities, and widening discretion, deterrence tactics may also have disparate effects in Black, Latino, and Native American communities.

The large literature examining the effects of police force size and policing tactics on crime consistently finds that higher staffing levels reduce crime rates with statistically and substantively significant impacts on homicide (the National Academies of Sciences, Engineering, and Medicine, 2018, see Chapter 7; Chalfin and McCrary, 2017). While fewer studies examine the impact on racial inequality, one recent paper analyzes the relationship between race-specific crime rates and the number of police officers in 242 large U.S. cities from 1981 to 2018 (Chalfin et al., 2020). The results indicate that on average, an increase in police staffing is associated with a reduction in homicide victimization, with the effect on homicides per 100,000 being twice as large for Black homicide rates relative to White homicide rates. The authors also find that higher police staffing levels lead to a significant *decrease* in index crime arrests (and presumably index crimes), with the decline in index crime arrests four to six times larger on a per-capita basis for Black suspects relative to White suspects. The authors interpret this finding in particular as strong evidence of a deterrence effect of policing and evidence of "double-dividend" in the form of both less crime and fewer arrests for the most serious offenses. However, the authors also find that the effects on homicide are smaller in cities with a higher percentage of Black residents. Moreover, analyzing quality-of-life arrests, the burden of low-level arrests found to be associated with an additional police officer is 70 percent greater in the Black population than for White people. The authors interpret the race-specific results as indicating that additional policing presents a mixed bag of benefits and costs, with African Americans experiencing the largest per-capita declines in homicide and Part 1 offenses, as well as declines in Part 1 arrests, but increases in quality-of-life arrests. Moreover, their estimates of the interaction terms between policing and the proportion of Black residents suggests that there are some predominantly Black cities in the country where the marginal benefits from having additional police are small if not zero.

Focused Deterrence

In contrast to the broad brush of low-level enforcement and a blanket police presence, a highly concentrated deterrence strategy, called focused deterrence, narrowly targets police attention on a relatively small number of people who are identified as at high risk of crime and victimization (the National Academies, 2018). Focused deterrence shares some attributes of community-based anti-violence strategies reviewed in Chapter 6. In contrast to these approaches, however, focused deterrence relies on the threat of serious formal sanctions from the criminal justice system as a tool to motivate behavior change among individuals and groups. Focused deterrence is a place-based strategy that aims to intervene with specific individuals or gang networks in an effort to head off serious crime before it occurs. As a police-based deterrence tactic, focused deterrence involves the direct communication of the consequences of continued criminal offending and the availability of social services to targeted subjects. Often this communication takes the form of a "call-in," a "forum," or a "notification," involving face-to-face meetings with police, service providers, and community representatives. Leading examples—such as Operation Ceasefire, which was first fielded in Boston and later replicated in Newark, Los Angeles, and other cities—are typically deployed in highly disadvantaged minority communities (see Box 8-1 for a description of Operation Ceasefire; see also Chapter 6).

The most successful focused deterrence programs are associated with significant reductions in shootings and other serious violence (Braga et al., 2018). In 1996, Operation Ceasefire in Boston reported a 63 percent reduction in youth homicide, and a 44 percent reduction in youth gun assaults in one high-risk district (Braga et al., 2018). However, these declines occurred

BOX 8-1
Focused Deterrence in Boston: Operation Ceasefire

Operation Ceasefire was implemented by the Boston Police Department during the mid-1990s to tackle rising youth gun violence. A small population of chronic offenders involved in neighborhood-based groups was identified as responsible for more than 60 percent of youth homicide in Boston. As part of the Operation Ceasefire Program, the police and their social service and community partners reached out directly to the identified gangs, explicitly warning them that violence would no longer be tolerated. The warnings were given teeth by applying every legally available enforcement response when violence occurred. For example, the police and other law enforcement agencies sought to

> . . . disrupt street drug activity, focus police attention on low-level street crimes such as trespassing and public drinking, serve outstanding warrants, cultivate confidential informants for medium- and long-term investigations of gang activities, deliver strict probation and parole enforcement, seize drug proceeds and other assets, ensure stiffer plea bargains and sterner prosecutorial attention, request strong bail terms (and enforce them), and bring potentially severe federal investigative and prosecutorial attention to gang-related drug and gun activity. (Braga and Weisburd, 2015, p. 57)

At the same time, gang members were offered constructive help from youth workers, probation and parole officers, and in time even churches and other community groups. But these service partners also reinforced the message that violence was no longer acceptable to the community and that gang members' typical justifications for violence were wrong. The partners in Operation Ceasefire delivered these messages across multiple venues for contact with gang members, including formal meetings (known as "forums" or "call-ins"), the contacts that individual police officers and probation officers had with gang members, meetings with gang members in detention at juvenile facilities, and service partners who worked directly through outreach to the gangs. In this way, the police focused on a narrow problem (gang violence) by targeting specific offenders (gang members).

SOURCE: Excerpted from the National Academies (2018).

as violent crime was also decreasing in other cities, including cities that did not adopt an Operation Ceasefire approach. Operation Peacekeeper in Stockton (CA) was associated with a 42 percent reduction in gun homicide (Braga et al., 2018). Ceasefire in Rochester (NY) was associated with a 25 percent reduction in homicides with Black male victims ages 15–30 and a 27 percent reduction in gun robberies for the same group; however, the total homicide rate and the gun assault rate were not reduced in Rochester (Braga et al., 2018). In the 24 observational evaluation studies identified by

Braga and his colleagues (2019), focused deterrence was found on average to have a "statistically significant, moderate crime reduction effect." The National Academies Committee on Proactive Policing reviewed the evaluative literature on focused deterrence and concluded that

> [e]valuations of focused deterrence programs show consistent crime-control impacts in reducing gang violence, street crime driven by disorderly drug markets, and repeat individual offending. The available evaluation literature suggests both short-term and long-term area-wide impacts of focused deterrence programs on crime. (the National Academies, 2018, p. 175)

A literature scan of focused deterrence programs from the Urban Institute Justice Policy Center uncovered the following themes in their implementation: the need for analysis-driven goal setting, the importance of strong partnerships with local communities to build trust and a sense of joint ownership, challenges with replication that require tailoring programs to the local context, and the need for consistent monitoring and reevaluation for sustainability (Matei et al., 2022). Qualitative researchers report that the success of focused deterrence depends on a belief in the legitimacy of the police among local community residents and a procedurally just approach to the call-in meetings by police (Braga et al., 2018).

A related set of strategies in which police resources are deployed in relation to an assessment of risk involves directed patrol at crime hot spots. Directed patrols aimed at gun violence deploy police in small areas where shootings have been concentrated. In some research sites, gun patrols were preceded by police outreach to local households informing residents of upcoming patrols. The patrols themselves typically involve proactive car and pedestrian stops aimed at gun interdiction. Like focused deterrence, directed patrol has been found to be effective at reducing gun violence, and experimental results indicate reductions in gun-related assaults, robberies, and homicides (the National Academies, 2018; Koper and Mayo-Wilson, 2006). As the National Academies report on proactive policing discusses, strategies like directed patrol that initiate intense police contact in small areas (in practice, often in Black and Latino neighborhoods) have been shown to reduce serious violence but also carry the risk of discriminatory treatment and community mistrust. This finding points to the possibility of a tradeoff between reducing crime and reducing racial disparity.

Such research on the effectiveness of directed patrols cannot be viewed in isolation from the substantial evidence we have reviewed on the discriminatory treatment of minority communities in police stops. As Webster (2022, p. 40) states, "Given the potential for abuse in proactive gun-law enforcement, police must have strong systems of internal and external accountability to ensure that practices are not only legal but minimize harms and are acceptable to community members." This observation is particularly relevant at the time of this writing when levels of gun violence and violent victimization have increased sharply among young men during the ongoing COVID-19 pandemic. To meet this challenge, the evidence we have reviewed suggests that time-limited and spatially focused directed patrols, in combination with strong safeguards, may provide one tactic in times and places in which gun violence has escalated. More generally, because police-based deterrence strategies can carry significant risks of racially disparate criminal justice contact, community collaboration (see Chapter 6) and social policy support (Chapter 7) offer important complementary approaches in a comprehensive strategy. Community collaboration has taken the form of civilian oversight, and community consultation and partnership with police. Complementary social policy has taken the form of behavioral health interventions, jobs and training programs, and community-based physical and mental health treatment. Combining police-based deterrence strategies with community partnership and social policy offers an evidence-informed approach to addressing gun violence in a way that protects against the risks of growing racial inequality in criminal justice involvement.

COURTS

Despite significant evidence, reported in Chapter 4, of racial disparities in court outcomes, little research has been conducted on reforms to reduce racial disparity in court processing. Several of the main efforts to reduce these disparities fall within three categories:

1. Pretrial release decisions and risk assessment;
2. Mitigation of fines and fees; and
3. Modifications of both judicial and prosecutorial discretion, specifically for crimes of poverty.

Many other areas of innovation have been active over the last decades, including specialty courts for specific populations, special procedures for diversion, and alternative approaches to accountability such as restorative justice. Although applications in many of these areas seek alternatives to the punitive approaches that characterized the era of high incarceration rates, programs are often small or lack detailed research that addresses our specific charge of reducing racial inequality.

Pretrial Release Decisions and Risk Assessment

Research indicates significant unwarranted racial disparities in pretrial release decisions (see Chapter 4). Pretrial detention is associated with a higher probability of a guilty plea and worse sentencing outcomes (Dobbie et al., 2018). Moreover, policy changes that inadvertently reduce racial disparities in pretrial detention have been found to reduce racial disparities in case outcomes (MacDonald and Raphael, 2020). Reducing disparities in pretrial detention thus holds the promise of reducing disparities downstream for sentencing and imprisonment.

Two main and inter-related approaches to reducing unwarranted racial disparities in pretrial processing have involved bail reform and the use of predictive tools to inform judicial decision making. Bail reforms have recently been adopted in New Jersey, New York, Vermont, and Washington (DC), as well as in localities such as Cook County (IL) and Atlanta (GA). Quantitative risk assessment has been widely adopted not just for making pretrial decisions but also in prison facilities and community corrections. Bail reform and risk assessment have often been implemented together, where the range of offenses where bail could be set is reduced and a risk-assessment instrument is introduced to inform the decision about pretrial detention.

A major statewide reform of this kind was adopted in New Jersey in 2017. New Jersey's criminal justice reform had five main components: (1) a reduction in the use of money bail; (2) the use of a risk tool and a decision process to inform release conditions; (3) a power of pretrial detention without bail; (4) a new pretrial monitoring program; and (5) speedy trial laws that set a schedule for the first court appearance and major milestones such as indictment. New Jersey's risk-assessment tool was a nine-item inventory based on the defendant's current age and criminal history that yielded one risk score for the likelihood of committing a new crime and another for the likelihood of failing to appear in court.

An evaluation of this bail reform in New Jersey compared court records in the period prior to the reform with those from the year in which the bail reform was adopted (2017). Bail reform was found to be associated with a reduction in the number of less serious arrests, and with large reductions in the number of jail stays—a 16 percent reduction in the number of jail stays of three days or more and a 36 percent reduction in jail stays of 10 days or more (Anderson et al., 2019). Between 2012 and 2018, the pretrial jail population declined by 44 percent, a decline of 6,000 detainees. This decline included 3,000 fewer Black defendants, 1,500 fewer White defendants, and 1,300 fewer Hispanic defendants, clear evidence of a disparate impact of the reform on Black and Hispanic defendants. Still, in 2018 Black defendants accounted for 54 percent of the pretrial jail population, the same proportion as before the reform (in 2012; Grant, 2019).

In 2018, the Philadelphia (PA) district attorney mplemented an advisory change to end monetary bail for defendants who were charged with certain low-level offenses. Ouss and Stevenson (2020) used a differences-in-differences approach and found that the policy was associated with a 22 percent increase in the likelihood that a defendant would be released with no monetary or supervisory conditions but had no effect on pretrial detention. The authors found no evidence to support the notion that cash bail or pretrial supervision has a deterrent effect on failure-to-appear in court or pretrial crime.

Risk-assessment Tools

Risk-assessment instruments for pretrial decision making have been a focal point for policy reforms that aim to reduce racial disparities and jail populations. Although quantitative predictive instruments hold the promise of eliminating judicial bias, as is evidenced by the New Jersey reform, the items comprising a risk tool such as age at first arrest and the number of prior convictions may themselves be subject to racial bias (Harcourt, 2015; Starr, 2015; Holder, 2014). The impact of risk tools on racial inequality thus remains an empirical question. Few jurisdictions have evaluated the validity of their risk tool, studied correlations with race and ethnicity, or modified risk assessment to remove racial correlates from the instrument. The impact of risk assessment on racial disparity thus remains an urgent question for research.

However, at least two jurisdictions, in Minnesota and New York State, have used and modified risk tools with a view to reducing racial disparity and have provided detailed assessments of the effort. The Fourth Judicial District of Minnesota, Hennepin County, has developed a reiterative process of assessing scale validity and mitigating racialized differences in bail decisions. Hennepin County first implemented the use of risk assessment in 1972, adopting and slightly modifying the well-known "Vera Scale." A 1992 evaluation studied the sensitivity of individual risk factors to the inclusion of race in an equation predicting pretrial failure to appear or risk to public safety. It found that race was significantly predictive, but only two of the seven variables included on the Vera Scale were also significant (Goodman, 1992). A new scale minimizing the importance of community affiliation was implemented in 1992 based on these findings. The 1992 assessment's validity was measured in 2006; while this tool was found to improve predictive power by three percent compared to the Vera Scale, only five of the nine variables were found to be significantly predictive, and three of the four found not to be predictive were correlated with race. These three factors were removed from the scale as a consequence, and a new iteration of the scale was implemented in 2007 (Podkopacz et al., 2006). The scale was again updated in 2015 and assessed for validity in 2018. Analysis by race showed that White defendants were about 50 percent more likely to fall in the low-risk category than non-White defendants. The failure rate for White people was about 10 percent higher than for non-White people, although the difference was not statistically significant (Podkopacz et al., 2018).

Like Hennepin County, New York City has also modified its pretrial risk-assessment instrument to reduce racial disparity. In 2003, the New York City Mayor's Office of Criminal Justice contracted the not-for-profit Criminal Justice Agency to create a pretrial release assessment tool, which it then implemented. In 2019, this tool was evaluated by the agency for disparate assessment by race and updated to reduce disparity. Under the 2003 tool, White defendants were recommended for release at a rate 7.6 percentage points higher than Black defendants (70.3% vs. 62.7%). To reduce racial disparity and create better predictive capacity, the Criminal Justice Agency updated its release assessment. In comparison to the 2003 tool, the 2019 tool significantly increased sum recommendations for release. If this newest version of the tool had been available and implemented with a 2014 sample, it would have recommended an additional 41,600 Black individuals, 19,800 Hispanic individuals, and 8,000 White individuals for release on their recognizance. Moreover, the new tool decreased the disparity in release recommendations for White and Black defendants to 4.3 percent (Luminosity and the University of Chicago, 2020).

There are relatively few academic studies that assess the impact of risk assessment on racial disparity. Kleinberg and colleagues (2018) analyze court data from New York City to assess machine learning predictive tools for pretrial decision making. In contrast to the simple risk-assessment scale, which typically takes a weighted sum of a dozen or so measures of criminal history and current charges, machine learning methods fit complex nonlinear functions of predictive variables on training data, which are then used in the field for out-of-sample prediction. For Kleinberg and colleagues, the input variables were similar to those regularly available to judges at New York City bail hearings and related to current offense and prior criminal history. Machine learning, however, constructs a potentially complex function of inputs to make predictions that balance model complexity and prediction error. The study also exploits the random assignment of judges, so the analysis can compare outcomes for defendants who are otherwise equal but vary in the judges' release decisions. Kleinberg and colleagues find that a machine learning algorithm will detain Black defendants at a higher rate than White people to reduce the rate of re-arrest or failure to appear. But the algorithm can be tuned to control racial disparity, with only a slight increase in pretrial failure. In short, pretrial failure can be minimized subject to a racial equity goal, but in that case, race must be explicitly taken into account in the pretrial detention decision.

In one of the few empirical studies of the impact of risk assessment on racial disparity, Stevenson and Doleac (2022) analyze data on judges' sentencing behavior in Virginia (see also Sloan et al., 2018, for pretrial release in Texas; Stevenson, 2018a, for pretrial release in Kentucky; and Berk, 2017, for parole decisions in Pennsylvania). Virginia courts began using a risk tool for nonviolent felony defendants from the early 2000s. With data on sentencing and risk scores, the research points to three key findings. First, like the findings in Hennepin County, New York City, and in many other studies, Black defendants, when compared to White defendants, are predicted to have a higher risk of court failure or re-offending. Second, the risk instrument directly conflicts with legal principle by assigning high-risk scores to young defendants who are often assessed as less culpable. Third, Virginia judges apply the risk scores in a racially disparate way, being more likely to follow the leniency recommendations of the score for White defendants than for Black defendants.

Fines and Fees Mitigation

Several jurisdictions have either taken an alternate approach to fee collection or pardoned outstanding debts in their entirety in an effort to reduce their disproportionate impact on Black, Latino, and Native American communities. The San Francisco Superior Court was the first in California to stop license suspension as a consequence of failure to pay. The expulsion of the practice is largely due to vocal advocates, who noted that court debt and its consequences fall disproportionately on poor people and Black, Latino, and Native American individuals, further exacerbating cycles of poverty. While no research has been conducted to see if disparity in the system has lessened as a result of this provision, one study found that this practice has had no negative impact on revenue collection (Brown et al., 2020). Another field experiment, conducted in a misdemeanor court in Oklahoma, repaid all current and past court debt for a randomly selected treatment group, and similarly found a very low level of debt repayment in the control group. The Oklahoma study found no racial differences in the effects of clearing court debt, but large racial disparities in the caseloads meant that the fewer warrants, debts in collection, and tax-refund garnishing enjoyed by the treatment group disproportionately benefited people of color (Pager et al., 2022).

Statewide efforts at legal debt relief have been undertaken in Minnesota and Iowa through programming that helps drivers set up a payment plan for outstanding balances and thus avoid license suspension (Bastien, 2017; Schwartztol, 2017). Some jurisdictions are also experimenting with warrant clearances: Atlanta Municipal Court, Milwaukee Municipal Court, and Montgomery Municipal Justice Center all have regular "amnesty periods," during which those with outstanding minor offenses and traffic violations can resolve cases from the year prior without fear of arrest or of being charged with additional failure-to-appear fees (however, persons are still responsible for paying prior debt; Bastien, 2017). Lastly, minority-majority districts, like New Orleans Parish, have experimented with bail reform, including mandating ability-to-pay evaluations and consideration of non-monetary bail alternatives (Sledge, 2021).

Modification of Judicial and Prosecutorial Discretion

In 2005, the Vera Institute of Justice created the Prosecution and Racial Justice Program, which aimed to "manage the exercise of discretion within their [prosecutor's] offices in a manner that reduces the risk of racial disparity in the decision-making process" (Davis, 2013, p. 837). The program partnered with Mecklenberg County (NC) and Milwaukee County (WI) and with their respective district attorney's offices to identify disparities in prosecutorial decision making and enact policies to reduce them.

Mecklenberg County reduced the number of drug charges they prosecuted by nine percent when they found defendants to be disproportionately Black. When Milwaukee County found that a large percentage of drug paraphernalia cases involved possession of a crack pipe by Black defendants in the city of Milwaukee, District Attorney John Chisholm instructed his office to decline prosecution and instead divert arrestees to drug treatment. Milwaukee also conducted an evaluation of prosecution against domestic violence charges and found that there was a 34 percent greater chance of prosecution when the defendant was Black and the victim was White than when both defendant and victim were White. Chisholm responded with department-wide, culturally conscious training around domestic assault in diverse scenarios (Davis, 2013).

Suffolk County (MA), which includes the Greater Boston Area, has also experimented with changing prosecutorial policy to reduce racial disparity. District Attorney Rachael Rollins, who was inaugurated in 2019, created an officewide presumption of non-prosecution for 15 nonviolent misdemeanor offenses, all of which were considered "crimes of poverty" and disproportionately charged against people of color. The "Rollins list" included disorderly conduct, drug possession, receiving stolen property, and shoplifting (Daniel, 2018). While there has been no evaluation of racial disparity post-implementation at this time, one study found that the presumption of non-prosecution instituted by Rollins's office was associated with a 47 percent decrease in new criminal complaints for nonviolent misdemeanor cases not on the Rollins list and a 56 percent decrease in new criminal complaints for all nonviolent misdemeanor cases (both statistically significant). The study also found that the new policy had no effect on reported crime (Agan et al., 2021).

Similar to Rollins, other efforts by a newly elected cohort of prosecutors who campaigned to reduce the negative effects of courts and incarceration have been implemented with the goal of reducing disproportionate system contact for Black, Latino, and Native American individuals.[12] While these efforts are race-neutral on the surface, they largely affect Black, Latino, and Native American individuals, either because these jurisdictions have large minority populations or because of racial disparities in court involvement. Additional research is needed to understand the relationship among these reform efforts, racial disparities, and impacts on community safety.

Lastly, one study has identified targeted racial disparities in judicial decision making when sentencing post-conviction. Scorecards that rated the extremity of disparity were calculated at the county level in New York State. These scorecards were made available to both county judicial leadership and the New York State Permanent Commission on Sentencing, but the commission was disbanded before action could be taken based on county-level scoring (Ridgeway et al., 2020).

SENTENCING AND CORRECTIONS

The great increase in correctional populations during the last quarter of the 20th century remains one of the most important and distinguishing characteristics of the U.S. criminal justice system. Over roughly two decades, the United States went from having per-capita correctional populations comparable to those of western European nations to having the world's highest incarceration rate. While U.S. incarceration rates have declined in recent years, and more so for Black Americans than for other groups, the country still incarcerates its citizens at rates that are high by both historical and international standards, with Black Americans incarcerated at rates many multiples those of other groups. Moreover, the increases in the nation's prison and jail populations have occurred hand-in-hand with increases in the population of individuals under community corrections. As discussed above, this interacts with policing in a specific manner, since individuals on community corrections are subject to additional scrutiny

[12]For example, during her first three years as Cook County (Chicago) state's attorney, Kim Foxx dropped felony charges against 30 percent of felony defendants, an increase of 10 percentage points compared to her predecessor. Foxx's office has adopted a range of measures to encourage dropping charges tainted by improper police procedure (Jackson et al., 2020). Prosecutors under Larry Krasner, Philadelphia County district attorney, have reduced requests for cash bail at arraignment (Booker, 2021). George Gascón has dismissed 60,000 marijuana convictions as Los Angeles County district attorney and 9,000 during his former post as San Francisco district attorney, all of which occurred recently but prior to marijuana legalization under CA Proposition 64 (Queally, 2021). Lastly, Brooklyn district attorney Eric Gonzalez established a 2020 action plan that would seal or expunge marijuana convictions and normalize prosecution's pursuit of non-jail resolutions at all case junctures, among other initiatives (Brooklyn County District Attorney's Office, 2020). Obstacles and risks associated with changes in prosecutorial policy are examined by Mitchell and colleagues (2022) and Hogan (2022).

and subject to warrantless search. Given racial disparities in rates of incarceration and rates of community corrections supervision, these disparities in community corrections involvement translate directly into disparities in invasive interactions with the police.

To reverse these trends and to narrow disparities in correctional supervision, one could pursue several alternative lines of analysis. One could investigate the specific policy changes that led to large increases in U.S. correctional populations, critically evaluate their impacts on communities in terms of both public safety and harms visited upon those bearing the brunt of the punishment, and then reverse the changes in sentencing policy that have done the most harm and generated the least benefit. Alternatively, one could look to recent experiences with reforms occurring at the federal and state levels, identify those that have had an especially strong impact in reducing correctional populations without affecting public safety, and then devise proposals that draw upon the lessons from these reforms.

The sentencing policy changes in the 1980s and 1990s that drove the increases in correctional populations are well known (see NRC, 2014, Chapter 3). During that period, sentencing policy across the states shifted from having relatively unstructured, indeterminate sentencing schemes in which individuals would receive a wide range of minimum to maximum sentences and correctional authorities would largely determine time of release, to more structured, determinate sentencing with legislatively prescribed sentences and administrative rules pertaining to good conduct credits determining release dates. Sentencing in general became more punitive, both in the widening range of offenses for which prison was prescribed and in the duration of sentences (Tonry, 2019). In many states as well as in the federal system, sentencing guidelines greatly reduced judicial discretion in admission to prison and parole board discretion at the end of a prison term.

Moreover, during this period state and federal lawmakers passed legislation mandating minimum sentences for specific offenses, imposed enhancements for second- and third-time prior convictions or enhancements for specific places or associations (e.g., school zones or gang membership), and added enhancements associated with specific conduct (e.g., use of a gun) or for specific criminal histories (e.g., enhancements for prior prison terms). Many states lengthened mandatory community correctional supervision time and often used technical violations of conditions of release to return people to prison without a new conviction. Moreover, many jurisdictions required that those sent to prison serve minimum percentages of their sentences regardless of conduct while incarcerated or efforts toward rehabilitation. The cumulative impact of these changes lengthened time served, especially for violent offenses; increased prison admission rates, particularly for lower-level drug offenses; increased racial disparities from the early 1970s to the late 1990s; and largely drove the five-fold increase in the nation's incarceration rate (NRC, 2014).

Given that U.S. sentencing occurs in the context of 51 different systems, the description above is stylized and the particulars of sentencing (the degree of indeterminacy, the use of enhancements, and the severity of sentences, for example) vary greatly across systems. However, some generalizations can be drawn from the past four decades that may guide reforms to reduce racial inequality. First, part of the growth in prison populations and in racial disparity from the early 1970s to the early 1990s is due to sentencing policies that impose terms of imprisonment and affect the rate of admissions to prisons. Mandatory minimum prison sentences and classification of offenses as felonies (which carry prison time) are examples of policies that tend to increase prison admission rates. Second, part of the growth in imprisonment and racial disparities is related to increases in the duration of sentences. Reforming sentencing policy to reduce racial disparity could thus focus on reducing prison admission rates, or on reducing the length of stay in prison, particularly for those serving long sentences.

Reducing Prison Admissions

Examples of sentencing reforms that have reduced prison admissions include changes in drug policy and "de-felonization" statutes that downgrade felony offenses to misdemeanors (Elderbroom and Durnan, 2018). California's Proposition 47 provides an important example of de-felonization. Passed in 2014, Prop 47 redefined some nonviolent property crimes, those where the value does not exceed $950, as misdemeanors. It also redefined some simple drug possession offenses as misdemeanors. The law also allows for past convictions for these charges to be reduced to misdemeanors by a court. Figure 8-1 documents arrest-age profiles for the one-year periods prior to and following the passage of Proposition 47. The figure presents felony arrest rates per 100,000 by single year of age for violent offenses, property crime offenses, drug offenses, and other offenses for African American, Hispanic, White, and Asian California residents. It shows that sizable changes occurred for all age categories and that racial disparities narrowed for most age groups for property felony and drug felony arrests. The declines in drug felony arrest rates are very steep and fairly evenly distributed across age groups. The declines in property crime arrest rates are also notable and particularly large for African Americans in their early 20s.

A number of other states have since followed California in reclassifying drug possession from a felony to a misdemeanor, including Utah, Connecticut, Oklahoma, and Alaska. In each case, simple drug possession (until a third conviction) was downgraded from a felony to a misdemeanor, and

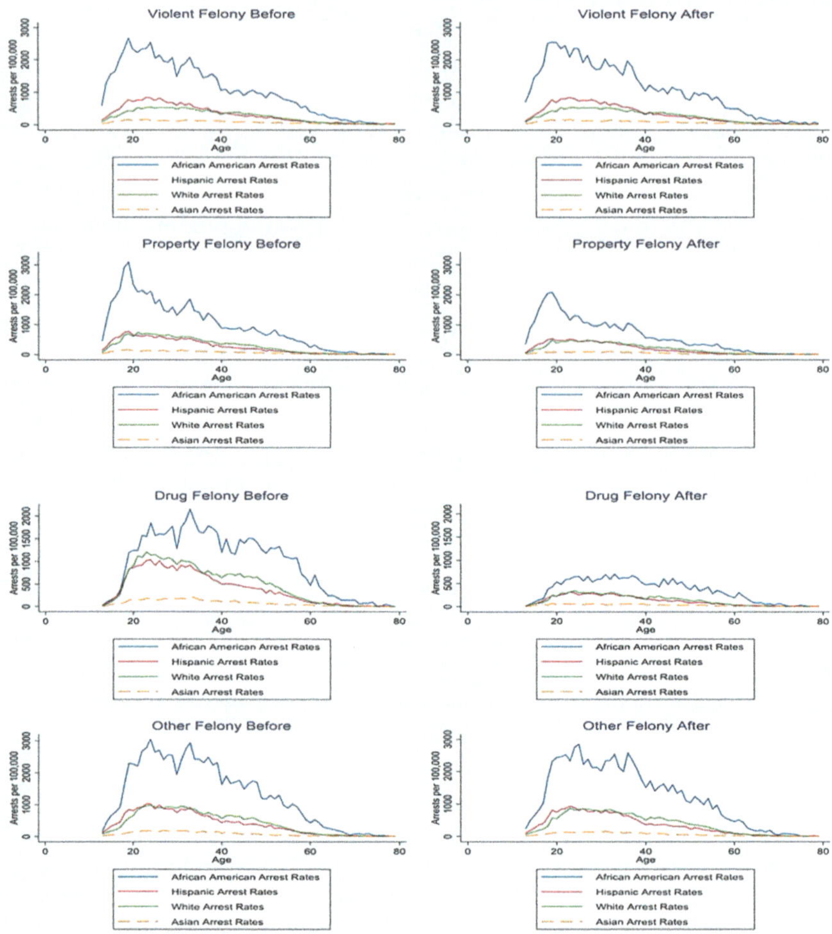

FIGURE 8-1 Felony arrests per 100,000 by race and single year of age for 12 months before and 12 months after the passage of Prop 47.
SOURCE: Lofstrom and colleagues (2020).

people convicted of drug possession could not be sent to prison. Moreover, these changes applied to virtually all controlled substances.

Similar sentencing reforms have been adopted that also reduce prison admission for drug possession, small sales of drugs, and other high-disparity offenses. In particular, reforms to narrow the application of mandatory minimum sentences have been adopted since the early 2000s. Legislative reforms have focused on drug sentencing. A 2014 report found that judges have been given discretion by state legislatures to depart from mandatory minimum drug sentences in six states: Connecticut (2001), Georgia (2013), Hawaii (2013), Louisiana (2012), Michigan (2002), and New York (2009; Subramanian and Delaney, 2014).

Reducing Long Sentences

As discussed earlier, the growth in prison populations and racial disparities was associated with increasing lengths of stay in prison, especially for violent crimes. The increase in the length of stay resulted from the proliferation of truth-in-sentencing, three-strikes, life-without-parole, and related reforms that concentrated their effects on violent offenses. Since African Americans are incarcerated at higher rates for violent offenses, murder and robbery in particular, the increase in the length of stay has tended to increase the racial disparity in imprisonment (Kazemian, 2022). Neal and Rick (2016), using data from seven states, find that for the violent crimes of murder and robbery, arrest rates declined from 1985 to 2005, yet incarceration in these offense categories increased. This occurred in part because of a slight increase in the risk of prison admission, given an arrest, but mostly because of an increase in the length of stay in prison. The proportion who were in state prison after 10 years increased during the period by 57 percent for murder and by 236 percent for robbery. Similar findings for length of stay were reported by Raphael and Stoll (2013) and Blumstein and Beck (2012; Beck and Blumstein, 2018). In 2020, more than 200,000 people were serving life sentences, and one in five imprisoned Black men were incarcerated on a life sentence (Nellis, 2021).

The increasing length of sentences has tended to prolong the incarceration of many, well past the age of being criminally active. Thus, studies of incapacitation, which estimate the counterfactual criminal involvement in free society of those who are incarcerated, find little to no crime-reducing effect of lengthening already long sentences (NRC, 2014, pp. 140–145). Deterrence studies also find little evidence of crime-reducing effects. Studies of gun crime enhancements (Raphael and Ludwig, 2003), greater penalties associated with moving from the juvenile to the adult justice system (Hjalmarsson, 2009; Lee and McCrary, 2009), and California's third-strike enhancement indicate that adding time to long sentences either has no effect on crime or, in some studies, only a small effect. Nagin (2013, p. 231) concludes, "The deterrent return to increasing an already long sentence is small, possibly zero." Largely based on this empirical evidence, the National Research Council panel on high incarceration rates concluded that long sentences could be reduced with very little effect on crime (NRC, 2014, p. 5). Reducing long sentences would also reduce absolute racial disparities because the conviction offenses of Black men disproportionately carry long sentences.

Unlike sentencing reforms that reduce prison admissions for drug possession and other low-level felonies, there are few significant examples of reducing long sentences. Exceptions include California's three-strikes reform, which greatly reduced the use of long sentences for third-time felonies and eliminated the sentence of mandatory life without parole for people committing homicide as juveniles—which had been ruled unconstitutional by the U.S. Supreme Court in 2012 (Daftary-Kapur et al., 2022). Reducing long sentences in both cases disproportionately benefited Black incarcerated people because of their relatively high incarceration rates, and it had no measurable effect on serious crime.

Another approach to the reduction of long sentences has involved so-called second-look provisions, which offer procedures for review after sentencing. In the Model Penal Code, a second-look review could reduce sentences for good conduct in prison, for advanced age or infirmity, or based on changed circumstances of the offense or the offender after the sentence was imposed (Frase, 2009). Under revisions in 2017, the Model Penal Code recommends legislature authorize judicial review of sentences after 15 years of imprisonment for adult crimes, and after 10 years for youth who commit crimes while younger than age 18. Second-look provisions have been adopted or are being considered in several jurisdictions (Porter, 2021). California's AB 2942 allows district attorneys to initiate re-sentencing, considering factors such as the applicant's prison disciplinary record and record of rehabilitation, and whether age, time served, or diminished physical condition has reduced the applicant's risk of future violence. In Washington (DC) the Second Look Amendment Act, 2020, allows those who committed crime as young adults (under the age of 25) to petition for resentencing after 15 years of imprisonment. Proposed legislation in New York State, known as the Elder Parole Bill, would allow people ages 55 and older who have served 15 years or more to receive a parole hearing. At the federal level, a Second Look Bill has been introduced that would allow people who have been incarcerated for at least 10 years in federal prison to petition a court for re-sentencing.

Although the details of second look provisions vary across jurisdictions, they offer a mechanism to reduce very long prison sentences, and they recognize that the risk of re-offending is relatively low for people in midlife or who are elderly. The provisions are consistent with a large body of research showing very low rates of criminal involvement for people in their thirties, forties, and older (Daftary-Kapur et al., 2022; Blumstein and Nakamura, 2009; Laub and Sampson, 2003; Hirschi and Gottfredson, 1983).

Repealing the Death Penalty

At the far end of sentencing severity lies the death penalty. Chapter 2 reports evidence of both racial disparity and racial bias in death penalty sentencing, and the committee sees death penalty abolition as an important initiative for reducing racial inequality. The U.S. Supreme Court, in the landmark case *Furman v. Georgia*,[13] invalidated all the states' death penalty statutes. *Furman,* which was decided 5–4, was a complex decision with no controlling opinion on which the majority could agree. In deciding with the majority, Justice Douglas spoke directly to the issue of racial inequality and observed that the death penalty was applied disproportionately to "the Negro, and the members of unpopular groups," noting that in the present cases the defendants were Black and the victims were White (Garland, 2010, p. 226). The sequel to *Furman*, *Gregg v. Georgia*,[14] reaffirmed the constitutionality of the death penalty with additional procedural safeguards.

Since *Gregg*, advocacy campaigns against the death penalty have appealed to a variety of rationales, including the incidence of wrongful conviction, the absence of a deterrent effect, the cost of capital cases, the evolving standards of decency, the cruelty of methods of execution, the arbitrariness of capital charging, and what Steiker and Steiker (2016, p. 110) have called the "unjust influence of race in the capital punishment process" (Breyer, 2016; Martin, 2009; see Garland, 2010, Chapters 9 and 10, for a discussion of the politics and culture of the death penalty after *Furman*).

Racial inequality thus figures as one of several arguments used against the death penalty, although experimental research also shows that presenting evidence of racial disparity can *increase* support for the death penalty among White people (Peffley and Hurwitz, 2007). In 2005, the U.S. Supreme Court in *Simmons v. Roper*[15] also banned the death penalty for juvenile offenders, citing the neuroscience of adolescent brain development. Thirty-seven states had re-established the death penalty after the *Furman* decision, but by 2020 repeals had been passed in 12 states, and moratoriums on the use of the penalty had been issued by governors in another three states. Many states, although having a death penalty, have not conducted an execution in years. The Death Penalty Information Center has found that official misconduct is extremely prevalent in death penalty cases—5.6 percent of all death sentences since 1972 have been exonerated due to prosecutorial misconduct. The most likely outcome of an individual's death sentence is that it will be overturned without being re-imposed. Since 1972, less than one in six death sentences have resulted in an execution (Death Penalty Information Center, 2022b). In 2020, the federal government carried out 10 of the 17 executions nationwide.

---

[13]408 U.S. 238 (1972). See https://supreme.justia.com/cases/federal/us/408/238/
[14]428 U.S. 153 (1976). See https://supreme.justia.com/cases/federal/us/428/153/
[15]543 U.S. 551 (2005). See https://supreme.justia.com/cases/federal/us/543/551/

COMMUNITY SUPERVISION

Probation and parole are systems of supervision that hinge on a high degree of discretion. Entry into probation and revocation for technical violations are both determined by a judge in a court hearing. Parole supervision also operates with a high level of discretion, such that a parole board first decides on early release from prison and later on return custody in the event of a violation. Research shows large racial disparities in the rates of both community supervision and revocation of community supervision, with Black and Hispanic people at greater risk of re-incarceration (Bradner et al., 2020; Steen et al., 2013; Grattet et al., 2009). Black parolees and probationers are regularly found to be at high risk of return to custody for violations of technical conditions of supervision and for new offenses (Bradner and Schiraldi, 2020; Lin et al., 2010; Steen and Opsal, 2007). The conditions of supervision are themselves often onerous, involving regular visits with probation and parole officers, drug testing, mandated programming, unannounced visits by officers to places of work and home, and the payment of supervision fees.

Recent reforms have reduced the disproportionate impact on minority parolees and probationers by limiting the duration of community supervision, limiting discretion to revoke parole or probation, and reducing the intensity of supervision. Reforms in all these areas appear to have had very little, if any, adverse effect on crime rates based on available research.

The largest recent reduction in the scale of community supervision can be found in California, as part of the process of realignment, initiated by a series of cases pointing to constitutional violations as a result of prison overcrowding. The court rulings and advocacy prompted legislation that reduced the scale of imprisonment and the extent of community corrections supervision. In 2009, the California legislature passed Senate Bill 678, the Community Corrections Performance Incentive Act,[16] which created incentives for counties to retain probation supervision for technical violations and eliminated parole for low-level offenses. In 2011, the California Public Safety Realignment Bill legislated that felony convictions for nonserious, nonviolent, and nonsexual offenses could no longer result in sentencing to state prison and parole but only to local jail and probation. Restricting community supervision in this way also meant that probation revocation would result in 90 days in jail and not in longer periods of imprisonment (Sundt et al., 2016). In 2014, California's Safe Neighborhoods and Schools Act (Proposition 47)[17] downgraded six felony offenses to misdemeanors, reducing the application of prison sentences (and subsequent parole) and

---

[16]See https://www.courts.ca.gov/documents/sb678.pdf

[17]See https://www.courts.ca.gov/prop47.htm

felony probation, and diverting people to shorter and often unsupervised periods of local probation. In 2020, Assembly Bill 1950[18] was passed, reducing misdemeanor probation in California from a maximum of three years to one, and reducing felony probation from five years to two. In the period from 2009 to 2020, California experienced steep declines in the probation revocation rate, which dropped from eight percent to 2.5 percent.

The California reforms, which were sustained over a decade, included a mix of sentencing reforms and administrative changes that diverted jurisdiction from the state to the local level. In many cases, reducing the severity of sentences—sometimes through sentence reductions and sometimes through de-felonization—had the effect of eliminating parole supervision or of shifting people from state felony probation to the less-punitive local misdemeanor probation.

A number of studies have examined the impact of these California reforms on the state's crime rates. During the period of declining community supervision in the 2010s, crime declined by 7.4 percent (Bartos and Kubrin, 2018), and "no measurable effect on violent crime" from the California reforms was found. Analyses of California Realignment and Proposition 47 similarly found no increase in violent crime and small declines in re-arrest and reconviction (Bird et al., 2018). While these analyses do not isolate the effect of reduced community supervision, they indicate that the overall scale of correctional supervision—institutional and community-based—has been reduced significantly with no adverse effect on serious crime.

A second case study of reducing the scale of community supervision is provided by New York City (Lopoo et al., 2022). In New York City, pretrial populations can be assigned to probation supervision, and misdemeanor convictions can result in a sentence of local probation. Beginning in the early 1990s, New York City greatly reduced the intensity of probation supervision, using reporting kiosks that followed a fingerprint reading with a few questions instead of the traditional meeting with a probation officer. The intensity of supervision was further reduced in the 2000s with "distance reporting," in which probationers could check in by phone or computer. Probation officers would request a reduction in the period of supervision for those completing distance reporting successfully. New York City also undertook a large-scale review of probation absconders, reviewing more than 15,000 records; if an absconding person had not been re-arrested, the arrest warrant for absconding was dismissed. Policy on probation revocation also shifted in the 2000s to discourage incarceration for violations of the conditions of supervision.

The cumulative effect of policy reforms in New York City, along with substantial reductions in felony arrests from the early 1990s to the 2000s,

[18]See https://leginfo.legislature.ca.gov/faces/billNavClient.xhtml?bill_id=201920200AB1950

resulted in a large decline in local probation supervision. In 2000, probation supervision in New York City peaked at 82,342. By 2021, the city probation population had shrunk to 11,531. The index crime rate fell as well, from 3,099 per 100,000 (in 2000) to 1,732 per 100,000 (in 2019) during the period of shrinking community supervision (Lopoo et al., 2022). The decline in the probation population also unfolded in a context in which advocacy groups raised public awareness about criminal justice reform, and an array of social services for job training, housing, educational assistance, and peer mentorship were made available to those involved in the criminal courts (Lopoo et al., 2022). These trends in New York City probation supervision, along with other research finding no crime-reducing effect of probation or parole, suggest that substantial reductions in community supervision are possible without adverse effects on public safety.

In sum, the experiences of California and New York City indicate large reductions in the probation and parole population, with substantial and disproportionate reductions in the community supervision of Black and Hispanic people. These reductions were achieved with a wide variety of policy changes, including reforms to sentencing those downgraded offenses from felonies to misdemeanors, that limited parole and probation periods and that shifted jurisdiction for supervision from the state to the local level. In addition to legislative shifts, policy change within probation departments has reduced the intensity of supervision, shifting from personal reporting to an officer to various forms of distance reporting. All these reforms were adopted during periods of significant reductions in crime.

These experiences, sustained in very large jurisdictions over several decades, indicate that substantial and disproportionate minority correctional supervision can be reduced through sentencing reforms that limit the numbers and duration of probation and parole supervision and that reduce revocation to incarceration for technical violations, as well as through agency policy changes that reduce the intensity of supervision.

The steady accumulation of sentencing reforms around the country since the early 2000s has contributed to reductions both in the prison population and in racial disparities. Changes in drug sentencing, notably the elimination of mandatory prison sentences, have reduced incarceration for drug crimes, reducing absolute racial inequality between Black and White people. Reducing long sentences also promises to reduce racial disparity, with Second Look provisions offering one important mechanism for reviewing long sentences. Several states have also reduced community supervision populations and curtailed the discretionary power of line officers and judges to return people on probation and parole to incarceration for technical violations. Reducing revocations for technical violations of community supervision is also likely to reduce racial disparities in incarceration.

CONCLUSION

The U.S. constitutional system embodies a principle of parsimony, of limited government, that is reflected in foundational restrictions on executive powers of search and seizure, the prohibition of cruel and unusual punishment, a positive right to counsel, and due process protections against group-based inequalities. In the era of mass criminalization and high incarceration rates, the principle of parsimony was subject to enormous stress. Many of the criminal justice reforms reviewed in this chapter restore the principle of parsimony by reducing police contact, the scale of incarceration, and arbitrary community supervision. In so doing, these measures also offer substantial promise for reducing racial inequality.

Although racial inequality in criminal justice contact remains high, a wide range of criminal justice reforms have been adopted across the country that have reduced the disproportionate involvement in disadvantaged communities. Reforms—variously imposed by courts, by federal monitors, through legislation, or through agency policy change—have changed the practice of policing, court processing, sentencing, and correctional supervision. Clear evidence of reduced racial inequality is associated with large reductions in the scale of police stops, the level of incarceration, and revocations of parole and probation supervision. In each of these cases, we see evidence of large reductions in absolute racial disparity at little or no cost to public safety.

Efforts at reducing relative disparity—whether with body-worn cameras, risk assessments, or anti-bias training—are not as strongly supported by the research evidence. This is in part because the evidence base is relatively thin, and in part because technical and human interventions may be underpowered in the face of the large structural inequalities in which the criminal justice system is embedded.

Throughout this review we have encountered the complex issue of possible tradeoffs between racial fairness and crime. Does reducing racial inequality come at the cost of more crime? In many cases, fairness is constitutionally mandated and in this sense is a dominant value for public policy. In some cases, the harms of criminal justice intervention are clear-cut, and reducing the scale of intervention both reduces racial inequality and promotes safety. The criminogenic effects and pains of long periods of incarceration is a leading example. But our review also points to examples, such as directed police patrols, where the goals of crime reduction and racial fairness—at least in the very short term—can sometimes be in conflict. In these cases, the risk of greater inequality can be addressed by designing criminal justice interventions (say, gun patrols) with strong safeguards against abuse and using them in a limited way in coordination with close community collaboration and social policy.

CONCLUSION 8-1: A wide variety of measures—including judicial bans on unconstitutional policing and incarceration, sentencing reform for drug offenses and de-felonization, bail reform, and reductions in the intensity and duration of community corrections supervision—have reduced the overall level of criminal justice contact, incarceration, and community supervision. Although in many cases relative disparities have not been reduced, these measures have had large effects on reducing absolute racial disparities, with little evidence across specific cases of an adverse effect on crime.

CONCLUSION 8-2: More targeted initiatives to reduce relative disparities—through, for example, federal oversight, diversity hiring, anti-bias training, or quantitative risk assessment—have been less clearly effective. In part, this is due to limitations of the research evidence, which should be further developed to effectively guide policy. Targeted initiatives also face resistance from criminal justice officials—police officers, police executives, and judges, for example—who may not view the initiatives as legitimate.

Although some jurisdictions have significantly reduced specific kinds of criminal justice contacts that have in turn reduced absolute disparities, substantial racial inequality in the criminal justice system remains.

RECOMMENDATION 8-1: Subject to the main goals of parsimony and community safety, states, localities, and the federal government should explore ways to reduce police stops and searches, jail detention, prison admissions, and long sentences, which would further reduce racial disparities. Examples of such efforts could include limiting jail detention to only those charged with serious crimes who pose a serious and immediate risk of harm or flight, pursuing further drug sentencing reform, establishing second-look provisions for long sentences, eliminating revocations of community supervision for technical violations, and eliminating the death penalty.

CONCLUSION 8-3: The research and policy experience reviewed here has often involved piecemeal and uncoordinated reforms that have affected racial disparity at specific stages of criminal processing but have had less effect on racial inequality that emerges across stages and in community contexts of racial inequality. Reducing racial inequality will involve coordinated reforms across stages of the criminal justice system that will reduce the racial disadvantage that accumulates from police contact, to court processing and sentencing, to correctional supervision.

RECOMMENDATION 8-2: Given evidence of how racial inequality in the criminal justice system partly results from structural inequalities in society and the cumulative effect of criminal processing, states, localities, and the federal government should explore ways to reduce racial inequality through coordinated reforms that work across the stages of the criminal justice system and also address structural inequalities in society.

9

The Federal Role

This chapter lays out a framework by which federal actors and policy makers can support communities in their work to promote safety and address the inequalities in their respective public safety systems. The goal of this framework is to strengthen the capacity of communities and local jurisdictions to promote safety while optimizing the footprint of the criminal justice system by reducing the scope of its harm. In this context, the emphasis on *growing* opportunities rather than repressing individual traits or behaviors, as described in Chapter 6, is critically important. The federal government can support growing opportunity through mechanisms such as *revenue sharing* or formula funding programs, allowing for local discretion, rather than tying aid to a particular solution through categorical grants-in-aid, which have made funding contingent on implementing policies/strategies deemed best by the federal agency (or the congressional appropriator).

This chapter opens with a discussion of the history of the first federal grant program for crime control, underscoring the role of the federal government in local crime control efforts. The critical importance of federal dollars in crime initiatives was outlined in a 2014 National Research Council report, *The Growth of Incarceration in the United States: Exploring Causes and Consequences*:

> In the 1980s and 1990s, state and federal legislators passed and governors and presidents signed laws intended to ensure that more of those convicted would be imprisoned and that prison terms for many offenses would be longer than in earlier periods. The increase in the use of imprisonment as a response to crime reflects a clear policy choice. No other inference can

be drawn from the enactment of hundreds of laws mandating lengthier prison terms. In the federal Violent Crime Control and Law Enforcement Act of 1994, for example, a state applying for a federal grant for prison construction was required to show that it: (A) has increased the percentage of convicted violent offenders sentenced to prison; (B) has increased the average prison time which will be served in prison by convicted violent offenders sentenced to prison; (C) has increased the percentage of sentence which will be served in prison by violent offenders sentenced to prison.

During the 1970s, experiments with voluntary sentencing guidelines were undertaken in many states, and all but one state enacted mandatory minimum sentence laws typically requiring minimum 1- or 2-year sentences or increases of 1 or 2 years in the sentences that would otherwise have been imposed. During the 1980s, the federal government and nearly every state enacted mandatory minimum sentence laws for drug and violent crimes, typically requiring minimum sentences of 5, 10, and 20 years or longer. During the 1990s, the federal government and more than half the states enacted truth-in-sentencing and three strikes laws. Almost all of the states now have life without possibility of parole laws. Voluntary guidelines and statutory determinate sentencing laws proved ineffective at achieving their aims of increasing consistency and diminishing racial and other unwarranted sentencing disparities.

Racial and ethnic disparities in imprisonment reached extreme and unprecedented levels in the 1980s and 1990s and have since remained at deeply troubling levels. They were partly caused and significantly exacerbated by recent sentencing laws aimed at achieving greater severity, certainty, and crime prevention and by law enforcement strategies associated with the war on drugs. They also resulted partly from small but systematic racial differences in case processing, from arrest through parole release, that have a substantial cumulative effect. And they were influenced by conscious and unconscious bias and stereotyping that remain pervasive in America despite the near disappearance of widespread beliefs about racial superiority and inferiority. (NRC, 2014, pp. 70; 101–102)

HISTORY OF FEDERAL GRANT MAKING FOR CRIME AND PUBLIC SAFETY

The Law Enforcement Assistance Administration (LEAA) was established by the Omnibus Crime Control and Safe Streets Act of 1968 (hereafter the Safe Streets Act) as the first federal program to distribute crime control grants to states. The LEAA functioned as the federal government's law enforcement consultant, promoting a national strategy on crime to the states and, through them, to local governments. The agency provided and arranged for technical assistance both directly and through contractors, consultants, and publications produced by its research arm, the National Institute of Criminal Justice. In its early years, the LEAA focused on improving the technological capacity of police departments and modernizing police operations. The Safe Streets Act's emphasis on interagency planning and coordination supported the LEAA in forging links between law enforcement and social agencies in urban centers as well as military and intelligence agencies, such as the Department of Health, Education, and Welfare; the Department of Housing and Urban Development; the Army; and the Central Intelligence Agency (CIA; Hinton, 2017).

The Safe Streets Act required states to develop long-term crime control strategies through criminal justice planning agencies and provided federal funding for such efforts at 90 percent of their cost. These state-level planning agencies acted as subgrantors between the federal government and municipalities. To be eligible for LEAA grants, governors had six months to organize local and law enforcement officials to craft a criminal justice improvement plan. Once the LEAA reviewed plans in areas such as training officers, detecting and apprehending criminals, and improving prosecution and the courts, each state received a grant of at least $100,000 with additional funds available based on their population (Hinton, 2017).

The various crime prevention programs the LEAA helped subsidize included the state-level acquisition of surplus military technologies such as carbine rifles, armored vehicles, and bullet-proof vests at up to 90 percent of their cost. Special tactical units such as SWAT teams, plainclothes forces, and undercover squads were funded by the agency at up to 75 percent of their cost. In addition to these hardware and patrol programs, the LEAA supported the development of police-community relations programs, which were eligible for federal funding at 40 percent of their cost. The LEAA also sought to make law enforcement into an attractive middle-class profession: the agency funded the tuition for some 50,000 officers enrolled in police science programs at more than 1,000 colleges and universities in mostly small suburban areas across the United States. Finally, LEAA funding incentivized the private sector to manufacture cutting-edge equipment such as walkie-talkies and develop technologies such as computerized criminal justice databanks, tasks that the LEAA viewed as crucial to modernizing American law enforcement (Hinton, 2017).[1]

The LEAA served as the centerpiece of the federal government's grant making and research arm within the Department of Justice through the 1970s. In 1969, the initial congressional allocation for the LEAA was only $63 million. The LEAA spent several months of its first year of operation building staff capacity before evaluating proposals and making awards.

[1]On the relationship between the LEAA and the Department of Housing and Urban Development, and between LEAA and the CIA and the army, see Hinton (2017). On the LEAA and public relations programs promoting the crime issue, see Carmody (1974) as cited in Hinton (2017) as well as Waugh (1969).

Once the LEAA was up and running, its funding grew rapidly during the early 1970s. Although the LEAA never became a key driver of overall spending on criminal justice, given that the vast majority of spending occurs at the state and local levels, it was a channel through which federal policy directly influenced local police. This influence (money, research, and technical assistance) was the reason why the LEAA was first created. Direct state and local expenditures on criminal justice also grew rapidly during the first half of the 1970s, and when the LEAA spending peaked at $895 million in 1975, the LEAA funds accounted for five percent of state and local spending on criminal justice (U.S. General Accounting Office, 1977).[2]

After a decade of operation, with billions of dollars in expenditures and a reputation for mismanagement and corruption, the influence of the LEAA was gradually phased out by federal policy makers. After spending more than a year reviewing the agency, in early 1978 the Carter administration devised a plan that maintained the agency's functions but divided it into three separate organizations, which would be phased into existence over a period of several years. The LEAA would continue to provide money to state and local law enforcement agencies, the National Institute of Justice would oversee all federal crime control research, and the Bureau of Justice Statistics would be a clearinghouse for the data that the LEAA and the Federal Bureau of Investigation (FBI) gathered. All three agencies would report to the Office of Justice Assistance, Research, and Statistics, which had been created in the summer of 1977 (Hinton, 2017).[3]

The Justice System Improvement Act, passed in December 1979, officially began to phase out the LEAA. The legislation gave state and local governments a three-year window during which they could receive federal crime control grants through the LEAA; thereafter; they were expected to operate their respective law enforcement programs independently. The act reduced the planning requirements that the Safe Streets Act had tied to federal funding so that states would no longer need to submit a criminal justice plan every year, and cities like Los Angeles (CA), Chicago (IL), Atlanta (GA), and Newark (NJ) now provided the federal government with one grant application a year for all criminal justice programs instead of separate proposals (Hinton, 2017).

From 1985 through the end of the 1990s, federal spending on crime policy expanded through the grants to local law enforcement and through increased allocations to the FBI, the Drug Enforcement Agency, anti-drug initiatives of the Department of Defense, and the Bureau of Prisons (Hinton, 2017; U.S. Department of Justice, 2002).

[2]In 1965, the nation spent $4.6 billion on criminal justice; by 1977, the figure had reached $23 billion, or just less than $12 billion in constant 1965 dollars.

[3]The LEAA's budget exceeded even the FBI's $513 million allocation by nearly a quarter of a billion dollars (Hinton, 2017).

Federal guidance for local law enforcement on law enforcement strategies also persisted in the absence of the LEAA. For example, the National Drug Policy Board that President Reagan convened by executive order in 1987 brought together the attorney general; the secretaries of Defense, State, Housing and Urban Development, Labor, and Education; the CIA director; the national security advisor; and other relevant cabinet officials and consultants to coordinate all activities concerning public safety needs. The strategies the board developed to fight the War on Drugs would play out in the lives of disproportionate numbers of low-income Black and Latino people (Hinton, 2017).

CURRENT GRANT PROGRAMS

In many ways, the federal administration's grant-making mechanisms of the 21st century reflect the system created under the LEAA. Despite a national push toward criminal justice reform that highlights community partnerships and strategies for addressing crime (Office of Community Oriented Policing Services, 2015) and victimization (Holder et al., 2013), as well as improving the outcomes of reentry populations (The National Reentry Resource Center, 2018), the many tenets of federal grant funding that led to calls for change in the 1970s and 1980s remain intact today.

Office of Justice Programs

The Office of Justice Programs, which replaced the LEAA and the Office of Justice Assistance, Research, and Statistics, serves as the primary agency vested with the oversight of the vast majority of federal grant programs for local, tribal, and state jurisdictions for reducing and preventing crime (U.S. Department of Justice, 2021). The assistant attorney general, who leads the Office of Justice Programs, provides oversight of four programmatic offices that manage federal public safety grants: the Bureau of Justice Assistance; the Office of Victims of Crime; the Office of Juvenile Justice and Delinquency Prevention (OJJDP); and the Office of Sex Offender Sentencing, Monitoring, Apprehending, Registering, and Tracking (SMART).[4] The offices' federal grants go to local, tribal, and state jurisdictions via various mechanisms including formula grants, congressionally directed awards, discretionary grants, and cooperative agreements.

Although unified in their mission to support local and state entities in reducing crime and advancing fairness and justice, these programmatic

[4]The Office of Justice Programs also houses the National Institute of Justice, the science agency of the Department of Justice, and the Bureau of Justice Statistics, and statistical agency of the Department of Justice.

offices are each responsible for their own budget planning, staffing, peer review of respective grant programs, and reporting to the Department of Justice, the President's Office, and Congress. The reach of the grant programs administered by these four offices is expansive. Grants support crime prevention, school safety, crime laboratories, crime victim services, policing operations, the conditions in correctional settings, reentry programs, investigations of wrongful convictions, and a missing persons program.[5]

Byrne Justice Assistance Grant Program

Today, the primary source of federal funding for local and state jurisdictions is the Byrne Justice Assistance Grant (Byrne JAG) program, which is housed within the Bureau of Justice Assistance. The formula-based grant program was created by the Consolidated Appropriations Act of 2005, which merged the Local Law Enforcement Block Grant program and the Edward Byrne Memorial Grant program (BJA, 2021a). These two grant programs were a continuation of LEAA efforts to support law enforcement agencies with crime control initiatives. The Edward Byrne Memorial Grant was established by the 1988 Anti-Drug Abuse Act to support local and state criminal justice systems in addressing violent and drug-related crimes, and encouraged multi-jurisdictional and multi-state collaborations to support drug control policies (Dunworth et al., 1997). The program was created in honor of a New York police officer who was killed in the line of duty. The Local Law Enforcement Block Grant program was created as part of the amendment to the Violent Crime Control and Law Enforcement Act of 1994 (Gist, 2000). The 1996 Appropriations Act directed the Bureau of Justice Assistance to fund local governments through the block grant program to reduce crime and improve public safety with a competitive grants program based on a jurisdiction's rate of violent crimes, as recorded in the Uniform Crime Report as Part 1 Violent Crimes (Bauer, 2004).

Like its predecessors, the Byrne JAG program is the federal administration's principal source of justice grants dedicated to reducing crime and improving public safety. While the origins of the program were dedicated to funding law enforcement, the current program provides local, tribal, and state jurisdictions with resources for a broad array of program areas, including prosecution and courts, corrections, drug treatment and enforcement, planning and evaluation, technology improvement, and mental health programs (BJA, 2021a). The grants offer support for personnel, equipment, supplies, contractual support, training, technical assistance, and criminal justice information systems. The Byrne JAG program, much like other

[5]See https://www.ojp.gov/funding

federal public safety grant programs over the years, has been criticized for its outdated grant structure and impact in addressing crime (Eisen, 2021; Crowley and Pearl, 2020). Despite recent changes to the program's areas of emphasis, which stress building strong criminal justice system and community collaborations for reducing violent crime and police policies that promote trust, transparency, and accountability (BJA, 2021c), the way local, tribal, and state jurisdictions use the funds is up to their full discretion. Importantly, the Byrne JAG program is only one of a host of federal grant programs within the Department of Justice that make up the complex web of resources dedicated to public safety.

Other Bureau of Justice Assistance Grant Programs

The Bureau of Justice Assistance administers the largest catalogue of grant programs dedicated to strengthening the criminal justice system (BJA, 2021d). In addition to the Byrne JAG program, its grant programs support law enforcement via programs such as the Smart Policing Initiative, Project Safe Neighborhoods, law enforcement and prosecution programs, and law enforcement and behavioral health collaborations (BJA, 2021e,f,g). The Bureau of Justice Assistance also supports local jurisdictions and states with grants to implement drug courts and reentry programs (e.g., Second Chance Act) and the reinvestment of resources to improve criminal justice efficiency and reduce recidivism (BJA, 2021h, 2018; Ames, 2019; D'Amico and Kim, 2018; Lindquist et al., 2018). While some of its program areas, like the Second Chance Act program, are authorized by Congress to be evaluated, the impact of other public safety grant programs that it manages remains relatively unknown.

Programs Supporting Juvenile Justice, Crime Victims, and Sex Offense Enforcement

OJJDP, as discussed in Chapter 5, is the federal agency responsible for supporting juvenile justice systems and juvenile delinquency prevention programs[6] (OJJDP, 2019). OJJDP is one of the few programmatic offices within the Office of Justice Programs to have its grant-making program externally reviewed. A 2013 review by the National Research Council found that OJJDP's grant-making capacity was limited given the agency's reauthorization status and decreased appropriations funding over the years to support its formula and block grants program, as well as additional authorized programs like the Missing Children's Assistance Act and the Victims of Child Abuse Act (NRC, 2013).

---

[6]Juvenile Justice and Delinquency Prevention Act, 1974, Public Law 93-415, 88 Stat. 1109.

The two additional programmatic offices within the Office of Justice Programs that administer federal grants serve specific sectors. These are the SMART Office and the Office for Victims of Crime. The SMART Office was authorized by the Adam Walsh Child Protection and Safety Act of 2006 to support jurisdictions with sex offender management efforts, in particular policies that enhance sex offender registration and notification.[7] The Office for Victims of Crime administers the Crime Victims Funds, which come from the fines and penalties paid by individuals processed in the federal system. With an annual budget of $2.1 billion in 2020, the Office for Victims of Crime supports victim compensation and assistance programs, as well as capacity-building efforts to serve diverse victims across communities.[8]

Separate Offices Administering Public Safety Grants

Outside of the Office of Justice Programs, two additional offices administer public safety grants. The Office of Community Oriented Policing Services (COPS) was created by the Violent Crime Control Act and Law Enforcement Act of 1994 to support law enforcement agencies with grants for technical training and assistance. This office also administers grants to hire additional officers through its COPS Hiring Program (Office of Community Oriented Policing Services, 2014). The Office on Violence Against Women, which was created to implement the 1994 Violence Against Women Act, administers both formula and discretionary grants for services dedicated to address and reduce domestic violence, dating violence, sexual assault, and stalking (Office on Violence Against Women, 2018). Nongovernmental entities, like nonprofit organizations and community-based organizations, as well as local, state, and tribal governments, are eligible to receive funding from the Violence Against Women Act, although it should be noted that not all nonprofit organizations are community-based, nor do all have significant community involvement in their operations. Furthermore, nongovernmental community-based initiatives may not be equipped to successfully obtain federal funding; grant mechanisms can be dauntingly complex to navigate.

Unfortunately, the federal administration's capacity to track and measure the impact of the various grant vehicles is limited at best. While some information about select federal grant programs is available from reports by the U.S. Government Accounting Office, investigations by the Office of Inspector General, program evaluations, and external stakeholders' reports of programs (e.g., Byrne JAG funds), both the full scope of where funds are being invested and their impact on crime reduction are unknown. Based on reports from the National Criminal Justice Association, it is estimated

---

[7]See https://smart.ojp.gov/about

[8]Victims Compensation and Assistance Act of 1984, Public Law 98-473, Section 20111.

that two-thirds of annual Byrne JAG funds are dedicated to supporting law enforcement (National Criminal Justice Association, 2021).

Formula-Funding and Categorical Grants-in-Aid

The Byrne JAG Program is a good example of a formula-funding program providing resources for states and local governments to address their own public safety needs. Funds appropriated by Congress for the Byrne JAG program are allocated among the states and U.S. territories based on each jurisdiction's share of violent crime (50%) and its share of the nation's population (50%). For the states, the program further stipulates that 60 percent of the total allocation be retained by the state government and 40 percent be set aside to be allocated to local governments. However, states may retain only award amounts that bear the same ratio of total expenditures on criminal justice by the state government in the most recently completed fiscal year to the total expenditure on criminal justice by the state government and units of local government within the state in such year. Data from fiscal year 2021 allocations indicate that 56 out of 64 total states and territories received Byrne JAG funding (BJA, 2021i). Data from 2020 show that 1,362 local governments were eligible for awards, either directly or through a joint award with other governments within their counties.

An example of categorical grants-in-aid is the Bureau of Justice Assistance's Smart Suite of grant programs. These competitive grants are made on a peer-reviewed basis within budgetary limits based on the congressional appropriation to each individual Smart Suite program. The bureau specifies the goals, objectives, tasks, and deliverables for each program. Applicants compete based on their problem statement, project design, applicant capabilities and competencies, and soundness of budget. These characteristics limit the opportunity of local communities to pursue their own goals and objectives, as many of the communities most in need of support lack the grant-writing skills, project management skills, and even the Internet access necessary to submit a viable proposal in a competitive arena.

ENHANCING THE FEDERAL SYSTEM TO ADDRESS RACIAL INEQUALITY IN THE SYSTEM

Aligning the Department of Justice's federal grant-making infrastructure with crime reduction and prevention programs that show promise in reducing inequality, as outlined in Chapters 3 and 4, would go a long way toward addressing the needs of communities and advancing criminal justice reforms. Enhancing the grant-making system will require addressing key features of the federal grants process that hinder an effective use of resources, including the limited access by non-criminal justice entities.

Barriers to Funding

Relative to other federal grant programs, the majority of the Department of Justice administrated grants are relatively small in size. For example, the Byrne JAG formula program has two categories for eligible units of local government: a category for less than $25,000 and a separate category for amounts of $25,000 or more (BJA, 2021a; NCJA, 2021). The total allocation for the 2020 Byrne JAG funding was approximately $244.2 million, of which $238.7 million went to states and $5.5 million went to U.S. territories and the District of Columbia (Cooper, 2021). While federal competitive grants provide jurisdictions with more resources to support specific areas like violence prevention and reentry programs, a competitive grant structure significantly favors jurisdictions with grant development capacity and a grant infrastructure, resulting in a disparate patchwork of federal support that benefits a select few jurisdictions and agencies.

The vast landscape of grant programs across various offices within the Department of Justice means each grant program is tied to a programmatic office with its own mission and funding priorities, as authorized by Congress and key stakeholders. The structure of the Department of Justice and the bureaus makes it so that grants largely go to these agencies, without any one bureau focused on community crime prevention. The siloed nature of the funding mechanisms for public safety leaves much room for inefficiency, duplication, and competing efforts. Given the expansive areas of federal support, programmatic offices may find themselves addressing the same problem (e.g., gun violence) but taking radically different approaches (The White House, 2021). Further, the varied sources of funding across offices create barriers for collaboration and coordination within the Department of Justice/Office of Justice Programs and across departments, like the Department of Health and Human Services and the Department of Education. Box 9-1 illustrates an example that shows how the positioning of federal responsibilities for a public safety issue can shape mission and approaches.

Despite a continued focus on community partnerships to reduce crime, community organizations have relatively few opportunities to receive Department of Justice grant dollars. As a result, the existing grant funding mechanisms hinder advancing community-based and community-led efforts to reduce crime that could offer alternatives to traditional crime policy responses. Since states or units of local government must serve as the lead agencies applying for key federal funding programs, like Byrne JAG grants, community organizations are in essence barred from assuming a leadership role in standing up programs geared toward reducing crime in their communities.

Readily accessible information on federal grants programs as reported by the Department of Justice/Office of Justice Programs is currently scant (Eisen,

BOX 9-1
Allocation of Federal Responsibilities: Human Trafficking

A fact too often neglected is that where a responsibility is lodged matters a great deal in shaping how that responsibility is discharged. This applies as well to parts of the federal government, where different organizations and their subunits have different visions, missions, and cultures; so careful placing of a program and its attendant responsibilities is important.

Consider a recent example. The Trafficking Victims Protection Act, as amended in 2003, established the Senior Policy Operating Group (SPOG), which consists of senior officials designated as representatives of the President's Interagency Task Force on Human Trafficking agencies. The SPOG brings together federal agencies that address all aspects of human trafficking. Five standing committees meet regularly to advance substantive areas of the SPOG's work: Research & Data, Grantmaking, Public Awareness & Outreach, Victims Services, and Procurement & Supply Chains.

Early in its operation, the SPOG addressed the question of administering the T-1 visa, created in October 2000 when Congress passed the Victims of Trafficking and Violence Protection Act, to protect victims of human trafficking. This status allows victims of human trafficking to remain in the United States to assist in investigations or prosecutions of human trafficking violators. Foreign citizens seeking T-1 nonimmigrant status must be physically present in the United States already, due to the risks of human trafficking.

The discussions on administering the T-1 visa program reflected strongly held department perspectives, each grounded in department vision, mission, and culture.

- The Department of Health and Human Services, true to its name, advocated for granting T-1 visa status immediately upon an individual declaring him- or herself to be a victim of human trafficking; the goal for HHS was to protect that individual, restoring health and safety through the prompt offer of needed human services.
- The Department of Homeland Security, true to its name, advocated a much more cautious approach to granting the T-1 visa, emphasizing the possibility of false claims of trafficking victimization by individuals seeking illegal entry to the United States for nefarious purposes, such as terrorism, gang violence, and/or drug trafficking—all of which place the homeland at risk.
- The Department of Justice, true to its name, preferred to leverage the granting of a T-1 visa to induce the trafficking victim to provide testimony against the trafficker, thus enabling successful prosecution and sentencing of the trafficker, bringing him or her to justice.

In sum, allocating responsibility to different agencies will produce different outcomes—a product of differing institutional visions, missions, and cultures.

2021; Crowley and Pearl, 2020). Data and other information about federal dollar investments and how those funds impact public safety and system-related processes and outcomes directly impact government and community-led strategies. For example, policy makers as well as community members need to have easy access to information about the type and the amount of federal dollars that have been awarded in their jurisdiction, the purpose of those funds, and the impact of those grant dollars on public safety. Information of this type is vital for strategic planning and effective responses for crime reduction. Without a transparent process that illustrates where grants for public safety are going, the federal grant-making process will remain a black hole of investment and continue to erode public trust.

Moreover, the Office of Justice Programs' process for budgeting and appropriations is fast paced, comprising a series of quick and continuous steps involving the Department of Justice, the Office of Management and Budget, the President, and Congress (Office of Justice Programs, 2021b). The planning of the budget and budget submission, known as Spring Call, runs from March through June. This process involves the planning of a budget two years into the future, which makes the allocation of funds for current and immediate matters for addressing public safety virtually impossible. Further complicating the appropriations process are continuing resolutions, known as CRs. This form of appropriations temporarily funds the federal government in the absence of a signed appropriations bill. The routine use of CRs results in programmatic offices being unable to spend their budgets as planned for a full year and consequently produces great uncertainty about funding allocation.

Further Implications of These Barriers

There are several important practical implications of the Department of Justice/Office of Justice Programs federal grant-making system. Much like the original LEAA program, current grant resources continue to overwhelmingly fund policies and programs that prioritize traditional system responses, such as apprehension, prosecution, and confinement. If jurisdictions are seeking funds to support such policies, the existing funding programs will advance such policies.

However, if jurisdictions are looking for funding to support policies and programs outside of the criminal justice system, current Department of Justice grant dollars will be limited. Consequently, by primarily funding government entities (i.e., criminal justice organizations), the Department of Justice is prioritizing those investments and de-emphasizing non-system interventions to reduce crime and inequality, in particular those created, led, and implemented by community organizations. Community organizations, including advocates, seeking alternatives to current criminal justice practices have limited access to resources despite the important role they play in preventing and reducing crime. In the end, the longstanding practice of funding criminal justice agencies, in particular law enforcement agencies, continues despite calls for alternatives to criminal justice system responses and community-led innovations to address crime.

Lastly, modifying existing grant conditions or structures to incentivize law enforcement agencies to partner with community organizations, collect and report data, or spend their funds in certain ways might face constitutional roadblocks. Generally speaking, agencies through their congressionally vested power may place conditions on federal funding given to states and private entities. However, courts reviewing the constitutionality of a condition will assess whether the imposed condition meets four general constitutional limits: (1) the statute provides clear notice of the condition; (2) the condition is related to the purposes of the underlying spending; (3) the condition does not coerce state or local governments; and (4) the condition does not violate any independent constitutional bar, or the related unconstitutional conditions doctrine (Killion, 2021).

Of these four criteria, conditions on Byrne JAG funding are most likely to run into coercion or anti-commandeering issues under the third prong, which derives from the 10th Amendment's reservation of certain legislative powers to the states.[9] Case law dictates that Congress may offer states sizeable incentives to carry out federal policies as long as states ultimately remain free to opt out by declining the federal funding. To preserve the dual federalist structure of government inherent in the Constitution, courts generally hold that Congress may not "compel" states to adopt certain policies by legislating on its behalf nor penalize states unduly by withholding federal funds. As the Supreme Court first clearly articulated in *South Dakota v. Dole*, sometimes the "financial inducement offered by Congress in the spending context might be so coercive as to pass the point at which pressure turns into compulsion."[10] When states lack legitimate choice to accept or forego federal funding, financial inducements and grant programs turn into unconstitutional compulsion.[11]

For example, Byrne JAG grant conditions imposed by the attorney general in fiscal years 2017 and 2018 were challenged for infringing on the anti-commandeering principles of the 10th Amendment. One set of challenges revolved around use of the certification condition of the Byrne JAG application to ensure compliance with 8 U.S.C. § 1373, which prohibits

[9] U.S. Constitution Amendment X.

[10] *South Dakota v. Dole*, 483 U.S. 203, 211 (1987; quoting *Steward Machine Co. v. Davis*, 301 U.S. 548, 590 (1937)).

[11] Id.; See also *New York v. United States*, 505 U.S. 144, 167 (1992) and *NFIB v. Sebelius*, 567 U.S. 519 (2012).

states and localities from restricting the exchange of information about an individual's citizenship or immigration status with federal authorities.[12] The certification aspect of the Byrne JAG application provides for "certification, made in a form acceptable to the Attorney General" that "the applicant will comply with all provisions" of the Byrne JAG statute[13] and "all other applicable Federal laws."[14] The Department of Justice argued that this language authorized the conditioning of Byrne JAG funds on compliance with 8 U.S.C. § 1373 because it was one such "applicable Federal law."[15] Appellate courts across the country were split on whether this Department of Justice grant condition was consistent with the underlying Byrne JAG statute. Some courts determined that the attorney general had exceeded his authority and violated the Constitution in imposing the certification condition.[16] Others found the move to violate neither the Department of Justice's statutory authority nor the constitutional separation of powers.[17]

In sum, federalism concerns cabin the ability to condition funding for states and localities, and any policy-oriented changes to Byrne JAG allocations may implicate constitutional challenges from recalcitrant states or local law enforcement agencies.

Opportunities

Today the nation finds itself at a moment in which it has a considerable opportunity to reduce racial inequality in the criminal justice system. As a result of significant investment in research and data collection, quite a lot is known about the causes and correlates of crime and criminal involvement, certainly enough to know the significance of mental health, substance abuse, poverty, family breakdown, and economic and housing insecurity, among other factors. A great deal is known, as well, about complements to policing. Investments in research and data have yielded insights into the onset of and desistence from involvement in criminal behavior as well as the intensity of such involvement.

---

[12]See 8 U.S.C. § 1373(a). ("Notwithstanding any other provision of Federal, State, or local law, a Federal, State, or local government entity or official may not prohibit, or in any way restrict, any government entity or official from sending to, or receiving from, the Immigration and Naturalization Service information regarding the citizenship or immigration status, lawful or unlawful, of any individual.")

[13]34 U.S.C. § 10151-10158.

[14]34 U.S.C. § 10153(a)(5)(D).

[15]See City of Chicago, 961 F.3d at 897. ("Under the Attorney General's reasoning, Congress itself incorporated § 1373 into the Byrne JAG program by requiring compliance with 'all other applicable federal laws.'")

[16]City of Providence, 954 F.3d at 39; City of Philadelphia, 916 F.3d at 291; City of Chicago, 961 F.3d at 931.

[17]*New York v. DOJ*, 951 F.3d 84, 111 (2d Cir. 2020).

As the preceding chapters have shown, the response to public safety challenges seems curiously "stuck." Funding from the Department of Justice still focuses on promoting public safety and community wellness through policing, prosecuting, adjudicating, and correcting. The Department of Justice should avoid the proliferation of criminal justice system silos that undermine coordination and, when coupled with complex and burdensome processes for accessing federal funding, place the locus of control in Washington bureaucracies. Even so, the Department of Justice could consider promulgating rules or using existing incentive structures, like the Byrne JAG program, to condition funds on compliance with existing anti-discrimination laws or reporting requirements. Although broad-sweeping financial modifications could face scrutiny in the courts, milder versions of rules that impact an overall small percentage of total funding would likely withstand legal challenges and constitutional scrutiny.[18]

While such financial incentives could result in justice (of a sort), public safety, community wellness, and racial equity may well depend more on community-based and community-led anti-violence programs funded through other executive departments, such as Health and Human Services, Housing and Urban Development, Labor, and Education, or through agencies such as the Substance Abuse and Mental Health Services Administration or Centers for Medicare & Medicaid Services. This is not an "either/or" choice; rather, it is a question of balance and relative emphasis.

However, it is important to note that executive agency actions also face anti-coercion and anti-commandeering obstacles similar to those discussed in the previous section. For example, the Department of Health and Human Services recently amended its Conscience Rule to explicitly allow enforcement of 30 federal "conscience and antidiscrimination" provisions through denial, temporary withholding, or termination of the federal funds it administers.[19] This new rule was challenged in three different district courts, all of which held the conditions to be invalid based on various separation of powers, clear notice, and anti-coercion concerns.[20] While the rule is currently being litigated, funding for community wellness structured to encourage voluntary participation should avoid legal challenges and ensure program longevity.

In addition to broadening the scope of funding sources beyond the Department of Justice, reducing the barriers to accessing funding, regardless

---

[18]In *South Dakota v. Dole*, Congress would initially withhold five percent of federal highway funding for states that did not maintain a minimum legal drinking age of 21. This percentage was deemed constitutional because it was only a small percentage of federal funding amounting to pressure but not undue coercion.

[19]2019 Conscience Rule, 84 Fed. Reg. at 23, 272.

[20]See *New York v. HHS*, 414 F. Supp. 3d 475, 532 (S.D.N.Y. 2019); *City & Cty. of San Francisco v. Azar*, 411 F. Supp. 3d 1001, 1024 (N.D. Cal. 2019); and *Washington v. Azar*, 426 F. Supp. 3d 704, 720 (E.D. Wash. 2019).

of source, is equally important to building community involvement. In the case of formula-funded programs, which agency receives the funds from the federal government and how transparent is the distribution process at the state or local level? Are community-based organizations able to apply for funding by themselves or only in partnership with a governmental entity? How burdensome are the application and accountability requirements? These questions apply equally to categorical grants-in-aid.

Illustrative Example: The Office of Juvenile Justice and Delinquency Prevention

The formation of the OJJDP in 1974 offered the federal government an opportunity to address the problem of crime and violence among young Americans by confronting related problems in urban public school systems, public housing, and low-income neighborhoods. Instead, the Juvenile Justice and Delinquency Prevention Act of 1974[21] shifted the federal government's approach to delinquency toward punishment, empowering law enforcement authorities to intervene in public institutions serving youth in low-income urban communities.

With an initial $380 million, three-year outlay for delinquency prevention and control programs, the Juvenile Justice and Delinquency Prevention Act of 1974 created the modern American system of juvenile justice. Prompted by new research on criminality among urban youth of color and concern that "wayward" White youth were being mistreated by the criminal justice system, the legislation supported the widespread implementation of juvenile prisons, foster and protective care programs, and shelter facilities. It also established the National Institute for Juvenile Justice and Delinquency Prevention to research and evaluate various programs, acting as a clearinghouse to guide state and local governments as they designed new youth detention and rehabilitation programs (*Congressional Quarterly Almanac* [1974] as cited in Hinton [2017]).[22]

---

[21]Public Law 93-415, 88 Stat. 1109.

[22]A special amendment to the 1974 act strengthened the influence of the federal government and private consultants at all levels of the prison system. The legislation created a National Institute of Corrections, which brought together an advisory board from the spectrum of federal law enforcement and criminal justice agencies and private-sector groups to set priorities within carceral institutions and award contracts to firms to implement those priorities. Designed to operate as a small consultant group appointed by the attorney general and removed from public accountability in the Bureau of Prisons, the institute served as an information clearinghouse and trained law enforcement and social service personnel. In order to equip penal authorities with stronger tools to manage unprecedented numbers of inmates, the institute supported research on a range of pressing issues, including correctional security, classification systems, and gang control programs. Along with the Office of Juvenile Justice and Delinquency Prevention, also created by the 1974 Act, the National Institute of Corrections has endured as a legacy of the punitive reforms of this period.

The debates that emerged in Congress about the purpose and targets of the federal government's youth crime intervention marked a critical turning point in the direction of the War on Crime, unearthing questions that had yet to be fully resolved about whether the federal programs should respond to delinquency as a social welfare or crime control issue. The Department of Health, Education, and Welfare had directed federal delinquency programs since the 1960s, and the House version of the legislation proposed that this department continue to anchor the national juvenile justice system. The Senate's more punitive vision for the nation's juvenile justice system ultimately prevailed, transferring juvenile justice authority to the LEAA.

According to Hinton (2017), the decision to place the Office of Juvenile Justice within the LEAA did not pass through Congress without vocal objections across party lines. New York's Democratic congresswoman Shirley Chisholm consistently pointed out that the LEAA itself was characterized by inefficiency and mismanagement. And on the day his fellow representatives conceded Health, Education, and Welfare (HEW) as the agency responsible for administering the juvenile justice system, Congressman William Steiger issued a grave warning. "By eliminating HEW," the Wisconsin conservative said on the House floor, "we have done serious damage to our efforts to prevent people from becoming delinquents instead of simply seeing them wound up in the juvenile justice system as it is now."[23]

However reluctant some members of Congress may have been about the decision to treat delinquency as a crime control problem rather than a social welfare concern, the final version of the bill reflected the ideas of an ever-growing consensus of policy makers, law enforcement officials, and scholars that the remnants of the War on Poverty had *worsened* the crime problem, that Black youth were responsible for the majority of the nation's crime, and that the focus on rehabilitation and prevention in previous delinquency programs had been misguided.[24]

The shift in control of anti-delinquency programs from Health, Education, and Welfare to the Department of Justice vastly enhanced the power and influence of the latter. OJJDP was charged with disbursing $600 million in block grants to the states—a striking increase over the

---

[23]Hearings before the Subcommittee on Equal Opportunities of the Committee on Education and Labor, House of Representatives, 93rd Cong., 2nd sess., on HR 6265 and HR 9298, held in Los Angeles, March 29, and Washington, DC, April 21, May 1, 2, 8, and 21, 1974, 434; see Hinton (2017).

[24]On July 1, an overwhelming majority (329 to 20) approved the bill. Albert H. Quie, a Republican from Minnesota, argued that "juvenile justice and delinquency prevention programs are not separate entities and should not be treated separately," and introduced an amendment that shifted responsibility to the LEAA from Health, Education, and Welfare. The House rejected the transfer, with only 114 Republicans and 30 Democrats supporting the measure (Congressional Quarterly Almanac [1974] as cited in Hinton [2017]).

initial $14 million Congress had allocated for delinquency programs in 1969. Congress proceeded to allocate nearly $900 million to national crime control in 1974, and the department enjoyed its largest-ever operating budget. To make youth crime control a national priority, all 50 states received a minimum of $200,000 to establish juvenile delinquency advisory boards that brought together relevant public and private figures to plan and implement programs—much like the state planning agencies the Safe Streets Act of 1968 has imposed on governors. Since previous experiences in block-grant funding demonstrated that states could not be relied upon to follow federal policy makers' preferred strategies for the War on Crime or to focus on low-income urban communities, the office awarded block grants to states based on age and income characteristics alone. States with larger youth populations and citizens living at or below the poverty level received a greater proportion of funds.[25]

With the 1974 Act, Congress deinstitutionalized status offenses, or crimes that applied only to minors (such as curfew violations and truancy), by supporting diversion programs, community-based detention, and foster care. Federal policy makers also encouraged these types of alternatives for nonviolent or minor offenders, whom they believed could be better rehabilitated outside of formal juvenile prisons. The Department of Health, Education, and Welfare funded these types of community-based rehabilitation programs for youth who had been labeled "troublesome" or "acting out"—the only aspect of the national juvenile delinquency program where the social welfare agency retained its authority. Yet in practice, rehabilitative institutions were widely implemented in suburban and rural communities, and the "troublesome" label was applied to White offenders on a far more frequent basis than to their Black and Latino counterparts (Weis and Sederstrom, 1981).[26] The lack of these sorts of viable community-based alternatives in low-income urban communities exacerbated the racial disparities in the sentencing and treatment of young offenders. Social service and law enforcement authorities had few options outside of processing young residents through the criminal justice system.

Indeed, the formal law enforcement system for young offenders that Congress designed in 1974 resulted in more Black and Latino youth

[25]This amounts to roughly $850 million in today's dollars (Juvenile Justice and Delinquency Prevention Act of 1974).

[26]The terms "hard core delinquent" and "acting out youth" are from the report *Rural Programs* (OJJDP, 1979). Health, Education, and Welfare funded 90 percent of the cost for special programs and facilities for runaways. Steven Nicholas, associate director of Focus Runaway House in Las Vegas, in House Committee on Education and Labor, Juvenile Delinquency Prevention and Runaway Youth Hearings before the Subcommittee on Equal Opportunities, 93rd Cong., 2nd session, held in Los Angeles, March 29; Washington, DC, April 21, May 1, 2, 8, and 21, 1974, 272.

receiving criminal justice records, interacting with the courts, and being formally incarcerated even though crime was increasing faster in suburban and rural areas in the mid-1970s.[27] Under the terms of the legislation, while the social welfare arm of the federal government treated White and middle-income youth, it was the punitive arm that handled young people from segregated urban neighborhoods.[28] In addition, the national anti-delinquency program generated an explosion of privately owned juvenile shelters and community-based custody facilities. By 1978, 90 percent of the delinquency prevention programs funded by the Department of Health, Education, and Welfare were administered by private groups, responsible for some 130,000 youth, or about one-tenth of the population of juvenile offenders detained in public facilities (U.S. Congress, Senate Committee on the Judiciary, 1980; U.S. Congress, House Committee on Education and Labor, 1978).

Although young people in the juvenile justice system tended to come from backgrounds marked by poverty, unemployment, and unstable families, Black and Latino youth came to experience this system in ways markedly different from their White counterparts. The federal programs supported by the 1974 legislation focused the majority of rehabilitative and prevention efforts on White status offenders, who had a much greater chance of being successfully diverted from state detention facilities. As the number of young people in private custody increased nearly 10 percent between 1975 and 1977, the population of Black youth in penal

[27]As measured by the FBI's crime index, large cities witnessed a 12 percent crime increase in 1974, while suburban and rural areas reported a 20 percent crime increase that year (Federal Bureau of Investigation, 1975, as cited in Hinton, 2017).

[28]The administration of the Runaway Youth Program (RYP) that was established in Title III of the 1974 legislation illustrates the way the policy exacerbated racial inequities in the criminal justice system. The RYP created local centers that provided runaway youths shelter and counseling while allowing them freedom of movement and, often, the opportunity to remain in school. They were also provided with meals, therapeutic counseling, clothing, transportation, medical care, legal counseling, job counseling and training, follow-up and aftercare services, placement services, and 24-hour hotlines. According to Hinton (2017), "Policymakers hoped the Runaway Youth Program would provide more humane and thrifty alternatives for young people. The constituency of the Runaway Youth Program shelters matched the gender and racial demographics of the United States in the mid-1970s to a far greater degree than other federal crime control programs. Approximately 60 percent of the young people served by the program were women, 73 percent were white, 14 percent were black, and 7 percent were Latino. Still, framing the problem as an issue that primarily affected middle-class young people gravely underserved black and Latino youth, who left home on a far more frequent basis than their white counterparts. Here was an instance where targeting urban youth of color might have been appropriate and beneficial. Instead, the federal government exacerbated existing discrepancies by locating most of the runaway youth programs in rural areas. The National Statistical Survey on Runaway Youth found that Latino youth had the highest incidence of running away, at a rate of 4.6 percent, with black youth following closely behind at a rate of 3.2 percent, and white youth the lowest at a rate of 2.9 percent (Opinion Research Corporation, 1975; Oversight Hearing on the Runaway Youth Act, 1978)."

institutions continued to rise. While Black youth constituted only one-fifth of all children under private supervision, they amounted to one-third of all youth in public facilities. Due to the targeted deployment of police patrols, Black youth were more likely than their White counterparts to have prior criminal referrals, to be charged with violent crimes, to face formal court proceedings, and to be institutionalized in secure, state-run detention facilities (Hinton, 2017). The legislation also led to the sentencing of disproportionate numbers of Black youths as adults beginning in the mid-1970s by lowering the age threshold for violent federal crimes, so that any 16-year-old whom the attorney general deemed to be particularly "dangerous to the community" could be tried as such—a provision that a number of states quickly adopted.[29] In effect, young White people experienced the system through treatment and prevention while children and teenagers of color were criminalized.

CONCLUSION

In the current context, the federal government has an important role to play in shaping the narrative around criminal justice reform efforts. The 2021 Executive Order on Advancing Racial Equity and Support for Underserved Communities through the federal government is a first step. The Department of Justice and similarly situated federal agencies with charges to support justice-involved populations should use their bully pulpit to disseminate findings about evidence-based programs that work to reduce racial and ethnic disparities, promote model jurisdictions implementing effective reforms, and support innovative solutions that could be tested, evaluated, and scaled. In doing so, they could emphasize that the pursuit of public safety requires addressing racial and ethnic disparities throughout the criminal justice system.

RECOMMENDATION 9-1: To improve the grant-making process for communities seeking to reduce racial inequalities in crime and justice, the Department of Justice should enhance performance measures, build in transparency mechanisms, and specify program areas.

Some settings—for example, in Indigenous communities—may require additional flexibility, and in these cases, block grants may be necessary to support innovation and tailored approaches to the community's needs.

[29]The Department of Labor defined "disadvantaged" as "those on public assistance and those whose family income levels are below the poverty guidelines established under criteria issued by the Office of Management and Budget" (Hinton, 2017).

10

Data and Research Opportunities

This report has outlined a vision for reimagining the criminal justice system in the United States and advancing racial equity. However, in order to sustain reform, significant investments in the collection and transparency of criminal justice data are needed. Without a viable data infrastructure, researchers, policy makers, and community members will be unable to track, monitor, and evaluate the effectiveness of new policies and their effects on racial and ethnic disparities. Data across the criminal justice system—from policing, to sentencing, to the jail and prison populations, and to probation and parole systems—are needed to illuminate the operation of the criminal justice system and its impact on inequality as well as to provide transparency and accountability and build trust.

With that need in mind, in this chapter we outline opportunities for building a data infrastructure that promotes integration across the criminal justice system and linkages with non-criminal justice data sources to better assess and support efforts to reduce racial inequalities. The chapter also highlights key areas where future research is needed to better understand racial and ethnic disparities in the criminal justice system and to evaluate promising policies and programs for reducing inequalities.

BUILDING A ROBUST CRIMINAL JUSTICE DATA INFRASTRUCTURE

A 21st century data infrastructure with timely, accurate collection, validation, curation, and dissemination is needed to reduce racial and ethnic inequalities in the criminal justice system at all levels of government. A data infrastructure would help improve public understanding of crime and victimization, as well as the operation of police, courts, and correctional agencies. Such an infrastructure requires attention to three main pillars:

1. Integration of data systems and cross-system linkages and collaboration;
2. Consistent reporting of racial and ethnic data; and
3. Incentives for improving data quality and transparency.

Integration of Data Systems and Cross-System Linkages

The most vexing public problems require person-centric, multi-sector solutions, yet most of government today functions in agency siloes, where any given agency is disconnected from adjacent departments and their data systems. For example, addressing the criminal behavior of an individual experiencing homelessness cannot be solved without integrating data about that individual's situation and needs across employment and education, health and mental health, or substance use sectors.

Linking data outside of the criminal justice area has the potential to deepen insight on racial and ethnic inequalities, yet most government authorities are unable to connect such data across public health, substance use treatment, homelessness, public safety, education, and the workforce, among others. Data and technology capacity, at the state and local levels in particular, is often inconsistent, ranging from high levels of sophistication, to paper-based data storage, to mainframe systems built over 40 years ago. Most state and local jurisdictions do not have staff dedicated to data management and analysis. These problems persist at the federal level as well.

Even more basic attempts to link person-level data *within* an agency can be difficult, much less linking person-level data across the system to track the individual's progress. Simple questions like "did the person spend the night in jail?" or "how long did they wait before trial?" can be difficult to answer. Even more difficult are questions that require linking more than one individual record, such as "How many people in this adult prison were once in the juvenile system?" Connecting all stages of an individual's experience through the criminal justice system in a jurisdiction, from the point of first encounter, through case processing and adjudication, through supervision, and finally to reentry *is* currently possible but only in a handful of jurisdictions, mainly those with grant-funded outside expertise.

In addition, existing data collections undertaken by the Bureau of Justice Statistics are mainly cross-sectional in nature and focus on relatively narrow, individual parts of the criminal justice system. These cross-sectional series often provide extensive coverage, but data on longitudinal flows and progressions through (and out of) the criminal justice system are rare.

That is, while criminal justice data systems regularly provide snap shots in time of different sections of the criminal justice system (often providing useful benchmarks), such data offer little insight into how individuals flow through the system or get released from it. The ability to follow persons from initial contact with a police stop to arrest and then through exit from the system is important for understanding the fairness and effectiveness of the criminal justice system at all stages of its operations, especially given the amount of discretion exercised throughout the system. Without longitudinal cohort data collections to track such "flow," it is difficult to analyze how fairly that discretion is exercised. Moreover, linking such longitudinal data among decision points and connecting events to places for spatial analysis would enable greater understanding of the impact of the criminal justice system on racial and ethnic inequalities across communities.

Moreover, data integration can enable the use of data systems as a tool to provide reliable information on the actions of criminal justice agencies and institutional actors, in addition to those who come into contact with the system. For example, early warning systems related to police use of force, tracking of sentencing patterns that may exhibit bias, and complaints generated by people incarcerated in jails and prisons could be useful data for those seeking to reduce racial inequalities. The successful integration of such data systems can enhance transparency and accountability, as well as empower communities to advocate based on their needs.

Data linkage also offers the opportunity of placing criminal justice involvement in the larger social contexts of demography and community. For example, linking criminal justice records to the census and many other federal data collections would greatly enrich the statistical portrait of criminal justice involvement. Such linked data would contribute not only to public understanding of the socioeconomic status of people moving through the criminal courts and the penal system but also to a better understanding of the prevalence of criminal justice involvement in community life. Which communities contend with the greatest levels and disparities in incarceration? What has changed, and where? To be sure, such efforts carry serious technical challenges of accurate record linkage and data security, but overcoming these challenges to develop a highly integrated criminal justice data system would provide an important tool for reducing racial inequality.

The Criminal Justice Administrative Records System is an example of a national-level data system built to follow individuals throughout the criminal justice system. This data system works to track the criminal justice process from an initial arrest to a final sanction outcome though linking U.S. Census Bureau and other survey and administration data.[1] Data are collected through a combination of publicly available data, purchased

[1]See https://cjars.isr.umich.edu/

public information, and data use agreements with agencies.[2] This project began in 2016, and the resulting data were made available to the public in 2020 through the Federal Statistical Research Data Center network.

Lastly, it should be acknowledged that the conversation on data integration should be paired with a serious engagement of the potential civil rights and privacy risks that come with this type of data tracking. While data integration is necessary for understanding the scope of and potential solutions for reducing racial inequalities in the criminal justice system, great care and consideration should be taken to avoid unnecessary surveillance that could be used in harmful ways.

Consistent Reporting of Racial and Ethnic Data

Further contributing to the difficulty in understanding racial and ethnic disparities in the criminal justice system is the inconsistent way racial and ethnic data are captured. Such data are not gathered in a standard way across agencies and regions, making it difficult to get an accurate national picture of racial disparity. Many policies that may have a disparate impact on Black, Latino, and Native American people or low-income individuals (e.g., fees, fines, voter disenfranchisement) are not well documented in existing data collection efforts.

For example, according to a survey of state criminal justice data conducted by the Urban Institute, 40 states reported race (e.g., "White," "Black," "other") in their arrest records, but only 15 states reported ethnicity (Eppler-Epstein et al., 2016). A state's failure to collect and report ethnicity data affects not only Latino people but the entire criminal justice system. States that only count people as "Black" or "White" likely label most of their Latino prison population "White," artificially inflating the number of "White" people in prison and masking the White/Black disparity in the criminal justice system (Eppler-Epstein et al., 2016).

Moreover, data on American Indians are also often difficult to obtain. A number of state and local data collections rely on an "other" race designation, which lumps together Asian Americans, Pacific Islanders, Native Hawaiians, and American Indians and Alaska Natives. Many also do not distinguish among tribes. This practice obscures differences between these groups and makes it difficult to determine how the criminal justice system plays a role in Indigenous communities (Daniel, 2020).

How official reports of race and ethnicity are actually recorded also remains poorly documented. Social-scientific understanding today views race and ethnicity as subjectively held identities that are best measured through self-reports. Historically, racial data were provided by census enumerators,

[2] See https://cjars.isr.umich.edu/overview/agency-partners/

but modern methods of data collection use self-reports. It is often unclear how data on race are obtained for prison, court, and other administrative records. Documenting methods of data collection would assist with interpretation and standardization.

Possible steps for improving the quality and consistency of reporting data on race and ethnicity include these:

- Meet current U.S. Census Bureau standards by collecting race and ethnicity data separately and allowing for a designation of more than one race. This would result in more descriptive and accurate subcategories, such as "non-Hispanic White," "Hispanic Black," and multi-racial categories.
- Allow race and ethnicity data to be self-reported. Self-identification within provided categories is consistent with U.S. Census Bureau data collection standards. However, it should be noted that the self-report of race in certain circumstances can potentially exacerbate stereotype threat, and therefore the risks associated with this method should be explored further.
- List Americans Indians and Pacific Islanders as distinct demographic groups rather than as members of an "other" category.

Relatedly, while urban American Indian populations may be growing they remain relatively small, which creates a problem for much quantitative research. Ethnographic research can fill some of the resulting gap, but new quantitative data efforts in areas with large American Indian populations—such as Albuquerque (NM), Phoenix (AZ), and Oklahoma City (OK)—are also needed. The exposure to crime and the criminal justice status of American Indians is generally poorly documented and therefore constitutes an important priority for data collection.

Incentives for Improving Data Quality and Transparency

Data challenges are present at the federal, state, and local levels. Across the 18,000 state and local law enforcement agencies and 50 state corrections departments, and among all the jails, courts, and prosecutors in the nation's 3,000-plus counties, data entry clerks and professional staff are recording data and agencies are creating systems to track data without standard ways of recording similar information. The use of standards would provide the possibility of far greater ability to share data within a jurisdiction across agencies, and for the comparison of outcomes across jurisdictions.

Adopting shared standards would be an ambitious and long-term undertaking, as it would rely on major investments in technology system upgrades, which are not only expensive but require procurement processes that may take months or years. Compounding these challenges is the fact that no single entity has responsibility for data quality across the system. Data omissions and errors in one part of the system create problems for accurately linking individual-level data across departments or agencies. At the same time, if data were linked, improving quality in one agency could help not only that agency but also the system.

The Department of Justice could incentivize state and local law enforcement and criminal justice agencies in collecting and sharing high-quality data, including both crime data and the operational and administrative data used internally, and in making the data more available for (1) sharing across agencies within a jurisdiction to aid in data-informed decision making, and (2) analysis by researchers, policy makers, and communities for insight. The federal government could also fund research and technical assistance on data quality metrics and how to implement them. More and better data will mean more state and local ability to manage with data and greater access for researchers, policy makers, and communities to gain insight and to advance the state of knowledge and evidence in the criminal justice system. While the Department of Justice currently requires collection of performance metrics on programs supported by federal grants, those data are reported only to the federal funding agency. The State Justice Statistics program, administered through the Bureau of Justice Statistics, also encourages data sharing and analysis. However, the program is limited, with average awards to state Statistical Analysis Centers amounting to roughly $60,000 per year.

Improving data quality and transparency also requires supporting federal statistical agencies mandated to collect criminal justice data with additional resources. As noted by the National Research Council (2009), the Bureau of Justice Statistics "is one of the smallest of the U.S. principal statistical agencies but shoulders one of the most expansive and detailed legal mandates among those agencies." Funding for the Bureau of Justice Statistics has declined 25 percent since 2010, and by 37 percent when accounting for inflation, with an additional 11 percent cut in the fiscal year 2022 budget (American Statistical Association, n.d.). This keeps the agency from completing its work in a timely fashion—most of its statistical series (64% of them) have lacked either data collection or publication of results for five years or more. The lack of sufficient funding also hampers the agency's ability to keep current with rapidly advancing analytics methodologies and modern tools for linking data across sources. It also hinders the Bureau of Justice Statistics from leading on advancing the state of science and from addressing key policy issues such as the difficulty in measuring racial bias in the criminal justice system. As a result, a modern data infrastructure—which is necessary for research, the advancement of evidence-based practices, and community trust—is missing.

From the perspective of the committee's charge—reducing racial inequality—it is important to see community organizations and residents as a key audience for public data and as an important partner in the design of data systems. The design and dissemination of public data collections are often dominated by agency staff and researchers with little role for community representatives, who may not have strong academic or government connections. Developing a data system that can help community representatives reduce racial inequality will involve positive efforts at outreach and engagement by agencies and researchers alike. The committee believes such efforts at community outreach and representation can strengthen the utility of public data for reducing racial inequality.

AN AGENDA FOR FUTURE RESEARCH

Additional research is needed to enhance understanding of racial and ethnic disparities in crime and victimization and the inequalities both in and outside the system driving those differences. Moreover, as jurisdictions across the local, state, and federal levels continue to implement policies and programs to reduce disparities in their systems, those reforms will need to be evaluated to measure performance and assess outcomes with scientific rigor. Key items for a future research agenda include the following:

- Research on how racialized inequalities in socioeconomic conditions play out to produce differences in crime, and the long-term consequences of heightened exposure to toxic neighborhood environments, including violence;
- Research that advances methodology on how to better account for the fact that Black and White populations do not reside in comparably disadvantaged places;
- Research that improves assessment of the nature of competing viewpoints and norms of control, leveraging what researchers have termed the "ecometrics" of community measurement;
- Research that moves beyond a Black/White paradigm, reflecting the increasing diversity of the U.S. population;
- Research on the resiliency of communities to help illuminate how pockets of resiliency emerge and thrive in disadvantaged communities in ways that undercut vulnerability to crime;
- Research to enhance understanding of the collateral consequences of police-citizen contact, which may be especially salient for particular neighborhoods and communities;
- Research to better understand how criminogenic forces and processes work in rural areas, as much of the country's Indigenous population resides in nonurban places;

- Research on alternatives to the criminal justice system, including community-driven efforts and place-based strategies, that identifies factors that can contribute to or impede effective and timely uptake and scalability of programs; this includes understanding system capacity for replicating evidence-based practices (e.g., by identifying training needs of professional staff and community members and providing adequate reimbursement) and other system incentives to ensure replication of evidence-based practices with fidelity (see Chapter 6);
- Research and data collection allowing for spatial analysis to better understand patterns of behavior across places and communities;
- Research and data collection to track historical changes in crime and criminal justice contact, so that progress and regress can be measured empirically; in combination with life-course and historical perspectives, this suggests the additional utility of tracking changes in crime and criminal justice contact across birth cohorts; and
- Research on language accessibility, including how language barriers for limited-English-proficient populations limit access to fair and just outcomes (see, for example, Ballard and Rodriguez, 2022).

Moreover, as discussed in Chapter 6, there is a need to broaden the research paradigm to be inclusive of other research methods beyond randomized controlled trials (RCTs). RCTs provide indispensable insight into the effectiveness of policies and programs, but they may not be an optimal or practical approach for evaluating multifaceted, often place-based social programs that may vary greatly in implementation and in the sites of implementation. From the perspective of developing a research agenda that can help reduce racial inequality, the committee supports a pluralistic approach that includes experiments along with observational studies, ethnographic and qualitative field research, and historical analysis. With such an agenda, researchers can employ methods from public health, demographic, sociological, qualitative, and participatory-action research in partnership with community members outside the research community.

RECOMMENDATION 10-1: Federal agencies and private foundations that support criminal justice research examining racial inequalities in the criminal justice system should draw upon the best available research—quantitative, qualitative, or mixed methods—to maximize knowledge and avoid the problem of limiting scientific research where empirical methods are not possible or constrained by the lack of quantitative data.

The incorporation of lived experience through the participation of directly impacted people in research design, implementation, and evaluation is critical to the inclusion of community voices, as they are often excluded from public policy making yet have invaluable direct knowledge of how existing systems cause harm and fail to prevent future harm.

Finally, a more robust and transparent data system is needed. Such a system could be an empowering resource for communities working to reduce racial inequalities. Community organizations and actors have typically been left out of the design of data systems. Ensuring that communities are included as a key constituency for data and research is an important next step for developing a scientific program that can positively contribute to reducing racial inequality.

References

Abdulkadiroglu, A., Angrist, J.D., Dynarski, S.M., Kane, T.J, and Pathak, P.A. (2011). Accountability and flexibility in public schools: Evidence from Boston's charters and pilots. *The Quarterly Journal of Economics, 126*(2), 699–748.

Abdulkadiroglu, A., Angrist, J.D, Hull, P.D, and Pathak, P.A. (2016). Charters without Lotteries: Testing takeovers in New Orleans and Boston. *American Economic Review, 106*(7), 1878–1920.

Adler, J.S. (2019). *Murder in New Orleans: The Creation of Jim Crow Policing*. University of Chicago Press.

Agan, A.Y., Doleac, J.L., and Harvey, A. (2021). *Misdemeanor Prosecution*. NBER Working Paper 28600. National Bureau of Economic Research. https://www.nber.org/system/files/working_papers/w28600/w28600.pdf

Agan, A.Y., and Starr, S. (2018). Ban the box, criminal records, and statistical discrimination: A field experiment. *Quarterly Journal of Economics, 133*, 191–235.

Aizer, A., and Currie, J. (2019). Lead and juvenile delinquency: New evidence from linked birth, school, and juvenile detention records. *Review of Economics and Statistics, 101*(4), 575–587.

Akinyemi, O.A., Ogunbona, O.B., Abodunrin, F.O, and Oni, O. (2021). Racial disparity in mortality rates among Black and White Americans with multiple myeloma. *Blood, 138*(1), 5009. https://doi.org/10.1182/blood-2021-148132

Alba, R. (2020). *The Great Demographic Illusion: Majority, Minority, and the Expanding American Mainstream*. Princeton University Press.

Ali, M.U., and Pirog, M. (2019). Social accountability and institutional change: The case of citizen oversight of police. *Public Administration Review, 79*(3), 411–426.

Alpert, G.P., and Dunham, R.G. (2004). *Understanding Police Use of Force: Officers, Suspects, and Reciprocity*. Cambridge University Press.

Alpert, G.P., McLean, K., and Wolfe, S. (2017). Consent Decrees: An approach to police accountability and reform. *Police Quarterly, 20*(3), 239–249.

Amato, M.S., Magzamen, S., Imm, P., Havlena, J.A., Anderson, H.A., Kanarek, M.S., and Moore, C.F. (2013). Early lead exposure (< 3 years old) prospectively predicts fourth grade school suspension in Milwaukee, Wisconsin (USA). *Environmental Research, 126*, 60–65.

American Anthropological Association. (1998). AAA Statement on "Race". https://www.americananthro.org/ConnectWithAAA/Content.aspx?ItemNumber=2583

American Bar Association. (2018). *ABA Task Force on Reversing the School-to-Prison Pipeline: Report, Recommendations, and Preliminary Report.* https://www.americanbar.org/content/dam/aba/administrative/corej/final-school-to-prisonpipeline.pdf

American Psychological Association. (2013). Gun violence: Prediction, prevention, and policy. https://www.apa.org/pubs/info/reports/gun-violence-prevention.aspx

American Statistical Association. (n.d.). *Federal Statistical Agencies—budgets since FY03.* https://docs.google.com/spreadsheets/d/1_xt8oI2neZyTwaZvtyQOtujzuHnjemZPwPuYVsEELr0/edit?usp=sharing

Ames, B. (2019). NIJ-funded research examines what works for successful reentry. *National Institute of Justice Journal.* https://www.ojp.gov/pdffiles1/nij/252734.pdf

Anderson, C., Redcross, C., Valentine, E., and Miratrix, L. (2019). *Evaluation of Pretrial Justice System Reforms That Use the Public Safety Assessment.* MDRC. https://www.mdrc.org/sites/default/files/PSA_New_Jersey_Report_%231.pdf

Anderson, D.M., Crost, B., and Rees, D.I. (2018). Wet laws, drinking establishments and violent crime. *The Economic Journal, 128*(611), 1333–1366.

Anderson, E. (2000). *Code of the Street: Decency, Violence and the Moral Life of the Inner City.* Norton, W.W. and Company, Inc.

________. (2015). The white space. *Sociology of Race and Ethnicity, 1*(1), 10–21.

________. (2022). *Black in White Space: The Enduring Impact of Color in Everyday Life.* University of Chicago Press.

Anderson, M.B. (1999). *Do No Harm: How Aid Can Support Peace—Or War.* Lynne Rienner Publishers.

Andersson, F., Haltiwanger, J.C., Kutzbach, M.J., Pollakowski, H.O., and Weinberg, D.H. (2018). Job displacement and the duration of joblessness: The role of spatial mismatch. *Review of Economics and Statistics, 100*(2), 203–218.

Angrist, J.D, Pathak, P.A, and Walters, C.R. (2013). Explaining charter school effectiveness. *American Economic Journal: Applied Economics, 5*(4), 1–27.

Annie E. Casey Foundation. (2011). *When a Parent Is Incarcerated: A Primer for Social Workers.* https://assets.aecf.org/m/resourcedoc/aecfWhenAParentIsIncarceratedPrimer-2011.pdf

Apel, R., and Horney, J. (2017). How and why does work matter? Employment conditions, routine activities, and crime among adult male offenders. *Criminology, 55*(2), 307–343.

Arnold, D., Dobbie, W., and Yang, C.S. (2020). Comment on Canay, Mogstad, and Mountjoy. https://oconnell.fas.harvard.edu/files/cyang/files/comment_cmm.pdf

Aslim, E.G., Mungan, M.C., Navarro, C.I., and Yu, H. (2022). The effect of public health insurance on criminal recidivism. *Journal of Policy Analysis and Management, 41*(1), 45–91.

Assari, S., Smith, J.R., Caldwell, C.H., and Zimmerman, M.A. (2015). Gender differences in longitudinal links between neighborhood fear, parental support, and depression among African American emerging adults. *Societies (Basel, Switzerland), 5*(1), 151–170.

Atkinson, D., and Travis, J. (2021). The power of parsimony. *The Square One Project.* https://squareonejustice.org/wp-content/uploads/2021/05/CJLJ8747-Square-One-Parsimony-Report-WEB-210524.pdf

Aukerman, M.J. (2005). The somewhat suspect class: Towards a constitutional framework for evaluating occupational restrictions affecting people with criminal records. *Journal of Law in Society, 7*(1), 1–65.

Ayres, I., and Waldfogel, J. (1994). A market test for race discrimination in bail setting. *Stanford Law Review, 46*(5), 987–1047.

Ba, B.A., Knox, D., Mummolo, J., and Rivera, R. (2021). The role of officer race and gender in police-civilian interactions in Chicago. *Science, 371*(6530), 696–702.

Bailey, M.J., Hoynes, H.W., Rossin-Slater, M., and Walker, R. (2020). *Is The Social Safety Net a Long-Term Investment? Large-Scale Evidence from the Food Stamps Program* (No. w26942). National Bureau of Economic Research.

Baldus, D.C., Pulaski, C., and Woodworth, G. (1983). Comparative review of death sentences: An empirical study of the Georgia experience. *The Journal of Criminal Law and Criminology, 74*(3), 661–753.

Baldus, D.C., Woodworth, G., and Pulaski, C.A. (1990). *Equal justice and the death penalty: A legal and empirical analysis.* Boston: Northeastern University Press

Balfour, M.E., Hahn Stephenson, A., Winsky, J., and Goldman, M.L. (2020). *Cops, Clinicians, or Both? Collaborative Approaches to Responding to Behavioral Health Emergencies.* National Association of State Mental Health Program Directors. https://www.nasmhpd.org/sites/default/files/2020paper11.pdf

Ballard, M.M., and Rodriguez, N. (2022). Police department websites and digital language accessibility: A platform for achieving effective communication between limited English proficient communities and the police. *Policing and Society,* 1–21. https://www.tandfonline.com/doi/abs/10.1080/10439463.2022.2071893

Balto, S. (2019). *Occupied Territory: Policing Black Chicago from Red Summer to Black Power.* UNC Press Books.

Banfield, E.C. (1970). *The Unheavenly City.* Little Brown and Company.

Banks, D., Hendrix, J., Hickman, M., and Kyckelhahn, T. (2016). *National Sources of Law Enforcement Employment Data.* U.S. Department of Justice, Office of Justice Programs, Bureau of Justice Statistics. NCJ 249680. https://bjs.ojp.gov/content/pub/pdf/nsleed.pdf

Banks, T.L. (1999). Colorism: A darker shade of pale. *UCLA Law Review, 47*, 1705.

Barry, D., Dianis, J.B., Cartagena, J., Crowley, M., Hayashi, K., Ho, M., James, T., Kang, J., Levison, J., Olquin-Tayler, J., Ramirez, L., and Robinson, R. (2017). *Being Heard: Voices from Marginalized Communities.* The Topos Partnership. https://www.topospartnership.com/wp-content/uploads/2017/09/TOPOS_Vulnerable-Communities_FINAL.pdf

Bartik, A.W., and Mast, E. (2021). *Black Suburbanization and the Evolution of Spatial Inequality Since 1970.* Upjohn Institute Working Paper, 21-355. W.E. Upjohn Institute for Employment Research. https://doi.org/10.17848/wp21-355

Bartos, B.J., and Kubrin, C.E. (2018). Can we downsize our prisons and jails without compromising public safety? Findings from California's Prop 47. *Criminology and Public Policy, 17*(3), 693–715.

Bastien, A. (2017). Ending the debt trap: Strategies to stop the abuse of court-imposed fines and fees. PolicyLinks. https://allincities.org/sites/default/files/ending-the-debt-trap-03-28-17.pdf

Bauer, L. (2004). *Local Law Enforcement Block Grant Program, 1996–2004.* Department of Justice, Bureau of Justice Statistics. https://bjs.ojp.gov/library/publications/local-law-enforcement-block-grant-program-1996-2004

Baumer, E.P. (2013). Reassessing and redirecting research on race and sentencing. *Justice Quarterly, 30*(2), 231–261.

Baumer, E.P., Vélez, M.B, and Rosenfeld, R. (2018). Bringing crime trends back into criminology: A critical assessment of the literature and a blueprint for future inquiry. *Annual Review of Criminology, 1*, 39–61.

Baumgartner, F.R., Johnson, E., Wilson, C., and Whitehead, C. (2015). These lives matter, those ones don't: Comparing execution rates by the race and gender of the victim in the US and in the top death penalty states. *Albany Law Review, 79*, 797–860.

Beaudry, G., Zhong, S., Whiting, D., Javid, B., Frater, J., and Fazel, S. (2020). Managing outbreaks of highly contagious diseases in prisons: A systematic review. *BMJ Global Health, 5*(11), e003201.

Beck, A.J. (2021). Race and Ethnicity of Violent Crime Offenders and Arrestees, 2018. NCJ 255969. U.S. Department of Justice, Bureau of Justice Statistics. https://bjs.ojp.gov/content/pub/pdf/revcoa18.pdf

Beck, A.J., and Blumstein, A. (2018). Racial disproportionality in US state prisons: Accounting for the effects of racial and ethnic differences in criminal involvement, arrests, sentencing, and time served. *Journal of Quantitative Criminology, 34*(3), 853–883.

Beck, B. (2020). Policing gentrification: Stops and low-level arrests during demographic change and real estate reinvestment. *City and Community, 19*(1), 245–272.

Beckett, K. (2018). The politics, promise, and peril of criminal justice reform in the context of mass incarceration. *Annual Review of Criminology, 1*, 235–259. https://doi.org/10.1146/annurev-criminol-032317-092458

Beckett, K., and Brydolf-Horwitz, M. (2020). A kinder, gentler drug war? Race, drugs, and punishment in 21st century America. *Punishment and Society, 22*(4), 509–533.

Beckett, K., and Francis, M.M. (2020). The origins of mass incarceration: The racial politics of crime and punishment in the Post–Civil Rights Era. *Annual Review of Law and Social Science, 16*, 433–452.

Beckett, K., and Herbert, S. (2009). *Banished: The New Social Control in Urban America.* Oxford University Press.

Beckett, K., Nyrop, K., and Pfingst, L. (2006). Race, drugs, and policing: Understanding disparities in drug delivery arrests. *Criminology, 44*(1), 105–137.

Beckett, K., Nyrop, K., Pfingst, L., and Bowen, M. (2005). Drug use, drug possession arrests, and the question of race: Lessons from Seattle. *Social Problems, 52*, 419–441.

Bell, M.C. (2020a). Anti-segregation policing. *New York University Law Review, 95*(3).

______. (2020b). Located institutions: Neighborhood frames, residential preferences, and the case of policing. *American Journal of Sociology, 125*, 917–997.

______. (2021). Next-generation policing research: Three propositions. *Journal of Economic Perspectives, 35*, 29–48.

Bellair, P.E., and McNulty, T.L. (2005). Beyond the bell curve: Community disadvantage and the explanation of Black-White differences in adolescent violence. *Criminology, 43*, 1135–1168.

Bellair, P.E., and Roscigno, V.J. (2000). Local labor-market opportunity and adolescent delinquency. *Social Forces, 78*(4), 1509–1538.

Bellair, P.E., Roscigno, V.J., and McNulty, T.L. (2003). Linking local labor market opportunity to violent adolescent delinquency. *Journal of Research in Crime and Delinquency, 40*(1), 6–33.

Benns, M., Ruther, M., Nash, N., Bozeman, M., Harbrecht, B., and Miller, K. (2020). The impact of historical racism on modern gun violence: Redlining in the city of Louisville, KY. *Injury, 51*(10), 2192–2198.

Berg, M.T., and Huebner, B.M. (2011). Reentry and the ties that bind: An examination of social ties, employment, and recidivism. *Justice Quarterly, 28*(2), 382–410.

Berk, R. (2017). An impact assessment of machine learning risk forecasts on parole board decisions and recidivism. *Journal of Experimental Criminology, 13*(2), 193–216.

Berk, R.A., and Campbell, A. (1993). Comment on McDonald and Carlson. *Federal Sentencing Report, 6*, 227.

Bertrand, M., and Mullainathan, S. (2004). Are Emily and Greg more employable than Lakisha and Jamal? A field experiment on labor market discrimination. *American Economic Review, 94*(4), 991–1013.

Beydoun, K.A. (2014). Antebellum Islam. *Howard Law Journal, 58*, 141.

Bick, J.A. (2007). Infection control in jails and prisons. *Clinical Infectious Diseases, 45*(8), 1047–1055.

Biderman, C., De Mello, J.M., and Schneider, A. (2010). Dry laws and homicides: Evidence from the São Paulo metropolitan area. *The Economic Journal, 120*(543), 157–182.

Billings, S.B., and Schnepel, K.T. (2018). Life after lead: Effects of early interventions for children exposed to lead. *American Economic Journal: Applied Economics, 10*(3), 315–344.

Bing, L., Pettit, B., and Slavinski, I. (2022). Incomparable punishments: How economic inequality contributes to the disparate impact of legal fines and fees. *RSF: The Russell Sage Foundation Journal of the Social Sciences, 8*(2), 118–136.

Binswanger, I.A., Stern, M.F., Deyo, R.A., Heagerty, P.J., Cheadle, A., Elmore, J.G., and Koepsell, T.D. (2007). Release from prison—a high risk of death for former inmates. *New England Journal of Medicine, 356*(2), 157–165.

Biondi, M. (2003). *To Stand and to Fight: The Struggle for Civil Rights in Postwar New York City.* Harvard University Press.

Bird, M., Lofstrom, M., Martin, B., Raphael, S., and Nguyen, V. (2018). *The Impact of Proposition 47 on Crime and Recidivism.* Public Policy Institute of California. https://www.rcrcnet.org/sites/default/files/useruploads/Documents/Barbed_Wire/June_15_2018/R_0612_MBR_Press.pdf

Bittner, E. (1967). The police on skid-row: A study of peace keeping. *American Sociology Review, 32*(5), 699–715.

Blake, J.J., and Epstein, R. (2019). *Listening to Black Women and Girls: Lived Experiences of Adultification Bias.* Georgetown Law Center on Poverty and Inequality, Initiative on Gender Justice and Opportunity.

Blamey, A.M., and MacKenzie, M. (2007). Theories of change and realistic evaluation: Peas in a pod or apples and oranges? *Evaluation, 13*, 439–455.

Bloom, H.S., Orr, L.L., Bell, S.H., Cave, G., Doolittle, F., Lin, W., and Bos, J.M. (1997). The benefits and costs of JTPA Title II-A programs: Key findings from the National Job Training Partnership Act study. *Journal of Human Resources, 32*, 549–576.

Bloom, J., and Martin Jr., W.E. (2013). *Black against Empire.* University of California Press.

Blumenson, E., and Nilsen, E. (1998). Policing for profit: The drug war's hidden economic agenda. *The University of Chicago Law Review, 65*(1), 35–114.

Blumstein, A. (1982). On the racial disproportionality of the US states' prison population. *Journal of Criminal Law and Criminology, 73*(3), 1259–1281.

Blumstein, A., and Beck, A.J. (1999). Population growth in US prisons, 1980-1996. *Crime and Justice, 26*, 17–61. https://www.journals.uchicago.edu/doi/abs/10.1086/449294

______. (2012). *Reentry as a Transient State between Liberty and Recommitment.* Cambridge University Press.

Blumstein, A., and Nakamura, K. (2009). Redemption in the presence of widespread criminal background checks. *Criminology, 47*(2), 327–359.

Boessen, A., and Chamberlain, A.W. (2017). Neighborhood crime, the housing crisis, and geographic space: Disentangling the consequences of foreclosure and vacancy. *Journal of Urban Affairs, 39*(8), 1122–1137.

Boessen, A., and Hipp, J.R. (2018). Parks as crime inhibitors or generators: Examining parks and the role of their nearby context. *Social Science Research, 76*, 186–201.

Bogar, S., and Beyer, K.M. (2016). Green space, violence, and crime: A systematic review. *Trauma, Violence, and Abuse, 17*(2), 160–171.

Boggess, L.N., and Chamberlain, A.W. (2021). Investing in neighborhoods: The mitigating role of home mortgage loans on intimate partner violence. *Journal of Interpersonal Violence, 36*(23-24), NP12783–NP12806.

Bogira, S. (2005). *Courtroom 302: A Year behind the Scenes in an American Criminal Courthouse.* Vintage.

Bonam, C.M., Bergsieker, H.B., and Eberhardt, J.L. (2016). Polluting Black space. *Journal of Experimental Psychology: General, 145*(11), 1561.

Bonczar, T.P., and Beck, A.J. (1997). *Lifetime Likelihood of Going to State or Federal Prison.* U.S. Department of Justice, Office of Justice Programs, Bureau of Justice Statistics.

Bonilla-Silva, E. (1997). Rethinking racism: Toward a structural interpretation. *American Sociological Review, 62*(3), 465–480.

_______. (1999). The essential social fact of race. *American Sociological Review, 64*(6), 899–906.

Booker, B. (2021). This D.A. won by a landslide. He's still mad. *Politico.* https://www.politico.com/newsletters/the-recast/2021/06/11/larry-krasner-philadelphia-district-attorney-election-policing-493220

Boppre, B., Dehart, D., and Shapiro, C.J. (2022). "The Prison System Doesn't Make It Comfortable to Visit": Prison visitation from the perspectives of people incarcerated and family members. *Criminal Justice and Behavior, 49*(10), 1474–1494.

Bottoms, A.E. (1999). Interpersonal violence and social order in prisons. *Crime and Justice, 26,* 205–281.

Boyd, R.W., Ellison, A.M., and Horn, I.B. (2016). Police, equity, and child health. *Pediatrics, 142*(1).

Boyles, A.S. (2015). *Race, Place, and Suburban Policing.* University of California Press. https://doi.org/10.1525/9780520958081

Bradner, K., and Schiraldi, V. (2020). *Racial Inequities in New York Parole Supervision.* Working Paper. Columbia University Justice Lab. https://justicelab.columbia.edu/sites/default/files/content/NY%20Parole%20Racial%20Inequities.pdf

Bradner, K., Schiraldi, V., Mejia, N., and Lopoo, E. (2020). *More Work to Do: Analysis of Probation and Parole in the United States, 2017–2018.* Columbia University Justice Lab.

Braga, A.A., Brunson, R.K., and Drakulich, K.M. (2019). Race, place, and effective policing. *Annual Review of Sociology, 45,* 535–555.

Braga, A.A., and Dusseault, D. (2018). Can homicide detectives improve homicide clearance rates? *Crime & Delinquency, 64*(3), 283–315.

Braga, A.A., Kennedy, D.M., Waring, E.J., and Piehl, A.M. (2001). Problem-oriented policing, deterrence, and youth violence: An evaluation of Boston's Operation Ceasefire. *Journal of Research in Crime and Delinquency, 38*(3), 195–225.

Braga, A.A., MacDonald, J.M., and Barao, L.M. (2021). Do body-worn cameras improve community perceptions of the police? Results from a controlled experimental evaluation. *Journal of Experimental Criminology,* 1–32.

Braga, A.A., and Weisburd, D.L. (2015). Focused deterrence and the prevention of violent gun injuries: Practice, theoretical principles, and scientific evidence. *Annual Review of Public Health, 36,* 55–68. https://doi.org/10.1146/annurev-publhealth-031914-122444

Braga, A.A., Weisburd, D., and Turchan, B. (2018). Focused deterrence strategies and crime control: An updated systematic review and meta-analysis of the empirical evidence. *Criminology and Public Policy, 17*(1), 205–250.

Braithwaite, J. (2000). Restorative justice and social justice. *Saskatchewan Law Review, 63,* 185.

Braithwaite, J., Deer, S., and Freedman, H.V. (2019). Barriers to justice for victims of sexual violence in Indian Country. *Family & Intimate Partner Violence Quarterly, 12*(1).

Branas, C.C., and MacDonald, J.M. (2014). A simple strategy to transform health, all over the place. *Journal of Public Health Management and Practice, 20*(2), 157–159.

Branas, C.C., South, E., Kondo, M.C., Hohl, B.C., Bourgois, P., Wiebe, D.J., and MacDonald, J.M. (2018). Citywide cluster randomized trial to restore blighted vacant land and its effects on violence, crime, and fear. *Proceedings of the National Academy of Sciences, 115,* 1–11. www.pnas.org/cgi/doi/10.1073/pnas.1718503115

Branscombe, N.R., Ellemers, N., Spears, R., and Doosje, B. (1999). The context and content of social identity threat. *Social Identity: Context, Commitment, Content*, 35–58. Blackwell.

Brayne, S. (2014). Surveillance and system avoidance: Criminal justice contact and institutional attachment. *American Sociological Review, 79*(3), 367–391.

Brennan, P.K., and Spohn, C. (2008). Race/ethnicity and sentencing outcomes among drug offenders in North Carolina. *Journal of Contemporary Criminal Justice, 24*(4), 371–398.

Brewer, S., Godley, M.D., and Hulvershorn, L.A. (2017). Treating mental health and substance use disorders in adolescents: What is on the menu? *Current Psychiatry Reports, 19*(1), 1–9.

Breyer, S. (2016). *Against the Death Penalty*. Brookings Institution Press.

Briggs, S.J., and Keimig, K.A. (2017). The impact of police deployment on racial disparities in discretionary searches. *Race and Justice*, *7*(3), 256–275.

Bronson, J., Stroop, J., Zimmer, S., and Berzofsky, M. (2017). *Drug Use, Dependence, and Abuse Among State Prisoners and Jail Inmates, 2007–2009*. U.S. Department of Justice, Bureau of Justice Statistics.

Brooklyn County District Attorney's Office. (2020). *Justice 2020: An Action Plan for Brooklyn*. Office of Brooklyn District Attorney Eric Gonzalez. http://www.brooklynda.org/wp-content/uploads/2019/03/Justice2020-Report.pdf

Brooks, L. (2008). Volunteering to be taxed: Business improvement districts and the extra-governmental provision of public safety. *Journal of Public Economics*, *92*(1-2), 388–406.

Brown, C., Stuhldreher, A., and Pakdaman, K. (2020). *Driving Toward Justice: How Ending Driver's License Suspensions for Unpaid Traffic Tickets Helps Communities Without Impacting Court Collections*. The Financial Justice Project of San Francisco.

Brunson, R.K., and Wade, B.A. (2019). "Oh hell no, we don't talk to police": Insights on the lack of cooperation in police investigations of urban gun violence. *Criminology and Public Policy, 18*(3), 623–648.

Brunson, R.K., and Weitzer, R. (2009). Police relations with Black and White youths in different urban neighborhoods. *Urban Affairs Review, 44*(6), 858–885.

Brunton-Smith, I., Sturgis, P., and Leckie, G. (2018). How collective is collective efficacy? The importance of consensus in judgments about community cohesion and willingness to intervene. *Criminology, 56*, 608–637.

Buchanan, K.S. (2007). Impunity: Sexual abuse in women's prisons. *Harvard Civil Rights-Civil Liberties Law Review, 42*, 45–87.

Buggs, S.A., Webster, D.W., and Crifasi, C.K. (2022). Using synthetic control methodology to estimate effects of a Cure Violence intervention in Baltimore, Maryland. *Injury Prevention, 28*(1), 61–67.

Bui, J., Wendt, M., and Bakos, A. (2019). Understanding and addressing health disparities and health needs of justice-involved populations. *Public Health Reports, 134*(1 Suppl.), 3S–7S.

Bulman, G. (2019). Law enforcement leaders and the racial composition of arrests. *Economic Inquiry, 57*(4), 1842–1858. https://doi.org/10.1111/ecin.12800

Burchard, E.G., Ziv, E., Coyle, N., Gomez, S.L., Tang, H., Karter, A.J., Mountain, J.L., Pérez-Stable, E.J., Sheppard, D., and Risch, N. (2003). The importance of race and ethnic background in biomedical research and clinical practice. *New England Journal of Medicine, 348*(12), 1170–1175.

Bureau of Justice Assistance (BJA). (2018). *Adult Drug Court Discretionary Grant Program*. Department of Justice, Bureau of Justice Assistance. https://bja.ojp.gov/sites/g/files/xyckuh186/files/Publications/adult-drug-court-disc-grant-program-fs-11-2018.pdf

______. (2021a). Edward Byrne Justice Assistance Grant (JAG) Program Fact Sheet. Department of Justice. https://bja.ojp.gov/sites/g/files/xyckuh186/files/media/document/jag-fact-sheet.pdf

______. (2021b). Edward Byrne Memorial Justice Assistance Grant (JAG) Program Frequently Asked Questions (FAQs). Department of Justice, Bureau of Justice Assistance. https://bja.ojp.gov/program/jag/frequently-asked-questions

______. (2021c). BYA FY21 Edward Byrne Memorial Justice Assistance Grant (JAG) Program-State Solicitation. Department of Justice, Bureau of Justice Assistance.

______. (2021d). Funding and Awards. Department of Justice, Bureau of Justice Assistance. https://bja.ojp.gov/funding

______. (2021e). Smart Policing Initiative (PSI). Department of Justice, Bureau of Justice Assistance. https://bja.ojp.gov/program/smart-policing-initiative-spi/overview

______. (2021f). Project Safe Neighborhoods Training and Technical Assistance Resource Catalog. Department of Justice, Bureau of Justice Assistance. https://psntta.org/wp-content/uploads/2021/05/PSN_TTA_ResourceCatalog_FINAL.pdf

______. (2021g). Body-Worn Camera Toolkit. Department of Justice, Bureau of Justice Assistance. https://bja.ojp.gov/program/bwc

______. (2021h). Justice Reinvestment Initiative (JRI). Department of Justice, Bureau of Justice Assistance. https://bja.ojp.gov/program/justice-reinvestment-initiative/overview

______. (2021i). Fiscal Year 2021 JAG State Allocations. Department of Justice, Bureau of Justice Assistance. https://bja.ojp.gov/sites/g/files/xyckuh186/files/media/document/FY21-State-JAG-Allocations.pdf

Bureau of Justice Statistics (BJS). (2020). Law Enforcement Officers Killed and Assaulted, 2019 – Tables. U.S. Department of Justice. https://bjs.ojp.gov/library/publications/law-enforcement-officers-killed-and-assaulted-2019-tables

Burt, C.H., Lei, M.K., and Simons, R.L. (2017). Racial discrimination, racial socialization, and crime: Understanding mechanisms of resilience. *Social Problems, 64*(3), 414–438.

Bushway, S.D., and Reuter, P. (2002). Labor markets and crime risk factors. *Evidence-based Crime Prevention,* 212–254. Routledge.

Butts, J.A., and Delgado, S.A. (2017). *Repairing Trust: Young Men in Neighborhoods with Cure Violence Programs Report Growing Confidence in Police.* The Research and Evaluation Center, John Jay College of Criminal Justice, City University of New York. https://academicworks.cuny.edu/jj_pubs/418/

Byers, R.K., and Lord, E.E. (1943). Late effects of lead poisoning on mental development. *American Journal of Diseases of Children,* 66(5), 471–494.

Bylander, J. (2015). Civil unrest, police use of force, and the public's health. *Health Affairs, 34,* 8. https://doi.org/10.1377/hlthaff.2015.0717

Bynum, T., and Paternoster, R. (1984). Discrimination revisited: An exploration of frontstage and backstage criminal justice decision making. *Sociology and Social Research,* 69, 90–108. https://www.ojp.gov/ncjrs/virtual-library/abstracts/discrimination-revisited-exploration-frontstage-and-backstage

California Department of Corrections and Rehabilitation Expert Panel on Adult Offender Reentry and Reduction Programs. (2007). California Department of Corrections and Rehabilitation Expert Panel on Adult Offender and Recidivism Reduction Programming Report to the California State Legislature: A Roadmap for Effective Offender Programming. https://ucicorrections.seweb.uci.edu/2007/06/29/cdcr-report-a-roadmap-for-effective-offender-programming-in-california/

California Judicial Council. (2016). Prop 47 Frequently Asked Questions, Updated November 2016. California Judicial Council, San Francisco, CA. https://www.courts.ca.gov/documents/Prop47FAQs.pdf

Camp, J.T. (2016). *Incarcerating the Crisis.* University of California Press.

Camp, N.P., Voigt, R., Jurafsky, D., and Eberhardt, J.L. (2021). The thin blue waveform: Racial disparities in officer prosody undermine institutional trust in the police. *Journal of Personality and Social Psychology, 121*(6), 1157–1171. https://doi.org/10.1037/pspa0000270

Campbell, C.A., Hahn, R.A., Elder, R., Brewer, R., Chattopadhyay, S., Fielding, J., and Task Force on Community Preventive Services. (2009). The effectiveness of limiting alcohol outlet density as a means of reducing excessive alcohol consumption and alcohol-related harms. *American Journal of Preventive Medicine, 37*(6), 556–569.

Campbell, M.C., and Schoenfeld, H. (2013). The transformation of America's penal order: A historicized political sociology of punishment. *American Journal of Sociology, 118*(5), 1375–1423.

Candipan, J., and Sampson, R. (2021). *The Consistency of White Advantage and the Heterogeneity of Nonwhite Disadvantage: Neighborhood Trajectories over Two Decades in the Lives of Multiple Birth Cohorts.* SocArXiv Papers. https://osf.io/preprints/socarxiv/2k9sh/

Carbado, D.W. (2002). (E) racing the Fourth Amendment. *Michigan Law Review, 100*(5), 946–1044.

Carey, G. (1994). Genetics and violence. *Understanding and Preventing Violence, 2,* 21–58. National Academy Press.

Carmichael, J., and Kent, S. (2014). The persistent significance of racial and economic inequality on the size of municipal police forces in the United States. *Social Problems, 61,* 259–282.

Carr, P. (2005). *Clean Streets: Controlling Crime, Maintaining Order, and Building Community Activism.* New York University Press.

Carrigan, W., and Webb, C. (2013). *Forgotten Dead: Mob Violence against Mexicans in the United States, 1848–1928.* Oxford University Press.

Carroll, L., and Gonzalez, M.L. (2014). Out of place: Racial stereotypes and the ecology of frisks and searches following traffic stops. *Journal of Research in Crime and Delinquency, 51*(5), 559–584.

Carson, A. (2020). *Prisoners in 2018.* NCJ 253516. Bureau of Justice Statistics, U.S. Department of Justice. https://bjs.ojp.gov/library/publications/prisoners-2018

______. (2021). *Prisoners in 2020—Statistical Tables.* NCJ 302776. US Department of Justice, Bureau of Justice Statistics.

Carson, E.A., and Cowhig, M.P. (2020). *Mortality in Local Jails, 2001–2016-Statistical Tables.* NCJ 251921. Bureau of Justice Statistics, U.S. Department of Justice, Office of Justice Programs. https://www.ojp.gov/ncjrs/virtual-library/abstracts/mortality-local-jails-2001-2016-statistical-tables

Carson, E.A., and Sabol, W.J. (2012). *Prisoners in 2011.* NCJ 239808. U.S. Department of Justice, Office of Justice Programs, Bureau of Justice Statistics. https://bjs.ojp.gov/library/publications/prisoners-2011

Casey Family Programs. (2018). *What Are Some Examples of Evidence-Informed Practices to Keep Children Safe and Promote Permanency?* https://www.casey.org/what-are-some-examples-of-evidence-informed-practices-to-keep-children-safe-and-promote-permanency/

Centers for Disease Control and Prevention. (2019). Leading Causes of Death - Males - Non-Hispanic Black - United States, 2016. https://www.cdc.gov/healthequity/lcod/men/2016/nonhispanic-black/index.htm

Chalfin, A., Hansen, B., Weisburst, E.K., and Williams, M.C. (2020). *Police Force Size and Civilian Race.* No. w28202. National Bureau of Economic Research.

Chalfin, A., and McCrary, J. (2017). Criminal deterrence: A review of the literature. *Journal of Economic Literature, 55*(1), 5–48.

Chanin, J.M. (2015). Examining the sustainability of pattern or practice police misconduct reform. *Police Quarterly, 18*(2), 163–192.

Charles, K.K., and Hurst, E. (2002). The transition to home ownership and the Black-White wealth gap. *Review of Economics and Statistics, 84*(2), 281–297.
Chatelain, M. (2015). *South Side Girls: Growing up in the Great Migration*. Duke University Press.
Chavez-Garcia, M. (2012). *States of Delinquency: Race and Science in the Making of California's Juvenile Justice System*. University of California Press.
Chen, E.Y. (2008). Impacts of "three strikes and you're out" on crime trends in California and throughout the United States. *Journal of Contemporary Criminal Justice, 24*(4), 345–370.
Chen, K.M., Christenson, K.L., John, E., Owens, E., and Shuo, Y. (2022). Smartphone Data Reveal Neighborhood-Level Racial Disparities in Police Presence. Unpublished manuscript.
Chesney-Lind, M. (1988). Girls and status offenses: Is juvenile justice still sexist? *Criminal Justice Abstracts, 20*(1), 144–165. https://www.ojp.gov/ncjrs/virtual-library/abstracts/girls-and-status-offenses-juvenile-justice-still-sexist
Chetty, R., Hendren, N., Jones, M.R., and Porter, S.R. (2020). Race and economic opportunity in the United States: An intergenerational perspective. *The Quarterly Journal of Economics, 135*(2), 711–783.
Chetty, R., Hendren, N., and Katz, L.F. (2016). The effects of exposure to better neighborhoods on children: New evidence from the Moving to Opportunity experiment. *American Economic Review, 106*(4), 855–902.
Children's Bureau. (2021). *Child Welfare Practice with Families Affected by Parental Incarceration*. U.S. Department of Health and Human Services, Administration for Children and Families. https://www.childwelfare.gov/pubPDFs/parental_incarceration.pdf
Chillar, V.F. (2022). The racial divide at micro places: A pre/post analysis of the effects of the Newark consent decree on field inquiries (2015–2017). *Journal of Research in Crime and Delinquency, 59*(2), 240–276.
Chin, G.J., and Vernon, C. J. (2014). Reasonable but unconstitutional: Racial profiling and the radical objectivity of Whren v. United States. *The George Washington Law Review, 83*(3), 882.
Chuang, E., and Wells, R. (2010). The role of inter-agency collaboration in facilitating receipt of behavioral health services for youth involved with child welfare and juvenile justice. *Children and Youth Services Review, 32*(12), 1814–1822.
Chung, H., and Little, M. (2005). The transition to adulthood for adolescents in the juvenile justice system: A developmental perspective. *On Your Own Without a Net: The Transition to Adulthood for Vulnerable Populations, 68*. University of Chicago Press.
Clair, M., and Denis, J.S. (2015). Sociology of racism. *The International Encyclopedia of the Social and Behavioral Sciences, 19*, 857–863.
Clarren, R. (2017). Native American peacemaking courts offer a model for reform. *InvestigateWest*. https://www.invw.org/2017/11/30/native-american-judge-shows-peacemaking-courts-offer-a-model-for-reform/
Clear, T.R. (2009). *Imprisoning Communities: How Mass Incarceration Makes Disadvantaged Neighborhoods Worse*. Oxford University Press.
Cloward, R.A., and Ohlin, L.E. (1960). *Delinquency and Opportunity: A Study of Delinquent Gangs* (1st ed.). Routledge. https://doi.org/10.4324/9781315007274
Clutter, J.E., Henderson, S., and Haberman, C.P. (2019). The impact of business improvement district proximity on street block robbery counts. *Crime & Delinquency, 65*(8), 1050–1075.
Cochran, J.C., Toman, E.L., Mears, D.P., and Bales, W.D. (2018). Solitary confinement as punishment: Examining in-prison sanctioning disparities. *Justice Quarterly, 35*(3), 381–411.

Cocozza, J.J., and Skowyra, K.R. (2000). Youth with mental health disorders: Issues and emerging responses. *Juvenile Justice, 7*(3).

Cohen, F. (2004). The limits of the judicial reform of prisons: What works; what does not. *Criminal Law Bulletin-Boston, 40*, 421–465.

Cole, R.B., and Call, J.E. (1992). When courts find jail and prison overcrowding unconstitutional. *Federal Probation, 56*(1), 29–39.

Cook, P.J., Braga, A.A., Turchan, B.S., and Barao, L.M. (2019). Why do gun murders have a higher clearance rate than gunshot assaults? *Criminology and Public Policy, 18*, 525–551.

Cook, P.J., Kang, S., Braga, A.A., Ludwig, J., and O'Brien, M.E. (2015). An experimental evaluation of a comprehensive employment-oriented prisoner re-entry program. *Journal of Quantitative Criminology, 31*(3), 355–382.

Cook, P.J., and Ludwig, J. (2006). The social costs of gun ownership. *Journal of Public Economics, 90*(1-2), 379–391.

Cook, P.J., and MacDonald, J. (2011). Public safety through private action: An economic assessment of BIDS. *The Economic Journal, 121*(552), 445–462.

Cooper, A. (2021). *Justice Assistance Grant (JAG) Program, 2020 Technical Report*. Department of Justice, Bureau of Justice Statistics. https://bjs.ojp.gov/sites/g/files/xyckuh236/files/media/document/jagp20.pdf

Cooper, R.S., Kaufman, J.S., and Ward, R. (2003). Race and genomics. *The New England Journal of Medicine, 348*(12), 1166–1170. https://doi.org/10.1056/NEJMsb022863

Copeland, W.E., Miller-Johnson, S., Keeler, G., Angold, A., and Costello, E.J. (2007). Childhood psychiatric disorders and young adult crime: A prospective, population-based study. *American Journal of Psychiatry, 164*(11), 1668–1675.

Corburn, J. (2021a). *Advance Peace Sacramento 2020*. University of California, Berkeley, Center for Healthy Global Cities. https://www.advancepeace.org/wp-content/uploads/2021/10/Advance-Peace-Sac-2020-Summary-Rev.pdf

______. (2021b). *Office of Neighborhood Safety Richmond*. University of California, Berkeley, Center for Healthy Global Cities. https://www.advancepeace.org/wp-content/uploads/2021/10/ONS-2020-summary-2pager-Rev-.pdf

Corburn, J., Boggan, D., and Muttaqi, K. (2020). *Advance Peace & Focused Deterrence: What Are the Differences?* Advance Peace, University of California, Berkeley. https://www.advancepeace.org/wp-content/uploads/2020/08/ap-focused-deterrence-v1-1.pdf

Corburn, J., and Fukutome, A. (2021). *Advance Peace Stockton: 2018–2020 Evaluation*. University of California, Berkeley, Center for Global Healthy Cities. https://www.advancepeace.org/wp-content/uploads/2021/02/advance_peace_stockton_eval_report_2021_final.pdf

Cordero, K., Garcia, S., and van Schilfgaarde, L. (2021). Tribal Healing to Wellness Courts: Intergovernmental Collaboration. *Tribal Law and Policy Institute*. http://www.wellnesscourts.org/files/Tribal%20Healing%20to%20Wellness%20Court%20Intergovernmental%20Collaboration%20May%2020%202021.pdf

Cornell, S., and Hartmann, D. (2006). *Ethnicity and Race: Making Identities in a Changing World*. Sage Publications.

Correll, J., Hudson, S.M., Guillermo, S., and Ma, D.S. (2014). The police officer's dilemma: A decade of research on racial bias in the decision to shoot. *Social and Personality Psychology Compass, 8*(5), 201–213.

Correll, J., Park, B., Judd, C.M., and Wittenbrink, B. (2002). The police officer's dilemma: Using ethnicity to disambiguate potentially threatening individuals. *Journal of Personality and Social Psychology, 83*(6), 1314.

______. (2007). The influence of stereotypes on decisions to shoot. *European Journal of Social Psychology, 37*(6), 1102–1117.

Correll, J., Wittenbrink, B., Park, B., Judd, C.M., and Goyle, A. (2011). Dangerous enough: Moderating racial bias with contextual threat cues. *Journal of Experimental Social Psychology*, *47*(1), 184–189.

Corsaro, N., and Engel, R.S. (2015). Most challenging of contexts: Assessing the impact of focused deterrence on serious violence in New Orleans. *Criminology and Public Policy*, *14*(3), 471–505.

Cottle, C.C., Lee, R.J., and Heilbrun, K. (2001). The prediction of criminal recidivism in juveniles: A meta-analysis. *Criminal Justice and Behavior*, *28*(3), 367–394.

Council of State Governments Justice Center. (2021). *Tips for Successfully Implementing a 911 Dispatch Diversion Program*. U.S. Department of Justice, Bureau of Justice Assistance, NCJ Number 303178. https://bja.ojp.gov/library/publications/tips-successfully-implementing-911-dispatch-diversion-program

Council on Criminal Justice. (2021). *Civilian Oversight: Policy Assessment*. Council on Criminal Justice Task Force on Policing. https://assets.foleon.com/eu-west-2/uploads-7e3kk3/41697/civilian_oversight.2690411fd370.pdf

Cox, R.J. (2015). *Where Do We Go from Here: Mass Incarceration and the Struggle for Civil Rights*. Economic Policy Institute. https://www.epi.org/publication/where-do-we-go-from-here-mass-incarceration-and-the-struggle-for-civil-rights/

Cox, W.T., and Devine, P.G. (2016). Experimental research on shooter bias: Ready (or relevant) for application in the courtroom? *Journal of Applied Research in Memory and Cognition*, *5*(3), 236–238.

Crenshaw, K.W., Ocen, P., and Nanda, J. (2015). *Black Girls Matter: Pushed Out, Overpoliced and Underprotected*. Columbia Law School. https://scholarship.law.columbia.edu/faculty_scholarship/3227

Crowley, M., and Pearl, B. (2020). *Reimagining Federal Grants for Public Safety and Criminal Justice Reform*. Center for American Progress. https://www.americanprogress.org/article/reimagining-federal-grants-public-safety-criminal-justice-reform/

Crutchfield, R.D. (2014). *Get a Job: Labor Markets, Economic Opportunity, and Crime*. New York University Press.

______. (2015). From slavery to social class to disadvantage: An intellectual history of the use of class to explain racial differences in criminal involvement. *Crime and Justice*, *44*(1), 1–47.

Crutchfield, R.D., Bridges, G.S, and Pitchford, S.R. (1994). Analytical and aggregation biases in analyses of imprisonment: Reconciling discrepancies in studies of racial disparity. *Journal of Research in Crime and Delinquency*, *31*, 166–182.

Crutchfield, R.D., Drakulich, K., Groninger, H., and Wadsworth, T. (2011). *Labor Force Participation, Labor Markets, and Crime*. DIANE Publishing.

Crutchfield, R.D., Glusker, A., and Bridges, G.S. (1999). A tale of three cities: Labor markets and homicide. *Sociological Focus*, *32*, 65–83.

Crutchfield, R.D., Matsueda, R., and Drakulich, K. (2006). Race, labor markets and neighborhood violence. *The Many Colors of Crime*. New York University Press.

Crutchfield, R.D., and Pitchford, S.R. (1997). Work and crime: The effects of labor market stratification. *Social Forces*, *76*, 93–118.

Crutchfield, R.D., Skinner, M.L., Haggerty, K.P., McGlynn, A., and Catalano, R.F. (2012). Racial disparity in police contacts. *Race and Justice*, *2*(3), 179–202.

Crutchfield, R.D., and Wadsworth, T. (2013). Aggravated inequality. *Economics and Youth Violence*, 152–180. New York University Press.

Cui, J., Jensen, S.T., and MacDonald, J. (2022). The effects of vacant lot greening and the impact of land use and business presence on crime. *Environment and Planning B: Urban Analytics and City Science*, *49*(3), 1147–1158.

Cunneen, C., and Tauri, J.M. (2019). Indigenous peoples, criminology, and criminal justice. *Annual Review of Criminology*, *2*, 359–381.

Cure Violence Global. (2021). *The Evidence of Effectiveness.* https://cvg.org/wp-content/uploads/2021/09/Cure-Violence-Evidence-Summary.pdf

Curry, C. (2016). *Do Parole Revocations Contribute to Racial Disproportionality in Imprisonment? A Multilevel Analysis of State Prison Admissions from 1990–2009.* Graduate Dissertation. https://scholarworks.uark.edu/etd/1573

Curtin, M.E. (2000). *Black Prisoners and Their World, Alabama, 1865–1900.* Rutgers University Press.

Curtis, L. (1975). *Violence, Race, and Culture.* D.C. Heath.

Curto, V.E., and Fryer Jr., R.G. (2014). The potential of urban boarding schools for the poor: Evidence from SEED. *Journal of Labor Economics, 32*(1), 65–93.

Daftary-Kapur, T., Zottoli, T.M., Faust, T., and Schneider, R. (2022). A first look at the reentry experiences of juvenile lifers released in Philadelphia. *Psychology, Public Policy, and Law, 28*(3), 400–413. https://doi.org/10.1037/law0000344

D'Amico, R., and Kim, H. (2018). *Evaluation of Seven Second Chance Act Adult Demonstration Programs: Impact Findings at 30 Months.* Social Policy Research Associates. https://www.ojp.gov/pdffiles1/nij/grants/251702.pdf

Daniel, R. (2020). Since you asked: What data exists about Native American people in the criminal justice system? *Prison Policy Initiative.* https://www.prisonpolicy.org/blog/2020/04/22/native/

Daniel, S. (2018). Rollins eases concerns over 'The List' at WSANA Monday. *The Boston Sun.* https://thebostonsun.com/2018/10/26/rollins-eases-concerns-over-the-list-at-wsana-monday/

Davis, A.J. (2013). In search of racial justice: The role of the prosecutor. *Legislation and Public Policy, 16,* 821–851.

Davis, E., Whyde, A., and Langton, L. (2018). Contacts between police and the public, 2015. *US Department of Justice Office of Justice Programs Bureau of Justice Statistics Special Report,* 1–33.

Davis, J.M., and Heller, S.B. (2020). Rethinking the benefits of youth employment programs: The heterogeneous effects of summer jobs. *Review of Economics and Statistics, 102*(4), 664–677.

Davis, R.C., Henderson, N.J., and Ortiz, C.W. (2005). *Can Federal Intervention Bring Lasting Improvement in Local Policing? The Pittsburgh Consent Decree.* Vera Institute of Justice.

Death Penalty Information Center. (2022a). *Innocence: Overview.* https://deathpenaltyinfo.org/policy-issues/innocence

______. (2022b). The Death Penalty in 2022: Year End Report. https://reports.deathpenaltyinfo.org/year-end/Year-End-Report-2022.pdf

Decker, S.H., Ortiz, N., Spohn, C., and Hedberg, E. (2015). Criminal stigma, race, and ethnicity: The consequences of imprisonment for employment. *Journal of Criminal Justice, 43*(2), 108–121.

Dee, T.S., and Pyne, J. (2022). A community response approach to mental health and substance abuse crises reduced crime. *Science Advances, 8*(23).

Delgado, S., Alsabahi, L., and Butts, J.A. (2017). *Young Men in Neighborhoods with Cure Violence Programs Adopt Attitudes Less Supportive of Violence.* The Research and Evaluation Center, John Jay College of Criminal Justice, City University of New York. https://johnjayrec.nyc/wp-content/uploads/2017/03/databit201701.pdf

Delgado, S.A., Alsabahi, L., Wolff, K.T., Alexander, N.M., Cobar, P.A., and Butts, J.A. (2017). *The Effects of Cure Violence in the South Bronx and East New York, Brooklyn.* John Jay College of Criminal Justice Research and Evaluation Center. https://johnjayrec.nyc/2017/10/02/cvinsobronxeastny/

Deshpande, M., and Mueller-Smith, M.G. (2022). *Does Welfare Prevent Crime? The Criminal Justice Outcomes of Youth Removed from SSI*. (No. w29800). National Bureau of Economic Research.

Desmond, M., Papachristos, A.V., and Kirk, D.S. (2016). Police violence and citizen crime reporting in the black community. *American Sociological Review, 81*(5), 857–876.

Devers, L. (2011). *Plea and Charge Bargaining: Research Summary*. Bureau of Justice Assistance, U.S. Department of Justice. https://bja.ojp.gov/sites/g/files/xyckuh186/files/media/document/PleaBargainingResearchSummary.pdf

Devi, T., and Fryer Jr., R.G. (2020). *Policing the Police: The Impact of "Pattern-or-Practice" Investigations on Crime*. Working paper 27324. National Bureau of Economic Research. https://doi.org/10.3386/w27324

Devine, P. G. (1989). Stereotypes and prejudice: Their automatic and controlled components. *Journal of Personality and Social Psychology, 56*, 5–18. http://dx.doi.org/10.1037/0022-3514.56.1.5

Deza, M., Maclean, J.C., and Solomon, K. (2022). Local access to mental healthcare and crime. *Journal of Urban Economics, 129*, 103410.

Dietrich, K., Douglas, R., Succop, P., Berger, O., and Bornschein, R. (2001). Early exposure to lead and juvenile delinquency. *Neurotoxicology and Teratology, 23*(6), 511–518.

Ditton, P.M., and Wilson, D.J. (1999). Truth in sentencing in state prisons. NCJ 170032. *BJS Special Report*. U.S. Department of Justice.

Dobbie, W., and Fryer Jr., R.G. (2011). Are high-quality schools enough to increase achievement among the poor? Evidence from the Harlem Children's Zone. *American Economic Journal: Applied Economics, 3*(3), 158–187.

______. (2013). Getting beneath the veil of effective schools: Evidence from New York City. *American Economic Journal: Applied Economics, 5*(4), 28–60.

______. (2015). The medium-term impacts of high-achieving charter schools. *Journal of Political Economy, 123*(5), 985–1037.

______. (2020). Charter schools and labor market outcomes. *Journal of Labor Economics 38*(4).

Dobbie, W., Goldin, J., and Yang, C.S. (2018). The effects of pretrial detention on conviction, future crime, and employment: Evidence from randomly assigned judges. *American Economic Review, 108*(2), 201–240. https://perma.cc/7NAN-S7HB

Dodson, J., Gleeson, B., and Sipe, N.G. (2004). *Transport Disadvantage and Social Status: A Review of Literature and Methods*. Griffith University, Urban Policy Program.

Doleac, J. L., and Hansen, B. (2020). The unintended consequences of "ban the box": Statistical discrimination and employment outcomes when criminal histories are hidden. *Journal of Labor Economics, 38*(2), 321–374.

Dollar, C.B., Donnelly, E.A., and Parker, K.F. (2019). Joblessness, poverty, and neighborhood crime: Testing Wilson's assertions of jobless poverty. *Social Currents, 6*(4), 343–360.

Dominguez-Rivera, P., Lofstrom, M., and Raphael, S. (2019). *The Effect of Sentencing Reform on Crime Rates: Evidence from California's Prop 47*. Working paper, University of California, Berkeley.

Donders, N.C., Correll, J., and Wittenbrink, B. (2008). Danger stereotypes predict racially biased attentional allocation. *Journal of Experimental Social Psychology, 44*(5), 1328–1333.

Donnelly, E.A., and MacDonald, J.M. (2018). The downstream effects of bail and pretrial detention on racial disparities in incarceration. *Journal of Criminal Law and Criminology, 108*, 775.

Donohue III, J.J., and Levitt, S.D. (2001). The impact of race on policing and arrests. *The Journal of Law and Economics, 44*(2), 367–394.

Dovidio, J.F. (2001). On the nature of contemporary prejudice: The third wave. *Journal of Social Issues, 57*(4), 829–849.
Dovidio, J.F., and Gaertner, S.L. (2004). Aversive racism. *Advances in Experimental Social Psychology, 36,* 1–52. Elsevier Academic Press. https://doi.org/10.1016/S0065-2601(04)36001-6
Dovidio, J.F., Gaertner, S.L., and Abad-Merino, S. (2017). Helping behavior and subtle discrimination. *Intergroup Helping: The Positive Side of Intergroup Behaviour.* Springer.
Dovidio, J.F., Kawakami, K., and Gaertner, S.L. (2002). Implicit and explicit prejudice and interracial interaction. *Journal of Personality and Social Psychology, 82*(1), 62–68.
Du Bois, W.E.B. (1899). *The Philadelphia Negro: A Social Study.* University of Pennsylvania Press.
Dubber, M.D. (2001). Policing possession: The war on crime and the end of criminal law. *Journal of Criminal Law and Criminology, 91,* 829.
Duck, W. (2015). *No Way Out: Precarious Living in the Shadow of Poverty and Drug Dealing.* University of Chicago Press.
Dunbar-Ortiz, R. (2014). *An Indigenous Peoples' History of the United States.* Boston University Press.
Dunworth, T., Haynes, P., and Saiger, A.J. (1997). *National Assessment of the Byrne Formula Grant Program.* Department of Justice, National Institute of Justice. https://nij.ojp.gov/library/publications/national-assessment-byrne-formula-grant-program-research-brief
Durlauf, S.N., and Heckman, J.J. (2020). An empirical analysis of racial differences in police use of force: A comment. *Journal of Political Economy, 128*(10), 3998–4002.
Duster, T. (2004). *Backdoor to Eugenics.* Routledge.
Eaglin, J.M., and Solomon, D. (2015). *Reducing Racial and Ethnic Disparities in Jails: Recommendations for Local Practice.* Brennan Center for Justice at New York University School of Law. https://www.repository.law.indiana.edu/facbooks/32
Eberhardt, J.L., Davies, P.G., Purdie-Vaughns, V.J., and Johnson, S.L. (2006). Looking deathworthy: Perceived stereotypicality of Black defendants predicts capital-sentencing outcomes. *Psychological Science, 17*(5), 383–386.
Eberhardt, J.L., Goff, P.A., Purdie, V.J., and Davies, P.G. (2004). Seeing black: Race, crime, and visual processing. *Journal of Personality and Social Psychology, 87*(6), 876.
Educational Fund to Stop Gun Violence, DC Justice Lab, Cities United, March for Our Lives, Community Justice Action Fund, Consortium for Risk-Based Firearm Policy, and Johns Hopkins Center for Gun Violence Prevention and Policy. (2022). Racial Equity Framework for Gun Violence Prevention. https://efsgv.org/wp-content/uploads/EFSGV_REIA_Framework.pdf
Edwards, F., Lee, H., and Esposito, M. (2019). Risk of being killed by police use of force in the United States by age, race–ethnicity, and sex. *Proceedings of the National Academy of Sciences, 116,* 16793–16798.
Egerter, S., Barclay, C., Grossman-Kahn, R., and Braveman, P.A. (2011). *Violence, Social Disadvantage and Health.* Robert Wood Johnson Foundation.
Eid, T.A., Ellis, A., Gede, T., Goldberg, C., Sandlin, S.H., Keel, J., Quasula, T., Pomeroy III, E.R., and Pouley, T. (2013). *A Roadmap for Making Native America Safer: Report to the President & Congress of the United States.* Indian Law & Order Commission. https://www.aisc.ucla.edu/iloc/report/index.html
Eipper, C. (1983). The magician's hat: A critique of the concept of ethnicity. *The Australian and New Zealand Journal of Sociology, 19*(3), 427–446.
Eisen, L.B. (2021). *The Federal Funding That Fuels Mass Incarceration.* Brennan Center for Justice at New York University Law. https://www.brennancenter.org/our-work/analysis-opinion/federal-funding-fuels-mass-incarceration

Elbers, B. (2021). *Did Residential Racial Segregation in the U.S. Really Increase? An Analysis Accounting for Changes in Racial Diversity*. https://osf.io/preprints/socarxiv/dvutw

Elderbroom, B., and Durnan, J. (2018). *Reclassified: State-Drug Law Reforms to Reduce Felony Convictions and Increase Second Chances*. The Urban Institute.

Engel, R.S., Smith, M.R., and Cullen, F.T. (2012). Race, place, and drug enforcement: Reconsidering the impact of citizen complaints and crime rates on drug arrests. *Criminology and Public Policy, 11*, 603.

Engel, R.S., Worden, R.E., Corsaro, N., McManus, H.D., Reynolds, D., Cochran, H., Isaza, G.T., and Calnon Cherkauskas, J. (2019). Implications and recommendations. *The Power to Arrest*, 141–162. Springer. https://link.springer.com/chapter/10.1007/978-3-030-17054-7_6

Enns, P.K. (2016). *Incarceration Nation*. Cambridge University Press.

Epp, C.R., Maynard-Moody, S., Haider-Markel, D.P., and Epp, C. (2014). *Pulled Over: How Police Stops Define Race and Citizenship*. University of Chicago Press. 10.7208/chicago/9780226114040.001.0001

Epperson, M.W., and Pettus-Davis, C. (2015). *Smart Decarceration: Guiding Concepts for an Era of Criminal Justice Transformation*. Center for Social Development, Washington University in St. Louis. Smart Decarceration Initiative. CSD Working Paper No. 15-53. https://openscholarship.wustl.edu/cgi/viewcontent.cgi?article=1573&context=csd_research

Eppler-Epstein, S., Gurvis, A., and King, R. (2016). The alarming lack of data on Latinos in the criminal justice system. *Urban Institute*. https://apps.urban.org/features/latino-criminal-justice-data/?language=english

Epstein, R., Blake, J., and González, T. (2017). *Girlhood Interrupted: The Erasure of Black Girls' Childhood. Center of Poverty and Inequality, Georgetown Law*. https://genderjusticeandopportunity.georgetown.edu/wp-content/uploads/2020/06/girlhood-interrupted.pdf

Erickson, C.D. (2012). Using systems of care to reduce incarceration of youth with serious mental illness. *American Journal of Community Psychology, 49*(3), 404–416.

Escobar, E. (1999). *Race, Police, and the Making of a Political Identity: Mexican Americans and the Los Angeles Police Department, 1900–1945*. University of California Press.

Eugene Police Crime Analysis Unit. (2020). *CAHOOTS Program Analysis*. Eugene Police Department Crime Analysis Unit. https://www.eugene-or.gov/DocumentCenter/View/56717/CAHOOTS-Program-Analysis

Everytown for Gun Safety. (2022). *Mass Shootings in America, 2009–2019*. https://everytownresearch.org/massshootingsreports/mass-shootings-in-america-2009-2019

Faber, J.W. (2018). Segregation and the geography of creditworthiness: Racial inequality in a recovered mortgage market. *Housing Policy Debate, 28*(2), 215–247.

______. (2020). We built this: Consequences of New Deal era intervention in America's racial geography. *American Sociological Review, 85*(5), 739–775. https://doi.org/10.1177/0003122420948464

Fagan, J., Braga, A.A., Brunson, R.K., and Pattavina, A. (2016). Stops and stares: Street stops, surveillance, and race in the new policing. *Fordham Urban Law Journal, 43*, 539.

Fagan, J. and Davies, G. (2000). Street Stops and Broken Windows: Terry, Race, and Disorder in New York City. *Fordham Urban Law Journal, 28*, 457. https://ir.lawnet.fordham.edu/ulj/vol28/iss2/2

Fagan, J., Davies, G., and Carlis, A. (2012). Race and selective enforcement in public housing. *Journal of Empirical Legal Studies, 9*(4), 697–728.

Fagan, J., and Geller, A. (2018). Police, race, and the production of capital homicides. *Berkeley Journal of Criminal Law, 23*, 261.

Fagan, J., Geller, A., Davies, G., and West, V. (2010). Street stops and broken windows revisited: The demography and logic of proactive policing in a safe and changing city. *Race, Ethnicity, and Policing: New and Essential Readings*. New York University Press, Columbia Public Law Research Paper No. 09-203.

Feagin, J., and Elias, S. (2013). Rethinking racial formation theory: A systemic racism critique. *Ethnic and Racial Studies, 36*(6), 931–960.

Federal Highway Administration. (2014). *Mobility Challenges for Households in Poverty: 2009 National Household Travel Survey*. U.S. Department of Transportation, Federal Highway Administration.

Fein, S., and Spencer, S.J. (1997). Prejudice as self-image maintenance: Affirming the self through derogating others. *Journal of Personality and Social Psychology, 73,* 31–44.

Feldmeyer, B., Steffensmeier, D., and Ulmer, J.T. (2013). Racial/ethnic composition and violence: Size-of-place variations in percent Black and percent Latino effects on violence rates. *Sociological Forum, 28,* 811–841.

Felitti, V.J., Anda, R.F., Nordenberg, D., Williamson, D.F., Spitz, A.M., Edwards, V., and Marks, J.S. (1998). Relationship of childhood abuse and household dysfunction to many of the leading causes of death in adults: The Adverse Childhood Experiences (ACE) Study. *American Journal of Preventive Medicine, 14*(4), 245–258.

Fernandes-Jesus, M., Mao, G., Ntontis, E., Cocking, C., McTague, M., Schwarz, A., Semlyen, J., and Drury, J. (2021). More than a COVID-19 response: Sustaining mutual aid groups during and beyond the pandemic. *Frontiers in Psychology, 12.* https://www.frontiersin.org/articles/10.3389/fpsyg.2021.716202/full.

Finlay, K., Mueller-Smith, M., and Street, B. (2022a). *Criminal Justice Involvement, Self-employment, and Barriers in Recent Public Policy*. https://sites.lsa.umich.edu/mgms/wp-content/uploads/sites/283/2022/03/CJARS_Self_Employment_PPP_20220302.pdf

______. (2022b). Measuring intergenerational exposure to the US justice system: Evidence from longitudinal links between survey and administrative data. *Criminal Justice Administrative Records*. https://brittanystreet.github.io/website/FinlayMuellerSmithStreet_CJARS_kidexposure_20220622.pdf

Finn, P. (2001). *Citizen Review of Police: Approaches and Implementation*. US Department of Justice, Office of Justice Programs, National Institute of Justice. https://www.ojp.gov/pdffiles1/nij/184430.pdf

Fisher, B.W., and Hennessy, E.A. (2016). School resource officers and exclusionary discipline in US high schools: A systematic review and meta-analysis. *Adolescent Research Review, 1*(3), 217–233.

Flamm, M.W. (2005). *Law and Order: Street Crime, Civil Unrest, and the Crisis of Liberalism in the 1960s*. Columbia University Press.

Flies-Away, J., and Garrow, C. (2013). Healing to Wellness Courts: Therapeutic jurisprudence. *Michigan State Law Review 2013, 2,* 403–439.

Flies-Away, J.T., Garrow, C., and Sekaquaptewa, P. (2014). *Tribal Healing to Wellness Courts: The Key Components* (2nd ed.). Tribal Law and Policy Institute. http://www.wellnesscourts.org/files/Tribal%20Healing%20to%20Wellness%20Courts%20The%20Key%20Components.pdf

Flores, E.O. (2013). Recovery from gang life: Two models of faith and reintegration. *God's Gangs: Barrio Ministry, Masculinity, and Gang Recovery,* 88–108. New York University Press. https://doi.org/10.18574/nyu/9781479850099.003.0004

Forman Jr., J. (2017). *Locking up Our Own: Crime and Punishment in Black America*. Farrar, Straus and Giroux.

Fortner, M.J. (2015). *Black Silent Majority*. Harvard University Press.

Foster, H., and Hagan, J. (2009). The mass incarceration of parents in America: Issues of race/ethnicity, collateral damage to children, and prisoner reentry. *The ANNALS of the American Academy of Political and Social Science, 623*(1), 179–194.

Franco-Paredes, C., Ghandnoosh, N., Latif, H., Krsak, M., Henao-Martinez, A.F., Robins, M., Barahona, L.V., and Poeschla, E.M. (2021). Decarceration and community re-entry in the COVID-19 era. *The Lancet Infectious Diseases, 21*(1), e11–e16.

Frantz, C.M., Cuddy, A.J.C., Burnett, M., Ray, H., and Hart, A. (2004). A threat in the computer: The Race Implicit Association Test as a stereotype threat experience. *Personality and Social Psychology Bulletin, 30*(12), 1611–1624.

Frase, R.F. (2009). Second look provisions in the proposed model penal code revisions. *Federal Sentencing Reporter, 21*(3), 194–202. https://www.jstor.org/stable/10.1525/fsr.2009.21.3.19

Frase, R.S. (2019). Forty years of American sentencing guidelines: What have we learned? *Crime and Justice, 48*(1), 79–135.

Frase, R.S., and Roberts, J.V. (2019). *Paying for the Past: The Case against Prior Record Sentence Enhancements*. Oxford University Press.

Freeman, L., and Botein, H. (2002). Subsidized housing and neighborhood impacts: A theoretical discussion and review of the evidence. *Journal of Planning Literature, 16*(3), 359–378.

Friedman, S. (2008). Do declines in residential segregation mean stable neighborhood racial integration in metropolitan America? A Research Note. *Social Science Research, 37*, 920–933.

Friedson, M., and Sharkey, P. (2015). Violence and neighborhood disadvantage after the crime decline. *The ANNALS of the American Academy of Political and Social Science, 660*(1), 341–358.

Frost, N.A, and Monteiro, C.E. (2016). *Restrictive Housing in the U.S.: Issues, Challenges, and Future Directions*. CHAPTER 1 Administrative Segregation in U.S. Prisons. https://www.ojp.gov/pdffiles1/nij/250316.pdf

Fryer Jr., R.G. (2019). An empirical analysis of racial differences in police use of force. *Journal of Political Economy, 127*(3), 1210–1261.

Fullilove, M.T. (2001). Root shock: The consequences of African American dispossession. *Journal of Urban Health: Bulletin of the New York Academy of Medicine, 78*(1), 72–80. https://doi.org/10.1093/jurban/78.1.72

Furr-Holden, C.D.M., Nesoff, E.D., Nelson, V., Milam, A.J., Smart, M., Lacey, K., Thorpe, R.J., and Leaf, P.J. (2019). Understanding the relationship between alcohol outlet density and life expectancy in Baltimore City: The role of community violence and community disadvantage. *Journal of Community Psychology, 47*(1), 63–75.

Garces, E., Thomas, D., and Currie, J. (2000). *Long Term Effects of Head Start*. National Bureau of Economic Research.

García, J.L., Heckman, J.J., Leaf, D.E., and Prados, M.J. (2020). Quantifying the life-cycle benefits of an influential early-childhood program. *Journal of Political Economy, 128*(7), 2502–2541.

García, J.L., Heckman, J.J., and Ziff, A.L. (2018). Gender differences in the benefits of an influential early childhood program. *European Economic Review, 109*, 9–22. https://doi.org/10.1016/j.euroecorev.2018.06.009

______. (2019). Early childhood education and crime. *Infant Mental Health Journal, 40*(1), 141–151. https://doi.org/10.1002/imhj.21759

Gardner, T.G. (2020). Police violence and the African American procedural habitus. *Boston University Law Review, 100*, 849.

Garland, D. (2010). *Peculiar Institution: America's Death Penalty in an Age of Abolition*. OUP.

Garrow, C., Cordero, K., and van Schilfgaarde, L. (2018). Tribal Healing to Wellness Court: Case management. *Tribal Law and Policy Institute*. http://www.wellnesscourts.org/files/HTWC%20Case%20Management.pdf

Gascón, L.D., and Roussell, A. (2019). *The Limits of Community Policing: Civilian Power and Police Accountability in Black and Brown Los Angeles*. New York University Press.

Gaston, S. (2019). Producing race disparities: A study of drug arrests across place and race. *Criminology, 57*(3), 424–451.

Gaston, S., and Brunson, R.K. (2020). Reasonable suspicion in the eye of the beholder: Routine policing in racially different disadvantaged neighborhoods. *Urban Affairs Review, 56*(1), 188–227.

Gaston, S., Brunson, R.K., and Grossman, L.S. (2020). Are minorities subjected to, or insulated from, racialized policing in majority-minority community contexts? *The British Journal of Criminology, 60*(6), 1416–1437.

Gelber, A.M., Isen, A., and Kessler, J. (2016). The effects of youth employment: Evidence from New York City lotteries. *Quarterly Journal of Economics, 131*, 423–460.

Geller, A. (2021). Youth-police contact: Burdens and inequities in an adverse childhood experience, 2014-2017. *American Journal of Public Health, 111*(7), 1300–1308.

Geller, A., and Fagan, J. (2010). Pot as pretext: Marijuana, race, and the new disorder in New York City street policing. *Journal of Empirical Legal Studies, 7*(4), 591–633.

Geller, A., Fagan, J., Tyler, T., and Link, B.G. (2014). Aggressive policing and the mental health of young urban men. *American Journal of Public Health, 104*(12), 2321–2327.

Geller, A., Goff, P.A., Lloyd, T., Haviland, A., Obermark, D., and Glaser, J. (2021). Measuring racial disparities in police use of force: Methods matter. *Journal of Quantitative Criminology, 37*(4), 1083–1113.

Gelman, A., Fagan, J., and Kiss, A. (2007). An analysis of the New York City police department's "stop-and-frisk" policy in the context of claims of racial bias. *Journal of the American Statistical Association, 102*(479), 813–823.

Gelman, A., and Imbens, G. (2013). *Why Ask Why? Forward Causal Inference and Reverse Causal Questions*. Working Paper no. w19614. National Bureau of Economic Research.

Gilfus, M.E. (2002). *Women's Experiences of Abuse as a Risk Factor for Incarceration*. VAWnet, a project of the National Resource Center on Domestic Violence/Pennsylvania Coalition Against Domestic Violence, 2017-08. https://vawnet.org/material/womens-experiences-abuse-risk-factor-incarceration

Gist, N.E. (2000). *A History of the Local Law Enforcement Block Grants Programs Supporting Local Solutions to Crime*. Department of Justice, Bureau of Justice Assistance. https://www.ojp.gov/pdffiles1/bja/179982.pdf

Glaze, L.E., and Maruschak, L.M. (2008). *Parents in Prison and Their Minor Children*. Bureau of Justice Statistics Special Report. NCJ 222984. U.S. Department of Justice, Office of Justice Programs.

Glenn, E.N. (2015). Settler colonialism as structure: A framework for comparative studies of US race and gender formation. *Sociology of Race and Ethnicity, 1*(1), 52–72.

Gobillon, L., Selod, H., and Zenou, Y. (2007). The mechanisms of spatial mismatch. *Urban Studies, 44*(12), 2401–2427.

Goel, S., Rao, J.M., and Shroff, R. (2016). Precinct or prejudice? Understanding racial disparities in New York City's stop-and-frisk policy. *The Annals of Applied Statistics, 10*(1), 365–394.

Goff, P.A., Jackson, M.C., Di Leone, B.A., Culotta, C.M., and DiTomasso, N.A. (2014). The essence of innocence: consequences of dehumanizing Black children. *Journal of Personality and Social Psychology, 106*(4), 526–545. https://doi.org/10.1037/a0035663

Goff, P.A., Lloyd, T.S., Geller, A.B., Raphael, S., and Glaser, J. (2016). *The Science of Justice: Race, Arrests, and Police Use of Force*. Center for Policing Equity.

Goff, P.A., Steele, C.M., and Davies, P.G. (2008). The space between us: Stereotype threat and distance in interracial contexts. *Journal of Personality and Social Psychology, 94*(1), 91–107.

Goldberg, C., Champagne, D., and Singleton, H.V. (2007). Final report: Law enforcement and criminal justice under Public Law 280. U.S. Department of Justice, National Institute of Justice. https://www.ojp.gov/pdffiles1/nij/grants/222585.pdf

Goldberg, C.E. (1997). Overextended borrowing: Tribal peacemaking applied in non-Indian disputes. *Washington Law Review, 72*.

Goldberg, D.T. (1992). The semantics of race. *Ethnic and Racial Studies, 15*(4), 543–569.

Goldstein, N.E., Cole, L.M., Houck, M., Haney-Caron, E., Holliday, S.B., Kreimer, R., and Bethel, K. (2019). Dismantling the school-to-prison pipeline: The Philadelphia police school diversion program. *Children and Youth Services Review, 101*, 61–69.

Goldstein, R., Sances, M.W., and You, H.Y. (2020). Exploitative revenues, law enforcement, and the quality of government service. *Urban Affairs Review, 56*(1), 5–31.

Goldstick, J.E., Cunningham, R.M., and Carter, P.M. (2022). Current causes of death in children and adolescents in the United States. *New England Journal of Medicine, 386*(20), 1955–1956.

Goodman, L.A., Epstein, D., and Sullivan, C.M. (2018). Beyond the RCT: Integrating rigor and relevance to evaluate the outcomes of domestic violence programs. *American Journal of Evaluation, 39*(1), 58–70. https://doi.org/10.1177/1098214017721008

Goodman, R. (1992). *Hennepin County Bureau of Community Corrections Pretrial Release Study*. US Department of Justice, National Institute of Justice. https://www.ojp.gov/pdffiles1/Digitization/153608NCJRS.pdf

Gordon, D. (2020). The police as place-consolidators: The organizational amplification of urban inequality. *Law and Social Inquiry, 45*(1), 1–27.

Gordon, N. (2018). *Disproportionality in Student Discipline: Connecting Policy to Research*. https://www.brookings.edu/research/disproportionality-in-student-discipline-connecting-policy-to-research

Gorsuch, M.M., and Rho, D.T. (2019). Police stops and searches of indigenous people in Minneapolis: The roles of race, place, and gender. *International Indigenous Policy Journal, 10*(3).

Gottfredson, D.C., Crosse, S., Tang, Z., Bauer, E.L., Harmon, M.A., Hagen, C.A., and Greene, A.D. (2020). Effects of school resource officers on school crime and responses to school crime. *Criminology & Public Policy, 19*(3), 905–940.

Gottlieb, K. (2005). *Process and Outcome Evaluations of the Hualapai Wellness Court, U.S. Department of Justice*. U.S. Department of Justice, National Institute of Justice. https://nij.ojp.gov/library/publications/process-and-outcome-evaluations-hualapai-wellness-court

Gottschalk, M. (2014). *Caught*. Princeton University Press.

Gough, E., Kempf, M.C., Graham, L., Manzanero, M., Hook, E.W., Bartolucci, A., and Chamot, E. (2010). HIV and hepatitis B and C incidence rates in US correctional populations and high risk groups: A systematic review and meta-analysis. *BMC Public Health, 10*(1), 1–14.

Graf, G.H.J., Chihuri, S., Blow, M., and Li, G. (2021). Adverse childhood experiences and justice system contact: A systematic review. *Pediatrics, 147*(1).

Graham, S., and Lowery, B.S. (2004). Priming unconscious racial stereotypes about adolescent offenders. *Law and Human Behavior, 28*(5), 483–504. https://doi.org/10.1023/B:LAHU.0000046430.65485.1f

Graham, S.R., and Makowsky, M.D. (2021). Local government dependence on criminal justice revenue and emerging constraints. *Annual Review of Criminology, 4*, 311–330.

Grant, A.G. (2019). *2018 Report to the Governor and the Legislature*. New Jersey Administrative Office of the Courts.

Grattet, R., Petersilia, J., Lin, J., and Beckman, M. (2009). Parole violations and revocations in California: Analysis and suggestions for action. *Federal Probation, 73*, 2.

Greenwood, P.W., and Petersilia, J. (1975). *The Criminal Investigation Process: Volume I: Summary and Policy Implications*. RAND Corporation. https://www.rand.org/pubs/reports/R1776.html

Grenier, J. (2005). *The First Way of War: American War Making on the Frontier, 1607–1814*. Cambridge University Press.

Gross, E.K. (1999). *Evaluation/assessment of Navajo Peacemaking*. Northern Arizona University. https://www.ojp.gov/ncjrs/virtual-library/abstracts/evaluationassessment-navajo-peacemaking

Gross, K.N. (2006). *Colored Amazons: Crime, Violence, and Black Women in the City of Brotherly Love, 1880–1910*. Duke University Press.

Gross, S.R., O'Brien, B., Hu, C., and Kennedy, E.H. (2014). Rate of false conviction of criminal defendants who are sentenced to death. *Proceedings of the National Academy of Sciences, 111*(20), 7230–7235.

Hadden, S.E. (2003). *Slave Patrols: Law and Violence in Virginia and the Carolinas*. Harvard University Press.

Hagan, J. (1974). Extra-legal attributes and criminal sentencing: An assessment of a sociological viewpoint. *Law and Society Review, 8*(3), 357–384. https://www.jstor.org/stable/3053080

Hagan, J., McCarthy, B., and Herda, D. (2022). *Chicago's Reckoning: Racism, Politics, and the Deep History of Policing in an American City*. Oxford University Press.

Haley, S. (2016). *No Mercy Here: Gender, Punishment, and the Making of Jim Crow Modernity*. UNC Press Books.

Hand, C.A., Hankes, J., and House, T. (2012). Restorative justice: The indigenous justice system. *Contemporary Justice Review, 15*(4), 449–467.

Haney, C. (2006). The wages of prison overcrowding: Harmful psychological consequences and dysfunctional correctional reactions. *Washington University Journal Law and Policy, 22*.

______. (2018). The psychological effects of solitary confinement: A systematic critique. *Crime and Justice, 47*(1), 365–416.

Haney López, I.F. (1994). The social construction of race: Some observations on illusion, fabrication, and choice. *Harvard Civil Rights-Civil Liberties Law Review, 29*, 1.

______. (2006). A nation of minorities: Race, ethnicity, and reactionary colorblindness. *Stanford Law Review, 599*(4), 985–1063.

Hannon, L. (2020). An exploratory multilevel analysis of pedestrian frisks in Philadelphia. *Race and Justice, 10*(1), 87–113.

Har, J. (2021). Oakland City Council backtracks, voting to add police as it grapples with rise in homicides. *Los Angeles Times*. https://www.latimes.com/california/story/2021-12-08/oakland-add-police-as-crimes-surge

Harcourt, B.E. (2015). Risk as a proxy for race: The dangers of risk assessment. *Federal Sentencing Reporter, 27*, 237–243.

Hardeman, R., Chantarat, T., and Karbeah, J. (2020). Police exposure as a determinant of structural racism: An exploration of the association between preterm birth in neighborhoods with high police exposure. *Health Services Research, 55*, 50–50.

Harding, D.J., Morenoff, J.D., Nguyen, A.P., and Bushway, S.D. (2017). Short-and long-term effects of imprisonment on future felony convictions and prison admissions. *Proceedings of the National Academy of Sciences, 114*(42), 11103–11108.

Harpalani, V. (2020). Civil rights in living color. *Maryland Law Review, 79*(4), 881–953.

Harper, S., Lynch, J., Burris, S., and Smith, G.D. (2007). Trends in the black-white life expectancy gap in the United States, 1983-2003. *JAMA, 297*(11), 1224–1232.

Harper, S., Rushani, D., and Kaufman, J.S. (2012). Trends in the black-white life expectancy gap, 2003–2008. *JAMA, 307*(21), 2257–2259.

Harrell, E., and Davis, E. (2020). *Contacts between Police and the Public, 2018–Statistical Tables. Bureau of Justice Statics Report.* NCJ 255730. Bureau of Justice Statistics, Office of Justice Programs, U.S. Department of Justice. https://bjs.ojp.gov/content/pub/pdf/cbpp18st.pdf

Harris, A. (2016). *A Pound of Flesh: Monetary Sanctions as Punishment for the Poor.* Russell Sage Foundation. http://www.jstor.org/stable/10.7758/9781610448550

Harris, A., Pattillo, M., and Sykes, B.L. (2022). Studying the system of monetary sanctions. *RSF: The Russell Sage Foundation Journal of the Social Sciences, 8*(2), 1–34.

Harris, C.I. (1993). Whiteness as property. *Harvard Law Review, 106*(8), 1707–1791.

________. (2000). Equal treatment and the reproduction of inequality. *Fordham Law Review, 69*, 1753.

Harris, C.T., and Ulmer, J.T. (2017). "Mighty Like A River": The Black Protestant Church and Violence in Black Communities. *Sociology and Criminology, 58*(2), 295-314. DOI: 10.1080/00380253.2017.1296336

Harris, D.A. (1997). Car wars: The Fourth Amendment's death on the highway. *The George Washington Law Review, 66*, 556.

Harvey, A., and Mattia, T. (2022). Reducing racial disparities in crime victimization: Evidence from employment discrimination litigation. *Journal of Urban Economics*, 103459.

Hassrick, E.M., Raudenbush, S.M., and Rosen, L. (2017). *The Ambitious Elementary School: Its Conception, Design and Implications for Educational Equality.* University of Chicago Press.

Hawken, A., and Kleiman, M.A.R. (2009). *Managing Drug-Involved Probationers with Swift and Certain Sanctions: Evaluating Hawaii's HOPE [NCJ 229023].* National Institute of Justice.

Heaton, P. (2012). Sunday liquor laws and crime. *Journal of Public Economics, 96*(1-2), 42–52.

Heckman, J., Pinto, R., and Savelyev, P. (2013). Understanding the mechanisms through which an influential early childhood program boosted adult outcomes. *American Economic Review, 103*(6), 2052–2086.

Heinz, A.M., Heinz, J.P., Senderowitz, S.J., and Vance, M.A. (1976). Sentencing by parole board: An evaluation. *Journal of Criminal Law and Criminology, 67*(1).

Heller, S. (2014). Summer jobs reduce violence among disadvantaged youth. *Science, 346*, 1219–1223.

______. (2021). *When Scale and Replication Work: Learning from Summer Youth Employment.* Report no. w28705. National Bureau of Economic Research.

Hellerstein, J.K., Neumark, D., and McInerney, M. (2008). Spatial mismatch or racial mismatch? *Journal of Urban Economics, 64*(2), 464–479.

Hemenway, D., Azrael, D., Conner, A., and Miller, M. (2019). Variation in rates of fatal police shootings across US states: The role of firearm availability. *Journal of Urban Health, 96*(1), 63–73.

Henderson, T.N.Y. (2016). Property, penality, and (racial) profiling. *Stanford Journal of Civil Rights and Civil Liberties, 12.*

Henggeler, S.W., and Sheidow, A.J. (2012). Empirically supported family-based treatments for conduct disorder and delinquency in adolescents. *Journal of Marital and Family Therapy, 38*(1), 30–58.

Hennekens, C.H., Drowos, J., and Levine, R.S. (2013). Mortality from homicide among young Black men: A new American tragedy. *The American Journal of Medicine, 126*(4), 282–283.

Herbert, S. (1996). *Policing Space: Territoriality and the Los Angeles Police Department.* University of Minnesota Press.

Herbert, S., Beckett, K., and Stuart, F. (2018). Policing social marginality: Contrasting approaches. *Law and Social Inquiry, 43*(4), 1491–1513.

Hernández, K.L. (2017). *City of Inmates: Conquest, Rebellion, and the Rise of Human Caging in Los Angeles, 1771–1965*. UNC Press Books.

Herring, C. (2019). Complaint-oriented policing: Regulating homelessness in public space. *American Sociological Review, 84*(5), 769–800.

Hess, F.M., and Henig, J.R. (2008). 'Scientific research' and policymaking: A tool, not a crutch. *Education Week, 27*.

Hessick, C.B. (2021). *Prosecutors and Voters*. The Oxford Handbook of Prosecutors and Prosecution.

Hetey, R.C., Monin, B., Maitreyi, A., and Eberhardt, J.L. (2016). *Data for Change: A Statistical Analysis of Police Stops, Searches, Handcuffings, and Arrests in Oakland, Calif., 2013–2014*. Stanford University, SPARQ: Social Psychological Answers to Real-World Questions.

Hickert, A., Bushway, S.D., Harding, D.J., and Morenoff, J.D. (2022). Prior punishments and cumulative disadvantage: How supervision status impacts prison sentences. *Criminology, 60*(1), 27–59.

Hicks, C.D. (2010). *Talk With You Like a Woman: African American Women, Justice, and Reform in New York, 1890–1935*. University of North Carolina Press.

Hindelang, M.J., Hirschi, T., and Weis, J.G. (1981). *Measuring Delinquency, 123*. Sage Publications.

Hinton, E. (2017). *From the War on Poverty to the War on Crime*. Harvard University Press.

Hinton, E., and Cook, D. (2021). The mass criminalization of Black Americans: A historical overview. *Annual Review of Criminology, 4*, 261–286.

Hipp, J.R. (2007). Income inequality, race, and place: Does the distribution of race and class within neighborhoods affect crime rates? *Criminology, 45*, 665–697.

Hirsch, A. (1983). *Making the Second Ghetto: Race and Housing in Chicago 1940–1960*. University of Chicago Press.

Hirschi, T., and Gottfredson, M. (1983). Age and the explanation of crime. *American Journal of Sociology, 89*, 552–584.

Hjalmarsson, R. (2009). Crime and expected punishment: Changes in perceptions at the age of criminal majority. *American Law and Economics Review, 7*, 209–248.

Hochschild, J.L., and Powell, B.M. (2008). Racial reorganization and the United States Census 1850–1930: Mulattoes, half-breeds, mixed parentage, Hindoos, and the Mexican race. *Studies in American Political Development, 22*(1), 59–96.

Hockenberry, S. (2021). Delinquency Cases Waived to Criminal Court, 2018. Juvenile Justice Statistics, National Report Series Fact Sheet. U.S. Department of Justice, Office of Justice Programs. https://ojjdp.ojp.gov/publications/delinquency-cases-waived-2018.pdf

Hoekstra, M., and Sloan, C. (2022). Does race matter for police use of force? Evidence from 911 calls. *American Economic Review, 112*(3), 827–860.

Hoeve, M., McReynolds, L.S., and Wasserman, G.A. (2013). The influence of adolescent psychiatric disorder on young adult recidivism. *Criminal Justice and Behavior, 40*(12), 1368–1382.

Hofer, P.J. (2019). Federal sentencing after Booker. *Crime and Justice, 48*(1), 137–186.

Hoffman, C., Heflinger, C.A., Athay, M., and Davis, M. (2009). Policy, funding, and sustainability: Issues and recommendations for promoting effective transition systems. *Transition of Youth and Young Adults with Emotional or Behavioral Difficulties: An Evidence-Supported Handbook*, 263–290. Paul H Brookes Publishing.

Hogan, T.P. (2022). De-prosecution and death: A synthetic control analysis of the impact of de-prosecution on homicides. *Criminology and Public Policy, 21*(3), 489–534.

Holder Jr., E.H., Leary, M.L., and Frost, J.E. (2013). *Vision 21: Transforming Victim Services Final Report*. Department of Justice, Office of Victims of Crime. https://ovc.ojp.gov/sites/g/files/xyckuh226/files/media/document/Vision21_Report.pdf

Holzer, H.J. (1991). The spatial mismatch hypothesis: What has the evidence shown? *Urban Studies, 28*(1), 105–122.

Homeboy Industries. (2020). *Annual Report 2020*. https://readymag.com/u18075929/3025033/

Hope, T. (1995). Community crime prevention. *Building a Safer Society*, 21–89. University of Chicago Press.

Houston Police Department. (2020). *Annual Report*. https://www.houstoncit.org/annual-report/

______. (2021). *Crisis Call Diversion Program* (CCD). https://www.houstoncit.org/ccd/

Howard, H., Clark, K., and Piltch, M. (2020). Support for mothers who are incarcerated: Impact of mutual aid support groups. *Urban Social Work, 4*(1), 77–93.

Howell, K.B. (2016). The costs of broken windows policing: Twenty years and counting. *Cardozo Law Review, 37*, 1059.

Hoyt, L. (2004). Collecting private funds for safer public spaces: An empirical examination of the business improvement district concept. *Environment and Planning B: Planning and Design, 31*(3), 367–380. https://www.casey.org/what-are-some-examples-of-evidence-informed-practices-to-keep-children-safe-and-promote-permanency

Huebner, B.M., and Bynum, T.S. (2008). The role of race and ethnicity in parole decisions. *Criminology, 46*(4), 907–938.

Huizinga, D., and Elliott, D.S. (1986). Reassessing the reliability and validity of self-report delinquency measures. *Journal of Quantitative Criminology, 2*(4), 293–327.

Hyatt, J.M., and Barnes, G.C. (2017). An experimental evaluation of the impact of intensive supervision on the recidivism of high-risk probationers. *Crime and Delinquency, 63*(1), 3–38.

Hyra, D.S., Squires, G.D., Renner, R.N., and Kirk, D.S. (2013). Metropolitan segregation and the subprime lending crisis. *Housing Policy Debate, 23*(1), 177–198.

Inlow, A.R. (2021). A comprehensive review of quantitative research on crime, the built environment, land use, and physical geography. *Sociology Compass, 15*(7).

Institute of Medicine. (2003). *Unequal Treatment: Confronting Racial and Ethnic Disparities in Health Care*. The National Academies Press.

Jackson, D., Lighty, T., Marx, G., and Richards, A. (2020). Kim Foxx drops more felony cases as Cook County state's attorney than her predecessor, Tribune analysis shows. *Chicago Tribune,* August 10. https://www.chicagotribune.com/investigations/ct-kim-foxx-felony-charges-cook-county-20200810-ldvrmqvv6bd3hpsuqha4duehmu-story.html

Jacobs, D. (1998). The determinants of deadly force: A structural analysis of police violence. *American Journal of Sociology, 103*(4), 837–862.

Jacoby, S.F., Dong, B., Beard, J.H., Wiebe, D.J., and Morrison, C.N. (2018). The enduring impact of historical and structural racism on urban violence in Philadelphia. *Social Science and Medicine, 199*, 87–95.

James, D.J., and Glaze, L.E. (2006). *Mental Health Problems of Prison and Jail Inmates*. US Department of Justice, Bureau of Justice Statistics.

Jannetta, J., Breaux, J., Ho., H., and Porter, J. (2014). *Examining Racial and Ethnic Disparities in Probation Revocation: Summary Findings and Implications from a Multisite Study*. Urban Institute.

Jarvis, J.P., and Regoeczi, W.C. (2009). Homicides clearances: An analysis of arrest versus exceptional outcomes. *Homicide Studies, 13*(2), 174–188.

Jee-Lyn García, J., and Sharif, M.Z. (2015). Black lives matter: A commentary on racism and public health. *American Journal of Public Health, 105*(8), e27–e30.

Jenness, V. (2004). Explaining criminalization: From demography and status politics to globalization and modernization. *Annual Review of Sociology, 30*, 147–171.

Jenness, V., Sexton, L., and Sumner, J. (2019). Sexual victimization against transgender women in prison: Consent and coercion in context. *Criminology, 57*(4), 603–631.

John Jay College Research Advisory Group on Preventing and Reducing Community Violence. (2020). *Reducing Violence Without Police: A Review of Research Evidence*. Research and Evaluation Center, John Jay College of Criminal Justice, City University of New York. https://johnjayrec.nyc/wp-content/uploads/2020/11/AV20201109_rev.pdf

Johnson, B.D. (2006). The multilevel context of criminal sentencing: Integrating judge-and county-level influences. *Criminology, 44*(2), 259–298.

______. (2019). Trials and tribulations: The trial tax and the process of punishment. *Crime and Justice, 48*(1), 313–363.

Johnson, B.D., Spohn, C., and Kimchi, A. (2021). Life lessons: Examining sources of racial and ethnic disparity in federal life without parole sentences. *Criminology, 59*(4), 704–737.

Johnson, C.L. (2010). *Police Use of Intelligence Networks for Reducing Crime*. NCJ 238321. LFB Scholarly Publishing. https://www.ojp.gov/ncjrs/virtual-library/abstracts/police-use-intelligence-networks-reducing-crime

Johnson, L.T., and Kane, R.J. (2018). Deserts of disadvantage: The diffuse effects of structural disadvantage on violence in urban communities. *Crime and Delinquency, 64,* 143–165.

Johnson, W. (2013). *River of Dark Dreams*. Harvard University Press.

Jones, C.P. (2002). Confronting institutionalized racism. *Phylon (1960-), 50*(1/2), 7–22.

Jones, N. (2010). *Between Good and Ghetto: African American Girls and Inner-City Violence*. Rutgers University Press. Project MUSE. muse.jhu.edu/book/6039

______. (2014). "The regular routine": Proactive policing and adolescent development among young, poor Black men. *Pathways to Adulthood for Disconnected Young Men in Low-Income Communities. New Directions in Child and Adolescent Development, 143,* 33–54.

______. (2018). *The Chosen Ones: Black Men and the Politics of Redemption*. University of California Press.

Jordan, A. (2021). *Uniformity and Multiplicity in Contract Law: Some Reflections on the Morality of Promises*. https://dx.doi.org/10.2139/ssrn.3908100

Jordan, A., Karger, E., and Neal, D.A. (2022). *Heterogeneous Impacts of Sentencing Decisions*. Working Paper No. 2021-113. University of Chicago, Becker Friedman Institute. https://cpb-us-w2.wpmucdn.com/voices.uchicago.edu/dist/6/3381/files/2022/02/SSRN-BFI-2-22.pdf

Justice, B., and Meares, T.L. (2014). How the criminal justice system educates citizens. *The ANNALS of the American Academy of Political and Social Science, 651*(1), 159–177.

Kaeble, D., and Alper, M. (2020). *Probation and--Parole in the United States, 2017–2018*. NCJ 252072. Bureau of Justice Statistics, Office of Justice Programs, U.S. Department of Justice.

Kahn, K.B., McMahon, J.M., and Stewart, G. (2018). Misinterpreting danger? Stereotype threat, pre-attack indicators, and police-citizen interactions. *Journal of Police and Criminal Psychology, 33*(1), 45–54.

Kane, R.J. (2002). The social ecology of police misconduct. *Criminology, 40*(4), 867–896.

Kaplan, R.M. (1984). The measurement of human aggression. In R.M. Kaplan, V.J. Konecni, and R.W. Novaco (Eds.), *Aggression in children and youth* (pp. 44–72). The Hague, The Netherlands: Martinus Nijhoff.

Kapoor, R., and Trestman, R. (2016). Mental health effects of restrictive housing. *Restrictive Housing in the US: Issues, Challenges, and Future Directions*, 199–232.

Katz, A.H. (1981). Self-help and mutual aid: An emerging social movement? *Annual Review of Sociology, 7*(1), 129–155.

Kaufman, J.S., Cooper, R.S., and Mcgee, D.L. (1997). Socioeconomic status and health in Blacks and Whites: The problem of residual confounding and the resiliency of race. *Epidemiology, 8*, 621–628.

Kazemian, L. (2022). *Long Sentences: An International Perspective.* Council on Criminal Justice. https://counciloncj.foleon.com/tfls/long-sentences-by-the-numbers/an-internationalperspective

Keels, M. (2021). What schools need now: Relational discipline. *Educational Leadership,* 79(2), 32–38. https://eric.ed.gov/?id=EJ1317122

Kennedy, D.M. (2011). *Don't Shoot: One Man, A Street Fellowship, and the End of Violence in Inner-city America.* Bloomsbury Publishing USA.

Kenney, M., Nolen, J., and Hernandez, C. (2021). 'They just shot my baby,' says father, moments after 7-year-old daughter killed at McDonald's in Homan Square. *Chicago Sun Times.* https://chicago.suntimes.com/crime/2021/4/18/22391068/7-year-old-girl-killed-man-seriously-hurt-homan-square-shooting

Kessler, J.B., Tahamont, S., Gelber, A.M., and Isen, A. (2021). *The Effects of Youth Employment on Crime: Evidence from New York City Lotteries.* NBER Working Paper No. 28373.

Killion, V. (2021). *Funding Conditions: Constitutional Limits on Congress's Spending Power* (CRS Report No. R46827). https://crsreports.congress.gov/product/pdf/R/R46827/3

King, R.D., and Johnson, B.D. (2016). A punishing look: Skin tone and Afrocentric features in the halls of justice. *American Journal of Sociology, 122*(1), 90–124.

King, R.D., Johnson, K.R., and McGeever, K. (2010). Demography of the legal profession and racial disparities in sentencing. *Law and Society Review, 44*(1), 1–32.

King, R.D., and Light, M.T. (2019). Have racial and ethnic disparities in sentencing declined? *Crime and Justice, 48*(1), 365–437.

Kirk, D.S. (2006). Examining the divergence across self-report and official data sources on inferences about the adolescent life-course of crime. *Journal of Quantitative Criminology, 22*(2), 107–129.

Kirk, D.S., and Papachristos, A.A. (2011). Cultural mechanisms and the persistence of neighborhood violence. *American Journal of Sociology, 116*, 1190–1233.

Kirk, D.S., Papachristos, A.V., Fagan, J., and Tyler, T.R. (2012). The paradox of law enforcement in immigrant communities: Does tough immigration enforcement undermine public safety? *The ANNALS of the American Academy of Political and Social Science, 641*, 79–98. http://www.jstor.org/stable/23218824

Kirk, E.M. (2020). Obstructing the American dream: Homeownership denied and neighborhood crime. *Housing Policy Debate*, 1–21.

______. (2021). Community consequences of mass incarceration: Sparking neighborhood social problems and violent crime. *Journal of Crime and Justice, 45*(1), 103–119. https://doi.org/10.1080/0735648X.2021.1887751

______. (2022). Untangling eviction, disadvantage, race, and social processes: Neighborhood factors influencing crime. *Crime and Delinquency, 68*(4), 594–612.

Kirshenman, J., and Neckerman, K.M. (2019). "We'd love to hire them, but...": The meaning of race for employers. *Race and Ethnic Conflict*, 152–161. Routledge.

Kizer, J.M. (2017). Arrested by skin color: Evidence from siblings and a nationally representative sample. *Socius.* https://doi.org/10.1177/2378023117737922

Kjellstrand, J.M., and Eddy, J.M. (2011). Parental incarceration during childhood, family context, and youth problem behavior across adolescence. *Journal of Offender Rehabilitation, 50*(1), 18–36.

Kleck, G. (1981). Racial discrimination in criminal sentencing: A critical evaluation of the evidence with additional evidence on the death penalty. *American Sociological Review,* 783–805.

Kleinberg, J., Lakkaraju, H., Leskovec, J., Ludwig, J., and Mullainathan, S. (2018). Human decisions and machine predictions. *The Quarterly Journal of Economics, 133*(1), 237–293.

Kling, J.R. (2006). Incarceration length, employment, and earnings. *American Economic Review, 96*(3), 863–876.

Kling, J.R., Ludwig, J., and Katz, L.F. (2005). Neighborhood effects on crime for female and male youth: Evidence from a randomized housing voucher experiment. *The Quarterly Journal of Economics, 120*(1), 87–130.

Klinger, D.A. (1997). Negotiating order in patrol work: An ecological theory of police response to deviance. *Criminology, 35*(2), 277–306.

Kneebone, E., and Raphael, S. (2011). *City and Suburban Crime Trends in Metropolitan America.* Brookings Institution Metropolitan Policy Program.

Knox, D., Lowe, W., and Mummolo, J. (2020). Administrative records mask racially biased policing. *American Political Science Review, 114*(3), 619–637.

Knox, D., and Mummolo, J. (2020). Toward a general causal framework for the study of racial bias in policing. *Journal of Political Institutions and Political Economy, 1*(3), 341–378.

Kohler-Hausmann, I. (2018). *Misdemeanorland.* Princeton University Press.

Kohler-Hausmann, J. (2017). *Getting Tough: Welfare and Imprisonment in 1970s America.* Princeton University Press.

Kondo, M.C., Andreyeva, E., South, E.C., MacDonald, J.M., and Branas, C.C. (2018). Neighborhood interventions to reduce violence. *Annual Review of Public Health, 39*, 253–271.

Kondo, M.C., Keene, D., Hohl, B.C., MacDonald, J.M., and Branas, C.C. (2015). A difference-in-differences study of the effects of a new abandoned building remediation strategy on safety. *PloS one, 10*(7).

Koper, C.S., and Mayo-Wilson, E. (2006). Police crackdowns on illegal gun carrying: A systematic review of their impact on gun crime. *Journal of Experimental Criminology, 2*(2), 227–261.

Kornhauser, R.R. (1978). *Social Sources of Delinquency: An Appraisal of Analytic Models.* University of Chicago Press.

Kretschmar, J.M., Butcher, F., Flannery, D.J., and Singer, M.I. (2016). Diverting juvenile justice-involved youth with behavioral health issues from detention: Preliminary findings from Ohio's Behavioral Health Juvenile Justice (BHJJ) Initiative. *Criminal Justice Policy Review, 27*(3), 302–325.

Krivo, L.J. (2014). Reducing crime through community investment: Can we make it work? *Criminology and Public Policy, 13*.

Krivo, L.J., Lyons, C.J., and Vélez, M.B. (2021). The US racial structure and ethno-racial inequality in urban neighborhood crime, 2010–2013. *Sociology of Race and Ethnicity, 7*, 350–368.

Krivo, L.J., and Peterson, R.D. (1996). Extremely disadvantaged neighborhoods and urban crime. *Social Forces, 75*, 619–648.

______. (2004). Labor market conditions and violent crime among youth and adults. *Sociological Perspectives, 47*, 485–505.

Krivo, L.J., Peterson, R.D., and Kuhl, D.C. (2009). Segregation, racial structure, and neighborhood violent crime. *American Journal of Sociology, 114*, 1765–1802.

Krivo, L.J., Vélez, M.B., Lyons, C.J., Phillips, J.B., and Sabbath, E. (2018). Race, crime, and the changing fortunes of urban neighborhoods, 1999–2013. *Du Bois Review: Social Science Research on Race, 15*(1), 47–68.

Krysan, M., and Crowder, K. (2017). *Cycle of Segregation: Social Processes and Residential Stratification.* Russell Sage Foundation.

Kubrin, C.E., and Wadsworth, T. (2003). Identifying the structural correlates of African-American killings: What can we learn from data disaggregation? *Homicide Studies, 7*, 3–35.

Kupchik, A. (2016). *The Real School Safety Problem*. University of California Press. https://doi.org/10.1525/9780520959842

Kupchik, A., and Ward, G. (2014). Race, poverty, and exclusionary school security: An empirical analysis of US elementary, middle, and high schools. *Youth Violence and Juvenile Justice, 12*(4), 332–354.

Kurlychek, M.C., and Johnson, B.D. (2019). Cumulative disadvantage in the American criminal justice system. *Annual Review of Criminology, 2*, 291–319.

Kutateladze, B.L., Andiloro, N.R., and Johnson, B.D. (2016). Opening Pandora's box: How does defendant race influence plea bargaining? *Justice Quarterly, 33*(3), 398–426.

Kutateladze, B.L., Andiloro, N.R., Johnson, B.D., and Spohn, C.C. (2014). Cumulative disadvantage: Examining racial and ethnic disparity in prosecution and sentencing. *Criminology, 52*(3), 514–551.

Labella, M.H., and Masten, A.S. (2018). Family influences on the development of aggression and violence. *Current Opinion in Psychology, 19*, 11–16.

Lacey, N., Soskice, D., and Hope, D. (2018). Understanding the determinants of penal policy: Crime, culture, and comparative political economy. *Annual Review of Criminology, 1*, 195–217.

Lacey, N., and Zedner, L. (2017). 2. Criminalization: Historical, legal, and criminological perspectives. *The Oxford Handbook of Criminology* (6th ed.). Oxford University Press.

Lacoe, J., and Betesh, H. (2019). *Supporting Reentry Employment and Success: A Summary of the Evidence for Adults and Young Adults*. Mathematica Policy Research.

LaFree, G. (1995). Race and crime trends in the United States, 1946–1990. *Ethnicity, Race, and Crime: Perspectives across Time and Place*, 169–219. State University of New York Press.

LaFree, G., Baumer, E.P., and O'Brien, R. (2010). Still separate and unequal? A city-level analysis of the black-white gap in homicide arrests since 1960. *American Sociological Review, 75*(1), 75–100.

Lageson, S.E. (2016). Found out and opting out: The consequences of online criminal records for families. *The ANNALS of the American Academy of Political and Social Science, 665*(1), 127–141.

______. (2020). *Digital Punishment: Privacy, Stigma, and the Harms of Data-Driven Criminal Justice*. Oxford University Press.

Lanfear, C.C. (2022). Collective efficacy and the built environment. *Criminology, 60*. https://doi.org/10.1111/1745-9125.12304

Lanfear, C.C., Beach, L.R., and Thomas, T.A. (2018). Formal social control in changing neighborhoods: Racial implications of neighborhood context on reactive policing. *City and Community, 17*(4).

Lanfear, C.C., Matsueda, R.L., and Beach, L.R. (2020). Broken windows, informal social control, and crime: Assessing causality in empirical studies. *Annual Review of Criminology, 3*, 97–120.

Lang, C. (2021). Hate crimes against Asian Americans are on the rise. Many say more policing isn't the answer. *TIME*. https://time.com/5938482/asian-american-attacks

Lang, K., and Kahn-Lang Spitzer, A. (2020). Race discrimination: An economic perspective. *Journal of Economic Perspectives, 34*(2), 68–89.

Langan, P.A. (1985). Racism on trial: New evidence to explain the racial composition of prisons in the United States. *Journal of Criminal Law and Criminology, 76*(33), 666–683.

Laniyonu, A. (2018). Coffee shops and street stops: Policing practices in gentrifying neighborhoods. *Urban Affairs Review, 54*(5), 898–930.

Laub, J.H., and Sampson, R.J. (2003). *Shared Beginnings, Divergent Lives: Delinquent Boys to Age 70*. Harvard University Press.

Lauritsen, J., Heimer, K., and Lang, J.B. (2018). The enduring significance of race and ethnic disparities in male violent victimization: An analysis of NCVS micro-data, 1973-2010. *Du Bois Review: Social Science Research on Race, 15*, 69–87.

Lautenschlager, R., and Omori, M. (2019). Racial threat, social (dis) organization, and the ecology of police: Towards a macro-level understanding of police use-of-force in communities of color. *Justice Quarterly, 36*(6), 1050–1071. https://doi.org/10.1080/07418825.2018.1480792

Lawton, M.M. (2015). State responses to the Whren decision. *Case Western Reserve Law Review, 66*(4), 1039.

Leadership Conference on Civil and Human Rights. (2015). *Civil Rights, Privacy, and Media Rights Groups Release Principles for Law Enforcement Body Worn Cameras*. Leadership Conference on Civil and Human Rights.

Leap, J., Franke, T., Christie, C., and Bonis, S. (2010). Nothing stops a bullet like a job: Homeboy Industries gang prevention and intervention in Los Angeles. *Beyond Suppression: Global Perspectives on Youth Justice*, 127–138.

Lee, D.S., and McCrary, J. (2009). *The Deterrent Effect of Prison: Dynamic Theory and Evidence*. Princeton, NJ: University of Princeton, Industrial Relations Section.

Lee, J.R.S. (2016). A trauma-informed approach to affirming the humanity of African American boys and supporting healthy transitions to manhood. *Boys and Men in African American Families*, 85–92. Springer International Publishing.

Lee, M.T., Martinez, R., and Rosenfeld, R. (2001). Does immigration increase homicide? Negative evidence from three border cities. *The Sociological Quarterly, 42*(4), 559–580.

Legewie, J., and Fagan, J. (2016). *Group Threat, Police Officer Diversity and the Deadly Use of Police Force*. Columbia Public Law Research Paper No. 14-512.

______. (2019). Aggressive policing and the educational performance of minority youth. *American Sociological Review, 84*(2), 220–247.

Lerman, A.E., and Weaver, V.M. (2014a). *Arresting Citizenship*. University of Chicago Press. https://doi.org/10.7208/9780226137971

_______. (2014b). Staying out of sight? Concentrated policing and local political action. *The ANNALS of the American Academy of Political and Social Science, 651*(1), 202–219.

Leslie, E., and Pope, N.G. (2017). The unintended impact of pretrial detention on case outcomes: Evidence from New York City arraignments. *The Journal of Law and Economics, 60*(3), 529–557.

Levchak, P.J. (2017). Do precinct characteristics influence stop-and-frisk in New York City? A multi-level analysis of post-stop outcomes. *Justice Quarterly, 34*(3), 377–406. https://doi.org/10.1080/07418825.2016.1162320

Leverentz, A. (2014). New parochialism and community dynamics: Benefits and possible collateral consequences. *Criminology and Public Policy, 13*, 217–224.

Levy, B.L., Phillips, N.E., and Sampson, R.J. (2020). Triple disadvantage: Neighborhood networks of everyday urban mobility and violence in US cities. *American Sociological Review, 85*(6), 925–956.

Light, M.T. (2022). The declining significance of race in criminal sentencing: Evidence from US federal courts. *Social Forces, 100*(3), 1110–1141.

Light, M.T., and Thomas, J.T. (2019). Segregation and violence reconsidered: Do Whites benefit from residential segregation? *American Sociological Review, 84*, 690–725.

Light, M.T., and Ulmer, J.T. (2016). Explaining the gaps in White, Black, and Hispanic violence since 1990: Accounting for immigration, incarceration, and inequality. *American Sociological Review, 81*, 290–315.

Lin, J., Grattet, R., and Petersilia, J. (2010). "Back-end sentencing" and reimprisonment: Individual, organizational, and community predictors of parole sanctioning decisions. *Criminology, 48*(3), 759–795.

Lindquist, C., Lattimore, P., Willison, J.B., Steffey, D., Stahl, M.H., Scaggs, S., Welsh-Loveman, J., and Eisenstat, J. (2018). *Cross-Site Evaluation of the Bureau of Justice Assistance FY 2011 Second Chance Act Adult Offender Reentry Demonstration Projects: Final Report.* RTI International. https://www.ojp.gov/pdffiles1/nij/grants/251703.pdf

Lipsitz, G. (2011). *How Racism Takes Place.* Temple University Press.

Lochner, L., and Moretti, E. (2004). The effect of education on crime: Evidence from prison inmates, arrests, and self-reports. *American Economic Review, 94*(1), 155–189.

Lockwood, S.K., Nally, J.M., Ho, T., and Knutson, K. (2015). Racial disparities and similarities in post-release recidivism and employment among ex-prisoners with a different level of education. *Journal of Prison Education and Reentry, 2*(1), 16–31.

Loeffler, C.E. (2013). Does imprisonment alter the life course? Evidence on crime and employment from a natural experiment. *Criminology, 51*(1), 137–166.

Lofstrom, M., Hayes, J., Martin, B., and Premkumar, D., and Gumbs, A. (2021). *Racial Disparities in Law Enforcement Stops.* Public Policy Institute of California. https://www.ppic.org/publication/racial-disparities-in-law-enforcement-stops/

Lofstrom, M., Martin, B., and Raphael, S. (2020). Effect of sentencing reform on racial and ethnic disparities in involvement with the criminal justice system: The case of California's Proposition 47. *Criminology and Public Policy, 19*(4), 116–1207. https://doi.org/10.1111/1745-9133.12527

Lofstrom, M., and Raphael, S. (2016). Incarceration and crime: Evidence from California's Public Safety Realignment reform. *The ANNALS of the American Academy of Political and Social Science, 664,* 196–220. https://www.jstor.org/stable/24756115

Lofstrom, M., Raphael, S., and Grattet, R. (2014). Is public safety realignment reducing recidivism in California. *Public Policy Institute of California.*

Logan, M.W., Dulisse, B., Peterson, S., Morgan, M.A., Olma, T.M., and Paré, P.P. (2017). Correctional shorthands: Focal concerns and the decision to administer solitary confinement. *Journal of Criminal Justice, 52,* 90–100. https://doi.org/10.1016/j.jcrimjus.2017.08.007

Lopoo, E., Schiraldi, V., and Ittner, T. (2022). How little supervision can we have? *Annual Review of Criminology, 6.*

Losen, D.J., Hodson, C.L., Keith II, M.A., Morrison, K., and Belway, S. (2015). Are we closing the school discipline gap? University of California, Los Angeles.

Loury, G.C. (2021). *The Anatomy of Racial Inequality: With a New Preface* (Vol. 4). Harvard University Press.

Love, M.C., Roberts, J., and Klingele, C.M. (2021). *Collateral Consequences of Criminal Conviction: Law, Policy and Practice.* Thomson Reuters.

Lucchesi, A., and Echo-Hawk, A. (2018). Missing and murdered indigenous women & girls: A snapshot of data from 71 urban cities in the United States. *Urban Indian Health Institute.* http://www.uihi.org/wp-content/uploads/2018/11/Missing-and-Murdered-Indigenous-Women-and-Girls-Report.pdf

Ludwig, J., Duncan, G.J., Gennetian, L.A., Katz, L.F., Kessler, R.C., Kling, J.R., and Sanbonmatsu, L. (2012). Neighborhood effects on the long-term well-being of low-income adults. *Science, 337*(6101), 1505–1510.

______. (2013). Long-term neighborhood effects on low-income families: Evidence from Moving to Opportunity. *American Economic Review, 103*(3), 226–231.

Ludwig, J., Duncan, G.J., and Hirschfield, P. (2001). Urban poverty and juvenile crime: Evidence from a randomized housing-mobility experiment. *The Quarterly Journal of Economics, 116*(2), 655–679.

Ludwig, J., Duncan, G.J., and Pinkston, J.C. (2000). *Neighborhood Effects on Economic Self-Sufficiency: Evidence from a Randomized Housing-Mobility Experiment.* Unpublished paper. Georgetown University.

Ludwig, J., Ladd, H.F., Duncan, G.J., Kling, J., and O'Regan, K.M. (2001). Urban poverty and educational outcomes [with comments]. *Brookings-Wharton Papers on Urban Affairs*, 147–201. http://www.jstor.org/stable/25058785

Lum, C., Koper, C.S., Wilson, D.B., Stoltz, M., Goodier, M., Eggins, E., and Mazerolle, L. (2020). Body-worn cameras' effects on police officers and citizen behavior: A systematic review. *Campbell Systematic Reviews, 16*(3).

Lum, C., and Nagin, D.S. (2017). Reinventing American Policing. *Crime and Justice, 46*, 339 - 393.

Luminosity and the University of Chicago's Crime Lab. (2020). *Updating the New York City Criminal Justice Agency Release Assessment: Maintaining High Court Appearance Rates, Reducing Unnecessary Pretrial Detention, and Reducing Disparity*. Criminal Justice Agency. https://www.nycja.org/publications/updating-the-new-york-city-criminal-justice-agency-release-assessment

Lynch, M. (2009). Punishment, purpose, and place: A case study of Arizona's prison siting decisions. In *Studies in Law, Politics and Society*. Emerald Group Publishing Limited.

Lyons, C.J., and Pettit, B. (2011). Compounded disadvantage: Race, incarceration, and wage growth. *Social Problems, 58*(2), 257–280.

Lyons, C.J., Vélez, M.B., and Krivo, L.J. (2022). The dynamic racial structure and disparities in neighborhood crime change. *Social Problems*. https://doi.org/10.1093/socpro/spac013

Ma, D.S., Correll, J., Wittenbrink, B., Bar-Anan, Y., Sriram, N., and Nosek, B.A. (2013). When fatigue turns deadly: The association between fatigue and racial bias in the decision to shoot. *Basic and Applied Social Psychology, 35*(6), 515–524.

MacDonald, J., Golinelli, D., Stokes, R.J., and Bluthenthal, R. (2010). The effect of business improvement districts on the incidence of violent crimes. *Injury Prevention, 16*(5), 327–332.

MacDonald, J., Nguyen, V., Jensen, S.T., and Branas, C.C. (2021). Reducing crime by remediating vacant lots: The moderating effect of nearby land uses. *Journal of Experimental Criminology, 18*(3), 639–664. https://doi.org.10.1007/s11292-020-09452-9

MacDonald, J., and Raphael, S. (2020). The effect of scaling back punishment in racial disparities in criminal case outcomes. *Criminology and Public Policy, 19*(4), 1139–1164.

MacDonald, J., and Sampson, R.J. (2012). Introduction: The world in a city: Immigration and America's changing social fabric. *The ANNALS of the American Academy of Political and Social Science, 641*, 6–15. http://www.jstor.org/stable/23218820

MacDonald, J.M., and Stokes, R.J. (2020). Gentrification, land use, and crime. *Annual Review of Criminology, 3*, 121–138.

Maclin, T. (1998). Terry v. Ohio's Fourth Amendment legacy: Black men and police discretion. *St. John's Law Review, 72*(3), 1271–1322.

Makowsky, M.D., and Stratmann, T. (2009). Political economy at any speed: What determines traffic citations? *American Economic Review, 99*(1), 509–527.

Makowsky, M.D., Stratmann, T., and Tabarrok, A. (2019). To serve and collect: The fiscal and racial determinants of law enforcement. *The Journal of Legal Studies, 48*(1), 189–216.

Manduca, R., and Sampson, R.J. (2021). Childhood exposure to polluted neighborhood environments and intergenerational income mobility, teenage birth, and incarceration in the USA. *Population and Environment, 42*, 501–523.

Manski, C.F., and Nagin, D.S. (2017). Assessing benefits, costs, and disparate racial impacts of confrontational proactive policing. *Proceedings of the National Academy of Sciences, 114*(35), 9308–9313.

Manza, J., and Uggen, C. (2006). *Locked Out: Felon Disenfranchisement and American Democracy*. Oxford University Press.

Mao, G., Drury, J., Fernandes-Jesus, M., and Ntontis, E. (2021). How participation in Covid-19 mutual aid groups affects subjective well-being and how political identity moderates these effects. *Analyses of Social Issues and Public Policy, 21*(1), 1082–1112.

Marable, M. (2001). Structural racism and American democracy: Historical and theoretical perspectives. *Souls, 3*(1), 6–24.

Martin, R.J. (2009). Killing capital punishment in New Jersey: The first state in modern history to repeal its death penalty statute. *University of Toledo Law Review, 41*.

Martinez, M.M. (2018). *The Injustice Never Leaves You: Anti-Mexican Violence in Texas*. Harvard University Press.

Martinez Jr., R., Stowell, J., and Iwama, J.A. (2016). The role of immigration: Race/ethnicity and San Diego homicides since 1970. *Journal of Quantitative Criminology, 32*, 471–488.

Maruschak, L.M., Berzofsky, M., and Unangst, J. (2015). *Medical Problems of State and Federal Prisoners and Jail Inmates, 2011-12*. US Department of Justice, Bureau of Justice Statistics.

Massey, D.S. (2004). Segregation and stratification: A biosocial perspective. *Du Bois Review: Social Science Research on Race, 1*(1), 7–25.

_______. (2007). *Categorically Unequal*. Russell Sage Foundation.

_______. (2016). Residential segregation is the linchpin of racial stratification. *City and Community, 15*, 4–7.

Massey, D.S., and Denton, N. (1993). *American Apartheid: Segregation and the Making of the Underclass*. Harvard University Press.

Massey, D.S., and Kanaiaupuni, S.M. (1993). Public housing and the concentration of poverty. *Social Science Quarterly, 74*(1), 109–122.

Massey, D.S., Rothwell, J., and Domina, T. (2009). The changing bases of segregation in the United States. *The ANNALS of the American Academy of Political and Social Science, 626*, 74–90.

Mastrofski, S.D., Reisig, M.D., and McCluskey, J.D. (2002). Police disrespect toward the public: An encounter-based analysis. *Criminology, 40*(3), 519–552.

Matei, A., Courtney, L., White, K., Robin, L., Thompson, P.S., Martinez, R., and Zweig, J. (2022). *Implementing Youth Violence Reduction Strategies: Findings from a Synthesis of the Literature on Gun, Group, and Gang Violence*. Urban Institute, Justice Policy Center. https://www.urban.org/sites/default/files/publication/105301/implementing-youth-violence-reduction-strategies_0.pdf

Matsueda, R.L., Drakulich, K., and Kubrin, C.E. (2006). Race and neighborhood codes of violence. *The Many Colors of Crime: Inequalities of Race, Ethnicity, and Crime in America*. New York University Press.

Mauer, M. (2011a). Addressing racial disparities in incarceration. *The Prison Journal, 91*(3), 87s–101s. https://doi.org/10.1177/0032885511415227

______. (2011b). Sentencing reform: Amid mass incarcerations—guarded optimism. *Criminal Justice, 26*(1) 27–36.

Maxwell, C.D., Garner, J.H., and Skogan, W.G. (2018). Collective efficacy and violence in Chicago neighborhoods: A reproduction. *Journal of Criminal Justice, 34*, 236–244.

Mazerolle, L., Wickes, R., and McBroom, J. (2010). Community variations in violence: Social ties and collective efficacy in comparative context. *Journal of Research in Crime and Delinquency, 47*, 3–30.

McConnell, A.R., and Leibold, J.M. (2001). Relations among the Implicit Association Test, discriminatory behavior, and explicit measures of racial attitudes. *Journal of Experimental Social Psychology, 37*(5), 435–442.

McCourt, A.D., Crifasi, C.K., Stuart, E.A., Vernick, J.S., Kagawa, R.M., Wintemute, G.J., and Webster, D.W. (2020). Purchaser licensing, point-of-sale background check laws, and firearm homicide and suicide in 4 US states, 1985–2017. *American Journal of Public Health, 110*(10), 1546–1552.

McDonald, D., and Carlson, K.E. (1993). *Sentencing in the Federal Courts: Does Race Matter? The Transition to Sentencing Guidelines, 1986-90*. NCJ 145328. U.S. Department of Justice, Office of Justice Programs, Bureau of Justice Statistics.

McGlynn-Wright, A., Crutchfield, R.D., Skinner, M.L., and Haggerty, K.P. (2022). The usual, racialized, suspects: The consequence of police contacts with Black and White youth on adult arrest. *Social Problems, 69*(2), 299–315.

McGuire, D.L. (2010). *At the Dark End of the Street: Black Women, Rape, and Resistance—A New History of the Civil Rights Movement from Rosa Parks to the Rise of Black Power*. Vintage.

McLafferty, S., and Preston, V. (1996). Spatial mismatch and employment in a decade of restructuring. *The Professional Geographer, 48*(4), 420–431.

McLennan, R. (2008). *The Crisis of Imprisonment: Protest, Politics, and the Making of the American Penal State, 1776–1941*. New York: Cambridge University Press.

McNulty, T. (2001). Assessing the race-violence relationship at the macro level: The assumption of racial invariance and the problem of restricted distributions. *Criminology, 39*, 467–490.

McNulty, T.L., and Bellair, P.E. (2003). Explaining racial and ethnic differences in adolescent violence: Structural disadvantage, family well-being, and social capital. *Justice Quarterly, 20*(1), 1–31.

McNulty, T.L., Bellair, P.E., and Watts, S.J. (2013). Neighborhood disadvantage and verbal ability as explanations of the Black–White difference in adolescent violence: Toward an integrated model. *Crime and Delinquency, 59*(1), 140–160.

McNulty, T.L., and Holloway, S.R. (2000). Race, crime, and public housing in Atlanta: Testing a conditional effect hypothesis. *Social Forces, 79*(2), 707–729.

Mead, L.M. (ed.). (1997). *The New Paternalism: Supervisory Approaches to Poverty*. Brookings Institution Press.

Meares, T., and Rizer, A. (2020). *The "Radical" Notion of the Presumption of Innocence*. The Square One Project. https://squareonejustice.org/paper/the-radical-notion-of-the-presumption-of-innocence-by-arthur-rizer-and-tracey-meares-may-2020/

Meares, T.L. (2014). The law and social science of stop and frisk. *Annual Review of Law and Social Science, 10*(1), 335–352.

Mears, D.P., and Bhati, A.S. (2006). No community is an island: The effects of resource deprivation on urban violence in spatially and socially proximate communities. *Criminology, 44*, 509–548.

Meehan, A.J., and Ponder, M. (2002). How roadway composition matters in analyzing police data on racial profiling. *Police Quarterly, 5*(3), 306–333.

Mehranbod, C.A., Gobaud, A.N., Jacoby, S.F., Uzzi, M., Bushover, B.R., and Morrison, C.N. (2022). Historical redlining and the epidemiology of present-day firearm violence in the United States: A multi-city analysis. *Preventive Medicine*, 107207.

Melton, A.P. (2005). Indigenous justice systems and tribal society. *Justice as Healing: Indigenous Ways*, 108–120. Writings on Community Peacemaking and Restorative Justice from Native Law Centre. Living Justice Press. https://www.nakani.org/uploads/1/3/3/2/133290057/indigenous-justice.pdf

Meltzer, R. (2012). Understanding Business Improvement District formation: An analysis of neighborhoods and boundaries. *Journal of Urban Economics, 71*(1), 66–78.

Mendelberg, T. (2017). *The Race Card*. Princeton University Press. https://doi.org/10.1515/9781400889181

Mendez, L.M. (2003). Predictors of suspension and negative school outcomes: A longitudinal investigation. *New Directions for Youth Development*, *2003*(99), 17–33.

Mentel, Z. (2012). *Racial Reconciliation, Truth Telling, and Police Legitimacy*. Department of Justice, Office of Community Oriented Policing Services.

Meservey, F., and Skowyra, K.R. (2015). *Caring for Youth with Mental Health Needs in the Juvenile Justice System: Improving Knowledge and Skills*. National Center for Mental Health and Juvenile Justice and Mental Health and Juvenile Justice Collaborative for Change, 1–8.

Messner, S.F., and South, S.J. (1986). Economic deprivation, opportunity structure, and robbery victimization: Intra-and interracial patterns. *Social Forces, 64*(4), 975–991. https://www.jstor.org/stable/2578789

______. (1992). Interracial homicide: A macrostructural-opportunity perspective. *Sociological Forum, 7*(3), 517–536. Kluwer Academic Publishers-Plenum Publishers. https://link.springer.com/article/10.1007/BF01117559

Mian, A., and Sufi, A. (2015). *House of Debt: How They (and You) Caused the Great Recession, and How We Can Prevent It from Happening Again*. University of Chicago Press.

Mikos, R.A. (2020). The evolving federal response to state marijuana reforms. *Widener Law Review, 26*, 1.

Milam, A.J., Buggs, S.A., Furr-Holden, C.D.M., Leaf, P.J., Bradshaw, C.P., and Webster, D. (2016). Changes in attitudes toward guns and shootings following implementation of the Baltimore Safe Streets intervention. *Journal of Urban Health, 93*(4), 609–626.

Milam, A.J., Furr-Holden, C.D., Leaf, P., and Webster, D. (2018). Managing conflicts in urban communities: Youth attitudes regarding gun violence. *Journal of Interpersonal Violence, 33*(24), 3815–3828.

Millenky, M., Bloom, D., Muller-Ravett, S., and Broadus, J. (2011). *Staying on Course: Three-Year Results of the National Guard Youth Challenge Evaluation*. Manpower Demonstration Research Corporation.

Miller, L.L. (2008). *The Perils of Federalism: Race, Poverty, and the Politics of Crime Control*. Oxford University Press.

______. (2016). *The Myth of Mob Rule: Violent Crime and Democratic Politics*. Oxford University Press.

Miller, R.J. (2021). *Halfway Home: Race, Punishment, and the Afterlife of Mass Incarceration*. Hachette, UK.

Minor-Harper, S. (1986). *State and Federal Prisoners, 1925-85*. Bureau of Justice Statistics, NCJ 102494. https://bjs.ojp.gov/library/publications/state-and-federal-prisoners-1925-85

Minton, T.D., Beatty, L.G., and Zeng, Z. (2021). Correctional Populations in the United States, 2019 – Statistical Tables. U.S. Department of Justice, Bureau of Justice Statistics, NCJ 300655. https://bjs.ojp.gov/sites/g/files/xyckuh236/files/media/document/cpus19st.pdf

Mintz, E. (2021). First of its kind police legislation database shows reforms gaining traction. *Arnold Ventures*. https://www.arnoldventures.org/stories/first-of-its-kind-police-legislation-database-shows-reforms-gaining-traction

Mishler, M. (2016). *Boundaries of Freedom: Abolition, Punishment, and the Atlantic Origins of Mass Incarceration*. Dissertation, New York University.

Mitchell, O., Mora, D.O., Sticco, T.L., and Boggess, L.N. (2022). Are progressive chief prosecutors effective in reducing prison use and cumulative racial/ethnic disadvantage? Evidence from Florida. *Criminology & Public Policy, 21*(3), 535-565. https://doi.org/10.1111/1745-9133.12598

Mobasseri, S. (2019). Race, place, and crime: How violent crime events affect employment discrimination. *American Journal of Sociology, 125*(1), 63–104.

Modestino, A.S. (2019). How do summer youth employment programs improve criminal justice outcomes, and for whom? *Journal of Public Policy Analysis and Management, 38*(3), 600–628. https://doi.org/10.1002/pam.22138

Mohler, G., Bertozzi, A.L., Carter, J., Short, M.B., Sledge, D., Tita, G.E., Uchida, C.D., and Brantingham, P.J. (2020). Impact of social distancing during COVID-19 pandemic on crime in Los Angeles and Indianapolis. *Journal of Criminal Justice, 68*.

Molina, O., and Chapple, R. (2017). "A safe home away from home": A mutual-aid group for Latino and Latina adolescent survivors of parental intimate partner violence. *Groupwork, 27*(1).

Monk Jr., E.P. (2022). Inequality without groups: Contemporary theories of categories, intersectional typicality, and the disaggregation of difference. *Sociological Theory, 40*(1), 3–27.

Mooney, A.C., Giannella, E., Glymour, M.M., Neilands, T.B., Morris, M.D., Tulsky, J., and Sudhinaraset, M. (2018). Racial/ethnic disparities in arrests for drug possession after California Proposition 47, 2011–2016. *American Journal of Public Health, 108*(8), 987–993.

Morenoff, J.D., and Harding, D.J. (2011). *Final Technical Report: Neighborhoods, Recidivism, and Employment among Returning Prisoners.* National Institute of Justice, Office of Justice Programs, U.S. Department of Justice. https://www.ojp.gov/pdffiles1/nij/grants/236436.pdf

Morenoff, J.D., Sampson, R.J., and Raudenbush, S.W. (2001). Neighborhood inequality, collective efficacy, and the spatial dynamics of urban violence. *Criminology, 39*(3), 517–558.

Morgan, R., and Truman, J. (2020). *Criminal Victimization, 2019.* Bureau of Justice Statistics. https://bjs.ojp.gov/content/pub/pdf/cv19.pdf

Morris, J.E. (2015). *Troubling the Waters: Fulfilling the Promise of Quality Public Schooling for Black Children.* Teachers College Press.

Morris, N. (1974). The future of imprisonment: Towards a punitive philosophy. *Michigan Law Review, 72*(6), 1161–1180.

Morrow, W.J., Berthelot, E.R., and Vickovic, S.G. (2018). Police use of force: An examination of the minority threat perspective. *Criminal Justice Studies, 31*(4), 368–387.

Mowen, T., and Brent, J. (2016). School discipline as a turning point: The cumulative effect of suspension on arrest. *Journal of Research in Crime and Delinquency, 53*(5), 628–653.

Moyle, P., and Tauri, J.M. (2016). Māori, family group conferencing and the mystifications of restorative justice. *Victims and Offenders, 11*(1), 87–106.

Mueller-Smith, M. (2015). *The Criminal and Labor Market Impacts of Incarceration.* https://www.irp.wisc.edu/newsevents/workshops/2015/participants/papers/10-Mueller-Smith-IRP-draft.pdf

Muhammad, K.G. (2010). *The Condemnation of Blackness: Race, Crime, and the Making of Modern Urban America.* Harvard University Press. https://doi.org/10.2307/j.ctvjsf4fx

______. (2011). Where did all the White criminals go? Reconfiguring race and crime on the road to mass incarceration. *Souls, 13,* 72–90. https://doi.org/10.1080/10999949.2011.551478

______. (n.d.). A Review of Recent Historical Scholarship on Racial Criminalization and Punitive Policy in the United States. Harvard Kennedy School. https://squareonejustice.org/wp-content/uploads/2020/01/Muhammad-RT-Paper.pdf

Muller, C. (2012). Northward migration and the rise of racial disparity in American incarceration, 1880–1950. *American Journal of Sociology, 118*(2), 281–326. https://doi.org/10.1086/666384

______. (2021). Exclusion and exploitation: The incarceration of Black Americans from slavery to the present. *Science, 374*(6565), 282–286. https://www.science.org/doi/10.1126/science.abj7781

Muller, C., and Roehrkasse, A.F. (2020). *Racial and Class Inequality in U.S. Incarceration in the Early Twenty-First Century*. Institute for Research on Labor and Employment, Working Paper No. 109-20. http://irle.berkeley.edu/files/2021/04/Racial-and-Class-Inequality-in-US-Incarceration.pdf

Muller, C., Sampson, R.J, and Winter, A. (2018). Environmental inequality: The social causes and consequences of lead exposure. *Annual Review of Sociology, 44*, 263–282.

Muller, E.R. (2021). Trends on security, safety and criminal justice in the Netherlands. In *International Security Management*, 55–64. Springer.

Mumford, K. (2008). *Newark: A History of Race, Rights, and Riots in America, 10*. New York University Press.

Mumola, C.J. (2005). *Suicide and Homicide in State Prisons and Local Jails*. NCJ 210036. Bureau of Justice Statistics Special Report, Office of Justice Programs, U.S. Department of Justice.

Murakawa, N. (2012). The origins of the carceral crisis: Racial order as "law and order" in postwar American politics. *Race and American Political Development*, 245–266. Routledge.

Murphy, S., Estes, A., and Ellement, J.R. (2022). Founder of Violence in Boston and husband charged with fraud in federal indictment. *Boston Globe*, March 15. https://www.bostonglobe.com/2022/03/15/metro/founder-violence-boston-husband-charged-federal-indictment-with-fraud/

Murray, P., and Eastwood, M.O. (1965). Jane Crow and the law: Sex discrimination and Title VII. *George Washington Law Review, 34*, 232–256.

Na, C., and Gottfredson, D.C. (2013). Police officers in schools: Effects on school crime and the processing of offending behaviors. *Justice Quarterly, 30*(4), 619–650. https://doi.org/10.1080/07418825.2011.615754

Nagel, W.G. (1977). On behalf of a moratorium on prison construction. *Crime and Delinquency, 23*(2), 154–171. https://doi.org/10.1177/001112877702300206

Nagin, D.S. (2013). Deterrence in the twenty-first century. *Crime and Justice, 42*(1), 199–263.

Nagin, D.S., and Sampson, R.J. (2019). The real gold standard: Measuring counterfactual worlds that matter most to social science and policy. *Annual Review of Criminology, 2*.

Naidoo, K., and Karels, M. (2012). Hate crimes against black lesbian South Africans: Where race, sexual orientation and gender collide (Part I). *Obiter, 33*(2), 236–259.

Najdowski, C.J. (2011). Stereotype threat in criminal interrogations: Why innocent Black suspects are at risk for confessing falsely. *Psychology, Public Policy, and Law, 17*(4), 562–591. https://doi.org/10.1037/a0023741

Najdowski, C.J., Bottoms, B.L., and Goff, P.A. (2015). Stereotype threat and racial differences in citizens' experiences of police encounters. *Law and Human Behavior, 39*(5), 463–477.

Nanda, J. (2019). The construction and criminalization of disability in school incarceration. *Columbia Journal of Race and Law, 9*.

Nash, G.B. (1988). *Forging Freedom: The Formation of Philadelphia's Black Community, 1720-1840*. Harvard University Press.

National Academies of Sciences, Engineering, and Medicine. (2017). *Communities in Action: Pathways to Health Equity*. The National Academies Press. https://doi.org/10.17226/24624

______. (2018). *Proactive Policing: Effects on Crime and Communities*. The National Academies Press. https://doi.org/10.17226/24928

______. (2019a). *The Promise of Adolescence: Realizing Opportunity for All Youth*. The National Academies Press. https://doi.org/10.17226/25388

______. (2019b). *Health Systems Interventions to Prevent Firearm Injuries and Death: Proceedings of a Workshop*. The National Academies Press. https://doi.org10.17226/25354

______. (2020). *Decarcerating Correctional Facilities during COVID-19: Advancing Health, Equity, and Safety*. The National Academies Press. https://doi.org/10.17226/25945

______. (2021a). *Addressing the Drivers of Criminal Justice Involvement to Advance Racial Equity: Proceedings of a Workshop—in Brief.* The National Academies Press. https://doi.org/10.17226/26151

______. (2021b). *Community Safety and Policing: Proceedings of a Workshop—in Brief.* The National Academies Press. https://doi.org/10.17226/26099

______. (2021c). *Reducing Racial Inequalities in Criminal Justice: Data, Courts, and Systems of Supervision: Proceedings of a Workshop—in Brief.* The National Academies Press. https://doi.org/10.17226/26192

______. (2022a). *The Limits of Recidivism: Measuring Success After Prison.* The National Academies Press. https://doi.org/10.17226/26459

______. (2022b). *Building Trust in Public Health Emergency Preparedness and Response (PHEPR) Science: Proceedings of a Workshop—in Brief.* The National Academies Press. https://doi.org/10.17226/26658

______. (2022c). *Policies and Practices to Minimize Police Use of Force Internationally.* The National Academies Press. https://doi.org/10.17226/26582

______. (2022d). *Engaging Socially Vulnerable Communities and Communicating About Climate Change—Related Risks and Hazards.* The National Academies Press. https://doi.org/10.17226/26734

National Advisory Commission on Civil Disorders. (2016). *The Kerner Report: National Advisory Commission on Civil Disorders: With an Introduction by Julian E Zelizer.* Princeton University Press.

National Congress of American Indians. (2021). Research Policy Update 2020 Census Results: Regional Tribal Land Data Summary. National Congress of American Indians. https://www.ncai.org/policy-research-center/research-data/prc-publications/2020_Census_Tribal_Lands_Region_Summary_9_14_2021_FINAL.pdf

National Criminal Justice Association (NCJA). (2021). Cornerstone for Justice: How States Use Byrne JAG Funding to Protect Public Safety, Prevent Crime and Reduce Recidivism. https://www.ncja.org/_files/ugd/cda224_15254f0636354cabba1c20a44054b148.pdf

National Reentry Resource Center. (2018). *Fact Sheet on Second Chance Act.* https://csgjusticecenter.org/wp-content/uploads/2020/02/July-2018_SCA_factsheet.pdf

National Research Council. (NRC). (1983). *Research on Sentencing: The Search for Reform. Panel on Sentencing Research.* Committee on Research on Law Enforcement and the Administration of Justice, Commission on Behavioral and Social Sciences and Education. National Academy Press.

______. (2004a). *Fairness and Effectiveness in Policing: The Evidence.* The National Academies Press. https://doi.org/10.17226/10419

______. (2004b). *Measuring Racial Discrimination.* The National Academies Press. https://doi.org/10.17226/10887

______. (2005). *Firearms and Violence: A Critical Review.* The National Academies Press.

______. (2009). *Ensuring the Quality, Credibility, and Relevance of U.S. Justice Statistics.* The National Academies Press. https://doi.org/10.17226/12671

______. (2013). *Reforming Juvenile Justice: A Developmental Approach.* The National Academies Press. https://doi.org/10.17226/14685

______. (2014). *The Growth of Incarceration in the United States: Exploring Causes and Consequences.* The National Academies Press. https://doi.org/10.17226/18613

Neal, D.A. (2018). *Information, Incentives, and Education Policy.* Harvard University Press.

Neal, D.A., and Rick, A. (2016). *The Prison Boom and the Lack of Black Progress after Smith and Welch.* Working paper 20283. National Bureau of Economic Research.

Needleman, H.L., McFarland, C., Ness, R.B., Fienberg, S.E., and Tobin, M.J. (2002). Bone lead levels in adjudicated delinquents: A case control study. *Neurotoxicology and Teratology, 24*(6), 711–717.

Needleman, H.L., Riess, J.A., Tobin, M.J., Biesecker, G.E., and Greenhouse, J.B. (1996). Bone lead levels and delinquent behavior. *JAMA, 275*(5), 363–369.

Neil, R. (2021). *The Ecological Sources of Racial Inequities in Proactive Policing*. Doctoral dissertation, Harvard University. https://nrs.harvard.edu/URN-3:HUL.INSTREPOS:37370140

Nellis, A. (2021). *No End in Sight: America's Enduring Reliance on Life Imprisonment*. The Sentencing Project. https://www.sentencingproject.org/app/uploads/2022/08/No-End-in-Sight-Americas-Enduring-Reliance-on-Life-Imprisonment.pdf

Nesbitt, L., Meitner, M.J., Girling, C., Sheppard, S.R., and Lu, Y. (2019). Who has access to urban vegetation? A spatial analysis of distributional green equity in 10 US cities. *Landscape and Urban Planning, 181*, 51–79.

Newton, N.J., Anderson, R., Goldberg, C., LaVelle, J., Royster, J.V., and Singer, J.W. (2012). *Cohen's Handbook of Federal Indian Law, 2012 Edition*. LexisNexis.

Nielsen, M.O., and Zion, J.W. (eds.). (2005). *Navajo Nation Peacemaking: Living Traditional Justice*. University of Arizona Press.

Nordberg, C., and Wrede, S. (2015). Street-level engagements: Migrated families encountering the local welfare state [Introduction]. *Nordic Journal of Migration Research, 5*(2), 54–57.

Norris, S., Pecenco, M., and Weaver, J. (2021). The effects of parental and sibling incarceration: Evidence from Ohio. *American Economic Review, 111*(9), 2926–2963.

Norwood, K.J.E. (2014). *Color Matters: Skin Tone Bias and the Myth of a Post-racial America*. Routledge/Taylor and Francis Group.

Novak, K.J., and Chamlin, M.B. (2012). Racial threat, suspicion, and police behavior: The impact of race and place in traffic enforcement. *Crime and Delinquency, 58*(2), 275–300.

O'Brien, R.M. (1987). The interracial nature of violent crimes: A reexamination. *American Journal of Sociology, 92*(4), 817–835. https://www.journals.uchicago.edu/doi/10.1086/228584

O'Connor, A. (2001). *Poverty Knowledge: Social Science, Social Policy, and the Poor in Twentieth-Century U.S. History*. Princeton University Press.

Office of Community Oriented Policing Services. (2014). *The COPS Office: 20 Years of Community Policing*. U.S. Department of Justice. https://cops.usdoj.gov/RIC/Publications/cops-p301-pub.pdf

______. (2015). *The President's Task Force on 21st Century Policing Implementation Guide: Moving from Recommendations to Action*. Office of Community Oriented Policing Services. https://cops.usdoj.gov/RIC/Publications/cops-p341-pub.pdf

Office of Hawaiian Affairs. (2010). *The Disparate Treatment of Native Hawaiians in the Criminal Justice System*. https://www.oha.org/wp-content/uploads/2014/12/ir_final_web_rev.pdf

Office of Justice Programs. (2021a). Homeboy Industries. National Gang Centers. https://nationalgangcenter.ojp.gov/spt/Programs/86

______. (2021b). *Significant Events in the Budget and Appropriations Process*. U.S. Department of Justice. https://www.ojp.gov/sites/g/files/xyckuh241/files/media/document/budget_process.pdf

Office of Juvenile Justice and Delinquency Prevention (OJJDP). (1979). *Rural Programs*. U.S. Department of Justice, Law Enforcement Assistance Administration. https://files.eric.ed.gov/fulltext/ED180733.pdf

______. (2017). *Tribal Juvenile Healing to Wellness Handbook: Practical Planning and Supportive Tools*. Indian Country Child Trauma Center, OJJDP Tribal Youth Training and Technical Assistance Center. https://ojjdp.ojp.gov/library/publications/tribal-juvenile-healing-wellness-handbook-practical-planning-and-supportive

______. (2019). *OJJDP Fact Sheet: Key Amendments to the Juvenile Justice and Delinquency Prevention Act Made by the Juvenile Justice Reform Act of 2018*. Office of Justice Programs. https://ojjdp.ojp.gov/sites/g/files/xyckuh176/files/pubs/252961.pdf

______. (2022). Racial and Ethnic Disparity in Juvenile Justice Processing: Literature Review: A Product of the Model Programs Guide. https://ojjdp.ojp.gov/model-programs-guide/literature-reviews/racial-and-ethnic-disparity#2

Office of the Assistant Secretary for Planning and Evaluation. (2021). *Freeing Children for Adoption within the Adoption and Safe Families Act Timeline: Part 1—The Numbers.* U.S. Department of Health and Human Services, Office of Human Services Policy. https://aspe.hhs.gov/sites/default/files/private/pdf/265036/freeing-children-for-adoption-asfa-pt-1.pdf

Office on Violence Against Women. (2018). *2018 Biennial Report to Congress on the Effectiveness of the Grant Programs Under the Violence Against Women Act.* U.S. Department of Justice, Office of Violence Against Women. https://www.justice.gov/ovw/page/file/1292636/download

O'Flaherty, B., and Sethi, R. (2019). *Shadows of Doubt: Stereotypes, Crime, and the Pursuit of Justice.* Harvard University Press.

Okonofua, J.A., and Eberhardt, J.L. (2015). Two strikes: Race and the disciplining of young students. *Psychological Science, 26*(5), 617–624.

Olson, D.E., and Lurigio, A.J. (2000). Predicting probation outcomes: Factors associated with probation rearrest, revocations, and technical violations during supervision. *Justice Research and Policy, 2*(1), 73–86.

Olson, J.C. (2016). Race and punishment in American prisons. *Journal of Public Administration Research and Theory, 26*(4), 758–768.

Omi, M., and Winant, H. (2014). *Racial Formation in the United States.* Routledge.

Opinion Research Corporation. (1975). Part 1. In *National Statistical Survey on Runaway Youth.* Prepared under contract for the U.S. Department of Health, Education, and Welfare. https://www.ojp.gov/pdffiles1/Digitization/55400NCJRS.pdf

Osgood, H.L., Keep, A.B., and Nelson, C.A. (1905). *Minutes of the Common Council of the City of New York, 1675-1776, 8.* Dodd, Mead and Company.

Oshinsky, D.M. (1997). *Worse than Slavery.* Simon and Schuster.

Oudekerk, B., and Kaeble, D. (2021). *Probation and Parole in the United States, 2019.* U.S. Department of Justice, Bureau of Justice Statistics. https://bjs.ojp.gov/sites/g/files/xyckuh236/files/media/document/ppus19.pdf

Ousey, G.C., and Kubrin, C.E. (2018). Immigration and crime: Assessing a contentious issue. *Annual Review of Criminology, 1,* 63–84.

Ouss, A. (2020). Misaligned incentives and the scale of incarceration in the United States. *Journal of Public Economics, 191.*

Ouss, A., and Stevenson, M.T. (2020). Bail, jail, and pretrial misconduct: The influence of prosecutors. *SSRN,* 3335138.

Owens, E., Weisburd, D., Amendola, K.L., and Alpert, G.P. (2018). Can you build a better cop? Experimental evidence on supervision, training, and policing in the community. *Criminology & Public Policy, 17*(1), 41–87.

Owens, E.G. (2017). Testing the school-to-prison pipeline. *Journal of Policy Analysis and Management, 36*(1), 11–37.

Pager, D. (2003). The mark of a criminal record. *American Journal of Sociology, 108,* 937–975.

______. (2007). The use of field experiments for studies of employment discrimination: Contributions, critiques, and directions for the future. *The ANNALS of the American Academy of Political and Social Science, 609*(1), 104–133.

Pager, D., Bonikowski, B., and Western, B. (2009). Discrimination in a low-wage labor market: A field experiment. *American Sociological Review, 74*(5), 777–799.

Pager, D., Goldstein, R., Ho, H., and Western, B. (2022). Criminalizing poverty: The consequences of court fees in a randomized experiment. *American Sociological Review.* https://justicelab.columbia.edu/sites/default/files/content/Criminalizing%20Poverty.pdf

Pager, D., and Shepherd, H. (2008). The sociology of discrimination: Racial discrimination in employment, housing, credit, and consumer markets. *Annual Review of Sociology, 34*, 181–209.

Painter-Davis, N., and Ulmer, J.T. (2020). Discretion and disparity under sentencing guidelines revisited: The interrelationship between structured sentencing alternatives and guideline decision-making. *Journal of Research in Crime and Delinquency, 57*(3), 263–293.

Paoline III, E.A., Gau, J.M., and Terrill, W. (2018). Race and the police use of force encounter in the United States. *The British Journal of Criminology, 58*(1), 54–74.

Paradies, Y., Truong, M., and Priest, N. (2014). A systematic review of the extent and measurement of healthcare provider racism. *Journal of General Internal Medicine, 29*(2), 364–387.

Parker, K.F., MacDonald, J.M., Alpert, G.P., Smith, M.R., and Piquero, A.R. (2004). A contextual study of racial profiling: Assessing the theoretical rationale for the study of racial profiling at the local level. *American Behavioral Scientist, 47*(7), 943–962.

Paternoster, R. (1984). Prosecutorial discretion in requesting the death penalty: A case of victim-based racial discrimination. *Law and Society Review, 18*, 437–478.

______. (2010). How much do we really know about criminal deterrence. *Journal of Criminal Law and Criminology, 100*(3), 765–823.

Paternoster, R., Brame, R., Bacon, S., Ditchfield, A., Beckman, K., and Frederique, N. (2003). *An Empirical Analysis of Maryland's Death Sentencing System with Respect to the Influence of Race and Legal Jurisdiction.* University of Maryland, College Park.

Patterson, E.J. (2010). Incarcerating death: Mortality in US state correctional facilities, 1985–1998. *Demography, 47*(3), 587–607.

Pattillo, M., and Kirk, G. (2021). Layaway freedom: Coercive financialization in the criminal legal system. *American Journal of Sociology, 126*(4), 889–930.

Pattillo, M.E. (1998). Sweet mothers and gangbangers: Managing crime in a black middle-class neighborhood. *Social Forces, 76*, 747–774.

Payne, B.K. (2001). Prejudice and perception: The role of automatic and controlled processes in misperceiving a weapon. *Journal of Personality and Social Psychology, 81*(2), 181–192.

Payne, B.K., Lambert, A.J., and Jacoby, L.L. (2002). Best laid plans: Effects of goals on accessibility bias and cognitive control in race-based misperceptions of weapons. *Journal of Experimental Social Psychology, 38*(4), 384–396.

Peacemaking Program of the Judicial Branch of the Navajo Nation. (2012). *Plan of Operations.* http://www.courts.navajo-nsn.gov/Peacemaking/Plan/PPPO2013-2-25.pdf

Peffley, M., and Hurwitz, J. (2007). Persuasion and resistance: Race and the death penalty in America. *American Journal of Political Science, 51*(4), 996–1012.

______. (2010). *Justice in America: The Separate Realities of Blacks and Whites.* New York, NY: Cambridge University Press

Perkins, K.L., and Sampson, R.J. (2015). Compounded deprivation in the transition to adulthood: The intersection of racial and economic inequality among Chicagoans, 1995-2013. *RSF: The Russell Sage Foundation Journal of the Social Sciences, 1*(1), 35–54. https://scholar.harvard.edu/kperkins/publications/compounded-deprivation-transition-adulthood-intersection-racial-and-economic

Perry, I. (2011). *More Beautiful and More Terrible: The Embrace and Transcendence of Racial Inequality in the United States.* New York University Press.

Persico, N. (2009). Racial profiling? Detecting bias using statistical evidence. *Annual Review of Economics, 1*(1), 229–254. https://doi.org/10.1146/annurev.economics.050708.143307

Petersen, N. (2017). Neighbourhood context and unsolved murders: The social ecology of homicide investigations. *Policing and Society, 27*(4), 372–392.

Peterson, B., Cramer, L., and Fontaine, J. (2019). Policies and practices for children of incarcerated parents: Summarizing what we know and do not know. *Handbook on Children with Incarcerated Parents,* 331–343. Springer.

Peterson, B., Fontaine, J., Cramer, L., Reisman, A., Cuthrell, H., Goff, M., McCoy, E., and Reginal, T. (2019). *Model Practices for Parents in Prisons and Jails: Reducing Barriers to Family Connections.* Bureau of Justice Assistance and the National Institute of Corrections. https://www.urban.org/research/publication/model-practices-parents-prisons-and-jails/view/full_report

Peterson, R.D., and Krivo, L.J. (2009). Segregated spatial locations, race-ethnic composition, and neighborhood violent crime. *The ANNALS of the American Academy of Political and Social Science, 623*(1), 93–107.

______. (2010). *Divergent Social Worlds: Neighborhood Crime and the Racial-Spatial Divide.* Russell Sage Foundation.

Petrocelli, M., Piquero, A.R., and Smith, M.R. (2003). Conflict theory and racial profiling: An empirical analysis of police traffic stop data. *Journal of Criminal Justice, 31*(1), 1–11.

Pettit, B. (2012). *Invisible Men: Mass Incarceration and the Myth of Black Progress.* Russell Sage Foundation.

Pettit, B., and Western, B. (2004). Mass imprisonment and the life course: Race and class inequality in US incarceration. *American Sociological Review, 69*(2), 151–169.

Pfaff, J. (2017). *Locked In: The True Causes of Mass Incarceration—and How to Achieve Real Reform.* Basic Books.

Pfeifer, M.J. (2021). Daniel F. Littlefield Jr.'s Seminole burning and the historiography of the lynching of Native Americans. *The Journal of the Gilded Age and Progressive Era, 20*(1), 81–86.

Phelps, M.S. (2011). Rehabilitation in the punitive era: The gap between rhetoric and reality in US prison programs. *Law and Society Review, 45*(1), 33–68.

Phillips, S., and Marceau, J. (2020). Whom the state kills. *Harvard Civil Rights-Civil Liberties Law Review, 55,* 585.

Picard-Fritsche, S., and Cerniglia, L. (2013). *Testing a Public Health Approach to Firearm Violence: An Evaluation of Crown Heights Save Our Streets, A Replication of the Cure Violence Model.* Center for Court Innovation. https://www.courtinnovation.org/sites/default/files/documents/SOS_Evaluation.pdf

Piehl, A.M., and Bushway, S.D. (2007). Measuring and explaining charge bargaining. *Journal of Quantitative Criminology, 23*(2), 105–125.

Pierson, E., Simoiu, C., Overgoor, J., Corbett-Davies, S., Jenson, D., Shoemaker, A., Ramachandran, V., Barghouty, P., Phillips, C., Shroff, R., and Goel, S. (2020). A large-scale analysis of racial disparities in police stops across the United States. *Nature Human Behaviour, 4*(7), 736–745.

Pinderhughes, H., Davis, R., and Williams, M. (2015). *Adverse Community Experiences and Resilience: A Framework for Addressing and Preventing Community Trauma.* Prevention Institute. https://www.preventioninstitute.org/sites/default/files/publications/Adverse%20Community%20Experiences%20and%20Resilience.pdf

Piquero, A.R. (2008). Disproportionate minority contact. *The Future of Children, 59–79.*

Piquero, A.R., Jennings, W.G., Jemison, E., Kaukinen, C., and Knaul, F.M. (2021). Domestic violence during the COVID-19 pandemic—Evidence from a systematic review and meta-analysis. *Journal of Criminal Justice, 74,* 101806. https://doi.org/10.1016/j.jcrimjus.2021.101806

Pittman, L. (2014). Doing what's right for the baby: Parental responses and custodial grandmothers' institutional decision making. *Women, Gender, and Families of Color, 2*(1), 32–56.

______. (2015). How well does the "Safety Net" work for family safety nets? Economic survival strategies among grandmother caregivers in severe deprivation. *RSF: The Russell Sage Foundation Journal of the Social Sciences, 1*(1), 78–97.

Plunk, A.D., Peglow, S.L., Harrell, P.T., and Grucza, R.A. (2019). Youth and adult arrests for cannabis possession after decriminalization and legalization of cannabis. *JAMA Pediatrics, 173*(8), 763–769.

Podkopacz, M.R., Braun-Lewis, J., Cardinal, M., Swayze, D.H., Johnson, M.A., and Salmonson, M. (2018). *Hennepin County 2015 Adult Pretrial Scale Revalidation.* Fourth Judicial District of Minnesota.

Podkopacz, M.R., Eckberg, D., and Kubits, G. (2006). *Fourth Judicial District Pretrial Evaluation: Scale Validation Study.* Minnesota Judicial Branch, Fourth District of Minnesota Research Division. https://www.mncourts.gov/mncourtsgov/media/assets/documents/4/reports/PreTrial_Scale_Validation_(2006).pdf

Popkin, S.J., Gwiasda, V.E., Olson, L.M., Rosenbaum, D.P., Buron, L., and Blank, R.M. (2000). *The Hidden War: Crime and the tragedy of public housing in Chicago.* Rutgers University Press.

Porter, N.D. (2021). Successes in criminal legal reforms, 2021. *The Sentencing Project.* https://www.sentencingproject.org/publications/successes-in-criminal-legal-reforms-2021/

Poteat, V.P., Scheer, J.R., and Chong, E.S. (2016). Sexual orientation-based disparities in school and juvenile justice discipline: A multiple group comparison of contributing factors. *Journal of Educational Psychology, 108*(2), 229–241.

Powell, J.A. (2008). Structural racism: Building upon the insights of John Calmore. *North Carolina Law Review, 86.*

Pratt, T.C., and Cullen, F.T. (2005). Assessing macro-level predictors and theories of crime: A meta-analysis. *Crime and Justice, 32,* 373–450.

Premkumar, D. (2019). Public scrutiny and police effort: Evidence from arrests and crime after high-profile police killings. *SSRN.* https://doi.org/10.2139/ssrn.3715223

Prendergast, C. (2021). *"Drive and Wave": The Response to LAPD Police Reforms after Rampart.* University of Chicago, Becker Friedman Institute for Economics, working paper.

President's Commission on Law Enforcement and Administration of Justice. (1967). *The Challenge of Crime in a Free Society: A Report by the President's Commission on Law Enforcement and Administration of Justice.* https://www.ojp.gov/sites/g/files/xyckuh241/files/archives/ncjrs/42.pdf

President's Task Force on 21st Century Policing. (2015). *Final Report of the President's Task Force on 21st Century Policing.* Office of Community Oriented Policing Services. https://cops.usdoj.gov/ric/Publications/cops-p311-pub.pdf

Prevention Institute. (2011). Fact sheet: Links between violence and health equity. https://www.preventioninstitute.org/unity/publications/fact-sheet-links-between-violence-and-health-equity

Proctor, J.L. (1999). The 'New Parole': An analysis of parole board decision making as a function of eligibility. *Journal of Crime and Justice, 22*(2), 193–217. https://doi.org/10.1080/0735648X.1999.9721100

Provine, D.M. (2011). Race and inequality in the war on drugs. *Annual Review of Law and Social Science, 7,* 41–60.

Prowse, G., and Goff, P.A. (2022). Why seeing the big picture in the study of public safety is necessary for combating racism within it. *The Oxford Handbook of Psychology and Law.* Oxford University Press.

Pryor, M., Buchanan, K.S., and Goff, P.A. (2020). Risky situations: Sources of racial disparity in police behavior. *Annual Review of Law and Social Science, 16*, 343–360.

Pullen-Blasnik, H., Simes, J.T., and Western, B. (2021). The population prevalence of solitary confinement. *Science Advances, 7*(48).

Queally, J. (2021). L.A. County D.A. to dismiss 60,000 past marijuana convictions. *Los Angeles Times,* September 27. https://www.latimes.com/california/story/2021-09-27/la-los-angeles-da-gascon-dismisses-nearly-60000-past-marijuana-convictions

Racial and Identity Profiling Advisory (RIPA) Board. (2020). *Annual Report.* https://oag.ca.gov/sites/all/files/agweb/pdfs/ripa/ripa-board-report-2020.pdf

Ramey, D.M. (2013). Immigrant revitalization and neighborhood violent crime in established and new destination cities. *Social Forces, 92*(2), 597–629.

Ramey, D.M., and Shrider, E.A. (2014). New parochialism, sources of community investment, and the control of street crime. *Criminology and Public Policy, 13*(2), 193–216.

RAND Corporation. (2022). *Focused Deterrence in Depth.* https://www.rand.org/pubs/tools/TL261/better-policing-toolkit/all-strategies/focused-deterrence/in-depth.html#:~:text=With%20focused%20deterrence%2C%20the%20police,deterrents%20for%20engaging%20in%20violence

Raphael, J., Rennison, C.M., and Jones, N. (2019). Twenty-five years of research and advocacy on violence against women: What have we accomplished, and where do we go from here? A conversation. *Violence Against Women, 25*(16), 2024–2046.

Raphael, S. (2021). The intended and unintended consequences of Ban the Box. *Annual Review of Criminology, 4,* 191–207.

Raphael, S., and Ludwig, J. (2003). Prison sentence enhancements: The case of Project Exile. *Evaluating Gun Policy: Effects on Crime and Violence.* Brookings Institution Press.

Raphael, S., and Rozo, S.V. (2019). Racial disparities in the acquisition of juvenile arrest records. *Journal of Labor Economics, 37*(S1), S125–S159.

Raphael, S., and Stoll, M. (2013). *Why Are So Many Americans in Prison?* Russell Sage Foundation.

Raphael, S., and Weiman, D.F. (2007). The Impact of Local Labor Market Conditions on the Likelihood that Parolees are Returned to Custody. University of California, Berkeley, Barnard College, Columbia University. https://citeseerx.ist.psu.edu/viewdoc/download?doi=10.1.1.603.5212&rep=rep1&type=pdf

Rastogi, A. (2021). Race and income in US suburbs: Are diverse suburbs disadvantaged? *Socius,* 7. https://doi.org/10.1177/23780231211033722

Rattan, A., Good, C., and Dweck, C. (2012). "It's ok — Not everyone can be good at math": Instructors with an entity theory comfort (and demotivate) students. *Journal of Experimental Social Psychology, 48*(3), 731-737. DOI: 10.1016/j.jesp.2011.12.012

Raudenbush, S.W., and Sampson, R.J. (1999). "Ecometrics": Toward a science of assessing ecological settings, with application to the systematic social observation of neighborhoods. *Sociological Methodology, 29,* 1–41.

Ray, V. (2019). A theory of racialized organizations. *American Sociological Review, 84*(1), 26–53.

Rehavi, M.M., and Starr, S.B. (2014). Racial disparity in federal criminal sentences. *Journal of Political Economy, 122*(6), 1320–1354. https://doi.org/10.1086/677255

Reiter, K., Ventura, J., Lovell, D., Augustine, D., Barragan, M., Blair, T., Chesnut, K., Dashtgard, P., Gonzalez, G., Pifer, N., and Strong, J. (2020). Psychological distress in solitary confinement: Symptoms, severity, and prevalence in the United States, 2017–2018. *American Journal of Public Health, 110*(S1), S56–S62.

Reiter, M.D. (2015). *Substance abuse and the family.* New York, NY: Routledge.

Reyes, J.W. (2015). Lead exposure and behavior: Effects on antisocial and risky behavior among children and adolescents. *Economic Inquiry, 53*(3), 1580–1605.

Richeson, J.A. (2018). The psychology of racism: An introduction to the special issue. *Current Directions in Psychological Science, 27*(3), 148–149.

Richeson, J.A., and Shelton, J.N. (2007). Negotiating interracial interactions. *Current Directions in Psychological Science, 16,* 316–320.

______. (2012). Stereotype threat in interracial interactions. *Stereotype Threat: Theory, Process, and Application*, 231–245. Oxford University Press.

Richeson, J.A., and Sommers, S.R. (2016). Toward a social psychology of race and race relations for the twenty-first century. *Annual Review of Psychology, 67,* 439–463.

Richie, B.E. (2012). *Arrested Justice*. New York University Press.

Ricks, A., and Esthappan, S. (2018). States are looking beyond the juvenile justice system to address school truancy. *Urban Wire: Crime and Justice*. https://www.urban.org/urban-wire/states-are-looking-beyond-juvenile-justice-system-address-school-truancy

Ridgeway, G. (2007). *Analysis of Racial Disparities in the New York Police Department's Stop, Question, and Frisk Practices*. NCJ 222604. RAND. https://www.rand.org/content/dam/rand/pubs/technical_reports/2007/RAND_TR534.pdf

Ridgeway, G., and MacDonald, J.M. (2009). Doubly robust internal benchmarking and false discovery rates for detecting racial bias in police stops. *Journal of the American Statistical Association, 104*(486), 661–668.

Ridgeway, G., Moyer, R.A., and Bushway, S.D. (2020). Sentencing scorecards: Reducing racial disparities in prison sentences at their source. *Criminology and Public Policy, 19,* 1113–1138.

Riggs, P. (2002). *Tribal Healing to Wellness Court: Program Development Guide* (draft). Tribal Law and Policy Institute. https://www.tribal-institute.org/download/Draft_Program_Development_Guide.pdf

Riley, A.R. (2016). Crime and governance in Indian Country. *UCLA Law Review, 63,* 1564–1637.

Ritchie, A.J. (2017). *Invisible No More: Police Violence against Black Women and Women of Color*. Beacon Press.

Roberts, A., and Lyons, C.J. (2011). Hispanic victims and homicide clearance by arrest. *Homicide Studies, 15*(1), 48–73.

Robertson, C., Baughman, S.B., and Wright, M.S. (2019). Race and class: A randomized experiment with prosecutors. *Journal of Empirical Legal Studies, 16*(4), 807–847.

Roithmayr, D. (2014). *Reproducing Racism: How Everyday Choices Lock in White Advantage*. New York University Press.

Rojas, R. (2020). One high school, five students fatally shot. *The New York Times,* April 22. https://www.nytimes.com/2021/04/23/us/knoxville-anthony-thompson.html

Rojek, J., Rosenfeld, R., and Decker, S. (2012). Policing race: The racial stratification of searches in police traffic stops. *Criminology, 50*(4), 993–1024.

Rolnick, A.C. (2011). The promise of Mancari: Indian political rights as racial remedy. *New York University Law Review, 86*, 958–1045.

______. (2016a). Assimilation, removal, discipline, and confinement: Native girls and government intervention. *Columbia Journal of Race and Law, 11*(3), 811–860.

______. (2016b). Locked up: Fear, racism, prison economics, and the incarceration of Native youth. *Scholarly Works, 55–92.* https://scholars.law.unlv.edu/facpub/991

______. (2016c). Tribal criminal jurisdiction beyond citizenship and blood. *American Indian Law Review, 39*(2), 337–449. https://digitalcommons.law.ou.edu/ailr/vol39/iss2/1

______. (2016d). Recentering tribal criminal jurisdiction. *UCLA Law Review, 63,* 1638–1690. https://scholars.law.unlv.edu/facpub/993?utm_source=scholars.law.unlv.edu%2Ffacpub%2F993&utm_medium=PDF&utm_campaign=PDFCoverPages

______. (2021). Assimilation, Removal, Discipline, and Confinement: Native Girls and Government Intervention. *Columbia Journal of Race and Law, 11*(3), 811-860.

Rose, D.R., and Clear, T.R. (1998). Incarceration, social capital and crime: Examining the unintended consequences of incarceration. *Criminology, 36*(3), 441–479.

Rose, E., Schellenberg, J., and Shem-Tov, Y. (2021). *The Effects of Teacher Quality on Adult Criminal Justice Contact*. Working Paper. https://www.lowe-institute.org/wp-content/uploads/2022/04/RoseSchellenbergShemtov2022.pdf

Rose, E.K. (2021). Who gets a second chance? Effectiveness and equity in supervision of criminal offenders. *The Quarterly Journal of Economics, 136*(2), 1199–1253.

Rose, E.K., and Shem-Tov, Y. (2021). How does incarceration affect reoffending? Estimating the dose-response function. *Journal of Political Economy, 129*(12), 3302–3356.

Rosen, D.L., Wohl, D.A., and Schoenbach, V.J. (2011). All-cause and cause-specific mortality among Black and White North Carolina state prisoners, 1995–2005. *Annals of Epidemiology, 21*(10), 719–726.

Rosenfeld, R., and Lopez, E. (2021). *Pandemic, Social Unrest, and Crime in U.S. Cities: September 2021 Update*. Council on Criminal Justice. https://counciloncj.org/wp-content/uploads/2021/10/Pandemic-Social-Unrest-and-Crime-in-US-Cities-September-2021-Update.pdf

Rosenfeld, R., and Wallman, J. (2019). Did de-policing cause the increase in homicide rates? *Criminology and Public Policy, 18*(1), 51–75. https://doi.org/10.1111/1745-9133.12414

Ross, C.T. (2015). A multi-level Bayesian analysis of racial bias in police shootings at the county-level in the United States, 2011–2014. *PloS One, 10*(11). https://doi.org/10.1371/journal.pone.0141854

Ross, C.T., Winterhalder, B., and McElreath, R. (2018). Resolution of apparent paradoxes in the race-specific frequency of use-of-force by police. *Palgrave Communications, 4*(1), 1–9.

Ross, L. (2010). *Inventing the Savage: The Social Construction of Native American Criminality*. University of Texas Press.

Rothenberg, K., and Wang, A. (2006). The scarlet gene: Behavioral genetics, criminal law, and racial and ethnic stigma. *Law and Contemporary Problems, 69*(1/2), 343–365.

Rothman, D.J. (1971). *The Discovery of the Asylum: Social Order and Disorder in the New Republic*. Trans-action Publishers.

Rothstein, R. (2017). *The Color of Law: A Forgotten History of How Our Government Segregated America*. Liveright.

Rousey, D.C. (1996). *Policing the Southern City: New Orleans, 1805-1889*. Louisiana State University Press.

Rucker, J.M., and Richeson, J.A. (2021). Toward an understanding of structural racism: Implications for criminal justice. *Science, 374*(6565), 286–290.

Rugh, J.S., Albright, L., and Massey, D.S. (2015). Race, space, and cumulative disadvantage: A case study of the subprime lending collapse. *Social Problems, 62*(2), 186–218.

Rugh, J.S., and Massey, D.S. (2010). Racial segregation and the American foreclosure crisis. *American Sociological Review, 75*(5), 629–651.

Ruiz, D.S., and Kopak, A. (2014). The consequences of parental incarceration for African American mothers, children, and grandparent caregivers. *Journal of Pan African Studies, 7*(6), 9–25.

Rushin, S. (2015). Structural reform litigation in American police departments. *Minnesota Law Review, 99*, 1343–1422.

______. (2017). *Federal Intervention in American Police Departments*. Cambridge University Press. https://doi.org/10.1017/9781316226476

______. (2021). Police arbitration. *Vanderbilt Law Review, 74*(4), 1023–1078.

Rushin, S., and Edwards, G. (2021). An empirical assessment of pretextual stops and racial profiling. *Stanford Law Review, 73*.

Ryan, J.B., Katsiyannis, A., Counts, J.M., and Shelnut, J.C. (2018). The growing concerns regarding school resource officers. *Intervention in School and Clinic, 53*(3), 188–192.

Sabol, W.J., West, H.C., and Cooper, M. (2009). *Prisoners in 2008*. NCJ 228417. U.S. Department of Justice, Office of Justice Programs, Bureau of Justice Statistics. https://bjs.ojp.gov/content/pub/pdf/p08.pdf

Sakoda, R.T., and Simes, J.T. (2021). Solitary confinement and the US prison boom. *Criminal Justice Policy Review, 32*(1), 66–102.

Sampson, R.J. (1984). Group size, heterogeneity, and intergroup conflict: A test of Blau's inequality and heterogeneity. *Social Forces, 62*(3), 618–639. https://doi.org/10.1093/sf/62.3.618

______. (1986). Crime in cities: The effects of formal and informal social control. *Crime and Justice, 8*, 271–311.

______. (2008). Moving to inequality: Neighborhood effects and experiments meet social structure. *American Journal of Sociology, 114*(1), 189–231.

______. (2009). Racial stratification and the durable tangle of neighborhood inequality. *The ANNALS of the American Academy of Political and Social Science, 621*(1), 260–280.

______. (2012). *Great American City: Chicago and the Enduring Neighborhood Effect*. University of Chicago Press.

______. (2019). Neighbourhood effects and beyond: Explaining the paradoxes of inequality in the changing American metropolis. *Urban Studies, 56*(1), 3–32.

______. (2022). Legacies of inequality, legacy lead exposures, and improving population well-being. *Proceedings of the National Academy of Sciences, 119*.

Sampson, R.J., and Bartusch, D.J. (1998). Legal cynicism and (subcultural?) tolerance of deviance: The neighborhood context of racial differences. *Law and Society Review, 32*, 777–804.

Sampson R.J., and Loeffler, C. (2010). Punishment's place: the local concentration of mass incarceration. *Daedalus, 139*(3), 20-31.

Sampson, R.J., Morenoff, J.D.. and Raudenbush, S. (2005). Social anatomy of racial and ethnic disparities in violence. *American Journal of Public Health, 95*(2), 224–232.

Sampson, R.J., and Raudenbush, S.W. (2004). Seeing disorder: Neighborhood stigma and the social construction of "Broken Windows." *Social Psychology Quarterly, 67*(4), 319–342.

Sampson, R.J., Raudenbush, S.W., and Earls, F. (1997). Neighborhoods and violent crime: A multilevel study of collective efficacy. *Science, 277*, 918–924.

Sampson, R.J., and Wilson, W.J. (1995). Toward a theory of race, crime, and urban inequality. *Crime and Inequality*, 37–56. Stanford University Press.

Sampson, R.J., Wilson, W.J., and Katz, H. (2018). Reassessing "Toward a Theory of Race, Crime, and Urban Inequality": Enduring and new challenges in 21st century America. *Du Bois Review of Social Science Research on Race, 15*, 13–34. https://nrs.harvard.edu/URN-3:HUL.INSTREPOS:37367775

Sampson, R.J., and Winter, A. (2016). The racial ecology of lead poisoning: Toxic inequality in Chicago neighborhoods, 1995-2013. *Du Bois Review: Social Science Research on Race, 13*(2), 261–283.

______. (2018). Poisoned development: Assessing lead exposure as a cause of crime in a birth cohort followed through adolescence. *Criminology, 56*, 269–301.

Saporu, D.F., Patton, C.L., Krivo, L.J, and Peterson, R.D. (2011). Differential benefits? Crime and community investments in racially distinct neighborhoods. *Race and Justice, 1*(1).

Sawyer, W., and Wagner, P. (2020). Mass incarceration: The whole pie 2020. *Prison Policy Initiative*. https://www.prisonpolicy.org/reports/pie2020.html

Schell, T.L., Cefalu, M., Griffin, B.A., Smart, R., and Morral, A.R. (2020). Changes in firearm mortality following the implementation of state laws regulating firearm access and use. *Proceedings of the National Academy of Sciences, 117*(26), 14906–14910.

Schlanger, M., and Shay, G. (2008). Preserving the rule of law in America's jails and prisons: The case for amending the Prison Litigation Reform Act. *University of Pennsylvania Journal of Constitutional Law, 11*, 139–154.

Schlesinger, T. (2005). Racial and ethnic disparity in pretrial criminal processing. *Justice Quarterly, 22*(2), 170–192.

Schneider, L.E., Vuolo, M., Lageson, S.E., and Uggen, C. (2021). Before and after ban the box: Who complies with anti-discrimination law? *Law and Social Inquiry*, 1–34.

Schnepel, K.T. (2018). Good jobs and recidivism. *The Economic Journal, 128*(608), 447–469.

Schochet, P.Z., Burghardt, J., and McConnell, S. (2008). Does Job Corps work? Impact findings from the National Job Corps Study. *American Economic Review, 98*(5), 1864–1886.

Schrader, S. (2019). *Badges without Borders*. University of California Press.

Schwalbe, C.S., Gearing, R.E., MacKenzie, M.J., Brewer, K.B., and Ibrahim, R. (2012). A meta-analysis of experimental studies of diversion programs for juvenile offenders. *Clinical Psychology Review, 32*(1), 26–33.

Schwartztol, L. (2017). The role of courts in eliminating the racial impact of criminal justice debt. *2017 Trends in State Courts: Fines, Fees, and Bail Practices: Challenges and Opportunities*, 14–19. National Center for State Courts.

Schwarz, P.J. (1988). *Twice Condemned: Slaves and the Criminal Laws of Virginia, 1705-1865*. The Lawbook Exchange, Ltd.

Sciandra, M., Sanbonmatsu, L., Duncan, G.J., Gennetian, L.A., Katz, L.F., Kessler, R.C., Kling, J.R., and Ludwig, J. (2013). Long-term effects of the Moving to Opportunity residential mobility experiment on crime and delinquency. *Journal of Experimental Criminology, 9*(4), 451–489.

Seguin, C., and Rigby, D. (2019). National crimes: A new national data set of lynchings in the United States, 1883-1941. *Socius: Sociological Research for a Dynamic World, 5*, 1–9. https://doi.org/10.1177/2378023119841780

Sellin, J.T. (1976). *Slavery and the Penal System*. New York: Elsevier Scientific Publishing Company.

Sellin, T. (1928). The Negro criminal: A statistical note. *The ANNALS of the American Academy of Political and Social Science, 140*(1), 52–64.

______. (1935). Race prejudice in the administration of justice. *American Journal of Sociology, 41*(2), 212–217.

Sewell, A.A., Feldman, J.M., Ray, R., Gilbert, K.L., Jefferson, K.A., and Lee, H. (2021). Illness spillovers of lethal police violence: The significance of gendered marginalization. *Ethnic and Racial Studies, 44*(7), 1089–1114.

Shannon, S., Huebner, B. M., Harris, A., Martin, K., Patillo, M., Pettit, B., and Uggen, C. (2020). The broad scope and variation of monetary sanctions: Evidence from eight states. *UCLA Criminal Justice Law Review, 4*(1), 269–281. https://escholarship.org/uc/item/64t2w833

Sharkey, P.T. (2008). The intergenerational transmission of context. *American Journal of Sociology, 113*, 931–969.

______. (2013). *Stuck in Place: Urban Neighborhoods and the End of Progress toward Racial Equality*. University of Chicago Press.

______. (2018). *Uneasy Peace: The Great Crime Decline, the Revival of City Life, and the Next War on Violence*. W.W. Norton and Company.

Sharkey, P.T., and Friedson, M. (2019). The impact of the homicide decline on life expectancy of African American males. *Demography, 56*, 645–663.

Sharkey, P.T., and Marsteller, A. (2022). Neighborhood inequality and violence in Chicago, 1965–2020. *University of Chicago Law Review, 89*(2), 349–381.

Sharkey, P.T., Tirado-Strayer, N., Papachristos, A.V., and Raver, C.C. (2012). The effect of local violence on children's attention and impulse control. *American Journal of Public Health, 102*(12), 2287–2293.

Sharkey, P.T., Torrats-Espinosa, G., and Takyar, D. (2017). Community and the crime decline: The causal effect of local nonprofits on violent crime. *American Sociological Review, 82*(6), 1214–1240.

Shavit, S., Aminawung, J.A., Birnbaum, N., Greenberg, S., Berthold, T., Fishman, A., Busch, S.H., and Wang, E.A. (2017). Transitions Clinic Network: Challenges and lessons in primary care for people released from prison. *Health Affairs, 36*(6), 1006–1015.

Shaw, C.R., and McKay, H.D. (1942). *Juvenile Delinquency and Urban Areas.* University of Chicago Press.

______. (1949). Rejoinder. *American Sociological Review, 14,* 608–617.

Shedd, C. (2012). What about the other 99%? *Key Issues in the Police Use of Pedestrian Stops and Searches*, 24–29. The Urban Institute.

______. (2015). *Unequal City: Race, Schools, and Perceptions of Injustice.* Russell Sage Foundation.

Sheftall, A.H., Vakil, F., Ruch, D.A., Boyd, R.C., Lindsey, M.A., and Bridge, J.A. (2022). Black youth suicide: Investigation of current trends and precipitating circumstances. *Journal of the American Academy of Child and Adolescent Psychiatry, 61*(5), 662–675.

Shelton, J.N., and Richeson, J.A. (2005). Intergroup contact and pluralistic ignorance. *Journal of Personality and Social Psychology, 88,* 91–107.

______. (2006). Interracial interactions: A relational approach. *Advances in Experimental Social Psychology, 38,* 121–181. Academic Press.

______. (2014). Interacting across racial lines. *APA Handbook of Personality & Social Psychology: Group Processes.* APA Books.

Shelton, J.N., Richeson, J.A., and Vorauer, J.D. (2006). Threatened identities and interethnic interactions. *European Review of Social Psychology, 17,* 321–358.

Shepley, M., Sachs, N., Sadatsafavi, H., Fournier, C., and Peditto, K. (2019). The impact of green space on violent crime in urban environments: An evidence synthesis. *International Journal of Environmental Research and Public Health, 16*(24). https://doi.org/10.3390/ijerph16245119

Shi, L. (2009). The limit of oversight in policing: Evidence from the 2001 Cincinnati riot. *Journal of Public Economics, 93*(1-2), 99–113.

Shibru, D., Zahnd, E., Becker, M., Bekaert, N., Calhoun, D., and Victorino, G.P. (2007). Benefits of a hospital-based peer intervention program for violently injured youth. *Journal of the American College of Surgeons, 205*(5), 684–689.

Shihadeh, E.S., and Shrum, W. (2004). Serious crime in urban neighborhoods: Is there a race effect? *Sociological Spectrum, 24*(4), 507–533.

Shoag, D., and Veuger, S. (2016). No woman no crime: Ban the box, employment, and upskilling. *SSRN.* https://papers.ssrn.com/sol3/papers.cfm?abstract_id=2782599

Shoub, K. (2022). Comparing systemic and individual sources of racially disparate traffic stop outcomes. *Journal of Public Administration Research and Theory, 32*(2), 236–251.

Shoub, K., Christiani, L., Baumgartner, F.R., Epp, D.A., and Roach, K. (2021). Fines, fees, forfeitures, and disparities: A link between municipal reliance on fines and racial disparities in policing. *Policy Studies Journal, 49*(3), 835–859.

Shrider, E.A., and Ramey, D.M. (2018). Priming the pump: Public investment, private mortgage investment, and violent crime. *City and Community, 17*(4), 996–1014.

Shufelt, J.L., and Cocozza, J.J. (2006). *Youth with Mental Health Disorders in the Juvenile Justice System: Results from a Multi-state Prevalence Study*, 1–6. National Center for Mental Health and Juvenile Justice.

Sidanius, J. (1993). The psychology of group conflict and the dynamics of oppression: A social dominance perspective. *Explorations in Political Psychology*, 183–219.

Sidanius, J., Liu, J.H., Shaw, J.S., and Pratto, F. (1994). Social dominance orientation, hierarchy attenuators and hierarchy enhancers: Social dominance theory and the criminal justice system. *Journal of Applied Social Psychology, 24*(4), 338–366.

Sidanius, J., and Pratto, F. (1999). *Social Dominance: An Intergroup Theory of Social Hierarchy and Oppression*. Cambridge University Press.

Siegel, M., Negussie, Y., Vanture, S., Pleskunas, J., Ross, C.S., and King III, C. (2014). The relationship between gun ownership and stranger and non-stranger firearm homicide rates in the United States, 1981–2010. *American Journal of Public Health, 104*(10), 1912–1919.

Siegel, M., Poulson, M., Sangar, R., and Jay, J. (2021). The interaction of race and place: Predictors of fatal police shootings of Black victims at the incident, census tract, city, and state levels, 2013–2018. *Race and Social Problems, 13*(3), 245–265.

Simes, J.T. (2021). *Punishing Places: The Geography of Mass Imprisonment*. University of California Press.

Simes, J.T., and Jahn, J.L. (2022). The consequences of Medicaid expansion under the Affordable Care Act for police arrests. *PLoS ONE, 17*(1).

Simoiu, C., Corbett-Davies, S., and Goel, S. (2017). The problem of infra-marginality in outcome tests for discrimination. *The Annals of Applied Statistics, 11*(3), 1193-1216.

Simon, T.R., Kegler, S.R., Zwald, M.L., Chen, M.S., Mercy, J.A., Jones, C.M., Mercado-Crespo, M.C., Blair, J.M., and Stone, D.M. (2022). Notes from the field: Increases in firearm homicide and suicide rates—United States, 2020-2021. *MMWR Morbidity and Mortality Weekly Report, 71*, 1286–1287. http://dx.doi.org/10.15585/mmwr.mm7140a4

Skiba, R.J., Michael, R.S., Nardo, A.C., and Peterson, R.L. (2002). The color of discipline: Sources of racial and gender disproportionality in school punishment. *The Urban Review, 34*(4), 317–342.

Skogan, W. (1988). Community organizations and crime. *Crime and Justice*, 39–78. University of Chicago Press.

Sledge, M. (2021). Cash bail a thing of the past? Not yet, but New Orleans judges agree to new rules. *Nola*. https://www.nola.com/news/courts/article_e5351460-a79f-11eb-86f-5-47ad1381e0f5.html

Sloan, C., Naufal, G., and Caspers, H. (2018). *The Effect of Risk Assessment Scores on Judicial Behavior and Defendant Outcomes*. IZA Institute of Labor Economics.

Smith, D.A. (1986). The neighborhood context of police behavior. *Crime and Justice, 8*, 313–341.

Smith, J.M., and Kinzel, A. (2021). Carceral citizenship as strength: Formerly incarcerated activists, civic engagement and criminal justice transformation. *Critical Criminology, 29*, 93–110. https://doi.org/10.1007/s10612-020-09538-w

Smith, J.R., and Patton, D.U. (2016). Posttraumatic stress symptoms in context: Examining trauma responses to violent exposure and homicide death among Black males in urban neighborhoods. *American Journal of Orthopsychiatry, 86*(2), 212–223.

Sobol, N.L. (2017). Fighting fines & fees: Borrowing from consumer law to combat criminal justice debt abuses. *University of Colorado Law Review, 88*, 841.

Solinas-Saunders, M., Stacer, M.J., and Guy, R. (2015). Ex-offender barriers to employment: Racial disparities in labor markets with asymmetric information. *Journal of Crime and Justice, 38*(2), 249–269.

Solomon, B., Katz, E., Steed, H., and Temkin, D. (2018). *Creating Policies to Support Healthy Schools: Policymaker, Educator, and Student Perspectives*. Child Trends.

Solomon, J., and Martin, A. (2019). Competitive victimhood as a lens to reconciliation: An analysis of the Black Lives Matter and Blue Lives Matter movements. *Conflict Resolution Quarterly, 37*(1), 7–31.

Soss, J., Fording, R.C., and Schram, S.F. (2011). *Disciplining the Poor: Neoliberal Paternalism and the Persistent Power of Race*. University of Chicago Press.

South, E.C., MacDonald, J., and Reina, V. (2021). Association between structural housing repairs for low-income homeowners and neighborhood crime. *JAMA Network Open, 4*(7), e2117067.

Spade, D. (2020). *Mutual Aid: Building Solidarity During This Crisis (and the Next)*. Verso Books.

Spohn, C. (2015a). Race, crime, and punishment in the twentieth and twenty-first centuries. In M. Tonry (ed.), *Crime and Justice: A Review of Research, 44*. University of Chicago Press.

______. (2015b). Evolution of sentencing research. *Criminology and Public Policy, 14*, 225–232.

Spohn, C., and Holleran, D. (2000). The imprisonment penalty paid by young, unemployed black and Hispanic male offenders. *Criminology, 38*(1), 281–306.

Starr, S.B. (2015). The risk assessment era: An overdue debate. *Federal Sentencing Reporter, 27*, 205–206.

Steen, S., and Opsal, T. (2007). "Punishment on the installment plan": Individual-level predictors of parole revocation in four states. *The Prison Journal, 87*(3), 344–366.

Steen, S., Opsal, T., Lovegrove, P., and McKinzey, S. (2013). Putting parolees back in prison: Discretion and the parole revocation process. *Criminal Justice Review, 38*(1), 70–93.

Steenbeek, W., and Hipp, J.R. (2011). A longitudinal test of social disorganization theory: Feedback effects among cohesion, social control, and disorder. *Criminology, 49*(3), 833–871.

Steffensmeier, D., Ulmer, J., and Kramer, J. (1998). The interaction of race, gender, and age in criminal sentencing: The punishment cost of being young, black, and male. *Criminology, 36*(4), 763–798.

Steiker, C.S., and Steiker, J.M. (2016). *Courting Death*. Harvard University Press.

Steiner, B., Ellison, J.M., Butler, H.D., and Cain, C.M. (2017). The impact of inmate and prison characteristics on prisoner victimization. *Trauma, Violence, and Abuse, 18*(1), 17–36.

Steinmetz, K.F., and Henderson, H. (2016). Inequality on probation: An examination of differential probation outcomes. *Journal of Ethnicity in Criminal Justice, 14*(1), 1–20.

Stevenson, M. (2018a). Assessing risk assessment in action. *Minnesota Law Review, 103*, 303–384.

______. (2018b). Distortion of justice: How the inability to pay bail affects case outcomes. *Journal of Law, Economics, and Organization, 34*(4), 511–542. http://dx.doi.org/10.2139/ssrn.2777615

Stevenson, M.T., and Doleac, J.C. (2022). Algorithmic Risk Assessment in the Hands of Humans. https://ssrn.com/abstract=3489440 or http://dx.doi.org/10.2139/ssrn.3489440

Stewart, E.A., and Simons, R.L. (2010). Race, code of the street, and violent delinquency: A multilevel investigation of neighborhood street culture and individual norms of violence. *Criminology, 48*, 569–605.

Stone, C., Fogelsong, T., and Cole, C.M. (2009). *Policing Los Angeles Under a Consent Decree: The Dynamics of Change at the LAPD*. Program in Criminal Justice Policy and Management, Harvard Kennedy School.

Strong, B.L., Shipper, A.G., Downton, K.D., and Lane, W.G. (2016). The effects of health care–based violence intervention programs on injury recidivism and costs: A systematic review. *Journal of Trauma and Acute Care Surgery, 81*(5), 961–970.

Struckman-Johnson, C., and Struckman-Johnson, D. (2000). Sexual coercion rates in seven midwestern prison facilities for men. *The Prison Journal, 80*(4), 379–390.

Stuart, F. (2016). Becoming "copwise": Policing, culture, and the collateral consequences of street-level criminalization. *Law and Society Review, 50*(2), 279–313.

Stults, B.J., and Baumer, E.P. (2007). Racial context and police force size: Evaluating the empirical validity of the minority threat perspective. *American Journal of Sociology, 113*(2), 507–546.

Stults, B.J., Parker, K.F., and Lane, E.C. (2010). A spatial and contextual analyis of policing: Examining Black, White and Hispanic stop rates. *Journal of Crime and Justice, 33*(1), 1–36.

Stuntz, W.J. (2006). The political constitution of criminal justice. *Harvard Law Review, 119*(3), 780–851.

Sturm, S.P., and Tae, H. (2017). Leading with conviction: The transformative role of formerly incarcerated leaders in reducing mass incarceration. *Columbia Public Law Research Paper*, 14–547. https://www.prisonpolicy.org/scans/justleadership/leading-with-conviction.pdf

Subramanian, R., and Delaney, R. (2014). *Playbook for Change: States Reconsider Mandatory Sentences*. Vera Institute for Justice.

Subramanian, R., Riley, K., and Mai, C. (2018). Divided justice: Trends in Black and White jail incarceration, 1990-2013. *Vera Institute of Justice*. https://www.vera.org/downloads/publications/Divided-Justice-full-report.pdf

Substance Abuse and Mental Health Services Administration (SAMHSA). (2006). *Results From the 2005 National Survey on Drug Use and Health: National Findings*. US Department of Health and Human Services, Substance Abuse and Mental Health Services Administration.

______. (2015). *Behavioral Health Trends in the United States: Results From the 2014 National Survey on Drug Use and Health*. US Department of Health and Human Services, Substance Abuse and Mental Health Services Administration.

Suddler, C. (2019). *Presumed Criminal: Black Youth and the Justice System in Postwar New York*. New York University Press.

Sugrue, T. (1996). *The Origins of the Urban Crisis: Race and Inequality in Post-War Detroit*. Princeton University Press.

Sullivan, M.L. (1989). Absent fathers in the inner city. *The ANNALS of the American Academy of Political and Social Science, 501*(1), 48–58.

Sundt, J., Salisbury, E.J., and Harmon, M.G. (2016). Is downsizing prisons dangerous? The effect of California's Realignment Act on public safety. *Criminology and Public Policy, 15*(2), 315–341. https://doi.org/10.1111/1745-9133.12199

Suttles, G.D. (1972). The defended community. *The Social Construction of Communities*, 21–43. University of Chicago Press.

Sutton, J.R. (2013). Structural bias in the sentencing of felony defendants. *Social Science Research, 42*(5), 1207–1221.

Swencionis, J.K., and Goff, P.A. (2017). The psychological science of racial bias and policing. *Psychology, Public Policy, and Law, 23*(4), 398–409. https://psycnet.apa.org/doi/10.1037/law0000130

Sykes, G.M. (1958). *The Society of Captives*. Princeton University Press.

Tanenhaus, D.S. (2004). *Juvenile Justice in the Making*. Oxford University Press.

Tannenbaum, F. (1938). *Crime and the Community*, 16–20. Columbia University Press.

Tasca, M., Rodriguez, N., and Zatz, M.S. (2011). Family and residential instability in the context of paternal and maternal incarceration. *Criminal Justice and Behavior, 38*(3), 231–247.

Task Force on Community Preventive Services. (2009). Recommendations for reducing excessive alcohol consumption and alcohol-related harms by limiting alcohol outlet density. *American Journal of Preventive Medicine, 37*(6), 570–571.

Tauri, J.M. (2014). An Indigenous Commentary on the Globalisation of Restorative Justice. University of Wollongong. Paper no. 3197. https://ro.uow.edu.au/sspapers/3197

Tehranian, J. (2000). Performing whiteness: Naturalization litigation and the construction of racial identity in America. *The Yale Law Journal, 109*(4), 817–848.

Teplin, L.A., Welty, L.J., Abram, K.M., Dulcan, M.K., Washburn, J.J., McCoy, K., and Stoke, M.L. (2015). *Psychiatric Disorders in Youth After Detention.* Juvenile Justice Bulletin. U.S. Department of Justice, Office of Justice Programs, Office of Juvenile Justice and Delinquency Prevention.

Terrill, W., and Reisig, M.D. (2003). Neighborhood context and police use of force. *Journal of Research in Crime and Delinquency, 40*(3), 291–321.

Terte, R.H. (1963). Slums and suburbs provide; Deprived need specialists; 'Total' attack begun to de-fuse 'social dynamite' in slums. *New York Times*, April 9.

Testa, A., Turney, K., Jackson, D.B., and Jaynes, C.M. (2022). Police contact and future orientation from adolescence to young adulthood: Findings from the Pathways to Desistance Study. *Criminology, 60*(2), 263–290.

The White House. (2021). *Fact Sheet: More Details on the Biden-Harris Administration's Investments in Community Violence Interventions.* https://www.whitehouse.gov/briefing-room/statements-releases/2021/04/07/fact-sheet-more-details-on-the-biden-harris-administrations-investments-in-community-violence-interventions/

Theriot, M.T. (2009). School resource officers and the criminalization of student behavior. *Journal of Criminal Justice, 37*(3), 280–287.

Thompson, H.A. (2010). Why mass incarceration matters: Rethinking crisis, decline and transformation in postwar American history. *Journal of American History, 101*(3), 703–734.

Toch, H. (1978). Social climate and prison violence. *Federal Probation, 42*, 21–25.

Tolnay, S.E., and Beck, E.M. (1995). *A Festival of Violence: An Analysis of Southern Lynchings, 1882-1930.* University of Illinois Press.

Tonry, M., and Melewski, M. (2008). The malign effects of drug and crime control policies on black Americans. *Crime and Justice, 37*(1), 1–44.

Tonry, M.H. (1994). Racial politics, racial disparities, and the War on Crime. *Crime and Delinquency, 40*(4), 475–494.

______. (1995). *Malign Neglect: Race, Crime, and Punishment in America.* Oxford University Press.

______. (1996). The effects of American drug policy on black Americans, 1980-1996. *European Journal on Criminal Policy & Research, 4*, 36–62.

______. (1997). *Sentencing Matters.* Oxford University Press.

______. (2019). Fifty years of American sentencing reform: Nine lessons. *Crime and Justice, 48*(1), 1–34.

Trangenstein, P.J., Curriero, F.C., Webster, D., Jennings, J.M., Latkin, C., Eck, R., and Jernigan, D.H. (2018). Outlet type, access to alcohol, and violent crime. *Alcoholism, Clinical and Experimental Research, 42*(11), 2234–2245. https://doi.org/10.1111/acer.13880

Trawalter, S., Richeson, J.A., and Shelton, J.N. (2009). Predicting behavior during interracial interactions: A stress and coping approach. *Personality and Social Psychology Review, 13*, 243–268.

Tribal Law and Policy Institute. (2015). *AI/AN Youth & Status Offense Disparities: A Call For Tribal Initiatives, Coordination & Federal Funding.* https://www.home.tlpi.org/_files/ugd/8305c9_43cbc81e552a4ed096e6ebfa5c70ddef.pdf

Turney, K. (2021). Depressive symptoms among adolescents exposed to personal and vicarious police contact. *Society and Mental Health, 11*(2), 113–133.

Turney, K., and Jackson, D.B. (2021). Mothers' health following youth police stops. *Preventive Medicine, 150.*

Turney, K., and Wakefield, S. (2019). Criminal justice contact and inequality. *RSF: The Russell Sage Foundation Journal of the Social Sciences, 5*(1), 1–23.

Turney, K., and Wildeman, C. (2015). Detrimental for some? Heterogeneous effects of maternal incarceration on child wellbeing. *Criminology and Public Policy, 14*(1), 125–156.

Tuttle, C. (2019). Racial disparities in federal sentencing: Evidence from drug mandatory minimums. http://econweb.umd.edu/~tuttle/files/tuttle_mandatory_minimums.pdf

Twinam, T. (2017). Danger zone: Land use and the geography of neighborhood crime. *Journal of Urban Economics, 100,* 104–119.

Tyler, T. (2017). Procedural justice and policing: A rush to judgment? *Annual Review of Law and Social Science, 13,* 29–53.

Tyler, T.R., and Boeckmann, R.J. (1997). Three strikes and you are out, but why? The psychology of public support for punishing rule breakers. *Law and Society Review,* 237–265.

Tyler, T.R., and Huo, Y.J. (2002). *Trust in the law: Encouraging public cooperation with the police and courts.* Russell Sage Foundation.

Uggen, C. (2000). Work as a turning point in the life course of criminals: A duration model of age, employment, and recidivism. *American Sociological Review,* 65, 529–546.

Uggen, C., Larson, R., Shannon, S.K.S., and Pulido-Nava, A. (2020). *Locked Out 2020: Estimates of People Denied Voting Rights Due to a Felony Conviction.* The Sentencing Project. https://www.sentencingproject.org/publications/locked-out-2020-estimates-of-people-denied-voting-rights-due-to-a-felony-conviction/

Uggen, C., and Stewart, R. (2014). Piling on: Collateral consequences and community supervision. *Minnesota Law Review, 99,* 1871–1910.

Uggen, C., Vuolo, M., Lageson, S., Ruhland, E., and Whitham, H.K. (2014). The edge of stigma: An experimental audit of the effects of low-level criminal records on employment. *Criminology, 52*(4), 627–654.

Ulmer, J., and Harris, C. (2013). Race and the religious contexts of violence: Linking religion and White, Black, and Latino violent crime. *The Sociological Quarterly, 54*(4), 610–646. https://doi.org/10.1111/tsq.12034

Ulmer, J., Painter-Davis, N., and Tinik, L. (2016). Disproportional imprisonment of Black and Hispanic males: Sentencing discretion, processing outcomes, and policy structures. *Justice Quarterly, 33*(4), 642–681.

Ulmer, J.T. (2012). Recent developments and new directions in sentencing research. *Justice Quarterly, 29*(1), 1–40.

Ulmer, J.T., and Bradley, M.S. (2018). Punishment in Indian country: Ironies of federal punishment of Native Americans. *Justice Quarterly, 35*(5), 751–781.

______. (2019). Criminal justice in Indian Country: A theoretical and empirical agenda. *Annual Review of Criminology, 2,* 337–357.

Ulmer, J.T., Kramer, J.H., and Zajac, G. (2020). The race of defendants and victims in Pennsylvania death penalty decisions: 2000–2010. *Justice Quarterly, 37*(5), 955–983.

Ulmer, J.T., Light, M.T., and Kramer, J.H. (2011). Racial disparity in the wake of the Booker/Fanfan decision: An alternative analysis to the USSC's 2010 report. *Criminology and Public Policy, 10,* 1077–1118.

Underwood, E. (2021). *Community Learning Session.* Presentation for Committee on Reducing Racial Inequalities in the Criminal Justice System workshop #2: Addressing the Drivers of Criminal Justice Involvement to Advance Racial Equity. March 11. National Academies of Sciences, Engineering, and Medicine.

United States Sentencing Commission. (2018a). *Federal Sentencing: The Basics.* https://www.ussc.gov/sites/default/files/pdf/research-and-publications/research-projects-and-surveys/miscellaneous/201811_fed-sentencing-basics.pdf

______. (2018b). *Guidelines Manual.* Chapter 5 – Determining the Sentence. https://www.ussc.gov/guidelines/2018-guidelines-manual/2018-chapter-5

______. (2019). *Primer: Criminal History*, 1–2. https://www.ussc.gov/sites/default/files/pdf/training/primers/2019_Primer_Criminal_History.pdf

______. (2020). *Federal Sentencing: The Basics.* https://www.ussc.gov/sites/default/files/pdf/research-and-publications/research-publications/2020/202009_fed-sentencing-basics.pdf

Unnever, J.D. (2018). The racial invariance thesis in criminology: Toward a Black criminology. *Building a Black Criminology: Race, Theory, and Crime.* Routledge.

Urban Labs. (2022). *READI Chicago: A Community-Based Approach to Reducing Gun Violence.* University of Chicago: Crime Lab.

U.S. Congress, House Committee on Education and Labor. (1978). *Oversight Hearing on the Runaway Youth Act, held before the Subcommittee on Economic Opportunity of the Committee on Education and Labor.* U.S. House of Representatives, March 7, 1978. https://www.ojp.gov/pdffiles1/Digitization/149939NCJRS.pdf

U.S. Congress, Senate Committee on the Judiciary. (1980). *Hearings on the Reauthorization of the Juvenile Justice and Delinquency Prevention Act of 1974, before the Committee on the Judiciary.* United States Senate, March 27–28. Serial No. 96-84. https://www.ojp.gov/pdffiles1/Digitization/149844NCJRS.pdf

U.S. Department of Justice. (2002). Budget Trend Data: From 1975 Through the President's 2003 Request to the Congress. Budget Staff, Justice Management Division. https://www.justice.gov/archive/jmd/1975_2002/2002/pdf/BudgetTrand.pdf

______. (2015). *Investigation of the Ferguson Police Department.* Office of Public Affairs. https://www.justice.gov/sites/default/files/opa/press-releases/attachments/2015/03/04/ferguson_police_department_report.pdf

______. (2021). *Organization, Mission, and Functions Manual: Office of Justice Programs.* https://www.justice.gov/jmd/organization-mission-and-functions-manual-office-justice-programs

U.S. General Accounting Office. (1990). *Death Penalty Sentencing: Research Indicates Pattern of Racial Disparities.* https://www.gao.gov/assets/ggd-90-57.pdf

Valentine, E.J., and Redcross, C. (2015). Transitional jobs after release from prison: Effects on employment and recidivism. *IZA Journal of Labor Policy, 4*(1), 1–17.

Van Cleve, N.G. (2016). *Crook County.* Stanford University Press.

Vargas, R. (2016). *Wounded City: Violent Turf Wars in a Chicago Barrio.* Oxford University Press.

Vélez, M.B. (2006). Chapter 5: Toward an understanding of the lower rates of homicide in Latino versus Black neighborhoods: A look at Chicago. *The Many Colors of Crime: Inequalities of Race, Ethnicity, and Crime in America*, 91–107. New York University Press. https://doi.org/10.18574/nyu/9780814768549.003.0009

______. (2009). Banks and the racial patterning of homicide: A study of Chicago neighborhoods. *International Journal of Conflict and Violence*, 3(2), 154–171.

Vélez, M.B., Krivo, L.J., and Peterson, R.D. (2003). Structural inequality and homicide: An assessment of the Black-White gap in killings. *Criminology, 41*(3), 645–672.

Vélez, M.B., and Lyons, C.J. (2014). Making or breaking neighborhoods: Public social control and the political economy of urban crime. *Criminology and Public Policy, 13*, 225–236.

Vélez, M.B., Lyons, C.J., and Santoro, W.A. (2015). The political context of the percent Black-neighborhood violence link: A multilevel analysis. *Social Problems, 62*(1), 93–119.

Villarreal, A., and Silva, B.F. (2006). Social cohesion, criminal victimization and perceived risk of crime in Brazilian neighborhoods. *Social Forces, 84*(3), 1725–1753.

Visher, C., Naser, R.L., Baer, D., and Jannetta, J. (2005). *In Need of Help: Experiences of Seriously Ill Prisoners Returning to Cincinnati.* The Urban Institute. https://www.urban.org/sigtes/default/files/publication/51531/311155-In-Need-of-Help.PDF

Vito, G.F., Higgins, G.E., and Tewksbury, R. (2012). Characteristics of parole violators in Kentucky. *Federal Probation, 76*, 19–23.

Vogler, J. (2020). Access to healthcare and criminal behavior: Evidence from the ACA Medicaid expansions. *Journal of Policy Analysis and Management, 39*(4), 1166–1213.

Voigt, R., Camp, N.P., Prabhakaran, V., Hamilton, W.L., Hetey, R.C., Griffiths, C.M., Jurgens, D., Jurafsky, D., and Eberhardt, J.L. (2017). Language from police body camera footage shows racial disparities in officer respect. *Proceedings of the National Academy of Sciences, 114*(25), 6521–6526. https://www.pnas.org/doi/epdf/10.1073/pnas.1702413114

Vorauer, J.D., Hunter, A.J., Main, K.J., and Roy, S. (2000). Metastereotype activation: Evidence from indirect measures for specific evaluative concerns experienced by members of dominant groups in intergroup interaction. *Journal of Personality and Social Psychology, 78*, 690–707.

Vorauer, J.D., and Kumhyr, S. (2001). Is this about you or me? Self versus other-directed judgments and feelings in response to intergroup interaction. *Personality and Social Psychology Bulletin, 27*, 706–719.

Vorauer, J.D., Main, K.J., and O'Connell, G.B. (1998). How do individuals expect to be viewed by members of lower status groups? Content and implications of meta-stereotypes. *Journal of Personality and Social Psychology, 75*, 917–937.

Wadsworth, T. (2000). Labor markets, delinquency, and social control theory: An empirical assessment of the mediating process. *Social Forces, 78*(3), 1041–1066.

Walfield, S.M. (2016). When a cleared rape is not cleared: A multilevel study of arrest and exceptional clearance. *Journal of Interpersonal Violence, 31*(9), 1767–1792.

Walker, S. (1998). *Popular Justice: A History of American Criminal Justice*. Oxford University Press.

______. (2022). The Justice Department's pattern-or-practice police reform program, 1994–2017: Goals, achievements, and issues. *Annual Review of Criminology, 5*, 21–42.

Wallace Jr., J.M., Goodkind, S., Wallace, C.M., and Bachman, J.G. (2008). Racial, ethnic, and gender differences in school discipline among US high school students: 1991-2005. *The Negro Educational Review, 59*(1-2), 47–62.

Walsh, A. (2016). States, help families stay together by correcting a consequence of the Adoption and Safe Families Act. *Prison Policy Initiative*. https://www.prisonpolicy.org/blog/2016/05/24/asfa/

Wang, E.A., Hong, C.S., Shavit, S., Sanders, R., Kessell, E., and Kushel, M.B. (2012). Engaging individuals recently released from prison into primary care: A randomized trial. *American Journal of Public Health, 102*(9), e22–e29.

Wang, E.A., Lin, H.J., Aminawung, J.A., Busch, S.H., Gallagher, C., Maurer, K., Puglisi, L., Shavit, S., and Frisman, L. (2019). Propensity-matched study of enhanced primary care on contact with the criminal justice system among individuals recently released from prison to New Haven. *BMJ Open, 9*(5), e028097.

Wang, X., Mears, D.P., and Bales, W.D. (2010). Race-specific employment contexts and recidivism. *Criminology, 48*(4), 1171–1211.

Ward, G. (2012). *The Black Child-Savers: Racial Democracy and Juvenile Justice*. The University of Chicago Press.

Ward, G., Farrell, A., and Rousseau, D. (2009). Does Racial Balance in Workforce Representation Yield Equal Justice? Race Relations of Sentencing in Federal Court Organizations. *Law & Society Review, 43*(4),757-805. https://www.jstor.org/stable/40538734

Warikoo, N., Sinclair, S., Fei, J., and Jacoby-Senghor, D. (2016). Examining racial bias in education: A new approach. *Educational Researcher, 45*(9), 508–514.

Washburn, K.K. (2006a). American Indians, crime, and the law. *Michigan Law Review, 104*, 709–778.

_____. (2006b). Federal criminal law and tribal self-determination. *North Carolina Law Review, 84*, 778–856.

Wasserman, G.A., McReynolds, L.S., Schwalbe, C.S., Keating, J.M., and Jones, S.A. (2010). Psychiatric disorder, comorbidity, and suicidal behavior in juvenile justice youth. *Criminal Justice and Behavior, 37*(12), 1361–1376.

Waugh, J.C. (1969). Mitchell hints plan for "massive citizen war on crime." *Christian Science Monitor*, February 12.

Weaver, V.M. (2007). Frontlash: Race and the development of punitive crime policy. *Studies in American Political Development, 21*(2), 230–265.

Weaver, V.M., and Lerman, A.E. (2010). Political consequences of the carceral state. *American Political Science Review, 104*(4), 817–833.

Webster, D.W. (2022). Public health approaches to reducing community gun violence. *Daedalus, 151*(1), 38–48.

Webster, D.W., Buggs, S.A.L., and Crifasi, C.K. (2018). *Estimating the Effects of Law Enforcement and Public Health Interventions Intended to Reduce Firearm Violence in Baltimore*. Johns Hopkins Center for Firearm Policy and Research. https://abell.org/wp-content/uploads/2022/02/JHSPH-Gun-Violence-in-Baltimore.pdf

Webster, D.W., Whitehill, J.M., Vernick, J.S., and Curriero, F.C. (2013). Effects of Baltimore's Safe Streets Program on gun violence: A replication of Chicago's CeaseFire Program. *Journal of Urban Health, 90*(1), 27–40.

Weis, J.G., and Sederstrom, J. (1981). *The Prevention of Serious Delinquency: What to Do?* U.S. Department of Justice, Office of Juvenile Justice and Delinquency Prevention, National Institute for Juvenile Justice and Delinquency Prevention.

Weisburst, E.K. (2019). Patrolling public schools: The impact of funding for school police on student discipline and long-term education outcomes. *Journal of Policy Analysis and Management, 38*(2), 338–365.

Weitzer, R., and Tuch, S.A. (2002). Perceptions of racial profiling: Race, class, and personal experience. *Criminology, 40*(2), 435–456.

Welch, K., and Payne, A.A. (2010). Racial threat and punitive school discipline. *Social Problems, 57*(1), 25–48.

Wellford, C., and Cronin, J. (1999). *An Analysis of Variables Effecting the Clearances of Homicides: A Multistate Study*. Justice Research and Statistics Association.

Welsh, R.O., and Little, S. (2018). The school discipline dilemma: A comprehensive review of disparities and alternative approaches. *Review of Educational Research, 88*(5), 752–794.

Wen, M., Zhang, X., Harris, C.D., Holt, J.B., and Croft, J.B. (2013). Spatial disparities in the distribution of parks and green spaces in the USA. *Annals of Behavioral Medicine, 45*(Suppl. 1), S18–S27. https://doi.org/10.1007/s12160-012-9426-x

Werthman, C., and Piliavin, I. (1967). "Gang Members and the Police." In *The Police: Six Sociological Essays*, edited by David Bordua. New York: Wiley.

Western, B. (2021). Inside the box: Safety, health, and isolation in prison. *Journal of Economic Perspectives, 35*(4), 97–122.

Western, B., Davis, J., Ganter, F., and Smith, N. (2021). The cumulative risk of jail incarceration. *Proceedings of the National Academy of Sciences, 118*(16).

Western, B., Kling, J.R., and Weiman, D.F. (2001). The labor market consequences of incarceration. *Crime & Delinquency, 47*(3), 410–427.

Western, B., and Pettit, B. (2010). Incarceration and social inequality. *Daedalus, 139*(3), 8–19.

Western, B., and Sirois, C. (2019). Racialized re-entry: Labor market inequality after incarceration. *Social Forces, 97*(4), 1517–1542.

Wheeler, A.P., Dae-Young, K., and Phillips, S.W. (2018). The effect of housing demolitions on crime in Buffalo, New York. *Journal of Research in Crime and Delinquency, 55*(3), 390–424.

White, M.D., Fradella, H.F., Morrow, W.J., and Mellom, D. (2016). Federal civil litigation as an instrument of police reform: A natural experiment exploring the effects of the Floyd ruling on stop-and-frisk activities in New York City. *Ohio State Journal of Criminal Law, 14,* 9–66.

Whitehurst, G.J., and Croft, M. (2010). *The Harlem Children's Zone, Promise Neighborhoods, and the Broader, Bolder Approach to Education.* Brown Center on Education Policy, The Brookings Institution. https://abfe.issuelab.org/resources/9543/9543.pdf

Whitesell, N.R. (2016). *Building Strong Evidence in Challenging Contexts.* Powerpoint presented at the conference, Building Strong Evidence in Challenging Contexts: Alternatives to Traditional Randomized Controlled Trials. U.S. Department of Health and Human Services, Office of Planning, Research, and Evaluation.

Wickes, R., and Hipp, J.R. (2018). The spatial and temporal dynamics of neighborhood informal social control and crime. *Social Forces, 97,* 277–308.

Wildeman, C., Goldman, A.W., and Turney, K. (2018). Parental incarceration and child health in the United States. *Epidemiologic Reviews, 40*(1), 146–156.

Wildeman, C., Turney, K., and Yi, Y. (2016). Paternal incarceration and family functioning: Variation across federal, state, and local facilities. *The ANNALS of the American Academy of Political and Social Science, 665*(1), 80–97.

Williams, D.R., and Collins, C. (2001). Racial residential segregation: A fundamental cause of racial disparities in health. *Public Health Reports, 116*(5), 404–416.

Williams, K., Healy, J., and Wright, W. (2021). "A Horrendous Tragedy": The chaotic moments before a police shooting in Columbus. *The New York Times.* https://www.nytimes.com/2021/04/21/us/columbus-police-shooting-bryant.html

Williams Jr., M.C., Weil, N., Rasich, E., Ludwig, J., Chang, H., and Egrari, S. (2021). *Body-Worn Cameras in Policing: Benefits and Costs.* Working paper, Becker Friedman Institute for Economics, University of Chicago.

Wilson, W.J. (1987). *The Truly Disadvantaged: The Inner City, the Underclass, and Public Policy.* University of Chicago Press.

______. (1996). *When Work Disappears: The World of the Urban Poor.* Alfred Knopf, New York.

Winant, H. (2000). Race and race theory. *Annual Review of Sociology, 26*(1), 169–185.

Winter, A.S., and Sampson, R.J. (2017). From lead exposure in early childhood to adolescent health: A Chicago birth cohort. *American Journal of Public Health, 107,* 1496–1501.

Wiseman, J., and Brasher, K. (2008). Community wellbeing in an unwell world: Trends, challenges, and possibilities. *Journal of Public Health Policy, 29*(3), 353–366.

Wolff, N., Blitz, C.L., Shi, J., Bachman, R., and Siegel, J.A. (2006). Sexual violence inside prisons: Rates of victimization. *Journal of Urban Health, 83*(5), 835–848.

Wolfgang, M.E., and Riedel, M. (1973). Race, judicial discretion, and the death penalty. *The ANNALS of the American Academy of Political and Social Science, 407*(1), 119–133.

Woodstock Institute. (2010). Paying More for the American Dream IV: The Decline of Prime Mortgage Lending in Communities of Color. *Woodstock Institute.* https://woodstockinst.org/wp-content/uploads/2013/05/payingmore4_may2010_collaboration_0.pdf

Wooldredge, J., Frank, J., Goulette, N., and Travis III, L. (2015). Is the impact of cumulative disadvantage on sentencing greater for Black defendants? *Criminology and Public Policy, 14*(2), 187–223.

Wooldredge, J., and Steiner, B. (2012). Race group differences in prison victimization experiences. *Journal of Criminal Justice, 40*(5), 358–369. https://doi.org/10.1016/j.jcrimjus.2012.06.011

Wooldredge, J., and Thistlethwaite, A.B. (2003). Neighborhood structure and race-specific rates of intimate assault. *Criminology, 41,* 393–422.

Woolfgang, M., and Ferracuti, F. (1967). *The Subculture of Violence: Towards an Integrated Theory of Criminology*. Travistock.

Worden, R.E., McLean, S.J., Engel, R.S., Cochran, H., Corsaro, N., Reynolds, D., Najdowski, C.J., and Isaza, G.T. (2020). *The Impacts of Implicit Bias Awareness Training in the NYPD*. The John F. Finn Institute for Public Safety, Inc. and The Center for Police Research and Policy at the University of Cincinnati.

Wright, J.P., Dietrich, K.N., Ris, M.D., Hornung, R.W., Wessel, S.D., Lanphear, B.P., Ho, M., and Rae, M.N. (2008). Association of prenatal and childhood blood lead concentrations with criminal arrests in early adulthood. *PLoS Medicine, 5*(5). https://doi.org/10.1371/journal.pmed.0050101

Wu, J. (2016). Racial/ethnic discrimination and prosecution: A meta-analysis. *Criminal Justice and Behavior, 43*(4), 437–458.

Xie, M., and Baumer, E.P. (2018). Reassessing the breadth of the protective benefit of immigrant neighborhoods: A multilevel analysis of violence risk by race, ethnicity, and labor market stratification. *Criminology, 56*, 302–332.

Yang, C.S. (2015). Free at last? Judicial discretion and racial disparities in federal sentencing. *The Journal of Legal Studies, 44*(1), 75–111.

______. (2017). Local labor markets and criminal recidivism. *Journal of Public Economics, 147*, 16–29.

Yazzie, R. (1994). Life comes from it: Navajo justice concepts. *New Mexico Law Review, 24*, 175–190. http://digitalrepository.unm.edu/nmlr/vol24/iss2/3

Yudell, M. (2014). *Race Unmasked*. Columbia University Press.

Yudell, M., Roberts, D., DeSalle, R., and Tishkoff, S. (2016). Taking race out of human genetics. *Science, 351*(6273), 564–565.

Zane, S.N., Welsh, B.C., and Drakulich, K.M. (2016). Assessing the impact of race on the juvenile waiver decision: A systematic review and meta-analysis. *Journal of Criminal Justice, 46*, 106–117.

Zane, S.N., Welsh, B.C., Mears, D.P., and Zimmerman, G.M. (2021). Pathways through juvenile justice: A system-level assessment of cumulative disadvantage in the processing of juvenile offenders. *Journal of Quantitative Criminology, 38*, 483–514.

Zavez, M. (2008). Use of the Adoption and Safe Families Act at 15/22 months for incarcerated parents. *Vermont Law Review, 33*, 187–199.

Zeng, Z. (2020). *Jail Inmates in 2018*. Bureau of Justice Statistics, U.S. Department of Justice. https://bjs.ojp.gov/library/publications/jail-inmates-2018

______. (2021). *Jail Inmates in 2019*. U.S. Department of Justice, Bureau of Justice Statistics, NCJ 255608. https://bjs.ojp.gov/content/pub/pdf/ji19.pdf

Zhang, R., Srinivasan, S., Kambath, A., Nnadi, V., Price-Tucker, A., Zhou, A., Charroux, A., Tenzin, C., Robertson, E., Abdalla, H., and Gu, J. (2019). *Successful Reentry: A Community-level Analysis*. Harvard IOP.

Zimring, F.E. (2006). *The Great American Crime Decline*. Oxford University Press.

Zimring, F.E., Hawkins, G., and Kamin, S. (2001). *Punishment and Democracy: Three Strikes and You're Out in California*. Oxford University Press on Demand.

Zion, J.W. (1998). The dynamics of Navajo peacemaking. *Journal of Contemporary Criminal Justice, 14*(1), 58–74.

Zoorob, M. (2020). Do police brutality stories reduce 911 calls? Reassessing an important criminological finding. *American Sociological Review, 85*(1), 176–183.

Appendix

Biosketches of Committee Members and Staff

Khalil Gibran Muhammad (*Co-Chair*) is a distinguished, multi-award winning professor of history, race, and public policy at Harvard Kennedy School and the Suzanne Young Murray Professor at the Radcliffe Institute for Advanced Studies. He is the former director of the Schomburg Center for Research in Black Culture, a division of the New York Public Library and the world's leading library and archive of global Black history. Before leading the Schomburg Center, Muhammad was an associate professor at Indiana University. His scholarship examines the broad intersections of race, democracy, inequality, and criminal justice in modern U.S. history. He is the author of *The Condemnation of Blackness: Race, Crime, and the Making of Modern Urban America,* which won the John Hope Franklin Best Book award in American Studies. Much of Muhammad's work has been featured in national print and broadcast media outlets, including the *New York Times, New Yorker, Washington Post, The Nation,* National Public Radio, *Moyers and Company,* and MSNBC. He has appeared in a number of feature-length documentaries, including the Oscar-nominated *13th* and *Slavery by Another Name.* Muhammad was Andrew W. Mellon fellow at the Vera Institute of Justice. He is a member of the Society of American Historians and the American Antiquarian Society. Muhammad is on the boards of the Vera Institute of Justice, The Museum of Modern Art, The New York Historical Society, and *The Nation* magazine, as well as the advisory boards of Cure Violence, Common Justice, The HistoryMakers, and the Lapidus Center for the Study of Transatlantic Slavery. Muhammad graduated from the University of Pennsylvania with a B.A. in economics and earned a Ph.D. in U.S. history from Rutgers University. He also holds two honorary doctorates.

Bruce Western (*Co-Chair*) is the Bryce Professor of Sociology and Social Justice and co-director of the Justice Lab at Columbia University. His research has examined the causes, scope, and consequences of the historic growth in U.S. prison populations. Western's current projects include a randomized experiment assessing the effects of criminal justice fines and fees on misdemeanor defendants in Oklahoma City, as well as a field study of solitary confinement in Pennsylvania state prisons. He is also the principal investigator of the Square One Project, which aims to re-imagine the public policy response to violence under conditions of poverty and racial inequality. Western was the vice chair of the National Research Council panel on the causes and consequences of high incarceration rates in the United States. He is the author of *Homeward: Life in the Year After Prison* and *Punishment and Inequality in America.*Western is a member of the National Academy of Sciences and the American Academy of Arts and Sciences. He has been a Guggenheim fellow, a Russell Sage Foundation visiting scholar, and a fellow of the Radcliffe Institute of Advanced Study. Western received his Ph.D. in sociology from the University of California, Los Angeles.

Daryl Atkinson is the co-director of Forward Justice, a non-partisan law, policy, and strategy center dedicated to advancing racial, social, and economic justice in the U.S. South. Prior to joining Forward Justice, he was the first Second Chance Fellow for the U.S. Department of Justice (DOJ). While at DOJ, Atkinson was an advisor to the Second Chance portfolio of the Bureau of Justice Assistance (BJA), a member of the Federal Interagency Reentry Council, and a conduit to the broader justice-involved population to ensure that BJA heard from all stakeholders when developing reentry policy. Atkinson was the senior staff attorney at the Southern Coalition for Social Justice where he focused on criminal justice reform issues, particularly removing the legal barriers triggered by contact with the criminal justice system, and he was a staff attorney at the North Carolina Office of Indigent Defense Services where he helped develop the Collateral Consequence Assessment Tool (C-CAT). C-CAT is an online searchable database that allows the user to identify the collateral consequences triggered by North Carolina convictions. He was recognized by the White House as a "Reentry and Employment Champion of Change" for his extraordinary work to facilitate employment opportunities for people with criminal records. Atkinson is a founding member of the North Carolina Second Chance Alliance and serves on the North Carolina Commission for Racial and Ethnic Disparities in the Criminal Justice System. He received a B.A. in political science from Benedict College, Columbia, and a J.D. from the University of St. Thomas School of Law, Minneapolis.

Robert D. Crutchfield is professor emeritus and department chair in the Department of Sociology at the University of Washington. His research is on labor markets and crime, alongside race, ethnicity, and the criminal justice system. Crutchfield is a fellow and former vice president of the American Society of Criminology; a University of Washington Distinguished Teaching Award winner; chair of the American Sociological Association's (ASA's) Crime, Law, and Deviance Section; and to the Council of the ASA. He is chair of the National Academies of Sciences, Engineering, and Medicine's Committee on Law and Justice and served on several National Research Council study panels, including the Committee to Improve Research and Data on Firearms, the Committee on Assessing the Research Program of the National Institute of Justice, and the Committee on the Causes and Consequences of High Rates of Incarceration. Crutchfield is a National Associate of the National Research Council of the National Academy of Sciences. He has been on the board of directors of The Sentencing Project, the Washington State Juvenile Sentencing Commission, and the Board for the Washington State Council on Crime and Delinquency, and he served on the Executive Committee of the U.S. Department of Justice Office of Justice Programs Science Advisory Board. Crutchfield is a former juvenile probation officer and worked as a parole agent for the Pennsylvania Board of Probation and Parole. He received his B.A. in sociology from Thiel College and his M.A. as well as his Ph.D. from Vanderbilt University.

Ronald L. Davis is a principal consultant at 21st CP Solutions, LLC. He served as the director of the U.S. Department of Justice Office of Community Oriented Policing Services (COPS Office) and was appointed to serve as the executive director of the President's Task Force on 21st Century Policing (Task Force). The final report of the Task Force now serves as a foundational document in American policing. Prior to serving as COPS director, Davis had a distinguished career in law enforcement serving as chief of police of East Palo Alto (CA) and with the Oakland (CA) Police Department. He was recognized for working collaboratively with the community to dramatically reduce crime and violence in a city once named as the murder capital of the United States. Davis also served as the interim city manager for East Palo Alto. He led the city through a national economic downturn and the state dissolution of all re-development agencies. Davis worked with stakeholders, including employee unions, to reduce costs while avoiding staff layoffs. He also led the city's adoption of an economic development strategy that has contributed to significant economic growth. Davis is the co-author of the publications *Race and Policing: An Agenda for Action* and *Exploring the Role of the Police in Prisoner Reentry*, and the U.S. Department of Justice publication *How to Correctly Collect and Analyze Racial Profiling Data: Your Reputation Depends on It*. He has a

B.A. from Southern Illinois University and has completed the Senior Executives in State and Local Government Program at the Harvard University Kennedy School of Government.

Bernice Donald is a judge on the United States Court of Appeals for the Sixth Circuit. She was nominated to that position by President Barack Obama and was confirmed by the Senate. Prior to her nomination, Donald sat on the U.S. District Court for the Western District of Tennessee. She previously served as judge on the U.S. Bankruptcy Court for the Western District of Tennessee and was also elected to the General Sessions Criminal Court, becoming both the first African American woman in the history of the United States to serve as a bankruptcy judge and the first African American woman to serve as a judge in the history of the state of Tennessee. Donald also served as adjunct faculty at the University of Memphis School of Law and as faculty for the Federal Judicial Center and the National Judicial College. Chief Justice Rehnquist appointed Donald to the Judicial Conference Advisory Committee on Bankruptcy Rules two different times. She is extremely active in the American, Tennessee, and Memphis Bar Associations, serving in vital leadership roles in key committees. She previously served as secretary of the 430,000-member American Bar Association. Donald has been the recipient of more than 100 awards for professional, civic, and community activities. She received her law degree from the University of Memphis School of Law, an LL.M. from the Duke University School of Law, and an honorary Doctor of Law degree from Suffolk University.

Francis (Frankie) Guzman is director of the California Youth Justice Initiative at the National Center for Youth Law. He leads a team of attorneys, policy advocates, and community organizers working to eliminate the practice of prosecuting and incarcerating children in California's adult criminal justice system, reduce incarceration and justice system involvement, and increase developmentally appropriate services in communities for youth. Raised in a poor, mostly immigrant community plagued by crime and drugs, Guzman experienced his parents' divorce and his family's subsequent homelessness at age three, experienced the life-imprisonment of his 16-year-old brother at age five, and lost numerous childhood friends to violence. At age 15, he was arrested for armed robbery and, on his first offense, was sentenced to serve 15 years in the California Youth Authority. Released on parole after six years, Guzman attended law school and became an expert in juvenile law and policy with a focus on ending the prosecution of juveniles as adults. Through partnerships with community organizations and advocacy groups, he has helped lead California's effort to reduce the number of youths prosecuted as adults and serving time in adult prisons by passing legislation that established Youth Offender Parole

Hearings, reformed Juvenile Transfer Hearings, and eliminated prosecutors' direct file authority. More recently, Guzman helped lead statewide efforts to eliminate California's practice of prosecuting 14- and 15-year-olds as adults and prohibit the incarceration of children younger than age 12 in the juvenile system; furthermore, he secured approximately $60 million to expand pre-arrest diversion programs and developmentally appropriate, culturally relevant community-based services for youth in California. Guzman received his J.D. from the University of California, Los Angeles, School of Law.

Elizabeth Hinton is associate professor of history and African American studies and professor of law at Yale University. Her research focuses on the problems of poverty, urban violence, and inequality in the 20th century United States. Hinton is the author of *From the War on Poverty to the War on Crime: The Making of Mass Incarceration in America*, which received the Ralph Waldo Emerson prize from the Phi Beta Kappa Society and was named to the *New York Times's* 100 notable books in 2016. Her articles and op-eds can be found in the pages of the *New York Times, The Atlantic, The Los Angeles Times, The Boston Review, The Nation,* and *Time*. Hinton earned her Ph.D. in U.S. history from Columbia University.

Nikki Jones is a professor in the Department of African American Studies at the University of California, Berkeley. She is also a faculty affiliate with the Center for the Study of Law and Society. Jones's areas of expertise include urban ethnography, race and ethnic relations, and criminology and criminal justice, with a special emphasis on the intersection of race, gender, and justice. She has published three books, including the sole-authored *Between Good and Ghetto: African American Girls and Inner City Violence* (www.betweengoodandghetto.com). Her research appears in peer-reviewed journals in sociology, gender studies, and criminology. Jones's next book, based on several years of field research in a San Francisco neighborhood, examines how African American men with criminal histories change their lives and their place in the neighborhood once they do. Her current research draws on the systematic analysis of video records that document routine encounters between police and civilians, including young Black men's frequent encounters with the police. Jones is the past-chair of the American Sociological Association's Race, Gender and Class Section. Jones has received awards for her research and publications including the William T. Grant Award for Early Career Scholars, the New Scholar Award from the American Society of Criminology's Division on Women and Crime, and the New Scholar Award from the American Society of Criminology's Division on People of Color and Crime. Before joining the faculty at the University of California, she was on faculty in the Department of Sociology at the

University of California, Santa Barbara. Jones earned her Ph.D. in sociology and criminology from the University of Pennsylvania.

Tracey Meares is the Walton Hale Hamilton Professor and a founding director of the Justice Collaboratory at Yale Law School. Before joining the faculty at Yale, she was a professor at the University of Chicago Law School, serving as Max Pam Professor and director of the Center for Studies in Criminal Justice. Meares was the first African American woman to be granted tenure at both law schools. She is a nationally recognized expert on policing in urban communities. Meares's research focuses on understanding how members of the public think about their relationship(s) with legal authorities such as police, prosecutors, and judges. She teaches courses on criminal procedure, criminal law, and policy as well as having served on the National Academies of Sciences, Engineering, and Medicine's Committee on Law and Justice, a standing committee, and the U.S. Department of Justice Office of Justice Programs Science Advisory Board. Meares is a member of the board of directors at The Joyce Foundation. She was elected as a member to the American Academy of Arts and Sciences and later appointed as a member of The President's Task Force on 21st Century Policing. She has a B.S. in general engineering from the University of Illinois and a J.D. from the University of Chicago Law School.

Derek A. Neal is the William C. Norby Professor at the University of Chicago. He studies labor, Black-White wage inequality, economics of crime, and education policy. Neal is the recipient of the Llewellyn John and Harriet Manchester Quantrell Award for Excellence in Undergraduate Teaching, a fellow with the Society of Labor Economists, president of the Midwest Economics Association, former co-editor of *Journal of Human Resources*, former editor-in-chief of *Journal of Labor Economics*, and former editor of *Journal of Political Economy*. He received his M.A. and Ph.D. in economics from the University of Virginia.

Steven Raphael is a professor of public policy at the University of California, Berkeley and is the James D. Marver chair at the Goldman School of Public Policy. His research focuses on the economics of low-wage labor markets, housing, and the economics of crime and corrections. Raphael's most recent research focuses on the social consequences of the large increases in U.S. incarceration rates and racial disparities in criminal justice outcomes. He also works on immigration policy, research questions pertaining to various aspects of racial inequality, the economics of labor unions, social insurance policies, homelessness, and low-income housing. Raphael, with Michael Stoll, is the author of *Why Are so Many Americans in Prison?* and *The New Scarlet Letter? Negotiating the U.S. Labor Market with a Criminal Record.*

He is a research fellow at the National Bureau of Economic Research, the California Policy Lab, the University of Michigan National Poverty Center, the University of Chicago Crime Lab, IZA (Bonn, Germany), and the Public Policy Institute of California. Raphael holds a Ph.D. in economics from the University of California, Berkeley.

Nancy Rodriguez is a professor in the Department of Criminology, Law, and Society at the University of California, Irvine. Her research interests include inequality (race/ethnicity, class, crime, and justice) and the collateral consequences of mass incarceration. Throughout her career, Rodriguez has engaged in use-inspired research and has been part of many successful collaborations with law enforcement, courts, and correctional agencies. Rodriguez was appointed by President Barack Obama to serve as the director of the National Institute of Justice (NIJ). As director of NIJ, she led the development of the agency's first strategic research plans in the areas of corrections, safety, health and wellness, and policing. She worked with federal partners to raise awareness of crime and justice research gaps and collaborated with federal partners to make investments in research and evaluation. Since leaving NIJ, Rodriguez has dedicated her time to advancing research in the areas of racial and ethnic disparities and prison violence (with the generous support from the John D. and Catherine T. MacArthur Foundation and Arnold Ventures).

Addie C. Rolnick is a professor of law at the University of Nevada, Las Vegas, William S. Boyd School of Law and a board member of the law school's program on race, gender, and policing. Her research investigates the relationships between sovereign power and Indigenous/minority rights in four main areas: the role of race and gender in the administration of criminal and juvenile justice, Native youth and juvenile justice, equal protection-based challenges to Indigenous rights, and tribal jurisdiction. Rolnick has investigated the impact of tribal, federal, and state juvenile justice systems on Native youth and regularly advises advocates, federal policy makers, and tribal governments on Native youth and juvenile justice. She teaches courses in criminal law, policing and race, civil rights, and Indian and tribal law. Prior to joining the University of Nevada, Las Vegas, she was the inaugural Critical Race Studies Law Fellow at University of California, Los Angeles (UCLA) School of Law. Before that, she represented tribal governments as a lawyer and lobbyist in Washington, DC. Professor Rolnick holds an M.A. in American Indian studies from UCLA and a J.D. with a concentration in critical race studies from UCLA School of Law.

Robert J. Sampson is the Henry Ford II Professor of the Social Sciences at Harvard University, affiliated research professor at the American Bar

Foundation, and founding director of the Boston Area Research Initiative. He has also taught at the University of Chicago and the University of Illinois. Sampson is an elected member of the National Academy of Sciences and a fellow of the American Academy of Arts and Sciences, the American Society of Criminology, the American Philosophical Society, as well as the American Academy of Political and Social Science. He served as president of the American Society of Criminology and received the Stockholm Prize in Criminology. Sampson was also elected as corresponding fellow of the British Academy and fellow of the John Simon Guggenheim Foundation. His research and teaching cover a variety of areas including crime, disorder, life course, neighborhood effects, civic engagement, inequality, "ecometrics," and the social structure of the city. Sampson is the author of three award-winning books and numerous articles. His last book, published by the University of Chicago Press, is *Great American City: Chicago and the Enduring Neighborhood Effect*, which is based on the culmination of more than a decade of research from the Project on Human Development in Chicago Neighborhoods, for which Sampson served as scientific director. He received his Ph.D. from the State University of New York at Albany.

Jeffrey Sedgwick is the executive director of the Justice Research and Statistics Association. He was appointed by President Bush as the director of the Bureau of Justice Statistics under the Office of Justice Programs (OJP). He was later appointed to serve as the acting assistant attorney general for the OJP. He is professor emeritus of political science at the University of Massachusetts-Amherst, where he has taught multiple courses, including policy analysis and evaluation as well as public policy. Sedgwick served on the National Research Council Committee on Modernizing the Nation's Crime Statistics. He also co-founded the consulting firm Keswick Advisors, which aides in developing program outcome and performance measures for a range of projects including an evaluation of youth crime prevention programs funded by the Office of Juvenile Justice and Delinquency Prevention. Sedgwick is the author of *Law Enforcement Planning: The Limits of an Economic Approach* and *Deterring Criminals: Policy-making and the American Political Tradition.* He received his M.A.P.A. in public administration and public policy and his Ph.D. in government and public affairs from the University of Virginia.

María B. Vélez is an associate professor at the University of Maryland. Her general interests are to understand how stratification along racial-ethnic, political, and economic lines shapes and is shaped by the uneven patterning of crime and justice outcomes. Key themes include investigating the influence of political conditions on crime patterns across neighborhoods, the dynamic nature of crime, and the consequences of mass incarceration and other forms of criminal justice contact for minority political behavior and the well-being of democracy in the United States. Vélez was a member of the Roundtable on Crime Trends in America for the National Academies of Sciences, Engineering, and Medicine's Committee on Law and Justice. She received her Ph.D. in sociology from The Ohio State University.

STAFF

Emily P. Backes serves as the deputy board director with the Committee on Law and Justice and the Board on Children, Youth, and Families in the Division of Behavioral and Social Sciences and Education at the National Academies of Sciences, Engineering, and Medicine. Backes has served as the study director for the following reports: *The Promise of Adolescence: Realizing Opportunity for All Youth*; *Birth Settings in America: Outcomes, Quality, Access and Choice;* and *Transforming the Financing of Early Care and Education*. Additionally, she has provided substantive analytical and editorial support to projects covering a range of topics, including policing, juvenile justice reform, forensic science, and illicit markets; children's cognitive and behavioral health; science communication and literacy; and science and human rights. She is a member of the District of Columbia Bar. Backes received an M.A. and B.A. in history from the University of Missouri, specializing in international law and human rights policy. She received a J.D. from the University of the District of Columbia's David A. Clarke School of Law, where she represented clients as a student attorney with the Low-Income Taxpayer Clinic and the Juvenile and Special Education Law Clinic.

Natacha Blain serves as the senior director of the Board on Children, Youth, and Families and the Committee on Law and Justice at the National Academies of Sciences, Engineering, and Medicine. She has experience working with policy makers and senior legislative officials on a variety of social justice issues and campaigns including serving as a Supreme Court Fellow, chief counsel to Senator Dick Durbin on the Senate Judiciary Committee, and lead strategic advisor for the Children's Defense Fund's Cradle to Prison Pipeline Campaign. Prior to joining the National Academies, Blain served as associate director/acting executive director of Grantmakers for Children, Youth and Families. There, she played a critical role in helping convene and engage diverse constituencies, fostering leadership, collaboration and innovation-sharing through a network of funders committed to the enduring well-being of children, youth, and families. Blain earned her Master of Science and Doctorate in clinical psychology from Allegheny University of Health Sciences and MCP—Hahnemann University (now Drexel University), respectively, and her Doctor of Jurisprudence degree from the Villanova University School of Law.

Yamrot Negussie serves as the senior program officer supporting the Committee on Law and Justice in the Division of Behavioral and Social Sciences and Education of the National Academies of Sciences, Engineering, and Medicine. Previously, Negussie worked in the Health and Medicine Division of the National Academies, facilitating consensus studies and supporting the Forum on Microbial Threats. Since joining the National Academies she has staffed three major consensus studies on the topics of implementing community-based interventions to promote health equity, reducing alcohol-impaired driving injuries and fatalities, and advancing equity in prenatal and early childhood development. Prior to joining the National Academies, Negussie conducted research at the Boston University School of Public Health, exploring topics such as intimate partner violence and gun ownership in relation to homicide rates in the United States. She was also a co-evaluator of a Centers for Disease Control and Prevention–funded prevention program in the greater Boston area, which trained residents living in public housing to be health advocates in their communities. Negussie interned for the Boston Public Health Commission, assisting in the implementation of a teen dating violence prevention program. She conducted surveillance and assisted with police investigations for a local Maryland department of public safety. She received her M.P.H. from Boston University with concentrations in epidemiology and social and behavioral health and her B.A. in criminology and criminal justice from the University of Maryland, College Park.

Ellie Grimes serves as the research associate with the National Academies of Sciences, Engineering, and Medicine's Committee on Law and Justice. Previously, she worked with the Committee on Population and the Committee on National Statistics as a senior program assistant. Since joining the National Academies, Grimes has supported consensus studies on rising midlife mortality rates and socioeconomic disparities and the transformation of retail trade, as well as supported numerous workshops and expert meetings on topics including forced migration, human trafficking, and family planning and women's empowerment. Prior to joining the National Academies, she worked in the House of Representatives as a staff assistant for a member of Congress who represents Louisville, Kentucky. Grimes received her B.A. from the University of Pennsylvania, where she studied health and societies with a concentration in health policy and law.

Stacey Smit serves as the program coordinator on the National Academies of Sciences, Engineering, and Medicine's Committee on Law and Justice, supporting consensus studies on the board. She has experience providing project management, administrative, and event planning support and has worked at various organizations in the area. In the past, she has supported the Division of Behavioral and Social Sciences and Education's Executive Office; the Decadal Survey of Social and Behavioral Sciences for Applications to National Security; the Committee on the Use of Economic Evidence to Inform Investments in Children, Youth, and Families; the Committee on Supporting the Parents of Young Children; the Forum on Children's Cognitive, Affective, and Behavioral Health; and the Committee on Increasing Capacity for Reducing Bullying and Its Impact on the Lifecourse of Youth Involved. She received her B.A. in sociology from the University of Maryland, College Park.